This modern text is designed to prepare you for your future professional career. While theories, ideas, techniques, and data are dynamic, the information contained in this volume will provide you a quick and useful reference as well as a guide for future learning for many years to come. Your familiarity with the contents of this book will make it an important volume in your professional library.

EX LIBRIS

Financial Institutions

Financial Institutions

Second Edition
1985

Peter S. Rose

Donald R. Fraser
both of
Texas A & M University

BUSINESS PUBLICATIONS, INC.
Plano, Texas   75075

ISBN 0-256-02882-6

Library of Congress Catalog Card No. 84–70682

Printed in the United States of America

1 2 3 4 5 6 7 8 9 0 K 2 1 0 9 8 7 6 5

To Kandy, Lyn, Eleanor,
Jason, Michael, and Robbie

Preface

THE SECOND EDITION of this book represents a very substantial revision of the material contained in the first edition—changes that go well beyond updating numbers and making minor, cosmetic additions. The revisions reflect the experience of the authors in using the book in the classroom, numerous comments by students on specific parts of the book, comments by colleagues at Texas A & M and other universities who have taught from the book, and last and certainly not least, the enormous revolution in the financial services industry that is rapidly transforming the role of individual financial institutions and the entire financial system. The speed with which the operations and regulation of financial institutions have been changing is remarkable and compounds the difficulty of writing a book that is current both in the state of the art in institutions management and in describing the regulations which constrain the behavior and performance of individual financial institutions.

The major changes made for this new edition include the following:

1. *The addition of four new chapters:* Reflecting the growing interest in performance measurement and financial analysis of financial institutions, one of the new chapters (7) is devoted to analyzing the financial statements of banks and other financial institutions. This includes measurement of the returns or profitability of financial institutions, a discussion of the institutional planning process, and also a treatment of interest sensitivity, or gap management. A second new chapter (16) is devoted to money market mutual funds—the newest of major financial intermediaries. This chapter considers the functions of money market funds, the reasons for their phenomenal growth, the effect their expansion has had on the financial system, and their probable future in a deregulated environment. A third new chapter (23) is devoted to electronic funds transfer systems, a technological innovation that is gradually revolutionizing the process by

which financial services are delivered. This chapter covers the various facets of electronic funds transfer systems, including automated teller machines, point-of-sale terminals, and automated clearing houses, and considers the implications of these technological changes for the functioning of financial institutions and the financial system. A fourth new chapter (24) covers international financial institutions and discusses the role of U.S. banks abroad as well as the participation of foreign banks in the United States. It also explores the functions of retail and wholesale multinational banking organizations and the important topic of risk in international lending.

2. *A substantial revision of the majority of chapters:* For example, the previous discussion of savings and loans and mutual savings banks has been revised and expanded to incorporate new regulations that relate to these organizations and the recent problems experienced by many of these firms. As a result of this more thorough treatment, each of these industries is discussed in a separate chapter (savings and loans in Chapter 13 and mutual savings banks in Chapter 14). Similarly, Chapter 12, Capital Management, has been extensively revised in order to incorporate the changes in capital adequacy standards announced by the regulatory authorities in December 1981. As in the revisions of other chapters, the attempt has been made to make the discussion as current as possible and at the same time provide perspectives on major trends that are affecting financial institutions, management, and regulation.

3. *A discussion of the deregulation movement is integrated throughout the book as is a treatment of the growing competition and overlap of functions between depository and nondepository financial institutions:* Both the Depository Institutions Deregulation and Monetary Control Act of 1980 and the Garn–St Germain Depository Institutions Act of 1982 are discussed in detail in all chapters of the book where they are relevant, particularly in Chapter 5 on the Federal Reserve System, in Chapter 8 on banking structure and competition, and in Chapters 13–16, which deal with thrift institutions. Chapter 25, while carrying the same title as in the first edition—Reform of the Financial System—is entirely different in content, concentrating on the background, causes, and consequences of financial deregulation.

4. *An updating and reformulation of the problems for discussion which require students to apply the principles they have learned to realistic financial management problems:* In addition, several new problems for discussion have been added to the book. Overall, the second edition contains 14 problems for discussion, whereas the previous edition contained only 9.

As with the first edition, the book is designed for use in undergraduate and beginning graduate courses dealing with the management of financial institutions. It may also be used as supplemental material in money and banking, money and capital markets, and financial markets courses. It has purposely been designed so that there are few necessary prerequisites for the student to be able to follow the discussion. The use of mathematical formulas is sparing, while numerous exhibits serve to reinforce major points covered in each chapter. Where needed, additional exposition of concepts underlying the discussion has been incorporated in explanatory footnotes. Questions suitable for discussion or testing follow each chapter and serve as a guide for reviewing the key points. In addition, as pointed out above, there are problems for class discussion following 14 of the chapters.

As noted by the authors in the first edition, this book has been written from the conviction that a student should not only be familiar with the framework of the financial system and the role that financial institutions play in that system but also should be able to view financial institutions from an internal, managerial perspective. All students play a role in the financial system and many pursue careers as managers of commercial banks, savings associations, insurance companies, and other financial intermediaries. In order to better understand the role of financial institutions in the economy of the nation, it is necessary to understand the principles which are relevant to the management of these institutions. Conversely, in order to effectively manage financial institutions, one must understand their role in the economy and financial system. It is thus the conviction of the authors that a blend of internal and external perspectives is the appropriate approach to understanding financial institutions.

We have attempted to blend these perspectives in this book by first setting forth a general description of the objectives of financial institutions and the decision variables which management should concentrate upon in achieving its objectives. This general model is then applied to each major financial institution active in the U.S. economy.

In summary, throughout the book we have attempted to emphasize the enormous changes which are taking place today in the nation's financial system and in the role of individual financial institutions. Chapters dealing with individual financial institutions contain a discussion of recent trends affecting that particular institution. The last three chapters of the book are devoted to the element of change in the regulation and operation of financial institutions and the financial system. While it is impossible to anticipate all significant developments, the student should be aware of these profound changes which impact upon career opportunities in the field and upon the role of the institutions themselves.

**ACKNOWLEDG-
MENTS**

We are grateful to James R. Booth of Arizona State University, Kenneth A. Dyer of University of Massachusetts, Harbor Campus, Larry A. Frieder of Florida A & M University, Paul Grier of State University of New York at Binghamton, and B. Perry Woodside of Clemson University for their careful reading and numerous editorial suggestions on an earlier draft of the manuscript. Naturally, all errors that remain are the sole responsibility of the authors. Finally, we would like to express our deepest appreciation to our families for their understanding and encouragement during the many months in which this book was in preparation.

Peter S. Rose
Donald R. Fraser

Contents

Capital. Other Approaches. Recent Regulatory Guidelines: *Comptroller/Fed Guidelines. FDIC Guidelines.* Determining the Amount of Capital Needed. Evaluation of Alternative Means of Raising Capital. Summary.

The Structure of the Savings and Loan Industry: *Chartering and Supervision. Stock versus Mutual Associations. Size Distribution of Savings and Loans. S&L Mergers. Branching Activity in the Industry. Trends in the Number of Associations.* Assets and Funds Sources for Savings and Loans: *Mortgages and Mortgage-Related Assets. Consumer Installment Loans. Holdings of Liquid Assets. Sources of Funds: Savings Accounts. Net Worth or Equity Capital. Federal Home Loan Bank and Federal Reserve Borrowings. Trends in Sources and Uses of Funds.* Earnings, Dividends, and Expenses of Savings and Loans. Regulation of Savings and Loans: *Reserve Requirements. Net-Worth Requirements. Regulations Governing Deposit Interest Rates.* Summary.

Structure of the Industry: *Regulation of the Industry. A Trend toward Consolidation in Savings Banking.* Savings Banks Introduce the NOW Account. Industry Sources of Funds: *Savings Deposits. The Impact of Deposit Interest-Rate Ceilings. Equity Reserves.* Uses of Savings Bank Funds: *Loans and Investments. Liquidity. Types of Loans. Other Assets. Long-Term Trends in the Industry's Uses of Funds.* Revenues, Expenses, and Taxes. Summary.

History and Structural Makeup of the Credit Union Industry. Size Distribution of Credit Unions: *The Dominance of Small Associations. New Savings Instruments. Declining Numbers and Increasing Size.* The Basis for Joining a Credit Union. How Credit Unions Are Organized: *The Owners and the Board of Directors. Credit Union Committees and Management. Organizational Structure of the Industry.* Deposits, Loans, and Other Services Provided by the Industry: *New Services and Advantages over Other Lenders of Funds. Role in the Payments System. Credit Function. Other Services.* Principal Sources and Uses of Funds for the Industry: *Sources of Funds. Uses of Funds.* The Industry's

PART ONE

Financial Institutions in the Economy

1. *The Nature and Role of Financial Institutions in the Economy*

THIS IS A BOOK about the behavior and characteristics of financial institutions in the American economy. These institutions are vitally important to the economic well-being and future growth of a market-oriented economy such as ours. As we will discuss in this and subsequent chapters, financial institutions receive approximately four-fifths of all savings dollars generated each year in the U.S. financial system. The liabilities of financial institutions are the principal means for making payments for goods and services, and their loans are the chief source of credit for all economic units in society—businesses, households, and governments. Moreover, the nature of individual financial institutions has been changing rapidly in recent years. For all of these reasons an understanding of the lending and borrowing activities, the portfolio behavior, the management policies, and the regulatory environment of financial institutions is essential for every serious student of the economic and financial system.

This book will acquaint the student with all the major types of financial institutions. We will focus in turn upon commercial banks, savings and loan associations, mutual savings banks, credit unions, money market funds, life insurance companies, property-casualty insurance companies, pension funds, finance companies, investment companies, and other financial institutions. We will examine closely the role of these institutions in the financial markets and the contribution each makes to the proper functioning of the economic and financial system. Our perspective will be that of the manager seeking to understand the role of each financial institution in the nation's financial system and to understand the unique management problems faced by all financial institutions today.

A financial institution is a business firm whose principal assets are financial claims—stocks, bonds, loans—instead of real assets like buildings, equipment, raw materials, and so forth. Financial institutions make

THE NATURE OF FINANCIAL INSTITUTIONS

loans to customers or purchase investment securities in the financial marketplace. They also offer a wide variety of other financial services, ranging from insurance protection and the sale of retirement plans to the safe-keeping of valuables and providing a mechanism for making payments and transferring funds.

Financial Intermediaries

We may divide financial institutions into two groups—financial intermediaries and other financial institutions (see Figure 1–1). *Financial intermediaries* acquire the IOUs issued by borrowers—primary securities—and at the same time sell their own IOUs—secondary securities—to savers. A commercial bank, for example, is happy to accept your checking or savings account, which, from your point of view, is a financial asset. To the banker it is debt—a secondary security—which can be used to make loans and investments by accepting primary securities (IOUs) from borrowers. The major types of financial intermediaries found in the United States are commercial banks, credit unions, mutual savings banks, savings and loan associations, money market funds, life insurance companies, property and casualty insurance companies, investment companies, finance companies, pension funds, real estate investment trusts, and leasing companies. All make heavy use of financial liabilities to attract savings and invest principally in financial assets in the form of borrower IOUs. This book is devoted primarily to a study of financial intermediaries.

Figure 1–1   Types of Financial Institutions

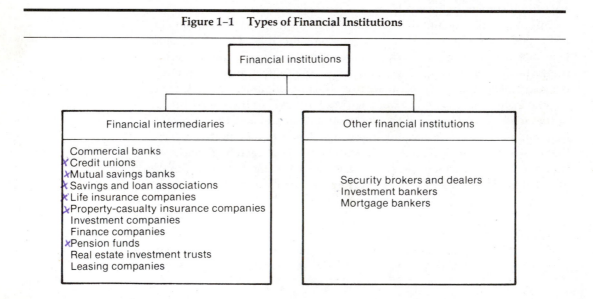

Other Financial Institutions

Not all financial institutions are financial intermediaries, however. Included in the category of other financial institutions are security brokers, dealers, investment bankers, and mortgage bankers.

Security *brokers* act as middlemen for buyers and sellers of securities, bringing the two groups together so that financial transactions can take place. In return for services rendered the broker charges a commission which reflects the cost of searching the market for suitable buyers and sellers of securities. Security *dealers* not only bring buyers and sellers of securities together, but they also purchase securities for their own accounts. Thus dealers in securities accept significant risk by buying securities outright in anticipation of being able to resell those securities profitably in future days and weeks. Both security brokers and dealers provide the essential services of creating a resale (secondary) market for financial instruments and improving the flow of information among financial market participants.

Related to the functions performed by security dealers are the services provided by investment bankers and mortgage bankers. These institutions provide a conduit for the offering of *new* securities in the financial markets. Investment bankers underwrite new issues of corporate stocks and bonds and state and local government debt securities, first purchasing the new securities and then lining up willing buyers to take these securities into their portfolios at a higher, more favorable price. A similar function is performed by mortgage bankers who acquire mortgage securities arising from the construction of new homes, apartments, and business firms and who eventually place those mortgages with long-term lenders (such as insurance companies, pension funds, and savings banks).

We note that security brokers and dealers, investment bankers, and mortgage bankers are clearly specialized kinds of financial institutions. However, they are *not* financial intermediaries like commercial banks, credit unions, or insurance companies. These institutions do not create their own IOUs (secondary securities) as true financial intermediaries do. Instead, brokers and dealers, investment bankers, and mortgage bankers merely pass securities issued by other institutions along to other investors.

Financial intermediaries and other financial institutions are part of a vast *financial system* which serves the public. The financial system is composed of a network of financial markets, institutions, businesses, households, and governments that participate in that system and regulate its operation.

As Figure 1–2 illustrates, the basic function of the financial system is to transfer loanable funds from lenders (or savings-surplus units) to borrow-

FINANCIAL INSTITUTIONS AND THE FINANCIAL SYSTEM

Figure 1–2 **Financial Intermediaries and Other Financial Institutions within the Financial System**

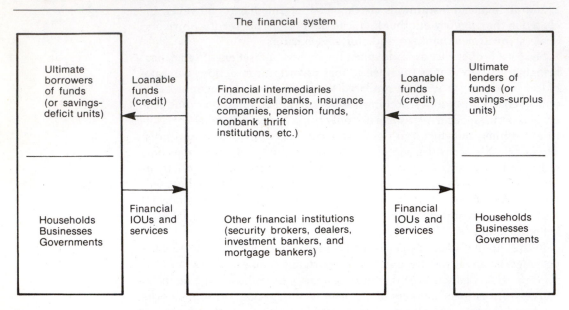

ers (or savings-deficit units). These funds are allocated by negotiation and trading in a wide array of financial markets which bring together individuals and institutions supplying funds with those demanding funds. As we will note in Chapter 2, most of the savings flowing through the financial system come from households, while the principal borrowers in the financial system are business firms and governments.

Functions of the Financial System

The financial system is one of the most important components of any nation's economy. It provides essential services without which a modern economy could not function.

The financial system supplies *credit* to support purchases of goods and services and to finance capital investment—the construction of buildings, highways, bridges, and other structures and the purchase of machinery and equipment. Investment increases the productivity of a nation's resources and makes possible a higher standard of living for its citizens.

The financial system supplies a *mechanism for making payments* in the form of currency, checking accounts, and other transactions media. In recent years, institutions operating in the financial system have developed many new payment services, including NOW accounts and share drafts—both types of interest-bearing checking accounts—telephone bill-paying services, and electronic machines which accept deposits and dispense cash. Slowly, but surely, the financial system is moving away from payment in paper form (especially checks) toward a system where funds are moved in microseconds via computer hookup.[1]

Through the services of supplying credit and providing a mechanism for making payments, the financial system makes possible the *creation of money*. While there are several different definitions and forms of money in use today,[2] all forms of money serve as a medium of exchange for purchasing goods and services. The existence of money avoids the necessity and inconvenience of having to barter for the goods and services we need. Money provides a standard unit of account, expressing the value of all goods and services in terms of a single unit of measure (such as the dollar) in order to simplify transactions and recordkeeping. Money also serves as a store of value until an individual or institution wishes to spend its money holdings for goods and services. In modern economies, all types of money are debt—IOUs, issued either by a financial institution or by some unit of government. For example, the checking account—still the principal form of money in most industrialized nations—represents the debt (promise to pay) of a bank.

Finally, the financial system provides a profitable *outlet for savings*. Both individuals and institutions save today in order to be able to consume more goods and services tomorrow. Saving really performs an essential economic function because it releases scarce resources from producing goods and services for current consumption in order to produce investment goods (buildings, equipment, etc.). However, there would be little incentive to save in the absence of a financial system. Through that system and the financial markets which are a part of it, savers can lend their surplus funds to borrowers and earn income in the form of interest, dividends, capital gains, and so forth. When borrowers need additional funds, the financial system sends out a signal to savers in the form of higher interest rates, encouraging savings-surplus units to save more and consume less. On the other hand, when fewer funds are required by borrowers, interest rates tend to fall and the flow of savings is reduced. Thus the financial system provides a mechanism for encouraging savings and providing funds for investment.

Methods of Moving Loanable Funds in the Financial System from Lenders to Borrowers

As we noted above, the basic task of the financial system is to transfer loanable funds from lenders (savings-surplus units) to borrowers (savings-deficit units). This transfer of funds takes place in markets—money

---

[1]The development of an electronic funds transfer system (EFTS) for making payments is discussed in detail in Chapter 23.

[2]See Chapter 5 for a discussion of alternative definitions of the nation's money supply.

and capital markets—which bring borrowers and lenders together. Actually, loanable funds can be exchanged between lenders and borrowers through three different routes.

Direct Extension of Credit by Ultimate Lenders to Ultimate Borrowers. For example, borrowers and lenders might communicate directly with each other without the aid of a financial intermediary or any other financial institution. With this so-called direct financing method once a deal is struck, the borrower gives to the lender a financial asset—stocks, bonds, notes, etc.—evidencing a claim against the borrower's resources or income in exchange for funds. Usually the borrower promises to make a series of payments to the lender in the future until the lender recovers all of his funds plus an added return for the risk of lending.

While the direct financing approach is obviously simple and straightforward, it has several drawbacks which severely limit the volume of lending and borrowing that otherwise might take place. Quite clearly, both lender and borrower must agree on the essential terms of the loan—its maturity, yield, collateral or security, potential marketability in advance of maturity, and other conditions normally included in the terms of credit. When there is lack of agreement on any credit terms and the difference cannot be resolved through negotiation, there can be no transfer of loanable funds. Credit cannot be created and the volume of borrowing in the economy will not expand.

The Intervention of Brokers and Dealers in the Lending Process. A popular alternative to the direct exchange of funds and financial claims between borrowers and lenders is the semi-direct financing technique. In this case borrowers and lenders rely upon the intervention of a third party—broker, dealer, investment banker, or mortgage banker—to complete the loan transaction.

A single borrower, such as General Motors Corporation or Shell Oil Company, may decide to issue thousands of securities bearing a range of maturity dates, collateral, and other terms and then rely on securities dealers, for example, to place the entire issue with a large diversified group of investors who may include households, banks, insurance companies, pension funds, mutual funds, and so forth. Analogous to the direct financing technique, however, investors (ultimate lenders) still must hold the securities issued by ultimate borrowers. But the dealer's intervention in this transaction has served to reduce transactions and information costs and improved the liquidity and marketability of securities created in the borrowing and lending process. In fact, one of the real contributions made by brokers, dealers, investment, and mortgage bankers to the functioning of the nation's financial system is to enhance the growth of secondary (resale) markets for securities issued by borrowers. Through the operation of secondary markets the lender of funds is no longer locked in to holding a security until it matures. Provided the borrower is sufficiently well-known to potential investors, his or her securities may be readily accepted for resale through a broker or dealer.

Clearly, while semidirect financing is an improvement in efficiency over direct financing, this method of borrowing and lending does not solve all the problems involved in credit transactions. For example, what do investors (ultimate lenders) do if they are concerned about risk—the safety of their funds—and all securities currently issued by ultimate borrowers are viewed as too risky? What do investors do who want to have access to their funds immediately if their only investment alternatives are stocks and long-term bonds, many of which have no active resale market? Moreover, many marketable securities are unstable in price, subjecting the investor to the risk of substantial capital loss. There is also the cost and inconvenience of contacting a broker or dealer who must then find another investor willing to accept the same terms of credit.

Financial Intermediation (Indirect Finance).   Perhaps not surprisingly, these shortcomings of direct and semidirect finance opened the door to a third method for carrying out financial transactions—financial intermediation, or indirect finance. With this method, both ultimate borrowers (savings-deficit units) and ultimate lenders (savings-surplus units) have their financial requirements satisfied through the efforts of a financial intermediary.

The classic example of a financial intermediary at work, meeting the needs of both ultimate borrowers and lenders, is the commercial bank. Many of its customers who walk in to open a checking account or savings deposit do so because they value highly the safety (minimal default risk), liquidity (minimal money risk), accessibility (minimum denominations in which saving can take place), and great convenience offered by a local banking institution. While it is true that, in nominal terms, the deposit customer may sacrifice some return (yield) for these advantages of safety, liquidity, accessibility, and convenience, the potential reduction in monetary return must be weighed against these other attractive features which have positive utility for the depositor. On balance, the customer may feel better off accepting the deposit IOU of a bank rather than the risks and inconveniences of securities offered through brokers, dealers, or investment bankers.[3]

---

[3]Of course, the attractiveness of the deposits offered by commercial banks and other depository institutions (such as credit unions, savings and loan associations, and mutual savings banks) is further enhanced by federal deposit insurance up to $100,000 and state and federal regulation of these intermediaries to promote safety of the public's money. As we will soon see, however, the financial institutions' sector (especially the depository institutions' portion) is gradually being deregulated, leading to greater freedom for management decision making but also greater risk for the institutions themselves and for at least some of their customers.

The foregoing analysis reminds us, then, that an essential part of the indirect financing (financial intermediation) process is the creation of financial claims attractive to ultimate lenders of funds. These claims are *secondary securities*, widely recognized by the public for their safety, liquidity, convenience, and accessibility. Secondary securities include, of course, not just bank deposits but also insurance policies to protect lives and property; pension plans to provide financial support in retirement; shares in money market funds and investment companies to provide an outlet for current savings; and deposits in credit unions, savings and loan associations, and mutual savings banks for storing liquidity and purchasing power.

Still, as Figure 1–3 shows, the issuing of secondary securities is only half of the indirect financing, or intermediation, process. The other half involves lending funds to ultimate borrowers. In this process the intermediary must be willing to accept risks and inconveniences not palatable to many ultimate lenders, particularly the small saver. In brief, the so-called primary securities issued by many borrowers and taken on by a financial intermediary often carry terms and features quite different from the secondary securities the intermediary offers to the ultimate lenders who trust their savings to that particular financial institution.

This *transformation of financial claims* lies at the heart of the indirect financing, or intermediation, process. Through the sale of secondary secu-

Figure 1–3   Nature of the Financial Intermediation Process

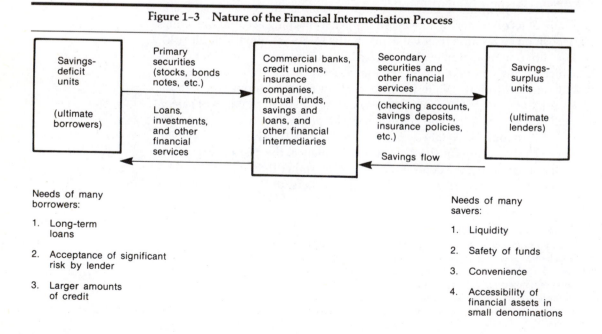

Needs of many borrowers:

1. Long-term loans

2. Acceptance of significant risk by lender

3. Larger amounts of credit

Needs of many savers:

1. Liquidity

2. Safety of funds

3. Convenience

4. Accessibility of financial assets in small denominations

rities to savers that are safe, convenient, liquid and accessible, while at the same time taking on what are often riskly, large-denomination, long-term, and illiquid primary securities from borrowers, financial intermediaries perform an indispensable function in the nation's economy. This intermediation process encourages saving, especially from those of limited means, and makes for a more optimal and efficient allocation of financial resources. It brings together and resolves the fundamentally different financing requirements of businesses, households, and governmental units, simultaneously transforming the nature of financial claims available in the nation's money and capital markets. This transformation of financial claims overcomes the inherent limitations of direct and semidirect financing in the borrowing and lending of money.

Financial intermediaries actually perform several different kinds of intermediation. These include (1) denomination intermediation, (2) default-risk intermediation, (3) maturity intermediation, (4) information intermediation, (5) risk pooling, and (6) economies of scale.

Denomination intermediation occurs when intermediaries accept small amounts of savings from individuals and others and pool these funds to make large loans, principally to corporations and governments.

Default-risk intermediation refers to the willingness of financial intermediaries to make loans to (acquire primary securities from) risky borrowers and, at the same time, issue relatively safe and liquid (secondary) securities in order to attract loanable funds from savers.

Maturity intermediation refers to the practice of borrowing comparatively short-term funds from savers and making long-term loans to borrowers who require a lengthy commitment of funds.

Information intermediation refers to the process by which financial intermediaries substitute their skill in the marketplace for that of the saver who frequently has neither the time to stay abreast of market developments nor access to relevant information about market conditions and opportunities.

Intermediaries also engage in *risk pooling* and take advantage of *economies of scale* in their activities. By investing in assets with a wide variety of risk-return characteristics, the benefits of financial diversification—greater stability in earnings and cash flow—are achieved, enhancing the safety of funds supplied by savers. As the intermediary increases in size, its operating costs per unit may decline, which can reduce the cost of many financial services supplied to the public.[4]

KINDS OF FINANCIAL INTERMEDIATION

---

[4]For a more complete discussion of these concepts see Kaufman [12], chap. 4; Van Horne [15], chap. 1; and Brill [3].

TYPES OR CATEGORIES OF FINANCIAL INTERMEDIARIES

While all financial intermediaries perform the same basic function—accepting primary securities from ultimate borrowers and issuing secondary securities to ultimate lenders—they are not all alike. Some may be labeled *depository intermediaries* because most of their secondary securities (sources of loanable funds) consist of deposits received from businesses, households, and governments. In this group are commercial banks, credit unions, savings and loan associations, and mutual savings banks. Other important intermediaries, designated as *contractual intermediaries*, enter into contracts with their customers to promote saving and/or financial protection against loss of life or property. Among the best known contractual intermediaries are life and property-casualty insurance companies and public and private pension funds. Still another group of institutions is known as *investment intermediaries* because they offer the public securities which can be held indefinitely as a long-term investment or sold quickly when the customer needs his or her funds returned. Investment intermediaries include mutual stock funds, bond funds, and money market funds. It is generally argued that cash inflows and outflows of contractual and investment intermediaries are more easily predicted than fund flows through deposit type intermediaries. This permits the former institutions to minimize short-term liquid investments and reach for longer-term investment assets with higher yields.

We may also distinguish between *mutual* and *stock* intermediaries. A mutual institution is owned by its customers, who receive a share of the institution's net earnings in the form of dividends. For example, most savings and loan associations today are mutuals; their depositors are really owners, receiving dividends on their deposits. Each depositor has a vote in any matter affecting the institution as a whole, such as a merger or reorganization. Mutuals are very important organizational forms in the savings and loan, savings bank, and life insurance industries.

Other intermediaries, such as commercial banks, are stockholder-owned financial institutions organized as regular business corporations. The shareholders in a stock financial institution are its owners, receiving a share of any net earnings and entitled to elect the board of directors and vote on any significant issues bearing on the whole organization. For example, in a stock savings and loan association the stockholders are the owners, while its depositors are not owners but creditors, receiving interest on their deposits and having first claim against the association's assets in the event of liquidation. Commercial banks are stockholder-owned corporations as are most property-casualty insurance companies and finance companies.

Financial intermediaries (whether stock or mutual, depository, contractual, or investment in form) are business firms organized and operated to achieve certain goals, such as maximum profitability. In this respect intermediaries share certain characteristics with other types of business firms. For example, like any other business firm, an intermediary uses inputs—land, labor, capital, and management skills—to produce units of output that customers demand. And like any other business firm the intermediary contributes organization to the production process, providing a location and a framework within which labor and capital can be combined with other resources to produce a product—financial services of various kinds (see Figure 1–4).

A Two-Stage Production Process

Actually, the operation of a financial intermediary is more complex than for most business firms. As noted by Haywood [11] in a recent study, the intermediary possesses a two-stage production process (see Figure 1–5). Inputs in the form of land, labor, capital, and management skills are first applied to stage I—the sources-of-funds stage—where savings are attracted by offers of interest-bearing deposits, insurance policies, safety deposit boxes, pension plans, and thousands of other financial services desired by the public. Then, once the intermediary puts aside a certain portion of its incoming funds in reserves to meet short-run demands for cash, the remaining funds (called loanable funds) go into stage II of the institution's production process—the uses-of-funds stage—where the main activity is the making of loans and other kinds of investments. In order to provide financial services in a competitive environment and to earn a satisfactory return on invested capital, the intermediary applies land, labor, capital, and other resources to produce the maximum volume of output of financial services at the lowest possible cost.

Figure 1–4   The Financial Intermediary as a Business Firm

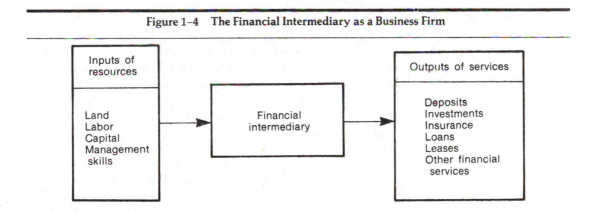

Figure 1–5   The Two-Stage Production Process of Financial Intermediaries

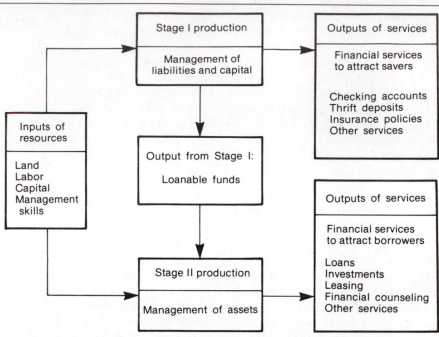

Source: Adapted from Charles F. Haywood, "Production of Consumer Financial Services," *Public Regulation of Financial Services, Costs and Benefits to Consumers*, phase I, interim report (Cambridge, Mass.: ABT Associates, 1977), vol. 1. This material is based upon research supported by the National Science Foundation under contract no. NSF-C76-18548. Any opinions, findings, and conclusions or recommendations expressed in this publication are those of the author and do not necessarily reflect the views of the National Science Foundation.

Two fundamentally different questions must be dealt with by the management of a financial intermediary in these two stages of production. In stage I, the sources-of-funds stage, the problem is to raise funds from savers at the lowest possible cost—that is, by offering the lowest rates of return necessary to attract the public's money. Management must decide what mix of fund sources will result in the lowest overall cost of funds raised. In stage II, the uses-of-funds stage, the problem is quite different. Management seeks that combination of loans and other assets resulting in the highest overall rate of return to the intermediary, consistent with regulations and other goals of the institution. In this sense the principal objective of stage I is minimum cost, and that of stage II, maximum return. Necessarily, though, these two stages are interrelated, and decisions made in one stage will affect decisions made in the other.

The goals of financial intermediaries are multidimensional. Some seek a larger share of the local market for savings, loans, and investments—that is, they try to be a bigger organization relative to their competitors. Others define their primary objectives as growth and service to the public. The more aggressive institutions emphasize maximization of the wealth of their shareholders or pursue the related goal of maximizing profits.

Areas for Management Decision Making

In pursuing its goals the management of a financial intermediary must consider five major areas of decision making (see Figure 1–6):

1. Management of assets (principally loans and securities).
2. Management of liabilities.
3. Management of capital (or net worth).
4. Expense control.
5. Marketing policy.

Figure 1–6   Areas for Management Decision Making and the Goals of a Financial Intermediary

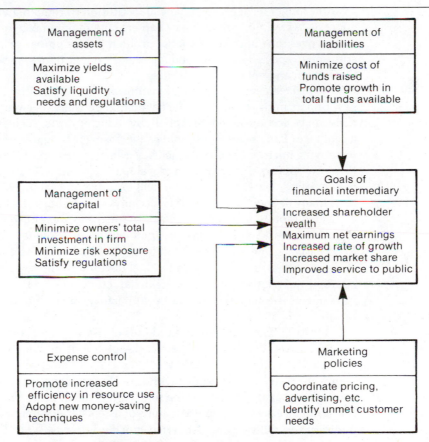

Managements of Assets, Liabilities, and Capital.   In the management of assets, liabilities, and capital, financial institutions must be especially conscious of the gap between the yields on their assets and the returns paid to savers for the loan of both debt and equity capital. (The difference between a financial intermediary's asset yield and cost of debt or equity capital is known as its spread, or *net interest margin.*) While the intermediary will try to offer the lowest returns possible to savers and lend funds to borrowers at the highest possible interest rates, it will be limited in its ability to do so by competition from other financial institutions operating in the same markets.

SPREAD.   Indeed, competitive forces in conjunction with economic and financial conditions may temporarily result in a negative spread, or negative net interest margin, between yields earned by the intermediary on its assets and the returns it pays to savers. Under normal circumstances, however, yields earned by the intermediary on assets will exceed the rates paid savers to attract funds, resulting in a positive spread, or net positive margin, between revenues and costs. In fact, a positive spread must exist over the longer term for the financial institution to remain a viable going concern. As we will see in later chapters, the maintenance of a positive spread over time has been a special problem for a number of financial institutions (especially savings and loans and savings banks) in recent years due to high and volatile interest rates.

The management of a financial institution must be continually alert to new opportunities to increase the net margin between revenues and costs. This can be accomplished, first of all, by reducing costs, such as by taking advantage of advances in technology, increasing the organization's size, or improving internal operating efficiency. Management may also be able to find new sources of revenue, by developing new services or penetrating new markets, for example. As we will examine in a later chapter of this text, many financial institutions (especially large commercial banks) have expanded rapidly into foreign countries for the express purpose of opening up new markets and, therefore, new sources of revenue.

Risk.   Management of assets, liabilities, and capital is also related to the degree of risk assumed by the individual institution. Indeed, the ability to appraise the relative return and risk characteristics of different financial instruments is essential to the successful management of a financial institution.

LIQUIDITY.   There are two major kinds of risk of importance to a financial institution. One is the risk of a cash-out—of being illiquid when cash is needed. A financial institution is liquid if it can meet all legitimate demands for cash (such as deposit withdrawals and requests from good customers for loans) precisely at the time cash is demanded. Unfortunately, this is not an easy task. Different kinds of assets vary dramatically in their liquidity (or ability to be converted quickly into cash with little risk of loss). Moreover, the need for liquidity varies significantly among different financial institutions, depending primarily on the stability and predictability of their sources of funds.

INSOLVENCY. The second major kind of risk which must be considered by the individual financial institution is the risk of insolvency, which is simply the inability to cover the intermediary's debts in the long run. If the market value of a financial institution's assets is less than the value of its aggregate liabilities, technically that institution is insolvent. Assets bearing greater default and market risk increase the probability that the institution will become insolvent. Similarly, liabilities that are more volatile and uncertain in amount and timing increase the risk that the institution's assets, when liquidated, will be inadequate to meet all legitimate demands from creditors. And there is a trade-off between the solvency and profitability of a financial institution. The highest-yielding assets generally carry the greatest risk of default. Management must carefully steer a course which maximizes returns to the intermediary's owners yet protects the fundamental solvency of the institution.

Capital. The risk of insolvency makes another area of financial institution management—the management of capital or net worth—especially important. In general, the institution's owners would prefer to keep net worth (which is an expensive source of capital) at minimum levels in order to permit maximum use of financial leverage. (Leverage is the use of relatively fixed-cost sources of funds, principally debt, in order to increase returns to the firm's shareholders.) While management desires to use maximum financial leverage to increase the expected return to equity shareholders of a financial institution, it must be careful that high levels of leverage, mainly through heavy use of debt as opposed to equity funds, do not significantly increase the institution's risk exposure. If a financial institution is perceived to be substantially more risky than in the past, it will usually have greater difficulty in attracting funds, will pay higher rates for any funds attracted, and will run a greater chance of illiquidity, insolvency, and ultimate bankruptcy.

Expense Control. Control of expenses also is important in protecting or increasing the profitability of a financial intermediary. In fact, expense control is the most important discriminating factor between profitable and unprofitable financial institutions. Until the mid-1960s salaries and wages were generally the largest expense item for a financial institution, especially for commercial banks and nonbank thrift institutions which accept the public's deposits. At that point, however, competition across industry lines began to intensify as one type of financial intermediary increasingly came into direct competition with another. For example, commercial banks found themselves in direct competition with savings and loan associations and credit unions for deposits. Insurance companies, mutual funds, and pension funds found themselves in direct competition for the available supply of long-term savings. At the same time, the public was becoming more and more financially sophisticated, demanding a greater rate of return on its savings, especially with the appearance of severe inflation during the 1960s and 1970s.

These forces combined to send the cost of raising funds to the highest levels in the 20th century. Indeed, so rapid was the escalation of interest rates during certain periods—especially 1966, 1969, 1973–74, and 1979–80—that these periods have been labeled credit crunches because of the sharply reduced availability and high cost of loanable funds. In this kind of environment financial intermediaries were compelled to offer substantially higher yields in order to attract savings. The result was that expenses associated with borrowed funds soon dominated all other costs.

Because interest costs are largely exogenous to the individual financial institution (i.e., are determined in the regional or national market for savings), management has been forced to find other ways of cutting expenses, such as by reducing labor costs and overhead expenses. Automation has entered the industry, principally through the use of computers and electronic terminals to process financial data and store and retrieve information important to management, resulting in some substitution of capital for labor and probably also reducing the need for more "brick and mortar" branch offices. At the same time, as we will see in later chapters, a consolidation movement toward larger (but fewer) independent financial intermediaries is occurring. In several industries—savings and loan associations, credit unions, mutual savings banks, life and property-casualty insurance companies, finance companies, and others—the number of firms is declining through mergers and consolidations. Not surprisingly, the median-size institution in each of these industries has been on the rise. To the extent that economies of scale exist in each instance, unit production costs of providing important financial services have fallen as a partial offset to the growing cost of attracting funds from the public. Most experts argue that these trends toward financial institutions of larger and larger size will continue and that expense control will become one of the most critical aspects of financial institutions management in the years ahead.[5]

---

[5] As we will see later, the cost squeeze which financial intermediaries have endured in recent years also has stimulated management to diversify the package of financial services offered. For example, credit unions, which historically have dealt only in savings deposits and made relatively short-term loans to individuals and families, now find themselves in many cases offering check-type deposits and financial counseling, selling credit-related insurance, offering home mortgage credit, and assisting in the purchase of mutual funds shares. Similar types of diversification have entered the savings and loan, savings banking, and commercial banking industries. These changes represent an attempt by individual financial institutions to utilize existing management more efficiently and to open up new markets in order to increase revenues and offset rising costs.

Marketing Policy. The final area of importance to financial institutions' management concerns marketing policies, including the pricing of financial services offered to the public. Financial institutions are more marketing-oriented today than at any time in their history. There is a greater emphasis today on researching customer needs and targeting specific markets for the advertising of new financial services.[6] The use of marketing research tools imposes the discipline of the marketplace upon every aspect of a financial intermediary's operations, especially on the making of loans and attracting the public's savings. Advertising, customer relations, prices of financial services, and the location of office facilities all must be coordinated to reach customers and meet their needs conveniently and efficiently. A good marketing strategy demands that each financial institution state its goals in measurable terms, formulate short- and long-range plans, and continually research the needs and requirements of its customers.[7]

The Constraints Imposed by Law and Regulation

Of course, in pursuing their goals, financial intermediaries are not completely free to behave as they choose. Acquisitions of loans, investments, and deposits, the management of capital, the territorial expansion of the institution, and sometimes the prices charged and interest rates paid are closely regulated by government. Financial intermediaries are thought to be of special importance to the welfare of society and to the health of the economy. Most savings of individuals, families, and businesses are deposited for safekeeping with these institutions. They are also the principal source of credit—a vital ingredient in maintaining a high standard of living today. And related to the credit-granting function is the process of creating money—a daily task performed historically by commercial banks and now, increasingly by nonbank depository institutions. The money creation process has profound effects on the economic health of the nation and especially on the rate of inflation.

For all these reasons, financial intermediaries face what to many appears to be a bewildering array of laws and regulations enforced by both

---

[6]The spread of marketing techniques among financial intermediaries has been accelerated by the cost-earnings squeeze and the resulting reduction in profit margins discussed earlier. The growth of branching activity, the penetration of international markets by the largest intermediaries (especially commercial banks), and the spread of consumerism and social responsibility legislation also have contributed to an increased emphasis on marketing strategies.

[7]A goal of increased growth, for example, is probably too vague for management planning purposes. To specify, however, that the institution wishes to increase its growth rate in total assets or sales from 8 percent to 10 percent a year gives management a target to shoot at and a way of measuring the institution's progress towards its self-determined goals. See Chapter 7 for a discussion of goals and performance measurement for a financial institution.

federal and state authorities. The majority of these rules and regulations—many of which owe their origins to the Great Depression of the 1930s—are specifically designed to guarantee that intermediaries protect the public interest in their management decisions and operations.

A few examples of laws and regulations which restrict the activities of financial intermediaries may help to clarify the importance of the legal and regulatory factor in financial institutions management. For example, savings and loan associations, in order to qualify for special federal tax concessions, were required in the past to devote all but a small percentage of their assets to residential mortgage loans. Until recently there were few other permissible outlets for their funds. As we will see in later chapters such restrictive regulations on savings and loans were gradually liberalized early in the 1980s when the viability of the S&L industry was threatened by a volatile economy and needlessly confining government rules.

The influence of federal tax laws may be seen most dramatically in commercial bank purchases of state and local government securities (municipals). Commercial banks have dominated this market as buyers during the postwar period, principally because interest income from municipal securities is exempt from federal income taxation. Because commercial banks are subject to the same federal income tax rates as nonfinancial corporations, they find municipals an extremely attractive use of their funds. Therefore, to fully understand the management practices of financial institutions, we need information concerning (1) the general principles of asset, liability, and capital management; (2) the sources and uses of funds received by each institution; (3) the level and nature of competition in each industry; (4) the current state of technology and the prospects for technological change; and (5) a knowledge of the laws and regulations which apply to individual financial institutions.

FINANCIAL DISINTERMEDIATION

Our discussion of the problem areas for financial institutions management would not be complete without mention of a serious problem that many intermediaries have encountered over the past three decades—financial *disintermediation*, that is, the removal of savings from financial intermediaries and the placement of those funds by savers in other investment vehicles, especially stocks, bonds, and other securities available in the open market. For example, a depositor in a savings and loan association or credit union may decide that he or she can receive a higher rate of return on those funds by withdrawing the deposit and purchasing corporate bonds or stock through a securities dealer. Disintermediation thus reduces the volume of funds flowing through financial intermediaries.

Disintermediation is prevalent when interest rates in the financial marketplace increase rapidly and approach or exceed record levels. This may create a crisis situation for management. For some financial institutions, assets (particularly mortgages and other long-term loans and invest-ments) simply don't turn over fast enough to generate more revenue; therefore insufficient funds are available to pay higher interest rates on savings accounts. In other instances, legally imposed interest-rate ceilings (especially Regulation Q) prohibit depository institutions from paying more interest to savers. In the meantime, interest rates on securities sold in the open market, uncontrolled by legal ceilings, continue to rise. The more interest-sensitive depositors (particularly large business depositors and wealthy individuals) withdraw their funds and make sizable pur-chases of stock, bonds, and money market instruments. Management then faces a liquidity crisis. Ultimately, if deposit withdrawals become massive the institution may be forced into bankruptcy.

The effects of disintermediation are many and varied. From a social point of view it certainly changes the *direction* of credit flows in the econ-omy—away from small borrowers (such as consumers) who depend heavily upon financial intermediaries for credit and toward governments and large corporations able to tap the open market for funds. It is not clear, however, that disintermediation reduces the aggregate supply of credit available in the economy. Rather, some groups—particularly the largest borrowers—benefit at the expense of others. From the point of view of financial intermediaries, however, the effects can be devastating. Net earnings often are reduced, squeezed by rising deposit rates, while liq-uid reserves melt away.

In recent years financial institutions have developed new techniques to reduce the potential severity of the disintermediation problem. The prin-cipal remedy is to make the returns on assets and, therefore, the revenues of intermediaries more sensitive to changes in interest rates. Floating or variable rates on mortgages, business loans, and even consumer install-ment loans are indexed to changes in interest rates or commodity prices. Moreover, the average maturity of loans and security investments ap-pears to have shortened significantly, giving lenders of funds greater flexi-bility and more liquidity. At the same time federal interest-rate ceilings on deposits are gradually being phased out and are scheduled to end no later than 1986. Unfortunately, many of these changes are coming almost too late for certain financial institutions that are locked in to huge amounts of fixed-return, long-term loans granted years ago when interest rates were much lower. A substantial number of these institutions have either failed or have been merged out of existence.

Before proceeding with our discussion of the vastly important role of fi-nancial institutions in the economy, it is appropriate to pause and look at a "road map" of where we are going. This text combines a substantial vol-ume of descriptive material and analysis to give the reader as complete a

THE OUTLINE OF THIS BOOK

picture as possible concerning the functions and behavior of all major kinds of financial institutions. However, the chapters emphasize, not facts and figures, but the application of the principles of financial management to individual financial intermediaries. These principles, hopefully, will serve readers well as they deal with financial intermediaries in their daily life and, in some cases, become employees of financial institutions and build careers in this field. In short, the book attempts both to discuss the role of each major financial institution in the financial system and also to illustrate the principles of financial management for individual financial institutions and their application to particular situations.

In order to accomplish these goals, however, a conceptual framework with which to analyze the functions of each major financial institution is needed. This part of the book (which includes Chapters 1 and 2) examines the place of individual financial institutions within the financial system. Chapter 2 provides an overview of the sources and uses of funds of individual financial intermediaries as well as a brief explanation of why each intermediary possesses a unique mix of funds sources and uses.

Part Two (Chapters 3–5) examines the economic and financial environment within which financial institutions operate, beginning with a discussion of how the rate of interest—the price of credit—is determined. Chapter 4 examines the major instruments that are traded in the money and capital markets and that are important to financial institutions management; it discusses how the yields (rates of interest) on money and capital market instruments are calculated. Part Two concludes with an explanation of the impact of government policies, especially monetary policy carried out by the Federal Reserve System and debt management policy by the U.S. Treasury Department, on the economy and the financial institutions' sector.

Characteristics of the commercial banking industry and key problem areas in the management of financial intermediaries are discussed in Part Three. Nonbank financial intermediaries—especially savings and loan associations, mutual savings banks, money market funds, insurance companies, finance companies, credit unions, mutual funds, and pension funds—are the focus of Parts Four, Five, and Six. Many of the chapters in Parts Three through Six are followed by short problems for discussion in which the reader must unravel a typical problem in financial institutions management. Thus not only are readers introduced to the fundamental principles of financial institutions management but they are also encouraged to apply those principles to specific problem situations.

Further understanding of the role of individual financial intermediaries is provided in Part Seven (Chapter 23, 24, and 25), which concentrates upon recent innovations in the use of electronic equipment to transfer funds, current and prospective reforms in the financial institutions field, and the spread of international financial intermediation. The emphasis in this section of the book is upon innovation and competition. Financial institutions in recent years have demonstrated a strong propensity to offer new services, penetrate new markets, and adopt new computer-based, labor-saving techniques in an effort to expand their earnings and shelter those earnings from excessive risk. Nowhere is this more evident than in the growing trends toward automation and internationalization in the financial institutions' sector.

We begin in the next chapter to build a conceptual framework for understanding the operations of our financial system and the special role of financial intermediaries within that system. The chapter focuses upon the *Flow of Funds Accounts*, prepared quarterly by the Federal Reserve System. These accounts provide comprehensive data on the flow of savings and the creation of financial assets in the American economy.

Questions

1–1. What is the basic purpose of the financial system in the economy? Explain the meaning of the terms *direct financing; semi-direct financing;* and *indirect financing,* or *financial intermediation.*

1–2. Define the following terms:

a. *Denomination intermediation.*
b. *Default-risk intermediation.*
c. *Maturity intermediation.*
d. *Information intermediation.*
e. *Risk pooling.*
f. *Economies of scale.*

1–3. In your opinion, does financial intermediation affect the growth of the economy and the nation's standard of living? Explain.

1–4. What is disintermediation? Can you think of reasons why disintermediation may be less of a problem in future years than it was during the 1960s and 1970s?

1–5. What basic trade-offs are involved in the financial management of an intermediary?

What are the different types of risk that financial intermediaries face?

1–6. Why is the proportion of liquid assets generally higher in a deposit-type intermediary, such as a commercial bank, than in a contractual-type intermediary, such as an insurance company, or investment-type intermediary, such as a mutual fund?

1–7. Explain the difference between stockholder-owned financial institutions and mutuals.

1–8. Financial intermediaries have a two-stage production process, involving the procuring of funds and the investing of those funds. Explain which of the five areas of financial institutions management discussed in this chapter (Figure 1–6) apply to stage one of the production process and which to stage two. Which management areas involve *both* stages of production?

References

1. Harless, Doris E. *Nonbank Financial Institutions*. Richmond: Federal Reserve Bank of Richmond, 1975.

2. Board of Governors of the Federal Reserve System. *Flow of Funds Accounts, 1946–75*. Washington, D.C., 1976.

3. Brill, Daniel H. "The Role of Financial Intermediaries in the U.S. Capital Markets." *Federal Reserve Bulletin*, January 1967.

4. Dougall, Herbert E., and Jack Gaumnitz. *Capital Markets and Institutions*. 4th ed. Englewood Cliffs, N.J.: Prentice-Hall, 1980.

5. Goldsmith, Raymond W. *The Flow of Capital in the Postwar Economy*. New York: National Bureau of Economic Research, 1965.

6. _____. *Financial Intermediaries in the American Economy since 1900*. Princeton, N.J.: Princeton University Press, 1958.

7. Gurley, John G., and Edward S. Shaw. "Financial Aspects of Economic Development." *American Economic Review*, September 1955.

8. _____. "Financial Intermediaries and the Savings-Investment Process." *Journal of Finance*, May 1956.

9. _____. "The Growth of Debt and Money in the United States, 1800–1950: A Suggested Interpretation." *Review of Economics and Statistics*, August 1957.

10. _____. *Money in a Theory of Finance*. Washington, D.C.: The Brookings Institution, 1960.

11. Haywood, Charles F. "Production of Consumer Financial Services." *Public Regulation of Financial Services, Costs, and Benefits to Consumers*, phase I, interim report. Cambridge, Mass.: ABT Associates, 1977, vol. I, NSF/RANN Grant NSF-C76-18548.

12. Kaufman, George G. *Money, the Financial System, and the Economy*. Boston: Houghton Mifflin, 1981.

13. Kuznets, Simon. *Capital in the American Economy: Its Formation and Financing*. Princeton, N.J.: Princeton University Press, 1961.

14. Polakoff, Murray E., et al. *Financial Institutions and Markets*. 2d ed. Boston: Houghton Mifflin, 1981.

15. Van Horne, James C. *Financial Market Rates and Flows*. Englewood Cliffs, N.J.: Prentice-Hall, 1978.

2. *Flow-of-Funds Analysis of the Borrowing and Lending Behavior of Financial Institutions*

Ｉｎ THIS CHAPTER we examine the kinds of financial assets issued and acquired by the major types of financial institutions. We wish to trace the flow of savings through financial institutions into the hands of borrowers. This funds flow through the financial marketplace, as we saw in the last chapter, gives rise to increased investment spending and to the creation of financial claims. Our principal goal in this chapter is to examine in some detail one of the main sources of data on financial transactions in the U.S. economy. Developed during the 1950s, the *Flow of Funds Accounts*, published quarterly by the Federal Reserve Board, provide a wealth of information on the behavior of financial institutions and other sectors of the economy.

CONSTRUCTION OF THE *FLOW OF FUNDS ACCOUNTS*

The steps in preparing the Federal Reserve's *Flow of Funds Accounts* are relatively simple. First, the economy is separated into groups of decision-making units, called *sectors*, which have similar financial characteristics. Second, balance sheets are prepared for each sector for the beginning and end of the period examined. Third, a sources-and-uses-of-funds statement is constructed for each sector of the economy from the beginning and ending balance sheets. Finally, the statements of sector sources and uses of funds are merged into a flow-of-funds matrix representing all units in the economy.

Sectors in the *Flow of Funds Accounts*

The major sectors of the economy represented in the *Flow of Funds Accounts* include (1) households, (2) businesses, (3) state and local governments, (4) the U.S. government, (5) federally sponsored credit agencies, (6) monetary authorities, (7) commercial banks, (8) private nonbank financial institutions, and (9) the rest of the world (i.e., the international sector). In addition, the Federal Reserve System provides data on the assets and liabilities outstanding for major groups of financial institutions as well as for other sectors.

Balance Sheets in Flow-of-Funds Construction

After an appropriate number of sectors is selected, *balance sheets* are constructed for each sector of the economy. These financial statements show the combined assets, liabilities, and net worth of all individuals or institutions in a particular sector on a given date. Indeed, for each economic unit and for each sector of the economy the basic balance sheet identity must hold

$$\text{Total assets} = \text{Total liabilities} + \text{Net worth} \qquad (2\text{--}1)$$

The left-hand, or asset side, of each sector's balance sheet contains financial assets (i.e., money and near-money assets) and real assets (such as automobiles, buildings, equipment, and homes). The right-hand side of the balance sheet contains liabilities and net worth. Thus the balance-sheet identity shown above may also be written:

$$\text{Financial assets} + \text{Real assets} = \text{Total liabilities} + \text{Net worth} \qquad (2\text{--}2)$$

For the economy as a whole the total of all liabilities must equal the sum of all financial assets. This holds because each liability (IOU) incurred by some unit in the economy must be matched by a financial asset (claim) held by some other unit, indicating that a loan has been made. Another way of expressing the same idea is to note that the volume of lending in the entire economy must always match the volume of borrowing that occurs.

Similarly, the value of real assets held by all units in the economy must match the total volume of net worth. As we will soon see, the net worth account on any balance sheet represents *accumulated savings*. In contrast, real assets—buildings, equipment, vehicles, homes, etc.—are built up through *investment*. Thus to state that for the entire economy the value of real assets held must equal the volume of net worth is equivalent to saying that the volume of accumulated savings must equal the volume of accumulated investment. This follows because saving and investment are merely different aspects of the same phenomenon—the transfer of resources from the production of consumer goods to the production of capital (investment) goods. When households and other economic units consume less and save more, this action enables producers to transfer labor, equipment, and other resources from turning out consumer goods to producing capital goods. In the long run, society is made wealthier because its productive capacity is increased.

The above equalities for financial assets and liabilities, real assets, and net worth hold only at the level of the whole economy, however. For any single business firm, household, unit of government, or, indeed, even for any one sector of the economy these equalities need not be true. For example, there is no particular reason why an individual business or household will hold financial assets exactly equal to its liabilities (debts) or hold accumulated real assets equal in value to its net worth. The only fundamental equality which must hold for all units and all sectors in the economy is the balance-sheet identity: total assets (financial plus real) must equal total liabilities plus net worth. (See Figure 2–1 for a summary of the relationships which exist between assets, liabilities, and net worth for individual units or sectors and for the economy as a whole.) These interrelationships between components of the balance sheet are reflected in the framework and structure of the Federal Reserve's *Flow of Funds Accounts.*

Constructing Statements of Sector Sources and Uses of Funds

After balance sheets are constructed for each sector of the economy, *sources-and-uses-of-funds statements* can be prepared. We note here that any balance sheet reflects *stocks* held of certain items—assets, liabilities, and net worth—on a given date. However, we must transform these stocks into *flows* in order to trace the flow of funds within the financial system. In simple terms, *a sources-and-uses-of-funds statement is a statement of financial flows covering a designated period of time.*

How can we transform balance sheets containing stocks into sources-and-uses-of-funds statements reflecting financial flows? The answer is, we merely need to calculate the *difference* in dollar amounts for each item

---

Figure 2–1   Fundamental Relationships for Units, Sectors, and the Financial System as a Whole

Relationships Applying to an Individual Unit or Sector of the Economy	*Relationships Applying to the Entire Financial System and Economy*
1. Financial assets + Real assets = Liabilities + Net worth	1. Financial assets + Real assets = Liabilities + Net Worth
2. Change in financial assets (lending) + Change in real assets (net investment) = Change in liabilities (borrowing) + Change in net worth (saving)	2. Change in financial assets (lending) + Change in real assets (net investment) = Change in liabilities (borrowing) + Change in net worth (saving)
3. Financial assets $\gtreqless$ Liabilities	3. Financial assets = Liabilities
4. Change in financial assets (lending) $\gtreqless$ Change in liabilities (borrowing)	4. Change in financial assets (lending) = Change in liabilities (borrowing)
5. Real assets $\gtreqless$ Net worth	5. Real assets = Net worth
6. Change in real assets (net investment) $\gtreqless$ Change in net worth (saving)	6. Change in real assets (net investment) = Change in net worth (saving)

shown on the balance sheets as of the beginning and end of the period under study. Thus if we know that the household sector held financial assets of $200 million at the beginning of the year (on its initial balance sheet) and $300 million at year's end (on its terminal balance sheet), then the difference of $100 million represents a net flow of $100 million into household sector holdings of financial assets during the year.

It is important to point out here that when an asset item *increases* between the beginning (initial) and ending (terminal) balance sheets, this represents a *use of funds*. Conversely, a *decrease* in holdings of certain assets between the initial and terminal balance sheets would be a *source of funds*. When a liability or net worth item *increases* in amount between two balance sheets it becomes a *source of funds*. Obviously, then, a decrease in any liability or net worth item would represent a *use of funds*.

Total uses of funds must always equal total sources of funds. As Figure 2–2 reflects, on a sources-and-uses-of-funds statement the sum total of all changes in assets (i.e., total uses) must be exactly matched by the sum total of all changes in liabilities and in net worth (i.e., total sources). Of course, to derive a sources-and-uses-of-funds statement for each sector of the economy we must *sum* the sources and uses of funds for each unit in that sector.

We may define any changes in financial assets as *net lending*; and changes in real assets as *net investment*.[1] Changes in liabilities represent *net borrowing*, while changes in net worth reflect *net saving*. In addition to borrowing or saving, a sector or economic unit can raise funds by selling financial assets (including the spending down of money balances) or by selling real assets. Principal uses of funds include purchasing financial assets or paying off any outstanding debt. The foregoing considerations suggest an alternative way of picturing a sources-and-uses-of-funds statement. This approach to such a statement is depicted in Figure 2–3.

One of the most important components of a sources-and-uses-of-funds statement is *saving*. As suggested in Figure 2–3, current saving by a unit or sector of the economy is captured by the current net change in the unit's or

---

[1]Frequently in discussions of funds-flow analysis, *money* is separated from other financial assets due to its unique properties as a perfectly liquid medium of exchange. Viewed in this context, a rise in money holdings would be defined as hoarding, while a decline in money holdings would be labeled dishoarding. The hoarding of money reduces the supply of loanable funds available for lending and investing, while dishoarding expands the quantity of loanable funds. In economic systems today it is becoming increasingly difficult to segregate money from other financial assets. For example, some money balances used to carry out transactions (such as NOW accounts and share drafts) bear interest. Moreover, virtually all forms of money in use today are the debt (liabilities) of some financial institution or governmental unit and are matched by financial assets held somewhere within the financial system. Accordingly, in the discussion that follows, we include money among holdings of financial assets.

Figure 2–2   Statement Containing the Sources and Uses of Funds for a Sector of the Economy

Uses of Funds	Sources of Funds
Net change in financial assets +	Net change in liabilities +
Net change in real assets	Net change in net worth
Total uses of funds	Total sources of funds

Note: The entries shown above assume that each change is *positive*. If any of the changes shown in the table are *negative* in amount, then an item normally listed under uses of funds in effect becomes a source of funds, while a source item would then become a use-of-funds item. For example, a positive net change in financial assets represents a use of funds by a unit or sector. However, if the net change in financial assets is *negative* for any given time period (i.e., holdings of financial assets decline), this would represent a source of funds for the unit or sector experiencing the decline. Similarly, a positive net change in liabilities is a source of funds, but a negative net change in liabilities represents repayment of debt and would then be a use of funds.

sector's net worth (equity) account. (The total amount of savings accumulated by a unit or sector in the current period and all prior periods, therefore, would be shown on the latest balance sheet as total net worth.) Because of the fundamental balance-sheet identity discussed earlier, it follows that:

$$
\begin{aligned}
\text{Current saving} \;=\; & \text{Net change in net worth} && (2\text{–}3)\\
=\; & \text{Net change in total assets}\\
& -\;\text{Net change in total liabilities}\\
=\; & [\text{Net change in financial assets}\\
& +\;\text{Net change in real assets}]\\
& -\;\text{Net change in total liabilities}\\
=\; & \text{Net lending} + \text{Net investment}\\
& -\;\text{Net borrowing}
\end{aligned}
$$

We usually think of saving as a residual quantity. It is the spread between a unit's or sector's receipts and its expenditures. When saving occurs, total assets may rise as a unit or sector acquires stocks, bonds, notes, and other assets. Alternatively, the unit may pay off some of its IOUs, resulting in a decline in outstanding obligations. Some units will use their

Figure 2–3   An Alternative View of a Sources-and-Uses-of-Funds Statement

Uses of Funds	Sources of Funds
Net lending (i.e., net change in financial assets)	Net borrowing (i.e., net change in liabilities)
Net investment (i.e., net change in real assets)	Net savings (i.e., net change in net worth)
Total uses of funds (i.e., net change in total assets)	Total sources of funds (i.e., net change in total liabilities and net worth)

savings to simultaneously acquire assets and retire debt. Either way, current saving must match the current net change in net worth.

Combining Sources-and-Uses-of-Funds Statements in a Flow-of-Funds Matrix

When the economy has been divided into sectors and sources-and-uses-of-funds statements constructed for each sector, we may bring these source-use statements together into a flow-of-funds matrix applying to the whole economic system. Changes in the assets, liabilities, and net worth of each sector will be represented in this matrix. It will show the total amount of saving and investment, the total volume of lending and borrowing, and the total amount of money issued in the economy over a given time (usually a quarter or a year).

An Example of Flow-of-Funds Construction

To more fully understand the method by which the flow-of-funds accounts are constructed, we present a simplified example. Suppose that we wish to construct a flow-of-funds matrix reflecting financial flows in the economy during the year 1983. Because we wish to construct the flow-of-funds accounts for the entire year, we need to prepare balance sheets for the beginning and end of the year for each sector into which the economy is divided.

An example of the balance sheets we might construct for the business sector is shown in Table 2–1. These financial statements show that the total assets of the nonfinancial business sector[2] were $655 billion at year-end 1982, but increased to $900 billion by year-end 1983. This growth in total assets was led by an increase in real assets (mainly buildings, equipment, and inventories) from $400 billion to $600 billion. At the same time, the business sector's net worth account, reflecting principally saving in the form of retained earnings, rose from $340 billion at year-end 1982 to $500 billion at year-end 1983. Liabilities outstanding rose from $315 to $400 billion, indicating that current saving (the change in net worth) provided most of the funds for the business sector's growth in total assets, but additional borrowings (external financing) also provided a substantial portion of the funds needed to support the purchase of assets during 1983. These changes in assets and liabilities for the nonfinancial business sector between year-end 1982 and year-end 1983 are captured in the sources-and-uses-of-funds statement shown at the bottom of Table 2–1.

We would need to construct similar balance sheets and sources-and-uses-of-funds statements for the remaining sectors of the economy and en-

---

[2]Nonfinancial businesses would be all private enterprises except financial institutions.

Table 2-1 An Example: Beginning and Ending Balance Sheets and a Sources-and-Uses-of-Funds Statement for the Nonfinancial Business Sector: 1983 ($ billions)

Nonfinancial Business Sector Balance Sheet
December 31, 1982

Assets		*Liabilities and Net Worth*	
Financial assets	$255	Liabilities	$315
Real assets	400	Net worth	340
Total assets	$655	Total liabilties and net worth	$655

Nonfinancial Business Sector Balance Sheet
December 31, 1983

Assets		*Liabilities and Net Worth*	
Financial assets	$300	Liabilities	$400
Real assets	600	Net worth	500
Total assets	$900	Total liabilities and net worth	$900

Nonfinancial Business Sector
Sources-and-Uses-of-Funds Statement
1983

Uses of Funds		*Sources of Funds*	
Change in financial assets	$ 45	Change in liabilities	$ 85
Change in real assets	200	Change in net worth	160
Total uses of funds	$245	Total sources of funds	$245

ter each of these in a flow-of-funds matrix. Let us suppose that our economic system contains just four sectors:

1. Households, including all individuals and families in the economic system,
2. Financial institutions, including banks and other financial intermediaries,
3. Nonfinancial business firms, including proprietorships, partnerships, and corporations but excluding financial institutions,
4. State, local, and federal governments all combined into a single sector.

We will assume there are no external transactions with the rest of the world. Of course, we have already constructed beginning and ending balance sheets and a sources-and-uses-of-funds statement for the nonfinancial business sector in Table 2–1. We will assume that the same has been done for the remaining sectors and that their sources-and-uses statements are as given in Table 2–2.

The contents of all four sector sources-and-uses-of-funds statements are summarized in the economy-wide flow-of-funds matrix shown in Table 2–3. This matrix clearly illustrates several of the fundamental relation-

Table 2–2   Sources-and-Uses-of-Funds Statements for the Household, Government, and Financial Institutions' Sectors, 1983 ($ billions)

Household Sector
Sources-and-Uses-of-Funds Statement

Uses of Funds		*Sources of Funds*	
Change in financial assets	$175	Change in liabilities	$120
Change in real assets	190	Change in net worth	245
Total uses of funds	$365	Total sources of funds	$365

Government Sector
Sources-and-Uses-of-Funds Statement

Uses of Funds		*Sources of Funds*	
Change in financial assets	$ 5	Change in liabilities	$ 25
Change in real assets	—	Change in net worth	−20
Total uses of funds	$ 5	Total sources of funds	$ 5

Financial Institutions' Sector
Sources-and-Uses-of-Funds Statement

Uses of Funds		*Sources of Funds*	
Change in financial assets	$ 25	Change in liabilities	$ 20
Change in real assets	10	Change in net worth	15
Total uses of funds	$ 35	Total sources of funds	$ 35

ships between lending and borrowing and saving and investment discussed earlier. We note, for example, that current saving (i.e., the net change in net worth) in the economy totaled $400 billion in 1983, an amount which exactly matched the volume of current net real investment. At the same time, current lending or, as it is sometimes called, financial investment (i.e., the net change in financial assets) amounted to $250 billion in 1983, which was exactly equal to current borrowing (i.e., the net change in liabilities). Within each sector, however, there are marked differences in saving, investment, lending, and borrowing.

Savings-Surplus and Savings-Deficit Sectors

Some sectors of the economy consistently year-in and year-out are *savings-deficit* sectors—their current volume of saving is less than the amount of their net investment in real assets. As a result, savings-deficit sectors must borrow from other sectors more than they lend to them. In Table 2–3 this description clearly fits the nonfinancial business sector. In 1983 this sector's net investment in real assets amounted to $200 billion, while its current savings were only $160 billion. Consequently, nonfinancial businesses were forced to borrow $85 billion in the current period, significantly more than the $45 billion they loaned to other sectors through

Table 2–3   Example of a Flow-of-Funds Matrix ($ billions)

Asset, Liability, and Net Worth Items	Sectors of the Economy									
	Households		Nonfinancial Business Firms		Financial Institutions		Fed., State, and Local Gov.		Total	
	Uses	Sources	Uses	Sources	Uses	Sources	Uses	Sources	Uses	Sources
Net change in net worth (current saving)		$245		$160		$20		–$20		$400
Net change in real assets (current real investment)	$190		$200		$10				$400	
Net change in financial assets (current lending or financial investment)	$175		$45		$25		$5		$250	
Net change in liabilities (current borrowing)		$120		$85		$15		$25		$250
Totals	$365	$365	$245	$245	$35	$35	$5	$5	$650	$650

Note: Net change in net worth = Current volume of savings = $400 billion.
  Net change in real assets = Current volume of real investment = $400 billion.
  Net change in financial assets = Current volume of lending = $250 billion.
  Net change in liabilities = Current volume of borrowing = $250 billion.

purchases of financial assets. State and local governments, along with the federal government sector, form another savings-deficit sector, on balance. This was especially evident as the 1980s began due to record budget deficits at the federal level, forcing the U.S. Treasury to borrow several billion dollars weekly in the financial markets. In Table 2–3 we show the government sector borrowing net $25 billion, while lending (net) just $5 billion.

In contrast to governments and business firms, other sectors of the economy typically are savings surplus sectors. This means that the volume of their savings exceeds their net investment in real assets and, therefore, their current lending exceeds their current borrowing. In our example the household sector provides a surplus of savings with current savings of $245 billion and current net real investment of just $190 billion. With excess savings, the household sector was able to acquire $175 in financial assets, compared to current borrowing of only $120 billion.

The financial institutions' sector, whose principal function is to attract the public's savings and to make loans, also normally reports a surplus of savings. As shown in Table 2–3, financial institutions reported net current savings of $20 billion and net real investment of $10 billion. Their current lending of $25 billion exceeded current borrowing of $15 billion. Among its many activities the financial institutions' sector is the principal source of money for all other units and sectors. In our example, money supplied to nonfinancial sectors would be included in the change-in-financial-assets account of each nonfinancial sector but would show up in the change-in-liabilities account of the financial institutions' sector.

WHERE FLOW-OF-FUNDS INFORMATION COMES FROM

In each issue of the *Federal Reserve Bulletin*, the Board of Governors of the Federal Reserve System presents flow-of-funds data for the entire U.S. economy. In addition, complete flows of funds for all sectors are reported quarterly by the Federal Reserve Board on both a seasonally adjusted and unadjusted basis. Annually, the Federal Reserve revises historical flow-of-funds data, introducing new sources of information and refining current figures as well as those for previous years.[3] In compiling flow-of-funds data, the Federal Reserve draws upon a wide variety of government and private industry sources, including the national income and product accounts of the U.S. Department of Commerce; Census Bureau surveys; Federal Trade Commission financial reports from manufacturing, mining, and trade corporations; monthly statements of receipts and expenditures by the U.S. Treasury Department; business tax returns filed with the Internal Revenue Service; statistical reports from the Securities and Exchange Commission and the federal bank regulatory agencies; and regular surveys carried out by such industry trade associations as the National Association of Mutual Savings Banks, the Institute of Life Insurance, the National Association of REITs, and the Investment Company Institute.[4]

Examples of the flow-of-funds reports provided regularly by the Federal Reserve Board are shown in Tables 2–4 and 2–5. To illustrate the kinds of important information contained in this data, we note in Table 2–4 that the net amount borrowed in the financial markets by all sectors of the U.S. economy amounted to $472.4 billion during 1982, of which financial institutions accounted for $64.3 billion. Domestic nonfinancial sectors (including nonfinancial businesses, households, and governments) raised $408.1 billion through borrowing and issuing stock. Now, the total of $408.1 billion raised by domestic nonfinancial units should be exactly equal to the total funds advanced to these units by lenders in the economy. And, as Table 2–5 reveals, total funds advanced through the credit markets to domestic nonfinancial sectors did total $408.1 billion in 1982.

In addition to borrowing funds, corporations can issue stock to secure the capital they need for growth and expansion. The bottom panel of Table 2–4 indicates that $26.7 billion in net equity shares were issued by cor-

---

[3]Examples of recent revisions in data are found in references [3], [4], and [5]. Historical data on a quarterly basis is available on computer tape from the Federal Reserve Board.

[4]For a more complete listing of the sources of financial data used in constructing the flow-of-funds accounts, see reference 2, table 8.

Table 2-4 Summary of Funds Raised in Credit Markets: ($ billions)

SEASONALLY ADJUSTED ANNUAL RATES *SEASONALLY ADJUSTED ANNUAL RATES*

	1978	1979	1980	1981	1982	1981 III	1981 IV	1982 I	1982 II	1982 III	1982 IV		
							Net Credit Market Borrowing by Nonfinancial Sectors						
1	368.6	388.8	355.0	391.1	408.1	386.5	372.7	344.9	385.2	473.0	429.1	Total net borrowing by domestic nonfinancial sectors	1
2	53.7	37.4	79.2	87.4	161.3	62.7	123.0	99.7	98.8	229.0	217.5	U.S. Government	2
3	55.1	38.8	79.8	87.8	162.1	63.1	123.4	102.2	99.1	229.3	218.0	Treasury issues	3
4	−1.4	−1.4	−.6	−.5	−.9	−.4	−.4	−2.5	−.2	−.3	−.5	Agency issues + mortgages	4
												Private domestic	
5	314.9	351.5	275.8	303.7	246.8	323.8	249.7	245.2	286.4	244.0	211.6	nonfinancial sectors	5
6	198.7	216.0	204.1	175.0	168.3	156.9	150.0	151.7	163.2	148.1	210.3	Debt capital instruments	6
7	28.4	29.8	35.9	32.9	60.7	26.3	35.0	39.9	66.3	51.7	85.1	Tax-exempt obligations	7
8	20.1	22.5	33.2	23.9	22.4	19.5	26.4	10.2	16.7	27.3	35.5	Corporate bonds	8
9	150.2	163.7	135.1	118.3	85.2	111.1	88.6	101.7	80.3	69.1	89.7	Mortgages	9
10	112.1	120.1	96.7	78.6	55.6	72.5	51.6	64.9	44.7	52.0	60.9	Home mortgages	10
11	9.2	7.8	8.8	4.6	7.9	4.1	4.2	9.8	7.3	3.2	11.5	Multi-family resid.	11
12	21.7	23.9	20.2	25.3	16.3	23.7	22.6	19.7	24.7	9.3	11.4	Commercial	12
13	7.2	11.8	9.3	9.8	5.3	10.8	10.2	7.3	3.6	4.6	5.9	Farm	13
14	116.2	135.5	71.7	128.8	78.5	166.8	99.6	93.5	123.1	95.9	1.3	Other debt instruments	14
15	48.8	45.4	4.9	25.3	14.4	34.2	8.3	5.5	23.4	6.0	22.8	Consumer credit	15
16	37.1	49.2	35.4	51.1	53.7	66.0	43.2	67.5	86.7	64.2	−3.4	Bank loans n.e.c.	16
17	5.2	11.1	6.6	19.2	−1.3	32.9	22.3	12.2	−3.4	−1.8	−12.3	Open-market paper	17
18	25.1	29.7	24.9	33.1	11.6	33.8	25.9	8.3	16.4	27.6	−5.8	Other	18
19	314.8	343.6	288.7	292.3	250.5	299.2	226.7	239.9	291.4	244.0	226.6	By borrowing sector:	19
20	19.1	20.2	27.3	22.3	47.2	14.8	24.3	27.2	55.8	35.9	70.0	State + local governments	20
21	169.3	176.5	117.5	120.4	85.1	128.1	71.1	78.8	88.3	76.4	96.8	Households	21
22	126.4	154.8	131.0	161.0	114.5	181.0	153.7	139.2	142.3	131.8	44.8	Nonfinancial business	22
23	14.6	21.4	14.4	16.4	9.3	16.1	9.6	5.6	11.3	12.3	8.1	Farm	23
24	32.4	34.4	33.8	40.5	28.2	40.1	38.5	30.5	39.3	17.3	25.7	Nonfarm noncorporate	24
25	79.4	99.0	82.8	104.1	77.0	124.8	105.5	103.1	91.7	102.1	11.0	Corporate	25
26	33.8	20.2	27.2	27.3	16.2	20.3	20.8	16.5	18.3	8.7	21.0	Fgn. net borrowing in U.S.	26
27	4.2	3.9	.8	5.5	6.5	3.9	11.3	3.0	1.4	12.8	8.9	Bonds	27
28	19.1	2.3	11.5	3.7	−5.0	8.3	−3.8	−5.6	4.8	−14.2	−5.1	Bank loans n.e.c.	28
29	6.6	11.2	10.1	13.9	9.5	4.2	10.1	16.4	8.5	.5	12.4	Open-market paper	29
30	3.9	2.9	4.7	4.3	5.2	4.0	3.2	2.8	3.7	9.6	4.9	U.S. Government loans	30
31	402.3	409.1	382.2	418.4	424.2	406.8	393.5	361.5	403.5	481.7	450.2	Total domestic plus foreign	31
							Net Credit Market Borrowing by Financial Sectors						
												Total net borrowing	
1	75.0	80.7	61.3	80.7	64.3	123.5	27.6	68.6	118.1	43.4	27.0	by financial sectors	1
2	36.7	47.3	43.6	45.1	60.6	65.4	30.1	45.3	73.3	69.5	54.1	U.S. Government-related	2
3	23.1	24.3	24.4	30.1	13.2	53.0	13.5	9.1	33.8	18.4	−8.4	Sponsored credit ag. sec.	3
4	13.6	23.1	19.2	15.0	47.4	12.3	16.6	36.2	39.5	51.1	62.6	Mortgage pool securities	4
5	—	—	—	—	—	—	—	—	—	.	—		5
6	38.3	33.4	17.7	35.6	3.7	58.1	−2.5	23.2	44.9	−26.1	−27.6	Private financial sectors	6
7	7.5	7.8	7.1	−.8	2.4	−3.3	4.1	−2.1	−4.7	8.4	8.1	Corporate bonds	7
8	.9	−1.2	−.9	−2.9	1.8	−3.9	−3.2	2.9	.8	3.2	.1	Mortgages	8
9	2.8	−.4	−.4	2.2	1.4	1.9	−.5	13.8	−2.1	2.2	−8.4	Bank loans n.e.c.	9
10	14.6	18.0	4.8	20.9	−2.7	38.1	−4.0	−5.3	37.2	−23.7	−18.8	Open-market paper	10
11	12.5	9.2	7.1	16.2	.8	25.2	1.2	14.0	13.5	−16.2	−8.1	Fed. Home Loan Bank loans	11
12	75.0	80.7	61.3	80.7	64.3	123.5	27.6	68.6	118.1	43.4	27.0	Total, by sector	12
13	23.1	24.3	24.4	30.1	13.2	53.0	13.5	9.1	33.8	18.4	−8.4	Sponsored credit agencies	13
14	13.6	23.1	19.2	15.0	47.4	12.3	16.6	36.2	39.5	51.1	62.6	Mortgage pools	14
15	40.8	36.6	24.9	44.1	25.4	63.2	7.3	41.9	59.5	3.2	−3.1	Private financial sectors	15
16	1.3	1.6	.5	.4	1.4	.1	1.0	.4	.8	1.5	2.6	Commercial banks	16

Table 2–4   (*concluded*)

SEASONALLY ADJUSTED ANNUAL RATES   *SEASONALLY ADJUSTED ANNUAL RATES*

	1978	1979	1980	1981	1982	1981 III	1981 IV	1982 I	1982 II	1982 III	1982 IV		
						Net Credit Market Borrowing by Financial Sectors							
17	7.2	6.5	6.9	8.3	.8	14.8	4.5	6.6	12.7	−15.7	−.4	Bank affiliates	17
18	14.3	11.4	6.6	13.1	−3.7	21.2	−7.4	20.8	12.4	−24.7	−23.1	Savings and loan assns.	18
19	18.1	16.6	6.3	14.1	5.7	21.9	.1	−4.2	19.4	13.3	−5.6	Finance companies	19
20	−1.4	−1.3	−2.2	.2	.1	.6	−.1	.1	.1	.1	.1	REITs	20
						Total Net Credit Market Borrowing, All Sectors, by Type							
1	477.4	489.7	443.5	499.1	488.5	530.3	421.1	430.0	521.6	525.1	477.2	Total net borrowing	1
2	90.5	84.8	122.9	132.6	222.0	128.2	153.2	145.1	172.2	298.6	271.8	U.S. Government securities	2
3	28.4	29.8	35.9	32.9	60.7	26.3	35.0	39.9	66.3	51.7	85.1	State + local obligations	3
4	31.8	34.2	41.1	28.5	31.4	20.1	41.8	11.1	13.3	48.6	52.4	Corporate + foreign bonds	4
5	151.0	162.4	134.0	115.2	86.8	107.1	85.3	104.5	81.0	72.2	89.7	Mortgages	5
6	48.8	45.4	4.9	25.3	14.4	34.2	8.3	5.5	23.4	6.0	22.8	Consumer credit	6
7	59.0	51.0	46.5	57.0	50.1	76.3	38.8	75.7	89.4	52.2	−16.9	Bank loans n.e.c.	7
8	26.4	40.3	21.6	54.0	5.5	75.2	28.4	23.3	42.4	−25.0	−18.7	Open-market paper	8
9	41.5	41.8	36.6	53.7	17.7	62.9	30.2	25.1	33.7	21.0	−9.0	Other loans	9
10	3.8	.6	−3.8	*	5.7	−7.5	−3.9	22.0	−28.8	42.1	−12.6	Memo: U.S. Govt. cash balance	10
						Totals net of changes in U.S. Govt. cash balances:							
11	364.8	388.2	358.8	391.1	402.4	394.0	376.6	322.9	414.0	430.9	441.7	Net borrowing by dom. nonfin.	11
12	49.9	36.8	83.0	87.4	155.6	70.2	126.9	77.7	127.7	186.8	230.1	By U.S. Government	12
						External Corporate Equity Funds Raised in U.S. Markets							
1	1.9	−3.8	22.1	−2.9	26.7	−20.9	−13.1	12.5	20.1	29.8	44.3	Total net share issues	1
2	−.1	.1	5.0	7.7	19.5	4.2	8.7	16.5	12.4	27.1	21.8	Mutual funds	2
3	1.9	−3.9	17.1	−10.6	7.2	−25.2	−21.7	−4.0	7.7	2.6	22.5	All other	3
4	−.1	−7.8	12.9	−11.5	3.7	−24.6	−23.0	−5.3	5.0	—	15.0	Nonfinancial corporations	4
5	2.5	3.2	2.1	.9	2.2	.8	1.2	2.1	2.3	2.2	2.3	Financial corporations	5
6	−.5	.8	2.1	*	1.3	−1.4	.1	−.9	.4	.4	5.3	Foreign shares purchased in U.S.	6

Note: IV/82 based on incomplete information.
Source: Board of Governors of the Federal Reserve System.

porations in the U.S. financial markets in 1982. And this figure for net new corporate stock issued matches exactly the amount of equity shares purchased net by financial institutions and other sectors of the economy in 1982, as shown in the bottom panel of Table 2–5.

We should note here that figures shown in the *Flow of Funds Accounts* do not always match so perfectly. Indeed, flow-of-funds data is really a series of estimated financial flows based upon partial data, so that small discrepancies often arise between funds demanded and funds supplied and in column totals. For this reason a *statistical discrepancy account* is included in most flow-of-funds tables, adding or subtracting the amount necessary to make account totals balance out. Percentagewise, the discrepancy figure is usually quite small.

Table 2–5 Direct and Indirect Sources of Funds to Credit Markets: ($ billions)

SEASONALLY ADJUSTED ANNUAL RATES   *SEASONALLY ADJUSTED ANNUAL RATES*

	1978	1979	1980	1981	1982	1981 III	1981 IV	1982 I	1982 II	1982 III	1982 IV		
1	368.6	388.8	355.0	391.1	408.1	386.5	372.7	344.9	385.2	473.0	429.1	Total funds advanced in credit markets to dom. nonfinan. sectors	1
												By Federal agencies and foreign	
2	101.9	74.6	95.8	95.9	115.7	89.3	97.0	65.3	118.8	152.8	125.8	Total net advances, by type	2
3	36.1	−6.3	15.7	17.2	23.9	−.3	37.3	−13.7	13.7	66.6	29.0	U.S. Government securities	3
4	25.7	35.8	31.7	23.4	59.9	23.8	27.2	40.1	54.7	65.8	78.8	Residential mortgages	4
5	12.5	9.2	7.1	16.2	.8	25.2	1.2	14.0	13.5	−16.2	−8.1	FHLB advances to S + L's	5
6	27.6	35.9	41.3	39.1	31.1	40.6	31.3	25.0	36.8	36.5	26.1	Other loans and securities	6
7	101.9	74.6	95.8	95.9	115.7	89.3	97.0	65.3	118.8	152.8	125.8	By type of lender:	7
8	17.1	19.0	23.7	24.2	18.9	20.5	21.8	10.3	17.7	22.1	25.6	U.S. Government	8
9	39.9	52.4	44.4	46.0	61.9	64.6	30.9	50.5	70.4	60.7	65.9	Spons. credit ag. + mtg. pools	9
10	7.0	7.7	4.5	9.2	9.8	17.7	26.5	−5.2	−7.5	39.0	12.8	Monetary authority	10
11	38.0	−4.6	23.2	16.6	25.1	−13.4	17.8	9.7	38.2	31.0	21.5	Foreign	11
												Agency and foreign borrowing not in line 1:	
12	36.7	47.3	43.6	45.1	60.6	65.4	30.1	45.3	73.3	69.5	54.1	Spons. credit ag. + mtg. pools	12
13	33.8	20.2	27.2	27.3	16.2	20.3	20.8	16.5	18.3	8.7	21.0	Foreign	13
												Private domestic funds advanced	
14	337.1	381.8	329.9	367.6	369.1	382.8	326.6	341.5	358.0	398.4	378.6	Total net advances	14
15	54.3	91.1	107.2	115.4	198.0	128.5	116.0	158.9	158.5	232.0	242.8	U.S. Government securities	15
16	28.4	29.8	35.9	32.9	60.7	26.3	35.0	39.9	66.3	51.7	85.1	State and local obligations	16
17	22.4	23.7	25.8	20.6	17.0	13.7	31.7	3.4	−3.3	30.3	37.6	Corporate and foreign bonds	17
18	95.5	92.0	73.7	59.7	3.6	52.6	28.5	34.4	−2.9	−10.7	−6.5	Residential mortgages	18
19	149.1	154.3	94.4	155.3	90.6	186.9	116.7	118.9	152.9	79.0	11.5	Other mortgages and loans	19
20	12.5	9.2	7.1	16.2	.8	25.2	1.2	14.0	13.5	−16.2	−8.1	Less: FHLB advances	20
												Private financial intermediation	
												Credit market funds advanced	
21	302.9	292.2	257.9	301.3	254.7	318.0	234.6	319.7	235.8	266.3	197.1	by private financial insts.	21
22	128.7	121.1	99.7	103.5	98.8	110.5	87.9	148.6	93.3	80.4	72.8	Commercial banking	22
23	73.6	55.5	54.1	24.6	24.2	16.6	−6.0	46.2	13.3	−2.0	39.5	Savings institutions	23
24	75.0	66.4	74.4	75.8	87.7	71.7	80.0	83.1	92.0	82.3	93.6	Insurance and pension funds	24
25	25.6	49.2	29.8	97.4	44.0	119.2	72.7	41.8	37.3	105.6	−8.8	Other finance	25
26	302.9	292.2	257.9	301.3	254.7	318.0	234.6	319.7	235.8	266.3	197.1	Sources of funds	26
27	141.1	42.5	167.8	211.2	161.9	216.4	204.2	196.7	120.0	208.3	122.7	Private domestic dep. + RP's	27
28	38.3	33.4	17.7	35.6	3.7	58.1	−2.5	23.2	44.9	−26.1	−27.2	Credit market borrowing	28
29	123.5	116.4	72.4	54.6	89.1	43.5	32.9	99.8	71.0	84.1	101.6	Other sources	29
30	6.3	25.6	−23.0	−8.8	−27.9	11.9	−45.6	−24.6	−11.8	−79.9	4.7	Foreign funds	30
31	6.8	.4	−2.6	−1.1	4.5	−1.2	−15.2	22.8	−32.6	22.5	5.4	Treasury balances	31
32	62.2	49.1	65.4	70.8	77.9	77.3	74.0	68.7	86.6	74.1	81.9	Insurance and pension res.	32
33	48.3	41.3	32.6	−6.4	34.6	−44.5	19.8	32.7	28.8	67.4	9.6	Other, net	33

Line:

1. Page 2, line 1.
6. Includes farm and commercial mortgages.
12. Credit market funds raised by Federally sponsored credit agencies + federally related mortgage pool securities.
14. Line 1 less line 2 plus lines 12 + 13. Also line 21 less line 28 plus line 34. Also sum of lines 29 and 48 less lines 41 and 47.
19. Includes farm and commercial mortgages.
27. Line 40 less line 41 and 47.
28. Excludes equity issues and investment company shares. Includes line 19.
30. Foreign deposits at commercial banks, bank borrowings from foreign branches, and liabilities of foreign banking offices to foreign affiliates, net of claims on foreign affiliates and deposits by foreign banks.
31. Demand deposits and note balances at commercial banks.
32. Excludes investment of these reserves in corporate equities.
33. Mainly retained earnings and net miscellaneous liabilities.

Table 2–5   (*concluded*)

	1978	1979	1980	1981	1982	1981 III	1981 IV	1982 I	1982 II	1982 III	1982 IV		
												Private domestic nonfinancial investors	
34	72.5	122.9	89.7	101.9	118.1	123.0	89.5	45.0	167.0	106.0	154.3	Direct lending in cr. markets	34
35	36.3	61.4	38.3	50.4	60.1	85.5	30.0	34.1	83.5	62.1	60.6	U.S. Government securities	35
36	3.6	9.4	12.6	20.3	47.5	17.7	17.8	22.0	61.6	37.1	69.3	State and local obligations	36
37	−2.9	10.2	9.3	−7.9	−11.7	−17.5	4.3	−17.0	−35.9	3.3	3.0	Corporate and foreign bonds	37
38	15.6	12.1	−3.4	3.5	−1.9	1.9	14.8	−14.1	29.8	−20.3	−2.9	Open-market paper	38
39	19.9	29.8	32.9	35.6	24.1	35.4	22.5	20.1	28.1	23.8	24.3	Other	39
40	152.3	151.9	179.2	221.0	167.3	217.5	229.2	189.3	127.5	212.7	139.6	Deposits and currency	40
41	9.3	7.9	10.3	9.5	8.3	4.4	22.1	.7	3.4	13.2	16.0	Currency	41
42	16.3	19.2	4.2	18.3	17.8	−11.0	31.1	38.2	−21.0	20.0	33.9	Checkable deposits	42
43	63.7	61.0	79.5	46.6	123.8	49.6	83.0	96.0	62.6	86.8	249.7	Small time + svgs. deposits	43
44	6.9	34.4	29.2	107.5	24.7	137.3	84.3	37.6	41.2	86.5	−66.4	Money market fund shares	44
45	46.6	21.2	48.3	36.3	1.8	54.2	−2.7	24.6	35.5	13.5	−66.4	Large time deposits	45
46	7.5	6.6	6.5	2.5	−6.1	−13.8	8.6	.3	1.7	1.6	−28.2	Security RP's	46
47	2.0	1.5	1.1	.3	−3.0	−3.2	2.8	−8.1	4.1	−8.8	.9	Foreign deposits	47
												Total of credit mkt. instru-	
48	224.9	274.8	269.0	322.8	285.4	340.5	318.7	234.3	294.6	318.7	293.9	ments, deposits, and currency	48
49	25.3	18.2	25.1	22.9	27.3	22.0	24.6	18.1	29.4	31.7	27.9	Public holdings as % of total	49
50	89.9	76.5	78.2	82.0	69.0	83.1	71.8	93.6	65.9	66.8	52.1	Pvt. finan. intermediation (%)	50
51	44.3	21.0	.2	7.8	−2.8	−1.5	−27.8	−14.8	26.5	−48.9	26.1	Total foreign funds	51

					Corporate Equities not Included above								
1	1.9	−3.8	22.1	−2.9	26.7	−20.9	−13.1	12.5	20.1	29.8	44.3	Total net issues	1
2	−.1	.1	5.0	7.7	19.5	4.2	8.7	16.5	12.4	27.1	21.8	Mutual fund shares	2
3	1.9	−3.9	17.1	−10.6	7.2	−25.2	−21.7	−4.0	7.7	2.6	22.5	Other equities	3
4	4.6	10.4	14.6	22.9	24.5	29.4	11.7	20.3	21.2	36.3	20.1	Acq. by financial institutions	4
5	−2.7	−14.2	7.5	−25.8	2.2	−50.4	−24.7	−7.8	−1.1	−6.5	24.3	Other net purchases	5

Note: IV/82 based on incomplete information.
Line:
   34. Line 14 less line 21 plus line 28.
35–39. Lines 15–19 less amounts acquired by private finance plus amounts borrowed by private finance. Line 39 includes mortgages.
   48. Lines 34 + 40. Also line 14 less line 29 plus lines 41 and 47.
   50. Line 21/line 14.
   51. Line 11 plus line 30.
Corporate Equities Line: 1 and 3. Includes issues by financial institutions.
Source: Board of Governors of the Federal Reserve System.

As Table 2–4 shows, the U.S. Treasury in 1982 borrowed net $162.1 billion, which was partially offset by net repayments and redemptions of securities by other U.S. government agencies amounting to $0.9 billion. In the private domestic nonfinancial sector, corporations borrowed far more money than they raised by issuing stock. Line 25 in the top panel of Table 2–4 reveals that corporate debt increased net $77 billion, while the bottom panel of Table 2–4 shows that nonfinancial corporations (line 4) issued $3.7 billion in net new stock. What did corporations do with the funds raised by debt and equity capital? A check of data provided by the *National Income Accounts*, compiled quarterly by the U.S. Department of

Commerce, shows that nonfinancial corporations invested just over $258 billion in new plant and equipment. Another $96 billion was invested in new residential structures to provide housing for individuals and families. Thus the roughly $80 billion in funds supplied by debt and equity securities issued by domestic nonfinancial corporations covered less than one fourth of the more than $350 billion invested by these companies in the U.S. economy during 1982. The remainder of the investment funds needed by American corporations in that year—about $270 billion—was supplied by retained earnings and depreciation reserves. These statistics remind us that borrowing in the financial markets (including loans made by financial institutions) is a *residual* source of funds for most businesses. The primary source of funds in most businesses is internal.

The *Flow of Funds Accounts* tell us the *types of securities* used to raise funds over an annual or quarterly period, *who issued* those securities, and *who acquired* the securities issued (i.e., loaned the funds). For example, Table 2–4 shows that state and local governments had net borrowings of $47.2 billion in 1982 (line 20 in top portion of the table). Who purchased these state and local government debt obligations? In most years commercial banks are the heaviest purchasers of municipal bonds; however, in 1982, as Table 2–5 clearly shows (line 36), domestic nonfinancial investors (in this case predominantly households) acquired net $47.5 billion in state and local government securities—$300 million more than were newly issued. The additional municipal securities purchased over and above new issues were acquired in the secondary market from other investors.

The flow-of-funds tables show quite clearly the critical role of financial intermediaries in providing funds (credit) to other sectors of the economy. The degree of intermediation (i.e., indirect finance) in the nation's financial markets has risen significantly during the postwar era as businesses, households, and governmental borrowers have turned increasingly to financial intermediaries for credit through the issue of mortgages, installment loans, notes, and bonds. At the same time businesses, households, and governments have found deposits and other financial claims offered by intermediaries an increasingly attractive investment alternative to purchasing stocks, bonds, and other securities in the open market. Holdings of credit market instruments by financial intermediaries represented slightly less than 70 percent of all such instruments in the early 1950s but averaged around 80 percent during the late 1970s and early 1980s (see Table 2–5, line 50). In 1982, however, with the economy in a recession and high interest rates available on securities purchased directly in the open market, many nonfinancial investors bypassed financial intermediaries and purchased securities through brokers and dealers (semidirect finance) or directly from security issuers (direct finance). The result was a decline to 69 percent in the share of credit market funds provided by financial intermediaries in 1982.

The potential uses of flow-of-funds data are numerous. The financial analyst can use the information to determine which sectors of the economy acquire certain kinds of financial assets and which sectors issue those assets. Movements of funds among the various sectors may be observed and some indication of the causes of major changes in interest rates determined. For example, by comparing the volume of securities issued in various periods of time, we can estimate trends in the demand for credit from various sectors and for the whole economy. If demand appears to be putting pressure on savings flows, interest rates would be expected to rise. When demand slackens, interest rates will tend to fall, other things being equal. Patterns in the demand and supply of various financial assets may be compared over time and estimates made for future periods. In some recent applications, econometric models have been constructed which attempt to explain security prices, interest rates, and the demand for and supply of credit on the basis of flow-of-funds data.

Assets and Liabilities of Various Sectors of the Economy

As we noted earlier, the *Flow of Funds Accounts* trace financial *flows* between points in time. The balance sheets of individual economic units and sectors from which the flow-of-funds data are derived, however, measure *stocks* of assets, liabilities, and net worth at a single point in time. Of course, these stocks reflect the sum of current and past flows. For example, accumulated savings (which are captured by total net worth on a unit's or sector's balance sheet) are a stock, whereas the amount of saving in the current period clearly is a flow of funds passing through the financial markets into the hands of borrowers. Similarly, the amount of total liabilities appearing on a sector's or unit's balance sheet is a stock, but borrowing in the current period is a flow of funds from lenders to borrowers.

Because of the interrelationships between stocks and flows, we can reconstruct the balance sheets—assets, liabilities, and net worth—of major sectors in the economy from flow-of-funds data. A recent example of such a reconstruction is shown in Table 2–6, which contains the financial assets and liabilities of the household sector. We note that households held a huge volume of financial assets at year-end 1982—more than $5 trillion (line 1). These assets far exceeded the debts (liabilities) of this sector, which totaled slightly more than $1.7 trillion in 1982 (line 25). The dominant financial asset held by households in 1982 was deposits held in financial intermediaries—over $1.9 trillion (line 3). Corporate stocks (equities) were in second place, with $1.3 trillion in household portfolios (line 18). The principal liability of this sector is home mortgages, amounting to almost $1.1 trillion (line 27). Installment debt taken on by households totaled $343 billion in 1982 (line 29). A check of previous years shows that both household mortgage and installment debt have risen rapidly, reflecting the combined effects of inflation, rising energy costs, and a greater

Table 2–6 Financial Assets and Liabilities for the Household Sector: ($ billions)

YEAR-END OUTSTANDINGS   *YEAR-END OUTSTANDINGS*

Households, Personal Trusts, and Nonprofit Organizations

#	1971	1972	1973	1974	1975	1976	1977	1978	1979	1980	1981	1982		#
1	2151.4	2388.4	2301.9	2206.3	2564.3	2905.3	3079.8	3373.1	3860.8	4555.0	4850.8	5385.1	Total Financial assets	1
2	872.4	972.9	1088.3	1199.3	1326.5	1477.9	1636.9	1826.1	2061.6	2294.7	2565.3	2795.9	Dep. + cr. instr. (1)	2
3	624.3	710.8	788.4	853.7	945.3	1068.5	1195.5	1325.9	1459.8	1625.3	1824.2	1986.3	Deposits	3
4	130.3	142.6	156.5	163.8	170.7	186.4	205.6	228.8	250.9	261.8	287.6	313.5	Checkable deposits + curr.	4
5	473.9	541.9	579.7	614.2	710.6	829.1	924.1	988.0	1049.7	1129.4	1176.0	1300.3	Small time + svgs. dep.	5
6	—	—	—	2.4	3.7	3.7	3.9	10.8	45.2	74.4	181.9	206.6	Money market fund shares	6
7	20.1	26.3	52.1	73.4	60.4	49.3	61.9	98.3	113.9	159.6	178.7	165.8	Large time deposits	7
8	248.1	262.0	299.9	245.5	381.2	409.4	441.4	500.2	601.8	669.4	741.1	809.6	Credit market instruments	8
9	93.5	93.9	112.8	134.1	152.9	163.0	182.2	211.7	264.7	293.1	329.9	344.4	U.S. Govt. securities	9
10	76.5	79.6	96.6	113.3	133.2	139.9	153.3	175.3	206.3	225.5	249.2	261.1	Treasury issues	10
11	54.4	57.7	60.4	63.3	67.4	72.0	76.8	80.7	79.9	72.5	68.2	68.3	Savings bonds	11
12	22.1	21.9	36.3	50.0	65.8	67.9	76.6	94.6	126.4	153.0	181.0	192.8	Other Treasury	12
13	17.0	14.3	16.2	20.8	19.7	23.1	28.9	36.5	58.5	67.6	80.7	83.2	Agency issues	13
14	46.1	48.4	53.7	61.9	68.1	70.1	70.1	72.7	82.7	94.6	115.0	161.8	State + local obligations	14
15	46.5	53.1	55.0	60.1	69.0	80.7	75.7	72.8	83.1	90.0	81.3	72.7	Corporate and fgn. bonds	15
16	54.1	60.5	63.1	70.0	76.2	83.6	91.7	105.9	126.0	148.4	171.6	188.9	Mortgages	16
17	7.9	6.2	15.3	19.5	15.1	12.0	21.7	37.1	45.3	43.3	43.4	41.9	Open-market paper	17
18	832.8	913.2	712.8	505.9	660.5	772.3	732.9	749.9	914.3	1225.6	1165.5	1310.8	Corporate equities	18
19	55.4	58.9	46.6	35.2	43.0	46.5	45.5	46.1	51.8	63.7	64.0	93.0	Mutual fund shares	19
20	777.4	854.2	666.1	470.7	617.5	725.8	687.4	703.9	862.6	1161.9	1101.4	1217.8	Other corporate equities	20
21	136.8	143.7	151.3	158.0	166.6	175.0	186.5	198.5	211.1	222.5	232.8	243.7	Life insurance reserves	21
22	275.8	322.3	310.6	302.5	365.7	427.7	465.2	531.1	598.6	727.1	793.8	924.9	Pension fund reserves	22
23	4.9	5.0	4.9	3.9	4.5	6.3	5.3	7.9	8.5	12.6	16.2	27.7	Security credit	23
24	28.7	31.3	34.1	36.8	40.6	46.0	52.9	59.5	66.7	72.4	77.1	82.1	Miscellaneous assets	24
25	550.7	621.1	697.3	750.9	805.3	902.7	1043.6	1215.2	1394.2	1526.3	1650.9	1732.5	Total liabilities	25
26	526.2	591.0	670.5	724.2	776.1	866.5	1004.1	1171.8	1349.0	1469.2	1589.3	1668.3	Credit market instruments	26
27	316.7	358.0	404.5	442.3	482.9	544.3	635.1	746.5	869.4	967.9	1049.0	1095.9	Home mortgages	27
28	20.3	21.5	22.6	23.7	24.8	25.6	26.7	28.1	29.6	31.4	33.5	34.8	Other mortgages	28
29	118.3	133.2	155.1	164.6	172.3	193.8	230.6	273.6	312.0	313.5	333.4	343.4	Installment cons. credit	29
30	39.5	44.5	48.6	49.0	50.9	54.8	58.6	64.3	71.3	74.8	80.2	84.6	Other consumer credit	30
31	9.2	10.1	13.5	15.2	13.7	14.6	17.4	19.9	20.8	26.8	27.7	36.5	Bank loans n.e.c.	31
32	22.3	23.6	26.2	29.4	31.5	33.4	35.7	39.5	45.9	54.8	65.6	73.0	Other loans	32
33	13.1	17.5	13.2	11.4	12.1	17.2	18.5	19.8	18.6	27.1	27.2	25.3	Security credit	33
34	6.0	6.6	7.3	8.3	9.4	10.5	11.7	13.2	14.9	17.0	19.7	22.4	Trade credit	34
35	5.4	6.0	6.4	7.1	7.7	8.4	9.3	10.3	11.7	12.9	14.7	16.5	Deferred and unpaid life insurance premiums	35

(1) Excludes corporate equities.
Source: Board of Governors of the Federal Reserve System.

willingness of consumers to take on debt to sustain their desired level of consumption.

The two financial statements—flow-of-funds and financial assets and liabilities—should be analyzed together for a complete understanding of long-run and short-run financial changes in the economy. One statement is incomplete without the other. The *Flow of Funds Accounts*—Tables 2–4 and 2–5—indicate short-run changes in financial assets and liabilities. In contrast, statements of financial assets and liabilities for the whole economy or for individual sectors, as in Table 2–6, reflect long-run changes (i.e., accumulated flows for past years) in balance sheets. Each statement contributes important and unique information not reflected in the other.

TYPES OF INSTRUMENTS TRADED BY FINANCIAL INSTITUTIONS IN THE FINANCIAL MARKETS

In Chapter 1, we presented a framework for analyzing the behavior of financial institutions. We pointed out that institutions select which financial assets and liabilities to acquire on the basis of certain factors. Specifically, their portfolio choices depend upon (1) the expected returns attached to various financial instruments which they are interested in acquiring or issuing, (2) the degree of default and market risk displayed by each financial instrument, (3) the probabilities of cash-out (illiquidity) due to unexpected changes in inflows and outflows of funds, and (4) the laws and regulations which limit the range of portfolio choices to those financial instruments deemed appropriate by society.

The acquisition of assets (uses of funds) by a financial institution also is heavily influenced by its choices of liabilities (sources of funds). Institutions which depend upon highly volatile, relatively risky fund sources usually seek assets which are liquid and readily marketable. Commercial banks are a good example of this kind of portfolio behavior. On the other hand, institutions with highly predictable and stable sources of funds typically find little need for substantial investments in liquid assets and usually remain almost fully invested in longer-term, higher-yielding assets, including bonds, mortgages, and stocks. Financial institutions with this kind of portfolio strategy include insurance companies and pension funds. Of course, the final portfolio choices made by a financial institution are also shaped by the *goals* of the organization. Clearly, a financial intermediary pursuing maximum earnings or maximization of the wealth of its stockholders would make somewhat different portfolio selections than one interested solely in growth and public service.

In addition to giving us a glimpse of savings flows among various sectors of the economy, the *Flow of Funds Accounts* provide information on the actual portfolio choices made by financial institutions. Through these social accounts we can follow changes in the sources and uses of funds of each type of institution. The *Flow of Funds Accounts* also provide information on the stocks of assets and liabilities held by financial institutions at any given point in time. And these accounts indicate flows of financial assets among the different kinds of institutions over a specific period of time and also show how the financial institutions' sector interacts with the remainder of the economic and financial system.

It is useful for us to examine in some detail the kinds of information on financial institutions available from the *Flow of Funds Accounts*. Stocks of financial assets and liabilities for each major kind of financial institution for the years 1969 to 1980 are shown in Tables 2–7 through 2–12. In

Table 2–7 Statements of Financial Assets and Liabilities for the Banking System: 1969–1980 ($ billions)

Sector Statements of Financial Assets and Liabilities

YEAR-END OUTSTANDINGS, 1969–80   *YEAR-END OUTSTANDINGS, 1969–80*

	1969	1970	1971	1972	1973	1974	1975	1976	1977	1978	1979	1980		
							Monetary Authority							
1	80.7	86.1	94.6	97.6	106.9	113.4	124.6	134.5	143.0	156.2	166.7	173.8	Total financial assets	1
2	12.3	10.9	10.1	10.5	11.5	11.6	11.7	11.7	11.7	13.2	13.6	16.2	Gold and foreign exchange	2
3	6.8	7.5	8.0	8.7	9.1	9.7	10.6	12.0	12.6	13.1	14.9	16.4	Treasury curr. + SDR. ctfs.	3
4	3.4	4.3	4.3	4.0	3.1	2.0	3.7	2.6	3.8	6.5	6.8	4.5	Federal Reserve float	4
5	.2	.3	*	2.0	1.3	.3	.2	*	.3	1.2	1.5	1.8	F.R. loans to domestic banks	5
6	57.2	62.2	71.1	71.3	80.6	86.7	95.3	105.1	112.2	119.2	126.9	131.4	Credit market instruments	6
7	57.2	62.1	70.8	71.2	80.5	85.7	94.1	104.1	111.3	118.6	126.2	130.6	U.S. Government securities	7
8	57.2	62.1	70.2	69.9	78.5	80.5	87.9	97.0	102.8	110.6	117.5	121.3	• Treasury issues	8
9	—	—	.6	1.3	2.0	5.2	6.2	7.1	8.5	8.0	8.7	9.3	Agency issues	9
10	.1	.1	.3	.1	.1	1.0	1.1	1.0	1.0	.6	.7	.8	Acceptances	10
11	—	—	—	—	—	—	—	—	—	—	—	—	Bank loans n.e.c.	11
12	.8	.9	1.1	1.1	1.4	3.2	3.2	3.0	2.4	3.0	3.1	3.6	Miscellaneous assets	12
13	80.7	86.1	94.6	97.6	106.9	113.4	124.6	134.5	143.0	156.2	166.7	173.8	Total liablities	13
14	22.1	24.2	27.8	25.6	27.1	25.8	26.1	25.2	26.9	31.2	29.8	27.5	Member bank reserves	14
15	7.3	7.0	7.5	8.6	10.7	11.6	12.3	12.1	13.9	15.5	18.5	19.8	Vault cash of coml. banks	15
16	48.9	52.0	56.4	60.4	65.0	71.9	82.5	93.1	98.0	104.3	112.5	121.5	Demand deposits and currency	16
17	2.0	1.6	2.5	2.2	2.9	3.3	7.8	10.9	7.5	4.4	4.6	3.5	Due to U.S. Government	17
18	.4	.3	.5	.4	.3	.5	.5	.6	.6	.7	.8	.5	Due to foreign	18
19	46.6	50.0	53.4	57.9	61.8	68.1	74.3	81.6	89.9	99.2	107.1	117.4	Currency outside banks	19
20	2.4	2.9	2.9	2.9	4.2	4.0	3.8	4.1	4.2	5.2	6.0	5.1	Miscellaneous liabilities	20
							Commercial Banking (1)							
1	465.7	504.9	562.3	640.7	728.8	799.9	834.3	905.5	1002.9	1146.8	1274.5	1386.3	Total financial assets	1
2	.3	.4	.5	.7	1.0	.8	.9	.7	1.3	1.5	2.2	2.9	Demand deposits and currency	2
3	423.4	460.5	511.7	587.0	668.2	732.8	764.3	830.6	920.5	1046.1	1164.2	1264.6	Total bank credit	3
4	65.7	76.4	83.6	90.0	88.8	89.5	119.5	139.6	138.5	139.0	146.5	172.1	U.S. Govt. securities	4
5	53.6	62.5	65.6	68.1	59.2	56.3	84.9	103.6	101.7	95.2	95.3	111.2	Treasury issues	5
6	10.1	13.9	17.9	22.0	29.6	33.2	34.6	36.0	36.8	43.8	51.2	60.9	Agency issues	6
7	59.5	70.2	82.8	90.0	95.7	101.1	102.9	106.0	115.2	126.2	135.6	149.2	State + local obligations	7
8	1.9	3.0	3.9	5.2	5.6	6.6	8.4	7.8	7.7	7.4	7.1	7.7	Corporate + foreign bonds	8
9	296.2	310.8	341.3	401.6	478.1	535.5	533.3	577.0	658.9	773.4	874.9	935.4	Total loans	9
10	73.5	72.8	82.5	99.3	119.1	132.1	136.2	151.3	179.0	214.0	245.2	264.6	Mortgages	10
11	63.4	65.6	74.3	87.0	99.6	103.0	106.1	118.0	140.3	166.5	186.4	176.7	Consumer credit	11
12	144.0	151.2	162.2	188.5	237.3	278.2	265.7	272.0	301.4	358.8	408.0	456.3	Bank loans n.e.c.	12
13	6.7	8.2	8.5	8.3	7.0	9.2	10.3	14.0	14.3	13.0	15.2	16.9	Open-market paper	13
14	11.5	13.0	13.8	18.6	15.2	13.0	15.0	21.7	23.9	21.0	20.2	20.9	Security credit	14
15	.1	.1	.1	.1	.2	.2	.2	.2	.2	.1	.1	.1	Corporate equities	15
16	7.3	7.0	7.5	8.6	10.7	11.6	12.3	12.1	13.9	15.5	18.5	19.8	Vault cash	16
17	22.1	24.2	27.8	25.6	27.1	25.8	26.1	25.2	26.9	31.2	29.8	27.5	Member bank reserves	17
18	12.7	12.8	14.8	18.8	21.8	28.8	30.8	36.9	40.4	52.4	59.7	71.6	Miscellaneous assets	18
19	436.2	473.6	528.7	604.2	688.1	755.8	787.4	852.5	944.6	1081.9	1202.1	1306.2	Total liabilities	19
20	180.5	189.8	202.9	222.6	235.4	235.2	242.8	256.1	280.6	305.9	332.4	341.9	Checkable deposits	20
21	5.1	7.9	10.2	10.9	9.9	4.8	3.1	3.0	7.3	14.1	14.5	11.9	U.S. Government	21
22	5.8	6.4	6.0	7.9	10.9	13.5	13.2	16.2	18.7	18.3	22.7	23.6	Foreign	22
23	169.6	175.5	186.7	203.8	214.6	216.9	226.5	236.9	254.6	273.5	295.3	306.4	Private domestic	23
24	164.3	177.7	205.4	229.0	239.5	254.9	294.2	351.1	379.2	390.1	421.1	462.0	Small time + savings dep.	24
25	30.9	55.3	69.1	87.9	128.2	170.3	161.0	143.4	169.5	220.2	232.2	282.9	Large time deposits	25
26	8.1	4.0	7.7	9.2	25.4	23.5	26.9	40.6	49.5	69.8	86.1	104.8	Fed. funds + security RP's	26
27	22.9	18.1	12.2	10.3	6.6	6.8	−5.2	−13.2	−18.0	−8.2	9.4	−20.3	Net interbank claims	27

(1) Consists of U.S.-chartered commercial banks, their domestic affiliates, Edge Act corporations, agencies and branches of foreign banks, and banks in U.S. possessions. Edge Act corporations and offices of foreign banks appear together in these tables as "foreign banking offices."

Table 2–7   *(concluded)*

Sector Statements of Financial Assets and Liabilities

YEAR-END OUTSTANDINGS, 1969–80   *YEAR-END OUTSTANDINGS, 1969–80*

	1969	1970	1971	1972	1973	1974	1975	1976	1977	1978	1979	1980		
						Commercial Banking (1)								
28	3.6	4.6	4.4	6.0	4.4	2.3	3.9	2.6	4.1	7.7	8.2	6.3	To monetary authority	28
29	2.4	3.1	2.0	−2.4	−1.8	.7	−3.1	−4.0	−9.4	−8.6	−10.1	−13.5	To domestic banks (2)	29
30	16.8	10.5	5.8	6.8	4.1	3.9	−6.0	−11.8	−12.7	−7.2	11.4	−13.1	To foreign banks	30
31	6.3	5.6	7.2	10.9	14.1	18.7	19.5	25.5	28.1	35.4	42.1	49.2	Credit market debt	31
32	2.0	3.2	5.2	8.3	9.2	10.4	10.8	17.7	18.9	19.6	21.7	23.2	Corporate bonds	32
33	4.3	2.3	2.0	2.6	4.9	8.3	8.7	7.9	9.1	15.8	20.4	25.9	Open-market paper	33
34	.6	1.0	.9	.7	.8	.9	.6	.6	.6	.9	1.4	1.9	Profit taxes payable	34
35	22.7	22.1	23.3	33.4	38.1	45.5	47.5	48.3	55.1	67.8	77.5	83.8	Miscellaneous liabilities	35
36	411.8	447.4	497.8	568.3	652.9	719.7	749.1	808.7	896.3	1025.0	1143.9	1243.6	Memo: Credit mkt. funds adv.	36

(1) Consists of U.S.-chartered commercial banks, their domestic affiliates, Edge Act corporations, agencies and branches of foreign banks, and banks in U.S. possessions. Edge Act corporations and offices of foreign banks appear together in these tables as "foreign banking offices."

(2) Floats and discrepancies in interbank deposits and loans.

Source: Board of Governors of the Federal Reserve System.

the following sections we ·present a broad overview of the sources and uses of funds among the major classes of financial institutions.

1. Commercial Banks and the Monetary Authorities.   In many ways the commercial bank may be regarded as *the* most important financial institution and intermediary. At year-end 1980, according to the flow-of-funds data in Table 2–7, total financial assets held by U.S. commercial banks (including their domestic affiliates, foreign banking agencies, and banks in U.S. possessions) totaled about $1.4 trillion, compared to about $2.4 trillion for all nonbank financial intermediaries combined. Throughout the postwar period, commercial banks have held about 40 percent of the assets of all U.S. financial institutions. The next most important type of financial institution—savings and loan associations—held $630 billion in financial assets, followed by life insurance companies with $470 billion (see Tables 2–8 and 2–9). Equally significant, liabilities of the banking system represent about four fifths of the nation's money supply, while commercial banks are the principal conduit for government monetary policy.

As Table 2–7 suggests, commercial banks derive the majority of their funds from two sources—time and savings deposits (a combined total of $744.9 billion in 1980, as shown in lines 24 and 25) and checkable deposits ($341.9 billion). On the uses-of-funds side, commercial banks hold substantial quantities of liquid assets (principally cash and government securities), including cash reserves required by the regulatory authorities. Included in bank holdings of liquid assets at year-end 1980 was approximately $172 billion in U.S. government securities and $149 billion in state and local government obligations. Loans totaled $935 billion of

Table 2–8 Statements of Financial Assets and Liabilities for Nonbank Thrift Institutions: 1969–1980
($ billions)

Sector Statements of Financial Assets and Liabilities

YEAR-END OUTSTANDINGS, 1969–80 · YEAR-END OUTSTANDINGS, 1969–80

Savings and Loan Associations

	1969	1970	1971	1972	1973	1974	1975	1976	1977	1978	1979	1980		
1	162.1	176.2	206.0	243.1	271.9	295.5	338.2	391.9	459.2	523.6	379.3	629.8	Total financial assets	1
2	140.0	149.8	173.4	205.2	231.7	249.3	278.6	323.0	381.2	432.0	475.7	502.8	Mortgages	2
3	2.9	3.4	3.7	3.5	6.5	7.4	8.2	9.3	10.8	11.0	14.0	17.5	Consumer credit	3
4	19.2	23.0	28.9	34.4	33.6	38.9	31.4	59.6	67.3	79.8	88.9	109.5	Other assets	4
5	1.4	1.2	.9	1.2	1.0	1.0	1.3	1.6	1.5	1.6	2.1	2.6	Demand deposits + currency	5
6	.2	.6	2.3	3.4	2.9	3.6	8.1	6.7	6.8	7.2	5.0	7.5	Time deposits	6
7	—	—	.5	.9	2.2	4.8	3.0	5.0	7.3	9.0	11.5	10.8	Fed. funds + security RP's	7
8	10.4	11.0	13.5	15.0	15.8	15.6	20.4	26.3	30.7	35.9	36.3	49.3	U.S. Government securities	8
9	8.1	6.8	6.3	5.4	3.9	2.5	3.2	8.4	7.9	8.6	5.1	9.9	Treasury issues	9
10	2.3	4.1	7.2	9.6	11.9	13.1	17.2	17.9	22.8	27.4	31.2	39.3	Agency issues	10
11	.1	.1	.2	.2	.2	.5	1.5	1.2	1.2	1.3	1.2	1.2	State + local obligations	11
12	.3	1.8	2.8	3.3	2.0	1.8	2.7	2.6	2.3	2.7	3.4	4.9	Open-market paper	12
13	6.7	8.2	8.7	10.4	9.6	11.6	13.6	16.2	17.6	22.1	29.4	33.3	Miscellaneous assets	13
14	150.9	164.2	192.4	227.9	254.8	277.1	318.5	369.9	434.1	494.6	546.7	596.5	Total liabilities	14
15	135.5	146.4	174.2	206.8	227.0	243.0	285.7	335.9	386.8	431.0	470.0	511.0	Deposits	15
16	—	—	—	.3	.3	1.8	1.9	1.8	3.8	5.9	6.4	8.5	Fed. funds + security RP's	16
17	12.3	14.1	14.1	15.7	21.7	26.5	24.2	24.3	34.2	48.5	59.9	66.7	Credit market instruments	17
18	—	—	—	—	—	—	.1	.1	1.3	2.0	3.4	3.7	Corporate bonds	18
19	2.5	3.1	5.0	6.2	4.7	3.2	5.1	6.8	9.9	10.7	9.5	8.8	Mortgage loans in process	19
20	.5	.4	1.1	1.5	1.9	1.5	1.2	1.4	2.8	3.1	5.2	5.2	Bank loans n.e.c.	20
21	9.3	10.6	7.9	8.0	15.1	21.8	17.8	15.9	20.2	32.7	41.8	49.0	Fed. Home Loan Bank loans	21
22	.1	.1	.2	.2	.2	.3	.4	.6	.9	1.3	1.8	2.5	Profit taxes payable	22
23	3.0	3.6	4.0	4.9	5.6	5.5	6.2	7.3	8.4	8.0	8.6	7.9	Miscellaneous liabilities	23
24	153.8	166.2	193.6	227.3	256.2	274.6	311.4	362.4	426.1	483.7	531.3	575.6	Memo: Total cr. mkt. assets	24

Mutual Savings Banks

	1969	1970	1971	1972	1973	1974	1975	1976	1977	1978	1979	1980		
1	74.5	79.3	90.1	101.5	106.8	109.1	121.1	134.8	147.3	158.2	163.3	171.5	Total financial assets	1
2	.9	1.0	.9	1.0	1.1	1.1	1.2	1.3	2.1	3.0	2.8	3.9	Demand deposits and currency	2
3	.1	.3	.5	.6	.8	1.0	1.1	1.1	.3	.7	.4	.4	Time deposits	3
4	.3	.4	.7	.8	1.5	1.2	1.1	1.5	2.1	3.0	3.1	3.7	Fed. funds + security RP's	4
5	2.5	2.8	3.5	4.5	4.2	3.7	4.4	4.4	4.8	4.8	4.7	4.2	Corporate equities	5
6	69.8	73.5	82.8	92.4	96.8	99.4	110.1	122.9	134.1	142.6	148.0	154.2	Credit market instruments	6
7	5.0	5.4	6.3	7.7	7.2	7.0	10.9	14.9	17.6	18.3	19.5	22.8	U.S. Government securities	7
8	3.2	3.2	3.3	3.5	3.0	2.6	4.7	5.8	5.9	5.0	3.9	5.3	Treasury issues	8
9	1.8	2.2	3.0	4.2	4.2	4.4	6.1	9.1	11.7	13.4	15.6	17.5	Agency issues	9
10	.2	.2	.4	.9	.9	.9	1.5	2.4	2.8	3.3	2.9	2.4	State + local obligations	10
11	6.9	8.1	12.0	14.2	13.1	14.0	17.5	20.3	21.5	21.6	20.5	21.2	Corporate + foreign bonds	11
12	56.1	57.9	62.0	67.6	73.2	74.9	77.2	81.6	88.1	95.2	98.9	99.8	Mortgages	12
13	1.2	1.4	1.5	1.6	1.9	2.1	2.3	2.6	3.1	3.9	3.9	4.1	Consumer credit	13
14	.3	.5	.7	.6	.5	.5	.6	1.0	1.0	.3	2.3	4.0	Commercial paper	14
15	1.0	1.3	1.7	2.1	2.4	2.6	3.2	3.6	3.9	4.1	4.4	5.0	Miscellaneous assets	15
16	68.7	73.3	83.3	93.6	99.0	101.6	112.6	125.8	137.3	147.3	151.9	160.1	Total liabilities	16
17	67.1	71.6	81.4	91.6	96.3	98.7	109.9	122.9	134.0	142.6	146.0	153.4	Deposits	17
18	1.6	1.7	1.8	2.0	2.6	2.9	2.8	2.9	3.3	4.7	5.9	6.7	Miscellaneous liabilities	18

Credit Unions

	1969	1970	1971	1972	1973	1974	1975	1976	1977	1978	1979	1980		
1	16.1	18.0	21.1	24.6	27.8	31.1	36.9	43.3	51.6	58.4	61.9	69.2	Total financial assets	1
2	.6	.8	.9	.9	.9	1.0	.9	.8	.8	.0	1.1	1.3	Demand deposits and currency	2
3	—	—	—	.1	.3	.5	1.0	.8	.9	.9	.8	.9	Time deposits	3

Table 2–8   (*concluded*)

Sector Statements of Financial Assets and Liabilities

YEAR-END OUTSTANDINGS, 1969–80   YEAR-END OUTSTANDINGS, 1969–80

	1969	1970	1971	1972	1973	1974	1975	1976	1977	1978	1979	1980		
							Credit Unions							
4	1.7	2.1	3.0	3.6	2.9	3.3	3.3	3.3	4.3	3.6	4.2	3.9	Savings and loan deposits	4
5	13.8	15.2	17.2	20.1	23.7	26.4	31.7	38.4	45.6	52.9	55.8	63.2	Credit market instruments	5
6	1.0	1.4	1.6	2.1	2.6	3.0	4.1	4.7	5.2	5.3	5.3	14.6	U.S. Government securities	6
7	.7	.8	.8	1.0	1.4	1.5	2.0	2.5	2.8	3.4	4.0	4.5	Home mortgages	7
8	12.0	13.0	14.0	17.0	19.6	21.9	25.7	31.2	37.6	44.3	46.5	44.0	Consumer credit	8
9	13.7	15.5	18.4	21.6	24.5	27.5	33.0	39.0	46.0	53.0	56.2	63.2	Credit union shares	9

Source: Board of Governors of the Federal Reserve System.

which loans to consumers amounted to about $177 billion. The remainder of the loan total included construction financing, short-term working capital loans, long-term credits to agriculture and nonfarm businesses, and loans to other financial intermediaries.

The banking system, as defined by the *Flow of Funds Accounts*, also includes the financial accounts of the *monetary authorities*—the Federal Reserve System and the U.S. Treasury. The Federal Reserve banks hold the reserve deposits of member banks (which totaled $27.5 billion—line 14—at year-end 1980) and the deposits of nonmember depository institutions and the U.S. Treasury (which amounted to $3.5 billion, as reflected in line 17 at the top of Table 2–7). Through its monetary policy tools the Federal Reserve System changes the level of interest rates and the level and growth of the nation's money supply.[5] The principal device used by the Fed to carry out its policies is open market operations—the buying and selling of securities in the money and capital markets. We note that the Fed held a substantial volume of securities for this purpose at year-end 1980, including $121.3 billion in U.S. Treasury obligations and $9.3 billion in the debt obligations of various federal agencies (lines 8 and 9).

2. Savings and Loan Associations.   Savings and loan associations (S&Ls)—often referred to as domestic building and loan associations—were started during the 1830s for the express purpose of channeling the savings of members into the financing of new homes. It is clear from Table 2–8 that savings and loan associations derive the bulk of their funds from the savings deposits (shares) of individuals, trust funds, and other organizations. Other important sources of funds include bank loans, advances from Federal Home Loan Banks (FHLB), reserves, and undivided profits.

[5]The principal monetary policy tools of the Federal Reserve include (1) setting reserve requirements for depository institutions, (2) setting the discount rate on loans to qualified depository institutions made through its discount window, and (3) buying and selling securities in the open market. These policy tools are discussed at length in Chapter 5.

Table 2-9   Statements of Financial Assets and Liabilities for Insurance Companies: 1969–1980 ($ billions)

YEAR-END OUTSTANDINGS, 1969–80   *YEAR-END OUTSTANDINGS, 1969–80*

	1969	1970	1971	1972	1973	1974	1975	1976	1977	1978	1979	1980		
						Life Insurance Companies								
1	191.3	200.9	215.2	232.4	244.0	255.0	279.7	311.1	339.8	378.3	420.4	469.8	Total financial assets	1
2	1.6	1.8	1.8	2.0	2.1	2.0	1.9	2.0	2.1	2.4	2.7	3.2	Demand deposits and currency	2
3	13.7	15.4	20.6	26.8	25.9	21.9	28.1	34.3	32.9	35.7	40.5	52.9	Corporate equities	3
4	167.6	174.6	182.8	192.5	204.6	217.7	234.6	258.3	285.8	318.9	352.3	385.2	Credit market instruments	4
5	4.5	4.6	4.5	4.6	4.3	4.4	6.2	7.7	9.3	11.4	14.3	17.0	U.S. Govt. securities	5
6	4.1	4.0	3.8	3.8	3.4	3.4	4.7	5.4	5.3	4.8	4.9	5.8	Treasury issues	6
7	.4	.5	.6	.7	.9	1.1	1.4	2.3	4.0	6.5	9.1	11.1	Agency issues	7
8	3.2	3.3	3.4	3.4	3.4	3.7	4.5	5.6	6.1	6.4	6.4	6.7	State + local obligations	8
9	72.7	74.1	79.6	86.6	92.5	96.4	105.5	122.4	141.2	158.5	170.1	178.8	Corporate + foreign bonds	9
10	72.0	74.4	75.5	76.9	81.4	86.2	89.2	91.6	96.8	106.2	118.8	131.1	Mortgages	10
11	1.4	2.1	2.8	3.0	3.0	4.1	4.8	5.2	4.9	6.3	8.0	10.1	Open-market paper	11
12	13.8	16.1	17.1	18.0	20.2	22.9	24.5	25.8	27.6	30.1	34.8	41.4	Policy loans	12
13	8.3	9.2	10.1	11.1	12.0	13.4	15.0	16.5	19.0	21.4	24.9	28.5	Miscellaneous assets	13
14	177.5	187.7	201.0	216.3	230.1	243.9	267.0	296.1	324.0	359.2	396.9	438.4	Total liabilities	14
15	117.8	123.1	129.4	136.1	143.5	150.1	158.6	166.8	178.1	189.8	202.0	213.5	Life insurance reserves	15
16	37.9	41.2	46.4	52.3	56.1	60.8	72.2	89.0	101.5	119.1	139.2	165.8	Pension fund reserves	16
17	.7	.8	.8	.8	.8	.8	.7	.9	1.3	1.9	2.8	4.0	Profit taxes payable	17
18	21.1	22.6	24.5	27.1	29.6	32.2	35.5	39.4	44.0	40.5	52.9	55.1	Miscellaneous liabilities	18
						Other Insurance Companies								
1	45.6	49.9	57.4	67.5	69.5	67.0	77.3	93.9	113.2	133.9	154.9	100.1	Total financial assets	1
2	1.3	1.4	1.5	1.5	1.5	1.6	1.7	1.9	2.2	2.6	2.9	3.3	Demand deposits and currency	2
3	13.3	13.2	16.6	21.8	19.7	12.8	14.2	16.9	17.1	19.4	24.8	32.3	Corporate equities	3
4	27.0	30.9	34.6	38.3	41.8	46.4	53.7	66.2	83.7	100.2	113.7	129.2	Credit market instruments	4
5	5.1	5.0	5.1	5.2	5.1	5.5	8.0	11.2	14.1	15.3	16.6	20.0	U.S. Government securities	5
6	3.4	3.4	3.2	2.9	2.8	2.9	4.7	7.3	9.8	10.5	10.7	13.2	Treasury issues	6
7	1.6	1.6	1.9	2.3	2.3	2.7	3.3	3.9	4.4	4.9	6.0	6.7	Agency issues	7
8	15.5	17.0	20.5	24.8	28.5	30.7	33.3	38.7	49.4	62.9	72.8	81.1	State + local obligations	8
9	6.3	8.6	8.9	8.1	8.0	10.0	12.2	16.1	19.8	21.6	23.6	27.1	Corporate + foreign bonds	9
10	.2	.2	.2	.2	.2	.2	.2	.3	.4	.4	.7	1.0	Commercial mortgages	10
11	3.9	4.4	4.7	5.8	6.5	7.0	7.7	8.9	10.2	11.7	13.6	15.4	Trade credit	11
12	30.9	34.4	38.0	42.9	47.7	52.6	58.8	69.2	81.0	96.1	111.1	127.0	Total liabilities	12
13	.1	.2	.2	.3	.3	.3	.3	.4	.5	.7	1.0	1.3	Profit taxes payable	13
14	30.8	34.2	37.8	42.6	47.4	52.3	58.5	68.8	81.4	95.4	110.2	125.7	Policy payables	14

Source: Board of Governors of the Federal Reserve System.

The majority of savings and loan funds are invested in residential mortgage loans and housing-related securities. As Table 2–8 indicates, savings associations held almost $503 billion in mortgages by year-end 1980. S&Ls also hold small amounts of cash (in the form of demand deposits and currency) and other liquid investments, such as time deposits and U.S. government securities. Because savings deposits have been relatively stable for most of the industry's history, S&Ls have faced relatively limited liquidity needs, though, as we will see in Chapter 13, this situation is changing due to the pressure of competition and rising costs.

3. Mutual Savings Banks.   Mutual savings banks are similar to savings and loan associations in both their sources and uses of funds. Founded in Scotland in the early 19th century, mutual savings banks operate mainly along the East Coast of the United States today. The principal focus of savings bank activity is attracting and channeling the savings of small and middle-income households and organizations into mortgages, corporate bonds, U.S. government and federal agency securities, and corporate stock. The *Flow of Funds Accounts* indicate that deposits placed in mutuals totaled $153.4 billion in 1980 (see Table 2–8). Historically, about 90 percent of the industry's funds have come from savings deposits, though a growing portion of mutuals' deposits are NOW accounts. Borrowing from banks and other intermediaries and various equity reserves account for the remainder of funds available to mutuals.

With relatively stable deposits, savings banks have relatively small liquidity needs, though they have had problems in maintaining adequate liquidity in recent years, just as have savings and loan associations. Their holdings of U.S. government securities (including federal agency obligations) totaled only $22.8 billion in 1980, or about one fifth of their mortgage holdings. Cash assets in the form of demand and time deposits and currency represented less than 3 percent of the industry's total resources. Clearly, the principal investment of mutuals is mortgages, which represented about three fifths of their total financial assets at year-end 1980. Industry holdings of corporate bonds ranked as the third most important investment security, amounting to about 12 percent of total industry financial assets.

4. Credit Unions.   Credit unions are cooperative associations whose membership consists of individuals with some common relationship— usually the same employer, club, union, or church. In return for their deposits, members receive shares in the association and are eligible to borrow, subject to certain rules. As revealed by the flow-of-funds data in Table 2–8, the bulk of credit union funds comes from member deposits (shares) and is loaned out to members (consumer credit). However, small amounts of funds are obtained also from bank loans and reserves.

As of year-end 1980, U.S. credit unions held $44 billion in consumer loans, representing about three fifths of their total financial assets. At year-end 1980, the industry also held $14.6 billion in U.S. government securities—about one fifth of its total financial assets. Holdings of share accounts at savings and loan associations, bank deposits, and currency and coin amounted to $6.1 billion, or about 9 percent of total assets. Beginning in 1977 credit unions chartered by the federal government were given permission to make certain types of long-term residential mortgage loans. However, as Table 2–8 shows, credit union investments in mortgages represented less than 7 percent of the industry's total assets in 1980.

5. Life Insurance Companies. Life insurance companies provide both an outlet for savings and protection against financial losses and reduced income associated with death and old age. Funds received from policyholders (i.e., insurance premiums) are usually invested in longer-term, higher-yielding assets, such as corporate bonds, stocks, and mortgages. As Table 2–9 shows, total financial assets of life companies amounted to almost $470 billion in 1980. The largest single category of assets was corporate bonds (about 40 percent of the total), followed by mortgages (making up close to 30 percent of industry financial assets). Holdings of U.S. government securities were small (less than 4 percent of assets) and have been relatively stable as a percentage of total assets during the past decade. Reflecting the industry's relatively small liquidity needs, holdings of cash (demand deposits and currency) totaled only $3.2 billion, or less than 1 percent of total financial assets in 1980.

6. Property-Casualty Insurance Companies. Similar to life insurance companies, property-casualty insurers protect their policyholders against risk—in this instance, the risk of damage to property or health from accidents, disease, fire, and other sources of harm. Benefit claims against property-casualty insurers are considerably less predictable than policyholder claims against life insurance companies. As a result, property-casualty companies must hold substantially larger liquid reserves than life insurance companies and also more marketable long-term assets. As Table 2–9 suggests, financial assets held by nonlife ("other") insurance companies are concentrated principally in state and local government obligations (municipals), corporate stocks (equities), and corporate bonds. Holdings of cash assets (demand deposits and currency) accounted for only about 2 percent of total resources, but investments in U.S. government securities (including U.S. Treasury issues and federal agency obligations)—the principal source of liquidity—represented slightly over 11 percent of industry assets in 1980.

7. Private Pension Funds. Private pension funds have been among the fastest growing financial intermediaries in the period since World War II. In 1980, total financial assets held by private pension funds amounted to almost $287 billion, compared to only $110 billion as recently as 1970 (see Table 2–10). Because liquidity requirements for pension funds are virtually nil—cash outflows are easily predicted—pension funds can remain almost fully invested in corporate stocks and bonds. The rising cost of pension fund operations has created a demand for common stocks as a hedge against inflation, with corporate bonds a distant second, as indicated in Table 2–10. Reflecting the extremely low liquidity needs of pension funds, cash holdings and investments in time deposits and U.S. government securities combined represented only about 15 percent of total industry assets.

Table 2–10   **Statements of Financial Assets and Liabilities for Private and State and Local Government Pension Funds: 1969–1980 ($ billions)**

YEAR-END OUTSTANDINGS, 1969–80   *YEAR-END OUTSTANDINGS, 1969–80*

	1969	1970	1971	1972	1973	1974	1975	1976	1977	1978	1979	1980		
							Private Pension Funds							
1	102.4	110.4	130.1	156.1	134.3	115.5	146.8	171.9	178.3	198.3	222.0	286.8	Total financial assets	1
2	1.0	1.1	1.3	1.6	1.4	1.3	1.5	1.6	1.7	1.8	1.9	1.9	Demand deposits and currency	2
3	.6	.7	.3	.3	1.1	3.7	2.4	2.3	4.8	10.3	8.9	10.3	Time deposits	3
4	61.4	67.1	88.7	115.2	90.5	63.3	88.6	109.7	101.9	107.9	123.7	175.8	Corporate equities	4
5	34.6	36.6	35.0	34.0	36.3	41.9	48.9	52.5	64.7	73.0	81.8	92.6	Credit market instruments	5
6	2.8	3.0	2.7	3.7	4.4	5.5	10.8	14.7	20.1	22.2	25.0	30.9	U.S. Government securities	6
7	2.2	2.1	2.1	3.0	3.1	3.0	7.4	11.1	15.9	17.5	19.4	24.1	Treasury issues	7
8	.6	.9	.6	.7	1.3	2.6	3.3	3.6	4.2	4.7	5.6	6.7	Agency issues	8
9	27.6	29.4	28.6	27.6	29.5	34.0	35.8	35.5	42.1	48.0	53.7	58.1	Corporate + foreign bonds	9
10	4.2	4.2	3.7	2.7	2.4	2.4	2.4	2.4	2.5	2.0	3.1	3.7	Mortgages	10
11	4.7	4.9	4.8	5.0	5.1	5.3	5.5	5.7	5.2	5.4	5.8	6.2	Miscellaneous assets	11
							State and Local Government Employee Retirement Funds							
1	53.2	60.3	69.0	80.6	84.7	88.0	104.8	120.4	132.5	153.9	169.7	198.1	Total financial assets	1
2	.5	.6	.7	1.0	1.3	1.8	1.4	1.4	1.7	2.7	4.0	4.6	Demand deposits and currency	2
3	7.3	10.1	15.4	22.2	20.2	16.4	24.3	30.1	30.0	33.3	37.1	44.3	Corporate equities	3
4	45.5	49.6	52.9	57.4	63.1	69.8	79.1	88.9	100.8	117.8	128.6	149.2	Credit market instruments	4
5	7.0	6.6	5.4	5.7	5.8	6.2	7.8	10.9	16.3	23.4	30.1	39.5	U.S. Government securities	5
6	5.4	5.1	3.9	3.6	2.5	1.6	2.5	4.1	6.8	9.5	14.7	20.9	Treasury issues	6
7	1.6	1.5	1.5	2.1	3.3	4.6	5.3	6.8	9.6	14.0	15.4	18.6	Agency issues	7
8	2.3	2.0	2.2	2.0	1.7	1.0	1.9	3.4	3.5	4.0	3.9	4.1	State + local obligations	8
9	30.6	35.1	39.0	43.2	48.4	54.9	61.8	66.9	72.9	81.9	85.0	94.7	Corporate + foreign bonds	9
10	5.6	5.9	6.3	6.5	7.1	7.7	7.5	7.7	8.0	8.6	9.6	10.9	Mortgages	10

Source: Board of Governors of the Federal Reserve System.

8. Government Pension Plans.   Like private pension funds, public (government) pension funds have also experienced very rapid growth during the postwar period. This growth reflects rising per capita incomes and the drive of Americans for increased financial security. As indicated in Table 2–10, total financial assets of state and local government employee retirement funds rose from only $50 billion in 1970 to $198 billion in 1980.

Corporate bonds are the most important asset held by this financial intermediary, representing almost half of its total financial resources. The next most important asset is corporate stock, representing about one fifth of total assets in 1980. Holding of mortgages ranked third, representing about 6 percent of the industry's total portfolio. The rapid growth of investments in common stock in recent years is closely correlated with increased inflation. The high yields available on good-quality corporate bonds also have attracted considerable interest on the part of fund trustees for both private and public pension funds.

9. Finance Companies. Purchases of automobiles, home appliances, industrial equipment, business inventories, mobile homes, and numerous other commercial and consumer goods are supported today by the lending activities of finance companies. These intermediaries raise their funds principally by issuing money market securities and bonds or by borrowing from banks. In turn, the funds raised are invested in consumer and business loans and, less frequently, in mortgages.

As shown in Table 2–11, total financial assets held by U.S. finance companies more than doubled between 1970 and 1980, rising to almost $200 billion in the latter year. Loans extended to consumers totaled $92.8 billion at year-end 1980 and were roughly equal to business credits (excluding mortgages). Finance companies also play a major role today in the leasing of equipment to business firms as a substitute for direct loans. Mortgages granted by finance companies ran a distant third as a use of funds, accounting for less than 10 percent of the industry's total assets. Finance companies stay fully invested and have only modest liquidity needs. At year-end 1980, for example, demand deposits and currency held by these intermediaries represented less than 3 percent of their total assets.

10. Real Estate Investment Trust. Created by an act of Congress in the early 1960s, real estate investment trusts (REITs) were set up to expand the flow of funds into the mortgage market and, hopefully, to improve the availability of funds for the construction of multifamily and single-family residences. The industry grew rapidly in the late 1960s and early 1970s due to a heavy demand for mortgage credit. The high point was reached in 1974, when REITs held total financial assets of $17.5 billion (see Table 2–11). Unfortunately, numerous bad loans were made, especially in support of commercial and apartment construction projects, and the market value of industry assets declined precipitously in subsequent years. Many REITs today are affiliated with banks and bank holding companies. These affiliations, coupled with more careful portfolio management practices, should help the industry to stabilize its financial affairs in future years.

11. Investment Companies. One of the simplest and most direct illustrations of the financial intermediation process is the operation of investment companies (often referred to as mutual funds). These intermediaries attract funds from thousands of small savers and reinvest those dollars in financial assets, principally corporate stock. The investment company pools the savings of many investors in order to acquire a diversified portfolio of securities at reasonable cost. Dividends and interest received on investments, and capital gains earned on sales of securities are paid to share holders as a return on their investment (less, of course, portfolio management fees and other costs). As Table 2–11 shows, open-end invest-

Table 2–11 Statements of Financial Assets and Liabilities for Miscellaneous Types of Financial Institutions: 1969–1980 ($ billions)

YEAR-END OUTSTANDINGS, 1969–80   *YEAR-END OUTSTANDINGS, 1969–80*

Finance Companies

	1969	1970	1971	1972	1973	1974	1975	1976	1977	1978	1979	1980		
1	61.6	64.0	69.4	79.2	90.8	96.0	99.1	111.2	133.0	157.5	184.5	198.6	Total financial assets	1
2	2.4	2.7	2.9	3.2	3.5	3.7	3.9	4.1	4.3	4.4	4.6	4.7	Demand deposits and currency	2
3	59.2	61.3	66.5	76.0	87.4	92.3	95.2	107.1	129.5	153.1	179.9	193.9	Credit market instruments	3
4	5.7	7.4	8.9	10.6	12.5	10.6	9.3	9.0	10.2	11.1	12.0	13.0	Mortgages	4
5	32.0	32.1	34.4	38.0	42.6	44.6	45.0	48.6	56.3	67.5	83.3	92.8	Consumer credit	5
6	21.5	21.8	23.2	27.4	32.3	37.2	40.9	49.5	63.0	74.5	84.6	88.1	Other loans (to business)	6
7	58.5	62.4	67.7	79.2	92.5	98.6	103.7	116.6	139.9	163.7	190.9	205.3	Total liabilities	7
8	49.0	51.7	54.3	61.1	70.7	76.2	76.7	81.2	97.9	116.2	132.8	138.7	Credit market instruments	8
9	15.1	17.2	19.7	23.3	26.2	28.0	30.7	33.8	41.6	48.0	52.3	57.7	Corporate bonds	9
10	11.0	10.9	11.5	16.0	20.6	20.6	18.0	16.1	16.7	20.8	19.7	20.8	Bank loans n.e.c.	10
11	23.0	23.6	23.1	21.9	23.8	27.4	28.0	31.3	39.6	47.4	60.9	60.2	Open-market paper	11
12	.2	.3	.3	.3	.3	.3	.3	.3	.3	.5	.9	1.6	Profit taxes payable	12
13	—	—	.6	3.0	4.3	5.0	8.4	14.7	14.2	16.9	22.4	26.8	Funds from parent companies	13
14	9.2	10.5	12.5	14.9	17.2	17.1	18.2	20.3	27.4	30.1	34.7	38.2	Other miscellaneous liab.	14

Real Estate Investment Trusts

	1969	1970	1971	1972	1973	1974	1975	1976	1977	1978	1979	1980		
1	.7	.9	1.4	2.5	3.2	4.3	7.3	8.9	8.6	7.6	7.1	6.3	Physical assets	1
2	.2	.3	.4	.8	1.1	1.4	2.4	3.0	2.8	2.5	2.3	2.1	Multi-family structures	2
3	.5	.6	.9	1.7	2.2	2.9	4.9	6.0	5.7	5.1	4.7	4.2	Nonresidential structures	3
4	2.0	3.9	6.4	11.4	17.0	17.5	14.0	9.8	7.2	6.8	6.7	5.8	Total financial assets	4
5	.2	.6	.8	1.2	1.9	1.7	1.4	1.1	.9	.7	.5	.4	Home mortgages	5
6	1.3	2.0	3.2	5.0	7.5	7.7	7.0	5.2	3.8	3.3	2.8	2.4	Commercial mortgages	6
7	.5	1.3	2.2	4.2	6.6	6.8	4.8	3.1	2.2	1.8	1.6	1.3	Multi-family mortgages	7
8	—	—	.2	1.0	1.0	1.4	.8	.5	.3	.9	1.8	1.6	Miscellaneous assets	8
9	1.5	2.2	4.1	8.8	14.4	16.6	17.8	16.0	13.0	11.5	10.2	8.1	Total liabilities	9
10	1.5	2.2	4.1	8.8	14.4	15.8	15.7	13.8	11.3	9.7	8.4	6.2	Credit market instruments	10
11	.4	.5	.7	1.2	1.5	1.6	2.0	2.4	2.4	2.5	2.6	2.4	Mortgages	11
12	.1	.2	.2	.4	.5	.5	.7	.8	.8	.8	.8	.8	Multi-family residential	12
13	.3	.4	.5	.8	1.0	1.1	1.4	1.6	1.6	1.7	1.7	1.6	Commercial	13
14	.1	.6	1.0	1.4	1.9	2.1	2.1	1.9	1.8	1.6	1.6	1.4	Corporate bonds	14
15	1.0	1.0	1.6	3.0	7.0	11.4	10.8	8.9	6.5	4.9	3.5	1.8	Bank loans n.e.c.	15
16	—	—	.8	3.2	4.0	.7	.8	.6	.5	.6	.8	.5	Open-market paper	16
17	—	—	—	—	—	.8	2.1	2.3	1.8	1.8	1.8	1.9	Miscellaneous liabilities	17

Open-End Investment Companies (Mutual Funds)

	1969	1970	1971	1972	1973	1974	1975	1976	1977	1978	1979	1980		
1	47.6	46.8	55.4	58.9	46.6	35.2	43.0	46.5	45.5	46.1	51.8	63.7	Total financial assets	1
2	.7	.7	.9	.9	.7	.5	.6	.7	.7	.7	.7	.8	Demand deposits and currency	2
3	40.9	39.7	48.6	51.7	38.3	26.3	33.7	37.3	31.9	31.7	35.4	42.4	Corporate equities	3
4	6.0	6.4	6.0	6.3	7.6	8.3	8.7	8.5	12.9	13.7	15.6	20.5	Credit market instruments	4
5	.7	.9	.6	.7	.7	1.1	1.1	1.1	1.8	1.6	1.5	1.9	U.S. Government securities	5
6	—	—	—	—	—	—	—	.5	2.2	2.7	4.0	6.4	State + local obligations	6
7	2.9	3.5	3.7	4.2	4.3	4.9	5.6	6.0	7.0	6.4	7.2	8.5	Corporate + foreign bonds	7
8	2.4	2.1	1.7	1.4	2.6	2.3	2.0	.9	2.0	3.1	2.9	3.8	Open-market paper	8
9	47.6	46.8	55.4	58.9	46.6	35.2	43.0	46.5	45.5	46.1	51.8	63.7	Total shares outstanding	9

Money Market Mutual Funds

	1969	1970	1971	1972	1973	1974	1975	1976	1977	1978	1979	1980		
1	—	—	—	—	—	2.4	3.7	3.7	3.9	10.8	45.2	74.4	Total assets	1
2	—	—	—	—	—	—	*	*	*	.1	.1	.2	Demand deposits and currency	2

Table 2–11   (concluded)

YEAR-END OUTSTANDINGS, 1969–80   *YEAR-END OUTSTANDINGS, 1969–80*

	1969	1970	1971	1972	1973	1974	1975	1976	1977	1978	1979	1980		
								Money Market Mutual Funds						
3	—	—	—	—	—	1.6	2.1	1.5	1.0	4.5	12.0	21.0	Time deposits	3
4	—	—	—	—	—	.1	.1	.1	.3	.3	2.4	5.6	Security RP's	4
5	—	—	—	—	—	—	—	—	*	.5	5.1	6.8	Foreign deposits	5
6	—	—	—	—	—	.8	1.5	2.1	1.9	5.1	24.9	39.8	Credit market instruments	6
7	—	—	—	—	—	.1	.9	1.1	.9	1.5	5.6	8.2	U.S. Government securities	7
8	—	—	—	—	—	.6	.5	.9	1.1	3.7	19.3	31.6	Open-market paper	8
9	—	—	—	—	—	−.1	−.1	−.1	−.2	.3	.7	1.1	Miscellaneous	9
10	—	—	—	—	—	2.4	3.7	3.7	3.9	10.8	45.2	74.4	Total shares outstanding	10

Source: Board of Governors of the Federal Reserve System.

ment companies[6] held almost $64 billion in total financial assets at year-end 1980. Investment company holdings of corporate equities totaled about $42 billion. Thus corporate stock represented about two thirds of the industry's financial assets.

12. Money Market Funds.   During the 1970s, in response to high and rising interest rates and federal interest-rate ceilings on bank deposits, a new type of financial intermediary appeared—the money market mutual fund. Money funds offered both small and large savers (including both businesses and households) high yields on their savings accounts (known as share accounts), easy access to those accounts (via telephone and wire transfers and written checks), and low risk. The money market mutual fund typically invests in high-quality, short-term money market securities—U.S. Treasury bills, large bank CDs, commercial paper, and bankers' acceptances. Table 2–11 shows money market funds holding about $75 billion in assets at year-end 1980. So rapid has been their growth, however, that money-fund assets climbed to about $200 billion during 1982, making them far larger in the aggregate than the traditional stock-oriented investment companies.

13. Security Brokers and Dealers.   Although they are not financial intermediaries, brokers and dealers in securities nevertheless remain one of the most important of all financial institutions. These institutions provide a channel to the financial marketplace for corporations and governments issuing new securities and offer the investor in securities a way of selling his or her holdings to generate additional cash (liquidity). Security dealers are especially important in the market for government securities because

---

[6]See Chapter 21 for a definition of open-end investment companies and a discussion of the different types of investment companies.

they represent the principal channel through which the U.S. government markets its debt and also the main route through which the Federal Reserve conducts its open-market operations to affect the supply of money and credit.

Table 2–12 indicates that the principal securities held by brokers and dealers include corporate stock, U.S. government securities, and corporate and foreign bonds. They also make a substantial volume of credit available to their customers (almost $20 billion at year-end 1980) to purchase debt and equity securities. Dealers and brokers today borrow heavily from commercial banks and large nonfinancial corporations to finance their operations.

A CONCLUDING NOTE

In this chapter we have examined the construction of the *Flow of Funds Accounts* which are prepared by the Federal Reserve. We have observed how this system of social accounting can provide us with important information concerning savings flows in the American economy and the lending and investing activities of major financial institutions.

The *Flow of Funds Accounts* show clearly that different financial institutions draw upon different sources of funds. Some, such as commercial banks, savings and loan associations, mutual savings banks, and credit unions, receive deposits from the public. Others receive payments from savers in return for risk protection, as in the case of insurance companies

---

Table 2–12 Statement of Financial Assets and Liabilities for Security Brokers and Dealers: 1969–1980 ($ billions)

YEAR-END OUTSTANDINGS, 1969–80   *YEAR-END OUTSTANDINGS, 1969–80*

	1969	1970	1971	1972	1973	1974	1975	1976	1977	1978	1979	1980		
						Security Brokers and Dealers								
1	15.4	16.2	17.6	21.9	18.3	15.2	18.5	26.8	27.7	28.0	28.2	33.5	Total financial assets	1
2	1.4	1.1	1.1	1.1	.9	.8	.7	.9	1.0	1.1	1.6	1.6	Demand deposits and currency	2
3	1.9	2.0	2.1	2.4	2.8	2.2	3.4	3.8	4.0	3.7	3.1	3.9	Corporate equities	3
4	3.7	6.0	4.6	5.0	5.5	4.8	5.8	8.9	8.5	7.3	6.7	8.2	Credit market instruments	4
5	1.7	3.4	1.8	2.0	2.0	2.3	2.2	4.6	3.8	3.1	5.0	3.6	U.S. Government securities	5
6	.4	.9	1.0	.9	1.1	.7	.6	.9	1.1	.9	1.0	1.1	State + local obligations	6
7	1.6	1.7	1.8	2.0	2.4	1.8	3.0	3.4	3.7	3.3	2.7	3.5	Corporate + foreign bonds	7
8	8.5	7.2	9.8	13.5	9.1	7.6	8.6	13.2	14.2	15.9	14.8	19.9	Security credit	8
9	13.3	14.3	15.4	19.7	16.2	13.2	16.1	24.1	25.0	25.1	25.1	30.2	Total liabilities	9
10	13.2	14.2	15.3	19.5	16.1	13.2	16.0	23.9	24.9	25.0	24.9	29.8	Security credit	10
11	6.7	8.6	9.3	13.0	10.3	8.4	10.8	16.8	18.2	15.7	15.0	16.2	From U.S.-chartered banks	11
12	.9	.9	.9	1.2	.6	.5	.4	.9	1.3	1.4	1.4	1.0	From foreign banking off.	12
13	5.7	4.7	5.2	5.4	5.2	4.2	4.8	6.3	5.3	7.9	8.5	12.6	Customer credit balances	13
14	.1	.2	.1	.2	.2	*	.1	.2	.1	.1	.2	.4	Profit taxes payable	14

Source: Board of Governors of the Federal Reserve System.

and pension funds, or for portfolio management services, as in the case of investment companies and money market funds. Different financial institutions also hold unique kinds of financial assets, influenced largely by the types of claims held by savers against their assets, by laws and regulations imposed by state and federal authorities, and by the relative yields (rates of return) available on different financial assets. In the next chapter, we look more closely at the factors which determine the yields on different financial instruments. Then, in Chapter 4, we will take a detailed look at the characteristics of financial instruments most frequently acquired by financial intermediaries.

Questions

2–1. How might the *Flow of Funds Accounts* be used to determine such things as

a. Future interest rates?
b. The general state of the economy?

2–2. Outline the steps involved in the construction of the *Flow of Funds Accounts.*

2–3. Define the following terms:

a. Lending.
b. Net investment.
c. Borrowing.
d. Saving.

Explain how these concepts are related to each other within the framework of the financial system.

2–4. What is a savings-deficit sector? How does it differ from a savings-surplus sector? Give examples of each.

2–5. Make a list of the kinds of information contained in the Federal Reserve Board's *Flow of Funds Accounts* for each sector of the economy. From where is this information derived?

2–6. Discuss the basic differences in terms of types of assets held and basic functions or services of

a. Commercial banks.
b. Savings and loan associations.
c. Life insurance companies.
d. Private and government pension funds.
e. Mutual savings banks.
f. Credit unions.
g. Property-casualty insurance companies.
h. Finance companies.
i. Real estate investment trusts.
j. Investment companies.
k. Money market funds.
l. Security brokers and dealers.

2–7. What factors appear to determine the kinds of financial assets and liabilities acquired by a financial intermediary? Can you explain the differences in asset portfolios held by life insurance companies versus property-casualty insurers? Commercial banks versus savings and loan associations? Pension funds versus credit unions?

References

1. Bain, A.D. "Surveys in Applied Economics: Flow of Funds Analysis." *Economic Journal*, December 1973, pp. 1055–93.

2. Board of Governors of the Federal Reserve System. *Introduction to Flow of Funds*. Washington, D.C., February 1975.

3. _____. *Flow of Funds Accounts, 1946–75*. Washington, D.C., December 1976.

4. _____. *Flow of Funds Accounts, Assets, and Liabilities Outstanding, 1965–76*. Washington, D.C., December 1977.

5. _____. *Flow of Funds Accounts, 2nd quarter 1978*. Washington, D.C., August 1978.

6. Cohen, Jacob. "Copeland's Moneyflows after 25 Years." *Journal of Economic Literature*, no. 1 (March 1972).

7. Copeland, M.A. *A Study of Moneyflows in the United States*. New York: National Bureau of Economic Research, 1952.

8. Freund, William C., and Edward D. Zinberg. "Application of Flow of Funds to Interest-Rate Forecasting." *Journal of Finance*, May 1963.

9. National Bureau of Economic Research. *The Flow-of-Funds Approach to Social Accounting*. New York: Princeton University Press, 1962.

10. Powelson, John P. *National Income and Flow-of-Funds Analysis*. New York: McGraw-Hill, 1960.

11. Ritter, Lawrence S. "The Flow of Funds Accounts: A Framework for Financial Analysis." In *Financial Institutions and Markets*, by Murray E. Polakoff et al. Boston: Houghton Mifflin, 1970.

12. Van Horne, James C. *Financial Market Rates and Flows*. Englewood Cliffs, N.J.: Prentice-Hall, 1978.

PART TWO

The Economic and Financial Environment within Which Financial Institutions Operate

3. Determination of Interest Rate Levels

THIS CHAPTER DEALS WITH THE FACTORS that determine the levels of interest rates over time. The concept of *the* interest rate as representative of the price of credit is, of course, an abstraction since there are literally thousands of interest rates on different financial contracts. Yet *the* interest rate is an extremely important concept, especially for financial institutions.

Existing levels of interest rates affect both inflows and outflows of funds at intermediaries. The major source of revenue for most intermediaries is the interest return on their loans and investments; and the major expense category, at least for depository intermediaries, is interest payments for borrowed funds (including deposits). Even intermediaries such as investment companies (mutual funds) and pension funds which have investments concentrated in equity securities (common and preferred stock) are influenced significantly by the level of short- and long-term interest rates. Indeed, there is considerable evidence that in recent years the level of stock prices has been substantially affected by changes in the general level of interest rates.[1]

Changes in interest rates and interest-rate expectations also affect the income and expenses of financial intermediaries. Rising rates squeeze the earnings of some intermediaries, especially those (such as savings and loan associations) that borrow short-term funds and make long-term loans. This happens because short-term interest rates tend to rise more

---

[1] The basis for this relationship is fairly simple. Common stock prices should reflect the present value of all anticipated dividends payable during the life of the firm, including a liquidating dividend at the termination of the life of the business. As interest rates generally increase, the discount rate used to determine the present value of that expected stream of dividends is raised and the present value of that stream (i.e., the current market price per share of the stock) is reduced, unless of course there is an offsetting increase in anticipated dividends. Conversely, as interest rates fall the discount rate is reduced and the present value of the cash flow (market price of the stock) is increased.

rapidly than long-term rates during periods of economic expansion. Interest-rate expectations also influence the earnings and the volume and composition of intermediary portfolios. Unanticipated movements in interest rates often create an unusually profitable or especially unsuccessful year for a financial intermediary. Indeed, sharp and unexpected increases in interest rates may destroy the viability of a financial intermediary. For all of these reasons, it is important that the management of financial intermediaries understand the determinants of interest-rate levels and movements in interest rates. Such an understanding is fundamental to forecasting interest-rate pressures in various segments of the financial markets.

While there are many alternative approaches to understanding changes in interest-rate levels, one approach used widely by industry practitioners in explaining and forecasting changes in interest rates—and the one that we concentrate on in this text—is based upon the *loanable funds theory.* This method, which is short-run in concept, concentrates on the magnitudes of financial flows from various sectors of the economy. It seeks to explain changes in interest rates by examining the combined demand for and supply of funds by the business, household, and government sectors.

Major emphasis in the loanable funds approach is placed on shifts in the demands of business firms for funds due to changes in inventory holdings, capital expenditures, or other factors. In addition, since government, particularly the federal government, is frequently a deficit unit, emphasis is often placed on this sector (especially during periods of recession and heavy deficit financing) as a net demander of funds.

The supply of funds represents the combined supply of the household, business, and government sectors. Since the principal net surplus-spending sector in the U.S. economy is the household sector, changes in the supply of loanable funds must take into account the behavior patterns of consumers. However, there is one important complicating feature. The supply of funds is not only a function of the volume of saving carried out by different sectors of the economy, but it also includes money created by the banking system. Since money creation is the result of actions by depository institutions in acquiring primary securities—and since the process is strongly affected by the Federal Reserve's monetary policy—there is substantial attention devoted both to depository institutions, especially commercial banks, and to the Federal Reserve in this approach.

The discussion is initially in terms of a world in which inflation does not exist and is not expected to exist. The influence of changing price levels on interest rates is then explored later in the chapter.

**DEMAND FOR
LOANABLE FUNDS**

The demand for loanable funds is composed of several parts and emanates from all sectors of the economy—businesses, households, and governments. Each of these sectors has a demand for loanable funds which derives from a different motivation. It is, therefore, important to explore separately these basic behavioral factors in seeking to understand the reasons for shifts in the overall demand for loanable funds. However, in the interest of simplicity, this section concentrates on the business and government sectors, which are usually net demanders of funds, and views the household sector, from a net position, as a net supplier of funds.[2]

Business Demand

An understanding of the motives for demanding loanable funds by *business* firms is especially important because the business sector is the principal borrower in most years. Moreover, and perhaps of greater significance for understanding changes in interest rates, business demand for loanable funds is highly unstable from year to year. Hence changes in interest rates are to a considerable extent associated with changes in business demand for funds. This is especially true of changes in short-term (money market) interest rates.

Effect of Investment Spending. Demands for loanable funds by business firms arise principally from a desire by firms to acquire real assets—plant and equipment and inventories. This act of investment is, in turn, assumed to be a function of the *expected* rate of return from making the investment (in a capital budgeting sense, the internal rate of return) and of the cost of obtaining the necessary funds (the rate of interest or, in a capital budgeting sense, the weighted average cost of capital). It is important to note that the return that is relevant is the profitability that business managers expect to obtain in the future from the commitment of funds today (as opposed to the actual return realized on investments currently or in the past). This return, therefore, is affected to some extent by psychological factors. Hence the state of business confidence may be of considerable significance in affecting the total volume of investment carried out by the business sector.

Inverse Relationship between the Interest Rate and Quantity of Funds Demanded. For any given investment demand schedule, the higher the cost of funds the lower the quantity of investment. If management were contemplating an investment in a plant to produce a particular consumer good and if that plant were expected to yield a rate of return of 10 percent, it would be financially desirable to make the investment only if the cost of

---

[2]This does not, of course, imply that households are not very important in affecting the demand for loanable funds and that business firms through their use of internally generated funds are not significant in affecting the supply of loanable funds. It merely simplifies the analysis by concentrating on the fact that, taking each economic sector as a whole, the household sector is a net supplier of funds and businesses are a net demander of funds.

funds were less than 10 percent, where the cost of funds is the "true" cost and represents the combined cost of debt and equity. However, if the cost of funds were to increase to 14 percent (or to any level above 10 percent), the project would not be financially attractive. Therefore the higher the cost of funds the greater the number of projects that will be eliminated as potentially unprofitable. The relationship between the cost of funds and the amount of investment spending is thus thought to be a negative one.[3]

Responsiveness of Quantity Demanded.   A second important aspect of the relationship between interest rates and the volume of investment spending is the degree of responsiveness of investment to changes in the cost of funds. It is one thing if small changes in interest rates produce large movements in investment; it is an entirely different matter if large changes in interest rates produce only small changes in investment. While there is some disagreement about this relationship, it appears that the degree of responsiveness of business investment demand for funds to changes in interest rates is relatively small. Economically, this relationship implies that business investment spending, and thereby the demand for loanable funds by business, may not be affected to a great degree by public policy measures, such as monetary policy which focuses upon changes in the rate of interest. This suggests that business investment spending may be much more affected by the availability of funds—credit rationing, for example—than by its cost, and by the outlook regarding future demand for goods and services.

Volatility of Quantity Demanded.   A third important feature of the business investment demand function is its volatility or shiftability. Since the investment demand function is affected by the state of business confidence (essentially psychological in nature), it may be subject to sudden changes. At the time when public policy is seeking to increase interest rates in order to curtail investment spending, the investment demand function may shift to the right due to optimism about the future. As a result, despite the higher interest rates, the total volume of investment may rise instead of decline. Similarly, in periods when public policy is attempting to increase investment demand by lowering interest rates, business confidence may sag and the investment demand function may shift to the left, resulting in less total investment spending at every possible rate of interest.

Components of Business Investment Demand.   Business investment demand is composed of two basic parts: the volume of inventory accumulation (i.e., changes in the quantity of inventory held) and the amount of in-

---

[3]It should be pointed out that the demand for loanable funds by the business sector is dependent upon other factors as well as the volume of investment. In particular, the demand for loanable funds from external sources is affected by the amount of internal funds available after the payment of cash dividends.

vestment in fixed assets. These different components of investment behave quite differently. For example, changes from quarter to quarter and year to year in inventory accumulation appear to derive primarily from differences between anticipated sales and realized sales. If actual sales fall short of expected sales, business firms are left with an undesired amount of inventory. In contrast, if actual sales exceed expected sales, these firms may have inventory levels that are small compared with the total volume of sales; they may be—and indeed frequently are—large when compared with the amount of original inventory levels. As a result, inventory fluctuations often are significant in affecting business demand for loanable funds.[4] Since accumulations of inventory are financed generally through short-term borrowings (usually at commercial banks and through trade credit extended to a firm by its suppliers), substantial changes in the volume of these inventories often cause much larger fluctuations in business demand for short-term funds and, thus, in short-term interest rates. Moreover, the rate of interest appears relatively unimportant in influencing changes in inventory levels.

The largest component of business demand for loanable funds is associated with spending for plant and equipment. These expenditures are more clearly determined by the joint influence of the expected profitability from the planned investment and by the cost of funds, since they usually result from careful deliberation by management over a substantial period. While this type of spending should be influenced by interest rates, the variation in total investment spending as a result of changes in interest rates has been relatively slight in most years (though, as with inventory holdings, spending for plant and equipment appeared to be substantially affected by the record interest-rate levels of 1981 and 1982). Hurdle rates established by many firms for investment projects appear in practice to be sufficiently above the cost of funds so that small changes in interest rates have limited effects on investment plans. Moreover, investment projects which are replacement in nature appear to be little affected by interest-rate levels.

Changes in the demand for loanable funds as a result of shifts in plans for the purchase of plant and equipment appear to be less variable than shifts in the demand for loanable funds as a result of changes in inventories. Since plant and equipment expenditures generally are financed with long-term funds, the demand for *long-term* loanable funds tends to be less variable than the demand for *short-term* loanable funds. This tends to create greater stability in rates in the long-term sector of the financial markets than in the short-term area.

---

[4]These inventory fluctuations also may have substantial effects on the entire economy. Indeed, most post–World War II recessions in the United States have been associated with inventory adjustments.

Government Demand

The other major sector which is frequently a net demander of funds in the financial markets is *government*—state, local, and federal. State and local government demands for loanable funds are principally for the purpose of constructing facilities for providing education and other governmental services. This demand is determined primarily by the growth rate in population, changes in the geographic location and age makeup of the population, and the willingness of citizens to bear taxes in order to obtain desired services. It is commonly accepted that this demand for loanable funds is affected to only a minor degree by changes in interest rates.[5] While there is some responsiveness in state and local government borrowing to changes in interest rates, it would be expected that the effect of variations in interest rates on this borrowing should be considerably less than in the case of business demand for loanable funds.

Federal government demand for loanable funds arises primarily from federal fiscal policy (i.e., tax and expenditure policy). The size of the federal budget is determined as the result of decisions concerning tax rates, federal expenditures for goods and services, and transfer payments. There are few reasons to believe that these decisions should be affected by changes in interest rates. Rather, it would be more reasonable to argue that federal fiscal policy is a determining factor in shaping the level and pattern of interest rates. It may be argued, therefore, that the demand for loanable funds by the federal government is almost completely unrelated to interest-rate levels (i.e., almost completely inelastic).

Summary: Demand Factors

The principal net demanders of loanable funds in the financial markets are business firms, state and local governments, and the federal government. The demand for loanable funds by business firms appears to be somewhat but not greatly responsive to interest rates. The quantity of funds demanded by state and local governments is slightly responsive to changes in interest rates. In contrast, the quantity of funds demanded by the federal government is almost completely unresponsive to interest changes. However, the demand curve of each of these sectors is subject to large shifts, up or down. This is especially true for the business sector.

The total demand for funds, then, by all of these sectors is the sum of the demands by businesses, state and local governments, and the federal government. This total demand for funds is illustrated in Figure 3–1.

---

[5]There is some evidence that the *timing* of the demand for loanable funds by state and local governments is influenced to some degree by periods of extremely high interest rates. It appears that these governmental units reduce their borrowing during such periods but that—due to the long lag between borrowing and capital expenditures—this postponement of borrowing has a minimal effect on real capital spending.

**Figure 3–1   Relationship between Interest Rates
and Funds Demanded**

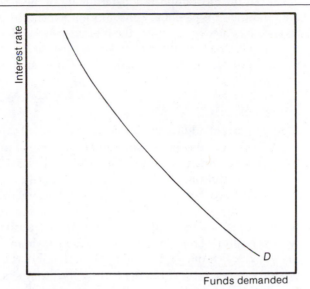

The supply of loanable funds is the result of the volume of saving and the amount of new money created. Since the only sector which consistently has a net surplus is the household sector, our discussion of the volume of saving and its influence will concentrate on examining the motives for household saving. As discussed above, we are viewing the household sector as a net supplier of funds after allowance is made for household demand for funds. In addition, since the amount of money is considerably affected by the Federal Reserve, it is necessary to include in the discussion a treatment of the monetary policy actions of the Fed.

**THE SUPPLY OF
LOANABLE FUNDS**

Saving

Saving refers to the postponement of current consumption. Saving is the act of abstaining from using current income for the purposes of acquiring goods and services. It is important to note that the act of saving and the act of investing in assets are different actions, motivated by different factors. Saving is important because it releases resources that can be used to expand the productive capacity of the economy. Those resources not used to produce goods for current consumption can then be employed to produce investment goods.

The volume of saving by individual consumers is a function of a number of factors, including the amount of current and expected income, the stock of wealth held by the individual, the level of interest rates, expectations concerning the future rate of inflation, as well as other variables. However, the most important determinant of the amount of personal saving (and thereby personal consumption expenditures) appears to be the level of income. In contrast, the interest-rate level—while it may have a substantial effect on the particular disposition of funds made available through saving—is thought to have only a small impact on the total volume of savings.

Money

An important addition to the potential flow of loanable funds from savings comes from the money supply. The volume of money is affected both by depository financial institutions and the Federal Reserve System. Depository institutions transform a given quantity of reserves into money through the process of making loans and investments. A multiple volume of money is created out of a given reserve base because only fractional reserves are required to support each dollar of deposits. However, the ability of depository financial institutions to make loans and investments and thereby create money is limited by the amount of these reserves, while the quantity of reserves within the entire depository system is determined by the Federal Reserve System in its role of conducting monetary policy.

The Federal Reserve uses its techniques of monetary control—open-market operations, changes in reserve requirements, and changes in the discount rate—in order to influence the volume of reserves and deposits. For example, if the Federal Reserve wishes to reduce the growth rate of the economy, it can curtail the volume of reserves through selling securities, increasing required reserves, and/or increasing the discount rate.

The quantity of new money created during a given period is essentially controlled by the Federal Reserve through its influence over the volume of reserves. There is no reason to expect that the volume of money is very sensitive to interest-rate changes, although there may be some influence of interest rates on the money stock, since depository institutions would be expected to use reserves more efficiently in a high, rather than in a low, interest-rate environment.

Summary: The Supply of Loanable Funds

The supply of loanable funds reflects the supply available to the financial markets through savings as well as the supply available from new money creation.[6] Other things being equal, increases in the volume of

---

[6]This analysis is abstracted from the influence of hoarding on the supply of loanable funds. Hoarding refers to the desire of economic participants to hold idle funds in the form of money balances. Naturally, saving or new money creation will increase the supply of loanable funds only if these funds are made available to the market (i.e., not hoarded).

saving will increase the supply of loanable funds and increases in the quantity of new money will increase the supply of loanable funds. The relationship between different interest rates and the quantity supplied of loanable funds is shown in Figure 3–2, that is the quantity of loanable funds supplied is presumed to increase with increases in the interest rate. This increase in the quantity supplied (though not in the supply schedule itself, which would reflect a shift in the supply curve rather than a movement along that curve) would result from substitution of future consumption for present consumption—that is, additional saving. Higher interest rates provide more reward for postponing current consumption. The positive slope of the supply curve would also result to some degree from more effective utilization of reserves by depository financial institutions at the higher level of interest rates.

The supply curve of loanable funds would *shift* if any of the basic determinants of supply change, other than the interest rate. For example, an increase in the desire to save from a given income level due to tax subsidies to savings or to rising income levels would produce a shift to the right in the supply curve. Conversely, concern about the future safety of funds provided by current saving might produce a downward shift in the volume of savings at each interest-rate level (which would be shown in Figure 3–2 by a shift to the left in the supply of loanable funds). Similarly, an increase in the quantity of reserves would shift the supply curve to the right, while a reduced quantity of reserves would shift it to the left.

Figure 3–2 The Supply of Loanable Funds

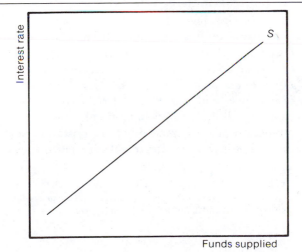

An Illustration. An understanding of the manner in which the supply and demand for loanable funds affects interest-rate levels can perhaps best be obtained through the use of a simple example. In interpreting this illustration, though, the reader should recognize that other factors besides those discussed influence the level of interest rates but in this context are implicitly held constant. Suppose that the economy is entering a period of slack business activity. It would be expected that the demand for loanable funds would fall. This decline in the demand for funds (shift in the demand schedule) might occur due to a reduction in inventory levels at business firms or for other reasons. As the recession intensifies, it might be expected that the amount of capital spending by businesses would fall as optimism concerning the future profitability of capital outlays is reduced. Both of these factors would shift the demand for funds to the left, indicating that at each rate of interest the quantity of loanable funds demanded might fall during this period.

Consumers may react to the recession by increasing their savings, perhaps by accelerating the repayment of their debt obligations or deferring the taking on of any new debts.[7] More importantly, perhaps, it would be expected that the Federal Reserve System would increase the quantity of reserves and that depository institutions would use these reserves to make new loans and investments, thereby expanding the nation's money stock. The increase in the supply of loanable funds, coupled with a decline in the demand for loanable funds, would be expected to lower the interest rate. Moreover, it would probably lower interest rates to a greater extent in the money than in the capital market, due to the combined effect of the sharp reduction in the demand for short-term inventory financing and the expansion in funds available through the commercial banking system, which is principally a short-term lender and investor. These relationships are illustrated in Figure 3–3.

The original level of interest rates was at r_1, while the original quantity of loanable funds bought and sold was at q_1. Responding to the increase in the supply (i.e., the supply curve shifts, from S_1 to S_2) and the reduction in the demand for loanable funds (i.e., the demand curve shifts from D_1 to D_2), interest rates fall from r_1 to r_2. It is important to note that the quantity of loanable funds traded is also reduced from q_1 to q_2. Moreover, these changes will, in turn, set in motion longer-term changes in income, government borrowing, and other responses in the economy. For example, the decline in interest rates might stimulate the economy and increase con-

---

[7]The repayment of debt is merely one way in which the consumer may dispose of savings. Consumers may also add to their holdings of financial assets or select some combination of debt repayment and additions to financial assets.

**Figure 3–3   The Interest Rate and Shifts in the Supply
and Demand for Loanable Funds**

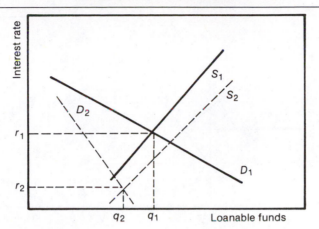

sumer and business spending, thereby leading to a rise in the demand for
loanable funds and to some increase in the interest rate.

As another example of the use of the loanable funds explanation of interest-rate changes, let us suppose that there is a sharp upsurge in the economy, which stimulates inflationary price movements. The demand for
loanable funds should expand as businesses desire to accumulate inventory and add to capital outlays. At the same time, the supply of loanable
funds should contract due to efforts by the Fed to restrict the availability
of reserves. Interest rates should therefore increase, reflecting both the increase in the demand for loanable funds and the decrease in the supply of
loanable funds. This scenario is illustrated in Figure 3–4, where r_1 represents the original level of interest rates and r_2 is the higher level, following
shifts in the supply and demand for loanable funds.

**INFLATION AND
THE INTEREST
RATE**

Our previous discussion of *the* interest rate was abstracted from changing prices, with the assumption that the price level was unchanged. Neither inflation (rising prices) nor deflation (falling prices) was allowed
within this model, either in terms of actual (realized) or expected price-
level changes. In fact, of course, price changes—particularly rising
prices—have become an integral part of the economic scene in the period
since World War II. Not only has inflation occurred but expectations of
further inflation have been built into the decision-making framework of
many individuals and businesses. This inflation has had a powerful impact on the level of interest rates. Indeed, in recent years a very substantial

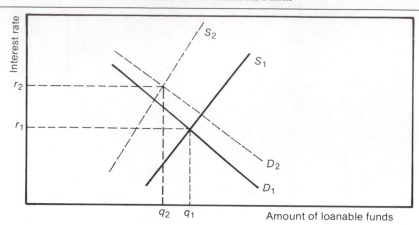

Figure 3–4   Relationship between Interest Rates and
the Amount of Loanable Funds

fraction of the interest rates on default–risk free securities may be explained in terms of the effect of inflation.

The Fisher Effect

As discussed originally by Fisher [4], once changing price levels are allowed for, the interest rate may be thought of as being composed of two elements: the real rate and the inflation premium. The real rate reflects underlying patterns of productivity and thrift and is thought to be relatively constant in the near term. The inflation premium is the compensation to the lender for accepting the risk of losing a fraction of his or her wealth through rising prices during the term of the contract (commonly referred to as purchasing power risk). As a result, the interest rate observed in the market—referred to as the nominal rate—may be thought of as follows:

$$i_n = i_r + p_e \tag{3-1}$$

where

i_n = Nominal rate of interest
i_r = Real rate of interest
p_e = Expected rate of change of prices over term of contract

It is important to note that the price variable is the *expected* change in prices rather than the actual rate at which prices have been advancing or declining over past periods. The realized rate of price-level changes is relevant only if it is a proxy or substitute for the expectation of inflation held by financial market participants.

A direct connection arises between the expectation of inflation or deflation and the nominal interest rate, once it is assumed that the real rate is constant. This connection is referred to as the *Fisher effect*. Under this assumption, the **nominal** rate may be viewed as ranging directly and precisely with expectations of inflation. It may then be said that the nominal rate contains an inflation premium. Hence, if the real rate is assumed to be 3 percent (this is in the area of most assumptions about the real rate), and if inflationary expectations are zero (that is, no inflation is expected over the term of the contract), the nominal rate should be 3 percent per year over the term of the contract. However, if prices are expected to rise by 7 percent per year, the nominal interest rate should be 10 percent. Further, if prices are expected to rise by 15 percent per year over the term of the contract, the nominal rate should be 18 percent.

It is relatively easy to explain the logic of the Fisher effect within the loanable funds framework. Recognizing the possibility of inflation, lenders are concerned about the potential loss of purchasing power over the life of their loan. Hence the supply of loanable funds will shift upward and to the left, as in Figure 3–5, indicating that lenders are unwilling to supply as many funds to the market at each nominal interest rate as before. S_0 represents the supply of loanable funds with no expected inflation, while S_s represents the supply of loanable funds with the expectation of inflation at a rate of 5 percent per year. It would be expected also that borrowers would see the opportunity to borrow at the previous rate of interest and to pay back the borrowed money with depreciated dollars. Hence the demand for loanable funds would increase, with the demand curve shifting from D_0 to D_s. As a result of a reduction in the supply of loanable funds and an upward shift in the demand curve, the nominal interest rate would rise from r_1 to r_2. According to the Fisher effect, the new equilibrium rate of interest (r_2) should be 8 percent. This 8 percent would be composed of a 3 percent real rate and a 5 percent inflation premium. At the 8 percent rate, lenders would be receiving a real return of 3 percent as they were at r_1 without inflation, and borrowers would be paying a real cost of 3 percent as they were at r_1.

Complications to the Fisher Effect

While there is considerable empirical evidence to suggest a strong association between inflation and the level of interest rates—for example, countries with high inflation rates usually have high interest rates—there is disagreement about whether the Fisher effect in its most stringent form is valid. Expectations of rising prices do apparently lead to higher nominal interest rates, but whether the change in nominal rates is rapid and fully reflects the extent of anticipated inflation is unknown. Questions have been raised, for example, about the stability of the real rate of interest. It

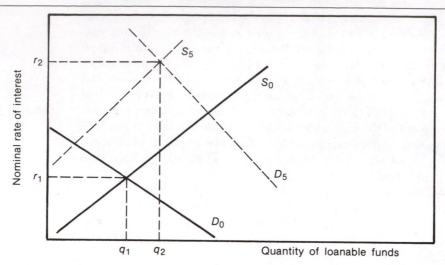

Figure 3–5   Inflation and the Interest Rate

appears that the *realized real rate*—the nominal rate less the actual rate of inflation over the time horizon for which the nominal rate is relevant— has been quite volatile, actually being negative in many periods in the 1970s and quite highly positive in some periods in the early 1980s (see Table 3–1). Yet instability of the realized real rate is not necessarily contradictory to the Fisher effect. The Fisher effect only holds that nominal rates are based upon expectations of inflation, not that these expectations are realized. The insistence that expectations actually be realized, so that the realized real rate would be constant is a much more severe assumption than that contained in the Fisher effect. Relatedly, some observers have questioned the speed with which the nominal rate adjusted to changes in inflationary expectations.[8] For example, if the nominal rate adjusts slowly to changes in inflationary expectations, the real rate would be unstable until the adjustment is complete and there would not be a direct connection between inflationary expectations and the nominal rate. This phenomenon might explain the persistence of negative real rates of return throughout the late 1960s and the 1970s, as investors in the United States have little historical experience with inflation. However, the continued existence of inflation may have sensitized investors sufficiently so that delayed reactions to changes in inflationary expectations may be less plausible today.

---

[8]See Darby [3] for a discussion of this phenomenon.

Table 3–1 Nominal and Estimated Real Interest Rates: 1960–1982

	Federal Funds Rate		90-Day T-Bill Rate		Prime Rate		Aaa Corporate Bond Rate		New Home Mortgage Yield		Inflation Rate†
	Nominal	*Real**	*Nominal*	*Real**	*Nominal*	*Real**	*Nominal*	*Real**	*Nominal*	*Real**	
1960	3.2	1.6	2.9	1.3	4.8	3.2	4.4	2.8	—	—	1.6
1961	2.0	1.1	2.4	1.5	4.5	3.6	4.4	3.5	—	—	0.9
1962	2.7	0.9	2.8	1.0	4.5	2.7	4.3	2.5	—	—	1.8
1963	3.2	1.7	3.2	1.7	4.5	3.0	4.3	2.8	5.9	4.4	1.5
1964	3.5	2.0	3.6	2.1	4.5	3.0	4.4	2.9	5.8	4.3	1.5
1965	4.1	1.9	4.0	1.8	4.5	2.3	4.5	2.3	5.8	3.6	2.2
1966	5.1	1.9	4.9	1.7	5.6	2.4	5.1	1.9	6.3	3.1	3.2
1967	4.2	1.2	4.3	1.3	5.6	2.6	5.5	2.5	6.5	3.5	3.0
1968	5.6	1.2	5.3	0.9	6.3	1.9	6.2	1.8	7.0	2.6	4.4
1969	8.2	3.1	6.7	1.6	8.0	2.9	7.0	1.9	7.8	2.7	5.1
1970	7.2	1.8	6.5	1.1	7.9	2.5	8.0	2.6	8.5	3.1	5.4
1971	4.7	− 0.3	4.4	− 0.6	5.7	0.7	7.4	2.4	7.7	2.7	5.0
1972	4.4	0.2	4.1	− 0.1	5.3	1.1	7.2	3.0	7.6	3.4	4.2
1973	8.7	2.9	7.0	1.2	8.0	2.2	7.4	1.6	8.0	2.2	5.8
1974	10.5	1.7	7.9	− 0.9	10.8	2.0	8.6	− 0.2	8.9	0.1	8.8
1975	5.8	− 3.5	5.8	− 3.5	7.9	− 1.4	8.8	− 0.5	9.0	− 0.3	9.3
1976	5.0	− 0.2	5.0	− 0.2	6.8	1.6	8.4	3.2	9.0	3.8	5.2
1977	5.5	0.3	5.3	− 0.5	6.8	1.0	8.0	2.2	9.0	2.1	5.8
1978	7.9	0.5	7.2	− 0.2	9.1	1.7	8.7	1.3	9.6	2.2	7.4
1979	11.2	2.6	10.0	1.4	12.7	4.1	9.6	1.0	10.8	2.2	8.6
1980	13.4	4.1	11.5	2.2	15.3	6.0	11.9	2.6	12.7	3.4	9.3
1981	16.4	7.0	14.1	4.7	18.9	9.5	14.2	4.8	14.7	5.3	9.4
1982‡	13.3	8.5	11.5	6.7	15.8	11.0	14.4	9.6	N.A.	N.A.	4.8

*The real interest rate shown equals the nominal rate minus the annual percentage change in the implicit price deflator.
†Annual percentage change in the implicit price deflator.
‡Through third quarter of 1982.
Source: G. J. Santoni and Courtney C. Stone, "The Fed and the Real Rate of Interest," *Monthly Review*, Federal Reserve Bank of St. Louis, December 1982, p. 9.

Application of the Fisher effect is also complicated by the existence of tax rates that are a function of nominal rather than real interest rates. In this situation, it may be shown that an increase in the expected inflation from 0 to 4 percent would produce an increase in the nominal interest rate by *more* than 4 percent. This must be the case since the lender must be compensated not only for the inflation but also for the higher taxes produced by the inflation. This phenomenon is sometimes referred to as the *Darby effect* [3].

Considerable interest exists in forecasting future interest-rate movements. This interest in the future level of interest rates is especially intense

**FORECASTING
INTEREST RATES**

at financial institutions, where borrowing and lending decisions today depend to a great degree on expectations of interest rates in coming weeks, months, and years. It has been heightened even further by the substantial volatility of interest rates after 1979 as the Federal Reserve reduced its attempts to stabilize interest rates.

There are a variety of different approaches used in forecasting interest-rate movements, ranging from very simple and subjective adjustments to extremely complicated financial models of the economy. One of the most widely used approaches makes use of the flow-of-funds concept within a loanable funds framework. Within this perspective, financial analysts project the supply and demand for loanable funds. The supply of loanable funds includes that provided by major financial institutions as well as by other sources (usually excluding individuals) while the demand for loanable funds reflects the demands from businesses, consumers, and governments. Projections of both supply and demand factors are based upon assumptions as to Federal Reserve monetary policy, the posture of fiscal policy, inflation, and other relevant variables. Comparisons are then made of the balance of anticipated supply and demand, given the assumption of the forecast. A large amount of excess demand—that is, a large gap or residual between the supply of funds (excluding the supply from individuals) and the demand for funds—implies upward pressure on interest rates, as individuals are induced to purchase securities (provide the credit) only by higher anticipated returns. In contrast, a lower gap between anticipated supply and demand would produce less pressure on interest rates.[9]

It is also possible to forecast interest rates indirectly through forecasting the future rate of inflation, provided of course that the analyst has confidence in the Fisher effect and its assumption of a constant real rate of interest. With this technique, anticipations of falling rates of inflation imply falling interest rates, while expectations of rising rates imply increasing interest rates. Such an approach could also incorporate expectations of changing inflation rates over time and, thereby, changing interest rates. For example, it might be expected that inflation would rise for the next three years and then decline gradually—an expectation which would have important implications for future levels of interest rates, as interest rates on financial assets with up to three years maturity would be higher than those with longer maturities.

Despite these many alternative approaches, the performance of financial analysts and others in forecasting interest rates has been quite poor.

---

[9]Salomon Brothers is perhaps the best known, though not the only user of this approach to forecasting interest rates.

Indeed, the record of professional forecasters has been so bad in anticipating interest-rate changes that it has been said that the most "important role for a forecaster is to forecast often and with as much ambiguity as possible." The poor record of forecasters is illustrated in a study by Fraser [5], who evaluated the forecast accuracy for the years 1974–76 of the consensus forecast by the National Association of Business Economists, Wharton Econometric Forecasting Associates, Chase Econometrics, as well as well-know individual forecasters and forecasting groups. He found that the average error in the forecasts of short-term rates was 23.7 percent of the actual level of rates in 1974, 19.6 percent in 1975, and 27.9 percent in 1976. Similar, though somewhat smaller, forecasting errors appeared for long-term rates. Of perhaps greater concern was the inability of forecasters to predict changes (or turning points) in interest rates. There appeared to be a considerable tendency for forecasters to predict rising rates in periods when rates had been rising and to predict falling rates when rates had been falling. For interest-rate forecasts to be useful, it is crucially important, of course, that such forecasts anticipate reversals in trend.

The Salomon Brothers Interest Rate Forecast

The Salomon Brothers approach to forecasting interest rates concentrates on the supply and demand for loanable funds. Separate estimates are made of the supply of credit provided by the major nonbank financial intermediaries, such as savings and loan associations, commercial banks, and other organizations such as finance companies, business corporations, state and local governments, and foreigners. The demand for credit is separated into the demand for long-term credit by nonfederal borrowers (including state and local government borrowing), the demand for short-term financing by business and consumers, and the demand for credit by the federal government (in connection with both the U.S. Treasury debt and federal agency debt).

The relative balance of these demand and supply factors is of substantial significance in explaining interest-rate movements. The difference between the net demand and the net supply of funds is the amount that individuals and miscellaneous investors must absorb. Since individuals generally place most of their surplus funds with financial intermediaries, it would be expected that increases in interest rates would be necessary in order to induce these individuals to provide a substantial amount of credit directly to the marketplace. Conversely, if the gap between the net demand for credit and the net supply of credit is relatively slight, the amount of securities that individuals must absorb is small and interest rates might be expected to fall.

This approach to interest-rate forecasts may perhaps best be explained by examining the Salomon Brothers' interest-rate outlook for 1983, as contained in its publication *1983 Prospects for Financial Markets*. Table 3–2 contains a summary statement of the data used in their analysis. Examining initially the net demand for credit, the forecast notably was for a substantial increase in the net demand for credit ($456.2 billion forecast for 1983 as compared to $399.4 billion in 1982). This increase in the forecasted demand for funds was predicated principally on the basis of an in-

Table 3–2   Summary of Supply and Demand for Credit ($ billions)

	Annual Net Increases in Amounts Outstanding							
	1976	*1977*	*1978*	*1979*	*1980*	*1981*	*1982*	*1983*
Net demand:								
Privately held mortgages	70.3	105.2	118.6	112.4	83.6	79.9	31.8	60.0
Corporate and foreign bonds	39.1	39.1	31.8	36.1	37.9	23.8	26.0	56.2
Subtotal long-term private	109.4	144.3	150.4	148.5	121.5	103.7	57.8	116.2
Short-term business	14.3	49.1	76.0	91.3	55.3	111.9	57.5	21.0
Short-term other	40.5	51.0	66.7	52.2	21.1	37.9	16.4	37.2
Subtotal short-term private	54.8	100.1	142.7	143.5	76.4	149.8	73.9	58.2
Privately held federal debt	73.3	75.5	82.6	77.4	118.5	123.0	215.8	224.0
Tax-exempt notes and bonds	17.6	28.9	32.5	27.9	33.0	32.2	51.9	57.9
Subtotal government debt	90.9	104.4	115.1	105.3	151.5	155.2	267.7	281.9
Total net demand for credit	**255.1**	**348.8**	**408.2**	**397.3**	**349.4**	**408.7**	**399.4**	**456.2**
Net supply:								
Thrift institutions	70.2	81.8	73.8	55.6	54.1	24.6	28.9	72.7
Contractual institutions*	49.2	68.2	73.2	63.5	70.3	69.0	89.3	96.4
Investment companies	2.8	7.1	6.4	25.2	22.8	72.4	48.3	42.8
Other nonbank finance	14.3	13.7	19.4	26.0	16.8	34.0	18.1	33.7
Subtotal nonbank finance	136.5	170.6	172.8	170.3	163.9	199.9	184.6	245.5
Commercial banks	60.9	84.1	105.9	104.0	83.3	100.7	81.6	103.4
Business corporations	9.1	−4.4	−0.8	7.4	−1.5	7.8	10.3	10.7
State and local governments	7.1	16.7	18.9	7.2	6.9	3.4	−0.2	8.4
Foreign	19.6	47.3	58.8	10.4	41.0	24.3	12.9	16.6
Subtotal	233.2	314.3	355.6	298.3	293.6	336.2	288.7	384.5
Residual (mostly households)	21.9	34.5	52.6	98.0	55.9	72.5	110.7	71.7
Total net supply of credit	**255.1**	**348.8**	**408.2**	**397.3**	**349.4**	**408.7**	**399.4**	**456.2**

*Insurance, pensions, etc.
Source: Salomon Brothers, *1983 Prospects for Financial Market*, December 6, 1982, p. 3.

crease in long-term private demands for funds, mainly the result of an expected sharp advance in the demand for mortgage credit and in the volume of corporate bonds. Federal government demand for funds was expected to remain substantial due to the continuation of a very large budget deficit.

While the demand for loanable funds was forecasted to expand considerably, the supply of loanable funds was expected to grow even more (from $288.7 billion in 1982 to $384.5 billion in 1983). The increase reflects a large rise in funds supplied by thrift institutions and commercial banks, due principally to a higher savings rate and an easier monetary policy. As a result of the greater expansion in the supply of funds, the residual—the amount that households would need to absorb through direct finance—was expected to fall (from $110.7 billion to $71.7 billion) exerting downward pressure on interest rates.

Analysis of the data contained in this forecast led Salomon Brothers to conclude that

> The implication for interest rates of these considerations and of the credit flow projections summarized below is a continued, irregular decline in both short- and long-term interest rates. Most of the decline will take place before midyear. Short-term rates will fall by 150–175 basis points and long-term rates will drop by 75–125 basis points. The sluggish pace of economic recovery, a high level of underutilized resources, a lower rate of inflation, and credit uncertainties will provide the Federal Reserve with sufficient reason to continue its accommodative posture. The huge U.S. Treasury borrowings will be facilitated by an increased rate of private saving and much lower private short-term financing. Long-term markets will benefit from an even steeper positive yield curve, lower inflation expectations and more receptive institutional investment strategies.[10]

SUMMARY

This chapter has discussed the importance of interest-rate movements for the behavior of individual financial institutions. Financial institutions are affected by interest-rate changes and conversely, through their behavior produce changes in interest rates. The chapter concentrates on the loanable funds explanation of interest-rate movements and on the basic sectors of the economy—business, government, and households—which are net suppliers and net demanders of funds. An understanding of the role of each of these sectors is crucial to understanding interest-rate developments and changes in the financial position of individual financial institutions. In addition, a distinction was made between the determinants of the interest rate with and without inflation. Further, various techniques used to forecast interest rates were discussed and the accuracy of interest rate forecasts was evaluated.

---

[10]Salomon Brothers, *1983 Prospects For Financial Markets*, December 6, 1982, p. 3.

Questions

3–1. What are the major elements of the demand and supply curves of the loanable funds theory? Explain the influence of the (*a*) business sector, (*b*) government sector, and (*c*) household sector.

3–2. Distinguish between a change in the supply of loanable funds and a change in the quantity supplied of loanable funds.

3–3. How might the Federal Reserve influence the supply of loanable funds? The demand for loanable funds?

3–4. Discuss the similarities between interest-rate theory and the general economic theory of supply and demand.

3–5. What is the Fisher effect? Is it valid?

3–6. Distinguish between nominal and real interest rates. What is the inflation premium?

3–7. How might interest-rate changes be forecasted?

References

1. Conard, Joseph W. *An Introduction to the Theory of Interest.* Berkeley: University of California Press, 1959.

2. Culbertson, John. *Money and Banking.* New York: McGraw–Hill, 1972.

3. Darby, Michael R. "The Financial and Tax Effects of Monetary Policy on Interest Rates." *Economic Inquiry,* June 1975, 266–76.

4. Fisher, Irving. *The Theory of Interest.* New York: Macmillan, 1930.

5. Fraser, Donald R. "On the Accuracy and Usefulness of Interest Rate Forecasts." *Business Economics,* Fall 1977.

6. Homer, Sidney. *A History of Interest Rates.* New Brunswick, N.J.: Rutgers University Press, 1963.

7. Keynes, John Maynard. *The General Theory of Employment, Interest and Money.* New York: Harcourt Brace Jovanovich, 1936.

8. Lutz, Frederick A. *The Theory of Interest.* Dordrecht, Holland: D. Reidel Publishing, 1967.

9. Polakoff, Murray, et al. *Financial Institutions and Markets.* 2d ed. Boston: Houghton Mifflin, 1981.

4. Money and Capital Markets: Instruments and Yield Relationships

MANAGERS OF FINANCIAL INTERMEDIARIES are heavily involved in transactions using financial instruments. Indeed, as was pointed out earlier, the distinguishing feature of financial intermediaries is that their principal assets are financial in nature. It is, therefore, important for management to be knowledgeable about the various characteristics of these financial instruments—short-term debt, long-term debt, and equity. Moreover, it is important for the managers of financial intermediaries to understand the factors which affect the price and yield relationships among different kinds of financial assets. The present chapter seeks to provide a brief discussion of the major instruments traded in the financial markets. Necessarily, the treatment of each financial instrument is quite general in nature. While money market instruments are discussed in some detail, discussion of capital market instruments is more limited, with emphasis on the general factors which influence the pattern or structure of yields. (For more specific information the reader should refer to the references listed at the end of the chapter.) In addition, there is a brief discussion of financial futures markets at the end of the chapter.

The chapter begins with a discussion of the measurement of the yield on a fixed-income instrument. Most of the financial instruments acquired by financial institutions are fixed-income instruments, such as bonds, notes, and mortgages. A critical question in the decision of a financial institution manager to acquire or sell fixed-income securities is, What is their yield or expected return to the institution?

Fixed-income instruments promise to pay to the holder a certain amount of interest periodically during the life of the instrument and to repay the principal or face amount at the maturity of the instrument. The return to the holder for such a fixed-income instrument is thus this cash flow expressed as a fraction of the value of the instrument. The simplest mea-

YIELD MEASUREMENTS

sure of the return (though not the best) is known as the *coupon rate*. The coupon rate is obtained by dividing the annual interest return on a bond or a note by the face or principal (or par amount) of the security, as in Equation 4–1:

$$\text{Coupon rate} = \frac{\text{Promised annual interest payment}}{\text{Principal value}} \qquad (4\text{–}1)$$

For example, a 10-year, $1,000 principal value bond that promised $50 per year would have a 5 percent coupon rate. The principal difficulty with using the coupon rate as a measure of the yield on a security is that the market value of a security such as a bond is often not equal to the principal value. In fact, the market value is generally equal to or very similar to the principal value only at the time the instrument is created. When the market value deviates from the principal value, the return to an investor on the investor's funds clearly is not accurately described by the coupon rate. In that case, the *current yield* divides the annual interest payment on the instrument not by the principal value but by the *market value* of the security, as shown in Equation 4–2:

$$\text{Current yield} = \frac{\text{Promised annual payment}}{\text{Market value of security}} \qquad (4\text{–}2)$$

The current yield and the coupon rate bear some important relationships to each other. For example, if the market value of the security exceeds the principal, or face amount (in which case the security is referred to as a *premium* instrument), the current yield will be less than the coupon rate. In contrast, if the market value of the security is less than the principal, or face amount (in which case the security is referred to as a *discount* instrument), the current yield will be greater than the coupon rate. Only in the case where the market value is equal to the principal amount will the current yield be equal to the coupon rate.

If the bond referred to above were to sell at a market price of $1,000, its current yield would be $50 ÷ $1,000, or 5 percent. If the market price was $900, then the current yield would be $50 ÷ $900 or 5.55 percent. Finally, if the market price was $1,100, the current yield would be $50 ÷ $1,100, or 4.54 percent.

While more meaningful than the coupon rate, the current yield also has important limitations as a measure of the return or yield on a financial asset. In particular, the current yield omits any gain or loss that may occur at the maturity of the instrument due to a difference between the original purchase price paid by the investor and the principal, or par value, at maturity. The return to the investor will be reduced if the investor has paid a price above par, while it will be increased if the investor has paid a price below par. This possibility is captured in the *yield to maturity* concept, which may be calculated as shown in Equation 4–3:

$$P = \frac{I_1}{(1+r)^1} + \frac{I_2}{(1+r)^2} + \ldots + \frac{I_n}{(1+r)^n} + \frac{PAR_n}{(1+r)^n} \quad (4\text{-}3)$$

where

I = Periodic cash payments during life of the instrument
P = Market value or price of the instrument
PAR = Par or principal value of the instrument payable at maturity
r = Yield to maturity

In simple terms the yield to maturity is the rate of discount that makes the present value of *all* cash flows from a financial instrument equal to its current market price. It takes into account both the interest payments during the life of the instrument and any capital gain or loss at maturity.

In the above example, with a market price of $900, the yield to maturity (assuming that interest is paid once per year) is 6.1 percent. At a price of $1,100 the yield to maturity is 3.9 percent.

The yield to maturity concept is, of course, not applicable to perpetual instruments such as common stock. While the current yield does provide some information on the return on common stock, a more relevant *measure* is the holding-period yield, which may be calculated as:

$$P = \frac{D_1}{(1+h)^1} \frac{D_2}{(1+h)^2} + \ldots + \frac{D_n}{(1+h)^n} + \frac{PR_n}{(1+h)^n} \quad (4\text{-}4)$$

where

P = Current market price
D = Amount of cash dividends
PR = Price at point of sale at end of holding period
h = Holding-period return

In concept, the yield to maturity and the holding-period return as calculated with the formulas specified are quite similar. However, for a common stock which by definition has no maturity, the expected price at time of sale replaces the principal or maturity value.

MONEY MARKETS AND CAPITAL MARKETS

The term *money market* refers to the market for short-term financial instruments with a time to maturity of one year or less. The term *capital market* refers to the market for long-term financial assets having actual maturities of more than one year. Distinctions between short and long are somewhat arbitrary, although one year is the most common dividing point. Both of these markets perform important services in the financial system. The focus of the money market is on providing a means by which individuals and business firms are able to rapidly adjust their actual liquidity position to the amount desired. The money market is the medium through which holders of temporary cash surpluses meet those with temporary cash deficits. Hence an individual with a temporary excess of investable funds is able to use the money market as a place where these funds may be "stored" for a short period of time at some positive rate of interest. Similarly, the individual or business firm with a temporary shortfall of liquidity can obtain funds in the money market for a short period of time. The money market then becomes important because of the lack of synchronization among inflows and outflows of cash at individual economic units. In both cases, the economic unit is using the money market—either as a supplier or as a demander of funds—as a means by which to adjust its liquidity.[1]

The capital market also plays a significant role in the financial system. Given the fact that savings and investment are vital for the growth of the economy and also that, in an advanced economy, the economic units which save are different from the economic units which invest, the capital market provides a bridge by which the savings of surplus units may be transformed into the investments of deficit units.[2] In this process, the capital market contributes to economic stability by matching savings and investment and to economic growth by expanding the total amount of savings and investment. In short, an efficient capital market contributes to a rising standard of living.

Comparison of the Roles of the Money and Capital Markets

While both the money and capital markets are significant in the financial system, it is important to recognize that these markets differ in a number of respects. As pointed out above, the money market primarily exists as a means of liquidity adjustment. In contrast, the capital market's principal function is to serve as a link between the ultimate surplus and deficit sectors (i.e., a conduit for savings and investment) and thereby to play an important role in the process by which "real" saving is transformed into "real" investment.[3]

---

[1]It is also important to observe that the holding of cash forces economic units to carry a significant opportunity cost, since cash deposits earn either no or a very low explicit rate of return. The money market serves to reduce the opportunity cost from holding liquid assets. This is especially important in periods of high and rising interest rates and during periods of severe inflation, when the opportunity cost associated with idle cash balances increases.

[2]Saving here refers to the postponement of current consumption, while investment refers to the purchase of real capital assets, such as new buildings and equipment.

[3]This does not, of course, mean that surplus units are only suppliers of funds in the money and capital markets and that deficit units are only demanders of funds in these markets. Indeed, surplus units may have to make very large (but temporary) demands on the money and capital markets for funds. Similarly, deficit units may provide very large (but temporary) supplies of funds to the money and capital markets.

The money and capital markets also differ in a number of other important respects. Many money market instruments, but not all, have strong *secondary markets;* that is, they can be sold to another investor prior to the maturity of the instrument. For example, the Treasury bill market is frequently referred to as one of the best secondary markets in the world. The relatively strong secondary market plus the short maturity of instruments and the low *default risk* provide substantial liquidity for these money market instruments. In contrast, many capital market instruments have a relatively weak secondary market.[4] For example, the market for home mortgages has traditionally been a relatively poor secondary market. The relatively weak secondary market plus the long period to maturity and (frequently) substantial default risk make capital market instruments generally unsatisfactory investments for liquidity purposes.

The money and capital markets also differ in terms of the volume of transactions. The total volume of transactions in the money market is extremely large when compared to the amount of capital market transactions. This reflects, to a substantial degree, the differences in the financial functions performed by these two markets. Since the money market principally serves as a vehicle for the adjustment of the liquidity position of economic units to expected and unexpected changes in cash flows, it is to a considerable extent a secondary market in which existing instruments are bought and sold. In contrast, since the capital market is principally a mechanism by which ultimate surplus units with excess funds are able to lock-up investments for long periods of time, this market is essentially a *primary* one—that is, a market for newly issued securities. This statement is, of course, much more correct for the mortgage and bond (both corporate and municipal) markets than for the equity market. But in general it is not too inaccurate to assert that money market instruments are bought to be sold as soon as cash is needed, while capital market securities are bought to be held as long-term investments. The rate of interest (yield) is the primary factor which motivates savers to part with their funds in the capital market, while the safety and liquidity of the financial instrument is at least as important as its rate of return or yield in the money market.[5]

Money and capital market instruments also differ greatly in terms of risk. Money market instruments generally carry low default and low interest-rate risk. As a general rule, only instruments issued by economic units of the highest standing qualify for entry into the money market. The very short maturity of money market securities and their good secondary market reduces the impact on price of changes in interest rates. In con-

---

[4]One obvious exception to this statement is the market for frequently traded stock, such as the New York Stock Exchange.

[5]The yield on a financial instrument does, of course, incorporate the safety and marketability of the instrument as well as other factors.

trast, both default and interest rate risk in the capital market are often substantial. Capital market instruments include both debt and equity. Equity issues represent claims on the earnings and assets of an individual firm which are inferior to those of debt instruments; necessarily, these equity issues carry more risk than debt instruments of the same firm. Moreover, debt quality ranges from U.S. government securities and highly rated corporate issues with limited default risk to unrated bonds of small and new business ventures and other securities with more substantial default risk. In addition, capital market instruments are long-term in nature, with the result that interest-rate changes have a substantial impact on the prices of these instruments.

The money market is dominated by one set of financial institutions—the commercial banks and the Federal Reserve System. The commercial banking system is by far the largest group of financial institutions in the nation. Moreover, because of the nature of their deposit liabilities and the regulations they face, commercial banks are heavily concentrated in short- and medium-term loans and investments. In addition, one of the major liabilities of the commercial bank—the large business ($100,000 and over) certificate of deposit (CD)—is one of the most important instruments by dollar volume in the money market. The behavior of the commercial bank is, in turn, affected and indeed controlled to a considerable extent by the Federal Reserve System. The Federal Reserve System supplies or withdraws reserves from the commercial banking system through its techniques of monetary control. It is, therefore, necessary for management to understand current monetary policy actions by the Federal Reserve in order to anticipate movements in interest rates and in the prices of financial assets. To some extent, especially in the short run, money market rates are principally what the Federal Reserve wishes them to be.

External influences on capital market rates and the prices of capital market instruments are much more complex. No single financial institution dominates the capital market. While individual financial institutions (such as savings and loan associations) may dominate certain subsectors of the capital market—such as the single-family residential mortgage market—no one financial institution can be said to dominate the capital market in the way that the commercial banks and the Federal Reserve influence the money market. As a result, the level of yields and pattern of yields among different financial instruments is much more complex. Certainly monetary policy influences are transmitted to the capital market. However, changes in inflationary expectations, corporate profits and liquidity, business spending for inventories and plant and equipment, and the relative inflows of funds into the major financial institutions are also important.

Finally, the capital market is dominant in terms of the *volume* of securities outstanding at any one time. This dominance reflects the differing maturities of the financial instruments traded in these markets. The money market instrument is, of course, short-term in nature. Its maturity is generally measured in days, weeks, or months. In contrast, capital market instruments are long-term in nature; their maturity usually is measured in terms of years. Moreover, common stock and most preferred stock—theoretically at least—have no maturity, though many corporations plan to retire their preferred stock issues when conditions are favorable.

It is important for the management of financial institutions to be knowledgeable about the specific financial characteristics of both money and capital market instruments as well as to understand the functions of the money and capital markets within the financial system. Financial institutions—whether bank or nonbank—participate actively in the money and capital markets. Commercial banks are active primarily in the money market, while nonbank financial institutions are active principally in the capital market. However, there is a considerable degree of overlap in the functions of different financial institutions. For example, while commercial banks are primarily short-term lenders, they also make a considerable volume of so-called term loans to businesses with maturities of five years or more. Moreover, commercial banks invest heavily in relatively long-term municipal securities. Similarly, while savings and loan associations have been principally long-term lenders, they also make a large amount of short-term construction loans for homes and other related purposes. Furthermore, while the major nonbank financial institutions are primarily long-term lenders, they all have a need for participation to a limited degree in the money market in order to adjust their liquidity positions. Certainly it should be kept in mind that financial institutions operate on both sides of the market—borrowing and lending—and frequently do so simultaneously. In addition, with the striking changes in the sources and uses of funds at the major financial institutions in recent years—and the expectation of greater changes in the future—the degree of overlap among these financial institutions will undoubtedly increase in the future.

Money and Capital Market Instruments

Table 4–1 provides information on the volume of the major money and capital market instruments outstanding in the U.S. financial system as of year-end 1981. As mentioned earlier, the volume of capital market instruments—particularly corporate equities ($1,493 billion) and mortgages ($1,542 billion)—far exceeds the volume of money market securities outstanding.[6] It is interesting to note that securities issued by governmental units do not dominate the U.S. capital market. Rather, private debt secu-

---

[6]Some distortion is introduced into these data since the volume of equity securities is measured at marker rather than book value.

rities—principally corporate equities and mortgages—are the most important financial instruments by volume in the U.S. capital market. In contrast, the securities of the U.S. government play a more important role in the money market. This reflects the enormous amount of deficit spending carried out by the U.S. government as well as the decision to finance this deficit principally with short-term securities.

MONEY MARKET INSTRUMENTS

U.S. Treasury Securities

Securities issued by the U.S. Treasury are important in both the money and capital markets. These securities are especially significant in the money market; indeed, Treasury securities (including agency securities) have historically played a dominating role in the U.S. money market. The average maturity of the Treasury's debt has fallen considerably in recent years, further increasing the role of these securities as money market instruments. U.S. Treasury securities are the major liquid asset held by a number of financial institutions.

Treasury securities (or "governments" as they are usually called) may be classified in a number of ways. One approach is to classify these instruments by their original maturity. By this method, governments may be divided into *bills* (with an original maturity of 1 year or less), *notes* (with an original maturity of 1 to 10 years), and *bonds* (with an original maturity

Table 4–1 Major Types of Money and Capital Market Instruments Outstanding as of December 31, 1981 ($ billion)

	Volume Outstanding
Major instruments of the money market:	
U.S. government securities	$ 340
Short-term municipal notes	20
Commercial paper	150
Bankers' acceptances	80
Large time deposits	386
Federal funds	130
	$1,106
Major instruments of the capital market:	
U.S. government securities	380
Mortgages	1,542
Municipal Bonds	314
Corporate equities	1,493
Corporate bonds	533
	$4,262

Source: Board of Governors of the Federal Reserve System, *Flow of Funds Accounts.*

of more than 10 years). All Treasury bills are money market instruments. Moreover, notes and bonds may be money market instruments if their maturity has become sufficiently short. However, short-term notes and bonds generally do not have the strong secondary market liquidity of bills. There also appears to be some difference in the bill market with regard to liquidity. Bills with a maturity of six months or less appear to have greater liquidity for secondary market trading than do bills with a maturity of more than six months.

Treasury bills differ from other government securities not only in terms of their original maturity but also in their return to investors. Treasury bills are discount instruments; that is, the return to the investor is derived from the difference between the original purchase price (at a discount from par) and the par value of the instrument. For example, an investor pays $9,500 for a bill but will obtain $10,000 for that bill (its par value) at maturity. The $500 increase in the value of the bill (taxable as ordinary income, not as capital gains) would constitute the return to the investor. In contrast, all other Treasury securities (except saving bonds) pay an explicit rate of interest in which the investor receives separate payment of interest.

Since Treasury bills are discount instruments, their yields cannot be compared directly with the returns on Treasury notes and bonds or on some other money market instruments. Bill yields are calculated on a "bank discount basis," which produces an estimate of the return to the investor that is different from and lower than the yield to maturity. For example, in the situation discussed above, (the purchase of a one-year bill at $9,500), the investor receives a total dollar return of $500. To calculate the rate of return, the investor would divide the absolute return (or discount), D, by the par value, P, and multiply by 360 divided by the number of days held (up to a maximum of 360 days). In symbols,

$$DR = \frac{D}{P} \times \frac{360}{H} \qquad (4\text{--}5)$$

where

DR = Discount or interest rate return to investor
D = Amount of discount in dollars
P = Par value of security
H = Number of days remaining until maturity

In the example given, the discount yield to the investor is

$$DR = \frac{\$500}{\$10,000} \times \frac{360}{360} = 5\%$$

This 5 percent return calculated on the bank discount basis is different from and lower than the true yield on a security for the following reasons:

First, the absolute amount of the discount is divided by par rather than by the purchase price of the instrument. Yet the investor only had to commit the amount of the purchase price (neglecting transaction costs), and it is this figure rather than par which is really relevant in determining the investor's return. Second, the return is calculated on a 360-day rather than a 365-day year. For all of these reasons, the discount yield is lower than the true yield to maturity. In order to convert the bill's yield (or indeed any other discount instrument's yield) from the bank discount yield to a bond-equivalent yield or yield to maturity, we may use the following formula:

$$\text{Investment return} = \frac{365 \times \text{Discount basis}}{360 - (\text{Discount basis} \times \text{Days to maturity})} \quad (4\text{-}6)$$

In the example cited above, the bank discount yield was 5 percent. The investment return or true yield was[7]

$$\text{Investment return} = \frac{365 \times 0.05}{360 - (0.05 \times 360)}$$

$$= \frac{18.25}{342}$$

$$= 5.336\%$$

Treasury bills are important not only because of their quantitative significance but also because of their use by a diverse group of financial and nonfinancial firms, as well as by the Federal Reserve System in its conduct of monetary policy. Treasury bills have been the traditional means for liquidity adjustment by commercial banks, and they have appeared frequently in the portfolios of manufacturing and other nonfinancial firms, as these firms have relied upon bills as a known storehouse of funds to pay dividends, taxes, and other short-term obligations. Also, of major significance, the Federal Reserve System conducts open-market operations primarily in Treasury bills. For all of these reasons, an understanding of the role of Treasury securities in general and of the Treasury bill in particular is important.

A more detailed view of the distribution of ownership of marketable Treasury securities is presented in Tables 4–2 through 4–4. Private investors (financial and nonfinancial) are the largest single holder of Treasury securities (Table 4–2). The Federal Reserve has also accumulated large amounts of Treasury issues. Table 4–3 shows the very short-term nature of the public debt. The average maturity of the Treasury debt is roughly

---

[7]For a useful discussion of yield computations on Treasury bills, see *Securities of the United States Government and Federal Agencies*, 28th ed. (New York: First Boston Corporation, 1978).

Table 4–2   Ownership of U.S. Government Marketable
Securities, March 1982 ($ millions)

	Total Outstanding
Held by U.S. government accounts	$ 8,001
Public issues held by Federal Reserve	135,589
Held by private investors	619,030
	$752,620

Source: *Federal Reserve Bulletin*, June 1982.

two years, while about two thirds of the debt matures within five years. Such short maturities may have inflationary potential and certainly lead to frequent refundings and some interference with monetary policy. Within the private sector, individuals, commercial banks, and foreign investors are the dominant investors (Table 4–4). Perhaps the most significant development has been the enormous accumulation of U.S. Treasury securities by the oil surplus countries in recent years.

Federal Funds

Another important subdivision of the money market is the market for federal funds. It is significant from a variety of perspectives and to a number of different economic units. To commercial banks, the federal funds market is an inexpensive and efficient way to obtain or dispose of extra reserves. Indeed, for very short-term purposes (i.e., one or two days) the federal funds market has become the dominant means of adjusting bank

Table 4–3   U.S. Government Marketable
Securities Classified by Maturity, March 1982
($ millions)

	Total Outstanding
By final maturity:	
Within 1 year	$357,073
1–5 years	242,354
5–10 years	60,785
10–20 years	46,399
20 years and over	46,010
	$752,620

Note: Components may not add to totals due to rounding.
Source: *Federal Reserve Bulletin*, June 1982.

Table 4–4   Ownership of U.S. Government
Marketable Securities by Private Investors:
March 1982 ($ billions)

	Total Outstanding
Held by:	
Commercial banks	$ 79.4
Savings and loans	4.8
Insurance companies	13.1
Mutual savings banks	4.5
Corporations	4.3
State and local governments	21.7
Other	624.8
	$752.6

Source: *Federal Reserve Bulletin*, June 1982.

reserves. Moreover, the federal funds market has become increasingly a source of permanent funds for larger banks and a means for permanent disposal of funds for smaller banks. The federal funds market has become significant in the implementation of monetary policy and in the interpretation by investors of monetary policy changes by the Federal Reserve System.

The term *federal funds* is a shorthand abbreviation for Federal Reserve funds, which are reserve balances at the Federal Reserve banks. Federal Reserve funds are both a financial asset and a liability, appearing on the balance sheets of two economic units. They appear on the books of the Federal Reserve banks as a liability of the Federal Reserve banks. Federal funds are an asset to the depositors who carry them on their balance sheet as "Deposits at the Federal Reserve." These reserve balances may be used to make loans or to purchase assets (such as currency and coin), much as individuals and businesses use checking accounts to carry out transactions.

Federal funds transactions are those which are accomplished in immediately available funds. Most such transactions involve the buying and selling of deposits at the Federal Reserve—either originated by the owning bank itself for its own purposes or by another party. These purchases and sales are generally for a one-day period but may be longer if desired. A loan made in federal funds is immediately available to the lending institution until repayment is made. This occurs because the transaction is carried out by wire and/or telephone communication between the banks involved and the Federal Reserve, and the funds are transferred by a simple bookkeeping entry from the account of one bank to the account of another. Contrast this with payment by check, where the recipient of funds normally does not have use of the money until the check passes through the check-clearing mechanism. If the writer of the check and the recipient are a considerable distance apart, funds transferred by check (usually referred to as clearinghouse funds) may take several days to reach their destination. The shortest time for a check to clear through most clearinghouse systems is one day, but even that is too long for banks, security dealers, and other institutions who trade daily in the financial markets, since each day that the transfer of funds is delayed is a day's interest income lost.

The federal funds market began in the 1920s and was confined almost exclusively to short (overnight) loans between major U.S. banks. In recent years, however, the number of institutions (both financial and nonfinancial) which use this market has expanded sharply, and commercial banks—especially large ones—have begun to employ the federal funds market for more permanent transfers of funds.

Commercial banks have used the federal funds market for many years as a temporary means for liquidity adjustment. Those banks with short-term surplus funds available have frequently found that the return from disposing of these funds in the federal funds market has exceeded the net return (after transaction costs) from investments in Treasury bills or other money market instruments. The federal funds market has also provided an attractive source of funds when the reserve position of banks is strained. The attractiveness of the federal funds market as a source of funds relative to attracting deposits (especially large certificates of deposit) was especially important in periods of tight money in the middle and late 1960s, since there is no legal limit on the rate a bank may pay to obtain federal funds, while there were and still are some limits on the amount banks can pay to obtain funds through the sale of deposits.[8]

In recent years, however, the federal funds market has been used by commercial banks of widely varying size as a more permanent source as well as a use of funds. Large, money center banks have arranged to acquire a given amount of federal funds from their correspondent banks on a daily basis. Through this means, the larger bank is able to acquire funds beyond its local deposit potential and to expand its earning assets (especially loans) beyond the volume that could be supported only through deposits. In some periods the cost of these funds is less than the cost of funds raised through deposits. For the smaller bank, the arrangement represents

---

[8]The attractiveness of federal fund transactions versus large CD operations was reduced when the Regulation Q ceiling on the maixmum rates payable to obtain funds was eliminated for large ($100,000 or over) CDs.

an assured use of funds that may be employed without "spoiling" the local loan market.

The number of nonbank participants in the federal funds market has broadened considerably in recent years. Many savings and loan associations, for example, now use the federal funds market as a means for meeting their liquidity needs, accomplishing these transactions through their correspondent banks. Moreover, U.S. government security dealers and many nonfinancial firms now use the federal funds market for a variety of purposes, particularly through the device of repurchase agreements on U.S. government securities payable in federal funds.

The federal funds market is of some importance as an indicator of the current posture of monetary policy. The Federal Reserve periodically announces specific growth-rate targets for the amount of money in circulation.[9] Through its open-market operations the Fed has then sought to increase or decrease the growth rate of the nation's money supply through altering the availability and cost of bank reserves. For example, should the Federal Reserve wish to expand the monetary growth rate, it may purchase securities in the open market, thereby increasing the availability of reserves and reducing the federal funds rate. Conversely, should the Fed wish to reduce the growth rate of money in circulation, it could sell government securities from its portfolio, thereby reducing the availabiltiy of reserves and increasing the federal funds rate. Since the Fed does not announce its policies until well after the fact, observers of monetary policy and Federal Reserve actions pay especially careful attention to day-to-day and week-to-week movements in the federal funds rate as published in major business and financial periodicals, as signals of changes in monetary policy. Such movements have substantial implications for the loan and investment policies of all financial institutions and especially for commercial banks. While the importance of the federal funds rate in this regard was reduced by the shift in October 1979 to a reserve-based operating target by the Fed, the federal funds rate is still watched closely.

Certificates of Deposit

One of the newest and most important money market instruments is the large ($100,000 or over) certificate of deposit. These obligations of commercial banks (and, to a lesser extent, of savings and loan associations) are relatively new as a money market instrument—in fact, not much more than 20 years old. Credit for the creation of the large certificate of deposit as a money market instrument is generally given to First National City

---

[9]See Chapter 5 for a discussion of alternative definitions of the money stock and the Federal Reserve's monetary growth targets.

Bank of New York (Citibank), one of the largest banks in the United States and considered by many to be the most innovative bank in the nation.

The large New York banks have traditionally been wholesale institutions, obtaining funds from demand deposits of businesses and concentrating their credit-granting activities in the field of commercial lending. They have not historically relied upon the small accounts of consumers. But with a period of relatively high interest rates (since World War II), the large corporate depositors of these banks have found it profitable to shift idle balances into interest-bearing assets and out of demand deposits. When this happened, the shift did, of course, affect the growth rates of deposits at all banks, but especially at the large New York banks, which relied so heavily on business demand deposits.

To compete effectively with the open market for funds and to prevent continued erosion of the importance of the banking system in the flow of funds, it was necessary for commercial banks to develop an instrument which had characteristics similar to other open-market financial instruments and yet would bring funds directly into the bank. The instrument would have to be short-term in nature, of very low credit risk, and have a good secondary market. When First National City Bank began to offer the large CDs in 1961 and when major dealers agreed to create a secondary market, a financial instrument with these desirable characteristics was created. The CDs have met with enormous success, so that by year-end 1982, more than $400 billion was outstanding in these money market instruments, making them the most important instrument by dollar volume in the U.S. money market.

The certificates of deposit which are considered money market instruments are negotiable and have a minimum denomination of $100,000 although a $1 million CD is a more standard denomination (a normal round lot for trading purposes is $1 million). The original maturity of the large CDs ranges from a minimum of only a few days to a maximum of over one year, although most have original maturities of less than six months. There is a good secondary market, especially for the instruments of the largest banks. CDs are generally classified as prime and nonprime. Prime CDs are those issued by a few banks which are generally very large and experienced in the CD market. Nonprime CDs are those issued by all other banks, generally at a higher interest rate.

It is important to understand the reasons for the sale of large CDs by major banks and also the reasons for the purchase of these money market instruments by investors. To understand why banks sell CDs, let us refer back to the traditional way in which banks managed their assets and to the development of liability-management techniques in the early postwar period. Historically, bank management has concentrated upon the control of assets and has regarded deposits as essentially determined by external factors outside the bank's control. Management decision making concentrated on the selection of specific assets in which to invest available funds. With the growth of large certificates of deposit and, indeed, with the development of the federal funds market, banks do not need to rely completely on assets for providing liquidity, nor do they need to view their deposits as totally beyond the control of management. With the development of CDs, banks could obtain funds not only by liquidation of their assets (such as by selling Treasury bills) but also by selling certificates of deposit. In the latter case the bank is using liability management to at least partially control its rate of growth and meet short-term reserve needs. Not only can banks use liability management to obtain relatively short-term funds, but they can also use the CD market for longer-term purposes; that is, they can raise funds through the CD market in order to expand their asset base. Moreover, the success of the CD encouraged major banks to develop new sources of funds subject to management decision making, such as Eurodollars and commercial paper.

Large CDs are purchased primarily by major business firms that wish to place temporarily available funds in a relatively safe instrument but would like a return which exceeds that available on Treasury bills. Risk involved in the investment in CDs is higher than with Treasury bills, as revealed by the failure of U.S. National Bank of San Diego and New York's Franklin National Bank, both of which had substantial amounts of CDs outstanding at the time of their collapse. In addition, the secondary market for large CDs is inferior to that of Treasury bills. For these reasons, market yields available to the investor on large CDs are slightly higher than those available on Treasury bills. As a general rule, the highest quality negotiable certificates of deposit offer a return of 50 to 100 basis points above those available on comparable maturity Treasury bills, although the differential varies widely over time as supply and demand forces shift in each market.

Eurodollars

A Eurodollar is a dollar-denominated deposit at a bank outside the United States. Most of these dollar-denominated deposits occur in banks in Europe, especially in London; hence the name Eurodollar. However, Eurodollar deposits occur throughout the world, with concentrations in Hong Kong and Singapore. It is also important to note that the Eurodollar market is a part of a broader market for deposits denominated in currencies other than that of the host country (i.e., Eurocurrencies).

The Eurodollar market is vast in size, with some estimates indicating that the total size of the market exceeds $1 trillion. It is principally a wholesale market, in which large denomination deposits are sold by bank participants, and loans are made in large denominations. Much of the market is interbank in nature; that is, major international banks buy and sell Eurodollars among themselves, though major participants in the market also are large multinational corporations, governments, and government agencies. Trading of Eurodollars among banks is done at the London interbank offering rate (LIBOR), and loans made by Eurodollar banks are usually made at the Eurodollar rate plus some premium. The rates are generally floating, with adjustments tied to changes in the LIBOR rate.

Eurodollar deposits include both time-deposit open accounts and certificates of deposit. Most are quite short-term, with many overnight in maturity. Movement of deposits from one Eurodollar bank to another occurs on the basis of small movements in interest rates offered by buying banks.

The Eurodollar market has expanded enormously in recent years. This expansion reflects the success of the market in offering attractive rates to market participants. In fact, Eurodollar banks have been able to offer rates on their deposit liabilities that typically have been higher than rates available on domestic deposits. At some points in the past this difference reflected the restraining influence of Regulation Q on the rates offered by domestic banks. More fundamentally, however, the differential has reflected the absence of regulation for Eurodollar banks and therefore the absence of the costs of regulation. At the time that the Eurodollar banks have been able to pay higher rates for dollar deposits they have been able to lend these dollars out at lower rates than many domestic competitors. This ability to offer competitive loan rates also reflects the absence of regulation, though the willingness of Eurodollar banks to operate on smaller spreads also plays a role.

Commercial Paper

Commercial paper consists of short-term promissory notes issued by large, established business firms with strong credit ratings. These firms include both financially oriented and nonfinancial enterprises, and, in fact, in recent years the commercial paper market has been used extensively by commercial banks as a source of loanable funds. Commercial paper notes are unsecured, though firms selling commercial paper often must arrange back-up lines of credit with commercial banks. They are issued for periods of no more than 270 days, since the Securities and Exchange Commission has ruled that longer-term paper must be registered. Commercial paper is sold at a discount, as are Treasury bills, and their yield is determined by the bank discount method. In contrast to Treasury bills and large CDs most commerical paper has no important secondary market; thus its liquidity is reduced. However, many borrowers have attached an informal buy-back arrangement, whereby the issuer will repurchase the paper if the buyer wishes to sell it prior to maturity. It is understood, though, that the buyer will use the informal buy-back arrangement only when there is a real need for funds and not merely to suit the investor's convenience.

There are two basic varieties of commercial paper. One form is sold by the very largest finance companies in the United States, such as General Motors Acceptance Corporation and CIT Financial. The paper issued by these firms is frequently referred to as finance company paper. It is sold directly to ultimate buyers of the financial instrument without the use of brokers or dealers. The issuers of this type of commercial paper are in the market almost continuously and have developed dependable sources of funds. The issuers usually post rates and stand ready to accommodate investors willing to accept the posted rates and maturities. In contrast, the second form of commercial paper is brought to the market by smaller, less well-known firms and businesses usually on an irregular basis. These firms include many industrial companies, a large number of electric and gas utilities, the smaller finance companies, and some banks (through their holding companies). This form of commercial paper typically is sold through brokers or dealers. The rate offered to the market for this dealer-placed paper is usually higher than for finance company paper, because dealers must be compensated for their services and because issuers of dealer-placed paper are perceived as somewhat more risky, perhaps because of their smaller size.

Commercial paper carries a number of significant advantages for both borrowers and lenders in this market. These advantages help to explain why the commercial paper market has been one of the fastest growing parts of the money and capital markets during the postwar era. One obvious reason for the use of commercial paper by many business firms is its cost. It is generally cheaper to finance short-term cash needs with commercial paper than by borrowing from a commercial bank. The commercial paper rate typically is lower than the prime rate on business loans at commercial banks. In addition, the cost of commercial paper is further enhanced, compared to borrowing at large commercial banks, by the absence of compensating balance requirements that add to the effective cost of the bank loan. The only mitigating element that reduces this cost spread between commercial paper and bank loans is the frequent requirement that issuers of commercial paper have a standing line of credit at a commercial bank.

There are other reasons, though, for the use of commercial paper by those firms which do have the option to issue it (i.e., the larger firms). One important justification is that a firm may be able to obtain a larger total volume of credit. If a business mixes both bank credit and commercial paper as sources of funds it may be able to obtain a larger total volume of short-term funds than if it used exclusively either commercial credit or bank credit. This, of course, assumes that the credit markets are imperfect.[10] Another advantage of commercial paper for the issuer is the added bargaining power it brings in dealings with banks. If the borrowing firm has an alternative source of credit it is less likely to be placed in a position of taking whatever deal the bank offers. Finally, there may be a certain element of prestige involved in selling commercial paper, since it has generally been sold only by the largest and most highly rated firms in the nation.

From the buyer's perspective, the two principal advantages of commercial paper compared with Treasury bills are yield and maturity. Commmercial paper generally carries a higher yield than Treasury bills, reflecting greater risk and reduced liquidity. In addition, the maturity of commercial paper may be tailored precisely to the needs of the investor while Treasury bills come in fixed maturities which may be less convenient to the lender.

As with other money market instruments, the commercial paper market is a wholesale market with a normal round lot of $1 million, although paper is often available in smaller denominations. Most commercial paper is purchased by nonfinancial firms. As a result, it is frequently argued that commercial paper is a financial device by which business firms finance other business firms and bypass the commercial banking system. The growth of the commercial paper market necessarily reduces the share of the total flow of credit which is captured by the commercial banking system. Indeed, some observers believe the commercial paper market has grown very rapidly in recent years due to basic inadequacies of the domestic banking system in meeting the credit needs of major corporations, especially during periods of tight money and high interest rates. Most industrialized nations today are served by a few very large banks operating hundreds of branch offices and possessing enormous credit-granting potential. In contrast, the U.S. banking system is composed of thousands of small and moderate size banks, many of which simply cannot accommodate the credit needs of large and rapidly growing corporations.

Bankers' Acceptances

One of the oldest and yet one of the smallest money market instruments by volume is the bankers' acceptance. The bankers' acceptance is a draft, or order to pay (a bill of exchange), a specified amount at a specified time.

---

[10]This is consistent with the fact that commercial banks are limited by their capital in the size of loans to a single customer.

It is drawn on an individual commercial bank by a business firm and becomes a bankers' acceptance when the bank stamps "Accepted" on the face of the draft. Bankers' acceptances are known as two-name paper, since they have the names of both the drawer and the drawee on their face. They are used primarily to finance the shipment of goods between different countries of the world. In addition to providing financing for foreign trade, however, bankers' acceptances also are used to finance the domestic shipment of goods, the domestic or foreign storage of readily marketable staples, and the provision of dollar exchange credit to banks in designated countries.

The workings of the bankers' acceptance as a tool of international commerce may best be explained by an example. Suppose that an American importer wished to purchase shoes from a Brazilian exporter. He could obtain an irrevocable letter of credit in favor of the exporter. This letter of credit would allow the exporter to draw a draft on the American bank. This draft would be an order to pay the Brazilian exporter a specified amount at a specified time in the future (a time draft as opposed to a sight draft). The exporter—probably acting through his bank—would then send the draft to the American bank. This draft would be stamped "Accepted" by the American bank, indicating its liability for payment at the maturity date of the draft. The acceptance may then either be returned to the Brazilian bank (in which case the Brazilian bank is the true source of credit for the transaction), held by the American bank (financing is then done by the American bank), or sold to an acceptance dealer (financing then is provided by the acceptance dealer).

The bankers' acceptance market provides a number of important functions. Perhaps most importantly it is an efficient means for the financing of international trade. In domestic commerce, where information on the creditworthiness of the buyer is readily available, trade credit (open account) provides the means for financing the flow of goods. In international commerce, where information about the buyer is much less readily available, the bankers' acceptance has provided an attractive financing device. Indeed, it is the only way to finance some international commerce. Moreover, it is a relatively low-cost means of financing. The interest rate on bankers' acceptances is generally only slightly higher than the rate on Treasury bills.[11] Finally, the bankers' acceptance offers a number of advantages to the accepting banks. If the bank chooses to dispose of the acceptance, it still is able to accommodate the credit needs of one of its customers and yet not use up any of its credit-creating capacity. On the

---

[11] The fee charged by the bank for creating the acceptance must, of course, be added to the bankers' acceptance rate in order to measure the true cost of financing with bankers' acceptances.

other hand, if the accepting bank chooses to hold the acceptance and thereby provides the financing, it holds a highly liquid money market instrument.

The bankers' acceptance has an excellent secondary market. There are a number of dealers who regularly hold sizable inventories of acceptances. Moreover, the Federal Reserve was instrumental in developing the bankers' acceptance market. Other than the acceptances held by dealers in their market-making capacity, most bankers' acceptances are held by foreign central banks and domestic bank investors (most of whom hold "own bills," which are acceptances created by the same bank that has purchased them).

CAPITAL MARKET INSTRUMENTS

Turning our attention from short-to long-term financing, we see that the capital market plays a vital role in the process of transferring savings from surplus sectors to deficit sectors in the economy. In this process, both direct and indirect securities are created. As revealed in Table 4–1, the volume of securities outstanding in the capital market is enormous. As of December 31, 1981, the total volume of capital market instruments was over $4 trillion. Of this total, the volume of mortgages and corporate equities was especially significant. These mortgages would, of course, include claims on singe-family residences, multi-family residences (apartment houses), and commercial buildings. The amount of mortgages outstanding is large not only because of the great amount of real estate activity in the post–World War II era but also because of the large amount of financial leverage which has been traditionally employed in financing construction.

Money versus Capital Market Instruments

There are a number of important similarities and differences among capital market instruments. The most obvious difference is that between debt and equity. All debt instruments represent a fixed claim on the issuer. In contrast, common stock represents a residual or variable claim on the issuer. The issuer of a debt instrument promises to make specific interest payments during the life of the issue and to return the principal to the lender at the maturity of the instruments. In contrast, there is no promise to pay any return to the investor in an issue of common stock nor even to return the investor's funds. While theoretically the owners of the common stock could force management to liquidate the company and thereby return to common shareholders the proceeds minus any amount due to creditors, in fact the separation of ownership and control that is characteristic of most publicly held corporations makes this impossible. Somewhere in between debt and common stock lies preferred stock, which has some features of debt and some features of equity.

Bonds and Notes

While all debt instruments are similar in that they represent a creditor-debtor relationship and a financial instrument that is a fixed obligation, individual debt instruments vary widely in their characteristics. For example, corporate, municipal, and U.S. government debt differ in terms of *denomination*. Corporate debt usually is sold in minimum denominations of $1,000. U.S. government debt, with the exception of Treasury bills and some note issues, also carries a minimum denomination of $1,000. In contrast, municipal issues are generally sold in minimum denominations of $5,000. These bonds also differ in terms of security. Some corporate bonds, which are referred to as *mortgage* bonds, have real assets, such as land or buildings pledged to guarantee payment of the bonds. Others have no specific asset pledged but only the general creditworthiness of the borrower. These are referred to as *debenture* bonds. Necessarily, all U.S. government securities are debentures. For municipal securities, more important than the pledge of specific collateral is the method of repayment. For some municipal bonds, the taxing power of the state or local government unit is pledged to secure payments. These are referred to as *general obligation* bonds. In contrast, some municipal bonds are secured only by the revenue-generating capacity of the project for which the funds are raised, a publicly owned electric generating plant, for example. These types of bonds are called *revenue bonds*. Bonds differ also in the method of sale in the primary or original issue market. Most municipal and U.S. government securities are sold through a competitive bid process, generally to professional security dealers who are said to *underwrite* the issue. In contrast, many corporate debt securities and some municipal bonds are sold through underwriters selected on a negotiation basis.

Mortgages

Mortgages represent a component of the debt market that is so distinct as to often be treated separately and independently of the other portions of the debt market. Mortgages themselves are quite heterogeneous in nature. Their denomination reflects the denomination of the underlying real property for whose transfer the mortgage is generally created. Moreover, the security of individual mortgages varies widely. While all mortgages convey a claim on real property, the nature of the claim varies (as it does with corporate bonds), with some mortgages (first mortgages) having first claim, with others (second mortgages) having second claim and with some mortgages having even lower claims. Mortgages also differ in the method of origination. Most mortgages are created in the sale of property. However, in recent years, a substantial number of mortgages have been created to allow property owners to realize a portion of the inflation-created buildup in the equity value of their property. The very substantial differences in the characteristics of mortgages are among the major reasons why the secondary market for mortgages has traditionally been quite poor. However, the development of pass-through certificates that are standardized contracts representing a share in a pool of mortgages has improved the secondary market for mortgages considerably.

Equity Securities

The greatest diversification in the nature of a given financial instrument probably occurs for equity. While all common stock represents a residual ownership interest in the earnings and assets of a business, the characteristics of individual common stock obviously vary tremendously. There is hardly any similarity at all between one share of common stock in AT&T and one share of common stock in a new, high-technology company, except that both represent an ownership interest. The AT&T share has traditionally been viewed by the marketplace almost like a bond (as is the case for most stocks, such as utilities, which are purchased for their dividends). Recent changes in the nature of the communications industry in general and in the structure of AT&T in particular, however, appear to be changing the nature of the security and increasing its degree of risk.

The equity market is almost entirely a secondary market in "used" stock. Very little new stock is created as firms choose to increase their equity base through the retention of earnings rather than the sale of new common stock, and as almost all external financing is done with debt. Similarly, very little preferred stock has been issued in recent years as companies have chosen debt with interest payments that are a tax-deductible expense to preferred stock with dividend payments that are not tax-deductible.

Growth of Capital Market Securities

While the outstanding volume of mortgages and corporate equities is quite similar in size, the rate of growth of these capital market instruments has been very different. The volume of corporate equities outstanding has grown very little in recent years for a variety of reasons. Perhaps most importantly, American business firms have found that the cost of raising funds through debt has been substantially less than obtaining funds with external equity.

In contrast to the enormous volume outstanding of mortgages and corporate equities, it is interesting to note that the amounts of U.S. government securities and municipal obligations outstanding are relatively modest. As previously discussed, the maturity of the debt of the U.S.

government has shortened considerably in recent years. The maturity has indeed been reduced to the point where U.S. government securities may be considered to be more of a money market rather than a capital market instrument. In contrast, municipal debt, while small compared to the amount of mortgages and corporate equities outstanding, has grown very rapidly in recent years. The substantial geographic shifts in population, coupled with an expansion in the role of state and local governments, have created an enormous expansion in the volume of municipal securities outstanding. With substantial demands for services in conjunction with resistance to tax increases, there has been a tendency for state and local governments to finance through borrowings rather than increased taxes, through the sale of general obligation bonds and especially through the marketing of revenue bonds for specific revenue-producing functions.

YIELD RELATIONSHIPS AMONG FINANCIAL MARKET INSTRUMENTS

Yield on money and capital instruments are affected by a number of different factors,[12] including, to name the major ones, *maturity, credit risk, marketability, callability,* and *taxability.* A brief analysis of each of these factors follows. It is important for the manager of a financial intermediary to be aware of how these factors affect the prices and yields on financial assets. Such knowledge may not only be used to reduce the possible loss on investment (a defensive strategy) but may also be useful in reaching for higher yields (an offensive strategy) and therefore greater earnings for the institution.

Time to Maturity

One of the most pervasive influences on the yield of financial market instruments is the time to maturity. As the time to maturity increases, the yield available on financial instruments usually rises, and, of course, the cost of raising funds through issuing these instruments increases. Conversely, as the time to maturity shortens, the yield available on these instruments usually falls, and, of course, the cost of raising funds through issuing such instruments decreases. The relationship between yield to maturity and time to maturity of a financial instrument is referred to as the yield curve, or the term structure of interest rates. For the investor, a normal yield curve indicates that a higher return on the investment may be obtained by seeking investments of longer maturity. Notice, however, that seeking investments of longer maturity means accepting greater inter-

---

[12]Our discussion of the influence of these factors on yield relationships concentrates on capital market instruments, where yield spreads are often quite large. The same factors, of course, influence money market yields; however, because money market instruments are quite homogeneous, their yield spreads are generally much less.

est-rate risk.[13] Of course, the issuer of securities must pay a higher cost in order to obtain the increased liquidity that goes with longer-term liabilities.

Yield curves may and do take a variety of shapes over the course of the business cycle. The normal yield curve is upward sloping. Sometimes, however, the yield curve is downward sloping, especially at or near peak levels of interest rates during periods of tight money. During some periods of tight money, the yield curve often takes on a hump in the middle. Each of these possibilities is illustrated in Figure 4–1.

There are a number of explanations for the yield-maturity relationship. Perhaps the most widely accepted view is the expectations hypothesis, which is that the current relationship between short- and long-term interest rates is determined by the expectations of market praticipants regarding future interest rates. For example, if investors feel that future interest rates will be higher than current interest rates, the yield curve would tend to have an upward slope. Conversely, if investors feel that future interest rates will be lower than current interest rates, the yield curve will tend to be downward sloping. Finally, if market participants expect that future interest rates will be the same as current interest rates, the yield curve should be flat, or horizontal.

One difficulty with a pure expectations explanation of the yield curve is that it does not explain satisfactorily the fact that the yield curve has displayed an upward slope more often than a downward slope. It would seem that there should be equal periods of upward and downward sloping yield curves unless investors are nearly always expecting increases in interest rates. To reconcile this problem some have argued—in a modified expectations hypothesis—that investors have a preference for liquidity and are willing to accept a lower rate of return in order to obtain greater liquidity in their investments. Therefore investors are willing to accept lower rates of return for shorter-term as opposed to longer-term securities because the former tend to be more liquid. Thus, even if the expectation is for unchanged interest rates in the future, the yield curve today should be upward sloping.

The expectations hypothesis relies heavily upon profit-maximizing behavior on the part of both lenders and borrowers, modifying financial decisions as expectations of future interest-rates change. It assumes that lenders and borrowers are indifferent with regard to the maturity of their assets (lenders) or liabilities (borrowers). It does not, however, take into account the institutional rigidities that exist in the financial system in which most primary securities are purchased by financial institutions,

---

[13]For a given change in interest rates, the price of longer-term securities fluctuates more than the price of shorter-term issues.

Figure 4–1   Yield Curves

A. Upward sloping yield curve

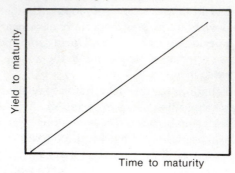

B. Downward sloping curve

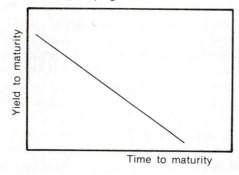

C. Humped yield curve

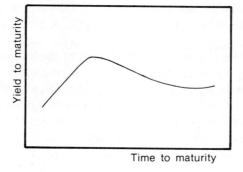

which are subject to significant legal and other restrictions on their investment behavior; nor does it take into account the desire by borrowers to issue securities of different maturities. This limitation of the expectations hypothesis has resulted in the development of the segmented markets (or hedging) explanation of the yield curve.

The segmented markets explanation of the yield curve is based upon the argument that financial institutions as investors and business firms as borrowers tend to specialize in the maturity of their investments. Commercial banks, for example, are purchasers principally of relatively short-term financial assets (money market instruments). In contrast, life insurance companies are involved primarily in long-term financial instruments of the capital market (principally corporate bonds and mortgages). Similarly, it is often good financial management practice for business firms which are temporarily building inventory to finance using short-term sources of funds and for business firms which are expanding their fixed assets to finance with long-term sources of funds.

The segmented markets explanation of the term structure would then explain a downward sloping yield curve as the result of a scarcity in the supply of funds from commercial banks (perhaps because of a tight money policy on the part of the Federal Reserve System) and a high demand for short-term funds (perhaps due to heavy inventory accumulation by business firms). Similarly, an upward-sloping yield curve may be explained by an easy monetary policy and slack business conditions.

The yield curve has a number of uses for financial managers. For those who accept the expectations hypothesis, or some variant of it, the yield curve may be used as a device to forecast future interest rates. For example, an upward-sloping yield curve suggests a rise in short-term interest rates. In addition, the yield curve may be useful in determining the best maturity of a security issue for the borrower and the best maturity for the lender. For example, a humped yield curve would indicate that, while there is a substantial interest-rate penalty for extending the maturity of an issue up to the peak of the hump, there is little or no penalty to the borrower for further extensions. This may suggest that the borrower should increase the maturity of a planned issue. Conversely, the existence of a humped yield curve might suggest to the investor that a purchase be kept near the short-term end of the maturity spectrum. As a third possible use of the yield curve, it may be possible (assuming some inefficiencies in the market) to find overpriced and underpriced securities through the use of the yield curve.

Default Risk

There are many other factors in addition to time to maturity which might be expected to affect the yield to maturity on a financial market instrument. One of the most important of these is default, or credit risk—the possibility that the principal and/or interest payments on a debt security will not be made in a timely fashion. It would be expected that the larger the default risk involved in the commitment of funds to a security, the higher must be the expected yield to maturity. The influence of default risk on relative yields is illustrated by the yields to maturity offered in the market for fixed-income securities. U.S. government securities—thought to carry no default risk—have the lowest return to the investor. In the corporate category, Aaa-rated securities have the lowest default risk and the lowest rate of return. Similarly, default risk and yield increase as the rating diminishes through Aa, A, and down to lower-grade issues. This relationship is known as the risk structure of interest rates.

Default risk on corporate municipal bonds is often represented by bond ratings. These evaluations are prepared by a number of private rating services, of which Moody's and Standard & Poor's are the best known. Table 4–5 shows the various classifications used by these two rating services. For example, for Moody's, the highest rating category is Aaa; while for Standard & Poor's, the highest rating category is AAA. The ratings then are reduced to Aa (Moody's) and AA (Standard & Poor's) to reflect greater risk of default. Securities in the first four rating categories are usually referred to as investment-grade securities and consist of those securities that do not have speculative characteristics. Moving down from these investment-grade issues produces a sufficient increase in default risk that the securities possess speculative characteristics. Not suprisingly, there is a strong correlation between the rating of a bond and its yield, with lower rating (higher default risk) producing higher yields.

Marketability

Another variable which does affect the yield to maturity on capital market securities is marketability. While investments in securities are generally planned for a considerable period in advance, it may be that, due to unforseen circumstances, the holder would want to liquidate the securities prior to maturity. In that case, the ability to eliminate the security from the portfolio quickly and with little impact on market price is an important factor to the investor. Among fixed-income securities, U.S. Treasury securities stand out as having the best secondary market. In contrast, municipal securities and corporate bond issues generally have a limited secondary market. At the extreme, investments in mortgages are generally quite illiquid. Among equity securities, the marketability of the issue varies widely. Equity investments in closely held corporations are often difficult to liquidate. In contrast, shares in a relatively stable security listed on the New York Stock Exchange are generally easier to liquidate, although

---

Table 4–5   **Bond Rating Categories Used by Moody's and Standard & Poor's**

	Ratings	*Description*
Moody's		
	Aaa	Highest quality
	Aa	High quality
	A	Higher medium quality
	Baa	Medium quality
	Ba	Some speculative elements
	B	Speculative
	Caa	Poor quality
	Ca	Speculative to a high degree
	C	Lowest grade
Standard & Poor's		
	AAA	Highest quality
	AA	High quality
	A	Upper medium quality
	BBB	Medium quality
	BB	Lower medium quality
	B	Speculative
	CCC-CC	Highly speculative
	C	Income bonds
	DDD-D	In default

---

the market price may be unsatisfactory due to variations in general market conditions.

Callability

Callability is another factor that may have some influence on market yields. Callability is defined as the ability of a borrower to retire a capital market instrument prior to maturity. The borrower may "call" the security at a previously specified price, thereby forcing holders of the security to exchange it for cash. Callability is an especially important feature for longer-term investors. Not only does the call of a security disturb the portfolio of the investor, but it also usually will reduce the yield of the portfolio. Most corporate bonds are callable. In contrast, most U.S. government securities and many municipals are not callable.

Since the call feature is undesirable to the investor (but desirable to the issuer), it would be expected that securities which are immediately callable would carry a higher yield than securities which are not callable or for which the call feature has been postponed or deferred for some period. However, the investor would demand a call premium only if there was some real possibility that the issue would, in fact, be called. Such a call would be most likely to occur when interest rates have fallen from higher levels when the security was first issued. In fact, studies have shown that the market requires a substantial call premium only in periods when interest rates are unusually high and are expected to fall.

Taxability

A final factor is taxability. Taxability refers to the tax status of the return from the security. The most publicized impact of the taxability feature occurs for municipal securities. The interest return on all issues of state governments and any instrumentality of the states, such as cities, counties, school districts, and other local governmental units, are exempt from the federal income tax. Moreover, the returns on these issues usually are exempt from the income tax of the area which has issued the security. For example, securities issued by the state of New York would be exempt from the New York state income tax. As a result of this tax exemption, municipal securities carry substantially lower yields in the market than corporate obligations. Capital gains realized on municipal securities, however, are taxable. As a result, municipal securities on which part of the investment return occurs in the form of capital gains must carry a higher yield than comparable securities in which the total return is in the form of interest. As a final and little noted feature, the interest income from U.S. government issues is exempt from state and local taxes.

Relative Yield Patterns

Some of the more important relationships among the money and capital markets which stem from the features discussed in this chapter are illustrated in Table 4–6. This table presents the market yield on selected money and capital market instruments for 1975, 1978, 1981, and 1983. A number of important observations can be made, based upon the information presented in this table. First, all three money market rates—rates on Treasury bills, large CDs and commercial paper—tend to cluster together, reflecting the substitutability of these instruments in investor portfolios. Second, yields on Treasury bills are lower than yields on other money market instruments, reflecting both the lower default risk on Treasury issues and their superior marketability. Third, the yield curve is upward sloping for each time period presented in the table. For example, in 1975 the yield on three-month Treasury bills was 5.80 percent, while the yield on 20-year U.S. government bonds was 8.19 percent. In the capital market, the structure of relative yields also reflects many of the factors discussed above. Yields on municipal bonds are below yields on either U.S. government or corporate issues, due to the taxability feature. Also, yields on U.S. government bonds are below yields on corporate bonds, in response to the reduced default risk on U.S. government issues and their greater marketability.

Table 4–6   Interest Rates on Selected Money and Capital Market Instruments (percent)

	1975	1978	1981	1983 (February)
3-month Treasury bills	5.80	7.19	13.14	8.11
Large CDs	6.43	8.20	15.14	8.54
90–119 day commercial paper	6.26	10.37	14.60	8.34
20-year U.S. government bonds	8.19	8.90	15.27	11.03
AAA municipal bonds	6.42	5.52	12.60	8.80
AAA corporate bonds	8.83	8.73	15.51	12.01
Federal funds	5.20	13.36	16.38	8.51
3-month Eurodollar deposit	N.A.	N.A.	16.79	9.14

Note: N.A. = Not available.
Source: *Federal Reserve Bulletin*, various issues.

The financial futures markets are one of the most innovative and rapidly growing segments of the financial markets. In this chapter we briefly discuss the meaning of financial futures and the reason for the explosive growth of financial futures trading. Discussion of the ways in which financial institutions may use the financial futures market is postponed until Chapter 11.

A futures market is an organized market in which a standardized contract is bought and sold for future delivery. It may thus be compared with the cash, or spot, market in which delivery of the item bought or sold is immediate. A number of organized financial futures markets have been created since the early 1970s (futures markets for agricultural products have existed for decades). The Chicago Board of Trade, the International Monetary Market, the New York Futures Markets, and London Futures Markets all trade futures contracts for delivery of money and capital market instruments. Trading occurs in Treasury bills, notes and bonds, bank certificates of deposit, as well as in other financial instruments. There even exists futures trading in stock market indexes such as the Standard & Poor's 500 Stock Index.

The financial futures markets are used by economic participants either as hedging or speculating vehicles. Hedgers wish to shift risk to others while speculators accept risk in the hope of earning large returns. For example, suppose that a financial institution holds a portfolio of long-term government bonds, and also suppose that this institution is concerned about an increase in the general level of interest rates (which would, of course, produce a decline in the value of the bond portfolio). It could hedge against this risk by establishing a position in the futures market that is the opposite of its position in the cash market. Since it is long in the cash market (an economic participant that owns a security is said to be long in

FINANCIAL FUTURES MARKETS

that security), the financial institution would take a *short* position in the futures market; that is, it would sell a futures contract. By this transaction it has hedged against the risk of rising interest rates. If interest rates do rise, the financial institution would have a loss on the long-term government bonds that it holds in its portfiolio (its cash position), but it would have a gain on its futures position. It could close out its position in the futures market by buying an equivalent futures contract at a lower price than it had sold the contract for (since interest rates have increased). Note, however, that the hedge not only reduces the risk of loss but also reduces the opportunity for gain. If interest rates were to decline, the investor would have a gain on a cash position but a loss on a position in the futures market.

Speculators, who willingly accept risk, play an important role in the futures markets. A speculator who expected interest rates to fall more than the consensus of market participants might purchase a futures market contract. If correct, the speculator would gain as the price of the futures contract advanced. The potential for gain (or loss) in futures market trading is enormous, since a contract may be purchased with a very small cash payment. For example, a $100,000 Treasury bond contract (a contract for future delivery of $100,00 of Treasury bonds) may be bought or sold with a cash payment (referred to as a margin) of only a few thousand dollars. In fact, a $1 million contract for Treasury bills may be obtained with a cash payment of $2,500. Of course, while speculation in financial futures may produce large gains, it also may produce large losses. Since the cash payment, or margin, represents a small fraction of the amount of the futures contract, small movements in the value of the contract will produce large changes in the value of the investor's funds.

SUMMARY   Money and capital market instruments are the vehicles by which financial transactions are accomplished. The money market refers to the market for short-term financial instruments with a time to maturity of one year or less. Money market instruments are primarily used for liquidity adjustment. The term *capital market* refers to the market for long-term financial instruments used for more permanent investment purposes. The money and capital markets differ in terms of the importance of secondary market transactions, the volume of transactions, default and interest rate risk, as well as other factors.

The principal money market instruments are U.S. Treasury securities, primarily Treasury bills, federal funds, certificates of deposit, Eurodollars, commercial paper, and bankers' acceptances. The principal capital market instruments are bonds issued by corporations, government (state, local, and federal), various types of mortgages, and equity securities in the form of common stocks. These financial instruments differ in terms of their maturity, default risk, marketability, callability, and taxability. These factors account for most of the range of interest rates observed on financial instruments.

Financial futures markets are markets in which standardized contracts for future delivery are bought and sold. These markets are used for both speculating and hedging. As we will note in Chapter 11, financial futures are increasingly used by financial institutions today to protect (hedge) the value of their security portfolios and to soften the blow of rising interest costs on borrowed funds.

Questions

4–1. Compare and contrast the differences between the money market and the capital market in terms of (*a*) purpose, (*b*) secondary market, (*c*) volume of transactions, (d) risk, (*e*) importance of different financial institutions, and (*f*) volume of financial instruments outstanding.

4–2. What are the characteristic financial instruments of the respective money market and capital market?

4–3. Note the different characteristics of U.S. Treasury bills, Treasury notes, and Treasury bonds. How are they different in terms of maturity?

4–4. What is a discount instrument? Which Treasury securities are discount instruments?

4–5. A U.S. Treasury bill is purchased for $9,350. It has a maturity of one year. What is its (*a*) bank discount yield and (*b*) bond equivalent, or true yield?

4–6. Differentiate between prime and non-prime certificates of deposit. How should this distinction affect the yield on these certificates?

4–7. What is the expectations hypothesis? The modified expectations hypothesis? The segmented markets, or hedging explanation of the yield curve?

4–8. Examine how the following factors may affect the yield of a security:
a. Maturity.
b. Credit risk.
c. Marketability.
d. Callability.
e. Taxability.

References

1. Federal Reserve Bank of Richmond. *Instruments of the Money Market*, 1981.

2. Henning, Charles; William Pigott; and Robert Scott. *Financial Markets and the Economy*. 3d ed. Englewood Cliffs, N.J.: Prentice-Hall, 1981.

3. Cooper, K., and D. Fraser. *The Financial Marketplace.* Reading, Mass.: Addison–Wesley Publishing 1982.

4. Homer, Sidney, and Martin L. Leibowitz. *Inside the Yield Book.* Englewood Cliffs, N.J.: Prentice-Hall, 1972.

5. Lendow, W. *Inside the Money Market.* New York: Random House, 1972.

6. Robinson, Roland, and Dwayne Wrightsman. *Financial Markets.* New York: McGraw-Hill 1974.

7. Van Horne, J.C. *Financial Market Rates and Flows.* Englewood Cliffs, N.J.: Prentice–Hall, 1978.

8. Woodworth, G.W. *The Money Market and Monetary Management.* New York: Harper & Row, 1972.

5. *Monetary Policy, Fiscal Policy, Debt Management, and the Financial System*

FINANCIAL MARKETS ARE AFFECTED by the monetary policy actions of the Federal Reserve (the Fed) and by the U.S. Treasury through the management of the public debt. Changes in the financial markets in response to monetary, fiscal, and debt management policies have important influences on the behavior of financial institutions. As discussed earlier, changes in interest rates in the money and capital markets influence the prices which financial institutions must pay to obtain funds and also the returns which these institutions can earn on their loans and investments. Moreover, the volume of funds flowing into financial institutions and the demand for these funds varies substantially over the business cycle. In periods of intense monetary restraint, the flow of funds into financial institutions (especially depository financial institutions) is often curtailed. Conversely, in periods of low interest rates and monetary ease, financial institutions frequently have large inflows of funds and find difficulties in investing these funds at reasonable rates of return. Since the Federal Reserve and the Treasury affect interest-rate levels and the flow of funds to such a large extent, it is important for managers of financial institutions to understand the role of these institutions in the marketplace. The impact of government financial policy falls most directly, although not necessarily more forcefully, on depository—as opposed to nondepository—financial institutions.

The Federal Reserve System is the principal organization in the United States for controlling the quantity and cost of money and credit. It is the nation's central bank, analogous in that role to the Bank of England and other central banks around the world. Created by Congress in 1913 to play a defensive role in eliminating "money panics," the Federal Reserve now plays a more aggressive role in seeking to achieve broad economic objectives, such as full employment, stable prices, economic growth, and

INFLUENCE OF THE FEDERAL RESERVE SYSTEM

balance in the international accounts of the United States. As a result of the more aggressive role of the Fed in carrying out these objectives, and its substantial influence on interest rates and funds flows, the day-to-day behavior of the Federal Reserve System is watched intently by the management of financial institutions and by other participants in the financial markets. In fact, many large financial institutions have a number of professional staff members whose principal function is to anticipate changes in monetary policy and to evaluate the implications of current and future monetary policy for the investment strategies of their institution.[1]

Organization of the Federal Reserve

In order to understand the particular organizational framework of the Federal Reserve (which is quite different from that of other major central banks around the world), it is necessary to remember that the central bank of the United States was established as an independent, politically neutral organization. It was the intent of the founders of the Federal Reserve System to isolate to a substantial extent the making of monetary policy from the political process. As a result, members of the board of governors—the chief administrative unit within the Federal Reserve System—are appointed for long, overlapping terms of 14 years. Moreover, the Federal Reserve was established as a system composed of a variety of different components, with a substantial degree of geographic diversification in order to prevent the centralization of power, especially on Wall Street. In addition, funds for operating the Fed were to come from its earnings and not from appropriations by Congress.[2]

The Board of Governors

The Federal Reserve System is composed of a large variety of important groups. These include the board of governors, 12 Federal Reserve banks, and the Federal Open Market Committee. The board of governors (locat-

---

[1]The principal focus of this chapter is with the monetary policy activities of the Federal Reserve. The Fed does, of course, also provide a number of service functions, such as clearing checks and other means of payment, providing currency and coin, and providing for safekeeping of securities. These service functions of the Fed are covered throughout the book in different chapters where most appropriate. The Depository Institutions Deregulation and Monetary Control Act of 1980 (DIDMCA) made a number of changes in the sevice functions of the Fed. Two in particular are especially important. First, DIDMCA mandated that the services be made available to *all* depository institutions. Second, DIDMCA required that the Fed *charge* for each of its services provided to depository institutions. Prior to DIDMCA, the Fed had provided these services only to member commercial banks and then usually without an explicit charge.

[2]Moreover, the Federal Reserve system's expenditures are not subject to audit by the General Accounting Office, although in recent years there has been increasing pressure to bring the Fed's expenditures under the scrutiny of this arm of Congress.

ed in Washington, D.C.) is composed of seven members appointed for 14-year terms by the president of the United States and confirmed by the Senate. The long terms (longer than the term allowed by law for any president) and the overlapping of terms for individual governors was designed to insulate the board from the influence of the president and the political process generally. This intent was strengthened by the features that, while the president has the power to appoint board members, the president does not have the authority to remove those members prior to the expiration of their terms. However, in practice, the political independence of the Federal Reserve System should not be overestimated. The chairman of the board of governors participates, usually actively, in the formulation of the economic policy of the current administration and is a regular member of major economic advisory committees within the administration. Moreover, it is unlikely that the Fed could stray too far from the desires of Congress. It is frequently said that the Federal Reserve System is independent *within* the government but not *of* the government.

The board of governors and its staff are primarily concerned with the formulation and implementation of monetary policy. Relying upon a large staff of professional economists, the board continually monitors current and forecasted developments in the financial and nonfinancial sectors of the economy. Current interest-rate movements in the money and capital markets are of great significance to the board; however, of even greater significance is the outlook for future interest rates, since interest rates, as we have seen, are closely linked to the volume of saving and investment in the economy and, therefore, the general level of employment and prices. Careful analysis is made of trends in production, prices, employment, and other important economic variables. Based upon an analysis of these economic data series, the board participates as a part of the Federal Reserve System in the conduct of monetary policy; and in the case of some specific techniques of monetary policy, the board is vested legally with total control. Of the major instruments of monetary policy, the board alone can determine the appropriate level of reserve requirements for depository institutions. It "reviews and determines" the discount rate established by the individual Reserve banks. The board also has a majority vote in the Federal Open Market Committee, the chief policymaking body of the system. It generally plays a particularly visible role in informing the economic and financial community about current Federal Reserve policy. In recent years the power of the board within the Federal Reserve System has grown at the expense of other components of that system.

The Reserve Banks

Congress wanted originally to create a decentralized system for conducting monetary policy, realizing that the central bank would possess great power and influence. Accordingly, 12 reserve banks (with 25 branch offices) were chartered, stretching from Boston to San Francisco. Each bank was to be responsible for keeping track of economic and financial conditions in its own specific region of the country and for regulating member banks in that area. Originally, each reserve bank was relatively autonomous and possessed the authority to set its own rate on discount loans to member banks without board approval. Over time, however, especially during the Great Depression of the 1930s, authority within the system became more centralized in the board of governors in Washington, D.C.

Today, the 12 reserve banks are concerned greatly with service functions, such as the clearing of checks, providing currency and coin, and handling wire transfer of funds. In addition, the individual reserve banks serve as a useful conduit of information from all regions of the nation to the board of governors and its staff. Moreover, the reserve banks increasingly have become active in the development of electronic funds transfer systems.

The reserve banks also play a significant role in the implementation of monetary policy. The individual reserve bank presidents are members of the Federal Open Market Committee, perhaps the most important organization operating within the Federal Reserve System. Concurrence of the reserve bank presidents is frequently sought by the board of governors prior to major changes in monetary policy.

The Federal Open Market Committee

The Federal Open Market Committee (FOMC) has become the focal point of Federal Reserve deliberation in recent years and its concerns include all aspects of monetary policy and every technique available to the Federal Reserve. The Federal Open Market Committee is composed of the 7 members of the board of governors and 5 reserve bank presidents—a total of 12 voting members. The chairperson of the board of governors also chairs the Federal Open Market Committee. The president of the Federal Reserve Bank of New York is always a voting member of the FOMC and serves as its vice chairperson. The other four positions for the reserve bank presidents are rotated on a yearly basis. While five of the reserve bank presidents are voting members of the FOMC at any one time, all of the reserve bank presidents (along with representatives of their staffs) are present at each of the meetings and participate fully in the discussion.

The FOMC meets roughly every month at the offices of the board of governors in Washington. At each meeting FOMC members hear presentations from the board's staff on the outlook for the economy and financial markets during the next few months as well as an evaluation of recent developments. Based upon its assessment of these economic and financial developments, the FOMC formulates a strategy to guide the trading desk of the New York Fed in the period until the next meeting of the committee. This strategy is embodied in a directive which reviews current and prospective economic and financial conditions and instructs the manager of the System Open Market Account, an official of the Federal Reserve Bank of New York, on the conduct of open-market operations.

While the Fed Open Market Committee has direct control only over the purchases and sales of securities for the System Open Market Account, the meeting of the committee is concerned with the whole range of monetary policy tools. Any changes in the discount rate or in reserve requirements are likely to be discussed at the FOMC prior to the decision by the board of governors to change any of these policy tools. The FOMC thus has become the heart of the policymaking function of the Federal Reserve System.

Reserve Requirements

TECHNIQUES OF MONETARY CONTROL

Reserve requirement changes are an infrequently used but powerful tool of monetary policy. Every depository institution is required to maintain a specified percentage of its deposits in the form of reserves, either as cash in the bank's vault or as deposits with the Fed (see Table 5–1). Changes in the percentage of reserves required by the Federal Reserve can have a substantial impact on the lending ability of the individual institutions and indeed on the total credit-creating power of the financial system. For example, the Federal Reserve could increase the reserve requirement ratio for either time or demand deposits if it wished to reduce the ability of a depository institution to expand credit. If depository institutions held excess reserves prior to the reserve requirement increase and

Table 5–1   Depository Institutions Reserve Requirements in Effect December 1983
(type of deposit and deposit interval)

	Percentage
Net transaction accounts	
0–$28.9 million	3
Over $28.9 million	12
Nonpersonal time deposits by original maturity	
Less than 1½ years	3
1½ years or more	0
Eurocurrency liabilities	
All types	3

Source: *Federal Reserve Bulletin*, January 1984.

thereby had unused lending capacity, the Federal Reserve could eliminate the excess reserves and prevent any further expansion of credit. For example, with deposits of $1,000, actual reserves of $100, and a reserve requirement ratio of 5 percent, $50 of excess reserves exist. This allows expansion of the amount of loans and investments by a multiple of the $50 of excess reserves. However should the Fed increase the reserve requirement ratio to 10 percent it would eliminate the excess reserves; and should it further increase the ratio to 15 percent it would cause a contraction in the amount of potential loans and investments, as depository institutions, short of reserves, are forced to raise additional funds.

Similarly, if the Federal Reserve wished to expand the availability of credit it could lower reserve requirements. If depository institutions had no excess reserves prior to the reduction in reserve requirements, the change in required reserves would place the individual firm in a position to expand its loans and investments (i.e., credit) and would allow for an increase in the total amount of credit by a multiple of the change in reserve requirements. Similarly, if the financial system did have excess reserves prior to the reduction in reserve requirements, the change in reserve requirements would allow further increases in credit extension.

Increasing versus Decreasing Reserve Requirements

There is one very important difference between lowering and increasing reserve requirements. An increase in reserve requirements can always have the desired result of lowering the volume of credit if that reserve requirement increase is sufficiently large. By increasing the amount of reserves required behind every dollar of deposits, the Federal Reserve can always force the management of commercial banks to curtail the growth of loans and investments. However, the impact of a reduction in reserve requirements may be quite different. The Federal Reserve, by supplying reserves, gives the financial system the capacity of expanding the quantity of credit, but the increase in credit will occur only if the depository system makes loans and investments rather than leave those reserves idle. The productive use of reserves depends upon many factors, including (1) the strength of the demand for loans, (2) interest rate levels on loans and investments, (3) the need for liquidity, and (4) the risk involved in making loans and purchasing securities. It has been argued, for example, that commercial banks did not respond to the availability of reserves provided by the Federal Reserve during the Great Depression of the 1930s because of a lack of loan demand and also because, with the wave of bank failures, management was concerned especially about maintaining satisfactory levels of liquidity. In that instance, reserves which were excessive from a legal perspective were not really excessive from the viewpoint of bank management.

Reserve requirement changes have been infrequently used both because of their excessive strength and because of their potentially uneven impact on individual member banks. Moreover, reserve requirements have been lowered more frequently than raised during the post–World War II period; the trend clearly has been toward a reduction in reserve requirements, especially on time and savings deposits. Part of the explanation for this trend lies in the need to provide more usable reserves in order to support a growing economy without adding further to the already large U.S. government security holdings of the Fed. Another important factor in past years was the Federal Reserve membership problem. Substantial numbers of banks withdrew from the Federal Reserve due principally to the large amounts of assets required by the Fed to be held in noninterest-earning form. The Fed responded to this change by gradually reducing the level of the required reserve ratio. However, the Depository Institutions Deregulation and Monetary Control Act of 1980 provided for uniform reserve requirements for all depository institutions.

Discount Rate

Another important technique used by the Federal Reserve in the conduct of monetary policy is the manipulation of the discount rate. The discount rate refers to the interest rate charged by the Federal Reserve to depository institutions when those institutions borrow from the Fed. Such borrowing is viewed by the Federal Reserve as a privilege of membership, rather than a right, and the loans are usually quite short-term (15 days or less). The discount rate (or the rediscount rate, as it is often called) is established by the individual reserve banks, subject to "review and determination" by the board of governors. In practice, the board has effective control over the discount rate.

When the Fed reduces its discount rate, investors in the marketplace usually interpret this as a move toward easier credit conditions. Such a change provides an incentive to depository institutions to obtain additional reserves and thereby may create additional lending capacity for these financial institutions. Conversely, should the Fed wish to curtail the pace of economic expansion, it could increase the discount rate. An increase in the discount rate might discourage any increase in reserve availability by raising the cost of reserves and might also serve as a signal to outside observers that the Fed wished to reduce the expansion rate of the nation's economy.

Reasons for Changes in the Discount Rate

Not all changes in the discount rate reflect the Fed's desire to bring about a change in policy. Many such changes represent reactions to other financial developments, some of which may be associated with the implementation of monetary policy by the use of one or more of the other techniques under the control of the Fed. For example, the Federal Reserve may have already used an increase in reserve requirements to curtail the quantity of bank reserves. This increase in reserve requirements, associated with the reduced availability of bank reserves, would be expected to result in an increase in interest rates. As the cost of alternative sources of funds to the individual financial institution increases relative to the discount rate, it would be expected that more firms would turn to the discount window. This change in the relative cost of funds might then create intense pressure on the Federal Reserve's discount window. If the Fed were to meet that demand and provide the reserves (even though only for a short period), this action might negate the credit tightening sought through an increase in reserve requirements. Moreover, the discount window would not be serving its principal function as a "lender of last resort." Borrowing would be stimulated by profitability rather than need. Hence, the Federal Reserve would raise the discount rate and seek to restore the more normal relationship between the discount rate and other interest rates in the market. Such a move, though, would not necessarily mean a change in monetary policy; rather the Federal Reserve in its announcement of the discount-rate change might state, as it frequently has in the past, that the change was made "for the purpose of bringing the discount rate into alignment with other open market rates."

The discount rate is one of the weakest monetary tools under control of the Federal Reserve. The discount rate does not affect the amount of required reserves at all, nor does it directly affect the total quantity of reserves. Of course, when a depository institution uses the discount window the quantity of reserves does change; however, the control is with the individual depository institution, in its decision to borrow, rather than with the Federal Reserve. As pointed out above, while there may be an announcement effect associated with discount-rate changes, the importance of this aspect of the technique is muted by the fact that changes in the discount rate may reflect adjustments to money market rates as well as other factors.

Open-Market Operations

By far the most important tool for the implementation of monetary policy is open-market operations. *Open-market operations* refers to the purchase and sale of securities (usually U.S. government securities) by the Federal Reserve in the open market. These transactions are implemented by the trading desk of the Federal Reserve Bank of New York for the entire Federal Reserve System. Such purchases and sales add to or subtract from a single account, referred to as the System Open Market Account. The trading desk of the New York Fed acts under the direction of the Federal

Table 5-2   Government Security Holdings of the
Federal Reserve: December 1983

	Holdings ($ millions)
U.S. government issues	
Bills	65,810
Notes	63,934
Bonds	20,814
Total	150,558
Federal agency obligations	8,645

Source: *Federal Reserve Bulletin*, January 1984.

Open Market Committee. For an understanding of the mechanics and impact of open-market operations, it is useful to examine how open-market transactions are carried out and the role of the Federal Open Market Committee.

The Federal Reserve System, acting through the trading desk of the New York Fed, will generally purchase securities if it wishes to expand the volume of credit (see Table 5–2). For example (refer to Figure 5–1), the trading desk of the New York Fed might place an order for $500 million of Treasury securities with the government security dealers with whom it transacts business. The purchase of these securities by the Fed would expand the volume of reserves by an equal amount. Following the transaction, the Federal Reserve would have added $500 million in government securities to its portfolio. Some dealer in government securities (either a large bank or a securities trader) would have $500 million less in government securities. This is simple and direct. But here is the important and

Figure 5–1   Purchase of $500 Million of U.S. Government Securities

Federal Reserve Banks ($ million)				Depository Institution ($ million)			
Government securities	+ 500	Deposits of depository institutions	+ 500	Reserves at Fed	+ 500	Deposit of dealer	+ 500

Dealer		
Government securities	− 500	
Deposit	+ 500	

less simple part of the transaction: the dealer's bank will receive credit on behalf of its customer (the dealer) for the U.S. government securities sold in the form of a credit to the bank's reserve account at the Federal Reserve. This credit would appear on the books of the commercial bank as an asset (reserves at the Federal Reserve) and on the books of the Federal Reserve as a liability (deposits of depository institutions). This item is sometimes referred to as high-powered money since $1 of reserves can create—due to the fractional reserve system—more than $1 of credit and money (deposits).

Where did the Federal Reserve get the money to pay for the government securities? It created the money. The Federal Reserve, through buying and selling securities, or, indeed, through any expansion or contraction of its assets creates or destroys high-powered money (i.e., reserves). In that instance, the Federal Reserve bought securities and thereby created high-powered money. And the creation of high-powered money usually leads to an expansion of the money supply held by the public. With the demand for money held constant, an expanded money supply typically results in increased demand (spending) for goods and services.

If the Fed had wished to curtail the volume of credit it might have *sold* securities. The impact of the sale of securities on the depository system is illustrated in Figure 5–2. In this case, the transfer of securities is from the Federal Reserve (its holdings fall by $500 million) to the dealer (whose holdings increase by $500 million). Payment for securities is again made by adjusting the reserve account of the dealer's bank at the Federal Reserve. The dealer's bank, in effect, writes a check payable to the Federal Reserve. Clearing of the check, which is instantaneous, then results in a $500 million decrease in reserves. This transaction appears on the books of the Fed as a $500 million reduction in the deposits of depository institu-

---

Figure 5–2   Sale of $500 Million in U.S. Government Securities

Federal Reserve Banks ($ million)		Depository Institution ($ million)	
Government securities − 500	Deposits of depository institutions − 500	Reserves at Fed − 500	Deposit of dealer − 500

Dealer	
Government securities + 500	
Deposits − 500	

tions and on the books of the dealer's bank as a $500 million decrease in reserves at the Fed. The importance of the transaction is that reserves are reduced by $500 million (i.e., high-powered money is reduced by $500 million) and the credit- and deposit-creating ability of the banking system will decline by more than $500 million.

Dynamic versus Defensive Operations

In viewing open-market operations, we should note two distinct categories: dynamic and defensive transactions. This distinction is based upon the Fed's motivation in conducting open-market operations. *Dynamic open-market operations* refers to the purchase or sale of securities in the open market for the purpose of implementing monetary policy objectives. *Defensive open-market operations* refers to the purchase or sale of securities for the purpose of preventing some external factor—such as a seasonal swing in currency demand by households and business firms—from having an undesired effect on the availability and cost of credit. For example, if the Fed desired to expand the economy's growth rate and lower the amount of unemployment, the FOMC might issue a directive to the trading desk of the New York Federal Reserve Bank which would result in the purchase of securities. These purchases would represent dynamic monetary policy—an attempt to change the status quo.

In contrast, defensive operations attempt to preserve the status quo. For example, around the Christmas–New Year's period there is usually a substantial outflow of currency and coin from commercial banks and other financial institutions. These outflows reduce (dollar for dollar) the amount of reserves and thereby curtail by a multiple amount the ability of depository institutions to create credit. The Federal Reserve would usually buy securities during this period in order to negate the impact of this important seasonal factor on monetary policy. Such purchases would represent defensive open-market operations and would be unrelated to any monetary policy actions.

Since purchases and sales of securities in the open market by the Federal Reserve may be either for defensive or dynamic purposes, it is not possible to interpret precisely the goal of monetary policy from examining the buying or selling behavior of the Fed. For example, in a period in which seasonal factors were draining reserves, the Fed might be tightening credit and yet also be buying securities. In this instance, of course, it would be buying a smaller amount of securities than the Fed would normally purchase if it wished to fully counteract seasonal factors draining reserves. For this reason as well as others, Federal Reserve policy is often difficult to interpret for those outside the system. Yet, understanding the current thrust of monetary policy is highly important to financial institutions, as interest rates and financial flows are closely correlated with the activities of the Federal Reserve System.

The major advantages and disadvantages of open-market operations and the other policy techniques are summarized in Figure 5–3. The flexibility of open-market operations and the adaptability of this technique to finetuning market conditions is especially notable. In contrast, for short-term psychological purposes, the discount rate is quite useful, especially for dealing with international financial disturbances. The use of the discount rate to "defend the dollar" in late 1978 and also in late 1979 are excellent examples of the use of this policy tool for international purposes.

Other Policy Tools

Interest-Rate Ceilings.   Two other techniques of monetary policy are worthy of mention: Regulation Q and moral suasion. Federal Reserve regulations governing the activities of member commercial banks are listed according to the letters of the alphabet—A to Z. Regulation Q governs the payment of interest on deposit accounts. By law, commercial banks can pay no explicit interest on demand deposits; banks do, of course implicitly pay interest on demand deposits through offering "free" checking accounts or some other type of bonus for the maintenance of checking balances. Moreover, the ability of commercial banks beginning in late 1978 to offer automatic transfers from savings to checking accounts created further latitude for banks to indirectly pay interest on demand deposits. The spread of negotiable order of withdrawal (NOW) accounts is a fur-

Figure 5–3   Principal Policy Tools of the Federal Reserve System

Item	Reserve Requirements	Discount Rate	Open-Market Operations
Purpose	Change level and growth of reserve availability, and cost of credit.	Same.	Same.
Method	Raise or lower percent of demand and time deposits which must be held in cash or on deposit, within limits set by Congress.	Raise or lower discount rate on short-term loans (up to 15 days)	Buy or sell securities through dealers.
Advantages	Affects entire system (nondiscriminatory) at once; works quickly; useful for major changes in policy.	Useful for international capital-flow problems; safety valve for Fed operations; aids depository institutions in trouble.	Flexible, changed quickly; suitable for fine tuning of market conditions; defensive versus dynamic.
Disadvantages	Too powerful and clumsy for fine-tuning credit and market conditions.	Fed has only partial control over borrowing; negative psychological effects.	Unable to effect massive changes in short period; some negative psychological effects.

ther innovation allowing banks to pay interest on transaction accounts, as is the development in 1983 of the super NOW account. Banks and other depository financial institutions do pay interest on time and savings deposits, but the rate of interest has been limited by the regulatory authorities. The maximum rate payable on time and savings deposits for member commercial banks is specified by Regulation Q. More generally, Regulation Q is frequently used to mean the maximum rates payable by all financial institutions on their deposit liabilities.

Regulation Q was used in the mid-1960s and early 1970s as a policy tool in periods of credit restraint. For example, if the Federal Reserve wished to place downward pressure on the lending ability of commercial banks, it would not increase Regulation Q ceilings at a time when other interest rates were increasing. With rising market yields but limited ceiling rates for time and savings deposits, investors would be expected to shift funds away from commercial banks. As a result, the lending ability of those banks which lost deposits would be reduced.

Interest-rate ceilings have diminished considerably in importance as a monetary policy tool. The Federal Reserve eliminated in the early 1970s the Q ceiling for negotiable time certificates of deposit of over $100,000 and has become much more flexible in adjusting other Q ceilings in line with market rates. Furthermore, (1) the recent ability of commercial banks and savings and loan associations to offer short-term certificates of deposit of relatively small denomination ($10,000 and up) at a rate tied to the Treasury bill rate and (2) the late 1982 introduction of money market deposit accounts without interest-rate ceilings further reduce the significance of Regulation Q. Finally, under the Depository Institutions Deregulation and Monetary Control Act of 1980 and the Garn—St Germain Depository Institutions Act of 1982, Regulation Q ceilings must be eliminated no later than 1986. In fact, control of deposit interest-rate ceilings is no longer in the hands of the Fed but is now under the control of the Depository Institutions Deregulation Committee. Voting members of this committee include the secretary of the Treasury, the chairman of the board of governors of the Federal Reserve System, the chairman of the Board of Directors of the Federal Deposit Insurance Corporation, the chairman of the Federal Home Loan Bank Board, and the chairman of the National Credit Union Administration; the comptroller of the Currency is a nonvoting member.

Interest-rate ceilings have discriminated against the small saver, forcing the saver to accept below-market rates of return. There is also considerable evidence that interest-rate ceilings were ineffective as a monetary policy tool; that is, interest-rate ceilings affect the allocation of credit but not its total amount. The financial markets have been quite innovative in devising new techniques to avoid artificial restraints, such as Regulation

Q, and many academic studies of the monetary policy process have opposed the use of Regulation Q on other than a standby basis. It also appears likely that the interest-rate prohibition on demand deposits will be eliminated in the near future.

Moral Suasion. Moral suasion refers to the public and/or private acts of officials of the Federal Reserve System which are taken with the purpose of achieving some particular monetary policy purpose. Moral suasion would encompass speeches given by the members of the board of governors or the Reserve bank presidents, telephone calls from Federal Reserve officials to bank officers and others, and letters from the Federal Reserve to commercial banks concerning monetary policy goals. An excellent example of the use of moral suasion occurred in August 1966. In that period, the Federal Reserve was attempting, through the use of a number of different policy techniques, to reduce inflation associated with the Vietnam War. Commercial banks were facing intense pressure for loans and sold municipal securities in order to raise funds to satisfy that loan demand. As a result, the municipal market was in turmoil and many banks were finding it extremely difficult to obtain the liquidity they needed. The Federal Reserve responded by sending a letter to each member bank stating, in effect, that if the bank would curtail its liquidation of municipal securities and practice moderation in satisfying its loan demand, loans from the the Fed's discount window would be available on a more liberal basis and borrowing could be made for longer periods of time.

Moral suasion is an especially important tool of monetary control in other industrialized countries. For example, in England the Bank of England is able to exercise considerable influence through using moral suasion. However, in England there are only a few banks, and direct, personal communication is relatively simple. In the United States, there are over 15,000 commercial banks, and the use of moral suasion is a much more complicated process.

MONETARY POLICY TARGETS

As pointed out above, open-market operations represent a particularly important technique of monetary policy. But the Fed has other, less significant weapons under its control, such as changes in reserve requirements and in the discount rate. The tools of policy are used to move the nation closer to its goals—relative price stability, full employment, economic growth, and balance-of-payments stability. However, in implementing its policy and seeking to achieve these objectives, the Fed must observe and react to changes in a number of variables which are intermediate between the ultimate objectives and the techniques. These variables, often referred to as intermediate targets, are especially important in the management of financial institutions, since they provide some evidence of the thrust of current monetary policy [11].

Characteristics of an Intermediate Target

An intermediate target should have a number of desirable characteristics. It should be closely associated with the ultimate goal; that is, the intermediate targets and the gross national product (GNP), the unemployment rate, and other economic goal variables should move together. In addition, the target should be a variable which is closely controlled and significantly influenced by monetary policy. It would, of course, be of little significance if there were some variable which was closely correlated with the ultimate targets but over which the Federal Reserve has little control. It is also necessary that the target be one that can be measured often. Even if there were some variable which was closely correlated with the GNP and also was one which the Fed could control within reasonable limits, it would not be a good target if the Fed did not know the value of the variable except after considerable lag. In addition, there must be a minimum feedback from the ultimate target to the intermediate target. For example, while changes in the target should affect the GNP, changes in the GNP should not affect the target. Otherwise, there would be no way to know if the movement in the monetary variable is the result of changes in policy or the effect of feedback from the ultimate goal. Conceptually, this problem is quite severe, since many, perhaps most, variables are associated with movements in the GNP, the most widely used goal variable. This problem is widely known as the "reverse causation" or "feedback problem."

Alternative Intermediate Targets

There are a number of monetary variables which, to one degree or another, have been suggested as meeting the criteria of a monetary target. These include measures of money market conditions, such as interest rates and marginal reserve positions (various measures of the difference between actual and required reserves, such as the net-free reserves position); aggregate reserve measures, such as the monetary base and reserve available for private deposits; and monetary aggregates, such as the money supply (variously defined) or total credit. Some of the more widely used targets are the following:

1. Money market conditions and marginal reserve measures:
   a. The free reserve position of depository institutions—total reserves less required reserves and borrowings from the Federal Reserve.
   b. Borrowings from the Federal Reserve.
   c. The three-month (or some other maturity) Treasury bill rate.
   d. The interest rate on federal funds.
2. Aggregate reserve measures:
   a. Total reserves of depository institutions.

     b. The monetary base—defined as the total of reserve balances at the Federal Reserve banks and the amount of currency in circulation and in the vaults of depository institutions.

     c. Reserves available for private deposits (RPDs)—total reserves minus the reserves required against U.S. government deposits and against net interbank deposits.

3. Monetary aggregates:

     a. The money supply narrowly defined (M1)—transactions accounts plus currency in circulation.

     b. The money supply broadly defined (M2)—M1 plus savings and small denomination time deposits at all depository institutions (including money market depsosits), overnight repurchase agreements at commercial banks, overnight Eurodollars held by U.S. residents other than at banks at Caribbean branches of member banks, and balances of money market mutual funds (general purpose and broker dealer).

     c. The money supply more broadly defined (M3)—M2 plus large denomination time deposits at all depository institutions and term RPs at commercial banks and savings and loan associations and balances of institution—only money market funds.

     d. Bank credit—loans and securities at commercial banks.

Monetary Policy: An Illustration

A more complete understanding of the influence of the Federal Reserve on the cost and availability of funds at financial institutions and upon the demand for credit could perhaps be supplied by tracing through the steps involved in the monetary policy transmission process—both the decision-making and implementation aspects of a particular policy. Suppose it appears that a substantial inflationary environment is developing within the economy. This event may be the result, for example, of an acceleration in defense spending at a time when the economy is already fully employed (the classic demand-pull inflation). How might the Federal Reserve react to such a development and how might its actions affect the cost and availability of funds at financial institutions? The Fed might increase the discount rate and/or increase reserve requirements. The board of governors would be expected to caution commercial bankers to proceed carefully in granting loan requests. However, since the primary focus of attention would be upon open-market operations, let us proceed with a detailed discussion of the formulation and implementation of open-market policy.

Role of the FOMC

As discussed above, the Federal Open Market Committee has the authority to formulate general policy and guidelines for the trading desk of the New York Federal Reserve Bank. While this group generally meets once a month, extraordinary circumstances might prompt an emergency meeting either in Washington or by telephone conference call. Prior to the regular monthly meeting the individual members of the board of governors and the Reserve bank presidents, assisted by their staffs, carefully review current and prospective economic and financial developments. The staffs of both the board and the Reserve banks have amassed a detailed evaluation of current and prospective developments, frequently including econometric forecasts of the gross national product and its components, as well as anticipated movements in short- and long-term interest rates. Moreover, the staff of the board of governors writes and makes available to all those concerned within the system a review of economic and financial developments.

Following a careful review of these and related sources of information, the members of the Federal Open Market Committee meet at the board's offices in Washington, D.C. Members present their views on the outlook for the economy and for the financial markets and make recommendations on the proper course of open-market operations until the time of the next meeting of the committee. The staff of the board has usually provided two or more alternative policy choices and their anticipated implications for the financial markets. A vote is then taken on these policy guidelines, and the one adopted (referred to as the directive) becomes the operating framework for the trading desk of the New York Fed.

For example, the domestic policy directive issued by FOMC to the Federal Reserve Bank of New York following its May 18, 1982, meeting reads as follows.[3]

> The information reviewed at this meeting suggests that real GNP will change little in the current quarter after the appreciable further decline in the first quarter, as business inventory liquidation moderates from last quarter's extraordinary rate. In April the nominal value of retail sales expanded, while industrial production and nonfarm payroll employment continued to decline. The unemployment rate rose 0.4 percentage point to 9.4 percent. Although housing starts edged up in March for the fifth consecutive month, they remained at a depressed level. The rate of increase in prices on the average appears to be slowing somewhat further in the current quarter; so far this year both the consumer price index and the producer price index for finished goods have risen little on balance, and the advance in the index of average hourly earnings has remained at a reduced pace.
>
> The weighted average value of the dollar against major foreign currencies, after rising somewhat further in early April, has fallen sharply over the past month, reflecting in part a decline in U.S. interest rates relative to foreign rates

---

[3]Board of Governors of the Federal Reserve System record of policy actions of the Federal Open Market Committee.

and market expectations of further declines. The U.S. foreign trade deficit in the first quarter was one-third less than in the preceeding quarter.

M1 increased sharply in April, but the expansion was concentrated in the first half of the month and was largely retraced later. Growth of M2 moderated somewhat, owing to a slackening of the expansion in the nontransaction component. Short-term market interest rates and bond yields on balance have declined since the end of March, and mortgage interest rates have edged down further.

The Federal Open Market Committee seeks to foster monetary and financial conditions that will help to reduce inflation, promote a resumption of growth in output on a sustainable basis, and contribute to a sustainable pattern of international transactions. At its meeting in early February, the Committee agreed that its objectives would be furthered by growth of M1, M2, and M3 from the fourth quarter of 1981 to the fourth quarter of 1982 within ranges of 2½ to 5½ percent, 6 to 9 percent, and 6½ to 9½ percent respectively. The associated range for bank credit was 6 to 9 percent.

In the short run, the Committee seeks behavior of reserve aggregates consistent with growth of M1 and M2 from March to June at annual rates of about 3 percent and 8 percent respectively. The Committee also noted that deviations from these targets should be evaluated in light of changes in the relative importance of NOW accounts as a savings vehicle. The Chairman may call for Committee consultation if it appears to the Manager for Domestic Operations that pursuit of the monetary objectives and related reserve paths during the period before the next meeting is likely to be associated with a federal funds rate persistently outside a range of 10 to 15 percent.

Changing Intermediate Targets

It is, of course, necessary to operationalize these general guidelines. Over the recent past, this has been done in a number of ways. In the early postwar period and through the 1960s, the variables which the Federal Reserve observed most directly and used to guide open-market operations were those involving money market conditions, especially the level of free reserves (i.e., excess reserves less borrowings from the Federal Reserve). If, for example, the level of free reserves was higher than desired, the Fed would generally sell securities to reduce the amount of actual reserves and, thereby, the level of free reserves. Conversely, if the level of free reserves was lower than desired, the Fed might buy securities. However, careful study has discredited the hypothesis that the amount of free reserves bears a close correlation with changes in the ultimate target variables, such as the gross national product.[4] Moreover, emphasis on the quantity of free reserves and other money market variables ignores the substantial evidence developed by economists concerning the importance

[4]For an excellent discussion and critique of money market conditions as a useful variable for Federal Reserve policy, see [10].

of the money supply in affecting the economy. Hence, in recent years the Federal Reserve has focused on two separate variables: the federal funds rate and the money supply (variously defined) as an intermediate target. The Fed would generally seek to specify that rate on federal funds which would, over the period until the next meeting of the FOMC, create the desired change in the money supply.

In seeking to restrain the economy, the FOMC might seek to create "moderate" growth in the money supply in an inflationary environment. As a result, it might be expected that the trading desk would be a net seller of Treasury securities (apart from seasonal factors). The resultant increase in interest rates and the reduction in reserves should have a number of important effects. The cost of credit to consumers and businesses should increase. While this might discourage borrowing to only a minor extent if the interest elasticity of the demand for borrowed funds is relatively low, there might be an even more important impact on the availability of credit. With smaller available reserves, the depository system would not be able to extend as much credit as it was able to do previously. As a result, the availability of credit to both consumers and business firms might be reduced. This rise in the cost and reduction in the availability of funds would be expected to reduce the spending of each sector of the economy (especially the private sector) and thereby reduce the inflationary pressures caused by excess demand.

It is also important to understand the implications of a tightening of monetary policy from the perspective of the management of an individual financial institution. It would be expected that the change in monetary policy, along with the economic conditions that produced that change, would significantly affect the financial position of the individual financial institution in a number of ways. First, the reduced availability of reserves and the slowdown in new money creation at the macro level should be reflected at the level of the individual financial institution in a reduction in the inflow of funds. From the viewpoint of the deposit type financial institutions, the growth rate of deposits would slow. From the viewpoint of nondepository financial institutions (such as life insurance companies and pension funds), the inflows of funds might also be reduced, although the impact on these "contractual" financial institutions would generally be smaller. Moreover, this reduction in funds inflows should be further accentuated by the increasingly unattractive comparison between the rates offered by financial institutions and the rates available in the market. Just as the inflow of funds to financial institutions was reduced by the tightening monetary policy, the demand for funds would be expected to rise. This increase should be especially pronounced for commercial banks with large amounts of inventory loans. The increase would be less at savings and loan associations and other real estate lenders, since the demand for mortgages varies less with the business cycle than does the demand for inventory loans.

In summary, the availability of funds at the individual financial institution would be reduced, but the demand for credit should be substantial. For some time, perhaps, financial institutions could meet the additional loan demand by liquidating securities and borrowing in the open market. At some point, however, these alternatives no longer become viable (the cost of funds sources becomes prohibitive), and financial institutions must curtail credit availability. Clearly, it is important for the management of the individual financial institution to be aware of and anticipate these changes in monetary policy which may have such a profound effect on the welfare of the institution.

The federal funds rate was used as the principal operating target for monetary policy during most of the 1970s. However, while the policy was reasonably successful in controlling the funds rate it was much less successful in producing the desired growth rate in the quantity of money. The growth rate of the money supply tended to alternate from excessively high to excessively low percentage rates. This led to substantial criticism of the Fed, especially from those who argued that the growth rate of money is the principal variable influencing the level of production, employment, and prices. In October 1979 the Fed announced that it was altering its approach to monetary policy. It would now place more emphasis in daily operations on controlling the quantity of bank reserves and less emphasis on short-term fluctuations in the federal funds rate. The purpose of this change was to achieve better control over the growth rate of money and bank credit. However, while the Fed has followed this reserves-based operating procedure since late 1979, in which primary emphasis is placed on the growth of a reserve aggregate, it is not at all clear that the procedure has in fact resulted in greater control over the money supply. In 1980, the first full year of the implementation of this new operating procedure, the money supply grew in an erratic fashion, exceeding target growth objectives in some periods and falling short in others.[5] Similar problems persisted in 1981 and 1982. In fact, beginning in August 1982, the Fed appeared to have de-emphasized the previous concentration on the growth of the monetary aggregates as its principal intermediate target.

INFLUENCE OF THE TREASURY: FISCAL POLICY AND DEBT MANAGEMENT

The portfolio behavior and profitability of financial institutions is also considerably influenced by the posture of fiscal policy and debt management. Fiscal policy refers to tax and expenditure changes by the federal government (as opposed to tax and expenditure changes by state and local governments) designed to achieve macroeconomic goals such as reducing

---

[5]See Gilbert [6] for a useful review of the experience of the Fed with this procedure in 1980.

the level of unemployment, stimulating economic growth, or lowering inflation. In contrast, debt management refers to alterations in the ownership and maturity of outstanding U.S. government debt in order to achieve these same macroeconomic goals. Fiscal policy is a very powerful technique of economic stabilization, while debt management has a much weaker effect on the economy. Yet the influence of debt management on the financial markets and on interest rates is quite direct, while the influence of fiscal policy is more indirect in nature.

Fiscal Policy

The theory of fiscal policy is reasonably simple and has not changed greatly since the British economist John Maynard Keynes provided theoretical justification in the 1930s for using government tax and revenue programs to achieve national economic objectives.[6] Tax cuts and expenditure increases should be used to stimulate the economy, and tax increases and expenditure reductions should be employed to restrain total spending. The tax cuts and expenditure increases would produce a deficit in the federal budget which would, on balance, add to the total demand and would therefore stimulate total employment, output, and income. In contrast, tax increases and expenditure reductions would be expected to produce a surplus in the federal budget which would, on balance, reduce total demand and thereby curtail inflationary pressures produced by excessive total spending. Following this prescription, the federal budget would be used in a countercyclical fashion and would alternate between periods of deficit and surplus. Over a long time, these deficits and surpluses might be expected to cancel each other out, so that the amount of the Treasury debt outstanding (the cumulative result of past federal budgets) would remain little changed.

Fiscal policy in practice has proved to be much more complicated to employ than most economists had thought would be the case. Stimulating the economy through tax cuts and expenditure increases has been relatively easy for Congress (the decision-making group with regard to fiscal policy) to accept. Raising taxes and cutting expenditures, however, has been much more difficult. As a result, the federal budget has developed a seemingly inherent tendency for expenditures to exceed revenues, both in periods of economic decline and expansion. In fact, in the 22 years from 1961 through 1983 the federal budget was in surplus only once. As a re-

---

[6]There are, of course, a number of implementation problems that complicate the use of fiscal policy. These include problems of conflicting and inconsistent goals—for example, high inflation and high unemployment—which make it necessary to establish priorities among the goals; there are also time lags between changes in taxes and expenditures and changes in the economy which make it important to base fiscal policy changes on forecasts (often unreliable) of future economic conditions.

sult, the federal debt has grown enormously (now exceeding $1 trillion), and this has placed great pressure on the Federal Reserve in its conduct of monetary policy. If the Fed were to monetize this debt by adding to its own portfolio, the amount of reserves and the money supply would expand excessively. On the other hand, if the Fed refuses to monetize the federal deficit, the sharp increase in the demand for loanable funds due to the increase in federal government borrowings would drive interest rates up substantially.

Debt Management

Treasury debt management refers to the conscious management of the maturity structure of the federal debt in order to achieve certain desired economic goals. Debt management is closely related to both fiscal and monetary policy but is less important than either. Fiscal policy is concerned with the impact of government spending and taxation on the level of employment, income, and other macroeconomic variables. Debt management, on the other hand, is concerned with the financial consequences of current and past fiscal policy actions. The decision by the federal government to run a budget deficit is a fiscal policy decision. However, that deficit must be financed by selling Treasury securities to the bank and nonbank public. Therefore the current level of the federal debt, (i.e., the total amount of Treasury securities outstanding) is the combined result of all past fiscal policy decisions. The Treasury in selling new debt to finance the current budget deficit or in selling new debt to refund existing debt created by past budget deficits must make a number of important choices, which we refer to collectively as the debt management decision. Probably the most important choice the Treasury must make with each security offering is what maturity of securities to offer—bills, bonds, or notes. This decision affects the maturity structure of the whole federal debt. It is this choice which is at the center of Treasury debt management. In essence, in conducting debt management operations, the Treasury is performing a central banking function.

As was pointed out earlier, government debt (over $1 trillion outstanding) is extremely short in maturity; the average maturity of the debt is approximately two years, while a substantial fraction of the debt is in the form of Treasury bills which have an original maturity of one year or less. In addition, in recent years the U.S. government has had substantial budget deficits (over $50 billion in some years), requiring a large volume of new debt financing. For all these reasons—to refinance the large volume of existing securities and to finance the current budget deficit requirements—the U.S. Treasury is often in the financial markets selling securities and raising new funds. As a general rule, bills are offered each week, while notes and bonds usually are sold quarterly.

In the process of financing the U.S. government the Treasury has a number of important influences on the financial system. One important influence is upon the Federal Reserve in its conduct of monetary policy. During the sale of a new issue of securities (excluding the regular marketing of Treasury bills), the Federal Reserve is under pressure to follow an even-keel policy, that is, the Fed does not make any major changes in monetary policy during the period of the Treasury financing. During periods of large budget deficits when the Treasury is constantly in the market offering new debt, the flexibility of the Federal Reserve may be reduced to some extent.

It is possible, however, to view the Treasury financing in a positive fashion. The Treasury can affect the total liquidity of the economy to a degree through the careful selection of the maturity of its newly issued debt. In a period of economic expansion, the Treasury should finance its need for funds with long-term securities. This action would shift the securities portfolio of the public and financial institution portfolios to longer-term assets, thereby reducing its liquidity and discouraging both consumption and investment spending. The great difficulty with this policy prescription from the perspective of the Treasury, however, is that this period would likely be one of high interest rates, and the Treasury would thereby commit itself to high interest payments for a considerable period of time. And there are legal restraints on the volume of long-term securities which the Treasury can sell. Except for a fixed amount authorized by Congress, the Treasury cannot sell bonds with an interest rate above 4.25 percent. Conversely, in periods of economic slack, proper debt management policy would emphasize the sale of short-term securities. By selling short-term securities the Treasury would add to the quantity of liquid assets held by the public and thereby encourage spending. However, in this period interest rates are likely to be low and there is some pressure for the Treasury to lock-in the lower long-term yields by selling bonds. There is a fundamental conflict between the goal of the Treasury to minimize the cost of the public debt (i.e., reducing interest payments as low as possible) and its goal of using the maturity of the debt as an instrument of economic stabilization. In the recent past, with few exceptions, the Treasury has emphasized financing the public debt at the least cost. Debt management policy has atrophied as an active tool of economic stabilization.

SUMMARY

Through monetary policy, the Federal Reserve attempts to influence the cost and availability of money. It does so within its organizational structure—the Board of Governors, the Reserve banks, and the Federal Open Market Committee—and with a variety of techniques. The major techniques used by the Fed are reserve requirements changes, discount rate changes, and open market operations. In addition, in the past it has used Regulation Q as a monetary policy tool, though with the scheduled phase-out of interest-rate ceilings no later than March 1986, Regulation Q has already become of limited significance. The Fed does, of course, always have some influence through moral suasion.

In seeking to affect the economy, the Fed works through various intermediate targets. These targets encompass money market conditions and marginal reserve measures, aggregate reserve measures, and monetary aggregates. During recent years the Fed has evolved from using a policy which focused on money market conditions and marginal reserve measures (initially free reserves and then the federal funds rate) to one based upon monetary aggregates. Beginning in October 1979, the Fed announced that it would place greater emphasis on aggregate reserves in an attempt to control the growth of the money supply.

Monetary conditions are also affected by fiscal and debt management policies. While fiscal policy could theoretically be used both to expand and contract the economy in a countercyclical fashion, it has, in practice, played an expansion role in recent years through large recurring deficits in the federal budget. Given the size of the federal debt created by these deficits, however, Treasury debt management becomes necessary. The immense size of the federal debt, coupled with its short maturity, means that Treasury financing is occuring on a regular basis, complicating to some degree the operation of monetary policy. However, Treasury debt management could be used in a positive way through altering the maturity of the federal debt, reducing the maturity in periods of economic decline, and lengthening the maturity in periods of excessive expansion.

Questions

5-1. What are the functions of the different components of the Federal Reserve System? What is the Fed's most important policymaking unit?

5-2. What are the different methods available to the Federal Reserve for influencing the availability and cost of money and how do they function? Discuss the strengths and weaknesses of each of the following policy tools:

a. Reserve requirements.
b. Discount rate.
c. Open-market operations.
d. Moral suasion.

5-3. What is the relationship between high-powered money and the fractional reserve depository institutions system?

5-4. In open-market operations, what is the distinction between dynamic as opposed to defensive transactions? Give an example of each.

5-5. What is debt management? Why has it fallen into disuse?

References

1. Ascheim, Joseph. *Techniques of Monetary Control.* Baltimore: Johns Hopkins University Press, 1961.

2. Blinder, Alan S., and Steven M. Goldfeld. "New Measures of Fiscal and Monetary Policy, 1958–1973." *The American Economic Review,* December 1976, pp. 780–96.

3. *Controlling Monetary Aggregates II: The Implementation.* Boston: Federal Reserve Bank of Boston, September 1972.

4. Davis, Richard G. "Implementing Open Market Policy with Monetary Aggregate Objective." *Monthly Review,* Federal Reserve Bank of New York, July 1973, pp. 170–82.

5. Gaines, Tilford C. *Techniques of Federal Debt Management.* New York: Free Press, 1962.

6. Gilbert, Alton R., and Michael F. Trebing. "The FOMC in 1980: A Year of Reserve Targeting." *Review,* Federal Reserve Bank of St. Louis, August/September 1981.

7. Holmes, Alan R. "A Day at the Trading Desk." *Monthly Review,* Federal Reserve Bank of New York, October 1970, pp. 234–38.

8. Lombra, Raymond, and Raymond L. Torto. "The Strategy of Monetary Policy." *Economic Review,* Federal Reserve Bank of Richmond, September/October 1975.

9. Mayer, Thomas. *Monetary Policy in the United States.* New York: Random House, 1968.

10. Meigs, A. James. *Free Reserves and the Money Supply.* Chicago: University of Chicago Press, 1962.

11. Saving, Thomas R. "Monetary Targets and Indicators." *Journal of Political Economy,* August 1967.

12. Van Horne, James E., and David A. Bowers. "Liquidity Impact of Debt Management." *Southern Economic Journal,* April 1968, pp. 526–27.

13. Wallich, Henry C., and Peter M. Keir. "The Role of Operating Guides in U.S. Monetary Policy: A Historical Review." *Federal Reserve Bulletin,* September 1979.

PART THREE

Commercial Banking and Problem Areas of Financial Institutions Management

6. *The Role of Commercial Banks in the Economy*

BY ALMOST ANY MEASURE the commercial bank is the most important financial intermediary serving the public today. For example, commercial banks hold far more assets than any other financial institution—about 40 percent of the aggregate resources of the financial sector. Banks also represent a vital link in the transmission of national economic policy (especially monetary policy carried out by the Federal Reserve System) to the remainder of the economy. When bank credit is scarce and expensive, spending in the economy slows and unemployment usually rises. On the other hand, when credit provided by banks is permitted to grow at a faster pace with more lenient terms, economic growth usually accelerates and employment rises. Fluctuations in the availability and cost of bank credit also have profound implications for inflation. This is not surprising since bank deposits represent the most significant component of the nation's money supply.

From the perspective of various groups in the economy, access to bank credit and other bank services is absolutely essential. Most consumer credit is supplied by the banking system, either in the form of direct negotiated loans and charges against bank-issued credit cards or indirectly through loans to retailers of automobiles, furniture, home appliances, and other consumer goods. Businesses in need of credit often consult a bank first, particularly when the need is for short-term funds to support purchases of inventory, pay taxes, or make repairs. Governments, too, look to the banking system as a source of credit when tax revenues fall short of current expenses. The federal government in particular, faced with huge financing needs, has placed billions of dollars in new debt with both large and small banks in recent years. Moreover, commercial banks through their trust departments are a major force in the equity and corporate bond markets.

This chapter gives a brief history of commercial banking and discusses the most important services offered by commercial banks today. In addition, recent trends in the sources and uses of funds of the commercial banking industry are discussed.

TYPES OF BANKS   What is a bank? The name *bank* is used very loosely today to describe a wide variety of institutions. For example, there are so-called *investment banks*, which specialize in underwriting corporate and government securities. These banks purchase securities from the issuer and attempt to resell them in the open market at a reasonable profit. There are *industrial banks*, which accept smaller consumer savings deposits and make certain types of loans, principally cash loans to wage earners. And there are *savings banks*, which draw upon individual and family savings as their principal source of funds and invest those funds mainly in mortgages, corporate bonds, and occasionally common stock.[1]

Complicating the issue of what a bank is are rapid changes now occurring in the financial services industry. Many financial firms, particularly insurance companies, brokerage firms, and mutual funds, are today offering traditional banking services. These services include liquid savings accounts and transactions accounts (checkable deposits) which can be drafted to make payments. Shares in a money market mutual fund are a well-known example of a recent service innovation by brokerage firms and mutual funds which compete directly with bank savings and transactions accounts.[2] Basically, a bank *is* what a bank *does*, regardless of the name given the institution by its owners or others.

When students in the field of financial institutions use the term *bank* they usually have a specific meaning in mind, however. A bank in the usual and traditional sense is a financial institution offering two major services to the public—(1) transactions accounts, which may be used to make payments for purchases of goods and services and are widely accepted by the public for that purpose; and (2) direct loans to businesses, individuals, and other institutions. The financial institution which comes closest to this definition is the *commercial bank*. Commercial bank checking accounts are the principal means of payment in the economy and are widely accepted as money. While commercial banks do purchase investment securities (such as corporate and government bonds) traded in the open market, their principal asset is *loans* made directly to business firms, individuals and families, securities dealers, and a host of other borrowers.

To be sure, banks offer many other services than just transactions accounts and loans. As discussed later on in this chapter, commercial banks offer such diverse financial services as time and savings deposits, lease financing, financial advice and counseling, portfolio management, the

---

[1]Savings banks are discussed in detail in Chapter 14.

[2]See Chapter 16 for an analysis of money market mutual funds.

safekeeping of valuables, transfer of securities, bookkeeping, and the guaranteeing of credit received from other lenders. Indeed, so numerous are the services offered today by commercial banks that these institutions are often called financial department stores. However, the essence of banking—what separates this particular financial institution from all the others—is the making of loans and the selling of transactions (or payments) accounts.

Incidentally, why is the adjective *commercial* used when referring to a bank? As we will see in the next section, when commercial banks got their start, they dealt almost exclusively with business firms, accepting deposits of money and other valuables from local merchants and discounting their commercial notes. Only in the 20th century did the commercial banking industry begin to aggressively compete for consumer accounts. Today, consumers are a principal source of deposits and represent one of the more rapidly growing sources of loans. In fact, commercial banks today are the leading consumer installment lending institution in the United States.

No one knows for sure when the business of banking began. One popular account traces the industry's origins to the shops of medieval goldsmiths (see Figure 6–1). These merchants accepted deposits of gold coins and other valuables for safekeeping and, in many cases, paid interest on those deposits. When a customer made a deposit of gold, a receipt was issued, indicating the amount and kind of metal left in the goldsmith's vault. Soon, gold depositors found it more convenient and safe to pay for goods and services using goldsmith receipts rather than gold itself. Thus the goldsmith's receipts—his promise to pay—began to circulate as money, the forerunner of modern-day checks.

THE ORIGINS OF MODERN BANKING

Goldsmiths soon discovered that the deposits left with them were relatively stable—while some customers were always withdrawing their funds from the goldsmith's vault, others were bringing in new deposits. At this point, so the story goes, an enterprising goldsmith discovered that, with stable deposits, he could make loans by issuing more receipts than he had gold reserves in the vault. It was at this point that the goldsmith became a banker because he was literally creating money. The concept of fractional-reserve banking was born.

While this is one appealing account of banking's origins, the history of banking actually goes back even earlier, to the money merchants who frequented the town markets of Asia, Europe, and the Middle East in ancient times. The Assyrians, Babylonians, ancient Greeks, and later the Romans employed money merchants to facilitate trade and commerce. Money merchants provided an essential service—changing one form of money into another—in an age when money consisted largely of metallic coins and every major nation and city-state issued its own coins. If an individ-

Figure 6–1   The Roots of Modern Banking

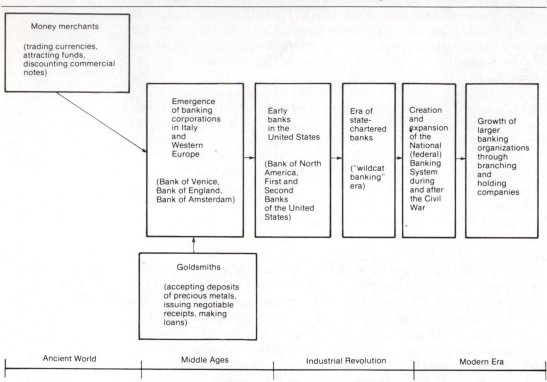

ual traveled to a large city (such as Alexandria, Athens, Jerusalem, or Rome) and wished to purchase food, clothing, or items for trading, this usually meant converting foreign coin into domestic coin. In some busy markets the business of exchanging coins became a full-time occupation and a few merchants began to specialize in financial services, including not only money changing but also accepting deposits for safekeeping and discounting notes from other merchants. In ancient Rome some money merchants specialized even further as bankers who made loans and bankers who traded foreign coin.

Banking institutions similar to the kind we recognize today first made their appearance in Italy during the Middle Ages and thereafter spread into Western Europe. As in the ancient world, the first European bankers were probably merchants changing one form of money for another as a sideline to their other commercial ventures. Frequently, these merchants would occupy a simple wooden bench in the market square and wait for customers to come by. Some scholars suggest that the term *bank* had its origins in the Italian word *banco*, meaning a bench. Others doubt the authenticity of this account, but it is at least a plausible story. Equally intriguing is the oft-heard suggestion that the foreboding term *bankrupt*—destroying a merchant's bench—came from the same source. Presumably, if one of the early bankers failed to serve his clients honestly and faithfully, he might well have found himself without customers and without any furniture either!

At some point during the Middle Ages the great potential of banks for creating (not just exchanging) money must have been noticed, particularly by beleagured governments. Indeed, as we will soon note, there has always been a close link between governments and banks, principally because banks exercise such a potent influence on the economy through their credit-granting and money-creating activities. There is historical evidence that a number of Italian cities (most notably Genoa and Venice) set up banks to accept deposits from local merchants, discount commercial notes, and, most importantly for some cities, make credit available for governmental activities (including preparation for war).

Slowly the practice of banking, especially the acceptance of deposits and the making of loans, began to spread from nation to nation. It did not happen overnight. Instead, the industry grew in a slow but steady evolution, reaching Western Europe in its more recognizable modern form about the time of the Industrial Revolution. This is not too surprising, because that revolution brought with it tremendous needs for both short- and long-term venture capital. At the same time a middle-class of consumers and savers began to emerge who, in later years, would supply a major share of bank funds.

Most authorities are agreed that the institutional father of modern banking was the Bank of England, chartered in 1694. This great institution was actually both a merchants' bank, accepting commercial deposits and lending against commercial notes, and an agent of the British government.[3] Today it plays an extremely important role in the conduct of economic policy in the British Isles, assisting in the management of govern-

---

[3]Some historians believe that banking in Great Britain began as a historical accident. The story here goes back to mid-17th century, when London merchants kept gold in the Tower of London for safekeeping. Allegedly, King Charles I, in need of more government revenue, began to tap the merchants' gold reserves. While the king only intended to borrow the money for a brief period, wary merchants appointed clerks or overseers to keep track of their deposits. The clerks, however, took a lesson from the king and began loaning the gold deposits out at interest to goldsmiths who turned around and made their own loans at a higher interest rate. In this way the goldsmiths stumbled on a key service of modern banking (especially among the largest, commercially oriented banks)—the brokering of money, borrowing from one individual or institution and lending to another at a profitable spread. Soon, the story goes, the goldsmiths dropped their secret borrowing from gold reserves in the Tower of London and turned to the more pedestrian practice of borrowing directly from the public through deposits that bore interest, promising safe return of the public's funds. (See especially *The Story of Banks* [2].)

ment debt, control of that nation's money supply, and influencing interest rates through changes in its own discount rate. (In some ways the central bank of the United States—the Federal Reserve System—was modeled after practices followed by the Bank of England.)

Banking in the United States began much as it had in Europe. First, local merchants began offering money changing and safekeeping services as a sideline. Later, some merchants began to specialize in accepting funds for deposit and making loans with those funds. Eventually the colonial governments became involved in establishing banks to promote commerce, expand the supply of credit, and assist in government financing. Just as their predecessors in Europe and the Middle East had been, U.S. banks were initially commercial-oriented, offering credit and deposit services primarily to business firms. But, governments, too, had critical financing needs, especially during the American Revolution. The Bank of North America—the first major banking institution in U.S. history—was chartered by the Continental Congress in 1781 in order to financially support the American War for Independence. After the Constitution was ratified by the states in 1789, Congress moved quickly to establish the First Bank of the United States in 1791 to promote a sound money and credit system in the early years of the American Republic. This federally chartered bank issued paper notes, which gave the nation a convenient source of circulating currency, and promoted the growth of private industry in order to reduce the nation's dependence on foreign imports. Later, in 1816, after the First Bank of the United States failed to win renewal of its charter, Congress chartered the Second Bank of the United States, to bring about orderly growth in the nation's supply of money and credit.

Unfortunately, banks have never been among the most politically popular institutions in the United States. Many prominent banking laws in U.S. history owe their origins to a misunderstanding of what banks do and fear of the financial power they seem to possess. This was certainly true of the First and Second Banks of the United States, both of which pursued policies calling for orderly and stable growth of money and credit at a time when the nation saw rapid growth and expansion (especially the development of western territories) as essential for its survival and prosperity. Accordingly, both of these government-sponsored banks failed to win Congressional renewal of their charters.[4] By the 1830s the federal government had ceased to be active in the chartering and regulation of

---

[4]A key feature of the credit policies followed by the First and Second Banks of the United States was to prevent inflation by limiting the growth of paper currency. Both banks stood ready at all times to redeem paper bank notes in gold and silver coin. This policy also applied to any bank notes issued by state-chartered banks. When the First or Second Bank of the United States received a note issued by a state-chartered bank, it would simply turn around and present the issuing state bank with its own note, demanding payment in silver or gold.

banks, leaving the door open for the states to manage the nation's banking system. And the states made the most of this opportunity by chartering a large number of banking institutions, most of which issued their own paper currency and provided a more ample supply of credit than had been true in the early years of the nation's history. Supported by aggressive bank lending policies, farming and ranching industries grew rapidly as did the manufacture of farm equipment, the railroads, and commercial shipping.

The era of exclusive state control over U.S. banking affairs ended with the Civil War, however. Many of the states failed to regulate the issue of paper bank notes carefully enough and neglected to actively supervise banking industry practices. In some areas, anyone with money or influence could secure a charter for a new bank, even if they possessed little or no experience at running a bank. Thousands of different bank notes appeared, many of which declined rapidly in value, making exchange difficult. Public outcry for reform, coupled with severe pressures on Congress to raise sufficient funds to finance the Civil War, brought the federal government back into the picture as an active regulator of the nation's banking system. In 1863 Congress passed the National Banking Act and initiated further amendments in that law a year later.

The National Banking Acts of 1863 and 1864 were landmark pieces of legislation which have continued to shape the character of American banking down to the present day. The acts created a new type of bank— federally chartered associations, known today as national banks—whose authority to operate came from a new federal office, the Comptroller of the Currency. The new national banks were required to pledge significant amounts of owners' (equity) capital to begin operations, to submit regular financial reports, and to undergo examination by members of the Comptroller's staff at least once each year. Determined to force as many of the state-chartered banks as possible into this new federal system, Congress levied a stiff tax against any notes issued by state banks, eliminating much of the profit from making loans. In turn, the new national banks could issue their own paper notes free of tax, provided they pledged U.S. government securities to back them up. The new federal bank notes were uniform in appearance and, with federal IOUs securing them, grew rapidly in popularity as a safe and convenient money medium. Moreover, the requirement that national banks buy government bonds to back bank notes gave the federal government an ample supply of funds to finance the Civil War.

The result was to limit growth of the nation's money supply and maintain interest rates at levels which appeared to be too high to those commercial interests counting on rapid economic expansion and rising land prices. The political unpopularity of such conservative credit policies culminated in the loss of a federal charter for the Second Bank of the United States in 1836.

For a time the federal bank note tax had the desired effect as scores of banks surrendered their state charters and became national banks. It looked as if the role of the states in regulating and supervising the nation's banking system might become a relic of history. However, the states came back into the picture during the latter part of the 19th century as deposit banking became increasingly popular with the average citizen. People were now more willing to accept and use deposits in a bank account as money instead of relying exclusively on bank notes. Checks became increasingly accepted as a medium of exchange. This made it possible for state-chartered banks to make loans, thereby creating deposits, without issuing taxable notes. The number of state-chartered banks grew rapidly again and eventually eclipsed the number of national banks.

This dramatic recovery of the state banking system has left us with an important legacy today—a dual banking system. Federal authorities (most notably the Comptroller of the Currency) have the primary responsibility for regulating and supervising national banks, while state authorities (usually in the form of state banking commissions) have primary responsibility for regulating and supervising state-chartered banking institutions. Yet, as we will discuss more fully in Chapter 8, both federal and state authorities have overlapping powers and responsibilities. A system of checks and balances seems to prevail today in which each unit of government—state and federal—possesses important powers which limit the decisions and actions of the other.

For example, the states may charter new banks at will, but no bank is likely to open its doors today without deposit insurance from the Federal Deposit Insurance Corporation in Washington, D.C., thus giving that federal agency an important measure of influence over the growth of state-chartered banks. Similarly, the states are empowered to set limits over the establishment of branch offices and the creation and growth of bank holding companies within their borders. While, as we will see in Chapter 8, this particular state authority is being challenged today at the federal level, it is currently an immensely powerful tool in the hands of state banking authorities (and, therefore, the state legislatures) in shaping the size and structure of the nation's banking system.

SERVICES OFFERED BY COMMERCIAL BANKS

Expanding the Money Supply through the Making of Loans and Investments

Commercial banks display all of the basic characteristics of financial intermediaries. Similar to insurance companies, mutual funds, and other intermediaries, they attract funds from savings-surplus units by issuing attractive financial assets (secondary securities) and lend those funds to borrowers or savings-deficit units. Still, banks are especially important financial intermediaries in one key respect: *commercial banks have the capacity to create money in the guise of new deposits by granting credit to borrowers*. Other financial institutions that cannot offer deposits used by the public to make payments (i.e., transactions accounts) cannot create a larger volume of funds than they receive from their customers. Banks and other depository institutions offering transactions accounts, however, can create a multiple amount of funds from any injection of new reserves into the banking system.

Individual banks receive deposits from a wide variety of sources. Households deposit their paychecks and other receipts in both demand (checking) accounts and time and savings deposits. Businesses, too, deposit their sales receipts, income from investments, and other funds in demand accounts and in time deposits. Both the federal government and state and local governments deposit tax collections and income from fees, fines, sales of securities, and other revenues received from the private sector. These deposits from businesses, households, and governments represent so-called *primary deposits* because they arise at the discretion of a bank's customers and the bank must place cash reserves behind these deposits, as required by the regulatory authorities.

In contrast to merely receiving primary deposits from their customers, commercial banks also have the capacity to create *secondary deposits*, which arise when they make loans and investments.[5] When a bank makes a loan to an individual or a business firm, for example, it merely creates a deposit on its books in favor of the borrower. Similarly, when a bank buys U.S. Treasury bills or other securities for its portfolio, deposits are created on behalf of the seller of those securities. Secondary deposits are, like all bank deposits, the IOUs of the bank that creates them. However, an important difference between a bank's IOU and that of other borrowers is that the bank's IOU is generally accepted as money—a medium of exchange that may be used to purchase goods and services.

Providing an Outlet for the Savings of Businesses, Households, and Governmental Units

Commercial banks provide an outlet for savings set aside by the public out of current income by offering financial assets with attractive rates of return. Time and savings deposits of commercial banks represent more than half of all thrift deposits held at depository institutions (commercial banks, credit unions, mutual savings banks, and savings and loan associations). Like the thrift deposits offered by credit unions, savings and loans, and savings banks, commercial bank time and savings deposits are regarded as a nearly riskless outlet for the public's savings, which can be cashed in almost immediately if funds are needed to meet an emergency.

---

[5]Secondary deposits are sometimes referred to as derivative deposits. For a good discussion of the process of money creation by banks see Hutchinson [6] or Board of Governors of the Federal Reserve System [1].

Federal insurance of bank deposits (up to $100,000) has further enhanced the desirability of these deposits, particularly to the small saver.

Offering a Means of Payment for Purchases of Goods and Services

Demand deposits (checking accounts) offered by banks serve as the principal medium of exchange with which to purchase goods and services. Until recently, banks had a clear field in the competition for demand deposits. No other financial institution offered an instrument with the unrestricted capacity to make payments to third parties immediately upon demand. Only in bidding for time and savings deposits did banks face stiff competition from nonbank financial institutions. However, state and federal laws and regulations governing the activities of savings banks and credit unions were liberalized during the 1970s and early 1980s, especially with passage of the Depository Institutions Deregulation and Monetary Control Act of 1980 and the Garn–St. Germain Depository Institutions Act of 1982. Today, thousands of nonbank thrift institutions throughout the nation offer third-party payments services which compete directly with commercial bank transactions accounts.

Among the most popular modern transactions accounts are NOW (negotiable order of withdrawal) accounts, offered by commercial and savings banks; and share drafts offered by credit unions, each paying a fixed rate of interest. Beginning in December 1982 money market deposit accounts (MMDAs) were authorized for federally regulated banks and nonbank thrift institutions. These new accounts can be drafted with checks but carry interest rates which float with current market conditions. MMDAs were set up to permit depository institutions to compete more effectively with shares offered by money market mutual funds, which can usually be accessed by check, by wire, or with a telephone call.[6]

Despite these new developments, however, commercial banks still play a central role in making funds available for the purchase of goods and services in a modern economy. Funds flow freely across state and national boundaries only because individual banks are willing to honor immediately any drafts made against them. A seller of goods in Cleveland is willing to accept a check from a buyer in San Diego because the seller knows that the bank will accept that check for deposit, route it through the banking system to the buyer's bank in San Diego, and receive payment within a very short time (typically two to three days). The whole system rests upon public confidence and a willingness to accept bank demand deposits (checking accounts) as a medium of exchange in payment for goods and services.

The payments system of the United States is presently in a period of

---

[6]See Chapter 16 for a more complete discussion of the transactions powers offered by money market mutual funds to their customers.

transition. The volume of checks written in the United States has expanded more than sixfold during the post–World War II period. However, with the exception of some relatively minor advances, our present check collection system is similar to that established more than 60 years ago. Many analysts, including Federal Reserve officials, are concerned with the increasing congestion of paper represented by checks and other cash items used to transfer funds. Moreover, the costs of handling the enormous volume of checks written each year in the United States have increased rapidly. The most promising remedies for this growing problem involve the computer and various electronic processing systems. We will discuss the new techniques for electronic movement of funds and computer processing of payments information along with their associated benefits and costs in Chapter 23.

Providing Fiduciary Services to Customers

A banking role of growing importance in the nation's financial system is providing trust or fiduciary services to businesses, individuals, and community organizations. In fact, bank trust departments administer the largest pool of investment funds of any financial institution in the United States. The trust function consists of managing the accumulated assets and financial affairs of an individual or institution for the benefit of that particular customer. It requires careful administration of the customer's financial affairs, continuing expert analysis of the customer's financial position, allocating funds for the customer's benefit, and protecting the customer's property. Modern bank trust departments rely upon the skills of economists, lawyers, and financial analysts to make decisions involving property that are of maximum benefit to their customers.[7]

It is exceedingly difficult, if not impossible, to list all of the services provided by a modern, fully staffed trust department at a major bank. Trust departments manage portfolios of stocks, bonds, and other securities for individuals and businesses. Acting under a power of attorney, a trust department may borrow money, pay bills, take out or renew insurance policies, execute leases, purchase real property, and endorse legal documents on behalf of a customer. Acting on behalf of a corporation, a bank trust department may retire or redeem securities issued by the firm, organize and manage its pension funds, distribute stock dividends to the corporation's owners (stockholders), supervise and protect assets pledged against bonds issued by the company, manage the sinking fund which may have been set up to gradually retire those bonds, and keep vital records on the company's financial affairs.

Bank trust departments also play a prominent role in managing the es-

---

[7]See Green and Schuelke [4] for a more detailed description of bank trust services and an analysis of their recent growth.

tates of deceased individuals. If appointed by a court of law or if specified in the deceased's will, a trust department can be granted the authority to protect the assets of a deceased person and liquidate those assets as needed to reimburse creditors and heirs specified in the deceased's will or as directed by court order. However, the same trust department will also be actively involved in managing securities, land, or other assets for the benefit of living persons. A prominent example of this kind of service arises when a father or mother places certain assets (often stocks or bonds) in trust to be managed by the bank until their children reach college age or start families of their own and need substantial amounts of money. In recent years bank trust departments also have been active in tax management issues on behalf of both business and household clients. Many families, for example, are concerned about tax exposure when gifts of property or other assets are made to children, either before or after the death of the original owner. Any transfer of funds which has tax implications may result in a bank trust department becoming actively involved in the transaction at the request of an individual or business customer.

THE SOCIAL RESPONSIBILITIES OF BANKING

In managing a financial institution, perhaps more than in any other industry, the stockholders, board of directors, and officers must chart a course that balances social goals and responsibilities with private interests. This is an especially difficult problem for commercial banks. As we have seen in the preceding sections of this chapter, banks provide services that profoundly influence the nation's economic and financial well-being. Recognizing this, banks are chartered by both federal and state authorities to serve the convenience and needs of the public and are closely regulated in virtually all of their activities. They are expected to cooperate with the monetary authorities to ensure that the growth of money and credit is consistent with national goals of full employment, sustainable economic growth, reasonable price stability, and equilibrium in the nation's balance of payments. Their lending, investing, and other business activities must be conducted in a reasonable and prudent manner that does not risk unduly the safety of depositor funds or reduce public confidence in the stability of the nation's financial system.

HOW BANKS ARE ORGANIZED

The organizational structure of the modern bank is arranged to provide the many services we have discussed in the foregoing paragraphs. Figure 6–2 provides a picture of how a large commercial bank might be organized. Of course, we hasten to note that every bank is organized somewhat differently, reflecting a somewhat different mix of services and varying management philosophies. *Size* also affects greatly the organizational

Figure 6–2   The Organizational Structure of a Commercial Bank

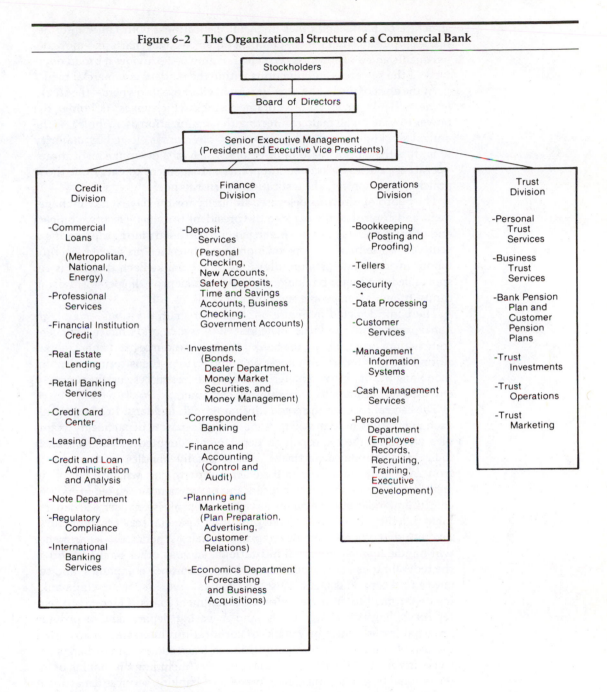

structure of banks and other financial institutions, with larger interme-diaries typically having more complex organizational charts and more de-partments and divisions. Nevertheless, Figure 6–2 provides a broad over-view of the key areas and functions within the modern commercial bank.

At the apex of the bank's organizational chart are its owners—the *stock-holders*. Banks issue mainly common stock which gives its holder the power to vote on all matters affecting the organization as a whole. At the annual stockholders' meeting a *board of directors* is elected by majority vote. It is the bank's board of directors which lays down the institutions' operating policies, selects and appoints management to carry out those policies, and monitors the institution's performance.

The board of directors delegates authority for the day-to-day manage-ment and control of the bank to the president (or chief executive officer) and other members of *senior management*. Included among the senior ex-ecutives of the bank are one or more executive vice presidents, each of whom oversees one or more divisions of the bank. Each division is re-sponsible for a major banking function, such as providing credit, raising funds, or managing people and physical facilities.

The bank depicted in Figure 6–2 has four main divisions—credit, fi-nance, operations, and trust. The first two—credit and finance—concen-trate mainly on managing the bank's financial resources and financial po-sition. The latter two—operations and trust—focus principally on managing the bank's own material and human resources and the property entrusted to the bank by trust division customers.

The central focus of the *credit division* is making loans. In a large bank each major type of loan will be handled in a separate department. Exam-ples would be the metropolitan department, devoted to local business loans; the national department, which usually handles credit requests from large corporations; and the energy department, which services the credit needs of oil and gas producers and other energy-oriented firms. Re-cently, a number of large banks have opened professional-service depart-ments, designed to provide loans and other financial services to doctors, lawyers, and other self-employed professionals. Other credit departments will handle loans to financial institutions, such as other banks (through the federal funds and Eurodollar markets), insurance companies, and se-curity brokers and dealers. Most large banks have a separate retail bank-ing department to dispense consumer installment loans, a credit card cen-ter for billings on charge cards, and a leasing department to provide financial leases, which go mainly to corporations interested in acquiring the use of equipment or property through lease contracts. For banks ac-tively involved in financial activities overseas (including the making of in-ternational business loans), an international banking services department will be organized to handle foreign business.

Analysis of loan and lease applications is typically done by a professional staff housed in the so-called *credit department*, or *credit analysis division*. Once a loan is made, however, a copy of the customer's signed note is filed in the records of the *note department*, which collects interest and installment payments from loan customers. The bank's credit function is closely monitored by state and federal regulatory authorities, since most of the risk in banking is centered in the making of loans. In recent years, comprehensive federal laws have been passed, prescribing the kinds of information banks must disclose to customers (especially consumers) who apply for loans and outlawing discrimination in the granting of credit.[8] Virtually all banks today have either an individual or a division responsible for monitoring the bank's credit-granting activities to make sure the institution is in compliance with state and federal regulations.

The *finance division* is responsible for raising funds which, in the main, flow on to the credit division for making loans. Most incoming funds are received through the *deposit services* department, which oversees checking, time, and savings accounts. Funds are also taken in from correspondent banks in return for services rendered (such as the clearing of checks or providing investment advice). The finance division also may house a bond or *investment department* which trades in both long- and short-term securities. Larger banks also have a *money desk*, or *money market division*, which is responsible for maintaining the bank's legal reserve position with the Federal Reserve bank in the region at the level required by law. The money market division also works at raising funds on an immediate basis (typically through offering money market CDs and borrowing in the Federal funds and Eurodollar markets) to insure that adequate reserves are available to make loans to preferred customers.

The finance division may also include a *planning and marketing department*, which sells existing services, develops new services, and plans for the bank's future growth and expansion. Large banks also house a staff of economists to assist in the planning function, to prepare forecasts of economic and financial conditions, to identify suitable new markets and new financially related businesses the bank may choose to acquire as it grows. The finance division may also house the *accounting department* and the *comptroller* of the bank, whose primary function is to keep and maintain the bank's financial records and make sure all funds flowing into and out of the bank are fully accounted for.

The *operations division* is responsible for managing and protecting the physical facilities owned or used by the bank and for the daily routine of *bookkeeping*—posting and proofing—for thousands of customer credit

---

[8]See Chapter 10 for a discussion of recent disclosure and antidiscrimination laws applying to banking.

and deposit accounts. The bank's computer facilities typically are operated and maintained by this division. Operations also frequently houses the *personnel department*, which keeps employee records and attracts and trains new employees. Human tellers and automated teller machines (ATMs) typically fall under the supervision of the bank's operations officer, as do the security guards. A role of growing significance for this division of the bank is the *cash-management department*, which aids corporations and other business firms in day-to-day management of their cash balances.

Finally, the *trust department* provides the many personal and business trust services discussed earlier in this chapter. Bank trust departments are playing a key role today in managing retirement (pension) accounts for the bank itself and for corporations, proprietorships, partnerships, and individuals. They also manage real property (i.e., land and buildings) owned by customers and, as we noted earlier, actively trade securities on behalf of their clients.

With so many divisions and departments, large commercial banks today offer a real challenge to management. Banking is slated to be one of the most dynamic growth areas in the economy for at least the next decade. Thus, the need for competent and efficient bank managers in all divisions, departments, and functions within the modern bank will almost certainly grow and intensify in the period ahead.

**SOURCES AND
USES OF FUNDS IN
BANKING: BANK
FINANCIAL
STATEMENTS**

Commercial banks in the United States submit two basic financial reports to the regulatory authorities each year: (1) the Report of Condition, or balance sheet and (2) the Report of Income, or statement of earnings and expenses.

Like the balance sheet of any corporation a bank's balance sheet—Report of Condition—reflects the assets, liabilities, and net worth (equity position) of the bank as of a particular day in the year. Assets represent *uses* of incoming funds to generate revenue for the bank, while liabilities and net worth (equity) are *sources* of bank funds.

In drawing upon borrowed funds and equity, the bank generates expenses but anticipates that revenues generated from working assets will more than compensate for the expenses associated with raising money. We can get a fairly detailed view of bank revenues and expenses from the Report of Income (or statement of revenues, expenses, and net earnings). This report is particularly important to investors in bank stock since it provides information on "the bottom line"—the net income from bank operations. As we will see in later chapters, net income from bank operations is a key source of long-term capital for the industry and a measure of how well depositors are protected against loss.

Principal Asset Items on a Bank's Balance Sheet

It is instructive to take a brief overview of the principal assets, liabilities, and net worth (equity capital) used or drawn upon by U.S. banks. Table 6–1 provides a listing of the principal assets held by all U.S. national (federally chartered) banks as June 30, 1979, and June 30, 1980. Table 6–2 enumerates the principal sources of borrowed funds (liabilities) and equity (net worth) drawn upon by the industry as of the same dates.

The most liquid asset held by any commercial bank is *cash*. Cash is held by banks to cover deposit withdrawals, meet emergency expenses, and to handle unexpected (unscheduled) credit demands from customers.[9] The cash account is listed on the Report of Condition as "Cash and Due from Depository Institutions." This asset item includes currency and coin held on the bank's premises to meet customer requests for pocket money. Cash

Table 6–1 Principal Assets Reported on the Balance Sheet of All U.S. National Banks
(Report of Condition for periods ended June 30, 1979 and 1980—$ millions)

Asset Items (uses of bank funds)	June 30, 1979 4,493 Banks Consolidated Foreign and Domestic	Domestic Offices	June 30, 1980 4,426 Banks Consolidated Foreign and Domestic	Domestic Offices	Change June 1979–June 1980 Fully Consolidated Amount	Percent
Cash and due from depository institutions	$170,239	$ 98,175	$195,697	$110,233	$ 25,458	15.0
U.S. Treasury securities	43,301	43,268	45,544	45,375	2,243	5.2
Obligations of other U.S. government agencies and corporations	22,800	22,790	26,680	26,549	3,880	17.0
Obligations of states and political subdivisions	68,788	68,427	74,189	73,554	5,401	7.9
All other securities	15,756	10,366	15,003	8,632	− 753	− 4.8
Total securities	150,645	144,851	161,416	154,110	10,771	7.1
Federal funds sold and securities purchased under agreements to resell	33,561	33,443	37,697	37,201	4,136	12.3
Total loans (excluding unearned income)	519,049	416,466	567,927	444,676	48,878	9.4
Allowance for possible loan losses.	5,163	4,996	5,815	5,652	652	12.6
Net loans	513,886	411,470	562,112	439,024	48,226	9.4
Lease financing receivables	7,115	6,036	8,855	7,312	1,740	24.5
Bank premises, furniture and fixtures, and other assets representing bank premises	13,114	12,384	14,604	13,711	1,490	11.4
Real estate owned other than bank premises.	1,440	1,313	1,347	1,212	− 93	− 6.5
All other assets.	38,138	37,443	53,283	52,930	15,145	39.7
Total assets	$928,139	$745,114	$1,035,011	$815,735	$106,872	11.5

Source: Comptroller of the Currency, Administrator of National Banks, *1980 Report of Operations*, Washington, D.C., Spring 1981.

[9]Banks try to anticipate customer demands for loans and other forms of credit in advance. Reserves held to accommodate expected near-term credit demands are placed mainly in interest-bearing marketable securities, not in cash, because the cash account earns no interest income for the bank. However, cash reserves aid the individual bank in covering immediate, unexpected credit requests.

Table 6–2   Principal Liabilities and Equity Capital (Net Worth) Items for All U.S. National Banks (Report of Condition—June 30, 1979 and 1980)

Liability and Equity Items (sources of bank funds)	June 30, 1979 4,493 Banks Consolidated Foreign and Domestic	Domestic Offices	June 30, 1980 4,426 Banks Consolidated Foreign and Domestic	Domestic Offices	Change June 1979–June 1980 Fully Consolidated Amount	Percent
Liabilities:						
Demand deposits of individuals, partnerships and corporations	$164,695	$164,695	$177,614	$177,614	$ 12,919	7.8
Time and savings deposits of individuals, partnerships and corporations	300,600	300,600	335,102	335,102	34,502	11.5
Deposits of U.S. government	1,627	1,627	1,624	1,624	−3	−.2
Deposits of states and political subdivisions	44,050	44,050	41,442	41,442	−2,608	−5.9
All other deposits	32,116	32,116	41,308	41,308	9,192	28.6
Certified and officers' checks	7,015	7,015	7,389	7,389	374	5.3
Total deposits in domestic offices	550,103	550,103	604,479	604,479	54,376	9.9
Demand deposits	206,658	206,658	228,206	228,206	21,548	10.4
Time and savings deposits	343,445	343,445	376,273	376,273	32,828	9.6
Total deposits in foreign offices	175,163	0	201,987	0	26,824	15.3
Total deposits	725,265	550,103	806,466	604,479	81,200	11.2
Federal funds purchased and securities sold under agreements to repurchase	79,597	79,464	86,697	86,546	7,100	8.9
Interest-bearing demand notes issued to U.S. Treasury	9,295	9,295	7,078	7,078	−2,217	−23.9
Other liabilities for borrowed money	16,795	9,569	17,481	8,511	686	4.1
Mortgage indebtedness and liability for capitalized leases	1,303	1,261	1,371	1,328	68	5.2
All other liabilities	40,560	40,345	54,911	47,059	14,351	35.4
Total liabilities	872,817	690,036	974,003	755,001	101,186	11.6
Subordinated notes and debentures	3,450	3,206	3,828	3,554	378	11.0
Equity capital:						
Preferred stock	30	30	33	33	3	10.0
Common stock	11,149	11,149	11,722	11,722	573	5.1
Surplus	17,407	17,407	18,295	18,295	888	5.1
Undivided profits and reserve for contingencies and other capital reserves	23,287	23,287	27,130	27,130	3,843	16.5
Total equity capital	51,873	51,873	57,180	57,180	5,307	10.2
Total liabilities, subordinated notes and debentures and equity capital	$928,139	$745,114	$1,035,011	$815,735	$106,872	11.5

Source: Comptroller of the Currency, Administrator of National Banks, *1980 Report of Operations*, Washington, D.C., Spring 1981.

assets also include the reserve account each bank (and today all federally insured depository institutions) must hold with the Federal Reserve bank in the region, demand and time deposits held with other depository institutions, and cash items in process. The latter are mainly uncollected checks written against accounts in other banks. Eventually (usually no more than two or three days hence) the bank receiving these cash items will receive credit for them either in its reserve account at the regional Federal Reserve bank or in the form of an increased deposit at a correspondent bank.

The second major asset item shown on the Report of Condition is *investments* in various kinds of securities (mainly bonds and shorter-term notes purchased in the open market). A portion of the securities held in this asset account are liquidity reserves—securities with low risk and ready marketability. Such reserves usually include money market instruments, such as U.S. Treasury bills, bankers' acceptances, federal funds loans, and commercial paper. They are the bank's second line of defense (after cash) against deposit withdrawals and other near-term liquidity needs.

The remaining securities in the investment account are held mainly for their income-earning power or advantages as a tax shelter. Such securities include U.S. government notes and bonds, federal agency securities, state and local government bonds and notes, and a small volume of corporate notes and bonds. State and local government (municipal) securities are particularly favored by U.S. banks interested in keeping their income-tax obligation as low as possible. Interest income from municipals is exempt from federal income taxation (though any capital gains received from these securities may be fully taxable).

Many banks today derive the liquidity they need by borrowing the necessary funds from other banks in the *federal funds* market.[10] Major banks both buy (borrow) and sell (loan) federal funds and, therefore, "make a market" for these reserve balances. Buyers of federal funds typically are banks that are in need of reserves required by the Federal Reserve or that have some other pressing, immediate need for money. Sellers of federal funds usually are banks with extra reserves beyond those needed to meet immediate loan demand or deposit withdrawals. In addition to trading in federal funds, many banks provide short-term loans to banks, securities dealers, and corporations through *repurchase agreements* involving marketable securities (principally U.S. government obligations). When engaging in a repurchase agreement with another institution, a bank may acquire securities (and thereby extend credit to a customer) but agree to sell back the securities to its customer after a certain period, usually a few days later.

Dwarfing in importance all other asset items on a bank's Report of Condition is *loans*—the direct extension of credit by a bank to its customers. We note that loans represented over half the assets of national banks in 1979 and 1980. Loans are nearly always made today simply by increasing the account balance of the customer—if he or she already owns a deposit

---

[10]As we saw in Chapter 4, federal funds include reserve balances of banks held with the regional Federal Reserve banks. Today the federal funds market also includes correspondent deposits that banks and other depository institutions hold with each other and any other deposits (such as those held by a securities dealer or corporation) which can be transferred and loaned immediately to some other institution. Thus, broadly speaking, federal funds are best defined as immediately available money.

account with the bank—or by setting up a new deposit account in the amount of the loan if the borrower is a new customer.

Banks make a bewildering array of loans for thousands of different purposes, ranging from the acquisition of assets (such as business inventories, automobiles, machinery, and motor homes) to the covering of expenses (such as arise from vacations, taxes, home repairs, and wage and salary costs). The most important type of loan made by banks (measured by dollar volume) is *commercial and industrial loans*, more commonly referred to as business loans. In second place are real estate loans, which represent extensions of credit to buy or build on real property (land) and include loans to support the construction or purchase of homes, factories, apartments, shopping centers, warehouses, and thousands of other structures.

Ranked third in dollar amount are loans to individuals, and they encompass credit extended to individual consumers in various forms. These loans may include outstanding charges on a credit card and direct cash loans negotiated between an individual and a bank loan officer. Growth in consumer-oriented loans has been rapid in recent years, with many households today battling inflation by making purchases on credit rather than waiting until later when prices are even higher. Other categories of bank loans—lesser in amount but still important to the sectors they serve—include loans to financial institutions, loans to individuals and security brokers and dealers to purchase securities, loans to farm and ranch (agricultural) operations, and a broad miscellaneous category.

The composition of a bank's loan portfolio varies with the bank's size and location. The smallest banks in rural and suburban communities tend to make more consumer and real estate credit available rather than business credit. These institutions are sometimes designated as *retail banks*, since they deal largely with the consumer. In contrast, the largest city banks make mainly business loans and are often called *wholesale banks*.

The remainder of the items on the asset side of the bank's balance sheet are relatively small in magnitude. These items include 'Premises, Furniture, and Fixtures," which represent the net value (after all depreciation charges) of the bank's fixed assets (buildings and equipment). Banks may also hold investments in properties not directly involved in offering bank services and which are entered under an account often labeled "Other Real Estate." As an alternative to making loans, banks also lease equipment to business firms. The expected lease payments constitute "Lease Financing Receivables." All other assets are listed in a miscellaneous account. These other assets may include investments in bank subsidiaries, which are financially related companies in which the bank holds some ownership interest. Another miscellaneous item is "Customers' Liability on Acceptances," which arises principally in the financing of international commerce when customers use their approved line of bank credit to authorize a draft on their account or when bills of exchange are issued in favor of the bank's customers to pay for imported goods.

Principal Liabilities on a Bank's Balance Sheet

The making of loans and the acquisition of securities and other assets requires banks to borrow heavily from the financial marketplace. Historically, most of the funds raised by banks have come from *deposits*. Equity capital (net worth) contributed by the stockholders is normally much smaller in amount than a bank's deposits. However, in recent years banks have turned increasingly to the money market (through federal funds and Eurodollar loans, for example) and occasionally to the capital market (through long-term notes and debentures) to raise the money required by their lending and investing activities.

Nevertheless, as Table 6–2 makes abundantly clear, *deposits* by businesses, households, and governments are still, far and away, the banking industry's chief funds source. These deposits may be categorized in several different ways. We may group them by (1) the type of customer who holds the deposit—individuals, partnerships, corporations, financial institutions, and federal, state or local governments—or by (2) deposit category—demand deposits and other transactions accounts, time deposits, or savings deposits. *Demand deposits* are payable by the bank as soon as someone designated by the deposit holder to receive funds presents a signed draft to the bank. The best-known demand deposit account is the *regular checking account*, which does not bear interest but permits the customer to write any number of checks desired (subject, of course, to some type of service or activity fee). However, there are other transactions accounts very similar to regular checking accounts, but these pay interest. A prominent example of an interest-bearing transactions account is the NOW (negotiable order of withdrawal), which carries a fixed rate of interest and is accessible by writing a check. Similar to NOWs, *money market deposit accounts* (MMDAs), first authorized in December 1982, permit limited check writing but generally pay a higher and more flexible rate of interest than NOWs. Both demand deposits and NOWs represent the chief method for making payments in the U.S. economy today.

Deposits not payable on demand may be either *time deposits* or *savings deposits*. The former have a fixed maturity and promised rate of return, while savings deposits promise the customer a particular interest rate but usually may be withdrawn without prior notice.

The composition of a bank's deposits is of considerable importance to its growth and earnings. The greater the proportion of demand deposits relative to time and savings deposits at an individual bank, the larger that bank's liquidity needs and the more concerned it usually is about cash withdrawals or unexpected demands for loans. However, in recent years the trend in banking has been toward a greater proportion of time deposits and smaller portions of both demand and passbook savings accounts. Unfortunately, time deposits carry the highest interest rates a bank can pay, which has the effect of driving up bank costs and placing considerable pressure on earnings.

Most banks today actively manage their liability accounts as well as their assets. Usually this requires supplementing deposits with nondeposit borrowings. These nondeposit sources of funds typically include short-term borrowings of reserves in the Federal funds and Eurodollar markets, through security repurchase agreements and short-term loans from the discount windows of the Federal Reserve banks. Banks also use long-term borrowings of funds, including mortgages and subordinated notes and debentures. The notes and debentures are frequently referred to as *debt capital* because they carry a maturity of at least seven years and are subordinated to the claims of depositors who are considered to be the primary creditors of a bank. A relatively new nondeposit liability item is "Interest-Bearing Demand Notes Issued to U.S. Treasury," which represents the bank's way of reimbursing the Treasury for U.S. government deposits left with the bank.

Equity Capital (Net Worth) on a Bank's Balance Sheet

Like any corporation, banks also draw upon their owners—the stockholders—for funds. This so-called *equity capital* is a relatively small proportion of total assets, as shown in Table 6–1. Commercial banks are highly leveraged organizations, relying mainly upon debt (principally deposits) to support their assets. Equity capital represents a cushion to protect the depositors against a decline in the value of a bank's assets. However, because the equity cushion is quite small, the soundness of a bank depends principally upon the competence and prudence of its management and the stability of the financial system. We note that the principal components of equity capital are undivided profits (i.e., retained earnings), capital reserves held for future contingencies, the par value of common and preferred stock issued, and surplus, which is the excess value of any stock issued above the stock's par value.

THE REPORT OF INCOME

We noted earlier that bank assets generate revenues, while the acquisition of funds through liabilities and equities creates expenses. How well the individual bank is doing in balancing its revenues against its expenses and generating adequate net income is reflected in the Report of Income. We have split this report for U.S. national banks into two parts, shown in

Table 6–3 Sources of Revenue (operating income) for All U.S. National Banks (Report of Income); Periods Ended June 30, 1979 and 1980 (amounts in $ millions)

Principal Source of Revenue (operating income)	June 30, 1979 4,493 Banks		June 30, 1980 4,426 Banks		Change June 1979–June 1980	
	Consolidated Foreign and Domestic	Percent Distri- bution	Consolidated Foreign and Domestic	Percent Distri- bution	Amount	Percent
Operating income:						
Interest and fees on loans	$28,666.6	68.8	$38,948.6	68.1	$10,282.0	35.9
Interest on balances with depository institutions	3,025.2	7.3	5,454.1	9.5	2,428.9	80.3
Income on federal funds sold and securities purchased under agreements to resell	1,523.7	3.7	2,346.2	4.1	822.5	54.0
Interest on U.S. Treasury securities and on obligations of other U.S. govern- ment agencies and corporations	2,598.1	6.2	3,108.7	5.4	510.6	19.7
Interest on obligations of states and political subdivisions in the United States	1,824.6	4.4	2,093.1	3.7	268.5	14.7
Income from all other securities (including dividends on stock)	368.5	.9	404.1	.7	35.6	9.7
Income from lease financing	351.5	.8	426.2	.7	74.7	21.3
Income from fiduciary activities	657.7	.6	753.7	1.3	96.0	14.6
Service charges on deposit accounts . . .	633.1	.5	790.5	1.4	157.4	24.9
Other service charges, commissions and fees	1,137.9	2.7	1,420.6	2.5	264.7	23.3
Other operating income	862.0	2.1	1,530.7	2.6	641.7	74.4
Total operating income	$41,649.0	100.0	$57,231.4	100.0	$15,582.4	37.4

Source: Comptroller of the Currency, Administrator of National Banks, *1980 Report of Operations*, Washington, D.C., Spring 1981.

Tables 6–3 and 6–4. Table 6–3 examines the principal sources of bank revenues (designated as operating income), while Table 6–4 tracks expenses and net income.

Most bank revenues are derived from the interest and fees charged for loans.[11] A much smaller, though still important, source of operating revenues is interest earnings on various security investments and deposits held by the bank. Leading this revenue category are income generated by investments in Treasury bills, bonds, and notes and income from munici-

---

[11]The reader will note that interest and fees on loans are lumped together on the bank's Report of Income. Actually, interest on a loan is the amount of dollars the borrower must pay for the actual use of bank funds. However, other fees and charges are associated with the making of loans. The most common example is a commitment fee levied when the bank agrees to extend credit to a borrower at a future date. Because the bank must stand ready to lend the funds when the borrower needs them, it will hold a liquid reserve (usually in the form of cash or readily marketable securities) until the commitment is exercised by the borrower. The rate of return on liquid assets held for this purpose is relatively low compared to loans and other assets, so that the commitment fee compensates the banker in some measure for maintaining extra liquidity.

Table 6–4   Expenses and Net Income for All U.S. National Banks (Report of Income); Periods Ended June 30,1979 and 1980

Principal Expense Items and Net Income	June 30, 1979 4,493 Banks Consolidated Foreign and Domestic	Percent Distri- bution	June 30, 1980 4,426 Banks Consolidated Foreign and Domestic	Percent Distri- bution	Change June 1979–June 1980 Amount	Percent
Operating expenses:						
Salaries and employee benefits	$ 5,976.6	16.3	$ 6,910.4	13.3	$ 933.6	15.6
Interest on time certificates of $100,000 or more (issued by domestic offices).	5,043.9	13.8	7,410.7	14.3	2,366.8	46.9
Interest on deposits in foreign offices	7,368.5	20.1	12,568.2	24.3	5,199.7	70.6
Interest on other deposits	7,333.2	20.0	10,418.9	20.1	3,085.7	42.1
Expense of federal funds purchased and securities sold under agreements to repurchase.	3,666.7	10.0	5,612.9	10.8	1,946.2	53.1
Interest on demand notes issued to the U.S. Treasury and on other borrowed money	836.2	2.3	1,408.3	2.7	572.1	68.4
Interest on subordinated notes and debentures. . . .	129.7	.4	144.1	.3	14.4	11.1
Occupancy expense of bank premises, net, and furniture equipment expenses	1,720.4	4.7	2,019.5	3.9	299.1	17.4
Provision for possible loan losses	1,041.0	2.8	1,243.4	2.4	202.4	19.4
Other operating expenses	3,564.1	9.7	4,055.8	7.8	491.7	13.8
Total operating expenses	36,680.3	100.0	51,792.1	100.0	15,111.8	41.2
Income before income taxes and securities gains or losses	4,968.7		5,439.3		470.6	9.5
Applicable income taxes	1,368.4		1,503.2		134.8	9.9
Income before securities gains or losses	3,600.3		3,936,1		335.8	9.3
Securities gains (losses), gross	− 113.6		− 237.1		− 123.5	108.7
Applicable income taxes.	− 52.3		− 79.0		− 26.7	51.1
Securities gains (losses), net	− 61.3		− 158.1		− 96.8	157.9
Income before extraordinary items	3,539.0		3,778.0		239.0	6.8
Extraordinary items, net	12.2		4.3		− 7.9	− 64.8
Net income.	$ 3,551.2		$ 3,782.3		$ 231.1	6.5
Cash dividends declared on common stock	$ 1,406.5		$ 1,359.6		$ − 46.9	− 3.3
Cash dividends declared on preferred stock.	1.1		3.0		1.9	172.7
Total cash dividends declared.	$ 1,407.6		$ 1,362.6		$ − 45.0	− 3.2
Recoveries credited to allowance for possible loan losses.	$ 370.3		$ 381.5		$ 11.2	3.0
Losses charged to allowance for possible loan losses.	995.3		1,339.1		343.8	34.5
Net loan losses	$ 625.0		$ 957.6		$ 332.6	53.2

Source: Comptroller of the Currency, Administrator of National Banks, *1980 Report of Operations*, Washington, D.C., Spring 1981.

pal bonds and notes. When we add earnings from deposits held with other financial institutions, income from other securities (mainly commercial paper and corporate notes and bonds), and earnings on funds sold in the Federal funds market and security repurchase agreements, the total revenue from all bank investments usually accounts for between one fifth and one fourth of bank operating income. In contrast, loans account for almost 70 percent of total operating revenues.[12]

While still relatively small in amount, a growing proportion of bank income in recent years has come from leases. Lease financing is a substitute for loans which carries significant tax advantages and avoids some of the disadvantages of ownership of any assets acquired. Under a typical lease granted by a bank the customer does not own the leased assets but only receives the right to use those assets for the period prescribed in the leasing agreement. However, most bank leases are really financial leases in which the customer makes sufficient lease payments to cover virtually the entire cost of any assets purchased (less scrap value) plus a profit for the bank. The bulk of bank leasing agreements today involves the purchase of business equipment. The leasing of such equipment brings substantial economic benefits to the bank as well as to the customer. Because the bank retains title to leased equipment, it also retains the right to capture tax-deductible depreciation expense on that equipment, thereby increasing the after-tax earnings from lease financing.

The remaining sources of bank revenue are generally quite small and include numerous miscellaneous items. One of these is income from trust services (i.e., fiduciary activities). The earnings of most bank trust departments are small at best and frequently negative at smaller banks. Trust department income at national banks in 1980 was less than 2 percent of their total operating income. Service charges on deposits are another relatively small source of bank income, roughly comparable to trust income. Charges are levied on demand deposit (checking) accounts based upon both the average balance in the account and upon the number of checks and other cash items processed through the account during a given month. Most banks do not levy a service charge on accounts with a minimum balance exceeding a certain figure and/or with an activity level below some stipulated amount. Some banks, in order to gain a foothold in a new market or to increase their share of an existing market, have offered checking accounts completely free of any service charges. In some instances this device has merely attracted numerous small accounts, added

---

[12]It is important to keep in mind here a point made earlier in this chapter. Loans are designed principally to generate income for the bank, while investments in securities fulfill several different roles—generating income, providing a reserve of liquidity, and sheltering a portion of net earnings from taxes. It is not surprising, then, that income from investments is substantially less than that on loans. Another reason for this difference in loan versus investment earning power, of course, is the fact that banks commit a much greater proportion of their total resources (assets) to loans than to investments. As Table 6–1 reflects, national banks hold over half their assets in the form of loans, but less than a fifth of their assets are committed to security investments.

more to costs than to revenues, and held down earnings from the deposit function.

At many banks in recent years, expenses of operation have grown faster than revenues, and, as a result, profits have been placed under severe pressure. Particularly noteworthy have been rising wage and salary expenses (including employee benefits) and interest paid on time and savings deposits. Commercial banks have responded to these cost pressures in a variety of ways. Larger banking units have been formed through branching, mergers, and holding companies in an effort to lower per-unit costs. The industry has developed new product lines, such as new savings plans, computer services, lease financing, management consulting, and so on, in order to boost its revenues. Electronic tellers and other computerized equipment have been given a greatly expanded role and have helped to offset some of the increases in other expense items.

As shown in Table 6–4, salaries, wages, and related costs represented about 13 percent of total national bank operating expenses in 1980. For most banks, salaries, wages, and fringe benefits—all personnel costs—are the second largest expense item (and a rapidly growing expense category in recent years). Personnel expenses are outdistanced by a wide margin by interest costs associated with raising funds. However, these interest costs come, of course, from selling time and savings deposits to the public and from nondeposit sources of borrowed funds (such as the Federal funds market, the Eurodollar market, and loans from the discount windows of the Federal Reserve banks). For all U.S. national banks operating in 1980, interest paid on certificates of deposit, savings deposits, and various nondeposit borrowings accounted for about 70 percent of all bank expenses.

A number of relatively small items appear at the end of the operating expense list, including occupancy expenses, equipment rentals, depreciation, and maintenance, provision for possible loan losses, advertising, deposit insurance fees, and office supplies. Occupancy expense includes the cost of maintaining and repairing bank properties, depreciation of buildings and equipment, insurance costs, and property taxes. The provision for possible loan losses shown on the Report of Income reflects the risk inherent in a bank's lending function. Banks are permitted to set up a reserve for losses on loans and to make periodic tax-free transfers into this reserve from operating income.[13]

The difference between total revenues (operating income) and operating expenses yields income before taxes and securities transactions—one measure of bank profitability. However, of more concern to stockholders is the figure for *earnings after taxes*. National banks paid income taxes of

---

[13]See Chapter 12 for a more complete discussion of the purpose and tax implications of the loan-loss account.

$1.5 billion through June 1980, leaving income after taxes but before securities gains (or losses) of $3.9 billion. Once net losses from securities transactions are taken out[14] (along with deductions for other tax payments and the addition of extraordinary income items) U.S. national banks were left with a net income of just under $3.8 billion as of midyear 1980.

Was this a high or low earnings figure? Was it an adequate profit rate? Questions like these are of extreme importance to bank stockholders, the regulatory authorities, and the public. We turn to such important issues in the next chapter, which looks at the methods used today to measure the performance of banks and other financial institutions. Our basic objective in the next chapter is to examine the financial firm from the point of view of a financial analyst concerned with measuring the efficiency and effectiveness of banks in serving the public.

SUMMARY

In many ways, commercial banks can be considered the most important financial institution. They hold the largest single amount of assets (resources) of any institution in the nation's financial system and provide the essential service of credit creation for businesses, consumers, and governments. However, the role of banks in the nation's economy is changing rapidly under the pressure of changes in technology (principally the use of computers and other electronic media) and regulation. There is a strong trend afoot today to gradually deregulate the banking industry and encourage greater competition between banks and their nearest rivals—the credit unions, savings and loan associations, savings banks, and money market funds.

These nonbank thrift institutions along with insurance companies, brokerage houses, and aggressive nonfinancial firms (such as Sears Roebuck) are making it increasingly difficult to distinguish banks from other financial institutions today. Historically, banks were unique in offering checking accounts and catering primarily to business (commercial) customers. That uniqueness, however, is gradually disappearing in the frantic rush of thousands of different nonbank businesses to get a piece of the action in traditional banking markets.

Banking has deep roots in history. Some scholars find the industry's origins in medieval goldsmiths who accepted deposits of gold and silver for safekeeping and made loans. Others see a much older forerunner in money merchants who changed one form of coin into another in the great marketplaces of the ancient world. Whatever the industry's true origins, it is clear that banking has been closely regulated and sometimes controlled by

---

[14]Banks are required to give special treatment to any gains or losses from trading securities, reflecting the fact that their principal function is to make loans.

government throughout most of its history. Banks are considered to be vested with the public interest, to be a repository of the public's savings, and to be the principal avenue through which the nation's money supply grows over time. Viewed from this perspective it is perhaps not too surprising that even in the United States, where most economic decisions are made in the free marketplace, banks face an imposing list of laws and regulations enforced by both federal and state governments.

The services provided to the public by the banking industry are almost too numerous to mention. They accept demand (checking) deposits, which serve as the primary means of paying for purchases of goods and services; they also accept interest-bearing time and savings deposits as a place for the public to hold reserves of liquid purchasing power. Banks create money by making loans and investments (through the setting up of so-called secondary deposits) and help their customers protect property and investments by providing trust services. While banks thus provide an imposing array of essential services, they are also private, profit-oriented corporations whose principal goal must be earning a satisfactory rate of return on capital invested by their stockholders.

Our understanding of the role of the banking industry in the economy can be greatly enhanced through a working knowledge of bank financial statements. The two principal financial statements which banking institutions must submit to federal and state regulatory authorities each year are the Report of Condition (balance sheet) and Report of Income (statement of earnings, expenses, and revenues).

Careful analysis of bank balance sheets reveals that their principal asset is loans, accounting for over half of all industry assets, followed by investments in securities. Banks are among the leading investor groups in their purchases of U.S. Treasury bills, notes, and bonds and of the bonds and notes issued each year by state and local (municipal) governments. The principal liability and source of funds for the industry is deposits, though a growing portion of banking's funds in recent years has come from nondeposit borrowings in the nation's money market. Leading the list here are purchases of federal funds and Eurodollars and borrowings from the Federal Reserve banks. Meanwhile, bank deposits increasingly have shifted toward interest-bearing time deposits (such as negotiable CDs), which carry the highest interest rates banks can pay.

Bank expenses have soared in recent years, led by rapid increases in interest costs on deposits and other borrowings and employee salaries and wages—the industry's two largest expense items. Many banks have managed to protect their profit margins in such a rising-cost environment by increasing their investments in (and therefore their earnings from) loans, by better tax management practices (principally the purchase of tax-exempt municipal bonds), and through greater use of financial leverage. The latter device has meant increased reliance on borrowed funds to support industry growth and less on equity capital from bank stockholders. To a largely indeterminant extent it may be that the riskiness of many banking organizations has increased in recent years. That issue and others focusing on the recent behavior of banks, however, we must leave to subsequent chapters in this book.

Questions

6-1. What is your understanding of the meaning of the word *bank*? How is the meaning of the word *bank* changing today?

6-2. Describe the beginnings of modern banking. To what extent did medieval goldsmiths actually perform the functions of banks? How about the ancient money merchants?

6-3. What institution is known as the "father of modern banking"? Explain why.

6-4. How have the relative roles of federal and state governments in U.S. banking changed over time? In your opinion, which level of government dominates the regulation of banking today? Explain.

6-5. What is unique about a commercial bank in terms of its ability to furnish credit?

How do banks differ from other financial institutions in this regard?

6-6. Discuss the following services offered by commercial banks:
a. Credit.
b. Deposit.
c. Clearing of checks.
d. Fiduciary.
Explain why each is important to the functioning of a modern economy.

6-7. List the principal items in a commercial bank's Report of Condition. Explain the function of each item listed.

6-8. List the principal items in a bank's Report of Income. What is the function of each item?

References

1. *The Federal Reserve System: Its Purposes and Functions*. Washington, D.C., 1972.

2. Federal Reserve Bank of New York. *The Story of Banks*. New York: Public Information Department, 1979.

3. _____. *The Story of Checks*. New York: Public Information Department, 1981.

4. Green, Donald S., and Mary Schuelke. *The Trust Activities of the Banking Industry*. Chicago: Trustees of the Banking Research Fund, Association of Reserve City Bankers, 1975.

5. Hempel, George, H., and Jess B. Yawitz. *Financial Management of Financial Institutions*. Englewood Cliffs, N.J.: Prentice-Hall, 1977.

6. Hutchinson, Harry D. *Money, Banking, and the United States Economy*. 2d ed. New York: Appleton-Century-Crofts, 1971.

7. Nadler, Paul. *Commercial Banking in the Economy*. New York: Random House, 1968.

7. *Analyzing the Behavior of Banks and Other Financial Institutions*

BANKS AND OTHER FINANCIAL INSTITUTIONS are becoming increasingly concerned today with the pursuit of goals and with their progress in achieving those goals. Many banks, for example, are keenly interested in earning maximum profits in order to provide the highest possible returns to their shareholders and to secure additional funds to support long-term growth. They realize that higher profits may instill greater confidence among depositors and investors, making it easier to raise capital in the future. This renewed concern over higher profits was especially evident among larger U.S. banks in the late 1960s and 1970s when many institutions paid closer attention to daily bank stock price movements. These banks saw rising profits, leading to higher stock prices, as an avenue permitting them to acquire more bank and nonbank affiliated firms and thereby expand into new markets.

While increased profitability ranks high on the list of goals for financial institutions, these institutions usually focus their attention on other measures of institutional behavior as well. For example, how risky is one financial institution compared to another? Is the institution we are studying using too much or too little financial leverage? Are recent *growth rates* in its customer accounts adequate compared to the competition? Is a financial institution managing its tax position carefully and effectively? How efficient is a given financial institution in generating loans and deposits from the personnel and resources it has at its command? Could employee productivity be improved? How does the composition (mix) of assets and liabilities compare with other institutions of comparable size and location? Are expenses rising too rapidly and does the financial institution we are studying carry too little or too much liquidity?

These and other behavior-oriented questions are heard in the board rooms and in management conferences among both large and small financial institutions today. They reflect the fact that the behavior of a financial institution and its success or lack of success depends upon many different factors—all of which management must monitor and, where possible, attempt to control. In this chapter we focus upon different measures of the behavior of banks and other financial institutions.[1] If, for example, profitability is a major goal for a financial institution, how can we measure its profitability? When profits fall, how can we decide what the cause might be or how management might respond to correct the problem? What are the various factors that affect the individual institution's degree of profitability? In addition to looking at measures of behavior we are also interested in this chapter in planning systems used by financial institutions. How do these institutions plan in order to improve their profits and to achieve other worthwhile goals?

THE GOALS OF FINANCIAL INSTITUTIONS

Banks and other financial institutions pursue many different goals today. Some stress, for example, *better service to the community*. For banks and many other intermediaries, their charter—license to operate—is a franchise granted by government to provide financial services to the public. Only a few such charters are issued, to protect certain financial institutions from 'excessive" competition. Because entry into financial industries is often closely controlled, performance that benefits the community, principally through an ample supply of credit and other financial services, is a key responsibility of the management of financial institutions. Although better service to the community as an institutional goal is extremely difficult to measure and track, public service nevertheless remains a key objective for the management of financial institutions.

Many financial institutions are *growth* and *market-share* oriented. Management asks, for example, How fast did customer accounts and earnings grow last year? Does the financial institution we are studying hold a larger or smaller share of the local market for checking accounts, money market CDs, consumer installment loans, small business credit, and so forth than it did five years ago? The basic argument here is that faster growth and a larger share of the local market may be tell-tale signs that the institution is, indeed, serving the community better. Also, more rapid growth results in a much larger institution with more resources available for the offering of new services, acquiring new subsidiaries, and constructing more modern facilities.

Growth and community service are, undoubtedly, worthwhile objectives for the management of a financial institution. However, economists and financial analysts usually argue that these goals must be secondary to one primary objective—*pursuit of maximum returns for the owners of the*

---

[1]This chapter is based, in part, upon an earlier study by one of the authors published in *The Canadian Banker and ICB Review*. See references [12], [13], and [14].

institution. In market-oriented economies, resources are most efficiently allocated and production of goods and services approaches optimal levels most closely where business firms operate to maximize rewards flowing to business owners. In the case of corporate financial institutions, this translates into greater returns on the stockholders' investment (equity capital). Presumably, those financial institutions offering services whose quantity and quality most satisfies public need will find their sales increasing and thereby will achieve greater net earnings. Those institutions either unable or unwilling to provide financial services most in demand will face declining sales, reduced availability of capital and other resources, and lower earnings, and perhaps ultimately they will exit the industry. In a competitive marketplace, improved service to the public usually leads to greater financial rewards for those who own and operate financial institutions.[2]

Key goals for many financial institutions are:

Satisfactory or maximum profitability.

Increased growth rate in assets, sales, funds sources, or credit accounts.

Better service to the community.

Maintenance of adequate capital.

Greater share of target markets.

Greater efficiency and productivity in the use of resources.

Greater diversification in services offered and market areas served.

If the most important goal for most financial institutions (especially those organized as corporations) is maximum returns to the owners of the business, how can we measure that return? How do we decide if current returns to the owners are adequate?

MEASURING THE REWARDS OF OWNERSHIP

In the case of a corporation whose stock is widely held and actively traded, the owners (stockholders) of the institution are clearly better off if the institution's stock price (i.e., its equity value in the marketplace) rises. We know that stock prices depend heavily on two factors—expected re-

---

[2]As we will suggest in more detail in future chapters, higher earnings for a financial institution can strengthen its position by reducing risk in the long run. Earnings retained in the business build up net worth, which provides an additional reserve against future financial difficulties. For banks and most other intermediaries, retained earnings are the principal source of growth in equity capital, which is the account that absorbs losses. An institution with a greater margin of equity capital has more time and resources to correct earnings problems and stay afloat. When earnings are high, more funds are available to take on new risks, such as through making more loans or developing and marketing new services.

As we will see in subsequent chapters, financial intermediaries have developed a wide range of new services in recent years—NOW accounts, money market CDs, variable-rate mortgages, universal life insurance, etc. Support for innovations of this sort, which are highly risky, comes from adequate profitability and well-trained management.

turns from the firm's operations and the riskiness of the firm as viewed by investors. Therefore if management of a financial institution can enhance investor expectations about future earnings or reduce the institution's perceived level of risk, the value of the firm's stock should rise, other things being equal. Expectations of future earnings might be raised by developing new financial services, penetrating new markets, initiating more effective cost-control methods, carrying out profitable mergers or acquisitions, and other favorable developments. Perceived risk can be reduced by leveling out fluctuations in earnings from year to year, perhaps as a result of more effective tax management, diversifying into new and different markets and services, or restructuring the sources of institutional capital away from volatile and expensive funds toward more stable and predictable sources of financing.

Unfortunately, there are thousands of financial institutions whose stock is not actively traded and whose stock prices, therefore, are often not an adequate barometer of risk and expected earnings. This is particularly true in the banking industry. For example, at year-end 1980 there were nearly 11,000 banks in the United States whose total assets were less than $50 million each. For most of these institutions there is, at best, a local market for their stock, and stock trades may be few and far between. There is no really reliable record of stock values that management or owners can rely upon as an index of success or failure. In this situation most financial analysts turn to key *financial ratios* as proxy measures of the returns flowing to the owners of the business.

Figure 7–1   Key Factors Affecting the Market Value of a Financial Institution's Stock

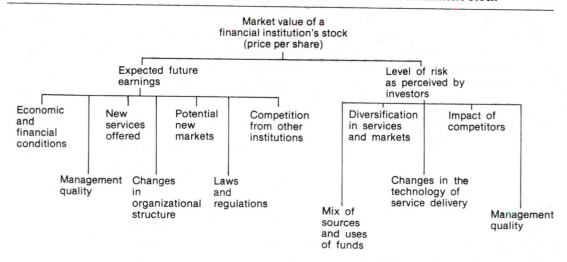

Each financial ratio consists of a numerator, expressed in dollars and drawn from either a financial institution's balance sheet or income statement, and a denominator, also expressed in dollars and drawn as well from either the institution's income statement or balance sheet.[3] The denominator of a financial ratio often serves as a scale factor to standardize that ratio so that it can be compared to the same ratio for another financial institution, or so that comparisons can be made over time to capture any trends. Commonly used scale factors are total assets, total deposits, total equity capital (net worth), total loans, total revenue (operating income), total expenses, and number of employees.[4]

ROA and ROE

Two of the most widely used measures of returns earned by a bank or other financial institution are the ratios

$$\text{Return on assets, or ROA (in percent)} = \frac{\text{Net income after taxes}}{\text{Total assets}} \times 100$$

$$(7\text{–}1)$$

$$\text{Return on equity, or ROE (in percent)} = \frac{\text{Net income after taxes}}{\text{Total equity capital}} \times 100$$

$$(7\text{–}2)$$

The numerator of both ratios—net income after taxes—is the "bottom line" on the earnings statement, measuring what's left over for payment of dividends to each institution's stockholders, any earnings retained in the business after *all* expenses (including taxes, securities gains or losses, and any extraordinary income or expenses) are accounted for. Total assets are a measure of the total resources available to the institution, while total equity capital normally includes the value of any stock issued (including surplus), retained earnings (i.e., undivided profits) and reserves held for future contingencies. It is usually good practice in calculating these or any other financial ratios drawn from a balance sheet to *average* the numbers.

---

[3]We recall from Chapter 6 that a balance sheet in the banking industry is also known as the Report of Condition, which must be submitted regularly to federal and state authorities. Income statements are known simply as the Report of Income.

[4]It is important to note that a single financial ratio viewed in isolation is really meaningless. Any ratio takes on meaning for management or financial analysts only when that ratio is compared with the same ratio from other time periods or from other financial institutions of similar size serving the same or similar markets. When comparisons are made over *time*, analysts generally refer to such comparisons as *trend analysis*. Comparisons of ratios among similar financial institutions is usually called *peer-group analysis*.

Thus we might use the total assets and equity capital figures for each quarter and average these over a full year to iron out any temporary or seasonal fluctuations.

Are ROA and ROE equally good proxies for the return to ownership of a financial institution? Does it matter which earnings ratio we use? The answer is yes, because ROA and ROE reveal *different* information about a bank or other financial institution. And, indeed, some institutions report comparatively high ROEs but modest ROAs, and vice versa.

ROA is a measure of *efficiency*. It conveys informaton on how well the institution's resources are being used in order to generate income. More efficiently run financial institutions tend to have higher ROAs. We can *compare* one financial institution against another in terms of resource efficiency using ROA. In contrast, ROE is a more direct measure of returns to the stockholders. Since rewards to the institution's owners are a key goal for the whole organization, ROE is generally superior to ROA as a measure of profitability. However, much depends on the particular kind of information—degree of efficiency or rate of return to stockholders—the financial analyst desires.

One point should be obvious here: ROE is strongly influenced by the capital structure of a financial institution—in particular, how much use it makes of equity financing versus debt financing. Management may be able to boost ROE simply by greater use of financial leverage—that is, increasing the ratio of debt to equity capital. This can be seen clearly if we note that

$$\text{ROE} \times \frac{\text{Total equity capital}}{\text{Total assets}} = \text{ROA} \qquad (7\text{--}3)$$

which means that

$$\text{ROA} \times \frac{\text{Total assets}}{\text{Total equity capital}} = \text{ROE} \qquad (7\text{--}4)$$

or, equivalently,

$$\text{ROA} \times \frac{\text{Total equity capital} + \text{Total debt capital}}{\text{Total equity capital}} = \text{ROE} \qquad (7\text{--}5)$$

Increased use of debt in place of equity capital may not improve ROA, but it will improve ROE. Thus undercapitalized financial institutions (i.e., those with high financial leverage through heavy use of debt) can increase their returns to equity owners. However, if the market perceives that their equity capital is too low, the institution will be viewed as more risky and its stock price may not rise. Indeed, with excessive risk, the institution's stock price is likely to fall.

The Elements Which Make Up ROE and ROA

It is interesting and sometimes useful to dissect ROE and ROA into their constituent parts in order to see why a financial institution's rate of return is either rising or falling. David Cole [3] has observed that ROE can be derived by multiplying together three other financial ratios: (1) the ratio of after-tax net income to total operating income (revenue), which is known as the profit margin; (2) the ratio of operating income to total assets, which measures asset utilization; and (3) the ratio of total assets to equity capital, which represents the equity multiplier. Thus Cole's formula for ROE is simply

$$\frac{\text{Net income after taxes}}{\text{Equity capital}} = \frac{\text{Net income after taxes}}{\text{Operating income}}$$

$$\times \frac{\text{Operating income}}{\text{Total assets}} \times \frac{\text{Total assets}}{\text{Equity capital}}$$

$$(7\text{--}6)$$

or

$$\text{ROE} = \text{Profit margin} \times \text{Asset utilization} \times \text{Equity multiplier}$$

The importance of the above formula is that it can aid management in pinpointing where the problem lies if a financial institution's ROE is low or falling. For example, if the institution's profit margin is falling, this implies that less net income is being recovered from each dollar of operating revenue received. A frequent cause here is lack of adequate expense control; other possible causes include below-par tax management practices, inappropriate pricing of services, and ineffective marketing strategies. Similarly, if ROE is low or declining due to a decreasing asset-utilization ratio, this often indicates the need to review the institution's asset management policies, particularly the yield and mix of its loans and security investments and the size of its cash or liquidity account. Finally, the equity multiplier sheds light on the financing mix of the institution—what proportion of assets are supported by owners' equity (principally stock and retained earnings) as opposed to debt capital. If the equity multiplier declines, management may wish to reconsider its policies regarding borrowings from deposit and nondeposit sources of funds.

A similar analysis can be carried out for ROA. As studies by Ford [7], Olson [10], Binder [2], Daniel [4] and others suggest, a bank's net after-tax income can, in most instances, be derived simply by adding and subtracting the following items:

Net income after taxes = Total interest revenues − Total interest expenses + Noninterest revenues − Noninterest expenses − Provision for possible loan losses − Taxes ± Income or losses from special nonrecurring transactions ± Securities gains or losses.

When we divide each of the above items by the institution's total assets and combine them as indicated, we derive ROA. By analyzing the changes over time in each component of ROA we can readily identify what has caused that earnings ratio to rise or fall. If the change is unfavorable, management can take remedial action.

Alternative Measures of a Financial Institution's Rate of Return

ROA and ROE do not exhaust the measures used by financial analysts to track the earnings records of banks and other financial institutions. For example, faced with increasing tax rates, many financial institutions have developed great proficiency at reducing their tax obligation through the use of allowable tax shelters. Examples include investments in tax-exempt municipal bonds, the leasing and depreciation of capital assets, the development of foreign sources of income which result in domestic tax credits, accelerated depreciation on bank assets, and tax-free allocations to reserves for loan losses and other future contingencies. The existence of such tax shelters often makes the true earnings picture of a financial institution from year to year difficult to detect. Ideally, financial analysts seek an indicator of an institution's net earnings that truly reflects the efficiency of the institution in generating revenues and in controlling expenses, independent of tax considerations.

Two possible earnings candidates which net out at least some of the impact of tax management decisions are the following:

$$\text{IBSG (in percent)} = \frac{\text{Income before securities gains or losses}}{\text{Total assets}} \times 100 \tag{7-7}$$

$$\text{RIBSG (in percent)} = \frac{\begin{array}{l}\text{Income before securities gains}\\\text{or losses} + \text{Provision for}\\\text{possible loan losses} - (\text{Losses}\\\text{charged to loan loss allowance} -\\\text{Recoveries on charged-off loans}\\\text{credited to loan loss allowance})\end{array}}{\text{Total assets}} \times 100 \tag{7-8}$$

The letters *IBSG* refer to income before securities gains (or losses); *RIBSG* stands for restated income before securities gains (or losses).

These earnings measures are particularly useful in analyzing bank financial statements because commercial banks are permitted to give special tax treatment to income from security and loan losses. Securities gains are treated as ordinary income (not capital gains) for tax purposes. However, losses on securities trading may first be deducted from any gains on securities as an offset to earnings from regular operations, helping the institutions to more closely achieve a desired level of net income. For example, a bank experiencing rapid growth in income from loans can frequently reduce its exposure to taxes by selling at a loss bonds held in its investment portfolio.

Similarly, a portion of bank revenues may be set aside each year in an account—allowance for possible loan loses—which appears on the asset side of a bank's balance sheet (Report of Condition). The amount set aside each year is somewhat arbitrary and is often changed from year to year by management to help achieve a specific target level of annual net income.[5] The annual amount of revenue set aside for possible losses in the loan portfolio is reported on the bank's income statement (Report of Income) as "Provision for Loan Losses." It is a tax-deductible expense item. When loan losses do occur, these are charged (net of any recoveries on loans in default) against the asset account, "Allowance for Loan Losses." Thus IBSG and particularly RIBSG give us a picture of bank earnings independent of certain expenses or portfolio manipulations designed to reduce the institution's tax exposure.

Another earnings measure which gives us some indication of the efficiency of operations and which nets out other tax-management effects is the net operating margin (NOM). This may be defined simply as

Net operating margin (in percent) =

$$\frac{\text{Total operating income} - \text{Total operating expense}}{\text{Total assets}} \times 100 \quad (7\text{--}9)$$

NOM is the ratio of the institution's net operating margin (i.e., how much total operating revenues exceed total operating expenses) to total assets, with total assets operating as a scale factor allowing us to compare one institution against another. NOM is a measure of operating efficiency—how well management controls expenses so that more revenues flow through to net income. Some analysts also see it as a reflection of the effectiveness of a financial institution's marketing program. Indirectly, it provides information relevant to such questions as: Are we pricing our services correctly? Is our marketing program reaching the customer?

A related measure favored by many analysts is the revenue-to-income ratio:

$$\text{RI} = \frac{\text{Total operating income}}{\text{Net income after taxes}} \quad (7\text{--}10)$$

---

[5]Recent tax reform legislation requires commercial banks to phase in a method for calculating allowances for loan losses based on their actual loan loss experience rather than setting aside an arbitrary amount of revenue in the loan-loss account.

This ratio gives us a further index of the effectiveness of the institution's cost-control program. It reflects how well management is able to squeeze net earnings out of each dollar of revenue received by the institution.

In considering various measures of earnings for a financial institution we need to bear in mind the basic function of such an institution: It borrows funds from surplus-spending units (ultimate savers) and lends those funds to deficit-spending units (ultimate borrowers). A key measure of the success of this intermediation function is certainly the spread between the yield on average earning assets (loans and investments) and the cost rate on interest-bearing sources of funds. That is, to measure the true cost of intermediation, we must look at

$$\text{Yield spread (in percent)} = \begin{array}{c} \text{Percent yield} \\ \text{on average} \\ \text{earning assets} \end{array} - \begin{array}{c} \text{Percentage cost rate} \\ \text{on interest-bearing} \\ \text{sources of funds} \end{array} \quad (7\text{--}11)$$

Related to this spread is the concept of net-interest margin (NIM). Basically, the net-interest margin is the difference between revenue generated by interest-bearing assets (loans and investments) and the interest cost of borrowed funds expressed as a percentage of either average total assets or, as some analysts prefer, average earning assets. Thus

NIM (in percent) =

$$\frac{\begin{array}{c} \text{Total income from interest-} \\ \text{bearing loans and investments} - \begin{array}{c} \text{Total interest cost} \\ \text{on borrowed funds} \end{array} \end{array}}{\text{Total assets}} \times 100 \quad (7\text{--}12)$$

Managers of banks and other financial institutions become concerned when the net-interest margin (NIM) falls, and they may reorient their investment policies or seek a cheaper mix of funds sources.[6]

---

[6]In calculating the net-interest margin it is important to place all forms of revenue—taxable and tax-exempt—on the same basis. This is usually accomplished by converting tax-exempt income (such as that generated by interest earnings on municipal bonds) into its taxable equivalent amount. Typically this can be done by multiplying the amount of tax-exempt income by the following quantity:

$$\frac{1}{100\% - t} - 1,$$

where t is the institution's marginal tax rate (i.e., the tax rate applying to the last dollar of income received during the year), and adding the resultant figure to tax-exempt income. Thus, if a financial institution is in the top 46% corporate tax bracket, we would multiply its tax-exempt income by

$$\frac{1}{100\% - 46\%} - 1 = 0.85$$

and add the resulting dollar figure to total tax-exempt earnings. (See Federal Deposit Insurance Corporation, *Bank Operating Statistics, 1980,* "Explanatory Notes.")

Many financial institutions, particularly those that accept deposits, have found their NIM squeezed more tightly in recent years due to rapidly rising interest rates on deposits. Federal regulation of interest rates on savings deposits (known as Regulation Q) has played a key role here. As market interest rates rose above federal deposit-rate ceilings, banks and other depository financial institutions have experienced higher interest margins because of rising loan rates which are not covered by legal ceilings. Conversely, in a period of falling rates, interest margins typically narrow as loan rates move down toward deposit rates. With gradual deregulation of deposit interest rates, as called for by the Depository Institutions Deregulation Act of 1980, however, this typical pattern in deposit and loan rates may change. Both loan rates and deposit rates will tend to move up or down in a highly correlated fashion. However, increased competition for deposits should result in a narrower margin over time, requiring financial institutions to become more efficient and to more effectively control their expenses.

A summary of the measures of return discussed in this section appears in Figure 7–2, while Figure 7–3 lists some benchmark values for each rate-

---

Figure 7–2   Frequently Used Measures of Rate of Return for Financial Institutions

$$ROA = \frac{\text{Net income after taxes}}{\text{Total assets}} \times 100$$

$$ROE = \frac{\text{Net income after taxes}}{\text{Total equity capital}} \times 100$$

$$IBSG = \frac{\text{Income before securities gains (or losses)}}{\text{Total assets}} \times 100$$

$$RIBSG = \frac{\begin{array}{l}\text{Income before securities gains (or losses)} \\ + \text{Provision for possible loan losses} \\ - \text{(Losses charged to loan-loss allowance} - \\ \text{Recoveries credited to loan-loss allowance)}\end{array}}{\text{Total assets}} \times 100$$

$$NOM = \frac{\begin{array}{l}\text{Total operating income} \\ - \text{Total operating expenses}\end{array}}{\text{Total assets}} \times 100$$

$$RI = \frac{\text{Total operating income}}{\text{Net income after taxes}}$$

$$NIM = \frac{\begin{array}{l}\text{Total income from interest-bearing assets} \\ - \text{Total interest cost of borrowed funds}\end{array}}{\text{Total assets}} \times 100$$

$$DIBSG = \frac{\text{Dividends paid to stockholders}}{\text{Income before securities gains (or losses)}} \times 100$$

$$DI = \frac{\text{Dividends paid to stockholders}}{\text{Net income after taxes}} \times 100$$

Figure 7–3   Measures of the Rate of Return Earned by Insured U.S. Banks: 1980 and 1982

Measures of Rate of Return	Average or Median for Industry		Average for Lowest 10% of All Banks		Average for Top 10% of All Banks	
	1980	1982	1980	1982	1980	1982
Return on equity (ROE)*	13.97%	12.89%	6.53%	2.02%	21.04%	20.63%
Return on assets (ROA)*	1.18	1.10	0.53	0.18	1.93	1.90
Income before securities gains or losses (IBSG)*	1.20	1.10	0.54	0.15	1.98	1.93
Restated income before securities gains or losses (RIBSG)*	1.25	1.15	0.58	0.20	2.04	2.00
Net operating margin (NOM)†	1.05	0.88	—	—	—	—
Revenue-to-income ratio (RI)†	13.62 times	17.24 times	—	—	—	—
Net-interest margin (NIM)†	2.96	3.57	—	—	—	—

*Median for insured commercial banks with balance sheet items averaged over four quarters of the calander year.
†Average based on year-end figures for all insured U.S. commercial banks.
Source: Federal Deposit Insurance Corporation, *Bank Operating Statistics, 1980 and 1982.* Calculations of some earnings measures by the authors.

of-return measure as reported by insured U.S. commercial banks in 1980 and 1982. The downward pressures on net-interest margins experienced by banks and other financial institutions in recent years have also shown up in the other earnings measures, particularly in returns on assets, net operating margins, and revenue-to-income ratios. Increases in interest rates on deposits and other borrowed funds (especially funds obtained in the money market) have been a key cause of earnings pressures in the financial institution sector; however, sharply rising wage and salary costs also have played an important role. So significant have been these cost increases that, as we noted in Chapter 1, expense control has become the major distinguishing feature between highly profitable and less profitable financial institutions. Interestingly, commercial banks have been among the most successful intermediaries at protecting their net earnings flowing to the stockholders (represented by ROE). This has been accomplished largely through greater use of financial leverage (i.e., lower ratios of equity capital to assets) and better tax management practices.

INTERNAL AND EXTERNAL FACTORS AFFECTING THE EARNINGS OF FINANCIAL INSTITUTIONS

The rate of return earned by a financial institution is affected by numerous factors. These factors include elements *internal* to each financial institution and several important *external* forces shaping earnings performance. The key external factors shaping earnings include:

Changes in the technology of service delivery.

Competition from bank and nonbank institutions.

Laws and regulations applying to financial institutions.

Government policies affecting the economy and financial system.

Management cannot control these external factors. The most it can do is to anticipate future changes in these outside influences and try to position the institution (especially the composition of its assets and liabilities) to take advantage of expected developments.

For example, if government economic policies and Federal Reserve monetary policies are expected to generate higher interest rates in the future, then each institution will want to adjust its loan and investment policies to take advantage of potentially higher interest income. This would involve perhaps more aggressive marketing of floating-rate loans, avoiding of heavy purchases of long-term bonds, and selected selling of bonds already part of the institution's security portfolio. Because deposit interest rates might also be expected to rise, it would be prudent to sell longer-term deposits with rates fixed at current levels and to reduce the institution's reliance on highly interest-sensitive sources of funds (such as negotiable CDs, Federal funds, and Eurodollar borrowings) with more emphasis upon less sensitive sources of funds (such as demand deposits, NOWs,

Figure 7-4   Factors Affecting the Earnings of Banks and Other Financial Institutions

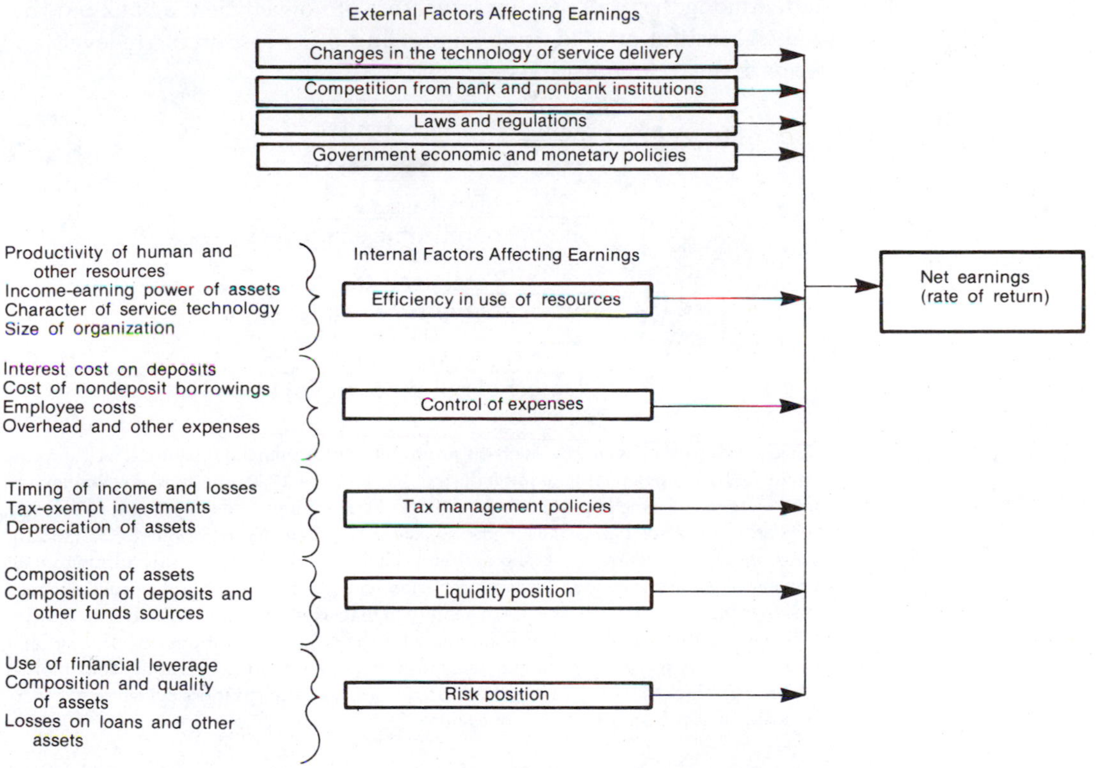

and small savings accounts). Of course, all of these strategic plans will be affected by the attitudes of customers and the response of competitors who generally limit how far any one institution can go in making adjustments in its financial and market position.

Control of Internal Factors

While the management of a financial institution may have difficulty in responding to external pressures on the institution's net earnings, it can change many internal factors to move the organization closer to its goals.

Improvements in Efficiency.   One possible management response is to improve the efficiency of the organization in managing its resources. This may mean installing new labor-saving machinery (such as computers and automated tellers) to increase the productivity of employees in processing accounts and transactions. It may also mean conscious decisions to expand the overall size of the organization to take advantage of any economies of scale.[7]

In general, greater efficiency is indicated by how well expenses are controlled relative to revenues and how productive each employee is in terms of revenues and income generated, assets managed, and accounts handled. Among the most popular indicators of how efficient a bank or other financial institution is in using human and other resources are levels and trends in the following ratios:

$$\frac{\text{Total operating expenses}}{\text{Total operating revenue}} \times 100$$

$$\frac{\text{Total assets}}{\text{Number of full-time employees}}$$

$$\frac{\text{Total deposits}}{\text{Number of full-time employees}}$$

$$\frac{\text{Total revenue}}{\text{Number of full-time employees}}$$

---

[7]Size can exert significant effects on the profitability of a financial institution. A good case in point is the commercial banking industry. Prior to the 1970s the most profitable U.S. banks were usually the largest institutions (over $100 million in deposits). More recently, however, top-earning banks have tended to cluster in the medium-size ranges ($10 to $100 million in deposits) with very small and very large institutions frequently turning in the worst earnings ratios. Among the most important causes of this shift in the profit-size relationship is the increasingly heavy use of liability management techniques (such as borrowing in the Federal funds and Eurodollar markets) by the largest institutions. Also, very large banks often have problems remaining in control of all facets of the operation. Still another problem is the lack of strong scale economies from growth, such as those evident in the manufacturing of automobiles or steel, for example.

$$\frac{\text{Net income after taxes}}{\text{Number of full-time employees}}$$

$$\frac{\text{Salaries and wages expense}}{\text{Number of full-time employees}}$$

$$\frac{\text{Interest and fees on loans}}{\text{Total loans outstanding}} \times 100$$

$$\frac{\text{Income from security investments}}{\text{Total security investments}} \times 100$$

The later two ratios measure the average return on loan and security investments—a measure of how efficient loans and investments are in generating revenue. Figure 7–5 provides an indication of the order of magnitude of these efficiency measures for all insured U.S. commercial banks in 1980 and 1982.

Control of Expenses. Related to efficiency is how well management can keep expenses under control in order to protect earnings. The greatest challenge in this area for the managers of financial institutions in recent years is control of the cost of funds—both deposit and nondeposit borrowings—and of salaries and wages (including fringe benefits). Both sets of costs increased dramatically during the past decade. Banks and other depository institutions saw their customers shift funds from checking accounts to high-cost savings plans (especially money market CDs). At the same time the general level of interest rates soared, raising the cost of all interest-bearing deposits and nondeposit borrowings from the Federal funds and Eurodollar markets and from other sources.

Figure 7–5 Measures of Efficiency for All Insured U.S. Banks: 1980 and 1982

Measures of Efficiency	Average for All Insured U.S. Banks	
	1980	1982
(Total operating expenses × 100) ÷ (Total operating revenue)	89.8%	92.6%
(Interest and fees on loans × 100) ÷ (Total loans outstanding)	12.14%	14.63%
(Income from security investments × 100) ÷ (Total security investments)*	6.90%	NA
(Total assets) ÷ (Number of employees)	$1,250.40†	$1,455.5
(Total deposits) ÷ (Number of employees)	$998.04†	$1,131.9
(Total revenue) ÷ (Number of employees)	$128.54†	$171.54
(Net income after taxes) ÷ (Number of employees)	$98.04†	$99.52
(Salaries and wages expense) ÷ (Number of employees)	$16.63†	$20.85

*Includes U.S. Treasury, federal agency, state and local governments and other marketable debt obligations. Balances held with other depository institutions, federal funds loans, and security RPs are excluded.
†Dollar figure times 1,000. Number of employees in ratio is the number of full-time equivalent employees.
Source: Federal Deposit Insurance Corporation, *Bank Operating Statistics, 1980 and 1982.* Calculations by the authors.

Among the most important expense-control indicator ratios are the following:

$$\frac{\text{Total interest expenses}}{\text{Total earning assets}^8} \times 100$$

$$\frac{\text{Total interest expenses}}{\text{Total time and savings deposits and nondeposit borrowings}} \times 100$$

$$\frac{\text{Interest on deposits}}{\text{Total operating expenses}} \times 100$$

$$\frac{\text{Interest on nondeposit borrowings}}{\text{Total nondeposit borrowings}} \times 100$$

$$\frac{\text{Payroll costs}}{\text{Total operating expenses}} \times 100$$

$$\frac{\text{Net occupancy, furniture and equipment expenses}}{\text{Total operating expenses}} \times 100$$

$$\frac{\text{Other operating expenses}}{\text{Total operating expenses}} \times 100$$

Figure 7–6 indicates average values of these ratios as reported by all U.S.-insured banks in 1980 and 1982. Significant increases in any of the above ratios normally would cause management to investigate the rea-

Figure 7–6 Expense Control Indicators for All Insured U.S. Banks: 1980 and 1982

Measures of Expense Control	Average or Median for All Insured U.S. Banks	
	1980	*1982*
(Total interest expense × 100) ÷ (Total earning assets)	5.98%*	8.16%*
(Total interest expense × 100) ÷ (Total time and savings deposits and nondeposit borrowings)	8.37%*	10.38%*
(Interest on deposits × 100) ÷ (Total operating expenses)	37.47%†	59.24%*
(Interest on nondeposit borrowings × 100) ÷ (Total nondeposit borrowings)	12.21%†	11.62%†
(Payroll costs × 100) ÷ (Total operating expenses)	14.41%†	13.13%†
(Net occupancy, furniture and equipment expenses × 100) ÷ (Total operating expenses)	4.29%†	4.19%†
(Other operating expenses × 100) ÷ (Total operating expenses)	8.55%	8.41%†

*Median for insured commercial banks with balance-sheet items averaged over four quarters of the calendar year.

†Average based on year-end figures for all insured U.S. commercial banks.

Source: Federal Deposit Insurance Corporation, *Bank Operating Statistics, 1980 and 1982*. Calculations by the authors.

---

[8] Earning assets include all the institution's assets except cash, fixed assets (i.e., buildings, furniture, and equipment), land, and miscellaneous assets not bearing interest.

sons behind the change and, if possible, to adopt policies which retard the growth in expenses.

Tax Management Policies.   As we noted earlier, tax shelters are extremely important to many financial institutions today as aids in achieving annual earnings targets. Management usually responds quickly to an increase in an institution's tax exposure by taking on additional tax-exempt investments, such as state and local government (municipal) bonds, or increasing tax-deductible expenses. Among the most widely used indicators of the effectiveness of tax management policies are the following ratios:

$$\frac{\text{Investments in tax-exempt assets}}{\text{Total assets}} \times 100$$

$$\frac{\text{Earnings from tax-exempt assets}}{\text{Total tax-exempt assets}} \times 100$$

$$\frac{\text{Total income tax payments}}{\text{Income before taxes}} \times 100$$

$$\frac{\text{Total income tax payments}}{\text{Total operating expenses}} \times 100$$

Figure 7–7 provides an indication of the mean size of the above ratios for insured U.S. banks reporting to the Federal Deposit Insurance Corporation in 1980 and 1982. In general, financial institutions have experienced rising effective tax rates in recent years, requiring their managers to become increasingly conscious of alternative methods for tax-sheltering net earnings.

Achieving a Desirable Liquidity Position.   As we noted in Chapter 1, one of the most pressing concerns for any financial institution is the prospect of a cash-out—not having sufficient cash available when it is demanded. Cash is drained from a financial intermediary by customer withdrawals

Figure 7–7   Tax Management Indicators for All Insured U.S. Banks: 1980 and 1982

Measures of Tax-Management Effectiveness	Average for All Insured U.S. Banks	
	1980	*1982*
Investments in tax-exempt assets × 100) ÷ (Total assets)	7.88%	7.07%
(Earnings from tax-exempt assets × 100) ÷ (Total tax-exempt assets)	5.59%	6.87%
(Total income tax payments × 100) ÷ (Income before taxes)	23.88%	19.00%
(Total income tax payments × 100) ÷ (Total operating expenses)	2.72%	1.53%

*Based on year-end figures. The only tax-exempt assets included here are state and local government bonds.

Source: Federal Deposit Insurance Corporation, *Bank Operating Statistics, 1980 and 1982*. Calculations by the authors.

and the closing of accounts, operating expenses, and demands for credit from good customers. A financial institution wants to be able to respond to each loan request from a valued customer and to take advantage of profitable investment opportunities that come along. In addition, some of its liabilities may be payable on demand (such as bank checking accounts), leaving it no choice except to have sufficient cash on hand. If it appears that withdrawals or credit demands will increase (perhaps due to seasonal factors or economic developments), the institution is likely to increase its holdings of cash and other liquid assets.

Liquidity policies are linked directly to earnings. Assets held to meet liquidity needs generally carry the lowest yields. Thus the maintenance of high levels of liquidity usually reduces earnings. An institution can often maximize its rate of return by minimizing holdings of liquid assets, but only by accepting a greater risk of a cash-out, which can be expensive to make up. Clearly, liquidity management hinges upon a careful choice of which assets to acquire and what sources of funds to draw upon.

The most liquid assets which financial intermediaries can acquire include cash and deposits with other financial institutions, U.S. government and federal agency securities, and very short-term loans (particularly those associated with federal funds transactions and repurchase agreements). Most loans are not liquid assets since repayment may be spread over a substantial period of time and the loan may not be salable (except perhaps at a significant discount) to other investors. However, certain types of loans are generally more liquid than others—for example, business loans (particularly those made to large corporations for purchases of inventory) generally have shorter maturities and usually are more marketable than loans to individuals or real estate loans. Therefore the particular composition, or mix, of a financial institution's loan portfolio has a significant impact on its need for liquidity. The same is true of the mix of its sources of funds. Demand deposits and borrowings in the money market through large CDs and other IOUs generate more liquidity needs than ordinary time and savings deposits, for example.

Important measures of the liquidity position of a financial institution include:

$$\frac{\text{Cash and deposits due from other institutions}}{\text{Total assets}} \times 100$$

$$\frac{\text{U.S. government securities}}{\text{Total assets}} \times 100$$

$$\frac{\text{Federal agency securities}}{\text{Total assets}} \times 100$$

$$\frac{\text{Money market assets}}{\text{Money market liabilities}^9} \times 100$$

$$\frac{\text{Total demand deposits}}{\text{Total time and savings deposits}} \times 100$$

$$\frac{\text{Large (\$100,000 and over) negotiable CDs}}{\text{Total deposits}} \times 100$$

Figure 7–8 presents recent values for the above financial ratios for all insured banks in the United States as of year-end 1980 and 1982.

Dramatic changes have occurred in recent years in the mix of both assets (uses of funds) and liabilities (sources of funds) drawn upon by financial institutions of all sizes. The general trend has been away from more liquid assets and toward higher-yielding but less liquid loans and investments. At the same time there has been much heavier use of money market borrowings to satisfy liquidity needs. Factors which have contributed to this trend include rising interest rates that have increased the opportunity cost of holding cash and liquid securities and rapid growth in the de-

Figure 7–8   Liquidity Measures for All Insured U.S. Banks: 1980 and 1982

Measures of Liquidity	Average for All Insured U.S. Banks, December 31, (in percent)	
	1980	1982
(Cash and deposits due from other institutions × 100) ÷ (Total assets)	17.98%	15.24%
(U.S. government securities × 100) ÷ (Total assets)	5.63	5.41
(Federal agency securities × 100) ÷ (Total assets)	3.18	3.48
(Money-market assets × 100) ÷ (Money-market liabilities)	NA*	NA*
(Total demand deposits × 100) ÷ (Total time and savings deposits)	57.11	36.07
(Large ($100,000 +) negotiable CDs × 100) ÷ (Total deposits)	NA*	NA*
(Nondeposit borrowings × 100) ÷ (Total liabilities)	10.20	11.55
(Total loans × 100) ÷ (Total Assets)	53.48	59.83
(Business loans × 100) ÷ (Total loans)	39.39	42.22
(Loans to individuals × 100) ÷ (Total loans)	18.88	16.66
(Real estate loans × 100) ÷ (Total loans)	27.17	25.77

*Not available.

Source: Federal Deposit Insurance Corporation, *Bank Operating Statistics, 1980 and 1982*; and Board of Governors of the Federal Reserve System, *Federal Reserve Bulletin*, recent issues.

---

[9]Money-market assets include holdings of U.S. Treasury bills, Federal funds loans, repurchase agreements in which securities are temporarily purchased, commercial paper and Eurodollar loans. Money-market liabilities include borrowings in the Federal funds and Eurodollar markets, repurchase agreements in which securities are temporarily sold, and sales of large ($100,000 and over) negotiable CDs.

mand for credit, especially from consumers, corporations, and state and local governments. Then, too, in recent years several periods of tight monetary policy have driven interest rates to record or near-record levels, encouraging financial institutions to become more efficient in the use of their funds. Also, there has been an increase in the ratio of more stable deposits (principally time and savings deposits) to less stable deposits (especially demand deposits), reducing the industry's need for cash and other liquid assets.

Establishing a Suitable Risk Position. One area of critical concern to the management of any financial institution is *risk*—the probability of substantial losses on loans and investments and the ultimate danger that the institution itself may fail. Contrary to popular belief, financial intermediaries carry a substantial element of risk in their daily operations, particularly in lending money. They can reduce risk to some extent by such devices as hiring competent management, spreading their loans and security investments over a large group of borrowers, selling their services in a variety of markets with different economic characteristics, and insuring against certain kinds of loss (such as embezzlement and theft). When all else fails, however, the ultimate defense against risk that a financial institution possesses is its equity capital (net worth).[10] If earnings turn into operating losses, the equity capital account absorbs those losses, giving management time to react to the problem. Thus a strong ratio of equity capital to total assets, loans, and total liabilities is a key barometer of a financial intermediary's protection against the ultimate disaster—insolvency and failure.

The account designated "Allowance for Loan Losses" is, as we noted earlier, another buffer against risk, particularly for commercial banks. Bad loans are charged against this account, net of any recoveries on loans previously written off and labeled as uncollectible. Therefore the size of the allowance-for-loan-losses account relative to the amount of the institution's loan portfolio and relative to the amount of the annual item ("Provision for Loan Losses") provides an index of the degree of protection a bank has built in against the risk of bad loans.

Among the more popular barometers of risk for banks and other financial institutions are the following ratios:

$$\frac{\text{Total equity capital}}{\text{Total loans}} \times 100$$

$$\frac{\text{Total equity capital}}{\text{Total deposits}} \times 100$$

---

[10]See Chapter 12 for a description of the functions of equity capital for a financial institution.

$$\frac{\text{Total equity capital}}{\text{Total assets}} \times 100$$

$$\frac{\text{Annual provisions for loan losses}}{\text{Annual net loan losses}} \times 100$$

$$\frac{\begin{array}{c}\text{Income before taxes and securities transactions}\\ + \text{Annual provision for loan losses}\end{array}}{\text{Annual net loan losses}} \times 100$$

$$\frac{\text{Net loan charge-offs}}{\text{Total loans}} \times 100$$

$$\frac{\text{Allowance for possible loan losses}}{\text{Total loans}} \times 100$$

Figure 7–9 illustrates the recent magnitude of these rates as reported for all insured U.S. commercial banks in 1980 and 1982.

Some Precautions in Using Financial Ratios.　In the foregoing paragraphs we have presented a number of financial ratios as measures of the behavior of financial institutions. These ratios serve as telltale indicators of possible problems which management may want to investigate. They help to pin down the area where a problem may be found.

Useful as they are, however, these ratios must be used with considerable caution. They are profoundly affected by the size and location of banks and other financial institutions. Therefore it is usually wise to compare these ratios across financial institutions of roughly the same asset or deposit size and serving the same or similar markets. Moreover, when a financial ratio changes over time, that change may be due to items contained in the numerator, the denominator, or in both terms of the ratio.

Figure 7–9　Indicators of Risk for All Insured U.S. Banks: 1980 and 1982

Risk Indicators	Averages for All Insured U.S. Banks, (in percent)	
	1980	*1982*
(Total equity capital × 100) ÷ (Total loans)	10.84%	10.79%
(Total equity capital × 100) ÷ (Total deposits)	9.02	7.55
(Total equity capital × 100) ÷ (Total assets)	5.80	5.87
(Annual provisions for loan losses × 100) ÷ (Annual net loan losses)	91.80	102.33
(Income before taxes and securities transactions + Annual provision for loan losses × 100) ÷ (Annual net loan losses)	491.58	420.61
(Net loan charge-offs × 100) ÷ (Total loans)	0.24	0.55
(Allowance for possible loan losses × 100) ÷ (Total loans)	0.45	0.70

Source: Federal Deposit Insurance Corporation, *Bank Operating Statistics, 1980 and 1982.*

The careful financial analyst would ascertain which components of the ratio have changed and then go on to find out, if possible, why the changes occurred.

PLANNING IN THE FINANCIAL INSTITUTIONS' SECTOR

The pursuit of increased profitability usually requires careful planning of a financial institution's future operations. And growing numbers of banks and other financial institutions have turned to formalized planning methods to achieve their goals.

While planning techniques vary widely in scope and design, many of the largest financial institutions today use *both* short-range and long-range plans. Short-range plans may include a monthly or weekly projected *cash budget* which tracks cash inflow and outflow and how the institution's level of cash reserves will vary over time if the projections turn out to be true. Planning over a year often is formalized in a so-called *profit plan*, which projects key items on the balance sheet and income statement for a 12-month period. Longer-range plans frequently include a *capital budget*, charting projected growth in facilities (such as branch offices, remote tellers, etc.), and a *strategic plan*. The latter forecasts the institution's future position in various target markets (such as checking accounts, consumer loans, energy loans, etc.), perhaps 5, 10, or more years into the future. Strategic plans also consider possible changes in the technology of service delivery or in the structure of the organization. For example, is a holding company organization desirable in the future? Will customers be more likely to patronize our institution if we offer in-home banking through small household computer terminals? In the making of a strategic plan, imagination is the key since virtually everything and anything is subject to change.

Components of Institutional Plans

Plans differ widely from financial institution to financial institution, but there are certain elements most have in common. All plans usually begin with a statement of *goals and objectives*, focusing, in most cases, on profitability, growth, and desired shares of certain markets where the institution offers or would like to offer its services. More detailed plans usually follow this statement with a careful *analysis of the institution's current environment*. What are our strengths and weaknesses inside the organization? What problems are apparent in asset, liability, and capital management? Has the institution's earnings and growth been satisfactory during the most recent period? Why or why not? And, what is happening and what is likely to happen in the period ahead to monetary policy, unemployment, loan demand, and interest rates? Are there any prospective changes in laws and regulations on the horizon?

With a careful statement of goals and a detailed analysis of present conditions and probable future developments as background, most plans then lay out a series of *policy decisions and actions* designed to move the institution closer to its announced goals. For example, the plan may call for a gradual increase in remote service units (RSUs), or automated tellers, located in local shopping centers to attract new customers and increase banking convenience for established customers. Management may also commit itself to gradually increasing the ratio of consumer loans to total loans to some target level by year's end, hoping to boost earnings. And service charges may be lowered on regular checking accounts but increased on NOW accounts to encourage customers to shift from one account to another. The final planning step, after all the foregoing actions have been taken, is to *analyze how well the institution did in achieving its goals.* For example, were the proposed earnings targets achieved? If not, why was there a shortfall in earnings and what does this suggest for next year's plan?

Risk in the Planning Process

A number of studies in recent years have suggested that planning works. That is, businesses using more sophisticated plans typically score higher (particularly in profits and growth) than those firms that either plan not at all or plan haphazardly.[11] But planning for a financial institution is not easy. These institutions are particularly sensitive to economic conditions, monetary policy, and interest rates which are continually changing. Moreover, banks and other intermediaries are heavily regulated, and their plans can be profoundly altered by new regulatory decisions.

Recent studies by Gup [8], Wood [16], and others point to certain mistakes in planning which often show up inside the institution. For example, management may fail to state clearly what the institution's goals are or fail to communicate these to the staff adequately. Frequently, plans are fragmented, applying only to one phase of operations, leaving large areas uncovered and subject to chance. Often a detailed plan is laid out by one or a few individuals without any involvement in the process by those who must carry out the plan's details. And there is evidence that senior executives and the board of directors often give only lip service to the institution's plans without a real commitment of interest, time, and resources.

---

[11]See especially the study by Wood and La Forge [17] in which 26 large U.S. banks with normal long-range planning systems were compared with banks chosen at random and with those with no formal planning systems. Net income grew significantly faster over the 1972–76 period at banks with comprehensive planning systems, and the comprehensive planning institutions also reported higher average returns on owners' equity.

The lesson here is that even the most elaborate plans are unlikely to be achieved if top officials in an organization remain on the sidelines, ignore the plan's requirements, and fail to hold themselves and other employees responsible for achievement of the plan's objectives.

Interest-Sensitivity Analysis

One of the devices used in recent years by many financial institutions (especially commercial banks and savings and loan associations) to aid in the planning process and particularly to protect profit margins is known as *interest-sensitivity analysis* (ISA). The goal of ISA is simply to protect (if minimum risk is the goal) or to maximize (if management is aggressive and willing to take on added risk) the *net-interest margin* between revenues from interest-bearing assets and the cost of interest-bearing liabilities.[12]

To illustrate the basic principle behind ISA, let's assume that the management of a financial institution wishes to insulate its net-interest margin from fluctuations in interest rates. By definition, the net-interest margin is

$$\frac{\text{Total income from interest-bearing assets} - \text{Total interest cost on borrowed funds}}{\text{Total assets}} \times 100$$

$$= \text{Net interest margin (in percent)} \tag{7–13}$$

Assume that currently the average yield on the institution's assets (i.e., the ratio of total income from interest-bearing assets to total assets) is 11 percent, while the average interest cost on borrowed funds (i.e., the ratio of total interest cost on borrowed funds to total assets) is 8 percent. Then the institution's average net-interest margin in percentage terms is

$$11\% - 8\% = 3\%$$

Obviously, if the average cost of borrowed funds climbs to 9 percent and the average yield on the institution's assets shows little or no change, the institution's net-interest margin will decline to only 2 percent. How can management adopt a fully hedged position which protects the 3 percent interest margin? Simply by keeping the volume of interest-sensitive assets and interest-sensitive liabilities approximately equal to each other. In other words, to *hedge* against interest-rate risk, the management of a financial institution would keep the ratio

$$\frac{\text{IS assets}}{\text{IS liabilities}}$$

[12]The ISA technique is sometimes called Gap management because it focuses upon the gap between interest earnings and interest expenses.

equal to or very close to 1. This could be done by insuring that the amount of floating-rate liabilities are roughly counter-balanced by the volume of floating-rate loans and investments. As interest rates rise, the cost of adjustable-rate liabilities goes up but so do revenues generated by floating-rate assets.

Another hedging strategy is to equalize the *maturity distribution* of assets with the maturity distribution of liabilities. This helps to insure that as liabilities come due, assets are rolling over into cash to provide the funds necessary to meet maturing debt. Thus a bank with $10 million in CDs maturing six months from today's date might also hold $10 million in Treasury bills and notes maturing on that same date.[13]

How do financial institutions today keep track of their relative quantities of interest-sensitive assets and liabilities? There are many different approaches to this question. However, one simple and useful method begins by simply classifying all of a financial institution's earning assets by the maturity range they occupy (e.g., assets immediately rolling over into cash, assets turning into cash 1 to 5 days from now, assets turning into cash 6 to 130 days, etc.). Then a weighted average yield on the assets in each maturity range is determined as well as the percentage of the institution's total earning assets falling in each maturity range. The foregoing information makes it easy to calculate maturity-weighted average yields on the institution's total earning assets.

Liabilities are treated the same way as assets. They are first grouped by maturity range (including those due and payable immediately), a weighted average cost is determined for each maturity range, and the percentage of the institution's total IS liabilities represented by each maturity range is computed. From this information, management can determine the average overall rate paid on total liabilities (including noninterest-bearing liabilities at a zero rate) and subtract the average liability rate paid from the average yield received on total earning assets to derive the institution's net-interest margin. The ratio of IS assets to IS liabilities is also calculated for each maturity range, so that management can determine if there is a rough balance between the two. A cumulative ratio of IS assets to IS liabilities may also be found simply by adding IS assets to IS liabilities for each maturity range, starting with the shortest maturities. This ratio would

---

[13]In general terms, we may say that a financial institution can hedge itself against interest-rate fluctuations by insuring that the volume of its borrowed funds subject to renegotiation of credit terms is matched by the volume of its interest-bearing loans and investments also subject to renegotiation of credit terms at the same time. If this is the case, then whether interest rates rise or fall, a financial institution can protect its net-interest margin by effective renegotiation of borrowing terms with those who supply loanable funds to the institution and by effective negotiation of credit terms with those who use loanable funds provided by the institution.

provide a measure of interest sensitivity across the institution's entire portfolio.

An Aggressive Interest-Sensitivity Strategy

As noted earlier, the management of a financial institution very concerned about the risk of changing interest rates would probably try to keep its ratio of IS assets to IS liabilities close to 1. Suppose, however, that a financial institution's management is highly aggressive and wishes to pursue the goal of maximum profitability. It might then adopt the following IS strategy:

1. If interest rates are expected to *rise*, move to a position in which

$$\frac{\text{IS assets}}{\text{IS liabilities}} > 1$$

(known as an asset-sensitive position).

2. If interest rates are expected to *fall*, move to a position in which

$$\frac{\text{IS assets}}{\text{IS liabilities}} < 1$$

(known as a liability-sensitive position).

Following this strategy, as interest rates rise, institutions whose interest-sensitivity ratio is greater than 1 will find revenues from assets increasing more than the cost of liabilities. Other factors held constant, profits will rise. Management might achieve such an asset-sensitive position by taking on more floating-rate loans than floating-rate deposits, shortening the maturity of assets while lengthening (or at least holding fixed) the maturity of liabilities, or by some combination of both actions. In contrast, financial institutions that adopt an IS ratio of less than 1 in a period of falling rates will find their liability costs dropping faster than their asset yields, and profits again will increase, *ceteris paribus*. Management might achieve such a liability-sensitive position by taking on more floating-rate liabilities than floating-rate assets, by lengthening (or at least holding fixed) the maturity of assets while shortening the maturity of liabilities, or by some combination of both actions.

Needless to say, the desires of customers must be considered in any such shifts in the interest-sensitivity of assets and liabilities, and customers who are well informed about current interest-rate forecasts will often resist these changes.[14] Customer resistance plus fundamental economic factors

---

[14]It is interesting to see how the particular IS ratio adopted by a financial institution will change with the business cycle. For example, interest rates normally rise during a business expansion and fall during the ensuing recession. As Olson and Simonson [11] have ob-

in a financial institution's principal market area probably permit management to make only gradual changes in the institution's IS ratio. For example, Olson and Simonson [11] in a survey of 45 U.S. banks covering the 1973–79 period found that most of these banks were neither significantly asset-sensitive nor significantly liability-sensitive. However, of the minority of banks that were interest-sensitive in one direction or the other, most tended to stay in the same position over the whole seven-year period. In recent years large numbers of financial institutions have been using interest-sensitivity analysis in the wake of highly volatile interest rates. Moreover, both floating-rate assets (especially loans) and floating-rate liabilities (especially CDs) have become much more common today than even a few years ago. Careful analysis and control of the margin between yields on assets and the cost of funds raised has become a more widely accepted management tool in the financial institutions' field.[15]

Financial institutions of all kinds have faced increasing competition in attracting funds from the public and in making loans and investments. Consequently, they have turned increasingly to analyzing their past track record and planning for more closely achieving their goals in the future.

SUMMARY

---

served, a financial institution holding its IS assets–IS liabilities ratio above 1 (i.e., in an asset-sensitive position) will find its spread moving *positively* with the cycle, rising in expansions and falling in business recessions. Conversely, if the IS ratio is less than 1 (i.e., a liability-sensitive position), its spread will move *counter* to the business cycle, falling during expansion periods and rising in recessions.

[15] A recent study by Flannery [6] supports this conclusion concerning the widespread use of bank portfolio strategies which balance interest-sensitive assets and liabilities. Flannery followed the earnings experience of 75 U.S. banks ranging in size from less than $25 million in assets to more than $1 billion. Predictably, he found that larger banks react more quickly (in terms of revenue and expense adjustments) to interest-rate changes than do smaller banks, probably because the larger institutions serve more interest-sensitive customers, on average. For banks with above $300 million in total assets, Flannery finds that their asset and liability maturities are roughly in balance so that revenues and costs react about the same to interest-rate changes in the short run. Thus, in the short run, the nation's largest banks do not reap significant gains in profits (or suffer significant losses) from rising interest rates. And, in the long run, U.S. banks with over $300 million in assets experience a slight decrease in operating margin as costs over the long pull increase slightly more rapidly than bank revenues.

In contrast, Flannery finds that smaller banks have assets that, on average, turn over more rapidly than their liabilities. The result is that asset returns of these banks respond more quickly to interest-rate changes than do liability costs. Interestingly, Flannery's study suggests that banks with below $100 million in assets benefit in average profitability from rising interest rates in the short run, and the same is true for banks with below $300 million in assets in the long run. Overall, however, U.S. commercial bank profits do not seem highly responsive to interest-rate changes due to the approximate balance maintained by the industry between its interest-sensitive assets and liabilities.

While higher profits appear to be the main goal of most institutions, other objectives—especially increased market share, more rapid growth, and better service to the public—also rank high as institutional targets. The profit goal (and a related objective—increasing the value of each institution's stock) is particularly important because profits are the principal source of capital to support long-term growth for most financial institutions.

Analyzing the behavior and future prospects for profitability of a financial institution is a complex task. Many factors affect each institution's profitability. Among the most important factors are the riskiness of loans and investments made, liquidity needs and the institution's provision for those needs, the effectiveness of tax-management practices, the level of efficiency in utilizing human and nonhuman resources, and the ability of management to control expenses (particularly interest expense and employee costs). All of the foregoing are *internal* factors, subject largely to management control. Even the best management decisions can be overwhelmed, however, by factors which the individual financial institution cannot control—changing technology, shifting competition, changes in laws and regulations, and variations in government policy affecting the health of the economy, credit, and interest rates. Management must try to anticipate changes in these factors and plan accordingly.

Planning has become an accepted part of the management process for the largest banks and other financial institutions. Cash budgets and profit plans are frequently used to guide short-run decisions (normally limited to a one-year horizon). Longer-term projections in the form of capital budgets and strategic plans may encompass periods of 3 years, 5 years, 10 years, or even longer. In the short-run plans the focus typically is upon current earnings, expenses, cash flows, and liquidity needs. Over a longer time, however, planning at most financial institutions centers upon changes in the technology of service delivery, the structure of the organization, the growth of equity capital needs, and the institution's share of key markets.

Regardless of their focus, however, all plans display common elements: (1) goals formulated, (2) problem areas within and outside the institution pinpointed, (3) strategies developed to move the institution closer to its goals, and (4) the institution's success or failure in achieving its goals carefully evaluated as a guide to the future. Effective planning, of course, does not guarantee high profits, but it increases the probability of success by permitting management to anticipate future events and their consequences. And in the fast-paced, constantly changing, volatile environment faced by financial institutions today, management must learn to *anticipate*, rather than merely react, to new developments.

Questions

7-1. List the principal goals and objectives pursued by financial institutions today. Which of these do you regard as most important? Explain why.

7-2. What are the principal measures of the rate of return of a bank or other financial institution? What aspect of the institution's behavior does each reflect? Which measures would you prefer and why?

7-3. List the *internal* factors affecting the earnings of a financial institution as discussed in this chapter. Explain exactly how each of these factors affects earnings.

7-4. List the *external* factors influencing the earnings of a financial institution. Explain how these factors could impact earnings behavior.

7-5. What types of plans typically are used in the financial institutions' sector?

7-6. List the key steps in the planning process. Explain what each involves and why that particular step is important in effective planning.

7-7. What is meant by the term *interest-sensitivity analysis*? What is the objective of the ISA technique?

7-8. Assume interest rates are expected to *rise*. Using ISA, what can management do to take advantage of rising rates to increase profits? Suppose rates are expected to *fall*. What strategy might be profitable in this case? Explain your reasoning.

References

1. American Bankers Association. *Bank Strategic Planning: A Guide for Organizing and Managing the Process*. Washington, D.C., 1977.

2. Binder, Barret F. "A Look at 1980 Commercial Bank Performance." *The Magazine of Bank Administration*, August 1981, p. 22.

3. Cole, David. "Return on Equity Model for Banks." *The Bankers Magazine*, Spring 1973.

4. Daniel, Donnie L. "Utilizing Industry Ratios to Assess and Improve Your Bank's Profitability." *The Magazine of Bank Administration*, April 1975, pp. 27–31.

5. Federal Deposit Insurance Corporation. *Bank Operating Statistics*, various annual issues.

6. Flannery, Mark J. "How Do Changes in Market Interest Rates Affect Bank Profits?" *Business Review*, Federal Reserve Bank of Philadelphia, September/October 1980, pp. 13–22.

7. Ford, William F. "Using High-Performance Data to Plan Your Bank's Future." *Banking*, October 1978, pp. 40–46, 48, 162.

8. Gup, Benton E. *Guide to Strategic Planning*. New York: McGraw-Hill, 1980.

9. Klein, Hans E. "The Impact of Planning on Growth and Profit." *Journal of Bank Research*, no. 2 (summer 1981), pp. 105–109.

10. Olson, Dennis A. "How High-Profit Banks Get that Way." *Banking*, May 1975, pp. 45, 50, 53–54, 58.

11. Olson, Ronald L. and Donald G. Simonson. "Gap Management and Market Rate Sensitivity in Banks." *Journal of Bank Research*, Spring 1982.

12. Rose, Peter S. "Planning: Elements, Steps and Strategies." *The Canadian Banker and ICB Review*, no. 3 (June 1982), pp. 50–55.

13. _____. "Performance Analysis: How Does Your Bank Measure Up? Part I." *The Canadian Banker and ICB Review*, no. 1 (February 1981), pp. 58–63.

14. _____. "Performance Analysis: What Separates the Leaders from the Also Rans." *The Canadian Banker and ICB Review*, no. 2 (April 1981), pp. 52–57.

15. Rose, Sanford. "Dark Days Ahead for Banks." *Fortune Magazine*, June 30, 1980.

16. Wood, D. Robley. "Long-Range Planning in Large United States Banks." *Long-Range Planning* (June 1980), pp. 91–98.

17. _____ and R. Lawrence La Forge. "The Impact of Comprehensive Planning on Financial Performance." *Academy of Management Journal*, XXII, no. 3 (1979), pp. 516–26.

Problem for Discussion

MERCHANTS NATIONAL BANK is a $200 million institution operating in a rapidly growing metropolitan area. It operates five branches—two in the downtown area and three in outlying suburbs which are high-income, growth areas. Management and the board of directors believe that achieving maximum profitability should be the bank's primary goal. However, there is concern among the bank's top officers and members of the board that Merchants is not as profitable as it could be. Comparisons of the bank's recent profitability with the profitability of its competitors has not put Merchants in a particularly favorable light.

The bank's executive committee is deeply divided as to the cause or causes of its lagging earnings record. Some members of the committee find fault with the bank's asset management and feel that both the loan and the investment portfolio are yielding less than is possible in today's market. Other members of the executive committee feel that expenses have not been adequately controlled, operating efficiency has suffered, and the bank is excessively liquid. Wade Allen, the bank's comptroller, argues that Merchants relies too heavily upon equity capital as a source of funds and is not managing its tax position effectively.

After reviewing the bank's latest earnings report, management has decided to get to the heart of the problem. Robert Fletcher, who joined the bank last year after graduating with a degree in business administration from State University, has just completed the bank's training program. He has had considerable prior training in economics, cost accounting, tax management, financial analysis, and marketing. The executive committee feels that Fletcher has the necessary skills to analyze the bank's recent financial statements and recommend corrective action.

Fletcher decided to assemble the bank's recent financial statements—Report of Condition and Report of Income—in the form of *spread sheets* to reflect recent trends in sources and uses of funds, revenues, and expenses. Information supplied by the Federal Deposit Insurance Corporation (FDIC) gives data for insured banks of comparable size in Merchants' home state. Fletcher reasons that if the bank's indicators of recent behavior compare unfavorably with those of similar size banks (especially those in the same state), then management needs to revise its operating strategies and policies if the bank's track record is to improve. Exhibits 7–1 and 7–2 contain recent balance sheets (Report of Condition) and income statements (Report of Income) for Merchants' National Bank for the period five years ago, the previous year, and the most recent year.[1] Exhibits 7–3 and 7–4 contain comparable data for all insured banks in Merchants' home state, while Exhibit 7–5 shows some key operating ratios for all insured banks over $100 million in assets headquartered in the home state.

As Fletcher begins to analyze Merchants' financial situation, he formulates several questions to be answered:

1. How profitable has Merchants National bank been in recent years? What is the trend in earnings?
2. How does the bank's profitability compare with other banks of comparable size in the state? Is there room for improvement?
3. What factors seem to account for the bank's recent earnings behavior? Are any of these factors subject to management control and influence?
4. Could earnings be improved? What specific steps should be taken to accomplish this?
5. Does the bank need a formal planning system? What form should it take?

---

[1]For purposes of analyzing this problem, the most recent year is considered to be 1980.

Exhibit 7–1   Balance Sheets (Report of Condition) for Merchants National Bank

Balance Sheet Items	Amounts for Year-End ($ millions)		
	Five Years Ago	*Previous Year*	*Most Recent Year*
Cash and due from depository institutions.	$ 17.5	$ 22.3	$ 18.3
U.S. Treasury securities	12.0	9.0	19.2
Federal agency securities.	1.9	5.3	4.0
State and local government securities	17.5	23.2	22.5
All other securities	2.0	2.0	2.1
Total loans and discounts	87.2	125.6	128.2
Real estate loans	31.9	48.8	52.7
Commercial and industrial loans	25.7	30.0	29.5
Agricultural loans	0.2	0.5	0.6
Security loans	0.0*	0.0*	0.0*
Loans to individuals	23.4	32.6	32.6
All other loans	6.0	13.7	12.8
Fixed assets	5.6	5.3	4.9
Other assets.	0.9	1.6	2.9
Total assets	$144.7	$194.3	$202.1
Total deposits	$124.4	$167.4	$171.5
Total demand deposits	52.7	56.4	51.6
Total time and savings deposits	71.7	111.0	119.9
Demand deposits, IPC.	44.2	48.3	44.4
Savings deposits	48.0	64.2	60.4
Other time deposits, IPC	17.8	40.6	54.9
Deposits of states and political subdivisions.	12.1	12.1	9.4
Deposits of U.S. Government	1.2	0.2	0.4
All other deposits.	1.1	2.0	2.0
Other liabilities	6.4	11.9	15.2
Total capital accounts	13.9	15.0	5.4
Total liabilities and capital.	$144.7	$194.3	$202.1

Note: Total loans and discounts are measured in gross terms and include federal funds sold and securities acquired under repurchase agreements. Other assets include direct lease financing. Other liabilities include Federal funds purchased, securities sold under repurchase agreements, interest-bearing demand notes, mortgage indebtedness, and other nondeposit borrowings. Total capital accounts include any subordinated notes and debentures outstanding, the par value of common and preferred stock issued, surplus, undivided profits, and capital reserves.

*Less than $100,000.

Source: Adapted from data published by the Federal Deposit Insurance Corporation.

Exhibit 7–2   Income and Expenses (Report of Income) for Merchants National Bank

Income Statement Items	Amounts for Annual Periods ($000)		
	Five Years Ago	*Previous Year*	*Most Recent Year*
Interest and fees on loans	$ 7,248	$11,991	$14,382
Interest on U.S. Treasury and federal agency securities	839	1,112	1,731
Interest on obligations of state and local governments	1,065	956	1,145
Interest and dividends on other securities	53	81	236
Income from fiduciary activities	689	755	860
Service charges on deposit accounts	384	641	599
Other operating income	326	509	506
Total operating income	10,604	16,045	19,459
Salaries and employee benefits	2,948	3,998	3,455
Interest on deposits	3,645	6,062	8,453
Interest on federal funds and other borrowed money	219	480	1,023
Interest on capital notes and debentures	—	—	—
Occupancy, furniture and fixture expenses	710	1,428	1,085
Provision for possible loan losses	149	245	165
Other operating expenses	2,112	2,348	2,829
Total operating expenses	9,783	14,561	17,010
Income before taxes and securities transactions	821	1,484	2,449
Applicable income taxes	− 18	320	731
Income before securities gains or losses	839	1,164	1,718
Securities gains, gross	6	—	− 120
Applicable income taxes	3	—	− 63
Securities gains, net	3	—	− 57
Net income before extraordinary items	$ 842	$ 1,164	$ 1,661
Extraordinary items, net of taxes	—	—	—
Net income	$ 842	$ 1,164	$ 1,661
Cash dividends paid on stock	$ 528	$ 395	$ 702
Number of full-time equivalent employees.	—	299	223

Note: Interest and fees on loans include Federal funds sold and securities purchased under repurchase agreements. Other operating income includes income from lease financing and service charges other than on deposit accounts. Interest and dividends on other securities also include interest on balances held with banks and other depository institutions.

Source: Adapted from data published by the Federal Deposit Insurance Corporation.

Exhibit 7–3   Balance Sheet (Report of Condition) for All Banks Combined in Merchants National Bank's Home State

Balance Sheet Items	Amounts for Year-End ($ millions)		
	Five Years Ago	Previous Year	Most Recent Year
Cash and due from depository institutions........................	$ 2,712.5	$ 6,380.2	$ 7,701.6
U.S. Treasury securities	1,461.4	2,674.0	2,782.9
Federal agency securities.................	507.0	893.7	1,031.4
State and local government securities........................	1,754.1	1,898.5	2,586.9
All other securities	239.9	403.4	595.1
Total loans and discounts	10,342.1	17,643.7	18,839.0
Real estate loans	1,977.6	3,548.4	3,946.9
Commercial and industrial loans	4,379.3	7,801.0	8,930.5
Agricultural loans	10.2	89.0	75.6
Security loans.......................	36.6	61.8	75.7
Loan to individuals....................	1,972.8	3,032.6	3,085.4
All other loans	1,965.5	651.0	2,147.6
Fixed assets.........................	398.4	485.5	555.0
Other assets.........................	1,108.9	1,752.7	2,111.6
Total assets	$18,524.4	$32,078.9	$36,205.5
Total deposits	14,934.7	24,353.2	27,772.3
Total demand deposits	7,387.7	8,984.5	8,754.5
Total time and savings deposits	7,547.0	10,230.1	12,872.5
Demand deposits, IPC..................	5,841.2	7,158.8	7,151.0
Savings deposits	3,029.2	4,437.9	4,377.8
Other time deposits, IPC	3,618.2	4,870.0	7,360.3
Deposits of states and political subdivisions........................	1,328.0	1,362.5	1,478.5
Deposits of U.S. Government	90.7	72.5	72.7
All other deposits.....................	1,027.4	6,451.4	6,145.3
Other liabilities	2,387.6	5,928.7	6,494.1
Total capital accounts	1,593.7	1,797.1	1,939.1
Total liabilities and capital...............	$18,534.4	$32,078.9	$36,205.5

Note: See Exhibit 7–1.

Source: Federal Deposit Insurance Corporation, *Bank Operating Statistics,* 1975, 1979, and 1980 editions.

Exhibit 7-4   Income and Expenses (Report of Income) for All Banks Combined in Merchants National Bank's Home State

Income Statement Items	Amounts for Year-End ($ millions)		
	Five Years Ago	Previous Year	Most Recent Year
Interest and fees on loans	$ 940.8	$2,181.7	$2,838.6
Interest on U.S. Treasury and federal agency securities	113.8	254.9	364.4
Interest on obligations of state and local governments........................	85.5	89.0	131.4
Interest and dividends on other securities	8.5	348.9	572.0
Income from fiduciary activities	68.5	114.7	136.4
Service charges on deposit accounts............	28.6	34.8	46.4
Other operating income	136.9	217.4	288.6
Total Operating Income..............	1,382.7	3,241.4	4,377.8
Salaries and employee benefits	328.3	530.3	641.6
Interest on deposits	441.2	1,324.3	1,961.9
Interest on Federal funds and other borrowed money	93.0	514.0	763.3
Interest on capital notes and debentures.........................	5.7	6.4	6.7
Occupancy, furniture and fixture expenses	71.4	160.5	188.5
Provision for possible loan losses	119.7	101.6	95.9
Other operating expenses	214.4	295.1	355.8
Total Operating Expenses..............	1,273.8	2,932.2	4,013.7
Income before taxes and securities transactions	108.9	309.1	364.1
Applicable income taxes...................	14.9	110.7	117.2
Income before securities gains or losses	94.0	198.5	246.9
Securities gains, gross	1.7	−10.4	−15.7
Applicable income taxes...................	—	−5.7	−8.4
Securities gains, net....................	1.7	−4.7	−7.3
Net income before extraordinary items.........................	95.7	193.8	239.6
Extraordinary items, net of taxes.............	$ 95.8	$ 194.7	$ 240.5
Net income	$ 95.8	$ 194.7	$ 240.5
Cash dividends paid on stock	$ 55.0	$ 79.8	$ 104.6

Note: Interest and fees on loans include Federal funds sold and securities purchased under repurchase agreements. Other operating income includes income from lease financing and service charges other than deposit accounts. Interest and dividends on other securities also includes interest on balances held with banks and other depository institutions.

Source: Federal Deposit Insurance Corporation, *Bank Operating Statistics*, 1975, 1979, and 1980 editions.

Exhibit 7–5　Key Operating Ratios for All Insured Banks with Assets of $100 Million or More in Merchants National Bank's Home State

Operating Ratio	Most Recent Year	Previous Year
Total loans to deposits	66.83%	69.50%
Total loans to assets	55.38	58.50
Equity capital to deposits	7.20	7.13
Income before securities gains to assets	0.86	0.79
Restated income before securities gains to assets	0.96	0.86
Net income to assets	0.86	0.78
Net income to equity capital	14.06	12.38
Dividends to net income	36.25	38.75
Interest expense to time and savings deposits and other borrowings	8.27	6.78
Return on total loans	12.31	11.25
Return on U.S. Treasury and federal agency securities	8.77	8.00
Return on all other securities	6.78	6.81
Net occupancy, furniture, and equipment expense to assets	0.64	0.65
Other operating expenses to assets	1.29	1.22
Average salary and benefits per employee	$15,008	$13,312
Assets (in thousands) per employee	$ 724	$ 676
Provision for possible loan loss to total loans	0.47%	0.61%
Loan loss coverage (times)	7.61	6.06

Source: Federal Deposit Insurance Corporation, *Bank Operating Statistics*, 1979 and 1980 editions.

8. Structure and Regulation of the Commercial Banking Industry

THE STRUCTURE OF THE AMERICAN BANKING INDUSTRY is one of the most unusual to be found anywhere in the world. There were more than 15,000 commercial banks in the United States operating at year-end 1983. This huge number of banks offering their services to the public stands in sharp contrast even to the banking industries of other developed Western countries. The United States' neighbor to the north, Canada, has only about six dozen banks today, of which only about one dozen are domestically chartered banks and the rest are foreign-owned. Mexico, prior to the nationalization of its privately owned commerical banks in 1982, had only a few more domestic banks than Canada. In short, the U.S. banking industry is decidedly unique in terms of its raw numbers of separately incorporated commercial banks.

The American banking industry is unique as well in its historical lack of emphasis on branch banking. While the growth of branch offices is one of the dominant trends in U.S. banking since World War II, U.S. banks operating branches are still slightly in the minority. Close to 8,000 American banks operate out of only a single full-service office. This situation stands in dramatic contrast to both Canada and Mexico, where most banks operate dozens or even hundreds of branches. For example, the average domestic bank in Canada has between 600 and 700 branch offices. With many banks operating and most without branches, it is not surprising that the average U.S. bank typically is much smaller than its counterpart in other countries. For example, at year-end 1982 about 70 percent of U.S. banks held assets of less than $50 million each. While most large banks abroad held at least $1 billion in assets, less than 2 percent of all U.S. banks fell into this largest size category. Yet, these largest U.S. banking institutions rank among the world's largest. For example, 6 of the 10 largest commercial banks in the world are located in the United States, including the 3 largest. And these few very large banking institutions control a major portion of U.S. banking resources. As we noted above, only about 2 percent of the total number of U.S. banks held $1 billion or more in total assets each. However, the assets held by these few banks were valued at over $1 trillion in 1982—more than half the industry's total assets. And so, while the U.S. banking system is dominated numerically by small banks, there is also a heavy concentration of market power in the hands of only a few institutions, not only at the national level but also at many local levels. Countless small towns outside the nation's major metropolitan areas contain only one, two, or three banks.

The U.S. banking structure has been changing in recent years at a rapid pace, reflecting forces operating within the industry and external developments. A gradual consolidation of resources into fewer but larger banking organizations seems to be underway, with these larger units offering a wider and wider array of financial services. Competition among banks themselves and among banks and nonbank financial institutions has intensified. Partly in response to increased competition, a trend toward diversification in financial services is underway to open up new markets and new sources of profitability for banks. And the development of many new services has necessitated the relaxing or liberalizing of some government regulations to permit innovation and greater competition. In this chapter we examine in some detail recent changes in U.S. banking structure and regulation and some of the reasons behind them.

THE IMPORTANCE OF BANKING STRUCTURE

What Structure Means

As we begin our study of the structure of U.S. banking, it is important to understand precisely what the term *structure* refers to and why it is important. Economists use the word *structure* in several different senses. For example, we may focus upon the structure of an *industry*, looking at how many businesses are present in that industry, their comparative sizes in assets or sales, their geographic locations, and their mix of products or services produced. We can also analyze the structure of a *market* where several firms compete in offering their goods and services. Again, we would focus upon how many firms serve the particular market under study; their comparative importance in that market, measured by such factors as the percentage of assets or sales each firm holds; their locations; and their mix of services offered.

Finally, we can look at the structure of an *organization*—how a firm is organized or arranged internally in order to produce and deliver its goods or services to the marketplace. In banking, several different organizational structures have emerged over time. One of the oldest is the *unit bank* which offers its full range of services from a single office. Unit banks operate no branches. In contrast, an increasing number of banks today are organized as *branch banks*, offering their services from multiple office locations. However, like unit banks, branch banks have a single board of directors, single capital structure, and one central management team no matter how many branches they operate. Branch and unit banks may form or be acquired by *bank holding companies*, which are corporations holding stock in one or more banks. The holding company may also own or control a number of nonbank subsidiaries, such as finance companies, mortgage companies, leasing firms, and so forth. This organizational type is characterized by multiple corporations and offices, multiple boards of directors, multiple capital structures, and, in some cases, multiple management teams brought together under one large corporate umbrella.

A related organizational form is the *symbiotic financial firm*. "Symbiotics" are large corporations which may operate or control simultaneously one or more financially oriented firms, such as a brokerage firm, real estate brokerage and development company, insurance company, investment banking house, or perhaps a money market fund. Many of the services offered by symbiotics today compete directly with services offered by commercial banks.

The Importance of Structure

Why is structure important? The answer is found in the almost universal belief among economists and regulatory authorities that the structure of industries, markets, and individual firms influences competition and efficiency.

Competition refers to interfirm rivalry—efforts by each firm serving a given market to earn greater profits and capture a larger share of available customers. *Efficiency* refers to the ability of a firm to produce its product or service at the lowest possible cost, perhaps passing those cost savings along to the customer in the form of lower prices.

In those markets where firms are both competitive and efficient, the public presumably is better served. Prices are lower, output of goods and services is greater, production costs are lower, and firms earn no more than a normal rate of return on their invested capital. On the other hand, when only one (monopoly) or a few (oligopoly) firms serve a market, competition may be reduced or completely eliminated and there is less incentive to be efficient in production. The result may be higher prices for the customer, less adequate service, and excessive or windfall profits. In brief, economic theory suggests that *structure affects competition and efficiency and that both competition and efficiency influence the performance of firms in serving the customer* (see Figure 8–1).

In our society the ideal is to approach "perfect competition" as closely as possible. However, in any practical situation this is virtually impossible to

Figure 8–1   The Importance of Structure

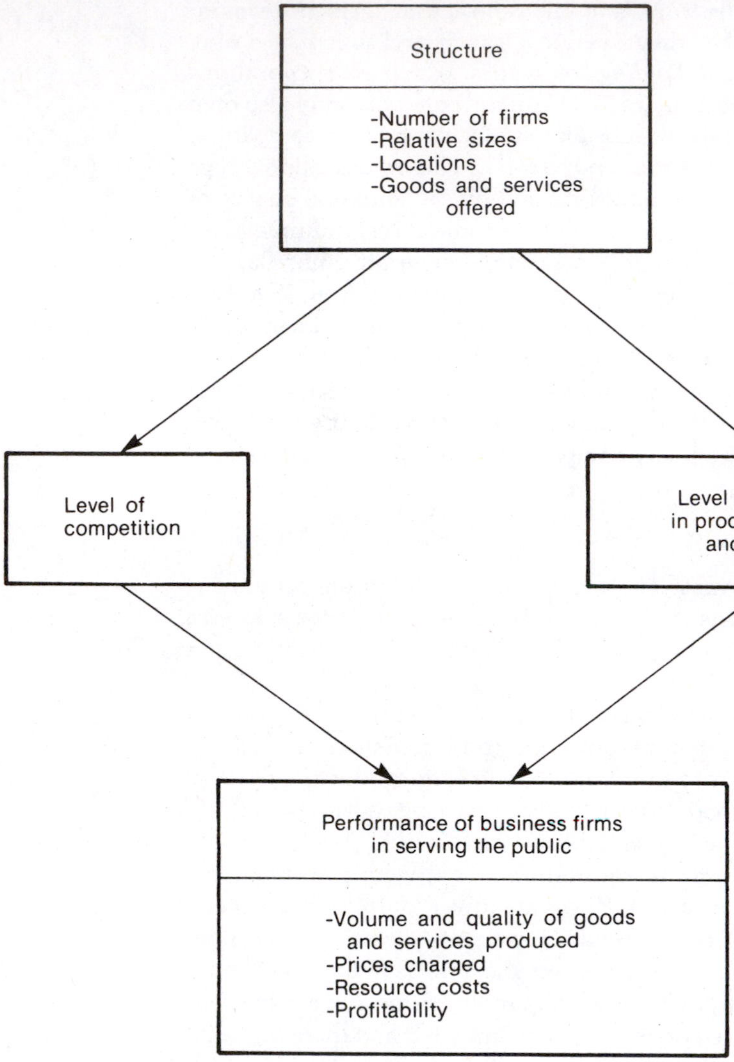

```
                    ┌─────────────────────────┐
                    │         Structure        │
                    ├─────────────────────────┤
                    │  -Number of firms        │
                    │  -Relative sizes         │
                    │  -Locations              │
                    │  -Goods and services     │
                    │         offered          │
                    └─────────────────────────┘
                      ╱                      ╲
                     ╱                        ╲
                    ▼                          ▼
    ┌──────────────────┐          ┌──────────────────────┐
    │    Level of      │          │  Level of efficiency │
    │  competition     │          │  in producing goods  │
    │                  │          │     and services     │
    └──────────────────┘          └──────────────────────┘
                 ╲                      ╱
                  ╲                    ╱
                   ▼                  ▼
         ┌────────────────────────────────────┐
         │   Performance of business firms    │
         │       in serving the public        │
         ├────────────────────────────────────┤
         │  -Volume and quality of goods      │
         │    and services produced           │
         │  -Prices charged                   │
         │  -Resource costs                   │
         │  -Profitability                    │
         └────────────────────────────────────┘
```

achieve since perfect competition requires (1) completely free entry of new firms in response to profitable opportunities, (2) free exit of inefficient firms or of those who refuse to compete, and (3) complete absence of collusion among existing firms which might result in price fixing or a division of the market. As a practical matter, we strive through law and regulation to promote as much competition as possible among banks and other financial institutions, consistent with other social goals. Beginning in the late 19th century the federal government and then the states enacted laws forbidding monopolies and restraint of trade. Today, these rules of the competitive game are enforced by the U.S. Department of Justice and the Federal Trade Commission for virtually all industries. In banking, federal and state regulatory agencies must give heavy weight to competition in deciding upon applications for new bank charters, new branch offices, mergers among existing banks, or the formation of bank holding companies. In general, mergers or other combinations among existing firms cannot be approved if they would adversely affect competition.[1]

Efficiency and Optimal Size

If competition is so desirable, why don't we charter a large number of banks and other financial institutions to serve each market, and completely forbid any mergers or other combinations among these firms? In most industries, including financial institutions, there is one particular size firm which is *optimal* in terms of producing goods or services at the lowest possible operating cost per unit. Firms smaller or larger than optimal size produce at higher unit costs and thereby waste resources. Such economies of scale (size) have been found to exist in commerical banking, savings and loan associations, and insurance companies, and they probably exist elsewhere in the financial institutions' sector. In the long run, individual firms tend to approach optimal size, or they exit from the industry.

The Department of Justice and most regulatory agencies in recent years have followed a relatively simple philosophy in dealing with economies of scale. The very largest banks and other financial institutions frequently are denied mergers with other firms in the same industry or market in order to discourage these companies from growing significantly beyond the least-cost (optimal) size. In contrast, smaller institutions, which presumably are below optimal size, may be encouraged to grow larger through favorable rulings on mergers, branch office applications, or the entering of new markets. At the same time these firms may be protected from the entry of new competitors by regulatory barriers, since the chartering of additional firms would make it more difficult for any one firm to approach optimal size. The purpose of such a policy, of course, is to reduce costs to the customer and thereby lower prices while at the same time improving the quantity and quality of output. Public policy attempts to reach a compromise in most industries so that effective competition pre-

---

[1]The exceptions to this rule center upon the convenience and needs of the public and the so-called failing firm doctrine. If a proposed merger, for example, would result in significantly improved service to the public or save a firm whose collapse would endanger the economic vitality of the local community, it may be approved even if the level of competition would be reduced.

vails, but it is not so strong as to prevent individual banks and other financial intermediaries from producing and selling their services at the lowest possible cost.

Safety and Soundness

The second reason why restraints are placed upon competition among financial institutions centers upon the issues of safety and soundness. A number of laws have been passed in the United States to restrict competition among banks and other financial institutions in order to reduce the probability of failure. These laws include the requirements that, before a new bank or other deposit-type intermediary can be chartered, the proponents of the charter application must prove the new institution will be profitable in a short period of time (usually two to three years), that there is a need for a new financial institution in the community, and that existing financial institutions will not be unduly harmed. Interest rates offered on deposits and rates on loans often have been subject to legal ceilings to reduce the likelihood of "destructive" price competition. Extensive restrictions are applied at both federal and state levels on the kinds of loans and securities that may be acquired by commercial banks, credit unions, savings banks, insurance companies, and pension funds. These laws and regulations are grounded in the belief that too much competition would increase the risk of a significant number of failures among intermediaries and threaten public confidence in the safety and soundness of the nation's financial system. Thus competition is tempered by regulation to protect the safety of individual financial institutions and by the desire for maximum economic efficiency in the production of financial services.

THE REGULATION OF COMMERCIAL BANKS

Commercial banks are closely regulated and supervised by various units of government. Extensive regulatory rules are applied at both federal and state levels to cover the chartering of new banks, the establishment of branch offices and the exercise of trust powers, the formation of holding companies and mergers, the offering of new financial services, the adequacy of bank capital, the quantity and quality of loans and investments, the level of cash reserves, the maximum rates payable on certain deposits, and the maximum rates that can be charged on loans in certain states. As we will see in Chapter 10, new federal laws and regulations dealing with consumer protection and civil rights have appeared during the 1970s, affecting the advertising of bank credit services, the types of information which can be requested of credit customers, the methods for reporting financial charges on loans, and the procedures for handling billing disputes between credit customers and their banks.

Why do we impose such extensive regulatory controls over bank behavior? Several arguments have been advanced over the years to justify these regulations. Commercial banks, as we have seen, are the principal source of the nation's money supply, which is closely linked to the growth and stability of the economy. Banks hold the public's savings, and imprudent practices might jeopardize those funds, adversely affecting the financial position of many businesses, families, and individuals. Access to bank credit directly affects the financial well-being and standard of living of many individuals and institutions—especially consumers, smaller businesses, and state and local governments. Finally, commercial banks, because of their unique combination of services, possess great financial power. The failure of a major bank in a local community can have disastrous consequences. And, if bankers get together and illegally agree not to compete on prices, rates, or services offered, the resulting damage to consumers of financial services could be tremendous.[2] Throughout U.S. history there has been considerable fear at both state and federal levels that banks working together, unregulated and unsupervised, could take actions which would have dire consequences for businesses and consumers who must rely on banks for essential financial services. This wide-spread fear of financial power and influence accounts for much of the law and regulation today governing branch banking, bank holding companies, and bank mergers.

The Dual Regulatory System

Banks and other financial intermediaries in the United States face a dual regulatory system with controls operating at both federal and state levels. There are three principal federal bank regulatory agencies—the Federal Reserve System, the Federal Deposit Insurance Corporation, and the Comptroller of the Currency (or Administrator of National Banks). Each of the 50 states, in turn, has a banking commission or department with powers generally paralleling those possessed by one or more of the three federal regulatory agencies (see Figure 8–2). With so many agencies overseeing the same industry it is not surprising that there is considerable over-

---

[2]Many of the same observations could be made about why financial institutions other than banks are so closely regulated. Virtually all financial institutions, directly or indirectly, hold and invest the public's savings, provide credit to businesses, consumers, or governments, and often possess great financial power. To leave the financial sector *completely* unregulated would appear to invite imprudent, excessively risky, and perhaps discriminatory practices which could have far-reaching consequences for the nation as a whole. Nevertheless, some deregulation of the financial services industry seems necessary today to stimulate greater competition and more financial innovation.

Figure 8-2   The Dual Regulatory System in U.S. Banking

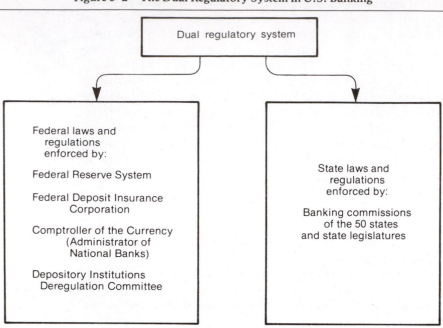

Principal federal and state regulatory
powers apply to:

-Chartering of new banks
-Branching, mergers, and holding companies
-Quantity and quality of loans and investments

-Offering of new services
-Adequacy of capital
-Level of cash reserves
-Interest rates paid and
 charged

lapping of regulatory powers, occasional conflicts among the agencies, and even competition from time to time.[3]

Federal Reserve System

The Federal Reserve System (the Fed) is one of the most important and powerful regulatory agencies in the federal government. As we saw in

---

[3]Two prominent examples of this competition and conflict among bank regulatory agencies: (a) the tendency of federal authorities in the past to charter federal banks in communities where state banks had previously received charters (and sometimes vice versa) and (b) a running controversy between the Comptroller of the Currency and the Federal Reserve System, on the one hand, and the Federal Deposit Insurance Corporation, on the other, regarding the measurement and minimum acceptable levels of bank capital. Chapter 12 discusses the disagreement over bank capital standards among these three federal agencies.

Chapter 5, the Fed's principal function is to carry out monetary policy—control over interest rates and the money supply in order to achieve the nation's economic goals. However, the Fed also exercises important supervisory powers over individual banks and the growth of banking organizations. It must approve or disapprove applications of bank holding companies to acquire bank and nonbank businesses and ensure that holding company organizations do not endanger the solvency or stability of the banks they acquire. The Fed supervises those commercial banks electing to join its system (so-called member banks), which include all 4,400 national banks and almost 1,000 state-chartered banks. It generally confines its detailed examinations of banking practices to state-chartered members of its system and secures examination reports on national banks from the Comptroller of the Currency. Finally, the Fed oversees member bank compliance with recent social responsibility laws and regulations, including truth-in-lending and equal-credit-opportunity laws.

Federal Deposit Insurance Corporation

The Federal Deposit Insurance Corporation insures the deposits of approximately 98 percent of all federal and state-chartered American commercial banks. Each depositor who keeps his or her funds in FDIC-insured banks is protected up to a maximum of $100,000—an amount which is satisfactory for most individuals and families but is of little help for major corporate depositors. The FDIC is responsible for the disposition of all failures among insured banks, paying off depositors up to the legal $100,000 maximum where necessary. While the FDIC is legally empowered to regularly examine all insured banks, it usually limits its examinations to insured banks not members of the Federal Reserve System. Generally, these examinations are conducted jointly with the state banking agencies to minimize the burden upon both the banks and the supervisory agencies. Insured commercial banks must submit to the FDIC financial statements containing a detailed breakdown of their assets, liabilities, capital, revenues, and expenses.

Comptroller of the Currency

The oldest of the federal bank regulatory agencies is the office of the Comptroller of the Currency, created by Congress in 1863. The comptroller's office is the source of certificates of association (i.e., federal charters) for groups wishing to organize new national banks. In order to secure a certificate authorizing the opening of a national bank, federal law and the comptroller's regulations require the bank's organizers to demonstrate a public need, pledge sufficient capital to protect the public's deposits, abide by all federal banking laws and regulations, demonstrate good moral character, and show that the new bank has reasonable prospects for success. The comptroller's office examines all national banks at least once a year on the quality of their loans, adequacy of capital, and competence of management. Since there are about 4,400 national banks, including most of the largest banks in the United States, this is a formidable task. To aid in its chartering, supervisory, and examination functions, the comptroller has set up several offices across the country staffed with attorneys, economists, and examiners. Each office is responsible for a different region of the nation.

Depository Institutions Deregulation Committee

With passage of the Depository Institutions Deregulation and Monetary Control Act of 1980, another federal regulatory authority was created whose decisions affect not only commercial banks but also credit unions, savings and loan associations, and mutual savings banks. This new regulatory group is known as the Depository Institutions Deregulation Committee (DIDC), composed of the heads of the Federal Reserve Board, the Federal Deposit Insurance Corporation, the Federal Home Loan Bank Board, the National Credit Union Administration, and the Secretary of the Treasury. (The Comptroller of the Currency is a nonvoting member of this committee.) The DIDC is responsible under the Depository Institutions Deregulation Act for "the orderly phaseout and the ultimate elimination of limitations on the maximum rates of interest and dividends that may be paid on deposits and accounts."[4] These legal maximum interest rates on time and savings deposits (known as Regulation Q ceilings, named after a decades-old regulation of the Federal Reserve Board) are to be phased out "as rapidly as economic conditions warrant" over a six-year period beginning March 31, 1980. The committee must vote no later than March 31, 1983, 1984, 1985, and 1986, on whether to increase the limitations on the maximum rates applicable to all categories of deposits and accounts by at least one half of a percentage point. It must report annually to Congress on its actions and their effects on thrift institutions, savers, and the housing industry. By March 31, 1986, the authority to impose interest-rate ceilings on deposits at the federal level will be automatically repealed and the DIDC will cease to exist unless Congress votes otherwise.

State Banking Commissions

Finally, the individual state banking commissions supervise and examine all state-chartered commercial banks in the United States. These state agencies must pass on applications for corporate charters to establish new

---

[4]See the Depository Institutions Deregulation and Monetary Control Act of 1980, Public Law 69–221, Title II.

banks, reviewing basically the same factors that the Comptroller's office considers in deciding whether to issue federal charters for national banks. In terms of sheer numbers, the states charter more banks than the Comptroller of the Currency, as shown in Table 8–1. However, in recent years adverse economic conditions have encouraged several states to adopt a go-slow policy in chartering new banks, while the Comptroller's office appears to have liberalized its chartering rules somewhat in order to increase the level of competition in many local banking markets. Also, organizers of a new bank located in a state which has strict banking regulations (particularly those applying to branch office expansion, reserve requirements, and loan interest-rate ceilings) are more likely to seek a federal bank charter.[5]

Each state maintains a staff of examiners who regularly review the operations of state-chartered banks operating within that state's borders. In addition, most of the state commissions must approve or at least be notified of any mergers or holding company acquisitions involving banks they charter and supervise.

Table 8–1   New U.S. Banks Chartered by Federal and State Authorities in Recent Years

Year	National Banks Chartered by the Comptroller of the Currency	Banks Chartered by the State Banking Commissions	Year	National Banks Chartered by the Comptroller of the Currency	Banks Chartered by the State Banking Commissions
1960	32	93	1972	54	184
1961	26	82	1973	88	245
1962	63	116	1974	97	292
1963	164	134	1975	74	181
1964	200	134	1976	65	107
1965	88	106	1977	39	148
1966	25	93	1978	37	137
1967	18	87	1979	42	182
1968	15	70	1970	61	173
1969	16	113	1981	100	149
1970	40	143	1982	198	41
1971	37	162			

Sources: Federal Deposit Insurance Corporation, *Changes Among Operating Banks and Branches*, various annual issues; and Susan F. Krause and Peter L. Struck, "The Bank Charter Decision: A Logit Analysis," staff paper, Comptroller of the Currency, 1982.

[5]There have been a few studies of how new banks fare after being chartered and what factors appear to contribute to the success of a new bank. One interesting observation is that the success or failure of a new bank is often heavily dependent on the ability of its organizers to seek out and attract large depositors and credit customers even before the bank is officially open for business. The capabilities of the organizers and board of directors also seem to have a significant impact on the success of a new bank. See Rose [21] for a useful summary of these bank charter studies.

At or near the top of the list of state supervisory powers over the nation's banking system is control over the ability of individual banks to set up branch offices. Federal law dictates that even national banks must conform to state rules regarding the establishment of branch offices and the permissible range of services which may be offered through those branches. In the past, most states have elected to restrict or prohibit branch banking, but today in one form or another it is gradually spreading across the nation. Frequently, banks skirt around state branching laws through the use of holding companies or special nonbank subsidiaries (such as loan production offices) which are not subject to branching rules.

The Goals of Federal and State Regulation

In summary, federal and state regulations have greatly expanded over the years, especially during and since the Great Depression of the 1930s, to achieve multiple and often conflicting goals in the banking field—competition, safety, public convenience, efficiency, and equity. Today, nearly all aspects of bank operations are covered by federal or state regulations administered by the Federal Reserve System, the Federal Deposit Insurance Corporation, the Comptroller of the Currency, and banking commissions in each of the 50 states. In the following sections we look more closely at recent changes in the structure and regulation of the commercial banking industry and at their implications for competition and for the safety and soundness of individual banks. We will pay special attention also to a gradual trend toward deregulation of the banking and financial services industry in order to promote greater competition and better service to the public.

BRANCH BANKING ### Growth of Branch Banking

The dominant trend in post–World War II U.S. banking is the spread of branch banking. For most of U.S. history the dominant banking organization was the single-office unit bank, independently owned and operated. Prior to the turn of the century, only a handful of American banks (less than 1 percent) operated branch offices. However, the serious agricultural recession of the 1920s and the Great Depression of the 1930s resulted in the failure of thousands of small unit banks, particularly those in rural areas and one-industry towns. Many unit institutions that did not fail were subsequently absorbed into larger banking organizations.

When prosperity returned after World War II, the consolidation of smaller banks into larger ones through mergers and acquisitions continued. Between 1945 and 1970, more than 3,000 unit banks disappeared, most of them caught up in a massive postwar merger movement. By 1982, almost half of all separately incorporated U.S. banks operated branch offices. Not unexpectedly, the number of branch offices themselves literally exploded. When World War II ended, the nation had less than 5,000 branch bank offices in operation; today the number of such offices approaches 40,000, though a decline in total branches began in the 1980s (see Table 8–2).

Despite the gradual replacement of unit banks by branching systems, the number of separately incorporated banks in the United States has increased since World War II. To be sure, the growth in bank numbers has been modest. For example, there were 14,142 commercial banks in existence at year-end 1945, and just 14,994 at the close of 1982. Most of the growth in new banks has occurred since 1960, reflecting rapid increases in income and population and the shifting of the nation's population from cities to suburbs and rural areas. There has also been a massive internal migration from northern and northeastern parts of the United States towards the west and south.

These economic and demographic forces have stimulated the demand for banking services and opened up new markets. They have created significant challenges for the management of existing banks in attempting to keep up with growth and population movements. For example, many metropolitan-based commercial banks have been forced to "chase after" their customers by opening scores of branch offices in suburban communities or by merging with smaller banks situated in more desirable locations. Rapid industrial growth also has intensified pressures on banks to expand in order to provide more credit, increase the stability of deposits,

Table 8–2   Recent Growth in Commercial Banks, Branch Offices, and Deposits (year-end figures)

Year	Number of Commercial Banks	Branch Offices	Volume of Deposits ($ billions)
1960	13,471	10,483	$ 229.8
1962	13,326	12,345	262.1
1964	13,760	14,601	307.1
1966	13,769	16,908	353.5
1968	13,679	18,777	435.2
1970	13,688	21.424	481.7
1972	13,928	24,850	616.6
1974	14.465	29,775	786.5
1976	14,697	31,403	841.9
1977	14,740	33,088	1,116.5
1980	14,836	38,779	1,194.0
1982	14,994	39,835	1,303.4

Sources: Board of Governors of the Federal Reserve System, *Federal Reserve Bulletin*; and Federal Deposit Insurance Corporation, *Annual Report*, selected issues.

and secure more efficient management control. Branch banking has offered a way for the banking industry to grow rapidly in areas where the market appears most promising.

Other factors explaining the growth of branch banking include rising operating costs and a squeeze on profit margins. Both factors have put commercial banks under pressure to expand their size, diversify, and seek new sources of revenue. As we saw in Chapters 6 and 7, interest-bearing sources of funds have increased relative to cheaper demand deposits, and more costly services (such as leasing, factoring, trust operations, and financial counseling) have been demanded by businesses and households. The result has been a major shift in bank policies in recent years away from the traditional position of being a short-term lender to business to a more aggressive, marketing-oriented banking operation, utilizing new techniques for attracting funds and placing greater emphasis upon consumer loans, leasing, mortgages, and nonfunds-using financial services. These developments have accelerated the need for larger and more diversified banking organizations in the form of branching systems.

The Effect of Branch Banking

Over the years there has been intense research interest in the impact of branch banking activity upon how and where individual banks provide their services to the public. State laws vary enormously on the type of branching activity permitted commercial banks within the borders of each state. As of June 1982, 22 states permitted branching *statewide*, subject only to minimal capital requirements and public necessity. These include such major states as Arizona, California, Connecticut, Maryland, New Jersey, New York, North Carolina, Oregon, and Washington. Nineteen states restricted branching activity to cities and counties. These typically are referred to as *limited branching* states and include such states as Alabama, Georgia, Indiana, Massachusetts, Michigan, Ohio, Pennsylvania, and Wisconsin. The remaining group of 9 states—usually labeled *unit banking* states—required that the business of banking be carried on in only one location, though remote drive-in or other limited service facilities may be permitted. States in this category include Colorado, Missouri, Oklahoma, and Texas.

There is a definite geographic pattern in branch banking laws. Unit banking states are prominent in the Midwest and South, while in the West statewide branching predominates. In areas east of the Mississippi River, limited branching and statewide branch banking are especially important. A number of states have changed their position on branching since World War II. Arkansas, Florida, Kentucky, Illinois, Iowa, Maine, Minnesota, New Hampshire, New Jersey, New York, and Virginia, for example, have loosened restrictive branching laws to permit banks to establish branch offices over wider areas. However, many of these states inserted a *home-*

office protection clause in their liberalized branching laws. A home-office protection rule restricts a bank from branching into a community or county where another bank has its home offices. Among other states changing their branching rules, Florida moved in 1979 to permit statewide branching. Even some unit banking states, while still prohibiting full-services branching, have allowed more liberal use of remote limited-service facilities. For example, Texas now permits off-premises automated teller machines (ATMs) as well as drive-in windows 500 to 2,000 feet from a bank's main office.

Proponents of branch banking claim that unrestricted entry into new markets through branching encourages competition and promotes efficiency in providing financial services. Because branching fosters larger and fewer banks, allegedly the consumer benefits by receiving financial services at lower cost due to economies of scale and greater productive efficiency. Opponents of branching, on the other hand, maintain that it results in greater concentration of resources and increased market power for the largest banks. Potentially, at least, the customer may have fewer real alternatives under a branch banking regime, and, therefore, prices charged for financial services may be higher. To some extent, acceptance of branch banking by the public may require a trade-off between competition (which may call for a market composed of many banks, each of only moderate size) and efficiency (which may necessitate fewer and larger banks serving the public).

A number of recent studies have examined the impact of branching on bank operating efficiency, the availability of banking services, prices, credit policies, mobility of funds, and market structure. Unfortunately, the results of these studies are much less than conclusive. For example, Horvitz and Shull [12] find that, compared with unit banking, branching results in more branch offices in rural areas but in fewer separately incorporated banks in metropolitan areas. Branching seems to result in more services, though research studies conflict as to whether these are offered at higher or lower prices.[6]

Branch banks do seem to make more credit available in local communities, especially to consumers. However, Edwards [8] finds some evidence that interest paid on time and savings deposits is lower and rates on many types of loans are higher at branch banks than at unit banks. Also, there is limited evidence of discrimination against small businesses in credit availability and in the pricing of loans under branch banking. Branching leads to fewer, but larger, commercial banks in a state, but frequently more total branch offices in metropolitan areas and in smaller communities, resulting in greater public convenience.[7] Finally, there is virtually no con-

---

[6]See, for example, Horvitz and Shull [12] and Weintraub and Jessup [32].

[7]See especially Edwards [8] and Jacobs [13].

crete evidence that the character of a state's branch banking laws affects income levels or rates of economic growth in local communities. We are still very much in the dark on the real long-run benefits of having a branch banking or a unit banking structure.

The McFadden Act and Interstate Banking

As we noted above, laws passed by the individual states determine whether banks can branch within their borders. This was not always the case. In fact, when federally chartered (national) banks were first authorized by Congress during the Civil War, it was commonly assumed that federal laws and regulations would determine where national banks could establish branches. When it appeared that national banks would be given more liberal branching rules than state-chartered banks, a number of bank trade associations vigorously objected. After years of debate and indecision, the McFadden Act was enacted by Congress in 1927, presumably settling the issue at least for a while.

The new law expressly prohibited branching across state lines (unless, of course, a bank already had such branches in place, which a few did). Within the boundaries of a single state, however, branching activity was to be controlled by state law, regardless of whether the banks involved were federally chartered. Thus an artificial barrier to the growth of banks through branching was created—a barrier consisting merely of lines drawn on a map. It didn't take a great deal of foresight to realize that a barrier of this sort would eventually be outmoded by changing technology and economic reality. Moreover, bankers, possessed of considerable ingenuity, would undoubtedly find a way around McFadden's restrictions if the economic incentives were strong enough.

The first serious cracks in the wall of branching restrictions erected by the McFadden Act appeared in the 1960s and 1970s. The pressures associated with rising costs, shifting populations, and broadening financial markets encouraged bankers to cast their eyes to distant territories and find ways to reach new markets. In some cases this could be done simply by pressing the state legislature to amend or eliminate antibranching rules. Where this was impossible or inadequate, new organizational forms were used—most notably, the bank holding company. As we will see more clearly in the next section, banks could legally set up a holding company organization and acquire nonbank businesses (such as a finance company or mortgage banking house) anywhere in the country (subject to Federal Reserve Board approval). These nonbank business outlets could be used to offer at least some banking services, especially on the credit side of the ledger, and create de facto interstate banking.[8]

---

[8]See especially Rhoades [18].

Another vehicle for skirting around the barriers created by McFadden was spawned by the internationalization of U.S. banking.[9] Around the time of the first World War, American banks received permission to establish subsidiaries (so-called Edge Act and Agreement corporations) whose principal business activities centered around international trade and commerce. In order to compete more effectively with foreign banks these internationally oriented subsidiaries were given much wider latitude in their financing activities than were granted domestic banks (including the acquisition of equity shares abroad) and were allowed to branch at home. The result has been that major banks on the East and West coasts have established Edge Act subsidiaries in several large U.S. cities scattered in different regions of the nation. Moreover, these "Edge Acts" have managed to make a large number of business contacts for the bank back home. At the same time, foreign banks were penetrating U.S. domestic markets in large numbers through agencies, affiliates, and branches, responding to the potential for business in the huge U.S. common market.

These efforts by the largest domestic and foreign banking institutions to skirt around the McFadden Act's prohibitions against widespread branching alarmed many individuals, especially the management and stockholders of many small banks and nonbank thrifts. Their complaints to Congress led ultimately to passage of the International Banking Act of 1978. This law, as we will note again in Chapter 24, placed foreign banks active in the United States under more strict regulation. At the same time, President Jimmy Carter was directed to review federal branching laws in cooperation with the federal banking agencies. Legislative recommendations soon appeared to lift, at least partially, the tight federal prohibitions against interstate branching.[10]

The recommendations which have subsequently appeared to loosen the legal restraints against branching have attracted at least their fair share of

---

[9]See Chapter 24 for a more complete discussion of the international activities of U.S. banks.

[10]A number of different proposals have since been made to expand the boundaries of permissible branching activity. One such proposal calls for identifying areas or regions of the nation, exclusive of state boundaries, where branching might produce beneficial results in terms of greater public convenience and the fostering of competition. For example, banks might be allowed to branch into distant cities within the same region.

Another, older proposal advocates reciprocal branching across state lines. For example, California and Oregon might agree to permit reciprocal branching between those two states; banks headquartered in Los Angeles and San Francisco might then set up branch offices in Portland, while Portland banks likewise would be permitted to open full-service branches in San Francisco and Los Angeles. Early in the decade of the 1980s a few states acted to permit branching in their territory by out-of-state banks. In April 1983, for example, the state of Washington agreed to let outside banking organizations acquire troubled Washington state banks. Delaware and South Dakota also made it easier for outside banks to enter their markets. In the New England area, regional interstate banking appears to be moving much closer to realization.

opposition. Many small banks in the Midwest, for example, foresee the day when perhaps the nation's largest banks as far away as New York and San Francisco might set up shop next door. This competitive entry might be in the form of a full-service branch or even a simple automated teller machine (ATM). If there are real scale economies in banking, the added competition might conceivably overwhelm the small-town financial institutions, especially as the U.S. financial system moves closer to an electronic, computer-oriented system which may well sharply increase operating costs and certainly will expand fixed costs. In this kind of environment, could the smallest financial intermediaries survive?

All sides to the branching issue—both pro and con—have hoped that it could be settled in a rational, step-by-step manner in which the benefits and costs were carefully weighed with all available research evidence brought to bear. Unfortunately, developments in the U.S. economy and financial system in 1981, 1982, and 1983 began to cast serious doubt that such a measured approach would be used. Persistent high interest rates, coupled with a sagging economy, threatened the viability of dozens of large financial intermediaries, particularly savings and loan associations—the principal lenders in the nation's critical housing market. So large were the losses racked up by the S&Ls heavily laden with old, low-yielding mortgages that emergency measures were taken by the Federal Savings and Loan Insurance Corporation (FSLIC) to protect depositors and preserve public confidence. Some of these measures took the form of mergers of savings and loans across state lines—in effect, creating interstate branching. This step raised eyebrows in the banking community because it seemed to grant (potentially, if not actually) an advantage to S&Ls over banks in entering new markets.

Two major developments in 1982 and 1983 in the banking industry itself appeared to further weaken restrictions against interstate branching. In September 1982 Citicorp of New York, one of the nation's leading bank holding companies, was authorized by the Federal Reserve Board to acquire the failed Fidelity Savings and Loan Association of San Francisco, one of the nation's largest savings and loans, holding close to $3 billion in assets. Then, in the spring of 1983, BankAmerica Corporation of San Francisco agreed to acquire Seafirst Corporation of Seattle, Washington, a large but troubled bank holding company, in return for a pledge from BankAmerica to pour $150 million in new capital into Seattle-First National Bank, the troubled company's principal affiliate. Thus, in both the Citicorp-Fidelity and the BankAmerica-Seafirst cases, federal banking authorities used the failing-firm doctrine to skirt around interstate branching rules. Many bankers predicted far-reaching changes in federal branching rules in the wake of these two interstate mergers.

One of the most serious dilemmas surrounding the branching issue is our comparative lack of knowledge regarding what would happen if branching were allowed over wider areas. This is all the more surprising because, as we saw earlier, research has been underway on the subject for many years. By itself, unrestricted branching seems to imply that new entry will occur in many new markets and the overall level of competition will rise. *Ceteris paribus*, the public will benefit from a wider array of better-quality financial services, offered at competitive prices, with minimal waste of resources and with reasonable profits. However, no one is in a position to *guarantee* that kind of outcome. Indeed, some opposite effects might occur. Suppose, for example, that many smaller financial institutions are absorbed by larger intermediaries, intent on expanding their branching network. Might the public wind up with fewer banking alternatives, less competition, and more failures among financial institutions? We need to know more about branching's effects.[11] The problem is that events, particularly the state of the economy and changing technology, may be bringing about banking-structure changes faster than our knowledge of the consequences can grow.

Characteristics and Growth

BANK HOLDING COMPANIES

Acquiring or absorbing banks and making them part of a branching network is one way for banking organizations to grow in size and market influence. Indeed, as we saw earlier, it is one of the dominant trends in the past century of U.S. banking. However, banks can also be linked through the multicorporate framework of the bank holding company. In this case, each bank acquired by the holding company retains its own corporate identity, but a portion (sometimes all) of its stock is controlled by a holding company organization. Often, the holding company is started by a large metropolitan bank and holds all of that bank's stock. Once started, the holding company will then use its capacity to borrow and issue stock to acquire other (usually smaller) banks and nonbank subsidiary firms. As we will soon see, banks acquired must be within the same state (with the exception of a small foothold purchase of less than 5 percent of the stock of out-of-state banks), but nonbank businesses (of a type approved by the Federal Reserve Board) can be located anywhere.

Holding company growth has been extremely rapid, especially since 1960. The reasons behind the growth of bank holding companies are generally agreed upon by authorities in the field. The bank holding company has been employed as a vehicle to (1) circumvent state laws and regula-

---

[11]A good sampling of recent research may be found in the studies by Rhoades [18] and Savage [25].

tions prohibiting or restricting branch banking, (2) allow banking organizations to diversify by entering new markets and offering new services, and (3) gain easier access to sources of capital. There is also evidence that holding companies realize economies of organization through centralized management and service facilities, especially in the fields of portfolio management, data processing, and liability management.

Chase and Mingo [5] in a recent study contend that holding company activity may result in important social benefits. By further pooling the risks of lending, these organizations may make the intermediation process more efficient. In general, holding companies are capable of greater portfolio diversification than single, independent commercial banks. Because these organizations typically are quite large, they may have an advantage in attracting highly qualified management personnel, resulting in more efficient operations and perhaps improved returns to their stockholders. On the negative side, bank holding company activity may lead to a greater concentration of financial resources in a handful of major banking organizations. Also, to the extent that holding company management is more prone to risk taking than is the management of smaller independent banks, the probability of failures among holding company–acquired banks may be increased. Unfortunately, only limited research evidence exists today on the benefits and costs of bank holding company activity. More preplexing still is the fact that research findings in this field frequently are mixed and contradictory.

Most holding company acquisitions of banks have occurred in the Midwest and South, where unit banking and limited branching laws domi-

Table 8–3   Expansion of Registered U.S. Bank Holding Companies: 1960–1980

Category	Year-End Figures						
	1960	*1970*	*1971**	*1974**	*1976**	*1977**	*1980**
Number of companies	47	121	1,567	1,752	1.913	2,027	2,905
Affiliated banks	4,267	895	2,420	3,462	3,793	3,903	4,954
Affiliated banks as a percent of all U.S. banks	3.2%	6.5%	17.%	23.9%	25.9%	26.5%	33.9%
Offices of affiliated banks	1,463	4,155	13,252	20,593	22,995	25,126	30,460
Affiliated bank offices as a percent of all U.S. bank offices	6.1%	11.8%	36.1%	47.6%	49.4%	52.4%	56.8%
Deposits of affiliated banks ($ million)	$18.2	$78.0	$341.0	$509.7	$553.7	$814.3	$1,125.0
Deposits of affiliated banks as a percent of all U.S. bank deposits	7.9%	16.2%	55.1%	67.9%	65.5%	72.9%	76.7%

*Figures beginning with 1971 include one-bank holding companies which were first required to register with the Federal Reserve Board in that year as well as multibank organizations which were required to register as early as 1957.

Sources: Board of Governors of the Federal Reserve System and the Federal Deposit Insurance Corporation.

nate. In fact, a study by Rose [19] indicates that nearly half of all holding company acquisitions of banks during the early 1970s were concentrated in the states of Florida, Missouri, Michigan, Ohio, and Texas. Three of these states have prohibited branch banking through most of their history, though Florida converted recently from unit banking to countywide branching and then to statewide branching by merger.

Holding companies generally have preferred banks in large metropolitan areas where population and personal income are growing rapidly. Presumably, these dynamic market areas offer holding company organizations higher expected returns on their investment and the opportunity to attract a greater volume of deposits. The result in the long run may be larger dividends to shareholders and an increase in overall firm size and share of the available market for financial services.[12]

Bank Holding Company Laws

Banking companies have been regulated by the federal government since the 1930s. Under the Banking Act of 1933, the Board of Governors of the Federal Reserve System was given limited powers to regulate some holding company activities. It was empowered, for example, to examine holding companies and their subsidiaries, to supervise their financial practices, and to set reserve requirements. But the Federal Reserve Board was not able to exercise effective control over the formation and expansion of bank holding companies or to prevent acquisitions that might adversely affect competition.

Effective power to regulate the postwar expansion of holding companies was granted to the Fed with passage of the Bank Holding Company Act of 1956. Under this act, a holding company which controlled either as much as a fourth of the voting stock of two or more banks or controlled the election of a majority of the directors of two or more banks was required to register with the Federal Reserve Board. Having thus become a registered holding company, the firm was required to divest itself of the control of corporations with interests not related to banking, submit to Federal Reserve regulation and examination, and receive Fed permission

---

[12]Holding company investments in banks have not always resulted in higher returns to shareholders. For example, Piper [16] examined 146 holding company acquisitions of banks during the 1960s and found that only about half were profitable. Excessive premiums paid for bank stock adversely affected the returns from many individual acquisitions. However, a recent study by Varvel [31] finds that holding companies experienced lower earnings during the initial period of reorganization and acquisitions, but, in later years, earnings grew at a more rapid pace for the holding company than would have been true if the holding company had not been formed. Similarly, Frieder and Apilado [10] after a review of numerous bank acquisitions recently concluded that holding company bank purchases were profitable for one through eight years and sometimes longer, regardless of the state of the economy.

before acquiring more than 5 percent of the stock of another bank. In considering an application to form a bank holding company, the Federal Reserve Board was required to consider the solvency of the company, its management and prospects for earnings, benefits to the public that might result from the transaction, and the possibility that the local banking market might become too concentrated.[13]

Ten years later, in 1966, the Bank Holding Company Act was amended to clarify the relative importance of *public convenience* and *competition* as matters to be examined by regulators in approving or denying holding company acquisitions. The 1966 amendments permitted the Federal Reserve Board to approve holding company acquisitions that might lessen competition, provided this effect was clearly outweighed by benefits to the public. However, the amendments did not require holding companies controlling only one bank to register. Due to this oversight in the law, the number of one-bank holding companies grew rapidly during the late 1960s and included some of the largest banks in the United States. These companies sought to diversify into new product lines and new geographic markets by acquiring a variety of nonbank businesses—mortgage companies, leasing firms, finance companies, data processing firms, and many others. Fearing that holding company penetration into areas other than banking would break down the traditional separation between banking and commerce, Congress passed the 1970 amendments to the Bank Holding Company Act.[14]

---

[13]It was expressly left to the states, however, to regulate holding company activity within their own borders if they so chose. A few states, such as Oklahoma and Louisiana, moved to restrict or prohibit the formation of multibank holding companies. Others, such as New Jersey, increased the potential for holding company growth by changing their laws to permit statewide expansion. (See especially Rose and Fraser [24]).

A key feature of bank holding company law at the federal level which affects the states is the so-called Douglas Amendment, which prohibits a holding company from acquiring more than 5 percent of the shares of a bank located outside the company's home state. The result of this restriction, which parallels the McFadden Act's prohibition of interstate branch banking, is to encourage holding companies to expand their interstate acquisitions of finance companies, mortgage and real estate companies, and other nonbank firms to be able to offer financial services regionally or nationally.

[14]Public policy in the United States since the 19th century has aimed at minimizing the interconnections between commercial banking and the industrial and manufacturing sectors of the economy. The fear that banks and their corporate customers, if linked by common ownership, would represent a formidable and undesirable concentration of economic and financial power is reflected in a host of federal and state banking regulations. Probably the most notable is the historic prohibition against commercial banks investing in common stock or underwriting new stock issues. This prohibition against banks underwriting corporate stock issues is one of the provisions of the Glass-Steagall Act passed by Congress in 1934.

The 1970 amendments had three main goals, each of which has significantly influenced the subsequent growth of U.S. bank holding companies. First, one-bank holding companies were no longer excluded from registration requirements. Now one-bank as well as multibank companies must register with the Federal Reserve Board and secure approval for any acquisitions of bank or nonbank businesses. Second, the definition of holding company *control* over individual banks was expanded. If a company was found to exercise a "controlling influence" over a bank, it might be required to register with the Federal Reserve Board as a bank holding company, regardless of what proportion of bank stock the company held. Finally, the nonbanking activities which a company could pursue were restricted to include only those "so closely related to banking or managing or controlling banks as to be a proper incident thereto . . . ." In addition to this so-called closely related test, the 1970 amendments imposed a public benefits test on all future bank holding company acquisitions of nonbank firms. Only those nonbank acquisitions that "can reasonably be expected to produce benefits to the public, such as greater convenience, increased competition, or gains in efficiency, that outweigh possible adverse effects, such as undue concentration of resources, decreased or unfair competition, conflict of interest, or unsound banking practices" may be approved.[15]

Nonbank Businesses Acquired by Bank Holding Companies

The provision of the 1970 amendments applying to nonbanking activities confined holding company acquisitions to business activities functionally related to banking. Beginning in 1971 the Federal Reserve Board conducted hearings on various nonbanking activities which holding companies were then seeking to acquire. Since then, the Board has added a substantial number of permissible nonbank activities to its approved list, including mortgage banking, full pay-out leasing, courier services, finance companies offering both consumer and commercial credit, credit life insurance, credit card companies, data processing companies, insurance agencies, factoring companies, industrial banks, trust companies, investment or financial advising firms, real estate appraisers, and real estate investment trusts. However, the addition of new nonbank activities has slowed significantly in recent years due to financial problems experienced by many banks and bank holding companies, a more conservative regulatory stance at federal and state levels, and the lack of sufficient numbers of skilled management personnel in the holding company field.

---

[15]Bank Holding Company Act, Section 4 (c) (8) as amended by the Bank Holding Company Act Amendments of 1970.

The acquisition of nonbank businesses through holding companies has been an attractive vehicle for growth among large banking organizations in recent years. As we noted earlier, nonbank acquisitions have served as a device to get around antibranching laws such as the McFadden Act. As Table 8–4 shows, in many cases holding companies have set up new (*de novo*) nonbank businesses instead of purchasing existing firms. However, the volume of acquisitions of existing nonbank firms also has been substantial in recent years, as Table 8–5 indicates.

Which nonbank businesses have bank holding companies preferred to acquire? Table 8–5 suggests that firms offering commercial and consumer credit, particularly consumer finance companies and mortgage banking companies, lead the list. Not far behind have been purchases of insurance agencies and underwriters to provide credit life insurance and other insurance services. Trust companies and data processing firms aiding in the storage and transfer of information also have ranked high as holding company targets for acquisition and expansion. Addition of these firms to a banking organization makes possible entry into new markets, greater diversification, and the offering of a more complete line of services to the customer.

CHAIN BANKING

Bank offices may be linked together through banking chains as well as through holding companies. Chain banking refers to the control of more than one bank by an individual or informal group of individuals. Due to the informal nature of most chain relationships, the extent of chain banking activity is extremely difficult to measure. However, substantial chain banking activity is known to exist in certain sections of the United States,

**Table 8–4   Number of De Novo
Nonbank Business Entries by
U.S. Bank Holding Companies: 1971–1977**

Year	Number of De Novo Entries into Nonbank Businesses
1971	71
1972	251
1973	495
1974	542
1975	297
1976	309
1977	471
Total	2,436

Source: Stephen A. Rhoades, "The Competitive Effects of Interstate Banking," *Federal Reserve Bulletin*, January 1980, p. 4.

Table 8–5   Number of Approved Acquisitions of Nonbank Firms by U.S. Bank Holding Companies: 1971–1977

Nonbank Business Activity	1971	1972	1973	1974	1975	1976	1977	Total Acquisitions by U.S. Bank Holding Companies
Mortgage banking	2	11	34	33	13	3	12	108
Consumer and commercial finance	2	26	231	160	8	58	14	499
Factoring	0	4	3	2	0	2	2	13
Insurance agencies	0	13	25	34	33	26	10	141
Insurance underwriting	0	0	13	13	13	17	8	64
Trust activities	1	1	4	1	3	3	1	14
Leasing	1	1	8	4	3	14	5	36
Community development	0	0	0	0	0	0	2	2
Financial advice	0	0	5	11	1	1	9	27
Data processing	0	1	6	6	4	4	16	37
Other activities	0	2	3	0	4	4	10	35
Total	6	59	332	264	82	138	95	976

Source: Stephen A. Rhoades, "The Competitive Effects of Interstate Banking," *Federal Reserve Bulletin*, January 1980, p. 4.

especially where there are large numbers of relatively small unit banks and branch banks.

A survey was carried out in the early 1960s by the Federal Reserve Board for evidence on the extent of chain banking in the United States.[16] A summary of the survey's results by Darnell [7] revealed that 19 percent of all member banks were then parts of chains having common ownership ties. In addition, an estimated 1,150 nonmember banks were operating in chains, bringing the total for all chain banks to about 2,300 institutions, representing nearly 18 percent of all insured U.S. commercial banks. These 2,300 banks held nearly $53 billion in assets, or close to 20 percent of the assets of all U.S. banks with insured deposits. A bank was defined as a member of a chain if it had a major stockholder (with 5 percent or more of total shares outstanding), director, or officer in common with one or more other banks.

Since the Bank Holding Company Act forces a company holding as much as 25 percent of the stock of at least one bank or, if less than 25 percent, having a controlling influence over at least one bank to register with the Federal Reserve, many companies have held their ownership interest in banks to slightly less than 25 percent of the outstanding shares, thus escaping federal registration requirements. Where control was required, these firms would bring together informal groups of stockholders who, collectively, would hold a controlling interest in the bank. Many large

---

[16]The full report on the Federal Reserve survey is contained in [30].

chain-banking organizations today consist of large metropolitan-based commercial banks with minority stock holdings in smaller affiliated banks in surrounding areas.[17] A number of holding company bank acquisitions approved in recent years have been designed merely to bring under the same corporate umbrella what had previously been accomplished through chain-banking organizations. Most of these chain-related acquisitions have occurred principally in states in the Midwest and South, where chain banking is still important.

THE SYMBIOTIC FINANCIAL FIRM

As the decade of the 1980s began, a new challenger to banking's preeminent position as a supplier of credit and funds-management services appeared on the scene.[18] The new competitors were quickly labeled "symbiotics" or "financial supermarkets"—conglomerate corporations embracing a large number of subsidiaries, many or all of which offered financial services to the public. (Figure 8–3 shows a hypothetical picture of a symbiotic financial firm and some of the subsidiary businesses it might choose to acquire.) Due to their large size and capable management, they pose a significant challenge to banks serving the same market area. In addition, while banks are heavily regulated in virtually all of their activities, the new symbiotics are not banks—at least, not legally speaking—and therefore they escape the regulations applicable to banks under both state and federal laws.

What are these firms? They include some of the leading financial and nonfinancial businesses in the United States that only recently have begun to grow even larger by acquiring subsidiaries in financial industries. While some symbiotics date back to the World War I era, 1981 was a high-water mark in the growth of symbiotics and in public awareness of their activities. In that year Sears Roebuck & Company, which had been involved in sales financing, real estate, and insurance activities for many years, announced its intention to acquire control of Coldwell Banker & Company, the leading real-estate broker in the United States. Also during 1981, Sears manuevered to purchase Dean Witter Reynolds Organization, Inc. a major securities broker. Not to be outdone, Prudential Insurance Company moved to add Bache Group, Inc., another major security brokerage firm, while American Express credit card company responded by linking up

---

[17]Early in 1978 the three federal banking agencies carried out a study of the number and amount of loans made by each bank to executive officers, major stockholders, and directors of other U.S. banks. A total of 6,721 commercial banks, or about 48 percent of all U.S. banks, reported having such loans outstanding as of September 30, 1977. Similarly, 902 banks reported loans secured primarily by the stock of other banks or bank holding companies totaling $2.7 billion. Thus chain banking still appears to be a substantial factor in U.S. banking (see, in particular [30]).

[18]This section depends, in part, on Rose [22].

Figure 8–3 How a Symbiotic Financial Company Might Be Organized

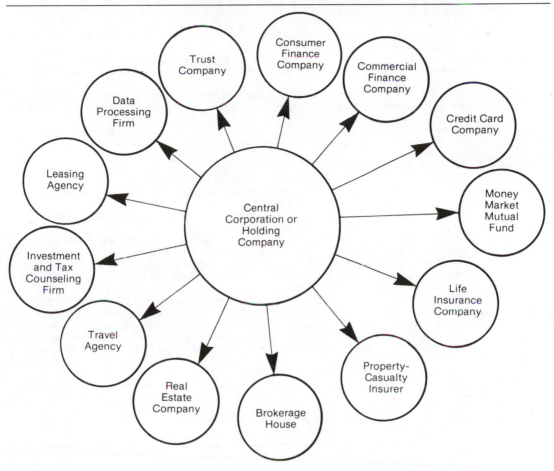

with the security brokerage firm of Shearson Loeb Rhodes, Inc. (See Figure 8–4 for some examples of recent acquisitions by symbiotic financial firms.)

The acquisitions made by Sears, Prudential, and American Express were important and had a dramatic impact on the financial community and especially on bankers. But as large as these companies are, they represent in a sense the tip of the financial iceberg. They were preceded by decades of financial adventurism by numerous other industrial firms, many of which had well-established captive finance companies that helped finance sales of their products. The best known examples are General Motors, which controls General Motors Acceptance Corporation, an auto financing company; and General Electric, International Harvester, Motor-

---

Figure 8–4   Examples of Recent Expansion or Expansion Plans by Symbiotic Financial Firms

April 1981	Prudential Insurance Company announces plans to acquire Bache Group, Inc., a major securities broker.
April 1981	American Express Company, a leading credit card firm, announces a proposed merger with Shearson Loeb Rhodes, Inc., a brokerage firm.
April 1981	New Equitable Life Assurance Society of the United States, which also operates a money market fund, asks the New York State Insurance Department for permission to offer corporate cash-management services.
June 1981	Baldwin-United Corporation, a firm with interests in mortgage banking, insurance, trading stamps, and the manufacture of pianos and organs, signs an option to purchase savings and loan associations in several states.
September 1981	National Steel Corporation arranges the largest merger of savings and loan associations in U.S. history, purchasing thrift institutions in Florida and New York and combining these with savings and loans in San Francisco.
October 1981	Sears Roebuck & Company agrees to acquire Dean Witter Reynolds Organization, Inc., a major securities broker, and Coldwell Banker & Company, a leading real estate broker.
October 1981	American Can Company announces plans to enter the financial services field by acquiring Associated Madison Companies, a life insurance marketer.
November 1981	BankAmerica Corporation announces its intention to acquire Charles Schwab Corporation, parent firm for the largest discount brokerage house in the U.S.
November 1981	Security Pacific Corporation announces that Security Pacific National Bank will establish a discount brokerage service in collaboration with Fidelity Brokerage Services, Inc.
August 1982	The Comptroller of the Currency grants approval to Security Pacific Corporation to create a discount brokerage unit as a subsidiary of Security Pacific National Bank—the first federal approval of bank entry into the discount brokerage business.
September 1982	Citizens and Southern National Bank, Atlanta, announces plans for a discount brokerage unit.
September 1982	Kemper Corporation, a diversified insurance company, agrees to buy 80 percent of Prescott, Ball & Tuben, a regional security brokerage firm, the third regional broker acquired by Kemper in 1982. Kemper Financial Services company announced it had initiated the development of a cash-management service which would encompass checking account services and stock purchases and sales.
September 1982	Citicorp, New York, a bank holding company, is granted approval by the Federal Reserve Board to acquire Fidelity Savings and Loan Association of San Francisco.
November 1982	Transamerica Corporation, a financial conglomerate with investments in insurance, equipment leasing, travel agencies, and manufacturing, offers to acquire Fred S. James & Company, the nation's fourth largest insurance broker.
April 1983	Merrill Lynch agrees, subject to regulatory approval, to acquire Raritan Valley Financial Corporation, which owns a New Jersey savings and loan association.

---

ola, Ford, and J. C. Penney, all of which have financial subsidiaries to facilitate their product sales. There are no legal or regulatory barriers preventing any of these firms or, for that matter, any other industrial or manufacturing company from branching out into new financial endeavors, bringing them into head-on competition with the nation's largest banks for financial service customers.[19] Indeed, as the 1980s began, this new fi-

---

[19]The challenge to banks posed by the symbiotics seems especially potent due to the fact that some of the symbiotics already have extensive branch office systems. For example, Merrill Lynch, the largest U.S. security broker, which recently has been offering checking services through a money market mutual fund and loans against a security holding account, has more than 300 office outlets nationwide. Sears operates more than 800 offices, a savings and loan association in California, and a car rental agency. Moreover, the well-known Allstate

nancial option was recognized clearly and acted upon by several companies which, unlike Sears, GM, GE, and Ford, for example, had no significant prior history in the financial services field. Thus Baldwin-United Corporation, known for its pianos and organs, moved to expand its operations in the savings and loan and insurance field as the 1980s began—a move followed by such industrial giants as American Can Company and National Steel Corporation.

The "Level Playing Field" Issue

The rapid growth of the symbiotics has brought into sharper focus a debate which has engulfed the banking community for several decades. The basic issue is one of *regulatory equity*—giving banks a "level playing field" in competition with nonbank thrift institutions and with the developing symbiotics.

During the post–World War II period, credit unions, savings and loan associations, and savings banks held a number of significant regulatory advantages over banks. Commercial banks generally faced stiff reserve requirements on their deposits (imposed by the Federal Reserve System or by the states) compared to lenient or no reserve requirements for nonbank thrifts. In addition, banks are subject to the same corporate tax rate that industrial and manufacturing corporations face, while the thrifts were either tax-exempt (as credit unions are) or given generous tax shelters (e.g., savings and loans). Commercial bankers argued that these regulatory differences placed the banks at a decided disadvantage in competing for loan and deposit business with nonbank thrifts. Many bankers were somewhat relieved when, in 1980, Congress passed the Depository Institutions Deregulation and Monetary Control Act. As we will note again in Chapters 13–15, this sweeping new law made credit unions, savings and loans, and other nonbank thrifts subject to federal reserve requirements just like commercial banks. While this regulatory change did not completely level the playing field for banks, it at least tilted the field a little more toward horizontal in the bank–nonbank thrift competitive game.[20]

Insurance Company, owned by Sears, operates out of well over 1,000 offices in all regions of the U.S. Added to this are the millions of Sears' credit customers who might someday be presented with the option of depositing funds through their credit cards.

[20]Not all analysts completely agree with this statement. While the Depository Institutions Deregulation Act of 1980 imposed uniform reserve requirements on all depository institutions, it also granted nonbank thrifts new powers. For example, these institutions were able to offer interest-bearing NOW accounts to compete with bank checkbook deposits and NOWs. Savings and loan associations were granted authority to offer credit cards, consumer, and business loans. (Other services permitted nonbank thrifts by the 1980 law are detailed in Chapters 13 and 14.) Thus, while the playing field where banks and nonbank thrifts competed looked a little more level after 1980, it also looked a bit more crowded with competitors.

A further step in expanding permissible service offerings of nonbank thrifts occurred in October 1982 when President Reagan signed into law the Garn–St. Germain Depository Institutions Act. This law extended to both banks and thrifts the power to offer savings accounts which would compete with high-rate money market fund accounts. The new law also sharply expanded the lending powers of federally chartered savings and loans which were authorized to offer commercial loans up to 10 percent of their assets after 1983, increase nonresidential loans up to 40 percent of their assets, and expand consumer loans up to a maximum of 30 percent of their assets. Thus savings and loans were granted credit powers similar to commercial banks.

Then the symbiotics began to enter the financial services field in a big way, offering services ranging from financial counseling, travel planning, real estate and security brokerage, investment underwriting, commercial and consumer credit, draftable (checking) accounts, and mutual funds. But these organizations under current law are not subject to reserve requirements, nor do the symbiotics face interest-rate ceilings, regular examination, continuous supervision, or the need to gain regulatory approval each time they wish to acquire a new subsidiary firm or open a new branch office. The future growth and expansion of symbiotics appears to be dependent entirely upon the decisions and resources of the symbiotics themselves, not upon the approval of regulators.

Therefore, the rise of the symbiotics has resurrected the level-playing-field issue all over again. Bankers typically argue that trying to compete against the unregulated symbiotics is like a boxer with one arm tied behind the back entering a match against a two-fisted opponent. Yet, in all fairness, the banking community has not been idle in developing a response to the growing symbiotics. Banks, especially the largest ones, are in the process of developing new services to compete with the symbiotics.

As Figure 8–4 suggests, several of the nation's largest banks have developed new subsidiaries to offer security brokerage services or aligned themselves with securities firms. One prominent example is the November 1981 acquisition of Charles Schwab Corporation, the largest discount brokerage house in the United States,[21] by BankAmerica Corporation, then the world's largest banking corporation. Other major U.S. banks have set up joint ventures with large brokerage houses to supply low-cost security brokering services to their customers. Examples include Crocker

---

[21]Discount brokerage houses began a period of rapid growth in the mid-1970s as a result of federal government pressure to halt the system of fixed security-trading commissions on the major stock exchanges. Discount brokers, which currently account for only about 10 percent of securities brokering, offer only to execute a customer's buy or sell order. They do not offer research or other securities-trading services as do the large brokerage companies. While discount brokers have only a small share of the trading market, their share may grow dramatically as banks offer the service.

National Bank of San Francisco, which began a brokerage program through Bradford Broker Settlement; and New York's Chemical Bank, linked with Pershing & Company for provision of brokerage services. Such acquisitions and joint ventures have been vigorously opposed by the Securities Industry Association, which views them as a possible violation of the Glass-Steagall Act of 1933. Bankers and the Comptroller of the Currency have argued that nothing in the Glass-Steagall Act prevents banks from buying and selling privately issued securities on behalf of their customers. Thus, while many bankers feel threatened by the rise of the symbiotics, others have elected to enter the competition by expanding the range of financial services offered through their holding companies.

One of the most important vehicles for change in banking structure during the postwar period has been the merger. Mergers have absorbed more than 3,000 separately incorporated U.S. banks since World War II. The pace of bank merger activity has slowed in recent years, however, due to tougher regulatory and antitrust restrictions, liberalization of branch banking laws in many states, the growth of bank holding companies, and difficulties in the stock market. Nevertheless, mergers still continue to be an important avenue for structural change in banking.

BANK MERGERS

Regulatory Controls over Bank Mergers

In the early years after World War II, bank mergers were regulated primarily by the states—a fact that contributed to a rapid increase in mergers, particularly during the 1950s. But with passage of the Bank Merger Act in 1960, Congress required that all mergers involving insured banks have the prior approval of their principal federal supervisory agency—the Comptroller of the Currency, the Board of Governors of the Federal Reserve System, or the Federal Deposit Insurance Corporation. The Bank Merger Act also enunciated the factors regulatory agencies must consider in approving a merger, such as its effects on competition and the convenience and needs of the public.

It was widely thought until the 1960s that, as part of a regulated industry, commercial banks were exempt from federal antitrust laws. This belief was dispelled in 1963 and 1965, however. In the Philadelphia National Bank and First National Bank of Lexington cases, the Supreme Court held that the impact on competition was the controlling factor in determining the legality of a bank merger and that the antitrust laws were fully applicable to commercial banking.[22] Congress responded to these court decisions

---

[22]See especially *United States* v. *Philadelphia National Bank et al.*, 210F Supp. 348 (1962)' 835 ct. 1715 (1963); and *United States* v. *First National Bank and Trust Co. of Lexington et al.*, 208F Supp. 456 (1962) 845 ct. 1033 (1964).

by passing the 1966 amendments to the Bank Merger Act. These amendments permit the regulatory authorities to approve a merger if its anticompetitive effects are clearly outweighed by a probable improvement in the convenience and needs of the public. The courts and bank regulatory agencies, however, continue to emphasize the competitive aspects of any proposed merger.

In 1968 the Department of Justice published a series of guidelines indicating at what point it would challenge a merger involving banks and other corporations under the Clayton Act's Section 7, which forbids mergers acting to restrain or restrict trade. In order to promote a market structure that is fully competitive, the Justice Department indicated it would probably challenge commercial bank mergers when a proposed acquisition would result in an excessive concentration of total deposits in a few large banking organizations. Justice was particularly concerned about markets where the four largest banks held 75 percent or more of the deposits. Mergers in these so-called highly concentrated markets were more likely to be challenged than in markets where the share of deposits held by leading banks was lower. In 1982 the Reagan Administration announced new merger guidelines. Markets across the country were to be divided into three groups—least concentrated, moderately concentrated, and highly concentrated. Similar to the original merger guidelines, a bank merger is most likely to be challenged in a highly concentrated market (roughly where the four largest banks have at least 70 percent of total deposits).[23]

Effects of Bank Mergers

The rapid pace of postwar U.S. bank mergers has raised a number of important public policy questions. For example, who benefits (if anyone does) from the merger of two banks? The public? Bank management? Bank employees? The stockholders? Moreover, there is a great deal of conflict in the existing research evidence concerning the real impact of mergers upon the behavior of individual banks. Some recent studies suggest that bank mergers have improved the quality of services offered, lowered prices charged, and resulted in greater public convenience. For example, Kohn [14] examined data for all commercial banks in New York State which had merged at least once during the 1950s. He found that the public generally was charged lower rates on loans and reduced service charges on deposits in the wake of a merger transaction. On the negative side, compensating balances required on loans to small business firms and rates on new car loans tended to be higher, as did service charges on special demand deposits. Horvitz and Shull [12] looked further into the issues raised

---

[23]See especially Gagnon [11].

by Kohn, studying the behavior of unit banks converted into branch offices after merger. They found that the policies of banks acquired by merger were soon made to coincide with those of the acquiring institutions. Higher interest rates on thrift deposits and lower rates on installment loans, mortgages, and business loans generally were the result. Credit policies regarding permissible loan maturities and down payments generally were liberalized in favor of the customer.

Not all studies of bank mergers come to such positive conclusions, however. For example, Cohen and Reid [6] observed that overall bank size rose, which contributed to the prestige of management but did little for stockholders or the public. Another study by Bacon [1] reviewed the effects of 15 bank mergers in Marion County, Indiana. Stockholders at these banks were given substantial premiums on their stock, while management salaries and fringe benefits improved. Finally, a study by Smith [27] found very few changes of any kind flowing from the merger of two banks. Total revenues increased following consummation of the merger transaction, but expenses climbed as well. As a result, bank earnings were generally unaffected by merger. Thus the true effects of mergers among commercial banks are in dispute and remain an open question awaiting further research.

MEMBERSHIP IN THE FEDERAL RESERVE SYSTEM

Another major structural change in U.S. banking in recent years has been the *withdrawal* of member banks from the Federal Reserve system. This exodus from the Fed has resulted in a decline in the total number of member banks and bank assets subject to direct Fed supervision and regulation. For example, in 1960 there were 6,174 member banks out of a total of 14,471 commercial banks, or 46 percent of the total. These member institutions held 84 percent of all U.S. bank deposits. By 1980, however, there were only 5,422 member banks, representing just 37 percent of the total industry population. At that time the share of industrywide deposits controlled by member institutions had shrunk to only 74 percent. Moreover, there is evidence that the speed of withdrawal from the Fed accelerated during the 1970s[24] (see Table 8–6).

The principal reasons banks left the Fed in such large numbers were the higher reserve requirements levied by the Federal Reserve Board against member-bank deposits compared to lower effective reserve requirements imposed by many states on state-chartered nonmember banks. In about half the states, percentage reserve requirements imposed on demand deposits were about the same as those called for by the Fed, and 15 states ac-

---

[24]See especially the discussion of causes and effects of the membership withdrawal trend by Rose [17].

Table 8–6   The Trend of Bank Membership in the Federal Reserve System

Year	Number of Member Banks	Percent of All U.S. Deposits Held by Member Banks
1945	6,884	86.3
1950	6.873	85.2
1955	6,543	85.2
1960	6,174	84.0
1965	6,221	82.9
1970	5,767	80.1
1975	5,787	57.2
1980	5,422	74.1
1981	5,471	70.9
1982	5,619	70.6

Source: Board of Governors of the Federal Reserve System.

tually levied higher percentage requirements than did the Federal Reserve. But there was a critical distinction prior to the decade of the 1980s between Federal Reserve and state reserve requirements in the definition of those assets eligible to be counted as *legal reserves*.

As we point out again in Chapter 9, legal reserves are simply those assets held by a commercial bank which the regulatory authorities permit it to count in meeting reserve requirements called for by law. The Federal Reserve System counts only vault cash held on bank premises and deposits with the Federal Reserve bank in the region as legal reserves. In contrast, individual state laws differed greatly in the assets which could be counted as legal reserves, with some states permitting their banks to count investments in interest-bearing U.S. government and municipal securities as meeting reserve requirements.

As we saw in Chapter 5, the differences between state reserve requirements and Fed reserve requirements were, for all practical purposes, eliminated with passage of the Depository Institutions Deregulation and Monetary Control Act of 1980. All federally insured or supervised depository institutions (including commercial banks, credit unions, savings and loan associations, and savings banks) offering transactions accounts (such as checking accounts and NOWs) or nonpersonal time deposits were made subject to reserve requirements set by the Fed. As a general rule, this new law meant that member banks would experience a reduction in required reserves while nonmember deposit-type institutions would face higher required reserves. To make adjustment to the new law as smooth as possible, an eight-year phase-in of new reserve requirements was allowed for nonmember institutions and four years for member banks. At the same time, all depository institutions keeping reserves at the Fed were granted access to loans from the discount windows of the Federal Reserve banks.

The Depository Institutions law has, for the time being, halted the exodus of banks from the Federal Reserve System. There is little incentive to leave the system, since deposit reserve requirements are uniform for members and nonmembers. Today, the distinction between member and nonmember institutions is relevant mainly for examination and supervisory purposes. The Fed has supervisory and examining powers only over banks that are members of its system.

It is interesting that the withdrawal of banks from the Fed generated many differing views as to its effects. To the Federal Reserve System it was a serious matter because, allegedly, the exodus hampered the Fed's ability to control the nation's money supply. As former Federal Reserve Board Chairman William Miller claimed in testimony before Congress:

> It is essential that the Federal Reserve maintain adequate control over the monetary aggregates if the nation is to succeed in its efforts to curb inflation, sustain economic growth, and maintain the value of the dollar in international exchange markets. The attrition in deposits subject to reserve requirements set by the Federal Reserve weakens the linkage between member bank reserves and the monetary aggregates.[25]

In the Fed's view the nonmember bank sector was growing faster than the member-bank sector, and thus the proportion of the nation's money supply directly under Federal Reserve control and supervision was shrinking. Nonmember institutions were not even obligated to report their deposits and loans to the Fed, though some did voluntarily. How could the nation's money supply—composed largely of bank deposits—be adequately controlled under these circumstances?

As passage of the Depository Institutions Deregulation and Monetary Control Act of 1980 indicated, Congress was persuaded by the Fed's arguments. All depository institutions not only came under common reserve requirements, but also were required to report their assets and liabilities according to schedules set by the Federal Reserve. However, were all of these rule changes really necessary? Did the Fed receive more regulatory power (at the expense of the states) than it really needed to carry out monetary policy?

Some analysts answer in the affirmative. After all, as we noted in Chapter 5, reserve requirements are not used very often as a tool of monetary policy, principally because their impact on the banking system is too powerful and difficult to control. Moreover, monetary policy in the United

---

[25]Statement by G. William Miller, Chairman of the Federal Reserve Board before the Banking Committee, U.S. House of Representatives, January 24, 1979.

States is carried out mainly through open-market operations conducted at the Trading Desk of the Federal Reserve Bank of New York. Open-market operations do not depend for their effectiveness on the level or distribution of bank deposits. However, the new rules in 1980 did bring about greater regulatory equity, at least as far as reserve and reporting requirements were concerned, among all depository institutions.

BANK FAILURES

Commercial banks in the United States are private corporations organized to provide maximum, or at least satisfactory, profits for their shareholders. Not all banks are successful, however, and a few are forced to close their doors each year. Indeed, in the absence of effective regulations to protect the public, substantial numbers of banks probably would fail each year. For example, prior to the imposition of federal and state controls over the chartering and operation of commercial banks, a massive number of U.S. banks collapsed during the 1920s and 1930s. Succumbing to the deepest economic recession in American history, the number of U.S. banks dropped from about 30,000 in 1920 to little more than 14,000 by 1940. In the wake of that calamity, Congress created a system of deposit insurance under the administration of the Federal Deposit Insurance Corporation. Banks were forbidden to underwrite corporate stocks, and maximum permissible interest rates were imposed on all categories of deposits, to mention only a few of the more important legal and regulatory changes. More recently, when the number of bank failures accelerated in the late 1970s and early 1980s, Congress responded with passage of the Garn–St. Germain Depository Institutions Act of 1982, permitting banks and savings and loans to acquire large failing financial institutions across state boundaries. In addition, the 1982 law permitted the Federal Deposit Insurance Corporation and the Federal Savings and Loan Insurance Corporation to accept net worth certificates from troubled banks and savings and loans they insure in return for agency-issued promissory notes which the troubled institutions can hold as assets. This major regulatory step, intended to reduce the drain on federal insurance funds, may serve to head off a number of bank and thrift institution failures.

Due to more stringent federal and state regulations and generally prosperous economic conditions, the number of failures during the postwar period has been relatively small—only about 1 to 2 percent of the total U.S. banking population. Between 1964 and 1980, only 214 U.S. commercial and savings banks failed, an average of just 6 bank failures each year (see Table 8–7). The relative sizes of these bankrupt institutions varied markedly. At one extreme was Franklin National Bank, headquartered in New York City, which was declared insolvent in 1974 while holding $1.4 billion in deposits. Franklin's failure occurred less than a year after U.S.

Table 8-7   Number of U.S. Failed Banks: 1946–1982

Year	Insured	Noninsured	Total	Year	Insured	Noninsured	Total
1946	1	1	2	1965	5	4	9
1947	5	1	6	1966	7	1	8
1948	3	0	3	1967	4	0	4
1949	5	4	9	1968	3	0	3
1950	4	1	5	1969	9	0	9
1951	2	3	5	1970	7	1	8
1952	3	1	4	1971	6	0	6
1953	4	1	5	1972	1	2	3
1954	2	2	4	1973	6	0	6
1955	5	0	5	1974	4	0	4
1956	2	1	3	1975	13	1	14
1957	2	1	3	1976	16	1	17
1958	4	5	9	1977	6	0	6
1959	3	0	3	1978	7	0	7
1960	1	1	2	1979	10	0	10
1961	5	4	9	1980	10	0	10
1962	1	2	3	1981	10	—	10
1963	2	0	2	1982	42	—	42
1964	7	1	8				

Source: Federal Deposit Insurance Corporation, *Annual Report*, various issues.

National Bank in San Diego closed its doors with over $900 million in deposits. However, two banks with less than $50,000 in deposits also were closed during the postwar period. Both the number of bank failures and the mean size of failed banks seem to have increased in recent years. For example, between 1970 and 1980, 86 U.S. banks failed—about 8 per year. And in 1982 a postwar record was set when 42 commercial and savings banks closed, the largest number for a single year since 1940, but even this record was exceeded in 1983. As Table 8–8 suggests, the average deposit size of failing banks appears to have increased significantly in recent years.

Reports issued by the bank regulatory agencies generally imply that the principal causes of bank failures are (1) self-serving loans to bank management or to the bank's owners; (2) general mismanagement of loans, defalcations, or embezzlements; and (3) miscellaneous manipulations of bank funds.[26] General economic conditions are not usually assigned a major role in causing recent bank failures; however, the number of U.S. bank failures has been slightly higher, on average, in periods of recession than in periods of prosperity since World War II. Another factor closely related to failures is the *size* of individual banks. The large majority of closings have occurred among relatively small banks. Close to 60 percent of U.S.

---

[26]See, in particular, the studies by Barnett [2], Benston [3,4], and Rose and Scott [23].

Table 8–8   Deposits of Banks Closed Because of Financial Difficulties: 1946–1982 ($000)

Year	Total Deposits for Insured and Noninsured Banks	Year	Total Deposits for Insured and Noninsured Banks
1946	$ 494	1965	$ 45,256
1947	7,207	1966	106,171
1948	10,674	1967	10,878
1949	9,217	1968	22,524
1950	5,555	1969	40,134
1951	6,464	1970	55,244
1952	3,313	1971	132,152
1953	45,101	1972	99,784
1954	2,948	1973	971,296
1955	11,953	1974	1,575,832
1956	11,690	1975	340,574
1957	12,502	1976	865,659
1958	10,413	1977	205,208
1959	2,593	1978	854,154
1960	7,965	1979	110,696
1961	10,611	1980	216,300
1962	4,231	1981	3,826,022
1963	23,444	1982	9,908,379
1964	23,867		

Source: Federal Deposit Insurance Corporation, *Annual Report*, 1982.

banks collapsing during the postwar years held $2 million or less in total deposits. Smaller banks appear to be more vulnerable to failure than larger institutions. The asset portfolios of the smaller institutions are not as well diversified, exposing them to more risk. Lack of geographic diversification also appears to affect the bank failure rate. Thus unit banks without branch offices appear to be more prone to failure than do branch banks, because the unit organizations appear to be more closely tied to the economic fate of one particular geographic area or local market.

Few efforts have been made until recently to predict bank failures. One of the more successful studies by Meyer and Pifer [15] used regression analysis in an attempt to discriminate between banks about to fail and paired sound banks operating in the same economic area. These researchers were successful in identifying the majority of failing institutions on the basis of a limited set of operating ratios. However, few financial ratios were able to forecast financial collapse more than a year or two before the event. Later, Sinkey and Walker [26] studied the behavior of banks identified by federal examiners as problem institutions. Statistical comparisons with sound banks revealed that the problem institutions had lower liquidity and were less efficient in controlling expenses. Examiners' ratings of individual banks also were the subject of a study by Stuhr and Van Wicklen [28]. The ratings are an overall index of each bank's financial condition, based upon information contained in bank examination reports. Variables used to sort banks into high- and low-rated categories included measures of the mix of assets, adequacy of capital, the competency of management, bank size, and organizational structure. The discriminant functions were quite satisfactory, correctly classifying more than 95 percent of all banks studied. These results seem promising as a possible forerunner of an early warning system for problem banks. However, the authors point out that more work needs to be done to determine if the results will still hold for other banks in other time periods.

Finally, a recent study by Rose and Scott [23] compared 69 U.S. commercial banks failing during the years 1965–75 with comparable size solvent banks serving the same countywide banking markets. Failing institutions were found to display greater risk exposure and lower proportions of liquid assets to total assets than solvent institutions. The failing banks also appear to have been beset by serious expense-control problems, which served to reduce their earnings significantly below industry norms for an extended time period. The authors concluded that the failing institutions were vulnerable over a considerable length of time before financial and other problems overpowered their weak defenses.

In brief, the question of whether bank failures and banks in financial trouble can be detected in advance and, presumably, helped is an interesting and unresolved issue. Limited evidence suggests that selected financial ratios—particularly those linked to earnings, efficiency, and liquidity— are able to distinguish between "normal" institutions and those with financial problems. Generally, however, there is not much advance warning— perhaps two or three years before a bank is in serious trouble and in need of closer supervision by the regulatory authorities. As in the past, the number of bank failures in future years will depend primarily on the competency and honesty of management and owners.

CONCLUSIONS

The structure of the American banking system has a profound impact upon the performance of individual commercial banks that operate within that system. The number and relative size of competitors that each commercial bank faces influence the makeup of its balance sheet, earnings, expenses, and growth. And, as we have seen, state and federal laws are a major determinant of the competitive environment faced by individual banks. Indeed, we can confidently make the same statement regarding all major financial intermediaries active today in the U.S. economy: *State and federal regulation is one of the most important elements in determining the structure of financial intermediation and, through structure, the degree of competition faced by individual financial institutions.*

We must not overemphasize the role of structure, however. Within the constraints imposed by law and structure there is still great latitude for the management of individual financial institutions, including commercial banks, to shape their performance. Whether a bank, savings and loan association, insurance company, or other financial institution is profitable, fast-growing, or public-service-oriented depends upon the quality and dedication of its management. More specifically, the success of the individual financial institution depends upon management's ability to solve key problems related to that institution's liquidity, capital adequacy, the composition of its assets and liabilities, and organizational makeup. In the ensuing chapters, we examine closely these problem areas faced by the management of all financial intermediaries.

Questions

8–1. Explain the meaning of the word *structure*. Of what importance is structure to the consumer of financial services?

8–2. Why has branch banking grown rapidly in importance during the post-World War II period in the United States? How has the trend toward increased branching affected the structure of the industry? The quantity and quality of service to the public?

8–3. What is a bank holding company? Explain why bank holding companies have grown so rapidly in recent years, particularly since 1970. What are the major potential advantages and disadvantages to the public of holding company expansion?

8–4. Give a brief history of U.S. bank holding company legislation. Can you explain why this legislation appears to be necessary?

8–5. What is a "symbiotic"? Why are symbiotics being formed today? What problems might they create for the banking community?

8–6. Explain what is meant by the term *chain banking*. In what part of the United States is chain banking most important, and why?

8–7. Why did so many member banks withdraw from the Federal Reserve System prior to 1980? Explain what the consequences of this withdrawal trend might be for effective control of the nation's money supply. How did the Depository Institutions Deregulation and Monetary Control Act of 1980 affect this withdrawal trend?

8–8. Explain why bank failures are of such concern to the public and the regulatory authorities. According to the regulatory agencies, why do most banks fail? Is there any evidence suggesting that impending bank failures might be predicted? Are there reasons for suggesting the proportion of bank failures might increase in the future?

References

1. Bacon, Peter W. "A Study of Bank Mergers in Marion County, Indiana, 1945–66." Doctoral dissertation, Indiana University, 1967.

2. Barnett, Robert A. "Anatomy of a Bank Failure." *The Magazine of Bank Administration*, April 1972, pp. 20–24, 313.

3. Benston, George. "Bank Examination." *The Bulletin*, New York University, nos. 89–90 (May 1973).

4. Benston, George J. "How Can We Learn From Past Bank Failures?" *The Bankers Magazine*, no. 1 (Winter 1975), pp. 19–25.

5. Chase, Samuel B., and John J. Mingo. "The Regulation of Bank Holding Companies." *Journal of Finance*, no. 2 (May 1975), pp. 281–92.

6. Cohen, Kalmen, and Samuel R. Reid. "Effects of Regulation, Branching, and Mergers on Banking Structure and Performance." *The Southern Economic Journal*, October 1976, pp. 231–41.

7. Darnell, Jerome C. "Chain Banking." *National Banking Review*, no. 3 (1966), pp. 307–31.

8. Edwards, Franklin. "The Banking Competition Controversy." *National Banking Review*, September 1965, pp. 1–34.

9. Eisenbeis, Robert A. "Regulation and Financial Innovation: Implications for Financial Structure and Competition Among Depository and Non-Depository Institutions." *Issues in Bank Regulation*, Winter 1981, pp. 1–23.

10. Frieder, Larry A., and Vincent P. Apilado. "Bank Holding Company Research: Classification, Synthesis and New Directions." *Journal of Bank Research*, Summer 1982, pp. 80–95.

11. Gagnon, Joseph. "The New Merger Guidelines: Implications for New England Banking Markets." *New England Economic Review*, Federal Reserve Bank of Boston, July–August 1982.

12. Horvitz, Paul M., and Bernard Shull. "The Impact of Branch Banking on Bank Performance." *National Banking Review*, no. 2 (December 1964), pp. 143–89.

13. Jacobs, Donald P. *Business Loan Costs and Bank Market Structure: An Empirical Estimate of Their Relations*. New York: National Bureau of Economic Research, 1971, Occasional Paper 115.

14. Kohn, Ernest. *Branch Banking, Bank Mergers and the Public Interest*. New York: New York State Banking Department, 1964.

15. Meyer, Paul A., and Howard W. Pifer. "Predictions of Bank Failures." *Journal of Finance*, September 1970, pp. 853–68.

16. Piper, Thomas R. *The Economics of Bank Acquisitions by Registered Bank Holding Companies*. Research Report No. 48. Boston: Federal Reserve Bank of Boston; March 1971.

17. Rose, John T. *An Analysis of Federal Reserve System Attrition Since 1960*. Staff Economic Study no. 93. Board of Governors of the Federal Reserve System.

18. Rhoades, Stephen A. "The Competitive Effects of Interstate Banking." *Federal Reserve Bulletin*, January 1980, pp. 1–8.

19. Rose, Peter S. "The Pattern of Bank Holding Company Acquisitions." *Journal of Bank Research* no. 3 (Autumn 1976), pp. 236–40.

20. _____. "Banker Attitudes Toward the Federal Reserve System: Survey Results." *Journal of Bank Research* no. 2 (Summer 1977), pp. 77–84.

21. _____. "Competition and the New Banks." *The Canadian Banker & ICB Review*, no. 4 (July–August 1977), pp. 61–66.

22. _____. "Symbiotics: Financial Supermarkets in the Making." *The Canadian Banker & ICB Review*, no. 2 (April 1982), pp. 77–84.

23. _____ and William L. Scott. "Risk in Commercial Banking: Evidence from Postwar Failures." *The Southern Economic Journal*, June 1978.

24. _____ and Donald R. Fraser. "State Regulation of Bank Holding Companies." *The Bankers Magazine*, winter 1974, pp. 42—48.

25. Savage, Donald T. "Developments in Banking Structure, 1970–81." *Federal Reserve Bulletin*, February 1982, pp. 79–85.

26. Sinkey, Joseph F., Jr., and David A. Walker. "Problem Banks: Identification and Characteristics." *Journal of Bank Research*, Spring 1975, pp. 208–17.

27. Smith, David L. "The Performance of Merging Banks." *Journal of Business*, April 1971, pp. 184–92.

28. Stuhr, David P., and Robert Van Wicklen. "Rating the Financial Condition of Banks: A Statistical Approach to Aid Bank Supervision." *Monthly Review*, Federal Reserve Bank of New York, September 1974.

29. U.S. Congress, House Committee on Banking and Currency, Subcommittee on Domestic Finance. *Twenty Largest Stockholders of Record in Member Banks of the Federal Reserve System*. 88th Congress, 2d session. Washington, D.C.: U.S. Government Printing Office, 1964.

30. U.S. Congress, Senate Committee on Banking, Housing and Urban Affairs. *Special Survey of Bank Stock Loans to Officials, and Major Stockholders of Other Banks, Insider Loans and Overdrafts*. U.S. Senate, March 16, 1978. Washington, D.C.: U.S. Government Printing Office, 1978.

31. Varvel, Walter A. "A Valuation Approach to Bank Holding Company Acquisitions." *Economic Review*, Federal Reserve Bank of Richmond, July–August 1975, pp. 9–25.

32. Wientraub, Robert, and Paul Jessup. *A Study of Selected Banking Services by Bank Size, Structure, and Location*. Subcommittee on Domestic Finance of the House Committee on Banking and Currency. Washington, D.C.: U.S. Government Printing Office, 1964.

Problem for Discussion

IN THIS PROBLEM for class discussion, background information is presented regarding an application to charter a new bank in a growing metropolitan community. As Chapter 8 explains, banks can be chartered in the United States either by state banking commissions or by an agency of the federal government, the Comptroller of the Currency. In this discussion problem, the student must consider the facts presented for and against chartering the proposed new bank and then reach a decision. As the facts below suggest, the government's decision to permit the creation of a new banking corporation is rarely an easy one, and there is often strong opposition to a new bank charter from established financial institutions located in the same community.

A new bank has just been proposed for Clifton, a rapidly growing city in the southeastern section of the nation. The Clifton area has made significant economic progress in recent years due to the influx of light industry, including several textile, construction, and electronics firms. In 1960 the two counties which contain the corporate limits of Clifton were designated as SMSA (i.e., standard metropolitan statistical area) by the Bureau of the Census. The combined two-county population then was 125,000. By 1970 the SMSA contained an estimated 175,000 residents, and by 1980 the Bureau of the Census counted 240,000 full-time residents in the Clifton metropolitan area.

Like so many large- and medium-size cities, Clifton's suburbs are expanding rapidly and commuter traffic into the central city each business day is heavy. There are four major banks headquartered in downtown Clifton, each with assets over $500 million. Six smaller banking institutions (with assets ranging from $50 million to $200 million) also serve the central city area. Full-service branches are forbidden by state law, though bank holding companies are permitted. In fact, all of the downtown banks have active holding company organizations. There are 15 banks in the surrounding suburbs, and all but five are affiliates of Clifton-based bank holding companies.

Banks are permitted to set up automated teller machines (ATMs) without legal restrictions. Eight of the 10 downtown banks have been aggressive in installing ATMs in the area's six largest shopping malls. These banks are now planning to install the newest, most efficient machines in the surrounding suburbs. Few of the suburban banks presently operate ATMs, though an attempt is being made to form a cooperative association among the five independent institutions and operate ATM networks in all area suburbs.

Most banks in recent years have been chartered on the east side of Clifton where the majority of new business firms have appeared. Since 1970, however, the west side of town has begun to take off. It is more cosmopolitan in character than Clifton's east side, with many more office buildings, car dealerships, planned communities, golf courses, and country clubs. Rather than being industrial in character like the east side, suburban communities on Clifton's west flank seem more like true bedroom communities, housing executives and office personnel who commute daily as much as 20 miles into the downtown area or to nearby businesses and office buildings.

Despite their rapid growth in recent years, however, communities on Clifton's west side have not yet attracted nearly as many new banks as has the east side of the city. The area still has a fairly low population density, with substantial open areas punctuated intermittently by pockets of industrial development, new homes, and office buildings. Driving times and distances between developed locations and into the central city are still fairly long. The half dozen banks serving this developing western fringe of Clifton are still quite jealous of their local market area and are especially concerned about the possible appearance of new competition.

It was in this kind of environment that a small group of organizers—10 businessmen who have been residents of the west side area for years—applied to charter a new national bank with the proposed name of Clifton National Bank. Several of the organizers have prior or current banking experience, and two are real estate brokers. All have successful businesses or professional careers and substantial personal net worth.

The proposed bank would be an affiliate of a small holding company which holds stock in four other banks, the largest of which has approximately $100 million in assets. The bank would be situated at the northeast corner of Wentworth Drive, a newly constructed suburban thoroughfare, and Highway 12, a state-maintained highway connecting Clifton with cities to the north and south of the metropolitan area. Thus the proposed site is a relatively new highway intersection. Immediately adjacent to the bank site is a 40,000-square foot office building, housing 93 employees—the first phase of a professional complex of four or five buildings.

To back up their application, proponents contracted with a consulting firm for a detailed economic study of the local banking market. This feasibility study, which was filed with the charter application, showed there were approximately 1,300 households in the primary service area (PSA) of the proposed bank.[1] This translated into an estimated PSA population of about 4,200. Within a quarter mile of the proposed bank site is a new and rapidly growing housing development known as Crestmont. Homes in the development are all priced well above average, with some approaching a market value of $250,000 to $300,000. Still relatively isolated, Crestmont is the scene of significant street construction activities at present. For example, an important new thoroughfare in the PSA should be completed in about 15 months. However, a full upgrading of existing county-maintained roads in the area is expected to take about five years. A shopping mall is included in the plans for future construction in Crestmont, but the date on which ground would be broken for the shopping mall is uncertain at this time.

Across the freeway and about half a mile to the south of the proposed bank site is another developing housing area, Shady Nook, which contains more modest, smaller homes. A major shopping center, Oak Village, lies 3 miles to the north along the same freeway. Traffic counts along the freeway and by the site show significant increases over the past three years and substantial projected increases. Only half a mile from the proposed bank site is a 400-acre stretch of land upon which a 3-million-square-foot industrial park eventually will be located. The projected completion date, however, is still six years away. A small number of firms are already moved in, with 1,200 employees working there. (Eventually, some 11,000 employees are expected to work in the park.) Some of these employees have complained about the lack of banking facilities in the area. The same complaint was received from employees of the office building immediately adjacent to the proposed bank site.

Within the past month, the completion of phase one of a new apartment and residential development, covering approximately 80 acres, was announced. The project is called Sunset Gardens and is 1¼ miles from the proposed bank site. About 300 apartments are completed, with 65 percent already under lease. A total of 720 apartments are planned for Sunset Gardens. Approximately 1 mile from the proposed bank site in the opposite direction is a small shopping center, with four retail shops under construction and an adjacent subdivision of 64 homes on the drawing boards. However, as proponents admitted during a public hearing on the charter application, the area around the bank site within a radius of approximately 2 miles is relatively undeveloped. They did argue strongly, however, that the area was undergoing rapid change and would look very different by

---

[1]The Comptroller of the Currency defines a bank's primary service area (PSA) as that geographic area from which the bank will receive at least three quarters of its customer accounts (mainly locally oriented deposits).

the time the proposed new bank opened (perhaps 18 months to 2 years after charter approval). Access to the bank allegedly would be good because of its proposed location along the freeway, and local county roads would soon be widened and improved to match the projected growth in new homes, apartments, office buildings, and retail stores in the service area.

As soon as the application to charter Clifton National was filed, the principal stockholders and management of the bank nearest the proposed site—Progressive National Bank—filed a formal protest with the Comptroller of the Currency and threatened to take legal action to block the proposed charter if necessary. Accordingly, following a field examination of the proposed bank site and the surrounding area, the Comptroller's regional office scheduled a public hearing to hear evidence from opponents and proponents of the charter. The hearing itself lasted just three hours, but it brought forth a number of arguments both supporting and denying the need for the new Clifton bank. Opponents of the charter hired professional legal counsel and an economic research firm to study the service area of the proposed new bank. After driving through the area, taking numerous pictures, and interviewing local residents, they concluded that the bank was likely to have such a small deposit base that it could not be profitable within a reasonable period of time (normally about three years). Opponents argued that substantial deposits would have to be drawn from nearby banks for the proposed new bank to survive and grow.[2] To them, this violated a basic requirement expressed in both federal and state banking laws that new banks should not be chartered in locations where they would work "undue harm" against the continued profitable operation of other banks already serving the local area.

Opponents to the charter argued that the organizers had based their projections of deposit growth and earnings upon the experience of other new banks in the Clifton area. However, opponents contended, this is a

---

[2]There was wide disparity among proponents and opponents of the new bank as to just how rapidly deposits might grow. Proponents, who are required by the Comptroller's regulations to submit a *pro forma* (estimated) balance sheet and income statement for the first three years of operation, argued that total deposits of the new bank would reach $13 million in three years. The opponents contended that $5¼ million was more likely because they believed the proposed bank's service area was far smaller than claimed by the proponents. The organizers claimed the new bank would be in the black by its second year of operation. In contrast, the opponents saw only losses for the first three years. Proponents countered with the claim that every one of the new banks chartered in the Clifton area over the past decade has grown even faster than their projections indicated. Furthermore, they promised an aggressive marketing program, drawing upon personal contacts and business relationships. Also, proponents claimed that the opponents overstated the projected expenses of the new bank, resulting in a forecast of unreasonably large earnings losses. Opponents had forecast a loss of about $530,000 by the proposed bank's third year of operation.

new bank in a new situation and no actual commitments for new accounts had been secured from prospective customers. Moreover, they pointed out that, in general, only one narrow road linked the proposed bank site with the principal residential areas within the bank's projected service area. Commuters and shoppers in the area had to pass by several other banks on their way to work and shopping. While the proposed bank would be situated along a freeway, opponents contended high-speed traffic passing along the freeway on their way to work or shopping would be highly unlikely to exit the freeway and stop at a bank not close to either shopping or to work. This is especially true, opponents argued, because there are several banks located near plants, office buildings, and shopping centers on Clifton's west side. In contrast, no major shopping or work facilities are currently adjacent to the proposed bank site.

Opponents placed heavy emphasis on two factors in objecting to the charter: (1) the lack of established shopping facilities and well-developed residential and commercial areas in the proposed bank's PSA, and (2) the inconvenience of reaching the proposed bank site as measured by substantial commuting time and distance, thus increasing customers' bank transactions cost. They saw the proposed bank's location as unlikely to coincide with the typical customer's daily route of travel to schools, shopping, and work. Implicit in the opposition's reasoning was the notion that convenience and driving time were the dominant factors in each customer's choice of which banks to trade with. They assumed that, other things being equal, the customer would always go to the nearest bank, particularly if the location of that bank coincided with the customer's daily shopping or commuting schedule. The lack of shopping facilities or major employers adjacent to the proposed site was a major source of controversy between proponents and opponents of the charter application. Other banks in the immediate area were, indeed, closer to developed shopping and work locations. During the public hearing there was considerable dispute over the boundaries of the proposed bank's primary service area and its population. Proponents estimated 4,800 people lived there. Opponents argued that the PSA population was more like 2,600 and that the actual PSA was a fraction of the size claimed by the proponents, due to the convenient locations occupied by other banks in the area.

As noted earlier, opposition to the new charter was centered mainly in one bank—Progressive National Bank, located about 2 miles from the proposed site. Officers and stockholders of that bank anticipated they might lose a substantial number of customers if a new charter were granted, and they believed that Progressive National's profitability and growth would be severely damaged. Proponents denied this prospect, pointing out that Progressive's net worth had roughly doubled in the five years since its charter date. The bank held between 9,000 and 10,000 customer accounts and had total deposits of $20.6 million.[3] Moreover, there was no evidence presented of any other bank in the area that had been as unprofitable or as slowly growing as opponents projected the new bank would be. Opponents countered that such information on the performance of Progressive National or other Clifton banks was irrelevant since the new bank would be in a different location, facing different circumstances.

Proponents claimed they would offer services not now available to residents in the primary service area, such as ATMs, longer hours of operation, and cash-management services. Opponents claimed there was no lack of such services in the area and that existing banks were aggressive competitors.

In summary, the Comptroller's office found itself faced with a hotly contested issue of whether to issue a charter for a new national bank. The law required the Comptroller, and the state banking commissions as well, to consider several key factors: (1) whether the new bank would be profitable in a reasonable period of time; (2) whether it would unduly harm other banks in the area; (3) whether there was a public need for a new bank; and (4) whether the organizers were financially responsible, of good moral character, and professionally qualified to operate successfully a new national bank. The Comptroller's office soon realized that in the Clifton case it indeed had a difficult charter decision to make.

---

[3]The consulting firm preparing the proponents' economic study pointed to recent statistics and annual reports which showed that Progressive's ROE and ROA for the past three years placed it among the leading banks in profitability in the Clifton area. The same was true of Progressive National Bank's growth rate.

9. *Liquidity Management*

MANAGEMENT OF LIQUIDITY is an important aspect of the financial management of every financial institution. Since all financial institutions engage in maturity intermediation—borrowing short and lending long—they are necessarily placed in a potentially illiquid position. Such potential illiquidity must be planned for, the amount of needed liquidity estimated, and a strategy developed for providing that liquidity in the amount required and at the necessary time. The basic concepts involved in liquidity management are common to all financial institutions—bank and nonbank, depository and nondepository, contractual and noncontractual—although the degree of the problem and hence its concern to management will vary considerably among different institutions. The discussion of liquidity management below is in terms of the commercial bank, but only minor modifications will need to be made to extend the analysis to most other financial institutions. Indeed, the needed modifications to this analysis for other financial institutions have diminished as some nonbank financial institutions have attained the legal authority to offer third-party payment services and have become more like commercial banks in other ways also.

One financial institution may have a large amount of liquid assets as compared to other firms and still be relatively illiquid, at least compared to its own needs for liquidity.[1] In contrast, another institution may have a relatively small amount of liquid assets (as compared to total assets) and still be quite liquid relative to its own needs. This distinction points up the difficulties involved for both internal management and outside analysts in

PERSPECTIVES ON LIQUIDITY

---

[1]An asset is usually considered highly liquid if it has good marketability and price stability and can be sold with low transaction costs in large quantity without markedly affecting the market price.

determining the amount of liquidity an individual financial institution should have. Indeed, determination of the *proper* amount of liquidity is not only difficult but also quite subjective.

The liquidity of an individual financial institution should also be distinguished from the liquidity of the financial system. Management of an individual financial institution, through careful planning and anticipation of deposit and loan changes, can control its liquidity to a substantial extent. Management may establish a policy of a relatively large or small amount of liquidity relative to anticipated needs for funds, depending upon risk preferences, risk factors, and other considerations. In creating such a policy, financial managers must naturally recognize the important trade-off between liquidity and profitability. Since the yield curve often is upward sloping—higher interest rates are associated with longer-term, less liquid financial assets and lower yields are associated with shorter-term, more liquid financial assets—management of a financial institution must decide if it wants to "sleep well or eat well." It can minimize the institution's liquidity, take the funds released from the sale of liquid assets, and invest longer term in order to gain a higher return (perhaps obtaining liquidity for unexpected needs through borrowed funds), but it will do so at greater risk, both in terms of having insufficient liquidity at a crucial time and also with regard to the interest-rate risk (and perhaps credit risk) associated with longer-term assets. Conversely, management can minimize the institution's risk of illiquidity by keeping large amounts of liquid assets relative to its anticipated needs, but earnings normally will be less.

While individual firm liquidity is a management decision variable, the liquidity of the financial system is not under the control of individual financial institutions. The liquidity of the financial system is determined basically by the Federal Reserve System. In the conduct of monetary policy the Federal Reserve may increase or decrease the system's liquidity. For example, if the Fed wished to accelerate the economy's rate of growth, the various techniques of monetary control—open-market operations, reserve requirement changes, and changes in the discount rate—could be used to increase the liquidity of the financial system. Conversely, if the Fed wished to curtail the expansion of the economy, it would be expected to reduce the liquidity level of the economy.

BANK LIQUIDITY

Table 9–1 presents information on selected liquid assets at commercial banks, expressed as a percentage of total assets: cash assets, U.S. Treasury securities, and other securities (primarily obligations of states and political subdivisions). Cash assets include a variety of different items: vault cash, deposits held by banks at Federal Reserve banks for purposes of meeting legal reserve requirements, deposits held by member and nonmember commercial banks at other commercial banks in order to buy services from the other banks, and cash items in the process of collection. U.S. Treasury securities include all issues which are direct obligations of the U.S. government, regardless of maturity, although most holdings at commercial banks are relatively short-term in nature. Securities of states and political subdivisions include all securities which are commonly referred to as municipals.

The data provided in Table 9–1 present only crude approximations to the liquidity position of individual banks. Not all securities are short-term in nature, nor are all cash assets (such as legal reserves) available to meet deposit withdrawals or loan demands. Moreover, liquidity can be provided from the loan portfolio as well as from other securities. And, perhaps especially important, liquidity can be provided by borrowings as well as through asset liquidation; that is, liquidity can be stored in assets or purchased through borrowings. Nevertheless, the data at least provide a basis for discussion of commercial bank liquidity.

As would be expected, given the deposit structure of commercial banks, the typical commercial bank maintains a substantial share of total assets in the form of cash and short-term securities. The amount of total funds devoted to these uses, is, however, a function of the size of the bank. The cash asset ratio rises sharply as bank size increases. The association of this ratio with bank size reflects the substantial role of larger banks in the clearing and collection of checks which, in turn, is reflected in large "cash items in the process of collection" balances.[2] In addition, the Federal Reserve requires larger commercial banks to maintain a higher proportion of demand deposits in the form of reserves. In contrast, U.S. Treasury security holdings diminish markedly as bank size increases. Large banks may be more conscious of minimizing their short-term securities portfolio, and this inverse relationship with bank size also reflects the greater use of purchased money (such as federal funds) as a means of providing liquidity at larger banks.

Table 9–1 Selected Liquidity Ratios for Insured Commercial Banks: July 1983

	All U.S. Banks
Cash assets ÷ Total assets	9.3%
U.S. Treasury securities ÷ Total assets	8.5
Other securities ÷ Total assets	12.3

Source: *Federal Reserve Bulletin*, August 1983.

[2]See Chapter 6 for a more thorough discussion of this point.

Trends in Liquidity Management

One of the most significant developments in commercial banking (and also at nonbank financial institutions) in the post–World War II period has been a sharp decline in liquid asset holdings and a change in the manner in which banks meet their liquidity needs. Commercial banks at the end of World War II had enormous holdings of U.S. government securities, reflecting their financing of the government's war effort. But in the postwar period, the banking system has been confronted with intense loan demand, rising costs of money and labor, and pressure on profit margins. Reflecting these factors, bank management has reduced to a substantial extent its holdings of short-term, highly liquid assets. Indeed, whereas U.S. Treasury bills were once central to bank liquidity management, today many commercial banks hold few U.S. Treasury securities beyond those required for pledging purposes.

Another important development has been a shift in emphasis away from *asset management* to provide liquidity towards *liability management*. Traditionally, sources of funds at commercial banks were viewed as being determined basically by factors external to management control. However, with the development of the federal funds market, CDs, and other sources of borrowed funds, commercial banks, especially large commercial banks, have increasingly relied upon nondeposit borrowed funds to provide liquidity. It is not an exaggeration today to assert that liquidity management at commercial banks encompasses total portfolio management, using assets and liabilities together as part of management planning. (This approach has sometimes been referred to as *funds management*. More will be said about asset, liability, and funds management later in this chapter.)

Primary and Secondary Reserves

Within an asset management perspective, liquidity requirements for commercial banks have been met traditionally from primary and secondary reserve holdings. *Primary reserves* refers to cash assets held to meet legal reserve requirements and for other operating purposes. While these assets are not all available to satisfy liquidity needs (since a large proportion must be held as legal reserves and as correspondent balances), primary reserves are still the first line of defense against daily demands for cash. Moreover, there is even some flexibility in legal reserve balances which the regulatory authorities require banks to hold. For example, reserve requirements for commercial banks must be satisfied only on a daily average basis for a reserve maintenance period. Hence a bank could use some of these cash assets during the period for liquidity needs as long as the average level of reserves for the entire time was satisfactory. Primary reserve holdings also include operating cash assets such as deposits at other commercial banks used to compensate these other banks for services rendered. There is some flexibility in the amount of these deposits also.

Most liquidity derived from the asset portfolio of a commercial bank is provided by secondary reserves. *Secondary reserves* refers to those assets which are primarily held for liquidity purposes; that is, those assets which can be converted into cash quickly with little risk of loss in value. While most secondary reserves take the form of short-term, marketable securities, such as U.S. Treasury bills, portions of the loan portfolio (such as commercial paper) may legitimately be viewed as secondary reserves. In addition, not all short-term marketable securities held by a financial institution should necessarily be included in secondary reserves. For example, during periods in which interest rates are expected to increase, it would be a reasonable portfolio policy to shift from long-term to short-term securities. These short-term securities would have high liquidity, but their primary function is to provide income rather than liquidity.

The money position of a commercial bank refers to those assets held to satisfy legal reserve requirements.[3] The goal of bank management should be to minimize holdings of these assets, since they earn no interest. For a large bank, specialized staff would ordinarily be employed in order to anticipate changes in the availability of reserves and to dispose of excess reserves at attractive rates in the federal funds market or in other money market investments. For small banks, the amount of interest lost through idle reserves is less significant and may not justify the use of a specialized staff. As a result, excess reserves at large banks are normally a much lower percentage of total reserves than at smaller banks, and frequently are zero or even negative, requiring the bank to purchase reserves from other banks overnight or for a few days in the federal funds or Eurodollar markets or from the Federal Reserve's discount window.

The legal restrictions on a commercial bank in the management of its money position should be understood, as they are basic to managing the money position.

THE MONEY POSITION IN LIQUIDITY MANAGEMENT

Federal Reserve Regulations

Throughout the 1970s and into the early 1980s, all financial institutions subject to reserve requirements set by the Federal Reserve Board followed

---

[3]This example is in terms of a commercial bank. However, since the Depository Institutions Deregulation and Monetary Control Act of 1980, reserve requirement regulations apply uniformly to all depository institutions offering transactions accounts or nonpersonal time deposits.

a system referred to as "lagged reserve requirements." Under this procedure, reserve requirements for a particular period are determined by deposit levels in an earlier period. However, the lagged reserve requirement
procedure has been criticized as reducing the degree to which the Fed is
able to control short-run fluctuations in the nation's money supply. As a
result, the Fed announced in late 1982 that—beginning in February 1984—
it would shift to *contemporaneous* reserve requirements for selected
groups of depository institutions.

A brief summary and comparison of lagged and contemporaneous reserve requirement procedures is provided in Figure 9–1. A discussion is
presented below of lagged reserve requirements, followed by a treatment
of contemporaneous reserve requirements. The principle features of the
lagged reserve requirement procedures are as follows:

1. The reserve requirement rules pertain to a given statement week. A
statement week is a seven-day period which begins on Thursday and ends
on Wednesday. Friday and Wednesday are especially important days—
Friday, since the bank's position as of the close of business on Friday

Figure 9–1   Timing of Lagged and Contemporaneous Reserve Accounting Systems

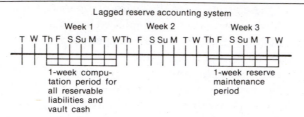

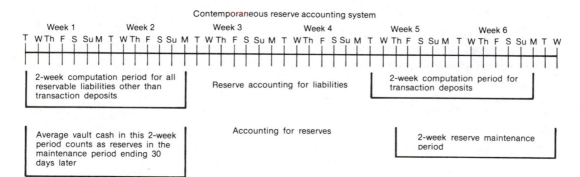

Note: A reserve maintenance period is a period over which the daily average reserves of a depository institution must equal or exceed its
required reserves. Required reserves are based on daily average deposit liabilities in reserve computation periods.

Source: R. Alton Gilbert and Michael E. Trebling, "The New System of Contemporaneous Reserve Requirements," *Review,* Federal Reserve Bank of St. Louis, December 1982, p. 4.

counts for Saturday and Sunday; and Wednesday, since it is the last day on which reserve adjustments may be made.

2. All important variables—deposits, reserves held at the Federal Reserve, and vault cash—are measured on a daily average basis over the seven-day statement week.

3. The reserve requirements which must be met during the current statement week are determined by the volume of deposits two weeks prior; that is, the amount of required reserves in the statement week (the reserve maintenance week) ending on Wednesday, June 15, depends upon the volume of deposits (on a daily average basis) in the statement week ending June 1. As a result of these lagged reserve requirements, the money manager for a depository institution holding reserves at the Fed knows at the start of the current reserve week what the institution's required reserves are for the entire week, since they are determined in the earlier reserve computation week.[4]

4. The amount of vault cash which may be used to satisfy reserve requirements this week is the quantity held two weeks earlier. Thus the amount of vault cash which can be used to satisfy reserve requirements in the statement week ending on Wednesday, June 15, is the amount of vault cash (on a daily average basis) which the bank maintained in the statement week ending June 1. Not only does the money manager know the amount of reserves that the bank must have this week, but the manager also knows the amount of vault cash that can be used to satisfy these requirements.

5. Any excess or deficiency in meeting required reserves during the current statement week can be carried over to the following statement week as long as that amount does not exceed 2 percent of required reserves. That is, excesses or deficiencies of up to 2 percent of required reserves in the statement week ending June 15 can be carried over and settled in the statement week ending June 22. Reserve deficiencies of more than 2 percent below the required reserve level would be assessed an explicit penalty in the form of an interest charge, while reserve excesses of more than 2 percent would incur an implicit penalty in potential lost income.[5]

The money manager for an individual commercial bank, then, has a number of factors to consider in the planning process: the volume of re-

---

[4] Some small depository institutions report their reserve on a quarterly basis. For these organizations, the seven-day maintenance period begins on the fourth Thursday following the end of the institution's computation period and ends on the third Wednesday after the close of the institution's next computation period.

[5] Under the Fed's regulation A, which spells out its reserve requirement rules, a penalty interest rate equal to the Federal Reserve's discount rate plus 2 percentage points is charged depository institutions on the amount of any reserve deficiences above 2 percent of required reserves.

quired reserves, the amount of vault cash which can be used to satisfy these requirements, and the amount of deposits at the Federal Reserve (which can, of course, also be used to satisfy legal reserve requirements). With lagged reserve requirements (where required reserves and vault cash in the current statement week are based upon past levels of deposits), the money manager knows the amount of required reserves for this statement week and the vault cash usable at the start of the week (on Thursday). Hence management of the money position really is narrowed to controlling the volume of bank deposits at the Federal Reserve so that, on average during the statement week, these deposits are just at the right level—neither so much as to produce excess reserves (which would result in loss of income) nor too little to produce a reserve deficiency, since that would incur a penalty charge (if the amount were outside the 2 percent limit set by the Federal Reserve for the carry-over privilege). At larger banks, with a multitude of transactions during a business day, this is a complicated and sometimes burdensome process. At smaller banks it is less so.

Contemporaneous Reserve Requirements

The contemporaneous reserve requirement regulations as adopted by the Federal Reserve Board in late 1982 became effective in February 1984. These regulations do not apply to all depository institutions but only to those with total deposits of $15 million or more (this limit though would encompass many commercial banks). As discussed above, under lagged reserve requirement procedures depository institutions must keep reserves in the current week based upon deposits two weeks earlier. With contemporaneous reserve accounting, the period over which reserves must be held is increased from one to two weeks; that is, the reserve maintenance period is lengthened from one to two weeks (refer to Figure 9–1). At the same time, the relevant deposit period for determining required reserves is altered. For transaction deposits, required reserves are based upon these deposits in the 14-day period ending two days before the end of the current maintenance period (i.e., the two-week period ending every other Monday). Hence, for transaction accounts, there is under contemporaneous reserve accounting only a two-day lag between determination of required reserves and maintenance of these reserves. For calculation of required reserves on nonpersonal time deposits and Eurocurrency liabilities the relevant period is the 14-day period ending 30 days before the end of the relevant maintenance period.

As with lagged reserve requirements, the only assets that may be used to meet required reserves are deposits at the Fed and in vault cash. The relevant deposits at the Fed under contemporaneous reserve requirements are those during the current 14-day maintenance period. However, the vault cash countable as reserves in the current maintenance period is the average amount of vault cash held during the 14-day period ending 30 days before the end of the current maintenance period.

The ultimate effects of contemporaneous reserve requirements are difficult to determine. The movement toward (partially but not completely) contemporaneous reserve requirements should make reserve management more difficult for depository institutions. However, this may be partially or totally offset by shifting the reserve maintenance period to 14 days, which should ease the burden of reserve management. Also, the effects of contemporaneous reserve requirements on the ability of the Federal Reserve to control the money supply remain to be seen.

Management Decisions

A volume of deposits at the Federal Reserve in excess of anticipated amounts may occur during the reserve maintenance period. This development may result from unanticipated deposit inflows, either directly or through a favorable clearing balance with other banks, or from prepayment of loans by businesses or consumers. Another possibility, especially for a relatively large bank, is that one of the bank's correspondents may have sold federal funds to the bank. If the bank is an accomodating bank, it would offer—as one of the services it provides to correspondents—to buy federal funds regardless of its own reserve position. In any case, the reserve balance at the Federal Reserve could become excessive for any of these reasons as well as for a large number of others.

Since the goal of reserve management is to keep the volume of excess reserves at a minimum, the money manager would wish to dispose of these reserves as soon as possible. There are, of course, a number of possible uses of these funds. The money manager could sell federal funds to other banks which were in need of reserves due to deposit withdrawals, adverse clearing balances, or other reasons; or the money manager could invest in other money market instruments, such as U.S. Treasury bills, bankers' acceptances, or commercial paper. The particular instrument chosen would depend upon the relative yields available on these money market instruments and upon other factors. However, it would be affected greatly by the amount of time the money manager expects the reserve position to be in surplus. Expansion of the loan portfolio generally would not be considered unless it was expected that the reserve surplus was permanent. In the converse situation—a reserve deficiency—the money manager would again look at the alternatives available. Traditionally, with asset management, attention would be focused on the use of short-term securities, especially U.S. Treasury bills. However, with liability management, reserves could be borrowed in the federal funds market if the cost were lower. Indeed, most such short-term reserve adjustments are made through borrowing federal funds rather than through asset liquidation.

If the reserve position of this bank was in surplus on Thursday and Friday but was expected to swing to a deficit on Tuesday and Wednesday of the same statement week, the implications for the investment strategy of the money manager would be quite different then if the reserve surplus is expected to persist for a number of weeks. In the former case, the amount of transactions costs associated with the purchase of Treasury bills today and their subsequent sale later in the same period probably would eliminate this particular money market instrument as a viable alternative and would also eliminate bankers' acceptances and commercial paper. In this circumstance, federal fund transactions would be the most liquid and appropriate money market instrument. Moreover, even though the money manager might anticipate a surplus to persist for some time, there is always a degree of uncertainty associated with any such expectation. As a result, the first course of action today for most banks is to dispose of surplus funds in the federal funds market and wait to see if the surplus continues. If the reserve surplus turns out to be longer term, then the money manager can make some permanent adjustment. In both cases—short-term adjustment and anticipated longer-term reserve adjustment—the money manager is likely to use the federal funds market as the primary means of initial reserve modifying actions.

As discussed briefly at an earlier point, reserve management techniques vary considerably with the size of the bank. Small banks often plan their reserve positions so that a surplus volume of reserves at the Federal Reserve builds up early in the statement week. As this excess develops, the smaller banks sell their excess reserves, thereby eliminating most or all of the reserve surplus by the end of the week. In contrast, many larger banks operate their reserve positions in a much more aggressive manner. These banks often plan their loan and investment policies so that a reserve deficiency will develop during the statement week. If the reserve deficiency does indeed occur as planned, it is eliminated by purchasing reserves in the federal funds market or, if the deficiency is expected to persist for a longer period, by reducing liquid asset holdings or selling large CDs to business firms. Moreover, many of these larger banks seek to increase returns by anticipating intraweek changes in the federal funds rate. For example, if the money manager expected that the federal funds rate would be high early in the statement week (Thursday and Friday) but low in the latter part of the statement week (Tuesday and Wednesday), additional returns on bank assets might be obtained by selling federal funds early in the statement week (and thereby deliberately creating a reserve deficit). This action is possible since legal reserve requirements do not have to be met each day, but only on an average over the statement period.

Management of the secondary reserve position of a commercial bank is closely related to the control of its money position. *Secondary reserves* refer to those assets—primarily short-term securities—which can or will be converted into cash in the near term. As such, secondary reserves automatically will become cash assets and thereby add to those assets which are usable to satisfy reserve requirements. Moreover, since most assets held as secondary reserves are highly liquid, these assets may be turned into cash prior to maturity at the discretion of management. Again, as with managing the money position, it should be kept in mind that liquidity can be provided through borrowing (liability management) as well as through liquidation of secondary reserves (asset management).

Estimating Liquidity Needs

There are a number of steps involved in the management of secondary reserves. The beginning of this process is the estimation of the amount of liquidity needed. While this is a subjective judgment, there are procedures which are useful in estimating the needed amount of secondary reserves. Once that is determined, management must then select the manner by which this need will be met. For example, it might be that during the next six months, management has estimated that the total liquidity needed is $1.5 million. This liquidity could be provided by selling Treasury bills, bankers' acceptances, or other money market instruments as well as by borrowing. A choice must be made among these particular instruments. Moreover, it may be that of the total $1.5 million, $250,000 is required in each month. Management could then invest in securities which mature at the time the liquidity is needed or it could invest for a longer term and sell the securities prior to maturity. Again, a choice must be made among these alternatives. As another possibility, management might not hold any particular assets to satisfy these anticipated liquidity needs but might buy the liquidity through liability management (probably in the federal funds market) at the time funds are needed.

Deposit Withdrawals and Increases in Loan Demand

In estimating the need for liquidity over some particular planning period, it is important to recognize that liquidity must be provided for deposit withdrawals *and* for any increases in loans, both anticipated and unanticipated. Naturally, the bank must meet the demands of depositors for their funds. Moreover, it should plan to honor all legitimate loan requests from credit customers regardless of its funds position. There are a number of reasons why loan demands may be viewed in the same context as depositor withdrawal requests. First, financial institutions, especially deposit type institutions, are chartered primarily to serve the credit needs of the local community. As such, each institution must be prepared for unanticipated demands for credit from businesses and consumers in its marketplace. Moreover, from a narrower perspective, a financial intermediary must be able to provide loanable funds to its customers in periods of stringency if it wishes to maintain their deposit accounts. Business firms especially tend to maintain a deposit account where they are able to obtain satisfactory continuing credit accommodation.

Sources and Uses of Funds

There are a number of approaches which might be employed in estimating the exact liquidity needs for an individual bank. The most comprehensive is the *sources-and-uses-of-funds* approach. It takes into account the liquidity required for deposit withdrawals and to satisfy loan demand.

This approach begins with the proposition that, for any given planning horizon of interest to management, it *is* possible to estimate anticipated changes in deposits and loans. Any withdrawal of deposits or increase in loans represents a *use* of funds. Conversely, any increase in deposits or any decrease in loans is a *source* of funds. This technique requires a coordinated forecast of deposit and loan changes over the appropriate planning period. Each fall, for example, management may wish to plan liquidity levels for the coming year. They might then forecast the amount of loans and deposits at the end of each month in the coming year. Month-to-month changes in these loans and deposits (added together) would then provide an estimate of liquidity needs over the annual planning period.

As we noted above, planning liquidity needs must also take into account *external factors* which are likely to affect the forecast of loans and deposits. For example, variations in business cycle conditions and monetary policy are especially significant variables in influencing the liquidity needs of an individual commercial bank. In periods of business expansion, inventory levels frequently move up substantially. Customarily, these business inventory accumulations are financed with short-term bank credit. As such, bank management should anticipate especially heavy short-term loan demand during periods of business expansion. Moreover, in these periods, especially if they are associated with inflationary price movements, monetary policy is usually taking steps to curtail the availability of bank reserves and reduce the growth of bank credit. At the individual bank level, this development might be reflected in a slowdown in the growth rate of deposits or even a decline in deposit levels. Hence bank management should be prepared for liquidity pressures to be especially severe in periods of economic expansion as loan demand rises and deposits fall off. In contrast, in periods of economic slack, liquidity pressures would usually be reduced as loan demand diminished and deposit growth expanded.

Management must also take into account local economic conditions. It may be that the national economic situation is buoyant and yet local loan demand may be weak due to the closing of a manufacturing plant in the local community or the existence of a drought if the local economy is agriculturally based. Conversely, the national economy may be weak and local loan demand may be buoyant. It is too often overlooked that the U.S. economy contains vast differences in types of local economies, so that national trends may be a poor source of information about developments in the service area of the financial institution.

An Example. The estimation of liquidity needs through the sources-and-uses-of-funds approach can perhaps best be explained through the use of a simple example. Table 9–2 provides data on anticipated loans and deposits for a six-month period for a hypothetical bank. The estimates might be provided by the research department of a large bank or by line officers in the case of a smaller bank. In any event, the estimates assume that all legitimate loan requests will be met during the planning horizon. We note from Table 9–2 that loan totals are expected to increase through March and then decline from April through June. Since increases in assets represent uses of funds, the increase in loans anticipated in February and March will require that funds be provided either by inflows of deposits or liquidation of other assets. It is anticipated that deposits will expand in February (although not by enough to provide the total funds needed for loans) and that, subsequently, deposits will fall in both April and June (as indicated under Change in Deposits). The net effect of all these movements is summarized in the last column ("Funds Required"). This shows that with loan and deposit movements taken together, the bank can anticipate a liquidity need of $500,000 in February and another $500,000 each in March and April. However, after April no further liquidity must be provided in May and June. Indeed, in May there will be excess liquidity amounting to $500,000.

Table 9–2 Estimation of Liquidity Needs ($000)

Month	Total Loans	Total Deposits	Change in: Loans	Change in: Deposits	Funds Required
January	$42,000	$60,000	$ —	$ —	$—
February	43,500	61,000	1,500	1,000	500
March	44,000	61,000	500	0	500
April	43,500	60,000	(500)	(1,000)	500
May	43,000	60,000	(500)	0	(500)
June	42,500	59,500	(500)	(500)	0

These estimates are, of course, subject to a wide margin of error, and they leave out the reserves required for deposit increases (and thereby understate liquidity needs). Perhaps more important, these estimates are usually made of funds needed and provided between the end of one month and the end of another month. Intramonth fluctuations in deposits and loans may require substantial liquidity even though month-end data indicate no important liquidity needs. Finally, there are substantial problems in accurately forecasting economic and financial variables.

The Structure-of-Deposits Method

Another approach to estimating the need for liquidity, referred to as the structure-of-deposits method, focuses on the stability of deposit liabilities. Under this approach, the deposits of the organization might be divided into categories on the basis of their probabilities of withdrawal, and different amounts of liquidity could be provided for the different types of deposits. For example, deposits could be divided into the following three different categories, depending on their probability of withdrawal over some given planning period: (*a*) *hot money*, (*b*) *vulnerable deposits*, and (*c*) *stable deposits*. Hot money would be those deposits which are almost certain to be withdrawn within the planning period. For example, a certificate of deposit held by a school district for the purpose of making a progress payment on a new school in the next 10 days would be classified as hot money within a 30-day planning horizon. Vulnerable deposits would be those deposits with some appreciable possibility of withdrawal, but in which deposit withdrawal would not be a certainty or a near certainty. All large deposits should probably be viewed as vulnerable, given their potential for disrupting the liquidity position of the organization. Stable deposits would be a residual, those that are neither hot money nor vulnerable.

Once the deposits have been categorized by probability of withdrawal, management must then determine the liquidity requirement for each of the categories. For example, the liquidity requirement for hot money would usually be 100 percent of the amount of the hot money less the reserve requirement against the deposits. Vulnerable deposits would have a lower liquidity requirement. While the exact liquidity requirement for each dollar of vulnerable deposits is subject to management discretion, a 20–25 percent liquidity requirement ratio is not uncommon. Finally, stable deposits would have an even lower liquidity requirement, with 5–10 percent as a reasonable number.

The structure-of-deposits method is significant as a liquidity estimation method because it requires management to focus attention on deposit volatility, the principal source of liquidity pressures. Yet this technique has a number of limitations. It is highly subjective in application, in terms of classifying deposits according to probability of withdrawal and also in determining the amount of liquidity required for the different types of deposits. There is nothing magical about the divisions established above nor about the liquidity requirements applicable to each category. Each is subject to management review and determination. In addition, even if this approach could correctly estimate the deposit-withdrawal potential over the planning horizon, as discussed earlier, liquidity must be provided *both* for deposit withdrawals and loan increases. This approach focuses exclusively on deposit changes and may therefore divert management attention from potential loan changes.

Forecasting Methods Used in the Banking Industry

According to a survey conducted by Giroux [5], the most common forecasting technique used in the banking industry is judgmental or subjective in nature. It might be expected, of course, that judgmental forecasting relies heavily on the experience of those involved in the forecasting process. Both loan-demand and deposit-level forecasts were reported as being based mainly upon judgmental factors, though other more quantitative techniques were also employed, such as econometric models, multiple regression, input-output models, and simulation. It is also interesting (but not surprising) to note that there was quite a difference in forecasting techniques used by banks of different sizes. Smaller banks relied much more on judgmental forecasts by management; while larger banks were more likely to use quantitative forecasting techniques, including models in which estimated deposit and loan growth are linked to changes in interest rates, business activity, and income flows in the economy.

It is not sufficient for a financial institution to merely determine the amount of liquidity which it must hold over some specified planning period. The individual financial institution must also develop a strategy for meeting anticipated and unanticipated demands. There are a number of different approaches to this problem that have been adopted by different financial institutions at different periods of time. As noted earlier, the traditional approach stresses asset management—that is, control of the mix of assets held both in terms of the nature of those assets (for example, loans versus securities) and the secondary-market characteristics of the assets (i.e., the ability to liquidate the asset prior to maturity). A more recent and more aggressive strategy is *liability management*—that is, control of the volume of liabilities, especially nondeposit liabilities, such as federal funds. In practice, most banks and an increasing number of nonbank financial institutions use *both* approaches (usually referred to as *funds management*). However, as a general rule, smaller financial institutions rely more heavily on asset management. Naturally, the appropriate

LIQUIDITY MANAGEMENT POLICIES

strategy in a decision situation will depend to a considerable extent upon the relative costs of the alternatives as well as the risk preferences of management and shareholders. For example, if borrowing from the federal funds market was a cheaper source of funds than liquidating Treasury bills, we would expect individual financial institutions to follow the former method in satisfying their liquidity needs.

Asset Management

A number of different asset management strategies have been developed over the years. One of the oldest is the *real bills doctrine*, or *commercial loan theory*. This approach maintains that a commercial bank should confine its loans principally to short-term, self-liquidating commercial loans. Since there will be a certain percentage of these loans maturing during any given period, the bank, it is argued, need not be concerned with the formal planning of its liquidity position. This strategy was, of course, more relevant to commercial bank liquidity management in earlier years, when bank assets were concentrated in loans to businesses and primarily in short-term loans. Its relevance to today's banking system, with a loan portfolio widely diversified as to type and maturity, is at best questionable.

Many commercial banks today rely upon the *money market approach* to managing liquidity through control of assets. This strategy calls for the meeting of liquidity needs by holding money market instruments, such as Treasury bills, commercial paper, or bankers' acceptances. The amount and maturity of these money market instruments should correspond to the amount and timing of expected liquidity needs. For example, if a commercial bank expected that it would need $1 million in March, $2 million in April, and $4 million in May, it might purchase Treasury bills with comparable maturities. The bills would then be maturing as funds were needed. Moreover, if estimates of liquidity were inaccurate and liquidity was needed prior to the anticipated dates, the Treasury bills could be sold since they have a very good secondary market. Similar investment strategies could be followed with commercial paper or bankers' acceptances, although commercial paper has a much weaker secondary market than either Treasury bills or bankers' acceptances.

While the easiest strategy is to match the maturity of liquid assets held with anticipated liquidity needs, this is not the only possible technique. For example, an aggressive commercial bank might seek to increase its yield on secondary reserves by "riding the yield curve." This strategy consists of buying securities which have a longer maturity than the expected holding period—that is, funds which are needed in March might be invested in securities which mature in October. The October maturing securities then would be sold in March prior to their maturity but at the time funds are needed. Such a strategy might increase yields since longer-term securities would be expected to carry a higher expected return (if the yield curve is upward sloping) than shorter-term securities. Moreover, the yield might be increased further since the bank may realize a capital gain on the sale of the securities if the structure of the yield curve did not shift to an appreciable extent. In contrast, however, the higher returns through riding the yield curve could be eliminated through transactions costs and potential capital losses which could be incurred if the yield curve shifted upward during the period in which the securities were held.

Liability Management

In recent years, as noted earlier, many commercial banks, especially the larger ones, have begun to manage their *sources* of funds (liability management) rather than only their uses of funds (asset management) in order to meet anticipated liquidity needs. This shift in strategy towards liquidity management has been part of a larger shift toward more aggressive financial management at commercial banks and other financial institutions. Instead of investing in particular money market instruments or being concerned about the liquidity of the loan portfolio, this strategy would not explicitly provide for liquidity *until* the funds are needed. At that time, the bank would buy liquidity in the money market by one of a number of different techniques. If the need was very short-term (one day or only a few days), the federal funds market would most likely be used. In contrast, if the funds needed were for a longer period (say three weeks), the bank could increase the rates paid on its large certificates of deposit and obtain funds through this device. As another possibility, larger banks could borrow funds in the Eurodollar market, probably through a London branch of a U.S. bank.

The main advantage of liability management is the potential increase in income. With liability management, the bank is able to keep a smaller quantity of funds, on average, committed to short-term investments in money market instruments and thereby can keep a larger quantity of funds invested in longer-term securities and loans. Since the yield curve is normally upward sloping, the bank should expect to increase its return on total assets. However, liability management also entails higher risk. Interest rates may be quite high at the time that the individual financial institution is seeking to acquire funds. This is especially likely if the funds requirement stems from business cycle conditions and the operation of monetary policy. Moreover, the individual commercial bank may find that funds are virtually unavailable in quantities desired by the bank. This may be especially true in periods of financial stress and concern about the stability of an individual bank. Probably the most appropriate policy for liquidity management for the majority of financial institutions is some judicious mixture of asset and liability management, depending upon relative cost, risk, and other considerations.

SUMMARY

Liquidity management encompasses both asset and liability management dimensions. When viewed within this context, liquidity management may appropriately be viewed as an important part of the entire funds management program of the financial institution. Such a program is vital for the viability and profitability of the individual financial institution. However, determination of the amount of liquidity that is adequate is quite difficult. Banks and many other financial institutions have been reducing their holdings of liquid assets—primarily cash assets and short-term securities—and increasingly using purchased funds (liability management) to meet their liquidity needs.

Looking at liquidity management only from an asset management perspective, liquidity management encompasses both primary and secondary reserves. Primary reserves are cash assets used to meet legal reserve requirements and for other operating purposes. Secondary reserves are assets held primarily for liquidity—principally short-term securities.

Managing the money position—an important part of liquidity management—refers to controlling the assets (cash and deposits at the Federal Reserve) used to meet legal reserve requirements. Money position management encompasses the regulatory framework for reserve control as well as management decision policies. The goal of management of the money position is to minimize reserve holdings (since they earn no interest), subject to legal reserve requirements. Such a goal must be pursued within the relevant regulations with regard to reserve requirements. As noted in this chapter, for many years the Federal Reserve System used a lagged reserve requirement system in which current reserve requirements imposed on the deposits of banks and other depository institutions were based upon their deposit levels two weeks earlier. Beginning in February 1984, however, the Fed drastically altered the reserve requirement system to one of contemporaneous reserve accounting, where required reserve deposits at the Federal Reserve banks are tied more closely to current deposit levels.

Management of secondary reserves involves estimating the amount of liquidity needed and providing for that liquidity. Such estimates may be made with the sources-and-uses-of-funds approach, which estimates liquidity needed both for deposit withdrawals and loan increases. Liquidity needs may also be estimated with the structure-of-deposits approach. Yet it is important to recognize that such secondary-reserves management must be carried out within the overall liquidity management policy of the financial institution.

Questions

9–1. What important trends exist in bank liquidity management? Do you expect those trends to continue? Why?

9–2. Differentiate between primary and secondary reserves. What are legal reserves? Excess reserves?

9–3. What does the money position of a commercial bank refer to?

9–4. What is a statement period? Show how it is related to a bank's money position.

9–5. Compare reserve accounting under lagged and contemporaneous accounting procedures? Which is preferable in your opinion? Explain why.

9–6. Differentiate between asset management, liability management, and funds management?

9–7. How would the liquidity demands placed upon a commercial bank differ over the course of the business cycle?

9–8. What are the risks and rewards involved in liquidity management?

References

1. Baughn, William H., and Charles E. Walker, eds. *The Bankers' Handbook.* Homewood, Ill.: Dow Jones–Irwin, 1978, pp. 411–32.

2. Beebo, Jack. "A Perspective on Liability Management and Bank Risk." *Economic Review*, Federal Reserve Bank of San Francisco, winter 1977, pp. 12–20.

3. Crosse, Howard, and George Hempel. *The Management of Bank Funds.* Englewood Cliffs, N.J.: Prentice-Hall, 1980, chaps. 9–10.

4. Gilbert, R. Alton, and Michael E. Trebling. "The New System of Contemporaneous Reserve Requirements." *Review*, Federal Reserve Bank of St. Louis, December 1982, pp. 3–7.

5. Giroux, Gary. "A Survey of Forecasting Techniques Used by Commercial Banks." *Journal of Bank Research*, spring 1980, pp. 50–53.

6. Jessup, Paul. *Modern Bank Management.* Minneapolis: West Publishing, 1980, chap. 8.

7. Laurent, Robert D. "Lagged Reserve Accounting and the Fed's New Operating Procedures." *Economic Perspectives*, Federal Reserve Bank of Chicago, June 1982, pp. 32–43.

8. McKinney, George. "A Perspective on the Use of Models in the Management of Bank Funds." *Journal of Bank Research*, summer 1977, pp. 122–27.

9. Woodworth, G. Walter. "Bank Liquidity Management." *The Bankers Magazine*, autumn 1967, pp. 66–78.

10. _____. "Planning Bank Liquidity Needs." *The Bankers Magazine*, summer 1968, pp. 22–32.

Problem for Discussion

THIS CHAPTER HAS DISCUSSED THE PROCEDURES by which a financial institution could estimate the amount of liquidity it needs and develop a strategy for meeting that requirement. The problem situation discussed below presents the student with an opportunity to apply the principles discussed in this chapter to liquidity analysis for a large commercial bank. The student should place himself or herself in the position of the bank's liquidity manager and, after reviewing the material, should address the following questions:

1. How much liquidity does the bank need? When does it need this liquidity?
2. Does the bank need additional liquid assets? If so, where should it get the added liquidity? If it has too much liquidity, what should it do with the excess funds?
3. How would interest-rate forecasts affect these decisions?

The Third National Bank is a multibillion dollar, full-service commercial bank located in a major metropolitan area. While it offers a complete range of banking services, it concentrates on business lending (wholesale operations), trust services (trust assets exceed bank assets), and international banking (branches in London, Paris, and Geneva as well as in other areas around the world where it is quite active in the Eurodollar market). But perhaps its most distinctive attribute is the bank's emphasis on *planning*. Senior management at Third National Bank is dedicated to thorough and complete profit planning.

Each fall the bank engages in an extensive review of the goals of the organization for the coming year and the specifics of how these goals are to be achieved. The process is approached with great seriousness by both junior and senior bank officers. Budgets are set with the active participation of department heads. Profit-center goals are established and each loan officer is viewed as a profit center. Moreover, at quarterly intervals during the year, variances (differences between the planned amount and the actual amount) for revenues and expenses are analyzed in order to isolate unfavorable factors before they have a serious impact upon the bank. These policies have met with some degree of success, although the bank has also benefited from location in an area with a robust economy. Earnings per share have increased each quarter (on a year-to-year basis) for more than five years, and the price of the bank's common stock has moved up substantially despite a lethargic stock market. The bank's price-earnings ratio is currently 8. Moreover, the loan loss experience of the bank in recent years has been quite good. Apart from a few problems with a commercial real estate development, the bank has encountered no real difficulties with the quality of its loan portfolio.

Third National Bank is located in one of the most rapidly growing areas of the sunbelt. Based upon heavy industry (especially oil refining and petrochemicals), the local economy has experienced vigorous growth throughout the post-World War II period. In recent years, however, the growth has accelerated as large numbers of corporate headquarters have moved into the area. As a result, the nature of the local population has changed markedly, with increased emphasis upon middle-class business and professional people and decreased importance of blue-collar workers. The growth in the local economy has meant that local demand continually presses on the lending capacity of the bank. Unlike most banks throughout the nation in this period, Third National did not have any shortage of loan demand; indeed, the bank was almost forced to ration loans even to its best customers. The major problem facing the loan function at Third National was the constant demand for loans from large manufacturing firms which exceeded the legal lending limit of the bank (see Exhibit 9-1). Since the capital base at the bank amounted to $180 million, the bank's total loans to any one customer could not exceed $27 million. Moreover, since the community served by Third National Bank consists mostly of relatively small banks, the major competition for these loans is out-of-state banks, and this makes loan participation with these same banks quite difficult.

Exhibit 9-1
THIRD NATIONAL BANK
Balance Sheet
December 31,19XX ($000)

Cash and due from banks	$ 250,000	Demand deposits (IPC)	$ 800,000
U.S. government securities	200,000	Demand deposits-banks	400,000
Federal agency securities	20,000	Other demand deposits	200,000
Obligations of states and political		Savings deposits	300,000
subdivisions	425,000	Time deposits	1,300,000
Loans	2,285,000	Capital:	
		Capital stock	60,000
Total assets	$3,180,000	Surplus	60,000
		Undivided profits	60,000
		Total liabilities and capital	$3,180,000

Liquidity management at Third National Bank is based principally upon forecasts of interest rates, deposit flows, and loan demands made by the Economic Research Department. The information provided for the coming year is summarized in Exhibits 9–2 and 9–3. It appeared that interest rates in the short-term money market were expected to fall moderately. The three-month Treasury bill rate was forecast to decrease from 11.5 percent yield in the fourth quarter of the current year to 9.0 percent in the fourth quarter of the next year, a decline of 250 basis points. Similar decreases were expected for other money market rates. However, long-term rates were expected to show smaller changes. The liquidity manager also received a list of short-term security holdings classified by type of security and maturity as of the current year (Exhibit 9–4). This list did not represent all the liquid assets held by the bank, as it omitted the liquidity of the loan portfolio (including $100 million in commercial paper) as well as the cash assets that could temporarily be drawn upon.

Exhibit 9–2   Third National Bank Interest-Rate Outlook
(prepared by Economic Research Department)

| | Annual Percentage Interest Rates Expected | | | | | |
| | Curent Year | | Next Year | | | |
	III	IV	I	II	III	IV
Short-Term Rates						
3-month Treasury bill	12.5%	11.5%	10.5%	10.0%	9.5%	9.0%
Federal funds	13.5	12.5	11.5	11.0	10.5	10.0
4–6-month prime commercial paper	14.5	13.5	12.5	12.0	12.0	11.5
Prime rate	16.0	15.0	14.0	14.0	13.5	13.5
Long-Term Rates						
AAA corporate bonds	15.0	14.8	13.6	13.5	13.4	13.3
U.S. government bonds	13.6	13.5	13.4	13.4	13.3	13.0
AAA municipals	11.7	11.7	11.8	11.9	11.8	11.9

| | Deposits and Loans (annual rate of change, in percent) | | | | | |
| | Current Year | | Next Year | | | |
	III	IV	I	II	III	IV
Money Supply, Deposits, Loans, and Investments						
M-1	5.2%	5.1%	6.3%	6.7%	6.8%	6.4%
Time and savings deposits	10.3	10.2	10.6	10.7	10.4	11.2
Total loans and investments	5.4	8.8	9.9	9.2	9.1	9.0

**Exhibit 9–3 Loan and Deposit Forecast for Third National Bank
(prepared by Economic Research Department)**

			Deposits ($000)	
Year and Quarter		*Loans ($000)*	*Demand*	*Time and Savings*
Current year	IV	$2,675,000	$1,525,000	$1,900,000
Next year	I	2,575,000	1,500,000	1,950,000
Next year	II	2,675,000	1,550,000	2,000,000
Next year	III	2,875,000	1,575,000	2,050,000
Next year	IV	3,000,000	1,600,000	2,150,000

**Exhibit 9–4 Third National Bank Short-Term Security Holdings:
December 31, 19XX (000s)**

U.S. Treasury Securities Maturing within:	
3 months	$10,000
3–6 months	75,000
6–9 months	80,000
9–12 months	25,000
12–15 months	10,000

Obligations of States and Political Subdivisions Maturing within:	
3 months	$10,000
3–6 months	10,000
6–9 months	10,000
9–12 months	10,000
12–15 months	10,000

10. *Lending Policies*

LENDING IS A VITAL ACTIVITY for most financial institutions. Not only do loans represent the largest commitment of funds for depository financial institutions, but they also produce the greatest share of the total revenue generated from all earning assets. Moreover, it is in the lending function where depository financial institutions generally accept the greatest risks. The failure of individual commercial banks and other depository financial institutions is usually associated with problems in the loan portfolio and is less often the result of shrinkage in the value of other assets.[1] In summary, most bank funds, as well as the funds of other depository financial institutions, are committed to loans, the bulk of their revenue is generated by loans, and the bulk of risk is centered in the loan portfolio.

Lending is not only significant quantitatively for the individual institution, but it also plays an important part in the social function which financial institutions perform in the economy. In terms of the model presented in Chapter 1, the lending function is at the center of Stage II of a financial institution's production process—the management of assets. Management must appraise the returns and risk characteristics of loans as compared to securities and must evaluate the relative attractiveness of different types of loans. This appraisal is complex since the loan function is central to the basic credit-granting role of the financial institution and also since loans differ widely in degrees of risk.

Lending is the basic reason-to-be for the commercial bank and other deposit-type financial institutions. Most financial intermediaries (especially the deposit type) are local in nature; their funds are drawn from a relatively

---

[1]This generalization must be modified to some degree due to the experience of some depository institutions, especially savings and loans, with the extra-ordinarily high interest rates in the 1980–82 period. These high interest rates caused severe problems for long-term, fixed-rate lenders who financed their assets with short-term, variable-rate deposits. Reflecting this mismatch of interest-sensitive assets and liabilities, many financial institutions experienced severe financial distress.

local market area and their loans are usually made within an even smaller geographic area. Local consumers and businesses depend essentially upon local financial institutions for credit. The fulfillment of this credit need by commercial banks and other depository financial institutions may be viewed as a social commitment or obligation of the institutions, subject, of course, to the constraints of profitability and risk. This social function performed by lending is perhaps even more significant for the other depository financial institutions, which, for the most part, have been mutual organizations designed to pool the funds of individuals with a common bond or purpose and make loans to these same individuals.

The present chapter initially presents basic information on the composition of the loan portfolio at commercial banks—the most important U.S. financial institution in the lending field. Since this composition cannot be understood within a historical vacuum, there is also some discussion of important trends in the loan portfolio. However, most of the chapter is devoted to the importance of a loan policy at a commercial bank and of the procedures involved in implementing that policy. As such, the discussion is quite general in nature and is essentially applicable to any lending institution, bank or nonbank.

Table 10–1 presents a percentage classification of loans at all insured commercial banks as of December 31, 1982. The traditional emphasis on lending to businesses by commercial banks is evident from the information presented in Table 10–1. Loans formally classified as commercial and industrial accounted for about 20 percent of total assets, while loans to finance agricultural production (which are also essentially business loans, though to a particular segment of the business community) accounted for

COMPOSITION OF THE LOAN PORTFOLIO

Table 10–1 Percentage Distribution of Insured U.S. Bank Loan Portfolios: December 31, 1982
(percent of total assets)

		Banks with Total Assets of ($ millions)					
Nature of Loan	All Banks	Under 5	5–9.9	10–24.9	25–99.9	100–299.9	300 or More
Real estate loans	14.0%	10.0%	13.2%	15.7%	18.0%	19.8%	12.3%
Loans to finance agricultural production	1.7	12.7	12.9	9.9	6.4	1.6	0.6
Commercial and industrial loans	22.0	9.1	9.9	11.3	12.6	17.0	26.2
Loans to individuals	9.0	10.2	11.7	12.2	12.6	12.7	7.7
All other loans	6.7	0.6	0.1	0.2	0.2	0.1	9.3
Total	54.4%	42.7%	47.8%	49.3%	49.8%	51.2%	56.1%

Source: Federal Deposit Insurance Corporation, *Bank Operating Statistics.*

about 2 percent of the total loan portfolio. Moreover, real estate loans, many of which are short-term interim construction loans to business, accounted for a very large fraction of the loan portfolio.

There are, of course, more detailed breakdowns of loans than those discussed above. For example, commercial loans include various types of temporary financing such as credit lines or revolving credit made available to individual borrowers. These types of loans, though, also include more permanent credit, such as the three- to five-year term loans or the permanent working-capital loan. Short-term loans for temporary credit needs are frequently not collateralized. In contrast, long-term loans for permanent credit needs generally carry specific collateral requirements.

The sharp differences in the composition of the loan portfolio at banks of different sizes are also evident from Table 10–1. For the largest size grouping (banks with total assets of over $300 million), the commercial and industrial loan was the largest single type of loan. These types of loans are not only extremely important at larger banks but are also quite cyclical. Much of this type of lending is done for inventory expansion by the borrowing firm. Since inventory holdings of businesses are highly unstable, loan demand also fluctuates markedly. In fact, changes in business inventories are one of the most important influences on short-term fluctuations in the volume of loans outstanding at larger banks.

In contrast, loans classified as commercial and industrial are much less important for smaller banking institutions. For example, at the smallest size group (banks with less than $5 million in total assets), about 13 percent of total assets were accounted for by farm loans. Many of these smaller banks are situated in rural areas where agriculture (including both farming and ranching) is the dominant industry. This type of lending involves both short-term production loans to farmers and ranchers as well as more permanent, long-term agricultural loans. However, most bank loans to farmers are relatively short-term in nature, perhaps because funds are available from government-sponsored credit agencies to provide permanent funds at attractive rates. Moreover, loans to individuals tend to be especially important at small and medium size banks, which frequently are located in residential areas and suburban communities. Loans to individuals encompass lending for the purchase of automobiles, bank credit card loans, and a variety of other types of credit directed at household needs.

Trends in the Loan Portfolio

The loan portfolio of commercial banks has changed drastically in recent years. In general, there has been a decreasing relative emphasis upon business lending and an increase in concentration on consumer and real estate lending. (Some of these trends are shown in Figure 10–1.) This dras-

Figure 10-1   Principal Classes of Loans—All Commercial Banks (semiannual call report dates, 1950–1973; seasonally adjusted, quarterly averages, 1973–1981)

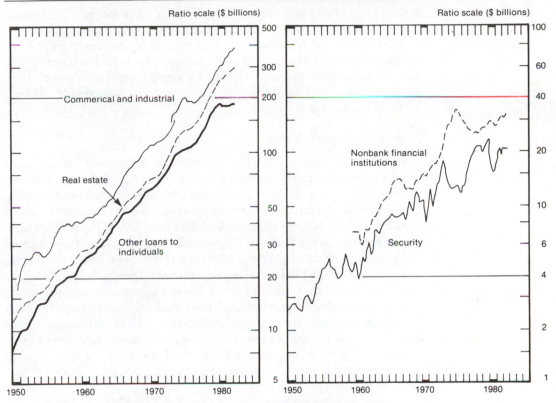

Source: Board of Governors of the Federal Reserve System, *Historical Chart Book, 1982.*

tic change reflects shifts in the economy and the financial system as well as in the relative rates of return on different types of loans. Bank liabilities, once primarily demand deposits, are now mostly time and savings accounts. Reflecting the longer-term nature of bank liabilities and also the more costly aspects of these sources of funds, banks have lengthened their loan portfolios and have increased their emphasis upon real estate related loans. As an example, term loans for the purchase of equipment and buildings are not of great significance at many banks. Also of considerable importance is the shift from fixed-rate to variable-rate lending. Many banks today have almost their entire loan portfolio on a variable-rate (or floating-rate) basis.

There has also been a revolution in the attitude of the financial system toward meeting the borrowing needs of consumers. At one time, consumer credit was viewed as a socially unproductive use of funds by a commercial bank. With the post–World War II emphasis on the consumption of durable goods and the need to finance these purchases, however, attitudes of bankers and others in the financial community have shifted. Commercial banks now actively solicit consumer accounts, both for the purchase of durable goods and for other uses. This change in the loan portfolio has brought commercial banks into active competition with a new group of financial institutions (particularly finance companies, credit unions, and savings banks) and has tended to blur the distinction among different kinds of financial institutions.

Regional Variations in Loans

Bank loan portfolios also reflect variations in geography. Banks located in rapidly growing portions of the nation and having substantial amounts of time and savings deposits place more emphasis on real estate lending than do banks operating in more mature economic environments and depending more heavily on demand deposits as a source of funds. For example, real estate loans made up 31 percent of total assets at commercial banks in Arizona as of year-end 1980. In contrast, real estate loans comprised only 4 percent of total assets at commercial banks in North Dakota as of the same date.[2] Also, banks in Texas and other energy-producing states often have a large fraction of their business loans concentrated in energy-related uses. These two states also vary widely in the degree of urbanization, the economic base, and hence the demand for different kinds of loans. To a very considerable extent the loan mix of an individual financial institution must reflect the nature of the economic base of the market area served by that institution.

LOAN POLICIES: DEVELOPMENT

In view of the importance of lending to the financial health of the individual financial institution and to the community it serves, every financial institution must carefully *plan* its lending operations. Careful consideration should be given to at least two major factors. The lending institution needs some general guidelines or loan policies to assist those involved in making loan decisions. Without such guidelines, individual loan officers are likely to make judgments which are inconsistent with the goals of the organization and which are inconsistent internally from loan officer to loan officer. Moreover, the development of a loan policy forces senior management to grapple with a number of complicated issues and to face significant concerns such as how much risk the institution is prepared to accept in its loan portfolio. Also, a loan policy can be an indispensable aid in the training of new employees. Beyond establishing a loan policy, how-

---

[2]Federal Deposit Insurance Corporation, *Bank Operating Statistics, 1980.*

ever, the institution needs to be concerned about how individual loan applications are evaluated. Here, the most common approach is to establish a set of criteria for evaluating each application. These criteria are usually referred to as the Cs of credit.[3]

Components of a Loan Policy

There are a number of important procedures involved in the establishment of a loan policy. The policy should be written, though the degree of formality of a written loan policy may be a function of the size of the financial institution. While it would be impossible to discuss all of the items which should be incorporated into a written loan policy, some of the most important ones should be mentioned. The policy should provide some general guidelines concerning the desired volume of lending. Since lending is the principal function of a commercial bank, for example, we would expect that the loan portfolio would dominate the asset structure. However, bank management must allocate funds to meet reserve requirements as well as to satisfy anticipated liquidity needs caused by deposit withdrawals. (The same problem is faced to varying degrees by savings banks and credit unions.) In addition, management may wish to hold a substantial amount of longer-term securities in order to achieve asset diversification as well as to minimize tax payments through municipal security investments. The size of the loan portfolio also will be affected by the credit needs of the community as well as the ability of the financial institution to meet those needs. For example, an intermediary may be located in an area of strong deposit potential but weak loan demand. Also important, the management of the institution may not have the expertise to service the particular kinds of loan demands provided by the local community. (For example, petroleum loans require the skill of petroleum engineers at some phase of the decision process.)

Mix of Loans

The loan policy should contain some reference to the *mix of credits* which the institution is to emphasize and what might be an appropriate balance of each type of loan in the loan portfolio. Such specification should be made with regard to the demand for credit in the local economy as well as the size of the intermediary and the expertise of its management. If the local economy is based on agriculture, the loan portfolio of the institution will necessarily be heavily weighted toward credits to farmers and ranchers and business firms serving the needs of farmers and ranchers. Moreover, a small financial institution normally faces a severe limit on the size of its loans to any one customer and this may, in turn, reduce the

---

[3]For a more complete review of these factors see [1], pp. 541–55. Also see [5], chap. 10, for a thorough review of loan policies.

proportion of its loans to business. For example, commercial banks chartered by the federal government (national banks) and many of those chartered by the state are restrained from lending more than 15 percent of their capital, surplus, and undivided profits to any one borrower. For many banks, especially in unit banking states which prohibit branching, this restriction may present an important constraint in the lending program and thereby reduce the long-term growth of the institution.

Charges for Loans

A loan policy would also include reference to customer *charges and fees* for loans and related terms associated with the loan contract.[4] There are a number of aspects of the interest-rate issue which are important. The institution must appraise the degree of credit risk and other factors which should affect the interest rate charged. An important issue concerns how to adjust the rate charged as the perceived risk of the loan varies. One possibility is to group loans into risk categories and vary the interest rate from category to category. The lending institution must also decide if it is to set a fixed rate or a floating rate on its loans. If the institution desires to establish a floating rate, it must decide what interest rate the loan contract rate should be related to. Short-term loans might be expected to have fixed rates, while longer-term loans are more likely to have floating rates, though the decision to establish a fixed or floating rate depends on other factors besides the maturity of the loan, such as the strength of loan demand. Traditionally, floating rate loans have been tied to the prime interest rate (the rate charged to the highest-quality customers for short-term loans). For example, the loan contract may specify that the loan rate will be equal to the prime plus 2 percentage points (200 basis points), in order to reflect credit risk considerations. This provision may run into the problem that in some periods of high interest rates, lenders, especially commercial banks, are under political pressure to hold down increases in the prime rate. In recent years, it has become common to tie loan rates to the London interbank offering rate (LIBOR) on Eurodollar deposits. In some cases, the loan rate might also be tied to the rate on U.S. government securities. It is not uncommon to tie the loan rate to more than one market index, with the borrower having the option to switch from one index to the other (though the frequency of such shifts is usually limited).

Other Factors

An integral part of the loan-pricing decision concerns compensating balance requirements. Compensating balances refer to noninterest-

---

[4]See [8], chap. 10 for an excellent discussion of loan pricing.

bearing deposits (some commercial banks allow time deposits to be used) which the borrower is required to maintain at the lending institution as a condition of the loan. Management must decide on the amount of compensating balance required and on what types of loan-compensating balances will be required. Moreover, decisions about the maturity of different kinds of loans must be made. For example, banks have increasingly been extending the maturity of their auto loans to four years or more. Such a movement reflects the increased cost of automobiles and the desire on the part of borrowers to prevent a sharp increase in monthly installment payments. Management must decide whether their institution should participate in this trend. As a part of this decision, it naturally needs to have some estimate of the implications for loan demand if lending is restricted to short-term car loans. Many banks incurred substantial losses on real estate–related loans in the mid 1970s. Does management wish to continue its participation in this type of lending at all? These are important questions that management must confront in a fast-changing financial environment.

Additional issues in the formulation and implementation of a loan policy involve the extent to which the lender will accept different kinds of credit arrangements. Are there certain kinds of collateral the lender will not accept? If so, under what conditions? How is the financial institution to decide the amount and the terms of these credit lines?

Another important aspect of the loan portfolio that bank management faces is structuring the administrative contact between the bank and the customer. Traditionally, loan officers have been assigned to certain types of loans. For example, a loan officer might be assigned to installment loans, real estate loans, or commercial loans. While this structure still dominates in commercial lending, an increasingly popular arrangement in installment lending is that of the personal banker. With this arrangement, all retail customers of the bank are assigned their own personal banker; that personal banker then handles all the relationships (not just loans) between the bank and the customer.

These are only a few of the issues that must be dealt with in the formulation of loan policy. Perhaps their greatest importance is that they force management to consider critical questions before the lending institution drifts into an undesirable position. Potential problems are less likely to become actual problems if the intermediary anticipates these problems.

Loan Policies: An Illustration

A sample loan policy for commercial banks has been provided by the American Bankers Association in its pamphlet "A Guide to Developing a Written Lending Policy" (1973). This pamphlet lists the following elements of a written loan policy: bank objectives, determination of lending policy, lending-policy administration, lending authorities, loan committee organization, experience and depth of loan staff, geographic limitations, interest rates, credit criteria, coping with grey areas, credit file requirements, credit life policies, and substandard loans. A brief discussion of the major items follows.

Clearly, the development of a loan policy must begin with the *objectives* of the institution. Development and reexamination of the loan policy provide the directors with an opportunity to evaluate the role of the bank (or other lending institution) in community economic development, its support of small business, and other important issues. Recognition must be made that the objectives of the institution are multifaceted, and some ranking of these objectives must be established. In fact, as discussed earlier, one of the major problems facing financial institutions management is reconciling different, and to some extent, conflicting objectives. Internal objectives such as earnings, liquidity, and acceptable risk levels must be specified. Once these goals have been determined, the board of directors must establish policies or rules which are consistent with the objectives. In doing this, it must be recognized that under both state and federal law, as well as common law established by judicial decisions, the board of directors remains ultimately responsible for the activities of the institution.

It is vitally important that procedures be established for the *efficient administration* of the lending function. The responsibility for administration of the lending function should be clear. Lending authorities for each individual and for the various committees in the institution should be specified. Most commercial banks, for example, have specific dollar limits or authority for different personnel. These limits generally increase as the responsibility and experience of the loan officer advance until—at some point—certain officials of the bank may have loan authority equal to the legal lending limit of the institution. A delicate balance must be reached between establishing too low and too high loan authorities for individual officers. Loan limits which are too low will discourage the progress of individual loan officers, force senior management (including the board of directors) to review an excessive amount of small-quantity loans, and perhaps drive away larger customers. Conversely, loan limits which are too high add risk to the institution's loan portfolio, in that inexperienced loan officers may commit the institution to undesirable loans. Certainly, it would be expected that the distribution of loan limits among individual loan officers would vary with the size of the lending institution.

The loan policy should also describe the *functions of the loan committee organization*. While there are no definite patterns for the organization of a loan committee, loan committees generally meet weekly or more frequently in order to consider loans that are in excess of some particular amount or outside the normal credit standards of the organization. The loan committee should be supported by a credit analysis group which has regular contact with the loan officers and also has access to all relevant credit files. At smaller commercial banks, for example, the size of the organization precludes setting up a separate credit analysis group, and loan officers must do their own investigation and analysis. At a few large banks, where a credit analysis department is feasible, operating policies still call for individual loan officers to perform their own credit investigation as a means of maintaining closer knowledge of the prospective borrower.

Loan policy should include some reference to the *trade area* of the lending institution. It might specify a primary trade area within which loans should be sought and also a secondary trade area which might be investigated more fully when loan demand from the primary trade area is weak. Naturally, the relevant trade area will vary with the size of the institution. A small financial institution generally should consider the local community and its immediate environment as the primary trade area. In contrast, a medium size lending institution may consider a particular region as its primary trade area while the largest institutions may consider the entire nation and even some foreign countries as falling within their trade area.

One important deficiency at many financial institutions in the past concerns the maintenance of *records* on borrowers, referred to as credit files. The exact credit file requirements for different kinds of loans should be specified in the written loan policy. Certainly the lender should have a credit file for every borrower and, in fact, may face serious difficulties with examiners if the credit files are not properly maintained. While the file may be large or small depending upon the particular characteristics of each loan, such as size and collateral, the file should provide all the important information necessary for the credit decisions, including complete financial statements for the prospective borrower. It is particularly important that the credit file contain sufficient information to justify the institution's decision on the loan application, whether that decision is positive or negative.

Commercial banks, as the most important lending institutions, have had substantial difficulty in recent years with the quality of their loans. Following the 1973–74 recession, loan losses at commercial banks mounted to particularly high levels and, at some banks, exceeded by a substantial margin the reserve for bad debts which the banks had amassed over a considerable period. Moreover, there was some evidence during this period that loan losses were not simply associated with the business cycle but also reflected improper lending standards of some institutions. Similar problems surfaced during the 1980–82 economic decline. Given these problems, it is vitally important that the individual financial institution include in the written policy some procedures for handling *substandard loans*.[5] While no financial intermediary makes loans which, before the fact, it knows to be substandard, all intermediaries can expect to have some loans that turn substandard after the fact. At larger lending institutions, the number of such loans may warrant the creation of a special department staffed with seasoned loan officers and other specialists who would be available to consult with other loan officers on problem cases or who might even assume responsibility for problem loans (in which case the loans would be transferred from the loan officer to the specialized department). Such a transfer policy does have the advantage of shifting problem loans to those with specialized knowledge (frequently the legal problems involved with these loans are great), but it has the disadvantage of not forcing the loan officer to live with prior mistakes. While such a policy would be impractical for a small intermediary, it is vital for every financial institution to have some established procedures for handling substandard loans and investments.

Loan Policies: Implementation

It is insufficient just to state a general lending policy. Those involved in the lending function must also take these general guidelines and apply them to a specific loan situation, making the final accept or reject decision based upon both quantitative and qualitative factors. The type of analysis which lies behind the loan decision varies widely from institution to institution. At relatively small commercial banks located in rural areas, for example, great importance is often placed on personal relationships between borrower and lender, and less significance is attached to financial statements and other objective sources of information. In contrast, in urban areas where personal relationships are frequently less stable, more reliance necessarily must be placed on hard evidence regarding the credit worthiness of different individuals and businesses. Moreover, in large-scale commercial lending, analysis of financial statements by the credit department of the organization becomes a vital factor.

A number of factors generally are emphasized in lending decisions. These are usually referred to as the Cs of credit. The number of Cs varies

---

[5]Bank examiners classify loans as substandard, doubtful, and loss. A substandard loan involves high credit risk and frequent monitoring. A doubtful loan has even higher credit risk, high enough that the final resolution of the credit problem cannot be predicted. A loan classified as loss is one that involves immediate loss to the institution and must be written off the books. This does not mean that loans classified as loss are never collected. Many such loans are ultimately collected in full.

from lender to lender, but the following three are commonly used: character, capacity to generate income, and collateral.[6]

Character refers to the personal traits of the borrower (completely apart from financial standing) which may be significant in the credit decision. Terms such as *ethical*, *honest*, and *integrity* are important in this regard. It is often said that character is the most important of the Cs of credit, since a dishonest borrower can always find a way to avoid the restrictions imposed by the lender in a loan agreement. Certainly, character should be one of the first factors examined by a loan officer. Given acceptable character, the other Cs of credit can be explored; but if it is found that this C is inadequate, further analysis would not be warranted. No matter how good the collateral or the financial position of the borrower, the lending institution should not provide a loan to anyone who does not meet its character standard.

Capacity to generate income refers to the ability of the borrower to generate sufficient funds either through liquidation of assets or earnings to repay the loan. Relevant to this question is the quality of management of the organization as distinct from the character of the individuals involved. In a long-term commitment, the lender would be inclined to look toward the earning potential of the borrower for repayment of interest and principal. Funds would be invested in permanent assets, and the cash flow generated from the operation of these permanent assets would be used to retire the debt. In contrast, funds for short-term loan repayment would come from liquidation of current assets, and, hence, the liquidity position of the firm would be crucial. For long-term loans, focus would be on interest-coverage ratio (profitability related to interest payments); while, on short-term loans, liquidity ratios would take on more importance. The financial analysis associated with loan applications concentrates on this C of credit.

The type of analysis which is used to evaluate capacity might best be explained through an example based on the procedures followed at a particular multibillion-dollar commercial bank in handling large commercial loan applications. The credit department of the bank receives a request from the loan officer to evaluate the financial characteristics of a particular loan applicant. The credit analyst then seeks information from a variety of sources. Financial statements of the applicant are essential but are not sufficient. Additional information comes from tax statements, news-

---

[6]Reed [10] refers to the five Cs of credit: capacity, character, capital, collateral, and conditions. *Capacity* refers to the legal ability of the borrower to obligate himself or herself as well as the organization the person purports to represent. *Conditions* refers to the general economic conditions beyond the control of the borrower that may affect the ability of the borrower to repay the loan.

paper clippings, and related sources. It is important to have information available on the industry in which the applicant operates in order to make good-bad evaluations. Many such sources are readily available. Government publications and industry trade periodicals are relatively easy to obtain. Financial ratios for various industries can be found in a number of places. One excellent source is the *Annual Statement Studies* published by Robert Morris Associates, a group of commercial loan officers working for commercial banks. In addition, Dun & Bradstreet publishes useful lists of financial ratios. It is important for the analyst to keep up with local business conditions, especially if the applicant is heavily dependent upon the local community for sales.

One of the most comprehensive sets of industry standards is provided by Robert Morris Associates. The *Annual Statement Studies* includes industry information on liquidity, coverage of fixed charges such as interest, and the current portion of long-term debt; leverage, including both operating leverage (as measured by the ratio of net fixed assets to tangible net worth) and financial leverage (as measured by the ratio of total liabilities to tangible net worth); various operating ratios that are designed to measure profitability and efficiencies in the use of assets; and expense ratios (see Table 10–2).

Once the data have been obtained, it is then possible to proceed with the credit analysis, which will culminate in a report to the loan officer. Such a report should include at least the following: (1) the purpose of the analysis (whether the request is for a short-term working capital loan or for a long-term capital loan), (2) the previous relationships of the customer with the lending institution (of substantial importance because management is interested in the profitability of the total customer relationship and not simply of one loan), (3) the business history of the firm, (4) the characteristics of the industry within which the firm operates, and (5) the financial operating factors relevant to the firm.

Analysis of financial operating factors is especially important in determining the ability of the borrower to repay the loan. Both income statement and balance-sheet ratios are calculated, sources and applications of funds are examined, and liquidity and leverage ratios are incorporated into the analysis. The report then concludes with a summary of the findings of the analyst.

Collateral is the third C of credit. This refers to the ability of the borrower to pledge specific assets to secure the loan. These assets may be fixed in nature, such as land and buildings, or working capital, such as inventory and accounts receivable. While collateral is important in reducing risk, it should not be viewed as a substitute for adequate earnings potential. Indeed, collateralized business loans generally carry higher interest rates than noncollateralized business loans. Low-risk loans are of-

Table 10–2   Principal Ratios Contained in Robert Morris Associates'
Annual Statement Studies

Ratio	Definition
A. Liquidity	
1. Current ratio	$\dfrac{\text{Total current assets}}{\text{Total current liabilities}}$
2. Quick ratio	$\dfrac{\text{Cash and equivalents} + \text{Accounts and notes receivable}}{\text{Total current liabilities}}$
3. Sales/Receivables	$\dfrac{\text{Net sales}}{\text{Accounts and notes receivable}}$
4. Cost of sales/Inventory	$\dfrac{\text{Cost of sales}}{\text{Inventory}}$
5. Sales/Working capital	$\dfrac{\text{Sales}}{\text{Net working capital}}$
B. Coverage ratios	
1. Earnings before interest and taxes (Ebit/Interest)	$\dfrac{\text{Earnings before interest and taxes}}{\text{Annual interest expense}}$
2. Cash flow/Current maturities long-term debt	$\dfrac{\text{Net profit} + \text{depreciation, depletion, amortization expenses}}{\text{Current portion of long-term debt}}$
C. Leverage ratios	
1. Fixed/Worth	$\dfrac{\text{Net fixed assets}}{\text{Tangible net worth}}$
2. Debt/Worth	$\dfrac{\text{Total liabilities}}{\text{Tangible net worth}}$
D. Operating ratios	
1. % Profits before taxes/Tangible net worth	$\dfrac{\text{Profit before taxes}}{\text{Tangible net worth}} \times 100$
2. Profits before taxes/Total assets	$\dfrac{\text{Profit before taxes}}{\text{Total assets}} \times 100$
3. Net sales/Net fixed assets	$\dfrac{\text{Net sales}}{\text{Net fixed assets}}$
4. Sales/Total assets	$\dfrac{\text{Net sales}}{\text{Total assets}}$
E. Expense-to-sales ratios	
1. % Depreciation, depletion, amortization/Sales	$\dfrac{\text{Depreciation, depletion, amortization}}{\text{Net sales}} \times 100$
2. % Lease and rental expense/Sales	$\dfrac{\text{Lease and rental expenses}}{\text{Sales}} \times 100$
3. % Officer's compensation/Sales	$\dfrac{\text{Officer's compensation}}{\text{Net sales}}$

Source: Robert Morris Associates, *Annual Statement Studies*.

ten made regardless of collateral. Higher risk is frequently offset to some extent by requiring collateral as well as by raising the rate of interest charged. However, especially high-risk loans should not be viewed as being made acceptable by collateral requirements. Such loans should not be made regardless of collateral possibilities. Collateral should be reviewed as a second line of defense (second to the ability of the borrower to generate cash flow from operations to repay the loan) in order to protect the lender.

The usefulness of collateral in the credit-granting process is affected by the nature of the collateral acceptable to the lender. For example, the lender may establish a policy of not accepting precious metals as collateral due to their frequently high price volatility as well as the difficulty of determining the true composition of the metal. If so, the lender may have to seek alternative collateral.

Loan Pricing and Profitability

Since interest revenue and fees on loans represent the bulk of the total revenue for most banking organizations, it is vitally important that loans be properly priced and an evaluation made of the different profitability of different types of loans. In order to do this, management must evaluate the following three factors:

1. The cost of making different types of loans.
2. The expected loan-loss ratio on different types of loans.
3. The interest rate charged on the loan.

The operating (as opposed to the funding or money) costs of making different types of loans vary widely. Those loans which are usually made in small denominations and which involve large amounts of time of clerical and management personnel for the bank are generally high cost per dollar of loans expended. In contrast, those loans which are made in large denomination and which involve small amounts of personnel time are

---

Table 10–3   Operating Expenses for Various Types of Loans (percent of funds used): 1981

Type of Loan	Size of Banks		
	Banks Up to $50 Million in Total Assets	Banks $50–100 Million	Banks over $200 Million
Real estate mortgage loans	.895%	.783%	.874%
Installment loans	3.407	3.372	3.304
Commercial and other loans	1.957	1.619	1.509

Source: Federal Reserve System, *Functional Cost Analysis, 1981 Average Banks.*

usually low cost per dollar of loans expended. Installment lending in general and credit card loans in particular fall into the former category and are high-cost types of loans, while large-volume commercial lending falls in the latter category and is a less costly type of lending. For example, it has been estimated that the cost of a credit card loan (as a fraction of the funds used) is almost *10 times* that of a commercial loan.

The profitability of loans or a class of loans also is affected by the loss experienced on loans. Unfortunately, as many banks found out in the early 1980s, the actual default experience on their loan portfolio sometimes is much higher than expected. But of particular importance to the loan allocation decision is the different default loss for different types of loans. For example, the actual default rate on credit card loans is often two or three or more times the default rate on commercial loans. Hence, when evaluating the desirability of making consumer, as contrasted with commercial loans, management should adjust (reduce) the interest return on the loans for the expected loan loss for each type of loan.

The profitability of loans is, of course, determined by the interaction of the cost of the loans, the expected default loss, and the interest rate that the bank can charge. The interest rate that is possible for the bank to charge is determined by competition. For large commercial loans to high-quality national or international borrowers, there is a single rate for credit, determined by competition among a large number of potential lenders. The individual lender for that loan is a price taker, not a price maker. The bank can look at its cost of funds, its operating costs of making the loan, the expected default loss, and the potential interest return on the loan and then determine whether or not it wishes to make the loan. In contrast, in most local and less competitive loan markets, the bank is a price maker; that is, the bank can set the price of the loans. In doing so, of course, the bank must recognize the "law of the downward sloping demand curve." It may set a higher price, but, if so, it will reduce the amount of funds that it may loan; and any excess funds will have to be disposed of in the securi-

Table 10–4 Loan Losses for Various Types of Loans (percent of funds used): 1981

	Size of Banks		
Type of Loan	*Banks Up to $50 Million in Total Assets*	*Banks $50–100 Million*	*Banks over $200 Million*
Real estate mortgage loans	0.46%	0.46%	0.51%
Installment loans	0.62	0.55	0.64
Commercial and other loans	0.410	0.356	0.339

Source: Federal Reserve System, *Functional Cost Analysis, 1981 Average Banks.*

ties markets, generally with a smaller return. The bank must also recognize that while all loan markets in which it is a price maker have a downward sloping demand curve, the elasticity of the demand curve may vary substantially from one type of loan to another. The quantity of some loans may be highly sensitive to changes in the interest rate while others (most with less elastic demand curves) may not be sensitive.

In summary, the profitability of different types of loans may be evaluated as follows:

$$P = I - O - F - D$$

where

I = Interest return (including fees associated with making the loan)
O = Operating costs associated with making the loan
F = The cost of funds
D = Expected default loss

GOVERNMENT RESTRICTIONS

It should also be recognized that lenders are increasingly constrained in their credit decisions by a variety of government regulations designed to assure equal access for all to sources of funds. While the impact of these restraints are greatest in the consumer credit area, they affect a variety of types of loans. Although usury regulations (limits on the maximum rates charged on loans) have been common for some time, the decades of the 1960s and 1970s have resulted in a large increase in the types of regulations applicable to loans made by financial intermediaries. These regulations have included disclosure requirements on interest rates under the Truth-in-Lending Act, substantial restrictions under the Equal Credit Opportunity Act, and important restrictions under other statutes.

The *truth-in-lending* law imposes substantial restrictions on lenders. The principle purpose of this legislation is to provide consumers with accurate information on the cost of credit in a uniform way, thereby allowing borrowers to more readily compare the charges from different credit sources. The law requires the lender to provide the total finance charge—the total amount of dollars paid by the borrower over the life of the loan—and the annual percentage rate (or APR) as it is frequently called. The annual percentage rate provides a means for the borrower to compare credit costs regardless of the amount of the costs or the length of time over which payments are made. Both the total finance charge (including any service charge or carrying charge) and the annual percentage rate must be displayed prominently on the forms and statements used by the lender. Such complete information on the credit terms must also be included in advertising by the lender (provided that any credit information is included).

The truth-in-lending law also affects the relationship between lender and borrower through the use of credit cards. For example, the law provides that consumer liability for lost or stolen credit cards is limited to $50. Moreover, for the lender to hold the borrower responsible even for that amount, the unauthorized use of the credit card must have occurred before the card issuer has been notified by the cardholder, who is not liable for any unauthorized use occurring after such notification. The law also prohibits card issuers from mailing a credit card to a potential customer unless the customer requested or applied for it.

The *Equal Credit Opportunity Act* also has important implications for lenders. This law prohibits discrimination against an applicant for credit because of age, sex, marital status, race, color, religion, national origin, or receipt of public assistance. It also prohibits discrimination because the potential borrower has made a good faith exercise of any of the rights granted under the federal consumer credit laws. It further requires that the borrower be notified in writing if credit is denied and gives the borrower the right to ask the reason for such a denial. In the event of an alleged violation of the Equal Credit Opportunity Act, the borrower may seek redress from the appropriate supervisory agency of the lender.

A number of other laws are also relevant to the credit process. The *Fair Credit Billing Act* requires the lender to promptly correct a billing error. This law is especially relevant for credit card purchases. It provides that on a credit card purchase the purchaser may withhold payment of any balance due on defective merchandise or service purchased with a credit card, provided the purchaser has made a good faith effort to resolve the difficulties with the seller. The *Fair Credit Reporting Act* establishes a procedure for the prompt correction of errors on credit records and requires that such records be kept confidential. The *Consumer Lending Act* (which applies only to personal property leased by an individual for a period of more than four months for personal, family, or household use) requires that borrowers be furnished with the facts about the cost and terms of leasing contracts. This allows the lessee to compare the cost of leasing with the cost of buying. It also limits any extra payments made by the lessee at the end of the lease and regulates lease advertising.

Two important laws affect the real estate lender in particular. The *Real Estate Settlement Procedures Act* requires that the buyer of real property be given information about the services and costs involved at settlement, when real property transfers from seller to buyer. The *Home Mortgage Disclosure Act* requires most lending institutions in metropolitan areas to let the public know where they make their mortgage and home-improvement loans.

The *Community Reinvestment Act* requires that the regulatory authorities take into account the extent to which the financial institution is meeting the credit needs of its community when evaluating branching, mergers, and holding company requests made by these institutions. The impact of the Community Reinvestment Act (as well as the other laws mentioned) on the quality of loans made by banks and other financial institutions is difficult to know, though these requirements obviously limit managerial discretion and increase lender cost. Moreover, the increases in costs associated with these programs may make it more difficult for small financial institutions to survive and may thereby lead to an even more rapid consolidation of the financial structure.

SUMMARY

Lending is critically important to the success of a financial institution. Loans provide most of the income for financial institutions, especially depository institutions, and it is in the loan portfolio where risk is concentrated. The composition of the loan portfolio for individual financial institutions varies with the demand for loans as well as the attitude and expertise of management. A loan policy is an important part of the management planning process. It should be written and cover at least the following factors: the volume of lending, the mix of loans, and the pricing system for individual loans. It may also discuss the objectives of the institution; the procedures for administering the lending function, including the functions of the loan committee organization; the trade area of the lending institution; the maintenance of records or credit files; and the procedures for dealing with substandard loans.

While it is necessary for efficient management of the lending function to develop a loan policy, it is also important to implement that policy. Such an implementation focuses on evaluating the quality of credit requests, with emphasis on the accept or reject decision. This usually involves the Cs of credit: character, capacity, and collateral. *Character* refers to the personal traits of the borrower, as contrasted with managerial talent. *Capacity* is the ability of the borrower to generate funds to repay the loan. *Collateral* refers to the ability of the borrower to pledge specific assets to secure the loan. In all of these decisions, the lender is constrained to some degree by government regulation, such as the Equal Credit Opportunity Act.

Questions

10-1. What are the major types of bank loans? How do they differ by bank size? Why?

10-2. What type of information might be found in a financial institution's loan policy?

10-3. What is a compensating balance? What role does it play in lending?

10-4. What is the difference between a fixed interest rate and a floating interest rate?

10–5. What are the relative merits of tying the price of a loan to the prime rate as compared to the LIBOR rate?

10–6. What is the purpose of a loan committee? Credit files?

10–7. What are the Cs of credit? Explain the characteristics of each.

10–8. What factors are considered in a credit analysis of a potential loan recipient?

10–9. What are the principal government restrictions on loan policies? Would they affect small and large institutions in the same way? If not, why not?

References

1. Baughn, William H., and Charls E. Walker, eds. *The Banker's Handbook* Homewood, Ill.: Dow Jones–Irwin, 1978, pp. 541–610.

2. Crosse, Howard, and George Hempel. *The Management of Bank Funds*. Englewood Cliffs, N.J.: Prentice-Hall, 1980, chaps. 11, 12.

3. Hester, Donald D. "An Empirical Examination of a Commercial Bank Loan Offer Function." *Yale Economic Essays*, spring 1962, pp. 3–57.

4. Hoeven, James A., and Jerone S. Oldham. "Commercial Loan Profitability-Pricing Analysis." *The Journal of Commercial Bank Lending*, June 1976, 44–57.

5. Jessup, Paul. *Modern Bank Management*. Minneapolis: West Publishing, 1980, chaps. 10–14.

6. Hodgman, D. R. *Commercial Bank Loans and Investment Policy*. Champaign, Ill.: Bureau of Economic and Business Research, University of Illinois, 1963.

7. Malone, Robert B. "Written Loan Policies." *The Journal of Commercial Bank Lending*, June 1976, pp. 18–24.

8. Mason, John M. *Financial Management of Commercial Banks*. Boston: Warren, Gorham & Lamont, 1979, chaps. 8–11.

9. Ponting, John T., and George R. Sanderson. "Profitable Loans, Risk, and the Loan officer." *The Bankers Magazine*, spring 1976, 68–72.

10. Reed, Edward W., Richard V. Cotter, Edward K. Gill, and Richard K. Smith. *Commercial Banking*. Englewood Cliffs, N.J.: Prentice-Hall, 1976, chaps. 8–16.

11. Wood, Oliver G. *Commercial Banking*. New York: D. Van Nostrand, 1978, pt. 4.

Problem for Discussion

THIS CHAPTER HAS DISCUSSED THE LENDING FUNCTION of financial institutions such as commercial banks. Lending not only produces most of the income of commercial banks but also accounts for most of the risk embodied in the bank's asset structure. As such, the evaluation of individual loan applications—in which management must evaluate the loan against its lending policies and perform a credit analysis of the loan—is crucial to the success of the enterprise. The problem situation provided by City National Bank presents students with an opportunity to engage in credit analysis. Students should place themselves in the position of the credit analyst and, after reviewing the material below, address the following questions:

1. What are the strengths and weaknesses of the loan application of Jones Manufacturing? What financial ratios are most relevant in evaluating the application? What types of industry ratios should be used for comparisons?
2. Should the loan be granted? If not, is there an alternative loan request which would be acceptable to the bank?

Jones Manufacturing is a family-owned firm engaged in the business of producing clothing of various types. Sales are primarily within the Southwest region and the output is marketed under the names of a number of large retailing organizations. The output of the firm includes slacks, shirts, and ready-to-wear suits, with casual and dress slacks accounting for about 50 percent of total sales volume. Founded by Fred Jones's father, George, immediately after World War II, the business has prospered during most of its life, although it experienced financial difficulties during some periods of adverse economic developments nationally. While the sales of Jones Manufacturing were affected to a moderate degree by national economic trends, they were subject to greater swings (as is true of the clothing industry generally) due to changes in taste, fashion, and technology.

Many clothing firms which were highly profitable 10 years ago are bankrupt today because they failed to adjust to the changing dimensions of the marketplace. As an example of these types of problems, Jones Manufacturing had recently experienced two successive unprofitable years in a row due to a shift in demand from cotton slacks to double knit polyester. Indeed, the most recent year had been the worst in the company's history. The senior management of the firm had failed to anticipate these developments and had been stuck with stagnating sales and substantial excess inventory, which it subsequently was forced to write down in value. Moreover, the shift in sales mix from cotton to polyester also caused production inefficiencies which has further reduced the profitability of Jones (see Exhibits 10–1 and 10–2).

Jones Manufacturing was founded by George Jones in 1946. The location in a moderate size city in south Texas was not attributable to any careful study of economic factors by the elder Jones but simply to the fact that he had served in the armed services during World War II at a local military base, had liked the city, and had chosen to stay and capitalize on his knowledge of clothing manufacturing acquired as a youth in New York City. In one sense, though, the location was fortuitous since there was an abundance of relatively cheap labor, which allowed a firm using a labor-intensive production process such as the manufacturing of clothing to gain a competitive edge over rivals from higher-cost locations. The firm had grown at a moderate rate, although episodes of rapid growth and high profitability had alternated with those of slow growth and diminished profitability. The instability inherent in the business had caused problems in the local community and especially with the firm's labor force. It seemed as if Jones Manufacturing was always hiring at a frantic pace or laying off at an equally frantic pace. Recently there had been some talk among the workers of attempting to unionize in order to stabilize working conditions.

George Jones had dominated the firm throughout its early life. From 1946 until 1968 he had served as president and chief executive officer and currently is chairman of the board of directors. In many respects, the financial position of the firm throughout its history reflected his conservative philosophy. Recognizing the cyclical nature of the business, he had always tried to create a strong balance sheet with high liquidity and low debt which would absorb the financial pressures placed on the firm during periods of adversity. He also hoped to begin times of economic decline with a strong cash position and little short-term debt. The only long-term indebtedness of the firm reflected the expansion of the plant (and the purchase of some adjacent land for future growth, which was completed about five years ago). The only exception to this conservative attitude concerned dividend policy. Jones Manufacturing Corporation had originally been financed through pooling the funds of George Jones and a number of his friends and relatives. George had remained grateful to these supporters and had increased the dividend almost every year regardless of the current profitability of the firm. Many of the original investors were now retired and depended to varying extents on the cash from these dividends for financial support. George Jones further defended this policy by saying that the dividends paid each year were dependent on the long-run profitability of the firm, not on the profits of any one year.

George Jones was playing a steadily diminishing role in the firm. Increasingly he participated only in the strategic decisions of the organization and left the tactical issues to others. In contrast, his son, Fred, who

Exhibit 10-1
JONES MANUFACTURING CORPORATION
Balance Sheets

Assets	19XX-2	19XX-1	19XX
Cash	$ 800,000	$ 600,000	$ 100,000
Accounts receivable	650,000	600,000	800,000
Inventory	1,600,000	2,300,000	2,600,000
Total current assets	3,050,000	3,500,000	3,500,000
Plant and equipment (net)	1,200,000	1,000,000	800,000
Total assets	$4,250,000	$4,500,000	$4,300,000

Liabilities and Capital	19XX-2	19XX-1	19XX
Accounts payable	$ 900,000	$1,435,000	$1,785,000
Notes payable—bank	300,000	350,000	750,000
Total current liabilities	1,200,000	1,785,000	2,535,000
Long-term debt	800,000	800,000	800,000
Capital stock	500,000	500,000	800,000
Surplus	500,000	500,000	500,000
Undivided profits	1,250,000	925,000	(335,000)
Total liabilities and capital	$4,250,000	$4,500,000	$4,300,000

Exhibit 10-2
JONES MANUFACTURING CORPORATION
Income Statements

	19XX-2	19XX-1	19XX
Sale (net)	$8,250,000	$8,500,000	$8,000,000
Cost of goods sold	6,400,000	7,200,000	7,400,000
Gross profit	1,850,000	1,300,000	600,000
General and administrative expenses	1,200,000	1,400,000	1,600,000
Net profit before taxes	650,000	(100,000)	(1,000,000)
Income taxes	280,000	0	0
Net profit after taxes	$ 370,000	$ (100,000)	$(1,000,000)
Dividends paid	200,000	225,000	250,000

had been appointed president and chief executive officer in 1976, was assuming a greater role in the major decisions of the firm. However, it remained clear to all those involved that George Jones retained a veto power over all major decisions. Fred Jones had been brought up to know the business from top to bottom. During the summers throughout high school and college he had worked on various phases of the firm's operations. Moreover, when he graduated from college he was given an intensive one-year training program in all aspects of the firm's activities. He seemed, however, to be most interested in the production side of the business (perhaps reflecting his engineering training in college) and often spent days working on schemes to reduce production costs. Moreover, there was speculation (completely unconfirmed) that George Jones was somewhat disappointed in his son's inattention to the details of the business. It was known that the younger Jones spent a considerable amount of time skiing and playing golf.

The specific proposal made by Jones Manufacturing to City National Bank was the following: City National would extend a five-year, $3 million term loan to Jones for the purpose of repaying existing short-term bank debt (which totaled almost $1 million at the time of the request) and to purchase new equipment required to produce a new blend of polyester fiber slacks.[1] The slacks—it was said by Fred Jones—resulting from the new blend were substantially superior to any existing material and could command a premium price. And the new production process would allow output to be established at about 10 percent per unit below existing costs. It was envisioned that within two years this new type of material would allow Jones Manufacturing to expand output by 25 percent and that the new material would make up almost 50 percent of the total output of the firm eventually. Currently, Jones Manufacturing is operating at less than 75 percent capacity. As Fred Jones said, "Once the production of our existing line gets back to normal and we add the increased output at lower cost associated with the new product, we should have no trouble servicing the debt. In fact, we might very well be able to pay the debt off before maturity."

---

[1]City National Bank is located 200 miles from the home of Jones Manufacturing. Jones Manufacturing does not maintain a deposit account with City National nor has it ever banked from City National. The request stemmed from the present friendship of Fred Jones and a senior vice president at City National.

11. *Investment Policies*

THE INVESTMENT PORTFOLIO at commercial banks and other financial institutions includes securities held principally to provide income, as opposed to those which are held principally for liquidity. For some financial institutions, such as mutual funds and insurance companies, securities represent the major proportion of their total assets. In contrast, for commercial banks and most other deposit type financial institutions, investments in securities typically take second place to loans and at times serve as substitutes for loans. For example, if banks are experiencing strong loan demand, few securities may be purchased and some securities previously purchased will be sold in order to fund new loans. When loan demand weakens, however, banks and other depository institutions typically will expand their security investments. This suggests that management of the security portfolio is an extremely difficult job and that losses are often substantial. For example, in a period of rising interest rates, securities held by a bank often must be sold subject to significant capital losses to accommodate rising loan demand.

Security investments are held by banks and other financial institutions for essentially four reasons: (1) income, (2) tax sheltering, (3) diversification to reduce risk when the need arises, and (4) liquidity. The dominant reason securities are held by most financial institutions is *income*, in the form of interest, dividends, and capital gains. For certain financial institutions (especially commercial banks and certain types of insurance companies), however, sheltering income from *taxes* is also a critically important reason for holding securities. For example, commercial banks are exposed to the full burden of the corporate income tax, and, since the bank's ability to reduce taxable income through loan loss provisions has been reduced in recent years, management has sought additional means to reduce the bank's effective tax rate.[1] While the loan portfolio offers only

---

[1]See Chapter 7 for a discussion of loan loss provisions and bank financial statements.

limited tax reduction opportunities (without taking actual losses), the purchase of municipal securities whose income is exempt from federal income taxes provides an excellent vehicle to shelter income. As a result, banks have invested heavily in the obligations of states and political subdivisions (municipals) regardless of the strength of local loan demand. The success of this policy can be judged by examining the extremely low effective tax rates of some of the nation's largest banks.

Most securities purchased by financial institutions have an active resale market, providing essential liquidity when additional funds are needed. In addition, through the investment portfolio, management is able to achieve the desired degree of diversification of assets and reduce the risk of failure associated with the faltering of the local economy.[2]

In the following discussion of investment portfolios and investment principles, we focus mainly upon commercial bank investments. However, the basic principles involved apply to many different kinds of financial institutions.

Table 11–1 presents information on the securities portfolios of large commercial banks in the United States. It should be noted that the balance sheet classification of securities is in terms of the borrower or issuer of the securities (U.S. government, municipal, etc.) and maturity, rather than functions (liquidity versus income), though maturity and function of the securities are often closely related. Not all of the over $100 billion in total securities should be considered as a part of the investment portfolio; a substantial share would qualify as liquid securities in that they are held primarily for liquidity purposes. While the dividing line between those securities held primarily for liquidity and those held principally for income is an arbitrary one, it is conventional to treat securities with a maturity of less than one year as a part of the liquid assets of the bank and those with a maturity of more than one year as a part of the investment portfolio.[3] By this criterion, at least $20 billion of the total securities portfolio (Treasury bills, notes, and bonds maturing in less than one year, and short-term

THE NATURE OF THE INVESTMENT PORTFOLIO

---

[2]For a portfolio of securities, the appropriate measure of risk for the individual assets is the covariance of returns on the assets with the existing portfolio rather than the variance or standard deviation of the returns on the individual assets. For institutions like banks, credit unions, and savings and loans that concentrate on making local loans, an additional loan drawn from the local market is likely to have a high covariance (high risk) with the existing portfolio. At some point, then, the risk-return mix for securities becomes superior to the opportunities available from the loan portfolio. Moreover, with municipal securities, the bank is able to obtain both a tax shelter and a financial asset with low covariance of returns (provided it is not a local municipal obligation).

[3]See Chapter 9 for a discussion of the distinction between investments and securities held for liquidity purposes.

Table 11–1   Investment Holdings of Large U.S. Commercial Banks: July 27, 1983 ($ millions)

U.S. Treasury securities:		$ 41,026
One year or less	13,654	
Over one through five years	24,648	
Greater than five years	2,524	
Other securities:		77,937
Obligations of states and political subdivisions	58,008	
One year or less	7,701	
Over one year	50,307	
U.S. government agencies	16,416	
Other bonds, corporate stocks, and securities	3,513	
Total		$118,963

Source: *Federal Reserve Bulletin*, August 1983.

municipals) would qualify as liquid assets, and the remaining securities would be a part of the investment portfolio (many agency securities also would qualify as part of the liquidity portfolio, though their maturity is not given in Table 11–1). In fact, as shown in Table 11–1, the average maturity of the U.S. government securities portfolio is considerably shorter than the average maturity of the municipal securities portfolio, suggesting that the U.S. government issues are held primarily for liquidity, while the municipal issues are held primarily for income and tax reasons.

Municipals

Those securities which qualify as a part of the investment portfolio today at most commercial banks and especially at large banks are principally obligations of states and political subdivisions (commonly referred to as municipals). Municipals include the debt securities of states, counties, cities, school districts, pollution control government units, and other similar governmental units. These debt securities may be either (1) general obligation bonds (GOs), in which case the "full faith and credit" (taxing power) of the governmental unit is available to secure payment of interest and principal; or (2) revenue bonds, whereby the revenue generated from the project (such as a public power authority) is used to pay principal and interest. Revenue bonds have grown faster than general obligation bonds as taxpayers have sought to limit increases in their tax burden.

Advantages and Disadvantages of Municipal Holdings

The major advantage of municipal obligations to the commercial bank is their exemption from the federal income tax. Many commercial banks have found the after-tax return from municipal securities to be quite attractive as compared to taxable instruments. For example, if a commercial bank can obtain a 10 percent pretax return (and the same after-tax return, since there are no federal income tax requirements on the interest) from these securities, and assuming that the bank is in the 46-percent tax bracket, it would have to earn 18.5 percent on a taxable debt instrument (corporate or U.S. government) to provide an after-tax return equal to that of the municipal. It is unlikely that the capital market would provide a return equal to 18.5 percent on taxables when tax-exempt securities are providing only 10 percent. Indeed, the spread between municipals and taxable securities of comparable quality is usually considerably less than the 8.5 percentage points in the illustration, although this spread does vary considerably over the business cycle. In October 1983, municipal Aaa-rated securities averaged 9.7 percent, while Aaa-rated corporate securities averaged 12.3 percent.

There is another compelling and related argument for the concentration of bank investment portfolios in municipals besides higher after-tax returns on these securities. Unlike ordinary investors, the commercial bank is able to borrow funds, deduct the interest paid on those borrowed funds and yet retain the tax exemption on the municipal securities in which the borrowed funds are invested. This possibility makes municipal investments especially attractive. For example, suppose that the commercial bank pays 10 percent for funds obtained through time and savings accounts. Assuming an effective tax rate of 46 percent, the after-tax cost of these funds is just 5.4 percent. As long as the bank can earn more than 5.4 percent on municipal securities, it would pay bank management to continue borrowing money (through selling CDs, for example) and to invest the funds in municipals. At some point, of course, the reduced taxable income would make the municipals unattractive compared to taxable investments, but that point would be where the bank held a large amount of municipals and had reduced its effective tax rate to a substantial extent.[4]

Municipal securities also carry some disadvantages relative to U.S. government and other taxable securities. In particular, municipals offer a lower pre-tax yield, such that a bank with little or no taxable income would not find the securities attractive. Also, municipals carry greater credit risk than the government issues. Even if a municipal security issuer does not default during the life of the issue (and the incidence of defaults has been quite low), there is also the risk that the credit quality of the issue may fall so that the holder will suffer a loss if the security must be sold prior to its maturity. Furthermore, municipal securities generally have less liquidity than governments, especially as compared with Treasury bills.

---

[4]This illustration does, of course, assume that the explicit interest rate is the only cost of attracting deposits. It also assumes that the bank has taxable income to shelter. Such a policy would probably be of little interest to a new bank, for example, which has insufficient net earnings to protect from taxation.

Reflecting these factors, commercial bank investments in municipals have grown substantially in recent years, as shown in Figure 11–1. The major impetus for the expanded role of municipals in bank portfolios appears to be the increase in the potential effective rate of return on these securities. With inflation and the growth of the economy, the total profits of

Figure 11–1   Principal Classes of Loans and Investments at All Commercial Banks (semiannual call report dates, 1950–1973; seasonally adjusted, quarterly averages, 1973–)

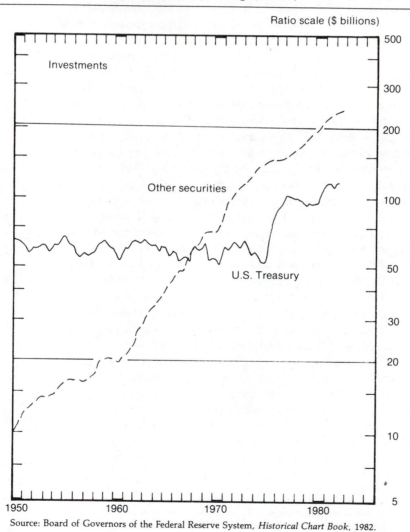

Source: Board of Governors of the Federal Reserve System, *Historical Chart Book*, 1982.

more banks have become subject to the higher levels of the corporate income tax. At these profit levels, the investment of large sums of money in municipal securities becomes desirable.

Banks and the Municipal Market

Concentration of bank investment portfolios in municipals has created a number of problems for that market and also for individual banks. These problems have centered on the dominance of the market by a few buyers, especially commercial banks. There are only three types of buyers of municipals who are quantitatively significant: commercial banks, property and casualty insurers, and high-income individuals (both directly and through tax-exempt mutual funds). Of the three, banks have been most important and have dominated the market. Many banks, however, have already used municipals to such a degree that their effective tax rate has been reduced to, or near, zero. Moreover, large banks in particular have found other means of reducing effective tax rates. For example, the invasion of the leasing business by commercial banking organizations has allowed some banks through the investment tax credit and accelerated depreciation associated with the ownership of real property to shield a substantial amount of income from taxes. Many of the nation's largest banks also receive a large share of their income from international banking activities. Taxes paid on foreign income create credits against tax liabilities domestically and thereby reduce the effective tax rate paid by these organizations and make municipal securities less attractive. In addition, as the result of the financial problems encountered in recent years by New York City, Cleveland, and by states and other political subdivisions, there appears to have been some shift in attitude by investors toward the credit risk involved in purchasing municipal securities. In the immediate post–World War II era, there seemed to be little differentiation among municipal issues on the basis of credit risk, and only a small credit risk premium was required by the market. In contrast, recently the market appears to be more discriminating about credit risk levels involved in different kinds of municipal securities, and the risk premium on municipals generally seems to have increased. Furthermore, a number of questions have been raised about the accuracy with which ratings by Moody's & Standard Poor's portray relative default or credit risk through bond ratings.

U.S. Government Securities

Banks have historically been large purchasers of U.S. government issues and today remain major holders. U.S. government and federal agency securities have a number of features that make them attractive to commercial banks. For banks seeking a low-risk portfolio, the U.S.

government offers a security free from credit risk and with great liquidity. These securities have great flexibility in use as they may be used for the purpose of pledging against public deposits of the bank and may also be used as collateral when the bank borrows from the Federal Reserve through its discount window.

As of July 27, 1983, large commercial banks held $24.6 billion in Treasury notes and bonds due in one to five years and almost $3 billion due in more than five years. However, the percentage of bank assets held in the form of direct U.S. government obligations has dropped substantially in recent years. Indeed, a large part of these securities held by commercial banks today are *pledged* to secure government deposits; that is, they are used as specific security for the deposits of the U.S. government and state and local governments. In contrast, commercial banks have become major lenders to various agencies of the federal government, such as the farm credit agencies, the federal home loan banks, and other government agencies designed to foster the flow of credit into specific sectors of the economy. As a result, holdings of U.S. government agency securities by these larger banks exceeded $16 billion, while holdings of other bonds, corporate stocks, and securities were only about $3 billion. The principal reason for the increased commitments of bank funds to agencies, as opposed to direct Treasury issues, is that the agency issues generally are treated by the regulatory authorities as equivalent to direct Treasury securities; have a somewhat higher yield, since they are not backed directly by the U.S. government; and also have liquidity characteristics which are almost as good as direct Treasuries. While Table 11–1 provides no information on the maturity composition of the agency issues, and while the maturity holdings will vary widely from one bank to another, holdings of agency issues at most banks are generally short-term in nature.

RETURN AND RISK IN THE MANAGEMENT OF THE INVESTMENT PORTFOLIO

Management of a financial institution must balance the return and risk characteristics of individual securities and of the entire portfolio. *Return* refers to the total return over the anticipated holding period of the security. *Risk* has a number of dimensions and encompasses credit or default risk, interest-rate risk, and liquidity risk. Naturally, an investment policy that stresses high total returns must accept relatively high risk. Conversely, an investment policy that will tolerate only a small amount of risk must be willing to accept a relatively low return.

Return

Any investor can anticipate the possiblity of two types of return from holding a bond: interest return and capital gain (or loss). For example, assume an investor purchases a corporate bond in the secondary market and further assume that the bond has a coupon of 12 percent, matures in the year 1995, and is purchased at a market price of $800. The investor will receive, assuming no default on the part of the issuer, interest payments of $120 per year on that bond. If the investor holds the bond for one year and then sells it at a price of $850 (perhaps because the general level of interest rates has fallen since the bond was purchased), the investor would receive a capital gain of $50, ignoring any transaction costs (the capital gain would be the difference between the purchase price of $800 and the sale price of $850). The total return to the investor over the holding period would then be equal to the $120 interest plus the $50 capital gain. Of course, this total return must be related to the amount of investment in order to determine the rate of return. In this case, the rate of return per year for the one-year holding period would be ($120 + $50) ÷ $800, or 21.25 percent. More generally, the rate of return (yield) can be calculated as:[5]

$$R = \frac{P_t - P_{t-1} + I}{P_{t-1}}$$

where

$$
\begin{aligned}
R &= \text{Rate of return} \\
P_t &= \text{Price of the security in period } t \\
P_{t-1} &= \text{Price of the security in period } t-1 \\
I &= \text{Interest payment}
\end{aligned}
$$

The above equation clearly shows the importance of price variability in influencing the rate of return that an investor obtains from a bond (or any other security for that matter). This raises the question of what causes the prices of bonds to vary, which actually is the question of what produces risk in investing in bonds.

Risk

The management of every financial institution should understand that the prices of bonds in a portfolio will vary with a number of factors. In particular, prices will be affected by the risk of default (credit risk), by changes in interest-rate levels (interest-rate risk), as well as by other considerations. These factors are important in influencing bank investment strategy.

Credit Risk.   Credit risk refers to the prospect that the issuer of a bond will be unable and/or unwilling to pay interest and repay principal as agreed. While the default rate for municipal and other bonds is generally

---

[5]Other ways to calculate yield are discussed in Chapter 4.

quite low, there is credit risk in all securities except those that are the direct obligation of the U.S. government. It is important also to recognize that the market price of the bond in the secondary market will vary inversely with *changes* in the perceived credit risk of the securities. For example, if the credit risk of a bond purchased by the bank increases after the bond is purchased, the bond can be resold (assuming unchanged interest rates) only at a reduced price. Such variations in credit risk then reduce the ability of the bank to adjust the portfolio with changing portfolio requirements.

The credit-risk quality of bonds is indicated by the rating categories assigned to municipal and corporate bonds by Standard Poor's & Moody's. For example, as shown in Figure 11–2, it is possible to categorize bond issues by credit risk into high quality, medium quality, lowest grade (or speculative issues), and defaulted bonds. By Standard & Poor's designation, A-rated bonds would be high quality, with very little credit risk. Moving down in credit quality (and up in terms of credit risk), B-rated issues are medium quality. (The three A-rated grades and the BBB-rated issues together are referred to as investment-grade issues.) These blend the characteristics of high quality and more speculative issues. In contrast, C-grade issues are purely speculative and clearly not appropriate for banks and other depository institutions, while D-grade issues are those in default and those issued by bankrupt companies.

Interest-Rate Risk.   Bond prices also vary because of changes in interest rates. The volatility of bond prices due to changing interest rates is re-

---

Figure 11–2   Bond-Rating Categories Employed by Moody's Investors Services and Standard & Poor's Corporation

Quality Level of Bonds	Moody's Rating Category		Standard & Poor's Rating Category	Risk Premium
High-quality or high-grade bonds	Aaa	AAA	Lowest	
	Aa	AA		
	A	A		
Medium-quality or medium-grade bonds	Baa	BBB		
	Ba	BB		
	B	B		
Lowest grade, speculative, or poor-quality bonds	Caa	CCC		
	Ca	CC		
	C	C		
Defaulted bonds and bonds issued by bankrupt companies	—	DDD	Highest	
	—	DD		
	—	D		

Note: See Chapter 4 for a more extensive description of bond ratings.

ferred to as interest-rate risk. There are two important aspects of interest-rate risk. First, prices of bonds move inversely with interest rates. Rising interest rates produce declines in bond prices, while falling interest rates produce increases in bond prices. Second the price volatility, or variance of bond prices, increases as the maturity of the bond increases; that is, interest-rate risk rises as maturity increases. Hence managers of financial institutions who wish to minimize interest-rate risk will hold a relatively short maturity portfolio, while managers who are willing to accept greater interest-rate risk will hold a longer-term portfolio. Since the U.S. government securities portfolio at most commercial banks has a shorter maturity than the municipal portfolio, the greater interest-rate risk in the investment portfolios at most commercial banks is located in their municipal portfolio.

Liquidity Risk. The third dimension of risk in the investment portfolio is liquidity risk, that is, the ability of the holder to sell or liquidate the asset without substantial fluctuation in its price. There are two aspects to liquidity risk. First, there exists the question of whether a secondary market for the security even exists. If no secondary market exists, then obviously the degree of liquidity risk is substantial. Second, even if a secondary market exists, the quality of the market may be highly variable. For example, the secondary market for Treasury bills is highly developed, while the secondary market for many long-term municipal issues is quite poor. While liquidity is a secondary consideration for the investment portfolio—income is the primary consideration—nevertheless, liquidity risk is a factor that must be considered in managing the investment portfolio.

INVESTMENT PORTFOLIO POLICIES

All banks and other financial institutions involved in purchasing securities should have a written policy governing the investment portfolio. Just as a written lending policy will contribute to the development of a rational and consistent approach to the loan function, so also a written investment policy will contribute to effective management of the securities portfolio. Such a policy will, of course, vary in terms of complexity and comprehensiveness from financial institution to financial institution. However, there are certain items which are central to every investment program.

Definition and Scope

The policy should specify precisely what is meant by the investment portfolio—that is, what assets compose the investment portfolio. Since bank balance sheets prepared for accounting purposes are generally divided into cash assets, loans, investments, and other asset categories rather than according to the function performed by the asset, it is not always easy to determine just what is meant by the term *investment portfolio*.

The objectives of the investment account and the types of assets which fall within the category should be discussed. As mentioned above, the investment portfolio usually consists of longer-term securities. However, there are periods when the investment portfolio will be comprised principally of short-term, highly liquid securities. For example, when interest rates are expected to increase, it would be desirable investment strategy for the financial institution to shift some of its investments from long- to short-term securities. This strategy is based upon the widespread argument by financial market participants that a portfolio should be lengthened in periods of rising prices (falling rates) and shortened in periods of falling prices (rising rates). The important consideration with regard to identifying the investment portfolio is not the maturity of the asset but rather the *purpose* for which the asset is held. If the asset is held primarily to generate income and as a substitute for the loan portfolio, even if the generation of income is viewed over the business cycle, it should be considered as a part of the investment portfolio regardless of whether the security is short- or long-term in maturity.

Credit Risk

Clearly one of the most important considerations in drafting a financial institution's investment policy should be the amount of credit risk which it wishes to assume. Management is constrained to a considerable degree in the selection of assets which are to be included in the investment portfolio. Yet, within these constraints, management must decide how much credit risk to assume. At one extreme, the financial institution could concentrate its holdings in U.S. government securities in which the credit risk is negligible. At the other extreme, low-quality municipal and corporate bonds could be purchased.

In making its credit-quality decision, management should keep the following factors in mind. First, as discussed earlier, commercial banks and many other financial institutions cannot purchase securities of a speculative character. This primarily limits the investment portfolio to those municipal and corporate securities rated investment grade or better, as defined by the major rating agencies. Yet there are substantial differences in quality among investment-grade issues. For unrated securities, the bank should maintain records which support its contention that the securities are not speculative in nature. Second, investment portfolio policy should be formulated with the understanding that the bank most likely is at a competitive disadvantage when seeking to obtain a high rate of return through its investment portfolio rather than its loan portfolio. In its lending function, the bank usually has detailed personal knowledge of its customer and may be operating in an imperfectly competitive market. In contrast, for the investment portfolio, the bank, especially the small bank, is frequently less knowledgeable than other, more sophisticated investors and is operating in a highly competitive and efficient market where excess returns are difficult to realize.

Risk and Return

There are a number of important generalizations concerning risk and return in the securities markets which might be useful to management in guiding the development of an investment policy with respect to credit risk. The obvious positive relationship between risk and expected return is an important consideration. If management wishes to obtain a higher return from its investment portfolio, it must be willing to accept a greater degree of risk. In an efficiently structured securities market there is no free lunch, especially for the small and relatively unsophisticated investor. This statement, however, should be modified in a number of ways. There is some evidence that the realized (*ex post*, or after the fact) return from lower-quality securities has been higher (indeed, considerably higher) than the realized return on higher-quality securities.[6] This is consistent with the notion that investors are risk-averse and must be compensated for bearing risk by additional return. However, the size of the greater return for bearing risk is also consistent with another hypothesis. It is sometimes argued that many institutional investors are constrained through legal and other means to confine their investments to higher-quality securities relative to lower-quality securities. As a result, it is argued, yields available on higher-quality securities are low relative to lower-quality issues (on a risk-adjusted basis). The market may not correctly price risk, and there may be an opportunity to increase return beyond what would be expected due to the greater risk by investing in lower-quality issues.

A second modifying comment to the expectation that risk and return are positively related in the capital market is the apparent instability over time of the risk premium. Differences between the yields available on high- and low-grade securities (the risk premium) appear to increase in periods of economic decline and to shrink in periods of economic expansion. This suggests that the market overprices risk in periods of economic decline and underprices risk in periods of economic euphoria. If so, investment strategy might be directed to purchasing lower-quality issues during recession and shifting to higher-quality issues when economic conditions have improved.

Interest-Rate Risk

Another important consideration is the degree of interest-rate risk which the bank is prepared to accept. As discussed earlier, interest-rate

---

[6]See especially Hickman [4].

risk—the volatility of the market price of the securities in the investment portfolio due to changes in interest rates—increases as the maturity of the portfolio expands. Also, while interest-rate risk does rise with longer maturity, the relationship between maturity and risk does not appear to be a linear one. Rather, equal additions to maturity appear to be associated with diminishing increments of interest-rate risk as maturity increases. Management should specify the degree of interest-rate risk it is willing to tolerate. This specification should be in terms of the maximum maturity it will allow in the investment portfolio for different categories of securities and also in terms of the maximum average maturity of the entire portfolio. For example, the investment policy might specify that no municipal security having a maturity longer than 10 years should be acquired and that the average maturity (weighted by the importance of different securities in the portfolio) should not exceed 5 years. Naturally, this decision would be heavily influenced by the sources of funds drawn upon by the individual financial institution.

Aggressiveness of Management

Commercial banks differ widely in terms of how aggressively the investment portfolio is managed. As a general rule, but with many exceptions, small banks do little explicit management of their investment portfolio, while larger banks are frequently heavily involved in active portfolio management.[7] To some extent, this reflects differences in the expertise of management. It may also reflect differences in risk preferences of the management and ownership of the bank. Different views on aggressiveness would affect both the maturity of the portfolio as well as the credit risk. In any case, the investment policy should contain some reference to the degree of aggressiveness considered appropriate by each institution.

At one extreme, many commercial banks have traditionally followed a spaced maturity policy (also called a staggered or laddered approach). With this policy, management establishes a maximum maturity of eight years or some other number, and then divides its investment portfolio equally among each of the yearly intervals. By this strategy, 12.5 percent of the total portfolio would be invested in securities with a maturity of eight years, 12.5 percent in securities with a maturity of seven years, and so on down to securities with a maturity of one year. Each year, as all the securities move one year forward in maturity, funds realized from the securities which have matured would be invested in issues with an eight-year maturity, and the average maturity of the portfolio would remain unchanged.

---

[7]Many small banks have their investment portfolio strategies determined by their large correspondents.

This policy has a number of advantages, not the least of which is the ease of management. It also smoothes interest income, though it does not necessarily maximize the return from a portfolio. It requires little or no expertise in security selection and, therefore, is especially suitable in small financial institutions. Similarly, management is not required to follow any particular interest-rate forecast. Moreover, this policy should provide an average return over the course of the business cycle. In addition, it is sometimes argued that this policy has the advantage of providing considerable liquidity, since a portion of the investment portfolio is quite short-term in nature. However, this advantage is of limited validity, since the purpose of the investment account is to provide income rather than liquidity. While this approach does have some advantages, it ignores the possibility that excess returns may be made by sophisticated investors through shifting maturity and credit quality in anticipation of changes in economic and financial conditions.

It is also possible for the bank to alter the amount invested in different maturity ranges. For example, the bank may put 100 percent of the portfolio in securities maturing in two years. This approach has sometimes been referred to as the front end–loaded maturity policy and, as reported by Hayes [3], appears to be very popular among banks. At the other extreme, the bank could put all its funds in long-term issues (the back end–loaded approach). A mix of these approaches (referred to as the barbell approach) would put large amounts of the portfolio in both short- and long-term securities and only small amounts in the intermediate range.

A much more aggressive portfolio policy would call for making major changes in the investment portfolio in response to changes in expectations regarding interest rates and security prices. When rates are expected to rise, the entire portfolio, or at least a substantial portion of it, would be moved toward short-term maturities. Not only would this allow the bank to avoid capital losses associated with the decline in long-term security prices as interest-rate expectations are realized, but it also would provide for the possibility of large capital gains when funds are later shifted long-term as interest-rate expectations are revised. While this type of policy provides the potential for large returns, it also opens the bank to potentially large losses. The success of the policy depends upon the accuracy of interest-rate forecasts, and evidence appears to suggest that experts have not been able to forecast either the direction or the magnitude of interest-rate changes with any degree of accuracy in recent years.

Organization and Responsibility

Certainly the investment policy should specify the line of authority within the organization for management of the securities portfolio. While the organizational form for investment management in a small organization may be simple and informal, in a large bank the line of authority will generally be quite complex. Such complexity makes the existence of a written investment policy even more important.

Other Factors

To the extent that there are other factors which should bear upon the investment portfolio, these should be included in the policy. For example, if it is the policy of the bank to bid actively for all securities issued by local governmental units in the primary service area of the bank, this should be included in the investment policy. Similarly, the position of the bank with regard to securities pledged to secure public deposits should be specified. Also, the bank policy on maintaining credit files on the investment portfolio should be specified. This is especially important for unrated issues, since regulations require that the bank be able to document the investment quality of unrated securities. For these issues, the bank may want information in the credit files on the population and economic base of the area served by the government unit that has issued the bond.

ARBITRAGE AND TAX SWAPPING

Financial institutions, especially commercial banks, frequently engage in both arbitrage and tax swapping through their investment portfolios. Within this context *arbitrage* refers to the attempt to earn high (or excess) returns made available by temporary distortions in the relative yields on different securities. For example, suppose that a large supply of new issues of Baa municipals was recently brought to market and that it had the effect of lowering the price (and thereby increasing the yield) on Baa municipals relative to A-rated issues. Suppose also that the increase in yields makes the difference between Baa and A-rated municipal yields much larger than normal. A financial institution that wishes to arbitrage then might sell its A-rated issues and buy Baa-rated issues. If its expectations were realized and the spread between yields on Baa- and A-rated issues returned to normal, the institution would be able to realize a gain on the transaction when it later sold the Baa and purchased A-rated issues. However, to be profitable the gain would have to exceed the transaction costs involved in the arbitrage.

Another way in which financial institutions attempt to increase the return to the institution from their investment portfolio is to engage in *tax swapping*. This refers to selling a security that is currently in the institution's portfolio and that has a market value below cost and replacing the security with an equivalent one. In recent years of high interest rates (and depressed bond prices), tax swapping has been quite common.

The process of tax swapping may be illustrated as follows: Suppose that a bank owns $1 million (face value) of Aaa municipal bonds that have been in its portfolio for the last seven years. Suppose further that these bonds have a coupon rate of 5 percent and currently have a secondary-market value of $800,000 (at the existing level of interest rates of 9 percent for Aaa municipals). If the bank were to sell the existing municipals in its portfolio, the sale would provide two benefits. First, the bank would realize a tax loss of $200,000. Such losses reduce taxable income and thereby reduce tax payments. Assuming the bank is in the 46 percent tax bracket (all bank security gains and losses are treated as ordinary income), the sale would reduce the bank's taxes by $92,000. Second, the bank is able to earn a higher income by reinvesting the proceeds at the now higher market interest rates. Against these benefits, however, must be compared the transactions cost involved in the tax swap. Also relevant in affecting the desirability of such a swap is the effect on the capital position and reported income of the bank. The swap reduces the bank's capital and may therefore lead the regulatory authorities to force the bank to raise additional capital. Also, the bank will—temporarily, at least—report reduced net income which may have an undesirable effect on the market's perception of the future of the organization.[8]

The development of futures contracts in principal financial instruments, such as Treasury bills, notes, and bonds (as discussed in Chapter 4), has substantially broadened the ability of commercial banks and other depository institutions to manage the interest-rate risk in their portfolios. For example, suppose that a bank has a large portfolio of long-term government securities that are pledged against public deposits. Suppose also that management is concerned about the potential for a sharp increase in interest rates and, thereby, a decline in the value of the government bond portfolio. It could reduce the risk of interest-rate movements by executing a *short hedge*, by which it would sell a contract for future delivery of government bonds. It would then be long in the cash, or spot, market and short in the futures market. If interest rates did in fact increase, the bank would have a loss on its holdings of government bonds (since the increase in interest rates would produce a decline in bond prices), when those bonds are sold as the public deposits are withdrawn. However, with the hedge, the loss in the cash market is partially or totally offset by the gain in the futures market. (There would be a gain, since the interest-rate increase produces a decline in the value of the futures contract and since the bank could now buy back the contract that it sold earlier, but at a lower price). This process is illustrated in Figure 11–3.

There are many other ways that financial institutions may use the futures market to hedge interest-rate risk. As one example, suppose that a

BANK USE OF THE FUTURES MARKET

---

[8]In an efficient market, however, such a transaction should not have any effect on the price of the bank's stock.

Figure 11–3   Illustration of a Short Hedge

	Cash Market	*Futures Market*
Today	Decision made to hedge portfolio of U.S. government bonds	Sale of bond futures contracts
Later	Sale of portfolio of U.S. government bonds	Purchase of bond futures contracts
Result	Loss	Gain

---

commercial bank expected a large inflow of deposit funds at some future period and suppose also that by then it expected interest rates to have fallen. The investor could then lock-in the current higher rates by executing a *long hedge*, by which it would buy a contract for future delivery. If, in fact, interest rates fall, the bank will incur a loss (an opportunity cost loss) by having to invest at the lower rates. This opportunity loss in the cash market, however, will be partially or totally offset by a gain on the sale of the appreciated futures contract.[9]

SUMMARY

This chapter has reviewed the nature of the investment portfolio at commercial banks, and the external risk factors that should shape the policies a bank follows toward its investments. To a considerable extent, the policies are applicable to other financial institutions also, especially other depository institutions. Securities held for income as well as securities held for liquidity play an important role in total portfolio management at financial institutions. The profitability of financial institutions can be substantially affected by the success of management in controlling the maturity and credit-risk levels of investment portfolios. While the principles discussed in this chapter should be helpful in portfolio management, it must be recognized that management must integrate the factors discussed here with those discussed earlier with regard to the management of liquidity (Chapter 9) and the management of the loan portfolio (Chapter 10). Indeed, the management of liquidity, loans, and investments must be accomplished within the framework of the management of the capital position of the bank as discussed in Chapter 12. While we necessarily discuss each aspect of portfolio management separately, it must be realized that portfolio management is best approached as an integrated strategy.

---

[9]Additional information on bank use of the futures market may be found in G. D. Koppenhaver, "A T-Bill Futures Hedging Strategy for Banks," *Economic Review*, Federal Reserve Bank of Dallas, March 1983, 15–28; and Glen Picou, "Managing Interest Rate Risk with Interest Rate Futures," *The Bankers Magazine*, May–June 1981, 76–81.

The commercial bank investment portfolio comprises those securities held primarily for income and only secondarily for liquidity. It thus encompasses principally long-term securities. Given its goal of producing income, the investment portfolio is competitive in the funds allocation process with the loan portfolio, though the loan portfolio is generally viewed as having higher priority. Investments do, however, provide certain tax and diversification benefits not usually available through the loan portfolio.

Securities eligible for inclusion in the investment portfolio include U.S. government issues, U.S. government agency issues, and municipals. In selecting among these securities, management must recognize the trade-off between risk and return. The risks relevant to this decision include credit risk, interest-rate risk, and liquidity risk. In formulating its investment policy, management must consider the definition and scope of the investment portfolio, the amount of risk it is willing to tolerate, and how aggressive it wishes to be in managing the portfolio. It should also examine the desirability of arbitrage and tax swapping.

Questions

11-1. Before any funds become available for a commercial bank's investment account, they are used to meet other funds needs and demands of the bank. What are these funds needs and demands? How do they affect the bank's investment account?

11-2. How do securities held for investment purposes differ from those securities held for liquidity purposes?

11-3. Why would a bank want to hold securities in an investment account? What if the returns were substantially below those on loans?

11-4. Differentiate between a general obligation bond and a revenue bond.

11-5. Differentiate between interest rate or market risk and credit risk. How do they affect bank portfolio management?

11-6. What is the difference between the current yield and the yield to maturity?

11-7. What are some of the factors that are important when considering the makeup of an investment policy?

11-8. In reference to commercial bank investment decisions, what is the spaced maturity policy?

11-9. How might a bank structure its investment policies over the business cycle?

11-10. What is arbitrage? What is tax swapping? How might a bank use each one?

References

1. Baughn, William H., and Charls E. Walker, eds. *The Banker's Handbook.* Homewood, Ill.: Dow Jones–Irwin, 1978, pp. 469–540.

2. Crosse, Howard, and George Hempel. *The Management of Bank Funds*. Englewood Cliffs, N.J.: Prentice-Hall, 1980, Chap. 13–14.

3. Hayes, Douglas A., *Bank Funds Management, Issues and Practices*. Ann Arbor: University of Michigan, 1980.

4. Hickman, W. Braddock. *Corporate Bond Quality and Investor Experience*. New York: National Bureau of Economic Research, 1958.

5. Hodgman, D. R. "The Deposit Relationship and Commercial Bank Investment Behavior." *Review of Economics and Statistics*, August 1961, pp. 257–68.

6. Hoffland, David L. "A Model Bank Investment Policy." *Financial Analysts Journal*, August 1966.

7. Jessup, Paul F. *Modern Bank Management*. Minneapolis, West Publishing, 1980, Chap. 9.

8. Lyon, Roger A. *Investment Portfolio Management in the Commercial Bank*. New Brunswick, N.J.: Rutgers University Press, 1960.

9. Wood, Oliver G. *Commercial Banking*. New York: D. Van Nostrand, 1978, Chaps. 15, 16.

Problem for Discussion

MANAGEMENT OF THE INVESTMENT ACCOUNT at commercial banks is a frequently neglected function, especially at small banks. Senior management at smaller banks usually has considerable expertise in lending—the bread and butter of banking—but often little or no knowledge of the securities markets. These banks often rely heavily upon larger banks, especially their correspondents, for investment advice. In the problem situation discussed below, the student is asked to assume the role of an outsider and evaluate the investment account of a small bank. After reviewing the material, the student should address the following questions:

1. Does the investment account at First National Bank conform to legal requirements?
2. Does the investment account at First National Bank appear reasonably balanced in terms of maturity, type of securities, and other significant characteristics?
3. What changes in the investment account would you recommend?
4. What additional services might a large bank offer to First National?

Wentworth National Bank—a multibillion dollar institution located in a regional financial center—has concentrated (with a great degree of success) its marketing effort for some years in the correspondent banking area. It has actively and aggressively promoted the services which it offers to smaller commercial banks in the area. These services include, to mention only a few, the following:

1. The clearing of checks for correspondents, where Wentworth maintains that its service is preferable to that provided by the Federal Reserve System for member banks, since Wentworth provides immediate credit for cash items and the Federal Reserve defers payment on many cash items for a period of up to two days and since Wentworth does not require expensive sorting and labeling (as the Fed does) of the cash items presented to it.

2. Participation in excess credit lines for its downstream correspondents while also serving these correspondents as an accommodating bank in the federal funds market. Senior management at Wentworth has told the correspondent banking officers that the message to the downstream correspondents should be "We trust your credit evaluation and will make a decision on an overline request within 24 hours." This policy has been quite successful. Of the total loan portfolio at Wentworth of over $2 billion, close to $500 million consists of loan participations with downstream correspondents. Loan losses in these participations have been minimal, substantially below the losses on the bank's direct loans.

   Serving as an accommodating bank has proven to be a successful policy for Wentworth. Most of the downstream correspondents have been consistent and predictable sellers of federal funds. While this occasionally has created some difficulties for the manager of the bank's money position, it has given the bank the opportunity to expand its loan portfolio (based on regular purchases of federal funds) by a substantial amount. Federal funds purchased by Wentworth from downstream correspondents recently averaged over $600 million per day.

3. Offering various types of data processing activities, an area which has disappointed management. It was hoped originally that the use of idle time on the data processing equipment of the bank to service correspondent accounts would prove highly profitable. However, the accounting department of the bank has regularly reported that the activity is unprofitable due to the heavy overhead costs.

The portion of correspondent banking in which Wentworth takes greatest pride is that of rendering financial advice. The marketing program at Wentworth for correspondent banking services stresses the ability of the bank to offer the advice of an expert in almost any area a downstream bank would need. For example, the bank maintains a fully staffed economic research department to offer opinions on the outlook for interest rates, loan demand, and other factors. Similarly, Wentworth has a large trust department, with experts on the accounting and legal aspects of trust activities, as well as management of the investment portfolio. While many of the downstream correspondents of Wentworth offer trust services, few have the specialized knowledge needed in these areas. Further, Wentworth has experts in particular areas of lending such as oil and gas, real estate, and farm and ranch loans which could be made available to assist correspondents on especially difficult loan applications. Wentworth recently placed an advertisement in *The Wall Street Journal* which gave the names and pictures of some of their personnel with specialized talent, their academic qualifications, and professional experience.

In view of the importance of correspondent activity to Wentworth (it is estimated that almost one half of total bank funds and more than 60 percent of total profits are associated with this activity), it is understandable that management reacted with some concern to a telephone call from Fred Hess, the president of First National Bank, on Wednesday, May 11. First National Bank had maintained more than $8 million in total deposits at Wentworth and had done so for some time. The account had relatively small activity and was therefore quite profitable for Wentworth. Moreover, this was the main correspondent account for First National, a bank with total deposits of about $70 million, located in a small, agriculturally

---

Exhibit 11–1 First National Bank Investment Portfolio: December 31, 19XX

Type	Cost
U.S. Treasury securities:	
Bills:	
Within 3 months	$ 570,000
3–6 months	1,220,000
6–9 months	1,410,000
9–12 months	1,800,000
Total	$ 5,000,000
Notes and bonds:	
Within 1 year	$ 500,000
1–5 years	2,500,000
5–10 years	1,000,000
10–15 years	3,000,000
Total	$ 7,000,000
Obligations of states and political subdivisions:	
Within 1 year:	
City of Dallas (AAA) GO*	$ 2,000,000
City of Houston (AA) GO*	2,000,000
1–5 years:	
Texas Municipal Power Authority (AA)	4,000,000
Essex Pollution Control Authority (AA)	3,000,000
Total	$11,000,000
Total investment portfolio	$23,000,000

*General obligation bond.

based city of approximately 15,000 people. Despite the size of the First National Bank account, Hess maintained that Wentworth had done nothing for First National except clear its checks. In particular, Hess, who had recently assumed the presidency of First National after the untimely and unexpected death of the previous president, was concerned about the investment portfolio.

Hess's concern had been prompted by a meeting the day before with a bond salesman from a brokerage house who had said that all forecasts were for sharply higher interest rates and that the bank should sell the bulk of its long-term securities and invest in short-term issues. But more generally, Hess was concerned with the quality of investments in terms of maturity, mix, and risk of the securities in the portfolio. His experience included 20 years of making small retail loans and agriculturally oriented credits, and he knew little of the tax and other aspects of managing a securities portfolio. He was therefore appalled to find that no one, except the previous president, had any real knowledge of investments. Moreover, most of the investments had been made by his secretary (presumably under instructions from the president, but no one knew for sure). There was no record of any communication about investment management between First National and Wentworth for at least the past five years. In closing, Hess said, "If this is the best you can do for us, then we just may take our deposits elsewhere. We expect more for our $8 million.

Officers of Wentworth decided to carefully evaluate the existing portfolio of the bank (Exhibit 11–1) with regard to any deficiencies in terms of maturity, mix of different kinds of issues, and quality of issues (see Exhibits 11–2, 11–3, and 11–4). For purposes of developing an investment policy, they took notice of the fact that First National Bank is the dominant bank in a two-bank town, that the economy of the area is stable and diversified, and that senior management expertise lies principally in the area of making loans. Moreover, the bank consistently follows a policy of keeping a small amount of excess reserves in order to reduce its risk exposure and prides itself on having sufficient liquidity to meet all loan requests of satisfactory quality.

Exhibit 11–2 First National Bank Selected Rates of Return (in percent)

	19XX–6	19XX–5	19XX–4	19XX–3	19XX–2	19XX–1	19XX
Return on U.S. Treasury securities	5.1%	5.4%	5.4%	10.0%	10.5%	12.4%	13.2%
Return on municipals	4.1	4.3	4.5	5.9	6.2	7.8	9.4
Average maturity of Treasury security portfolio (in years)	1.8	2.4	2.6	3.0	2.9	2.8	2.6
Average maturity of municipal security portfolio (in years)	1.7	1.8	2.0	2.1	2.2	2.1	2.1

Exhibit 11–3
FIRST NATIONAL BANK
Balance Sheet
December 31: 19XX
($000)

Assets		*Liabilities and Capital*	
Cash and due from banks	$12,000	Demand deposits	$29,000
U.S. government securities	12,000	Time and savings deposits	25,000
U.S. government agencies.	—	Other liabilities	1,000
Obligations of states and political		Capital.	7,000
subdivisions	11,000		
Loans.	27,000	Total liabilities and capital	$62,000
Total assets	$62,000		

Exhibit 11–4
FIRST NATIONAL BANK
Income Statement
19XX

Total revenue	$6,480,000
Expenses	
Interest on deposits	2,480,000
Wages and salaries.	1,280,000
Provision for loan losses	540,000
Other expenses	920,000
Total expenses	5,220,000
Net profit before taxes.	1,260,000
Applicable taxes	380,000
Net profit after taxes	$ 880,000

12. *Capital Management*

THE SUBJECT OF CAPITAL MANAGEMENT is one of the most important and most controversial topics in the financial institutions' field, especially among commercial banks and other depository institutions. Management and the regulatory authorities are frequently in dispute about the appropriate amount of capital. Management, concerned with the rate of return on the owners' investment in the business, has often desired to reduce the ratio of capital to assets. In fact, historically there has been a sharp reduction in the volume of capital relative to loans and other risky financial assets, particularly at larger commercial banks and at savings and loans and savings banks. In contrast, the regulatory authorities, concerned with the stability of the financial system and the failure problem, have sought to maintain relatively high capital ratios.

PURPOSES OF CAPITAL

The basic functions performed by capital must be kept in mind in order to understand the debate surrounding the capital adequacy issue. Capital exists to provide a *buffer to absorb losses* and to allow the institution to remain viable as a going concern during the period when problems are being corrected. From this perspective, capital is important for all financial intermediaries. This function may be viewed from a variety of perspectives. From a static point of view, capital exists to provide a cushion to absorb the risk of loss in the value of loans and investments on the books of the institution. Hence, if the ratio of capital to assets is only 5 percent, the institution cannot allow its assets to depreciate in value by more than 5 percent before the institution is insolvent.[1] In contrast, with a capital-to-

---

[1]To some extent, this problem is reduced in the banking industry by accounting principles which carry loans and securities at cost rather than market value as long as there is reasonable probability that the assets are sound. For securities especially, the ability to state value on the bank's books at cost rather than market has been important in maintaining at least an appearance of adequate capital for commercial banks.

asset ratio of 10 percent, the assets of the institution could depreciate by a much larger amount before it is technically insolvent. From a broader perspective, capital exists to provide assurance to the depositors and other creditors of the institution that it can continue to function as a viable economic unit during a period of adversity (and, of course, to provide protection in the event of failure). The capital account would then be able to absorb losses until additional capital could be obtained from the generation and retention of earnings.[2]

While there undoubtedly is validity to these arguments about the role of capital, it still remains true that from a broader perspective it is not capital which provides safety and stability to the banking and financial system but the ability of monetary and fiscal policy to maintain a reasonably stable economic and financial environment. In a period of great economic distress, such as the 1930s, even a relatively large capital base may be unable to absorb losses. Conversely, in periods of relatively stable economic conditions, such as the period since World War II, the number of bank failures has been much reduced despite a sharply reduced capital base.

Risk and Bank Capital

From any perspective, the amount of capital should be related to the degree of risk accepted by the banking industry in fulfilling its basic functions. For example, as observed earlier, the basic function of the commercial bank is to provide credit to local customers to meet legitimate credit needs. Necessarily, providing credit entails risk. Expected cash flow of the borrower may be insufficient to repay principal and interest at the agreed-upon times. Indeed, it is in the loan portfolio where the commercial bank should concentrate its risk taking.

There are, however, other areas in which commercial banks accept risk. For example, any commitment of funds to securities involves risk. This risk encompasses both credit or default risk and interest-rate risk. Again, as with the loan portfolio, there is the possibility that the borrower will be unable to repay principal and interest in a timely fashion. In addition, with relatively long maturity securities held for income, there is substantial risk of changes in the value of these securities as interest rates fluctuate. While the value of all securities fluctuates with changing interest rates, the price of a security fluctuates more the longer the maturity of that security for a given change in rates. In periods of very high interest rates, those institutions which have heavy commitments to long-term securities face a large risk of depreciation in the value of their portfolios. While this

---

[2]Capital may also be viewed as a funding source just as deposit and nondeposit borrowings are a funding source. Of course, for a new bank, capital provides the initial source of funds.

depreciation is not recognized in the carrying value of the securities on the balance sheet, it does reduce the liquidity of the bank and increase its risk of insolvency. Finally, there is always the risk of fraud and thievery. For example, commercial banks handle large amounts of funds, including substantial amounts of currency and coin. The danger of theft of currency and coin by lower-level officials is more difficult to detect and to protect the bank against. Numerous bank failures in recent years have resulted from the manipulation of funds by some members of the organization's senior management. Perhaps the best example was the 1973 failure of the billion-dollar U.S. National Bank of San Diego.

The definition of capital in the banking industry is somewhat different from that in other lines of business. Definitions of bank capital often include the following: capital stock, surplus, undivided profits, reserves, preferred stock, and subordinated notes and debentures.[3]

WHAT IS BANK CAPITAL?

Equity Capital

Capital stock, surplus, and undivided profits need only a brief discussion. In total, they represent the amount of funds the owners have directly contributed through the purchase of common stock or indirectly contributed through retention of earnings. The amount in the capital stock account is equal to the number of shares outstanding multiplied by the par value of the stock. Hence, if there are 1 million shares outstanding and the par value is $10 per share, then the capital stock value should be $10 million. The surplus, or, as it is more commonly referred to in accounting terminology, *paid in capital in excess of par value*, refers to the amount of funds committed by shareholders when they purchase common stock in excess of the par value of that stock.[4] Hence, in the previous example, if the common stock were purchased at $20 per share, the surplus would be $10 million. The total contribution for 1 million shares would be $20 million. Finally, the undivided profits (or retained earnings, as they are more frequently called) refer to the earnings generated from the operations of the bank which have not been distributed to shareholders in the form of cash dividends. The importance of this division of total owners' equity among capital stock, surplus, and undivided profits is significant in affecting the legal ability of the bank to declare dividends.

---

[3]Preferred stock has seldom been used by banks and, hence, is not discussed explicitly here. However, it is worth noting that in 1982 and 1983 there was an increase in preferred stock issues in the form of variable-rate preferred.

[4]Increases in capital and surplus may also occur due to stock dividends which (in an accounting sense only) transfer funds from retained earnings to capital and surplus.

Reserves

The subject of reserves perhaps needs a more complete explanation. As discussed earlier, commercial banks face risks in their normal lending and investing activities. Such risk should properly be recognized and reserves established to provide for these losses. In actuality, the establishment of reserves is complicated by taxes and other considerations. The reserves created by commercial banks are currently divided into three groups: (1) valuation reserves, (2) contingency reserves, and (3) deferred tax reserves. Only a portion of these reserves should be viewed as part of the capital account. *Valuation reserves* refers to the reserves created to protect the bank from anticipated losses on loans. These reserves are increased by a charge to current income—provision for loan losses—on the income statement. They are reduced by write-offs of existing loans and are increased by recoveries of loans which earlier had been deemed uncollectible. Each year (or more frequently if necessary) management determines an amount which may be viewed as an expense provision for loan losses on the income statement. Such an expense adds to valuation reserves. When losses actually occur, they do not directly affect current income. Rather, determination that a loan is uncollectible results in a decrease in the amount of loans and a decrease in the valuation reserves and has no income consequences. Similarly, recovery of a loan previously deemed uncollectible usually affects reserves but not income. These valuation reserves—which represent the bulk of loan loss reserves—are *not* treated as a part of the capital account. Rather, they are carried on the asset side of the balance sheet and are used to reduce gross loans to a net basis (net of valuation reserves).

There are substantial limitations on the amounts which banks can charge off on their income statement for tax purposes. In recent years, the amounts which banks could expense for tax purposes have often exceeded the provision for loan losses which, in the judgment of management, was necessary to provide an adequate level of reserves. The added expense for tax purposes reduces taxable income and hence reduces taxes. This increases after-tax income and results in the creation of two additional reserve accounts: the contingency reserve, which *is* viewed as a part of the capital account, and the deferred tax reserve, which is *not* viewed as a part of the capital account but rather is carried on the balance sheet as "other liabilities." In short, the added expense beyond that needed to maintain an adequate valuation reserve results in funds that are not taxed in the current period. These funds have two components: (1) the portion which would have been paid in taxes if the expense had not been taken, which is added to the deferred tax reserve, and (2) the remainder after the deferred taxes have been subtracted, which is added to the contingency reserve.

Subordinated Notes and Debentures

Bank capital is not limited only to the capital provided by common shareholders. Beginning in the early 1960s, national banks were allowed to count preferred stock and subordinated notes and debentures in meeting their capital requirements. Since dividend payments on preferred stock are not deductible for tax purposes, however, the amount of preferred stock sold has been relatively slight. But the amount of subordinated notes and debentures sold has been substantial. Subordinated notes and debentures have grown immensely in importance in the capital structure of banking organizations, especially those of substantial size, for a variety of reasons. These debt securities provide a convenient and relatively inexpensive way to meet the needs for more capital imposed by the bank regulatory authorities and yet not create the dilution of earnings per share which would be associated with the sale of new common stock.

Since the interest expense is deductible for tax purposes, this source of funds becomes relatively inexpensive, especially as compared to preferred stock. However, these subordinated notes and debentures must meet certain conditions if they are to be considered as a part of bank capital: They must be at least seven years in original maturity or they will be viewed as deposits by the regulatory authorities. If viewed as deposits, they will be subject both to Federal Deposit Insurance Corporation (FDIC) assessments, reserve requirements, and Regulation Q limitations on the maximum rates payable on all deposit liabilities. If viewed as capital, not only do they count as part of the capital structure of the bank, but they also do not require FDIC assessment, they do not affect required reserves, and there are no limitations on the maximum rates payable to obtain funds through this device. The regulatory authorities have imposed a maturity limitation in order to prevent commercial banks from using the notes and debentures as substitutes for deposits. In addition, the notes and debentures must be subordinated to the deposit liabilities of the bank. If the subordinated notes and debentures are to provide protection from risk to the depositors, they must necessarily be inferior in claim on the assets of the organization in case of bankruptcy.

There has been considerable controversy surrounding the use of subordinated notes and debentures as a part of the capital structure of individual commercial banking organizations. Some have argued that it is inappropriate to view a debt instrument as a part of the capital structure since the sale of the debt instrument imposes fixed obligations on the bank. Indeed, it may be argued that the sale of subordinated notes and debentures might increase the risk of failure due to the fixed nature of these obligations. This controversy has permeated the regulatory authorities, with differing views among different bank supervisory authorities about the suitability for capital adequacy purposes of subordinated notes and debentures. (Differences in the attitudes of the regulatory authorities with regard to subordinated notes and debentures as embodied in current capital standards are discussed below.)

CAPITAL TRENDS   Capital ratios at banks, especially those related to risk assets, have undergone substantial declines over a period of some decades.[5] For example, the ratio of total capital to total assets fell sharply during the 1930s, stabilized in the immediate postwar period, and then began to fall again after the mid-1950s. Recently, however, the ratio of capital to total assets has stabilized, though the ratio of capital to loans and other risky assets has continued to decline, as shown in Table 12–1. Moreover, the mix of total

Table 12–1   Capital Ratios for Insured U.S. Commercial Banks

	Ratio		
Year	*Total Capital* / *Total Assets*	*Equity Capital* / *Total Assets*	*Equity Capital* / *Risk Assets*
1945	5.5	5.5	10.1
1950	6.8	6.8	10.8
1955	7.2	7.2	10.5
1960	8.1	8.1	11.8
1965	8.0	7.5	11.0
1970	6.9	6.6	9.0
1971	6.8	6.3	8.6
1972	6.4	6.0	8.0
1973	6.1	5.7	7.5
1974	6.1	5.6	6.8
1975	6.3	5.9	7.3
1976	6.6	6.1	7.6
1977	6.4	5.9	7.3
1978	6.2	5.8	7.0
1979	6.1	5.7	7.5

Source:Federal Deposit Insurance Corporation.

[5]Capital ratios at savings and loan associations declined dramatically in the early 1980s reflecting the losses experienced by these organizations. These declining capital ratios prompted Congress to include a net-worth certificate program as one provision of the Garn–St Germain Depository Institutions Act of 1982. Under this program, the FSLIC and FDIC are permitted to purchase net-worth certificates from distressed real estate–oriented banks and thrift institutions in exchange for promissory notes. These certificates are treated as capital for regulatory purposes. By this device, regulators are able to increase the capital position of distressed institutions.

bank capital has changed enormously, as debt capital has become much more important.

For the entire banking system, total capital averaged almost 50 percent of bank assets throughout the first half of the 19th century. By the second half of that century the ratio of capital to assets had declined to 30 percent or less. Further declines occurred during the 20th century, with the ratio of capital to assets falling to well under 10 percent by the 1970s. Numerous factors account for this persistent decline. Rapid expansion of the economy and of deposits made it simply impossible to achieve commensurate increases in capital. Declining profit margins made it desirable for bank management to allow the capital ratio to fall in order to maintain the return on equity. And, perhaps most important, greater stability of the economic environment has allowed the banking system to operate with reduced capital. Not only has the total quantity of capital changed relative to the size of the banking system, but the composition of bank capital has been altered, especially in the post–World War II era, with an increased role for retained earnings and subordinated debt. In contrast, capital stock and surplus have fallen in significance. Banks have found external equity to be an expensive source of funds and have concentrated on re-

Table 12–2   Ratio of Equity Capital to Total Assets for All Insured U.S. Commercial Banks

	Asset Size					
Date	Less than $100 Million	$100 Million– $300 Million	$300 Million– $1 Billion	$1 Billion– $5 Billion	More than $5 Billion	All Banks
Year-end:						
1969	7.64%	7.21%	7.14%	6.54%	5.58%	6.77%
1970	7.63	7.11	7.08	6.15	5.34	6.58
1971	7.41	6.88	6.83	5.91	5.10	6.32
1972	7.22	6.66	6.43	5.43	4.71	5.95
1973	7.33	6.72	6.27	5.25	4.14	5.67
1974	7.64	6.85	6.43	5.51	3.82	5.65
1975	7.65	6.88	6.58	5.81	4.13	5.87
1976	7.94	7.10	6.78	6.03	4.51	6.11
1977	7.85	6.91	6.61	5.91	4.32	5.92
1978	7.98	7.06	6.53	5.78	4.13	5.80
1979	8.21	7.23	6.55	5.83	4.03	5.75
1980	8.45	7.34	6.77	5.68	4.12	5.80
1981	8.52	7.40	6.78	5.70	4.21	5.83
June:						
1981	8.71	7.57	7.09	5.77	4.12	5.89
1982	8.75	7.56	6.92	5.86	4.30	5.98

*Beginning in 1976, equity capital includes the contingency portion of reserves that was previously included in a separate reserve item. If the percentages shown above for 1976 and thereafter were adjusted for the definitional change, they would be about 2 percent smaller. For example, the percentage for all banks in June 1982 would be 5.86 percent rather than 5.98 percent.

Source: Samuel H. Talley, *Bank Capital Trends and Financing*, Board of Governors of the Federal Reserve System, February 1983, p. 2.

tained earnings as an internal source to bolster equity, and debt as an external source. This has been especially true for larger banks.

A closer look at capital trends of insured commercial banks during the decade of the 1970s is provided in Table 12–2. This table shows the ratios of equity to total assets for various size groups of banks in each year from 1969 through 1982. It is evident that, during that period, capital ratio trends varied widely among banks of different sizes. Banks with total assets of $300 million or less experienced *increases* in the ratio of equity capital to total assets. For example, banks with total assets of $100 million to $300 million averaged a 7.2 percent equity capital to total asset ratio in 1969 but had an average ratio of 7.56 percent in 1982. The capital-to-asset ratio at banks with total assets of $300 million to $1 billion remained about unchanged during the period. In contrast, banks with total assets of $1 billion experienced declining ratios during this period. The reduction in the capital-to-asset ratio was especially pronounced at banks with over $5 billion in total assets.

Additional information on capital trends is provided in Table 12–3. This table shows the number of issues and dollar amount of funds raised by banks through the sale of capital notes and debentures, preferred stock, and common stock in the period from 1967 to 1981. (Not included, of course, are additions to equity capital through the retention of earn-

Table 12–3   Capital Securities Issued by U.S. Banks (000s)

	Public Issues of Capital Notes or Debentures		Private Issues of Capital Notes or Debentures		Preferred Stock		Common Stock	
	Issues	Amount	Issues	Amount	Issues	Amount	Issues	Amount
1967	9	$ 248,000	6	$ 7,385	0	0	24	$ 36,438
1968	8	317,549	13	24,994	0	0	39	82,007
1969	14	221,851	7	39,880	1	30,446	26	68,762
1970	17	116,234	3	9,900	0	0	26	103,352
1971	56	1,535,500	8	36,500	1	1,980	26	125,533
1972	57	2,109,850	32	305,180	2	6,804	36	214,958
1973	19	760,144	29	263,350	0	0	26	87,448
1974	22	1,181,250	12	113,300	1	10,000	14	35,486
1975	30	1,298,750	9	147,500	3	77,500	4	37,853
1976	29	1,235,500	43	896,451	0	0	8	349,252
1977	21	1,539,100	57	720,700	4	355,000	10	176,957
1978	20	717,000	48	348,620	11	147,755	20	428,466
1979	20	2,179,500	13	98,154	1	53,475	21	120,981
1980	20	873,000	4	93,300	14	343,944	19	185,341
1981	10	514,000	9	81,800	2	26,500	36	793,291

Note: Figures for each year are totals.
*Excludes floating-rate notes which are redeemable at the holder's option after two years.
Source: Selected issues of *Capital Securities Issued: Commercial Banks*, Irving Trust Co., New York.

ings.) Also, publicly issued capital notes and debentures are distinguished from private placements of these securities. The domination of external capital financing by debt issues is shown in this table, principally reflecting the lower after-tax cost of debt as compared to equity. In contrast, the amount of common stock issued was relatively small, except in 1981 when bank stock prices moved up.

Capital exists to absorb losses stemming from making loans and investments, as well as to protect against other risks faced by the banking firm. Since the amount of risk cannot be specified precisely, it is impossible to determine exactly how much capital is adequate. There are, however, a number of approaches to determining capital adequacy which have traditionally been used by both management and the regulatory authorities. These include the use of ratios, such as the capital-asset ratio; other formal procedures, such as the Form for Analyzing Bank Capital, which has been used by the Federal Reserve; and more subjective approaches, such as those employed by the Comptroller of the Currency in its supervision of national banks.

MEASURES OF CAPITAL ADEQUACY

Capital-Asset and Capital-Deposit Ratios

The capital-asset ratio and the capital-deposit ratio are the simplest and oldest measures employed to ascertain capital adequacy. The total of all those items which count as capital—capital stock, surplus, undivided profits, contingency reserves, and perhaps preferred stock and subordinated notes and debentures—are added together and divided by the total amount of bank assets or deposits. There are, however, a number of limitations to the capital-asset ratio which make it quite difficult to use as an efficient means to judge capital adequacy. The most important limitation of this ratio is that it makes no attempt to relate the amount of capital to the amount of risk carried by the banking organization. Rather, the capital-asset ratio completely ignores the risk structure of the bank's assets. For example, suppose there were two banks with identical ratios of capital to assets, but one bank had all its funds invested in cash and short-term U.S. Treasury securities, while the other had all of its funds except required reserves invested in speculative forms of loans. The capital-asset ratio would indicate that these banks are identical in terms of capital adequacy; yet, clearly, the capital adequacy of the first bank is much greater than that of the second.

Capital-Risk Asset Ratio

In order to remedy some of these deficiencies, the ratio of capital to risk assets was developed, where risk assets are defined as total assets less cash and U.S. government securities. It is also interesting to observe that the capital–risk asset ratio became commonly used by the regulatory authorities during and immediately after World War II, when the capital-asset ratio at many banks had declined below the norm and when the banks were expanding vigorously their holdings of U.S. government securities to finance the war. This ratio clearly represents a step forward from the capital-asset ratio in that it recognizes that capital adequacy is a function of the riskiness of assets. However, it also has a number of deficiencies, and two in particular should be noted. First, it assumes that U.S. government securities, known also as governments, are riskless assets. While governments may indeed carry no credit (default) risk, these securities do carry interest-rate risk, and for long-term governments especially, the risk is substantial. Second, this approach assumes that all assets except cash and U.S. government securities are equally risky. This last assumption also may be highly questionable. These other assets would include federal funds sold; commercial paper; bankers' acceptances; short- and long-term municipals; and all varieties of loans, with respect to maturity and purpose. Clearly, these assets differ greatly in the degree of risk, with some perhaps having little more or no more risk than U.S. government securities.

Form for Analyzing Bank Capital

Perhaps the most comprehensive quantitative technique is the Form for Analyzing Bank Capital (FABC), which was developed by the Federal Reserve System. The FABC provides a comprehensive breakdown of the assets of the bank and also provides for the addition of extra capital if the liquidity position of the institution is inadequate. Hence the FABC recognized that risk in banking may come from a variety of sources and provides capital for these different types of risk.

The FABC classifies the asset structure of the bank into six categories: (1) primary reserves (cash assets and federal funds sold); (2) secondary reserves (commercial paper, bankers' acceptances, and securities maturing within 1 year); (3) minimum risk assets (securities maturing in 1 to 5 years); (4) intermediate assets (securities maturing from 5 to 10 years); (5) portfolio assets (loans and long-term securities); and (6) fixed, classified, and other assets. Since default and/or interest-rate risk increases as we move from category 1 through category 6, the capital required behind each dollar of assets also increases.

The analyst may then calculate the total capital required to cover the credit and market risk embodied in the asset structure. To this the analyst should add an adjustment factor for the importance of trust activities to the bank and capital required for other special reasons. Finally, consideration should be given as to whether additional capital is needed in order to cover liquidity deficiencies. A bank with a deficient liquidity position is more likely to have to sell illiquid securities at distress prices and, therefore, to require additional capital. In order to make these estimates, the analyst should calculate a required liquidity number based upon the composition of deposits. For example, demand deposits would require more liquidity than savings deposits. Total required liquidity is then calculated. If the total liquidity so calculated is particularly large for this type of bank, then extra capital would be required.

Other Approaches

Clearly the use of ratios and formulas such as the capital-asset ratio, the capital-risk asset ratio, and the FABC can only serve as guidelines. Final judgment as to capital adequacy must depend upon the subjective evaluation of a variety of factors. In fact, during the early 1960s the office of the Comptroller of the Currency abandoned the use of ratios such as capital to assets for the determination of capital adequacy for national banks and, instead, relied upon the *subjective* judgment of the supervisory process, based upon a wide variety of factors. For example, national bank examiners based capital evaluations upon the following factors: the quality of management, the liquidity of assets, the history of earnings (including the proportion retained), the quality and character of ownership, the burden of meeting occupancy expenses, the potential volatility of deposits, the quality of operating procedures, and the ability of the bank to meet the financial needs of its trade area.

Each of the tests of capital adequacy discussed above concentrates on the balance sheet of the individual commercial bank. Moreover, each is essentially static in nature. In recent years a number of additional tests have been proposed. One suggestion made by George Vojta is based upon the earnings of the bank. Moreover, the balance sheet measure would relate capital directly to the loan losses which capital exists to protect against. Under this capital adequacy approach, the earnings of the bank would be related to the expected losses on loans and securities, and the capital of the bank would be related to past levels of realized losses.[6]

Another interesting approach would utilize the information provided by the financial markets in evaluating the adequacy of bank capital. Conceptually, it would be expected that the cost of funds would be higher for banks that are undercapitalized. In the equity market, the cost of new funds raised through the sale of stock should be higher; and in the debt market, the cost of borrowed funds through deposits and subordinated debentures should also be higher. While an appealing concept, the market approach is hampered in its application by the fact that deposit insurance

---

[6]See Vojta [14].

at commercial banks and other depository financial institutions interferes with the association between risk and the cost of funds. Moreover, the concept would be difficult to apply to smaller organizations where no market exists for their debt and equity securities.

RECENT REGULATORY GUIDELINES

Consistent with the confusing and complex history of capital standards, the regulatory agencies adopted in December 1981 new guidelines for determining bank capital adequacy. The initial goal was to achieve uniformity in capital adequacy standards among the three federal bank regulatory agencies—the Comptroller of the Currency, the Federal Deposit Insurance Corporation, and the Federal Reserve System. In past years, these agencies had used different measures of capital and had required different levels of capital. Moreover, there were sizable differences—as pointed out in Table 12–2—in capital ratios among banks of different sizes. Unfortunately, the goal of establishing uniform and consistent capital standards for all commercial banks was not achieved. The Comptroller of the Currency and the Federal Reserve Board jointly adopted a set of guidelines to be used in assessing the adequacy of bank capital. The Federal Deposit Insurance Corporation, however, adopted its own set of guidelines.

In announcing the adoption of new guidelines, the Comptroller of the Currency and the Federal Reserve indicated that the standards adopted would permit somewhat lower capital ratios for the smaller banks than currently existed. The smaller banks had been complaining for many years against the "discriminatory" treatment by the regulatory agencies which allowed large banks to operate with much lower capital ratios than small banks. At the same time, the program would be structured to improve the capital positions of very large multinational banking organizations—at that time including 17 institutions with assets in excess of $15 billion.

The Comptroller and the Federal Reserve guidelines are relevant for assessing the capital of "well-managed national banks, state member banks, and bank holding companies."[7] The FDIC guidelines are relevant for state-chartered banks which are not members of the Federal Reserve.

Comptroller/Fed Guidelines

The Comptroller and the Federal Reserve announced that they would use two principal measures of capital in evaluating the capital adequacy of well-managed national banks, state member banks, and bank holding companies: (1) primary capital to total assets and (2) total capital to total assets. These capital measurements are applied differently for different

---

[7]*Federal Reserve Bulletin*, January 1982, p. 32.

types of organizations. Primary capital consists of common stock, perpetual preferred stock, capital surplus, undivided profits, reserves for contingencies and other capital reserves, mandatory convertible instruments, and allowance for possible loan losses. Total capital includes the primary capital components plus limited-life preferred stock and qualifying subordinated notes and debentures.

Institutions affected by the guidelines are categorized as (1) multinational, (2) regional (those with assets in excess of $1 billion), or (3) community organizations (less than $1 billion in total assets).

Capital guidelines for the small number of large multinational organizations are formulated and monitored on an individual basis. There is an attempt made, however, to halt and reverse the trend toward diminishing capital. A minimum primary capital to total assets ratio of 5 percent is usually expected.

Capital ratios for regional and community organizations are more quantitative in nature. Minimum acceptable ratios of primary capital to total assets are 5 percent for regional organizations and 6 percent for community organizations, though these organizations are generally expected to operate above the minimum levels. Guidelines were also established for ratios of total capital to total assets as follows:

Zone	Regional	Community
1	Above 6.5	Above 7.0
2	5.5 to 6.5	6.0 to 7.0
3	Below 5.5	Below 6.0

As a general rule, the nature and intensity of the supervision of the capital position of the organization is determined by the zone within which an institution falls. For those organizations operating in zone 1, the Comptroller of the Currency and the Federal Reserve presume adequate capital if the primary capital ratio is satisfactory and above the minimum level. For those organizations operating in zone 2, the regulatory agencies presume that the institution may be undercapitalized, especially if the primary and total capital ratios are at or near the minimum levels specified in the guidelines. These organizations receive extensive contact from the regulatory authorities and are required to submit comprehensive capital plans acceptable to the regulatory authorities. For the organizations operating in zone 3, the regulatory authorities have a very strong presumption that the bank is undercapitalized. The regulatory authorities maintain frequent contact with the bank and require a comprehensive capital plan, including a plan to expand the amount of capital.

It is important to note that those guidelines are administered in a flexible manner. The assessment of capital adequacy is made on a case-by-case basis that considers both quantitative and qualitative factors.

It is also interesting to note that the capital guidelines are generally administered on a *consolidated* basis in the case of a bank holding company organization; that is, the guidelines apply to the entire (consolidated) holding company organization. However, for bank holding companies of less than $150 million in consolidated assets, the capital guidelines apply to the bank only if the company engages in a nonbanking activity involving significant leverage and if no significant debt of the parent company is held by the general public.

FDIC Guidelines

Capital adequacy standards adopted by the Federal Deposit Insurance Corporation differ to some extent from those of the Comptroller of the Currency and the Federal Reserve. (A comparison of the two sets of guidelines is provided in Table 12–4.) The FDIC relies upon only one ratio, that of equity capital to total assets. Equity capital, as defined by the FDIC, is similar to primary capital as defined by the Comptroller and the Federal Reserve. However, the amount of equity capital is reduced by the amount of assets classified as loss and by one-half of the assets classified as doubtful. The FDIC also does not accept limited-life preferred stock and subordinated notes and debentures as a part of capital for purposes of determining capital adequacy.

More specifically, the FDIC announced in December 1981 its statement of policy on capital. This statement was designed to "formalize internal guidelines previously established by the Board of Directors, promote greater uniformity among the various FDIC regions, and provide guid-

Table 12–4   Comptroller/Fed and FDIC Capital Definitions

Type of Capital	Comptroller/Fed		FDIC
	Primary Capital	Total Capital	Equity Capital
Common stock	X	X	X
Captial surplus	X	X	X
Undivided profits	X	X	X
Perpetual preferred stock	X	X	X
Limited-life preferred stock	—	X	—
Reserves for contingencies and other capital reserves	X	X	X
Allowance for possible loan losses	X	X	X
Mandatory convertible instruments	X	X	X
Qualifying subordinated notes and debentures	—	X	—

Note: The FDIC reduces the amount of equity capital by the amount of assets classified as loss and by one half of the amount of assets classified as doubtful.

ance to affected institutions on the corporation's attitude toward this important issue."[8]

The capital measure used by the FDIC in assessing the adequacy of bank capital is equity (minus assets classified as loss and one half of assets classified doubtful) expressed as a percentage of total assets (minus assets classified as loss and one half of assets classified as doubtful). Equity capital is defined to include common stock, perpetual preferred stock, capital surplus, undivided profits, contingency reserves, mandatory convertible instruments, and reserves for loan losses.

In the FDIC procedures, the determination of a bank's capital adequacy begins with a *qualitative* evaluation of the critical variables that are useful in assessing the overall financial condition of a financial institution. These variables encompass the quality, type and diversification of assets, current and historical earnings, provision for liquidity with particular emphasis on asset-liability mismatches, and market depreciation in the portfolio of assets, the quality of management, and the existence of other activities which may expose the bank to risk.

While the FDIC capital adequacy assessment begins with these qualitative factors, it also has some specific *quantitative* guidelines that foster objectivity in appraising capital adequacy. For example, the FDIC established a threshold level for adjusted equity capital for all insured nonmember banks at 6 percent of adjusted total assets. If the adjusted equity capital ratio falls below this level, the FDIC requires submission of a comprehensive capital plan from the management of the bank. The FDIC also established minimum acceptable levels of adjusted equity capital at 5 percent of adjusted total assets. If the adjusted equity capital ratio falls below this level, the FDIC insists that bank management provide a specific program for promptly eliminating the capital deficiency.

It is important to recognize that these guidelines apply to sound, well-managed, and diversified institutions that have historical records of adequate capital. The guidelines apply regardless of size of bank or holding company affiliation. Also, individual state banking departments may require higher capital requirements.

DETERMINING THE AMOUNT OF CAPITAL NEEDED

A bank is able to project the amount of capital that it needs to raise externally once it has specified the following variables:

1. The desired leverage ratio, where the leverage ratio is the amount of assets divided by the amount of capital.

---

[8]Federal Deposit Insurance Corporation, *FDIC Statement of Policy on Capital*, December 17, 1981.

2. The return-on-assets ratio, where this ratio is defined as the ratio of after-tax profits to total assets.
3. The retention ratio, defined as the ratio of retained earnings for a period (that is, net income minus cash dividends) divided by net income.

Given these three variables, management can determine the amount by which the bank can expand without reducing the capital ratio by use of the following equation:

$$\begin{array}{ccccc} \text{Leverage} & \times & \text{Rate of return} & \times & \text{Earnings} & = & \text{Internal capital} \\ \text{ratio} & & \text{on assets} & & \text{retention} & & \text{generation rate} \\ & & & & \text{rate} & & \end{array}$$

For example, assume that the leverage ratio is 20 (indicating a ratio of capital to assets of 5 percent), the return on assets is 1 percent, and the retention ratio is 0.7 (indicating that 30 percent of earnings are paid out to shareholders in the form of cash dividends). Given these assumptions, the internal capital generation rate is 14 percent. This 14 percent is the maximum rate that total assets can expand without reducing the capital ratio.

This simple model can be used by bank management in a number of ways. It provides a number of decision variables that can be used in order to avoid the need to raise external capital. For example, suppose that management expects the bank's assets to grow at a 15 percent annual rate over the next five years and yet it does not wish to raise external capital. Assuming further that the 5 percent capital-to-asset ratio that currently exists is the desired ratio (or the minimum allowed by the regulatory authorities), management knows that it can prevent the need for raising capital externally by either increasing the return on assets or increasing the retention ratio (reducing the payout ratio) or both. An increase in the earnings ratio of 1.10 percent (from 1.00 percent) would raise the internal capital generation rate to 15 percent and avoid the need to raise external capital. The same result could be achieved by increasing the retention rate to 0.75 percent, without a gain in the return-on-assets ratio.

The model can also be used to estimate the amount of external capital required, providing that it is neither possible nor desirable to close the capital gap (the difference between the internal capital generation rate and the projected asset growth) by increasing the earnings or retention ratios. For example, suppose that the bank currently has total assets of $100 million and total capital of $5 million. Given an internal capital generation rate of 14 percent and a projected asset expansion of 20 percent (for example), management can anticipate the need to raise $300,000 in new capital. This figure is obtained by applying the 20 percent asset growth rate to the $100 million in original assets, producing year-end assets of $120 million; and applying the 14 percent internal capital generation rate to the $5 million in original capital, producing a year-end capital position of $5.7 million. On a year-end asset base of $120 million, the bank must maintain capital equal to $6 million. Hence, the bank has a projected $300,000 shortfall in capital. In this situation, then, the question is how best to raise the capital.

Commercial banks have found it necessary in recent years to raise substantial amounts of new capital externally. This need has resulted from a combination of factors. Rapid inflation has produced a large increase in the dollar volume of bank deposits. While inflation has a number of influences on commercial banks as well as on other types of business organizations, one of the most significant is the sharp increase in the dollar size of the institution. Banks which were once $100 million institutions become $500 million in size, while $500 million banks quickly become $1 billion-plus in size with inflation of the currency. Yet the increase in deposit growth does not automatically produce a comparable advance in the capital account.

EVALUATION OF ALTERNATIVE MEANS OF RAISING CAPITAL

All rapidly growing business firms have difficulty in providing an adequate equity base. Growth in the commercial banking.industry, though, has created special difficulties for bank management, as it has occurred at a time of intense pressure on profit margins. With growing costs of money and labor, particularly of money, commercial banks have found it increasingly difficult to maintain their profit margins. The decline in margins has not only reduced the ability of commercial banks to build capital through the retention of earnings but also has reduced the willingness of banks to add to capital, since it is possible to blunt the impact of falling margins on the return on capital to some extent by allowing the capital-asset ratio to fall. In addition, there is some evidence that many bank stocks have traditionally been held by investors for dividend or income purposes, and there has been a reluctance on the part of management to reduce the dividend payout ratio to shareholders. Reflecting all of these factors, capital ratios for many banks have declined and there has been intense pressure on management to raise capital externally. The pressure has been especially intense on commercial banks subject to regulation by the Federal Reserve System. For a number of holding company acquisitions, the Board of Governors of the Federal Reserve has conditioned its approval on the infusion by the holding company of equity capital into acquired banks.

The capital management decision is a vitally important one as management seeks to maximize the value of the firm to its shareholders.[9] In raising

---

[9]Decisions about capital (debt versus equity, for example) affect the financial risk of the banking organization. In contrast, asset management decisions determine the level of business risk. Total risk is the sum of business and financial risk.

capital from external sources, bank management has essentially the following options: common stock, preferred stock, and subordinated notes and debentures. In addition, in some instances. it may be possible to satisfy the capital requirements of the regulatory authorities by selling the fixed assets of the bank and then leasing them back.[10] In reaching its decision, management should focus on a number of different factors, such as income, risk, control, timing, and flexibility.[11]

Earnings per Share.   One of the most important factors involved in the financing decision by management is the impact on the earnings per share of the organization. In general, debt should have the least unfavorable (or the most favorable) effect on earnings per share, because raising capital through selling subordinated notes and debentures does not create any additional shares of common stock. It does increase the amount of interest expense, but the effect of that change on after-tax earnings is reduced by the tax deductibility of interest. Moreover, once the earning power of the funds raised through the sale of subordinated notes and debentures is taken into account, the earnings per share after the sale of new capital should be higher than before. The earnings per share will be greater as compared to the before-sale situation, as long as the funds are invested to earn a greater after-tax return than the after-tax cost of money raised. In other words, if leverage is favorable, there will be an incentive from an income perspective to proceed with financing through debt. A similar argument prevails for preferred stock except that dividend payments are not tax-deductible. Hence the unfavorable impact on earnings of preferred stock dividends are more pronounced than for debt, and similarly it takes a greater return on the funds invested to create favorable financial leverage.[12]

---

[10]The sale and lease-back of fixed assets became quite important in 1981 and 1982, especially for savings and loans and mutual savings banks. Such a sale allowed the institutions to realize the gains embodied in the appreciated value of the real estate as well as to reinvest the funds at the then high interest rates. It also bolstered the capital accounts of the institutions, since accounting rules don't allow the fixed assets to be carried at market value.

[11]It must also be recognized that the capital adequacy guidelines established by the regulatory authorities in late 1981 also affect this decision. Common stock, preferred stock, and debentures provide a funding source for all banking organizations, though whether this satisfies the minimum capital positions of the regulatory authorities depends upon the nature of the financial instrument and the nature of the regulatory authority. For example, for the FDIC, the principal regulator of smaller banks, only equity counts toward providing adequate capital. However, for national banks and larger state banks (which are more likely to be member banks), debentures count as secondary capital, though not as primary capital.

[12]Favorable leverage would be created through the use of either subordinate notes and debentures or preferred stock.

In contrast, the sale of common stock produces immediate dilution of earnings per share, since existing earnings must be spread over a larger number of shares. Moreover, even taking into account the income generated on the funds invested, earnings per share with the sale of common stock will be less than with preferred stock or debt financing as long as favorable financial leverage results. Over the longer term, of course, as funds invested begin to generate income, the earnings per share with common stock financing should exceed the earnings per share without that financing; or, from an income perspective, there would be no incentive to raise additional funds.

Risk. Different means of raising funds not only have different effects on income but also on risk. Risk in this context may be viewed from two different perspectives. The most tangible perspective is that of bankruptcy. The other is the effect on the market price of the bank's stock. The latter is less tangible but in many cases may be the most important impact from different financing alternatives. It is usually argued that risk is greatest when debt is added to the capital structure, and least when financing is done with common stock. Preferred stock falls somewhere between these two extremes.

Addition of debt to the capital structure increases the fixed charges (payment of interest and repayment of principal) faced by bank management. As such, the addition of debt can be viewed as adding to the risk that the organization will fail. However, the significance of this factor is reduced to some extent by the tax-deductibility of interest (so that the after-tax cost of a $1 million interest payment is only $540,000 if the bank is in the 46-percent tax bracket, assuming of course that the bank remains profitable during the term of the bond) and by the fact that bank management has numerous other fixed commitments, such as CDs; thus the addition of debt does not add greatly to the total fixed cash outflow which management is confronted with. However, an equally and perhaps more important factor is the effect on the market's perception of the risk involved in investing in shares of the organization. The additional debt may cause the price-earnings ratio of the bank's shares to decline, since the earnings available to common shareholders will be more variable with debt and since shareholders are presumed to dislike variability in the earnings and dividend stream. Hence debt may add to the income (earnings per share) of the organization but may not increase shareholder wealth if the price-earnings ratio reduction more than offsets the impact on share value of higher earnings. However, studies have indicated that—at least up to the debt ratios prevalent through the mid-1970s—the addition of subordinated debt to the capital structure did *not* reduce the price-earnings ratio. This would suggest that management should continue to employ debt in the capital structure as long as debt increases the bank's earnings per share and as long as the price-earnings ratio does not fall.

Preferred stock also adds risk to the banking organization, but the risk is of a somewhat different nature from that of debt. Dividends payable on preferred stock do not represent a legal obligation of the bank. In periods of diminished cash flow, bank management could quite legally reduce or eliminate preferred stock dividends. However, the payment of preferred stock dividends by a bank would generally be viewed as a moral commitment on the part of the bank and is therefore to be preferred from a risk perspective.

Control.   Control refers to the possibility that an individual or group of individuals who currently have control of the bank may lose their authority as the result of the means of financing chosen. Under this criterion, common stock is the least favorable choice since it creates additional voting shares.[13] The additional shares could fall into the hands of a new group and, along with shares already held, could be used to change control of the organization. To some extent, this threat is reduced by the preemptive right of existing shareholders. Under this arrangement, existing shareholders must be offered enough shares to allow them to maintain their proportionate interest in the organization. However, existing shareholders—particularly the control group—still face the difficulty of raising sufficient funds in order to buy the shares offered.

Problems with control are less pronounced with the sale of preferred stock or subordinated notes and debentures, since no additional voting securities are created. However, this is not meant to imply that control is not an issue with these securities. Frequently, it is necessary for the borrower to agree to certain restrictions prior to the sale of preferred stock and/or debt instruments and especially with debt securities. These restrictions might include limitations on management salaries and on dividends payable to common shareholders, to name only a few. Moreover, the borrower faces the loss of control should there be a failure to conform to the full terms of the contract under which the preferred stock or debt securities were issued. At the extreme, the board of directors could be dominated by a lender should the borrower experience financial difficulties.

Timing.   Timing refers to the question of whether the present is a particularly desirable or undesirable period to sell one of the securities under debate. For example, bond prices may be unusually high, in which case bond interest rates would be unusually low. In contrast, stock prices might be unusually low. In this circumstance, the present would be a de-

---

[13]If there is a good secondary market for the stock, however, the group seeking control also could acquire additional shares through open-market purchase of existing shares.

sirable time to raise funds with debt securities. However, it may be that for some reason the stock of the individual bank is selling at a historically high price-earnings ratio, in which case the timing criterion would suggest that funds should be raised with the sale of common stock. Given the enormous changes in the prices of financial assets in recent years, timing has become a consideration of great importance.

Flexibility. In a growing economy, and particularly in an inflationary environment, it is unlikely that bank management will be able to finance only once and fulfill its capital requirements for all time. Rather, in making the capital decision today, management should recognize that additional financing probably will be needed a number of times in the future. Within this context, it is important for management to consider how its financing decision today will affect the bank's ability to borrow in the future; from this perspective, common stock is clearly the preferred alternative. While the sale of debt securities today reduces future debt opportunities available to the firm and thereby reduces future financial flexibility, the sale of common stock does not use up any existing debt capacity. In contrast, the sale of common stock adds to the debt capacity of the firm by building its equity base.

Other Factors. Finally, management must consider all other relevant factors not specifically covered in those above. For example, the sale of debt securities may satisfy the capital requirements of the regulatory authorities but may not add to the legal lending limit of the organization. If the legal lending limit is a matter of great importance, then this factor should be given weight in the discussion. Similarly, management may wish to expand the common stock holdings of one group, perhaps representatives of large firms in the area. In any case, there are clearly other variables to consider in making the financing decision involved in raising the required amount of capital.

SUMMARY

Capital management is not only one of the most important areas of bank management; it is also one in which substantial conflict frequently exists between bank management (often desiring to reduce the capital ratios) and the regulatory authorities (desiring to increase the capital ratios). While capital serves a number of functions, its principal role is to provide a buffer to absorb losses and to allow the institution to remain viable as a going concern during the period when problems are being corrected. The definition of capital within the banking industry usually includes some or all of the following: capital stock, surplus, undivided profits, reserves, preferred stock, and subordinated notes and debentures.

Capital ratios at banks, especially those ratios that relate capital to risk assets, have declined substantially over recent decades. The reduction in capital ratios has been especially pronounced for large banks. In contrast, for smaller banks, most capital ratios remained roughly constant, or increased slightly during the decade of the 1970s. Most external capital raised by banking organizations has taken the form of subordinated notes and debentures, reflecting the lower after-tax cost of debt as compared with equity.

A number of measures of capital adequacy have been used. These include the capital-asset and capital-deposit ratios, the capital-risk asset ratio, the Form for Analyzing Bank Capital, as well as market-related measures. Subjective judgment of the quality of management and other factors associated with risk also play a role in assessing capital adequacy.

Regulatory guidelines for assessing bank capital adequacy were modified in December 1981. The Comptroller of the Currency and the Federal Reserve adopted one set of guidelines while the FDIC adopted a related, though separate, set of guidelines. The Comptroller/Fed guidelines, which are applicable for national banks, state member banks, and bank holding companies, use two sets of capital ratios: primary capital–total assets, and total capital–total assets. The FDIC uses only one ratio, equity capital–total assets.

External capital needs of banks have been substantial and have been met by the issuance of common stock, preferred stock, and subordinated notes and debentures. In deciding what types of capital to issue, management should focus on the effects of different capital sources on earnings per share, risk, control, timing, and flexibility.

Questions

12–1. What is the basic conflict over the subject of capital adequacy between management and the regulatory authorities?

12–2. What is capital? What is it composed of? What changes have recently occurred in the composition of capital?

12–3. What has been the relationship of capital-to-risk assets over time for the last 50 years?

12–4. What are some of the measures used in judging capital adequacy? What are their advantages and disadvantages?

12–5. How is the FABC (Form for Analyzing Bank Capital), developed by the Federal Reserve, constructed?

12–6. What factors influence the structure of capital? Why have banks relied heavily on borrowed capital?

12–7. Can a bank have too much capital?

References

1. Crosse, Howard, and George Hempel. *Management Policies for Commercial Banks*. Englewood Cliffs, N.J.: Prentice-Hall, 1980, chaps. 5, 6.

2. Gallant, Richard A. "Approaches to Capital Planning." *Journal of Bank Research*, autumn 1975, pp. 173–76.

3. Hahn, Phillip J. *The Capital Adequacy of Commercial Banks*. New York: American Press, 1966.

4. Hempel, George. *Bank Capital: Determining and Meeting Your Bank's Needs*. Boston: Bankers Publishing, 1976.

5. Jessup, Paul F. *Modern Bank Management*. Minneapolis: West Publishing, 1980, chap. 15.

6. Landow, Wesley. "Bank Capital and Risk Assets." *National Banking Review*, September 1963, pp. 29–46.

7. Maisel, Sherman J. *Risk and Capital Adequacy in Commercial Banks*. Chicago: University of Chicago Press, 1981.

8. Mock, Edward J. "Banks Find New Ways to Raise Capital." *Banking*, November 1964, pp. 47, 58–62.

9. Nadler, Paul S. "Can Debentures Save the Smaller Bank?" *Banking*, November 1964, pp. 43–44, 98.

10. Pettway, Richard H. "Market Tests of Capital Adequacy of Large Commercial Banks." *The Journal of Finance*, June 1976, pp. 865–75.

11. Sharpe, William F. "Bank Capital Adequacy, Deposit Insurance, and Security Values." *Journal of Financial and Quantitative Analysis*, November 1978, pp. 701–18.

12. Taggart, Robert A. "Regulatory Influence on Bank Capital." *New England Economic Review*, Federal Reserve Bank of Boston, September, October 1977, 37–46.

13. Talley, Samuel H. *Bank Capital Trends and Financing*. Board of Governors of the Federal Reserve System, Washington, D.C., February 1983.

14. Vojta, George J. *Bank Capital Adequacy*. New York: Citicorp, 1973.

Problem for Discussion

WITH RAPID DEPOSIT GROWTH in recent years placing pressure on capital positions, many commercial banks have been faced with the need—either because of regulations or management decision—to raise additional capital. Moreover, the alternative sources of capital funds available to commercial banks today are much greater and more complex than in previous periods. The problem situation discussed below provides the student with the opportunity to analyze the impact of alternative capital sources on the financial position of a large bank. After reviewing the material below, the student should address the following questions:

1. What are the advantages and disadvantages of each alternative?
2. How will the earnings per share of the bank be affected by each of the alternatives?
3. What might be the impact on the market value of the bank's common stock?
4. Which alternative would you recommend?

First National Bank presently serves a dynamic community of about 500,000 population. Area growth has been spurred by a heavy influx of new residents and new businesses seeking a warmer climate and by the development of new industries centered upon space technology, electronics, and commercial and residential construction. First National has captured a significant share of new business accounts and, by careful selection of branch office sites, has successfully penetrated the growing suburban consumer market.

First National's rapid growth has not been an unmixed blessing, however. For one thing, loan losses associated with the newest commercial accounts have been higher than average, principally because many of the newest firms are in relatively volatile industries subject to extreme business-cycle fluctuations. These conditions have also affected the bank's consumer loans, where losses have been higher than anticipated due mainly to the bank's limited experience with many of its household customers. A second major problem is that First National frequently finds it cannot meet the total credit requirements of its commercial customers. This is due, in large part, to the legal lending limit which the federal banking agencies have placed on both secured and unsecured loans to a single borrower. Under the terms of the Garn–St Germain Depository Institutions Act of 1982, unsecured loans made by a national bank to a single borrower are limited to 15 percent of unimpaired capital and surplus. Secured loans carry a limit of 25 percent of capital and surplus. When the bank receives a customer request for credit beyond its lending capacity, the overline typically is handled by sharing the loan with another bank or group of banks. (This is referred to in the banking business as "participating out" the loan.) Another important factor limiting the bank's lending power is the antibranching law imposed several years ago by the state legislature. A bank may establish branch offices only within the county where its headquarters is located. Thus deposits and other local sources of loanable funds must come from a relatively restricted geographic area, and this has limited First National's growth.

Last week, officials from the regional office of the Comptroller of the Currency visited with management and the board of directors. The officials had indicated only a year ago that the bank's capital position was relatively weak. This time, however, these officials insisted that steps be taken to remedy the capital deficiency—estimated to be in the neighborhood of $10.5 million. The Comptroller's office expressed concern about the volatile nature of the local economy, the limited availability of long-term nondeposit sources of funds to a bank of First National's size, the bank's modest earnings record compared to other banks of about the same size, its relatively low degree of geographic and portfolio diversification, and the intense competition in the local market area. The officials observed that First National's ratios of capital (net worth) to total assets, risk assets, loans, and deposits were substantially below comparable ratios for similar size banks. The board of directors agreed to study the situation and do whatever was necessary.

Four major alternative sources of new capital were considered by management: (1) issuance of common stock; (2) sale of capital notes and debentures; (3) sale of preferred stock; and (4) reduction of dividends and, therefore, greater retention of earnings. Management realizes the difficulty of its task, for the raising of new capital can be an inordinately difficult problem for small and medium-size banks, principally because several avenues open to larger banks are, for all practical purposes, closed to smaller institutions. The most satisfactory approach from the point of view of the regulatory authorities is the sale of stock, since this directly increases the bank's equity position. However, the sale of stock is one of the most expensive sources of capital and results in a dilution of earnings per share of common. Moreover, the market for the stock of smaller banks is both limited and highly imperfect. At present, First National's stock is selling for $39 per share, or about $2\frac{1}{2}$ times earnings per share. Management has determined that First National can sell its stock at $35 per share, net of any underwriting cost. Management has carried out a survey of key stockholders and found that only about 30 percent of the projected equity issue could be absorbed by current shareholders.

For most banks, retained earnings are the major source of growth in capital. First National's expenses have grown rapidly in recent years, due to its aggressive program of establishing new suburban branches and the rising cost of attracting deposits in a highly competitive banking market. These factors, coupled with above-normal loan losses, have squeezed the bank's earnings. Management estimates that earnings in the near term will provide only a small part of the necessary increase in capital. Moreover, the bank has followed a policy since its founding in 1921 of paying an automatic dividend of 8 percent. Reduction of this dividend to build up the bank's net worth might be desirable from a capital adequacy standpoint but would be likely to have a negative impact upon the value of the bank's stock. Reduction of dividends would lower the present value of expected dividend flows in future years and might be a signal to investors that First National's earnings were subject to more risk than in the past. Either way, a decline in the bank's stock price and price-earnings ratio would follow quickly. All factors considered, management feels that it must raise at least $9 million net in capital through some form of security (debt or equity) issue within the next six months.

Some consideration is being given by management to issuing preferred stock. A number of options are available, such as making the preferred issues callable at a fixed price at the bank's option or allowing conversion into common stock at a predetermined price at the investor's option. Convertible-preferred could probably be issued at a much lower dividend yield. The bank presently has no preferred issues outstanding. Conversations with investment bankers suggest the bank could issue preferred stock, provided it is willing to pay a guaranteed annual dividend of at least 10 percent with some provision for participation in future earnings. The new preferred shares could be sold for about $40 per share.

In recent years, banks have made widespread use of senior capital (i.e., notes and debentures) subordinated to deposits. This is particularly appropriate where local economic conditions are favorable to the bank's continuing growth, but equity capital simply has not grown rapidly enough to keep pace with the growth of loans and deposits. When the debt can be issued at relatively low rates, favorable financial leverage will result, increasing earnings per share on common stock. Management has investigated the option of selling debentures and found that a seven-year capital note with a coupon of 12 percent probably could be sold in a private placement. If a debenture issue that is convertible into common stock is offered, the interest rate could probably be reduced another percentage point. However, underwriting fees are significantly higher on convertible issues.

In choosing which way to go, management and the board of directors have in mind two main objectives: (1) the total amount of capital to be raised must be, at minimum, sufficient to satisfy the regulatory authorities, and (2) the method chosen to raise new capital should enhance the stockholders' position by maximizing their rate of return. During the past year, First National Bank received total revenues of $21.1 million and had total operating expenses of $16,401,800. Its effective income tax rate is 46 percent. The bank's stock has a par value of $20 with 150,000 shares outstanding. First National Bank held $550 million in total assets and $500 million in total deposits at year-end 1983. Its equity capital totaled $32.5 million at the end of 1983, or 6.5 percent of total deposits.

PART FOUR

Thrift Institutions

13. *Savings and Loan Associations*

SAVINGS AND LOAN ASSOCIATIONS are among the most important financial intermediaries in the American economy. These institutions serve mainly individuals and families, accepting savings and payment accounts from households and devoting most of their assets to home mortgage loans. And, because adequate housing is deemed to be of critical importance in the United States, savings and loans are closely regulated in both their deposit-taking and lending activities with many of the regulations aimed at insuring a large and stable flow of funds to the housing market. As we will note in this chapter, however, not all of the regulations confronting savings and loans have been successful in achieving their purposes, and some have severely restricted the ability of these institutions to compete with other, less closely regulated intermediaries, threatening the long-term viability of the industry. The key to the future viability of savings and loan associations lies in their ability to diversify services, enter new markets, and perhaps align themselves with other financial institutions (such as bank holding companies) which are in a stronger financial position. New federal laws and more lenient regulations have recently been developed to aid the industry in achieving these objectives.

The first savings and loan association was formed in the United States in 1831. It was called the Oxford Provident Building Association and was headquartered in Philadelphia County, Pennsylvania. Like thousands of other savings and loans set up across the country in later years, Oxford Provident was really a cooperative savings and home-financing association, composed of neighborhood individuals and families. Each member of the association was expected to contribute his or her savings into a common pool. Eventually, each member became eligible to borrow from the association's pooled resources to purchase a home.

In many ways, the modern savings and loan association resembles the earliest ones. It still devotes a large percentage of its assets to home financ-

THE STRUCTURE OF THE SAVINGS AND LOAN INDUSTRY

ing and, as we will see later in this chapter, draws most of its funds from the savings deposits of individuals and families. But the industry has grown and diversified its operations in recent years, bringing in high-quality professional managers and offering a wide array of consumer financial services. Also, unlike the early S&Ls, many people who keep their deposits in a modern savings and loan do not borrow there to purchase a home.

Chartering and Supervision

Like commercial banks, savings and loan associations must secure a charter from either federal or state authorities in order to open an office and receive deposits from the public. A savings and loan receiving a federal charter comes under supervision, regulation, and examination by the system of Federal Home Loan Banks (FHLBs). In the past, however, most savings and loans have sought state charters and are supervised by state banking commissions or savings and loan departments.[1] (Approximately three fifths of all S&Ls today have state charters; the remainder belong to the federal system.)

Both federally chartered and state-chartered associations may apply for federal insurance of their deposits through the Federal Savings and Loan Insurance Corporation (FSLIC) which protects each deposit account holder up to $100,000. Federally chartered S&Ls must secure FSLIC insurance coverage, while state-chartered S&Ls can elect to seek federal insurance if they so desire. Several states provide deposit insurance for thrifts chartered within their borders. Like the FSLIC, state insurance plans assess member institutions an insurance fee equal to a specified percentage of the amount of deposits to be insured. The fee usually varies with the loss experience of the insuring agency.

Stock versus Mutual Associations

The organizers of a new savings and loan can choose to structure their institution as a mutual association or as a stockholder-owned corporation. *Stock associations* are similar to any other business corporation; owners receive shares of stock and are entitled to dividends voted by the board of directors. *Mutuals*, on the other hand, issue no stock; their de-

---

[1] While federally chartered savings and loans must be members of the Federal Home Loan Bank (FHLB) system, state-chartered associations have the option of electing to join or not join this federal sytem. In this respect, the option of joining the FHLB system for state-chartered S&Ls is much like the option confronting state-chartered commercial banks in deciding whether or not to become members of the Federal Reserve System. Membership brings some prestige and may help attract or retain large business or household depositors as well as correspondent business from other depository institutions.

positors are legally the owners of the association, receiving dividend income at a stipulated rate based on their deposit balances. Individuals who deposit funds in a stockholder-owned S&L, in contrast, are creditors of the association, not owners.

Size Distribution of Savings and Loans

On December 31, 1981, there were 4,347 savings associations operating in the 50 states, the District of Columbia, Puerto Rico, and Guam. Of this total, 3,464 were mutuals and 883 were stockholder-owned S&Ls. The industry as a whole has witnessed a sharp decline in the total number of savings and loans, reflecting a massive consolidation trend. The number of stockholder-owned S&Ls, however, has been increasing, while the number of mutual associations has been declining. Really, the number of stock associations has grown in response to rapid population increases in areas of the nation where stockholder-owned S&Ls are important, principally the Midwest and western United States, and due to some regulatory encouragement at the federal level to convert from mutual to stock form.[2] Assets held by mutual associations amounted to an estimated $465 billion in 1981, while stock associations held estimated resources of $198 billion. Thus stockholder-owned associations controlled 30 percent of the industry's assets in 1981, yet represented only about 20 percent of the total number of S&Ls. By this reckoning it is obvious that stock savings and loans are larger, on average, than mutual associations.

The distribution of assets among large and small savings and loans reflects considerable concentration in the industry's resources. A large num-

---

[2]Stockholder-owned S&Ls have more options in raising funds since they may issue stock as well as offer deposits. In addition, two of the most rapidly growing states—Texas and California—permit the chartering of stock associations. Of the 883 permanent stock associations operating at year-end 1981, 129 were headquartered in California and 218 in Texas. California's stock associations dominated in asset size, holding about 46 percent of the assets of all stockholder-owned S&Ls in the United States. See, in particular, the United States League of Savings Associations [20].

Limited research suggests that stock savings and loans tend to be more aggressively managed than mutuals. This is evidenced by the stocks' stronger emphasis on profitability and market-share goals, heavier use of advertising, higher savings deposit rates, and faster rates of growth in resources and operating income, as suggested, for example, in a study by Nichols [15]. A more recent paper by Verbrugge and Goldstein [22] finds that stock S&Ls consistently earned higher average rates of return on their assets than mutuals (over the 1974–76 period). These researchers found that mutual associations preferred to hold a 'safer" loan portfolio than did stock associations and averaged higher operating costs, due in part to the absence of owner influence. Verbrugge and Goldstein believe their findings support recent trends in the industry for mutual associations to convert to stock form. Under the terms of the Garn–St Germain Depository Institutions Act of 1982, thrift institutions were authorized to freely change their organizational form between stock and mutual if they chose and to switch from state to federal charters, or conversely.

ber of relatively small S&Ls hold a minor proportion of all industry assets (see Table 13–1). At year-end 1981, for example, 730 associations (or about one sixth of the total in the industry) held total assets of less than $10 milion apiece, but controlled less than one half of 1 percent of the industry's resources. The few largest associations with $500 million or more in total assets held more than half of all industry assets. However, there has been dramatic growth in the number of associations moving into larger asset size categories. The average size S&L roughly quadrupled in assets over the decade of the 1970s.

S&L Mergers

The number of mergers involving savings and loans have accelerated in recent years. For example, between 1970 and 1981, there were more than 1,200 mergers among savings associations belonging to the Federal Home Loan Bank system. This acceleration in merger activity reflects, in part, increasing costs (particularly the cost of raising funds) and an attempt by individual associations to reach for greater economies of organization and operation. In addition, the increasing complexity of the savings and loan business has made it more difficult for individual associations to find capable management.

While the above-mentioned factors have played a major role in the long-term trend of savings and loan merger activity, a more potent factor of late has been the actual or impending financial collapse of a number of associations. Thus, as interest rates rose to record levels repeatedly during the 1970s and early 1980s, a large number of S&Ls, locked into old fixed-rate, low-yielding mortgages and confronted with sharply higher interest costs on deposits, saw their profits plummet and, in many cases, turn into

Table 13–1   Distribution of Savings Associations by Asset Size: December 31, 1981

Asset Size Category ($ millions)	Number of Associations	Percent of Total	Total Assets ($ millions)	Percent of Total
Under $10 million	730	16.8%	$ 2,586	0.4%
$10 and under $50 million	1,520	35.0	43,064	6.5
$50 and under $100 million	854	19.6	64,904	9.8
$100 and under $500 million	1,001	23.0	212,562	32.0
$500 million and over	242	5.6	340,728	51.3
Total	4,347	100.0%	$663,844	100.0%

Note: Columns may not add to totals due to rounding error.
Sources: Adapted from the United States League of Savings Associations, *'82 Savings and Loan Sourcebook* (Chicago, 1982), table 57, p. 39.

substantial losses. For example, in July 1982, H. Brent Beesley, director of the FSLIC, estimated that close to 80 percent of all federally insured savings and loans were experiencing losses.[3] Faced with a potentially staggering drain on the FSLIC's insurance fund from the claims of insured depositors, that federal agency began to aggressively seek out stronger associations as merger partners for troubled S&Ls. A number of FSLIC-directed mergers combined savings and loans in different states—a practice generally frowned upon in the past. Moreover, when Fidelity Savings and Loan Association of San Francisco began floundering, S&L regulatory authorities and the Federal Reserve Board agreed to the acquisition of Fidelity by Citicorp in New York, one of the nation's leading bank holding companies. These and other mergers have contributed to a 20 percent decline in the total number of savings and loans over the past decade. In 1982, for the first time in many years, the total assets of the savings and loan industry declined but still exceeded $600 billion on December 31 of that year, ranking the industry second in total resources only to commercial banks.

Branching Activity in the Industry

While the number of S&Ls has been declining, spurred on by financial troubles, many new branch offices have been set up in recent years. For example, there were about 17,000 savings and loan branch offices in 1980, roughly four times the number open in 1970. In 1967, federally chartered associations were permitted to operate mobile branches serving communities not large enough for full-time branch offices. During the early 1970s the Federal Home Loan Bank Board (FHLBB) authorized the establishment of satellite offices, more commonly known as minibranches, which are located principally in retail stores and shopping malls. Minibranches may be completely automated or manned by tellers.

The growth of branching activity in the industry can be explained by many of the same forces propelling the growth of merger activity. Rising costs, the risks of developing and marketing new services, and a shortage of qualified managers all have played a role in the growth of branch offices. As the decade of the 1970s drew to a close, however, branching activity slowed under the pressure of financial problems. Many of the really good sites for branch offices were now taken, and the poor financial health of many firms in the industry reduced its ability to handle the substantial costs associated with branch construction. Moreover, like banks, S&Ls began to make greater use of automated teller machines both at their branch office sites and through remote service units (RSUs) in shopping

---

[3]See "S&Ls Seen Posting Profit in '83 if Drop in Rates is Sustained," *The Wall Street Journal*, September 10, 1982.

centers, retail stores, and in other convenient locations. The expansion in RSUs reduced the need for full-service branches.

Trends in the Number of Associations

Reflecting the large number of mergers and more liberal branching rules, the total number of savings and loans has been declining since 1960. As shown in Table 13–2, there were nearly 2,000 fewer associations in 1980 than in 1960 and over 1,300 less than in 1970. As we noted earlier in this chapter, the decline in S&L numbers is the work of a number of powerful forces. Increased competition between commercial banks, savings and loans, and credit unions in conjunction with a more restrictive chartering policy have played important roles. The states have been far less liberal, historically, in granting new charters than have federal chartering authorities, and the number of state-chartered savings and loans has been declining for more than two decades. However, overriding all of these pressures toward consolidation is the industry's financial problems in an environment of high and often rising interest rates.

Savings and loans are particularly sensitive to an inverted yield curve (when short-term rates exceed long-term rates).[4] Their deposits are principally short-term while their assets are mainly long-term. An inverted yield curve typically results in deposit costs exceeding loan revenues, with a resultant loss in earnings and a decline in the net worth of individual associations. In such an adverse environment, state and federal authorities are obviously hesitant to charter new savings and loans.[5]

Table 13–2   Number of Savings and Loan Associations by Type of Charter (year-end figures)

Year	Federally Chartered Associations	State-Chartered Associations			Industry Totals
		Total	FSLIC Insured	Noninsured	
1950	1,526	4,466	1,334	3,132	5,992
1960	1,873	4,447	2,225	2,222	6,320
1970	2,067	3,602	2,298	1.304	5,669
1980	1,985	2,607	2,017	590	4,592
1981	1,907	2,440	1,872	568	4,347

Sources: Adapted from Federal Home Loan Bank Board; and United States League of Savings Associations, *'82 Savings and Loan Sourcebook* (Chicago, 1982), table 54, p. 37.

---

[4]See Chapter 4 for a detailed discussion of the yield curve and the factors that influence its shape or slope.

[5]Interestingly, *new* savings and loans chartered during the record interest-rate period of the early 1980s often benefited from the high and rising rates. The new S&Ls held no low-rate mortgages from earlier years and were able to make new loans at record rates. As a result, an interesting dichotomy emerged in the earnings distribution of the S&L industry.

Mortgages and Mortgage-Related Assets

Because savings and loan associations are specialists in financing the construction of homes and apartments, it is no surprise that mortgage loans are their principal asset. At year-end 1981, for example, conventional mortgage loans aimed mainly at financing the purchase of single-family homes represented about four fifths of the industry's total resources and amounted to $518 billion (see Table 13–3). Indeed, the industry's ratio of home mortgages to total assets has changed little since the 1930s.[6]

Table 13–3   Assets (uses of funds) for U.S. Savings and Loan Associations (figures as of year-end 1981)

Industry Uses of Funds	Amount ($ billions) 12/31/81	Percent of Asset Total
Conventional mortgage loans	$518.4	78.1%
Mortgages insured by FHA-VA and mortgage-backed securities	33.5	5.0
Loans secured by mobile homes	4.0	0.6
Loans for home improvement projects	5.9	0.9
Loans secured by savings accounts	5.2	0.8
Loans to support education	1.6	0.2
Miscellaneous consumer loans	2.5	0.4
Liquidity reserves: cash and security investments	48.5	7.3
Other security investments	14.2	2.1
Federal Home Loan Bank stock	5.3	0.8
Service corporation investments	3.8	0.6
Buildings and equipment	9.3	1.4
Real estate owned	2.8	0.4
Miscellaneous assets	8.8	1.3
Total industry assets (uses of funds)	$663.8	100.0%

Note: Components may not add to column totals due to rounding error.
Sources: United States League of Savings Associations, *'82 Savings and Loan Sourcebook* (Chicago, 1982), table 67, p. 42.

Older associations frequently reported record losses, while new associations in many instances showed strong earnings.

[6]A recent study by Kawallen and Freund [10] suggests that the attachment of savings and loans to mortgage lending, encouraged by regulation, is indeed strong. These researchers' model of quarterly mortgage commitments by the industry suggests that S&Ls allocate incoming funds to mortgages "largely on the basis of convention and institutional reasons" ([10], p. 42). Moreover, in the past the industry appears to have allocated its assets without significant sensitivity to interest-rate changes. Rather, Kawallen and Freund conclude that changes in interest rates have affected savings and loan asset allocation decisions *indirectly* through interest-rate effects on deposit flows. Moreover, these researchers found little evidence that the mix of S&L deposits between high-rate and low-rate accounts affected the volume of funds flowing into mortgages. It will be interesting to see if industry asset allocation decisions become more sensitive to interest-rate movements with the advent of greater deregulation.

While conventional housing loans account for the bulk of S&L assets, other asset items have grown much faster of late. These rapidly growing asset items include mortgage participation certificates (known as PCs) and mortgage-backed securities authorized by government agencies. PCs are financial instruments representing an undivided interest in a relatively large and geographically diversified portfolio of high-quality mortgages. The most well-known issuer of PCs is the Federal Home Loan Mortgage Corporation (FHLMC, or "Freddie Mac"), established by the Federal Home Loan Bank Board in 1970.[7] First introduced in 1971, PCs are sold today in denominations of $100,000, $200,000, $500,000, and $1 million and are freely transferable. They are attractive to savings and loans because they are exempt from federal lending limitations and qualify as mortgages on real property for calculating the tax deductions granted to S&Ls. PCs also may be used as collateral when a member savings and loan wishes to borrow reserves from the Federal Home Loan Banks to shore up its liquidity position.

A related type of investment of growing importance to savings and loans and other thrift institutions consists of mortgage-backed securities. The most familiar type are supervised by the Government National Mortgage Association (GNMA, or "Ginnie Mae"), which guarantees these securities. GNMA was set up in 1968 to improve the secondary market for housing-related mortgages and to help stabilize the residential mortgage market.[8] Mortgage-backed securities are issued against a pool of mortgages held by federally approved lenders and are retired as repayments on

---

[7]The Federal Home Loan Mortgage Corporation was created as a result of Congressional passage of the Energy Home Finance Act of 1970. "Freddie Mac" was designed to increase the flow of funds into the residential mortgage market and to encourage the development of a viable secondary market for home mortgages. In addition to issuing PCs, FHLMC raises funds by borrowing from the Federal Home Loan Bank System and by selling bonds and certificates. It uses these funds to carry on an active program of purchasing both conventional and government-guaranteed (FHA-VA) mortgages and participations in conventional mortgages from thrift institutions and other lenders.

Under federal law, FHLMC may deal only with government-supervised lending institutions, which essentially means depository institutions. It is also authorized to do business with mortgage bankers who conform to the rules and regulations of the Federal Home Loan Bank Board (FHLBB). FHLMC purchases FHA-VA and conventional mortgage loans and loan participations from these institutions, both over-the-counter and on a forward commitment basis. In 1979, FHLMC added interests in secured home-improvement loans and pledged-amount mortgage packages to its purchase list. The majority of funds used by Freddie Mac to carry out its purchases comes from selling FHLMC-guaranteed participation certificates and mortgage certificates.

[8]GNMA is a corporate organization wholly owned by the U.S. government and supervised by the Department of Housing and Urban Development (HUD). The Secretary of HUD sets the policies followed by GNMA. See especially United States League of Savings Associations [19 and 20].

mortgages in the pool are made. The most common type of GNMA mortgage-backed security is the "pass-through" certificate, which pays interest and principal monthly to the holder. GNMA mortgage-backed securities have grown dramatically in response to heavy demands for mortgage credit in recent years.[9]

Savings and loans also provide credit for the purchase of mobile homes. Such loans were first authorized for federally chartered associations by the Housing and Urban Development Act in 1968. Mobile home loans totaled $4 billion at year-end 1981 but still represented less than 1 percent of industry assets.

Consumer Installment Loans

There is a definite trend toward more diversified lending by S&Ls where state and federal regulations allow. Some states permit associations to make consumer installment loans for the purchase of automobiles, home appliances, and other durable goods. In recent years, however, it has been the federal government which has most dramatically broadened the lending and investing policies of federally supervised savings and loans. Major steps were taken toward loosening the restraints on asset diversification by S&Ls with passage of the Depository Institutions Deregulation and Monetary Control Act of 1980 and the Garn–St Germain Depository Institutions Act of 1982.

Under the terms of the 1980 Deregulation and Monetary Control Act, savings and loans with federal charters could offer trust services, issue credit cards, and acquire corporate bonds, commercial paper, and consumer loans. However, the 1980 law limited such loans and investments to just 20 percent of S&L assets. The Depository Institutions Act of 1982 greatly expanded this percentage-of-assets limitation. Federal S&Ls were granted permission to accept secured or unsecured commercial loans up to 5 percent of their assets and leases up to 10 percent of their assets (after 1983), consumer loans up to 30 percent of total assets (including loans to

---

[9]GNMA has been cooperating in recent years with another federal agency, the Federal National Mortgage Association (FNMA, or "Fannie Mae"), to help reduce the risks of lending through mortgages. The two agencies have pursued so-called tandem programs. With this approach GNMA may issue a commitment to a mortgage-lending institution, such as a savings and loan, to purchase a mortgage at a set price. GNMA then sells the mortgage to FNMA at its current market price. With fixed-rate mortgages in a period of rising interest rates, GNMA probably will have to sell the mortgage at a discount from its face value. This discount will be absorbed by GNMA as part of its so-called special assistance function. Since 1974, GNMA has also issued commitments to private lenders, such as S&Ls, to purchase conventional low interest-rate mortgages. In this instance, the actual purchase is made by FNMA or FHLMC, with GNMA absorbing any discount. The low rates on such conventional mortgage loans must be passed along to private borrowers.

businesses to acquire inventories of consumer goods), and commercial real estate loans up to 40 percent of assets. Federal associations may also purchase municipal revenue bonds as well as general obligation municipal securities and make overdraft loans. Those savings associations taking advantage of these liberalized loan and investment rules would obviously begin to look more and more like commercial banks.

Holdings of Liquid Assets

Due to the ever-present possibility of large deposit withdrawals and other immediate demands for cash, savings and loan associations must hold substantial liquidity reserves in the form of readily marketable assets or in the form of lines of credit with private lenders (especially commercial banks) or government agencies. Indeed, this need for liquidity has grown in recent years due to increasing competition from money market funds, commercial banks, and other intermediaries, the danger of runs on savings and loans which appear to be in deep financial trouble, and increasing deposit volatility of S&Ls. Historically, savings associations have held most of their liquidity reserve in the form of cash and readily marketable securities (such as Treasury bills and notes, federal agency obligations, bankers' acceptances, short-term municipal securities, and bank deposits). The amount of liquid assets held by savings and loans is closely monitored by the Federal Home Loan Bank System.

Sources of Funds: Savings Accounts

Savings and loans are thrift institutions and, therefore, their principal funds source is savings accounts. These accounts include both low-rate passbook accounts and higher-rate certificates of deposit. At year-end 1981, savings associations held a total of nearly $525 billion in savings deposits, representing about 80 percent of all funds raised by the industry (see Table 13-4).

The proportion of total S&L funds represented by savings deposits, while dominant in size, has by no means been stable. Fluctuations in interest rates, changes in economic activity, and changes in government credit policies have produced significant changes in the ability of savings and loans to attract deposits and to retain the deposits they already hold. During 1966-67, 1969-70, and 1978-81, for example, there were large federal budget deficits, rapid inflation, and restrictive money and credit policies which pushed interest rates in the money and capital markets to record levels. Savers reacted to this unsettling environment by transferring funds out of their savings accounts into other investments (including marketable securities and money market funds). During 1972 and 1976-77, in contrast, there were unprecedented increases in savings funds, particularly in the larger certificate type, interest-sensitive deposits, as the economy

Table 13–4   Liabilities and Equity (sources of funds) for U.S. Savings and Loan Associations (figures as of year-end 1981)

Industry Sources of Funds	Amount ($ billions) 12/31/81	Percent of All Funds Sources
Savings accounts:		
Earning regular rate or below	$101.8	15.3%
Earning in excess of regular rate	422.6	63.7
Advances from the Federal Home Loan Banks	62.8	9.5
Other sources of borrowed funds	26.3	4.0
Loans in process	6.4	1.0
All other liabilities	15.6	2.4
Total industry liabilities	$635.5	95.9%
Equity (net worth) of savings associations	28.4	4.3
Total industry sources of funds (liabilities and net worth)	$663.8	100.0%

Note: Components may not add to column totals due to rounding error.
Source: United States League of Savings Associations, *'82 Savings and Loan Sourcebook* (Chicago, 1982), table 67, p. 42.

slowly recovered from a recession and interest-rate increases remained relatively moderate.

In response to competitive pressures, regulatory actions, and market conditions, savings and loans frequently have changed the mix of savings plans offered the public, especially during the past decade. For most of the postwar period, passbook savings accounts, which generally permit the saver to withdraw funds at will, were the dominant type of S&L deposit. These accounts carried a maximum interest rate of 5.50 percent in 1982. Within the past few years, however, new regulations have permitted S&Ls to offer a much broader array of savings instruments, varying in the rates of interest paid, maturity, and minimum amounts. The most important is the certificate of deposit (CD), issued in fixed amounts with a set maturity not to exceed 10 years. While there are many different types of CDs, one of the most popular in recent years has been the money market CD (MMC), whose interest rate attached to *new* certificates fluctuates with the discount rate on six-month U.S. Treasury bills. MMCs proved to be an extremely popular savings instrument. They grew rapidly following their authorization by the Federal Home Loan Bank Board (FHLBB) in June 1978. By the end of 1981, about one third of S&L deposits were in MMCs. Also authorized by the FHLBB in 1978 were $100,000-plus ("jumbo") CDs. These large time deposits carry no legal interest-rate ceilings and in most cases carry a maturity of one to three months. In 1979 the FHLBB authorized the offering of small-saver certificates (SSCs) with 30-month maturities, carrrying a maximum rate tied to the average yield on 2

½-year U.S. Treasury notes at time of issue. An advantage of the SSCs is their small denomination. Commercial banks and savings and loans usually offer SSCs for an initial deposit as low as $100.

While these various forms of savings accounts have aided S&Ls in retaining deposits when interest rates rise, they do not fully protect the industry from the ravages of competition with money market mutual funds, which got their start during the mid-1970s.[10] Featuring high-rate, liquid share accounts which could be drafted by telephone, wire, or by check, the money funds grew into a $200-billion industry in the early 1980s. A substantial portion of the funds attracted by money market funds came from deposits in savings and loans. Larger savings associations and banks lobbied heavily in Congress for a new type of account combining the features of a savings and a checking account which would compete effectively with money market fund shares. These lobbying efforts finally paid off when Congress passed the Garn–St Germain Depository Institutions Act in October 1982. This new law authorized the Depository Institutions Deregulation Committee (DIDC) to develop and permit federally regulated depository institutions to offer a money market deposit account "directly equivalent to and competitive with" share accounts offered by money market mutual funds. The new money market deposit account (MMDA), which first appeared in December 1982, carries no minimum maturity. It may be drafted by check or by preauthorized automatic transfer. Each MMDA must be opened for at least $2,500, and its yield floats with prevailing money market yields.

Many savings and loans as well as commercial banks quickly moved to offer the new account. And it has been of benefit to S&Ls in retaining old deposits and in attracting new ones. However, a substantial amount of funds housed in the old, lower-yielding thrift accounts have merely been shifted by customers to the new, more costly accounts. These deposit transfers constitute a simple cost increase for S&Ls which has not been fully offset by a concomitant increase in returns on loans and investments. As a result, S&L earnings have been severely squeezed in many cases, preventing adequate growth of equity capital (net worth) which protects depositors. Yet, if the new deposit accounts had not been authorized by the regulatory authorities, it seems clear that the industry would have suffered even greater loss of deposits (disintermediation), reducing its efficiency and perhaps creating even more damaging earnings, liquidity, and solvency problems.

Net Worth or Equity Capital

The second largest source of funds for savings and loans is net worth, representing about 4 percent of all funds raised. Net worth includes re-

---

[10]See Chapter 16 for a discussion of money market funds.

tained earnings (i.e., undivided profits), paid-in surplus, and reserves. The net worth account is designed to protect depositor funds, since it absorbs any operating losses. Net worth has declined relative to borrowings and deposits as a source of industry funds in recent years. The huge operating losses recorded by many S&Ls as the 1970s ended and the 1980s began seriously eroded their net worth positions. Each month that interest costs on borrowed funds exceeded the yields on mortgages and other earning assets, the industry's equity (net worth) account was further reduced. After months of financial squeeze, many S&Ls were simply forced into bankruptcy or merger. As we noted earlier, the industry's insurance agency, the FSLIC, was forced to arrange a large number of mergers between failing S&Ls and solvent ones.

In 1982, Congress finally acted to aid S&Ls whose net worth was precariously low. Under provisions of the Depository Institutions Act of 1982, associations in trouble could issue net worth certificates with FSLIC backing to bolster their equity capital, provided the net worth of the issuing association had declined to 3 percent or less of total assets and it had a record of continuing losses. At the same time, the new law nullified state laws which limited S&L enforcement of due-on-sale clauses present in many home mortgages. These old state laws allowed many home buyers to simply assume older, low-rate mortgages and prevented S&Ls from rolling over their low-rate home loans into new higher-rate loans. The states were given three years from the law's passage to decide how to deal with old mortgage loans on existing homes.

Federal Home Loan Bank and Federal Reserve Borrowings

For many years, savings and loans faced with severe liquidity pressures have borrowed from the Federal Home Loan Bank headquartered in their district. These advances from the industry's chief supervisory agency represented almost 10 percent of total S&L funds in 1981. Savings and loans use FHLB advances as a *residual* source of funds, borrowing more heavily in periods when deposit growth slackens and repaying their borrowings when deposit growth accelerates.[11]

With passage of the Depository Institutions Deregulation and Monetary Control Act of 1980, federally supervised S&Ls gained still another

---

[11]Savings and loans also use the mortgage-backed bonds discussed earlier as a source of funds, issuing these securities against pools of previously acquired mortgages. Regulations limit the use of this source of funds to a maximum of 5 percent of an S&L's savings deposits. Mortgage-backed bonds are sold in the open market by larger S&Ls, while smaller associations tend to use private placements. Both government-guaranteed and conventional mortgages serve as collateral for these bonds.

borrowing source—the discount windows of the Federal Reserve banks.[12] While most loans from the Fed's discount window cover only a few days, the Federal Reserve banks also operate an Extended Credit Facility (ECF) which permits solvent depository institutions experiencing liquidity problems to borrow for periods as long as 12 months. A borrowing institution must demonstrate, however, that it is under sustained liquidity pressure, even after making all reasonable efforts to secure funds from other, traditional sources.

Trends in Sources and Uses of Funds

Data from the Federal Reserve's Flow of Funds Accounts highlight a number of important trends in S&L sources and uses of funds in recent years (see Table 13–5). Savings inflows have become much more volatile in response to fluctuations in interest rates and economic conditions. For a period stretching from the end of World War II through 1965, the industry grew rapidly, but the rate of deposit growth was relatively stable. Beginning, however, in the late 1960s and continuing to the present day, marked fluctuations in interest rates, government credit policy, and economic conditions frequently have led to abrupt changes in the inflow or outflow of savings deposits. In years of high and rising interest rates, savings deposits at S&Ls have become less attractive compared to other market investments, forcing a sharp cutback in mortgage lending and industry growth. In contrast, during periods of lower rates and stimulative monetary policy, rates offered on S&L deposits look more attractive, and frequently funds flow in large volume into associations' savings deposits. These marked fluctuations in savings deposits have forced savings and loans to draw more heavily upon nondeposit sources of funds, particularly borrowings from the Federal Home Loan Banks. This phenomenon of shifting fund sources between savings deposits and borrowings suggests the importance today for S&L financial managers of forecasting interest rates, especially short-term rates associated with deposit flows. Indeed, the need for better forecasting procedures at S&Ls should increase when federal deposit interest-rate ceilings are finally phased out completely and all savings deposit rates are determined by competition and market conditions rather than by regulation.[13]

---

[12]After 1980, all depository institutions offering nonpersonal time deposits or reservable transactions accounts (i.e., demand deposits, NOW accounts, or automatic funds transfer services (ATS)) are permitted to request loans of reserves from the Federal Reserve banks.

[13]As noted earlier in this book, the Depository Institutions Deregulation and Monetary Control Act of 1980 set up a new regulatory body, the Depository Institutions Deregulation Committee, composed of the heads of the federal banking agencies and the Secretary of the Treasury. This committee is charged with the responsibility of gradually phasing out Regulation Q deposit-rate ceilings by 1986.

**Table 13–5   Fluctuations in Deposit Flows and Mortgage Loans
at Savings and Loan Associations: 1971–1980
($ billions seasonally adjusted annual rates)**

	Funds Received or Loaned Out during:									
Item	*1971*	*1972*	*1973*	*1974*	*1975*	*1976*	*1977*	*1978*	*1979*	*1980*
Deposits	$27.8	$32.6	$20.2	$16.0	$42.8	$50.2	$50.9	$44.2	$39.1	$41.0
Mortgage loans	23.6	31.8	26.5	17.6	29.5	44.4	58.2	51.6	43.1	27.7

Source: Board of Governors of the Federal Reserve System, *Flow of Funds Accounts, Third Quarter 1981*, pp. 22–23.

A glance at the sources of income for savings and loan associations shows clearly the key historical role of this institution as a mortgage lender and thrift deposit institution. Income from mortgages represented about three quarters of S&L revenues in 1980. This percentage has declined in recent years due to the increasing importance of nonmortgage loans (especially consumer installment loans) and other interest-bearing assets. Other major revenue sources for the industry include income from service corporations and interest earned on security investments (see Table 13–6.)

Just as interest income from mortgage loans is the leading revenue item for savings and loan associations, interest paid on time and savings deposits is their principal expense. And, as Table 13–7 suggests, the interest cost on deposits has spiraled upward, particularly after the introduction of

EARNINGS, DIVIDENDS, AND EXPENSES OF SAVINGS AND LOANS

**Table 13–6   Total Operating Income of Savings and Loan Associations
(percentage distribution)**

	Interest on:		*Loan Fees and Discounts*	*All Other Operating Income*
Year	*Mortgage Loans*	*Investments*		
1960	83.3%	5.1%	– – – – – 11.6% – – – – –	
1965	86.8	5.4	3.5%	4.3%
1970	84.3	7.7	3.7	4.3
1975	81.6	8.6	4.1	5.7
1976	80.5	7.6	4.7	7.2
1977	80.8	6.8	5.0	7.4
1978	80.5	7.5	4.4	7.6
1979	78.8	9.1	3.7	8.4
1980	77.1	10.0	3.2	9.6
1981	75.5	12.0	2.4	10.1

Note: Figures for 1981 are preliminary.
Sources: United States League of Savings Associations, *'82 Savings and Loan Sourcebook* (Chicago, 1982), table 62, p. 40.

Table 13–7   Statement of Operations for All U.S. Savings and Loan Associations (figures in $ millions)

Year	Operating Income	Operating Expense	Net Operating Income	Interest on Savings Deposits	Interest on Borrowed Money	Net Income before Taxes	Taxes	Net Income after Taxes
1960	$ 3,711	$ 811	$ 2,900	$ 2,250	$ 81	$ 581	$ 4	$ 577
1965	7,081	1,366	5,715	4,486	237	978	157	821
1970	11,039	1,967	9,072	7,187	785	1,152	248	904
1975	24,193	3,979	20,214	16,420	1,640	2,135	650	1,485
1976	28,878	4,689	24,189	19,537	1,425	3,294	992	2,302
1977	34,623	5,443	29,180	23,034	1,539	4,710	1,442	3,268
1978	41,409	6,302	35,107	26,550	2,720	5,832	1,835	3,997
1979	49,554	7,227	42,327	32,778	4,383	5,299	1,608	3,691
1980	57,188	8,068	49,120	42,404	5,909	1,215	417	798
1981	65,618	9,036	56,582	55,415	8,191	− 6,197	− 1,564	− 4,633

Note: Figures for 1981 are preliminary.
Source: United States League of Savings Associations, *'82 Savings and Loan Sourcebook* (Chicago, 1982), table 61, p. 40.

higher-yielding CDs, such as money market CDs and small-saver certificates. The result has been a dramatic squeeze on the industry's net income before and after taxes, as reflected in Tables 13–7 and 13–8. By 1981, net income for the industry as a whole was negative. As shown in Table 13–9, profit margins, return on equity, and return on average assets all began a sharp decline in 1979 and turned negative as the 1980s began.

As Vrabac [23] observed in his recent study of S&L earnings problems, the principal reasons for the decline in industry profitability are "the inability of savings and loan associations to earn market rates of return on new mortgages, the slow turnover of older, lower yielding mortgages, and the rapid escalation in the cost of deposits due to a greater responsiveness to increases in short-term interest rates."[14] An additional depressing factor has been the secular rise in the industry's tax burden—a trend common to most depository financial institutions in recent years. Beginning in 1951, savings associations were brought under the same federal tax rules as commercial banks and other business corporations. However, the industry was granted an exemption in the form of tax-free additions to reserves for losses on assets. As a result of this privilege, few associations paid any taxes until the early 1960s, when permissible additions to reserves were significantly reduced. The Tax Reform Act of 1969 further restricted tax-

---

[14]See D. J. Vrabac [23], p. 18. An additional depressant on S&L earnings, as pointed out in a recent study by Verbrugge, Shick, and Thygerson [21], is state usury laws limiting rates and fees on loans. Verbrugge et. al. find that S&L profit performance is significantly shaped by cost-control procedures, control over the composition of the loan portfolio, and use of the secondary market to trade existing mortgages. Thus well-trained, highly motivated management still appears to be a key factor in determining the performance level of S&Ls even in the face of powerful market and regulatory factors.

Table 13–8   Income and Expense Ratios for All U.S. Savings and Loan Associations

Item	1978	1979	1980	1981	Annual Changes 1979	1980	1981
Operating income	8.60%	9.20%	9.65%	10.21%	0.55%	0.45%	0.56%
Operating expenses	1.32	1.34	1.36	1.41	0.02	0.02	0.05
Net operating income	7.33	7.86	8.29	8.80	0.53	0.43	0.51
Interest on savings deposits	5.55	6.08	7.15	8.68	0.53	1.07	1.53
Interest on borrowed money	0.57	0.81	1.00	1.22	0.24	0.19	0.22
Nonoperating income and expense (net)	0.00	0.02	0.07	0.11	0.02	0.05	0.04
Net income before taxes	1.22	0.98	0.21	−0.99	−0.24	−0.77	−1.20
Taxes	0.38	0.30	0.07	−0.24	0.08	−0.23	−0.31
Net income after taxes (return on assets)	0.84%	0.68%	0.13%	−0.75%	−0.16%	−0.55%	−0.88%

Note: Components may not add to column totals due to rounding error. Figures for 1981 are preliminary.
Sources: United States League of Savings Associations, *'82 Savings and Loan Sourcebook* (Chicago, 1982), table 65, p. 41; and *'81 Savings and Loan Sourcebook* (Chicago, 1982), table 66, p. 41.

deductible additions to reserves, gradually lowering the allowable percentage of net income transferable to loss reserves in order to more closely approximate actual loss experience. In addition, taxes were imposed upon so-called preference items, such as accelerated depreciation on real property and capital gains on assets. As Table 13–7 shows, the industry's tax burden has risen dramatically in recent years, and its *effective* tax rate is on a par with —or, in certain years, even greater than—that faced by commercial banks and many nonfinancial corporations.[15]

Table 13–9   Earnings Ratios for U.S. Savings Associations

Year	Profit Margin	Return on Equity	Return on Average Assets
1960	15.44%	12.26%	0.87%
1965	11.57	9.76	0.67
1970	8.56	8.01	0.57
1975	6.06	7.85	0.48
1976	7.87	11.14	0.64
1977	9.32	13.99	0.79
1978	9.57	14.91	0.84
1979	7.37	12.11	0.68
1980	1.38	2.45	0.13
1981	−7.22	−15.03	−0.75

Note: The industry's profit margin is defined as net after-tax income divided by total income. Return on equity equals net after-tax income divided by average net worth, while the return on average assets is net after-tax income divided by average assets (net of loans in process). Figures for 1981 are preliminary.
Source: United States League of Savings Associations, *'82 Savings and Loan Sourcebook* (Chicago, 1982), table 64, p. 41.

[15]As indicated in Table 13–7, actual taxes paid by all S&Ls began to fall in 1979 due to the sharp decline in the industry's net taxable income.

REGULATION OF SAVINGS AND LOANS

Reserve Requirements

Savings and loans are subject to reserve requirements on their deposits and minimum capital (net worth) requirements just like commercial banks. With passage of the Depository Institutions Deregulation and Monetary Control Act of 1980, common reserve requirements were imposed on transactions deposits and nonpersonal time deposits offered by savings and loan associations, commercial banks, and other depository institutions. These reserve requirements have been set by the Federal Reserve Board at 12 percent of all transactions deposits over $28.9 million, and 3 percent of nonpersonal time deposits not exceeding 1½ years to maturity. While these reserve percentages became effective in the 1980s, only a few nonbank institutions were subject to them initially. Instead, a long-term phase-in of the new reserve requirements is planned because these requirements are generally much higher than previously experienced by S&Ls and other nonbank thrifts. When fully effective for all institutions, however, the new set of requirements will place all depository institutions on an equal footing. They also will have the effect of giving the Federal Reserve System greater control over credit creation by savings and loan associations and other nonbank thrifts.

Net-Worth Requirements

S&Ls must also hold minimum levels of net worth (i.e., equity capital), designed primarily as a cushion to protect depositors. Savings and loans choosing to hold more risky loans must also hold greater levels of net worth for the protection of their depositors and other creditors. In general, associations supervised by the Federal Home Loan Bank Board must maintain a level of net worth equal to 4 percent of all other liabilities except net worth. The FHLBB can vary member associations' net-worth requirement between 3 and 6 percent.

Regulations Governing Deposit Interest Rates

Interest paid on deposits by savings and loans was brought under federal regulation with passage of the Interest Rate Adjustment Act of 1966. Under this law, the FHLBB had the responsibility to set maximum rates that could be offered on time and savings accounts. These rate ceilings were modified a number of times to preserve competitive equality with rates offered by commercial banks and other depository institutions and to keep abreast of open-market interest rates. Then, with passage of the Depository Institutions Deregulation Act in 1980, the responsibility for setting maximum legal rates on consumer type savings accounts and certificates of deposit was turned over to the Depository Institutions Deregulation Committee, which includes the chief administrators of all federal bank regulatory agencies; the Secretary of the Treasury; and the chairperson of the FHLBB, representing the savings and loan industry. The DIDC, under Congressional mandate, must phase out federal deposit-rate ceilings by early 1986. The committee proceeded cautiously at first, gradually liberalizing or eliminating the rate ceilings due to the financial problems of savings and loans. Later, in 1983, as S&L gained firmer ground the DIDC moved more aggressively to phase out the remaining federal deposit-rate ceilings.

For many time and savings deposit plans, savings and loans were authorized to pay an interest rate one-quarter percentage point higher than commercial banks could pay on deposits of comparable maturity. This deposit-rate advantage of savings banks over commercial banks was created by passage of amendments to the Interest Rate Adjustment Act in 1969. The purpose of this rate differential was to increase the flow of loanable funds through S&Ls and other savings banks in order to provide more funds for home mortgage loans. However, the Garn–St Germain Depository Institutions Act mandated the elimination of these rate differentials between banks and savings and loans as of January 1, 1984.[16]

SUMMARY

As this book was going to press, the future of the saving and loan industry was clouded by numerous cross currents. High interest rates on deposits, coupled with an industry portfolio crammed with low-interest, fixed-rate mortgages, threatened a continuing squeeze on net earnings and, in many cases, long-term operating losses. Numerous S&Ls across the nation were forced into interstate mergers and others into outright bankruptcy. While several different solutions have been proposed to deal with the industry's problems, it is not clear at this point which solutions are both feasible and in the public interest.

Many observers see the root cause of the industry's problems in restric-

---

[16]It is interesting to speculate as to the possible effects of removal of the legal interest-rate differentials between commercial bank and S&L deposits and, ultimately, the elimination of all federal deposit-rate ceilings. Most authorities have concluded that the impact of deposit-rate deregulation on S&L earnings and common-stock values will be negative, at least in the short run. For example, a recent study by Dann and James [7] finds that stockholder-owned savings and loans generally experienced declining equity market values when federal authorities announced the removal of rate ceilings on small-saver accounts and when money market CDs were introduced. These authors contend that S&Ls "have earned economic rents from the restrictions on interest rates paid to smaller saver accounts, and that relaxation of interest-rate ceilings has reduced these rents." ([7], p. 1,274.) Still, it is not clear that the long-run impact of deposit-rate deregulation on industry earnings or equity values will be negative. If savings and loans can pass on any added costs to their customers, increase the volume of their business by offering more highly competitive deposit accounts, and increase their efficiency in a deregulated environment, their earnings and market values may be preserved and even improved.

tive government regulations. S&Ls emerged from the economic debacle of the 1930s a tightly regulated industry, insulated from most competitive pressures by restrictive federal and state chartering policies which severely limited outside entry into the savings and loan business. Moreover, federally imposed deposit interest-rate ceilings limited the ability of commercial banks to bid savings deposits away from S&Ls. At the same time, the industry was handed significant tax advantages provided it would devote the majority of its assets to home mortgages. Thus savings and loans were specifically encouraged to borrow short-term savings deposits and make long-term mortgage loans with the assurance of government favor and protection.

The protective government umbrella developed severe leaks in the 1960s and 1970s due, in large measure, to changes in the financial marketplace. Inflation and large federal government deficits drove interest rates to record levels and often led to an inverted yield curve, where short-term deposits cost more than the yield on long-term mortgages. The high interest rates also dampened the public's demand for home ownership and thus reduced the growth of mortgage loans—the industry's chief source of revenue. Another consequence of high interest rates was to encourage strong competition for the industry's principal source of funds—consumer savings accounts. Particularly damaging was the appearance of money market mutual funds in the mid-1970s which attracted away billion of dollars in short-term, liquid deposits. At the same time, the federal government and the states began loosening the bonds of regulation to allow new and more costly savings instruments. This trend toward deregulation culminated, as we have seen, with passage of the Depository Institutions Deregulation and Monetary Control Act of 1980 and the Garn–St Germain Depository Institutions Act of 1982.

The long history of government support and involvement in the savings and loan business suggests to many that the government should bail out troubled associations. And, indeed, with passage of the 1980 and 1982 Depository Institutions laws, several major steps were taken to support troubled savings and loans. As we recall, the Depository Institutions Deregulation and Monetary Control Act of 1980 authorized S&Ls to borrow from the Federal Reserve banks when in need of reserves. The Garn–St Germain Act authorized S&Ls to issue net worth certificates backed by the FSLIC when their net worth dropped to 3 percent or less of total assets.[17] And, as we noted earlier in this chapter, in certain cases federal reg-

---

[17]To be eligible to issue the net-worth certificates, a savings and loan must put at least 20 percent of its loan portfolio in residential mortgages and display a track record of earnings losses. When an S&L issues net-worth certificates to the FSLIC, that agency will issue promissory notes to the S&L, which holds the notes as assets.

ulators have permitted interstate mergers between troubled and profitable S&Ls or allowed bank holding companies to acquire a few savings associations.

On a longer-term basis, broader loan and investment powers for S&Ls are likely to be a more effective solution for many of the industry's problems. Most savings and loans are likely to become more like commercial banks, offering transactions deposits and making a wide array of consumer and commercial loans.[18] Since most of these loans carry much shorter maturities than conventional home mortgage loans, the move toward nonresidential loans will increase the flexibility of S&L portfolios and revenue flows, enhancing the industry's ability to cope with changing interest rates and customer credit needs.[19] There is some concern by policymakers, however, that as a result of these changes the supply of credit to the critical home mortgage market will be reduced. This might well increase the cost of housing to millions of families, particularly those seeking single-family homes. However, the rapid growth of multifamily housing (apartments, condominiums, and so forth) in recent years allows for an expanded supply of dwelling units at a lower cost per unit and lower credit demand per unit than is true of the traditional single-family home. Moreover, for those S&Ls that continue to place heavy emphasis on mortgage lending, state and federal authorities permit greater use of adjust-

---

[18]While it appears likely that many, if not most, savings and loans have elected to become more like commercial banks, a variety of other institutional transformations are also underway. Some S&Ls have opted to become more like mortgage banks, actively trading mortgages in the secondary market and quickly selling any mortgage loans they make to other lenders. Often, on a mortgage that it sells, the S&L will retain the servicing contract, under which it will represent the new mortgage holder in collecting any loan payments due, inspecting the mortgaged property to see that it is being properly maintained, and providing other services as required under the mortgage loan agreement. Other S&Ls have organized highly diversified holding companies with interests in real estate development, leasing of commercial and personal property, and numerous other business activities. Still other associations are well along in the process of becoming family financial centers with extensive consumer loan portfolios and substantial resources devoted to individual checking or NOW account services, tax counseling, life insurance sales, household savings and retirement plans, and even travel planning. Whatever the option selected by individual associations, it seems clear that the "typical" savings and loan of the future will be very different from the traditional S&L which began more than a century ago.

[19]In effect, these new loans allow S&Ls to more effectively use interest-sensitivity analysis (ISA). As we noted in Chapter 7, ISA involves seeking a rough balance between interest-sensitive sources of funds (mainly deposits) and interest-sensitive uses of funds (mainly loans). One way to bring about such a balance is to match maturities of assets and liabilities. However, the financial futures market also offers a potentially important way of hedging against interest-rate fluctuations. Accordingly, in July 1981 the FSLIC authorized insured S&Ls to deal in a broad range of financial futures contracts. See Chapter 4 for a discussion of the uses of financial futures contracts by financial intermediaries.

able-rate and adjustable-term mortgage loans.[20] The result is a home-financing instrument that brings added flexibility to the revenue flows of savings and loan associations.

Questions

13–1. How may a savings and loan association be chartered? What is the difference between a mutual and a permanent stock association?

13–2. What is the most important regulatory agency in the savings and loan industry? What are its principal powers?

13–3. What are the major assets and liabilities of savings and loan associations? Can you explain why savings and loans invest in each of the major kinds of assets they hold?

13–4. What is a variable-rate mortgage? What potential advantages could it offer the management of savings associations?

13–5. Why do you think savings and loans are interested in becoming more active participants in the payments mechanism along with commercial banks? What benefits and costs do you think this move entails?

13–6. The number of savings and loan associations has been declining in recent years. Explain why this is happening. Do you think this trend will continue?

13–7. The growth of savings and loans has become much more volatile in recent years, leading to greater uncertainty in the financial management of these institutions. List the principal factors which have led to more volatile changes in the assets and deposits of these institutions. In what ways can management deal with this problem effectively?

13–8. What impact did passage of the Depository Institutions Deregulation and Monetary Control Act of 1980 and the Garn–St Germain Depository Institutions Act of 1982 have upon savings and loans? What new powers did the industry acquire? Can you foresee problems as well as benefits from these new powers? Explain your reasoning.

References

1. Benston, George J. "Savings Banks and the Public Interest." *Journal of Money, Credit, and Banking*, February 1972, pt. II, pp. 133–225.

[20]In April 1981, federally chartered savings and loans were authorized to grant adjustable mortgage loans to their customers. These so-called AMLs carry fluctuating interest rates that can change as often as monthly depending on the behavior of open-market rates. Such rate changes may be reflected in the home buyer's monthly mortgage payment, principal amount owed, mortgage loan maturity, or some combination of the three. However, the borrowing customer must be given 30 days' notice of any changes affecting his or her adjustable mortgage loan. Further liberalization of federal S&L mortgage lending powers occurred in the fall of 1981, when balloon-payment (i.e., nonamortized or partially amortized mortgages) were authorized. Many states have moved to allow similar powers for state-chartered associations.

2. Biederman, Kenneth R., and John A. Tuccillo. *Taxation and Regulation of the Savings and Loan Industry*. Lexington, Mass.: D.C. Heath, 1976.

3. Board of Governors of the Federal Reserve System, *Flow of Funds Accounts*, various quarterly and annual releases.

4. Bronwyn, Brock. "Mortgages with Adjustable Interest Rates Improve Viability of the Thrift Industry." *Voice*, Federal Reserve Bank of Dallas, February 1981.

5. Carlson, John B., and K. J. Kowalewski. "Thrifts, Extended Credit, and Monetary Policy." *Economic Commentary*, Federal Reserve Bank of Cleveland, September 7, 1981.

6. Daly, George G. "Financial Intermediation and the Theory of the Firm: An Analysis of Savings and Loan Association Behavior." *Southern Economic Journal*, January 1971, pp. 283–94.

7. Dann, Larry Y., and Christopher M. James, "An Analysis of the Impact of Deposit Rate Ceilings on the Market Values of Thrift Institutions." *Journal of Finance*, no. 5 (December 1982), pp. 1259–75.

8. Friend, Irwin. *Study of the Savings and Loan Industry* 1–4. Washington, D.C.: Federal Home Loan Bank Board, 1969–70.

9. Harless, Doris E. *Nonbank Financial Institutions*. Richmond: Federal Reserve Bank of Richmond, October 1975.

10. Kawallen, Ira, and James Freund. "Mortgage Lending at Savings and Loan Associations: A Further Inquiry." *Business Economics*, January 1981, pp. 39–49.

11. Lapp, John S. "Market Structure and Advertising in the Savings and Loan Industry." *Review of Economics and Statistics*, no. 2 (May 1976), pp. 202–8.

12. Loeys, Jan G. "Deregulation: A New Future for Thrifts." *Business Review*, Federal Reserve Bank of Philadelphia, January/February 1983, pp. 15–26.

13. Moran, Michael J. "Thrift Institutions in Recent Years." *Federal Reserve Bulletin*, December 1982, pp. 725–38.

14. Morrissey, Thomas F. "An Analysis of Quarterly Mortgage Loan Repayments in the Savings and Loan Industry." *Journal of Business of Seton Hall University*, no. 2 (May 1974), pp. 25–32.

15. Nichols, Alfred. "Stock versus Mutual Savings and Loan Associations: Some Evidence of Differences in Behavior." *American Economic Review*, May 1967, pp. 341–45.

16. Pratt, Richard T. "The Savings and Loan Industry: Past, Present and Future." *Federal Home Loan Bank Board Journal*, no. 11 (November 1982), pp. 3–8.

17. Shows, E. Warren. "Conversions of Savings and Loans: Some Aspects of Equity in the Transition." *Atlanta Economic Review*, January/February 1974, pp. 31–34.

18. Stigum, Marcia. "Some Further Implications of Profit Maximization by a Savings and Loan Association." *Journal of Finance*, no. 5 (December 1976), pp. 1405–26.

19. United States League of Savings Associations. *'81 Savings and Loan Sourcebook*. Chicago, Ill.

20. _____. *'82 Savings and Loan Sourcebook*. Chicago, Ill.

21. Verbrugge, James A., Richard A. Shick, and Kenneth J. Thygerson. "An Analysis of Savings and Loan Profit Performance." *Journal of Finance*, no. 5 (December 1976), pp. 1427–42.

22. _____ and Steven J. Goldstein. "Risk, Return and Managerial Objectives: Some Evidence from the Savings and Loan Industry." *Journal of Financial Research*, no. 1 (Spring 1981), pp. 45–58.

23. Vrabac, Daniel J. "Savings and Loan Associations: An Analysis of the Recent Decline in Profitability." *Economic Review*, Federal Reserve Bank of Kansas City, July–August 1982, pp. 3–19.

24. Zumpano, Leonard V., and Patricia M. Rudolph. "Another Look at Residential Mortgage Lending by Savings and Loans." *Journal of Financial Research*, no. 1 (Spring 1981), pp. 59–67.

Problem for Discussion

AS WE HAVE SEEN IN THIS CHAPTER, savings and loan associations make thousands of residential real estate (mortgage) loans each year. This is one of the most complicated areas for the lending of funds because home mortgage loans typically carry 20- to 30-year maturities, and both the borrower and the lending institution face substantial risks over this long period. Property values may decline or borrowers may suffer financial reverses and be forced to give up their homes. The risks of home mortgage lending have led many financial institutions active in this field to prefer FHA- or VA-insured mortgages, though most home mortgage loans granted today are conventional, not government-guaranteed loans.

In this problem, suppose you are a loan officer employed by Hardy Building and Loan Association to interview prospective mortgage borrowers. You have recently interviewed Mr. and Mrs. Robert Warren concerning the application they submitted last week for a conventional residential mortgage loan on a newly constructed three-bedroom home. You must decide whether to recommend to the association's loan committee if a mortgage commitment should be made to the Warrens.

The construction company has priced the one-story, three-bedroom structure, which has 1,500 square feet, at $70,000. The Warrens have been residents of the local community for about three years, but have been renting a home during that period. Their monthly rental is $525, significantly less than what the monthly mortgage payments would be on their new home. In the market area served by Hardy Building and Loan Association, mortgage loan rates on 90 percent loans have ranged in recent weeks between 15½ and 16 percent. The monthly mortgage payments associated with these two loan rates and various loan maturities from 20 to 35 years are shown in Exhibits 13–1 and 13–2.

Mr. Warren works as a salesman for an auto insurance company. His salary is about $35,000 annually, grossing about $2,900 per month. He has held his present job—his first full-time job after college—for about three years. Sally Warren works part-time as a secretary, a position she has held for eight months, and grosses about $375 per month. The Warrens have two children attending public school.

An appraisal report on the property and a credit check also have been made. A member of Hardy's credit appraisal staff estimates that the new home has a current market value of about $71,000. Two weeks ago the Warrens applied for a conventional mortgage loan at the First National Bank but were told the bank could lend no more than 80 percent of the property's appraised value with a maximum maturity of 10 years. Because Mr. Warren graduated from college only three years ago and the family has had little opportunity to build its savings, they can come up with no more than a 10 percent down payment. A check of the Warren's financial statements shows little additional financial strength beyond the family's two monthly paychecks. Mr. Warren carries a $30,000 term insurance

---

Exhibit 13–1   Monthly Payments Necessary to Amortize a Mortgage Loan with a 15½ Percent Interest Rate

Amount of Loan	Maturity of Loan				
	20 Years	*25 Years*	*29 Years*	*30 Years*	*35 Years*
$50,000	$676.95	$659.88	$653.35	$652.26	$648.80
55,000	744.64	725.86	718.68	717.49	713.68
60,000	812.33	791.85	784.01	782.72	778.56
65,000	880.03	857.84	849.35	847.94	843.44
70,000	947.72	923.83	914.68	913.17	908.31

Exhibit 13–2 Monthly Payments Necessary to Amortize a Mortgage Loan
with a 16 Percent Interest Rate

	Maturity of Loan				
Amount of Loan	*20 Years*	*25 Years*	*29 Years*	*30 Years*	*35 Years*
$50,000	$695.63	$679.45	$673.38	$672.38	$669.24
55,000	765.20	747.39	740.71	739.62	736.16
60,000	834.76	815.34	808.05	806.86	803.09
65,000	904.32	883.28	875.39	874.10	870.01
70,000	973.88	951.23	942.73	941.33	936.93

policy and holds a few corporate and government bonds valued at $3,500. The family's two-year-old Chevrolet station wagon is valued at $3,300. Their passbook savings account, held at First National Bank, has a balance of $1,200. The family is covered by a health insurance group plan through Mr. Warren's employer, but Mr. Warren has no disability insurance.

Hardy Building and Loan Association normally would prefer to make a conventional mortgage loan in this instance because of its greater flexibility. Currently, government-guaranteed Federal Housing Administration (FHA) loans carry a ceiling rate of 15½ percent. In contrast, there is no legal interest-rate ceiling applying specifically to conventional mortgages. For the 90 percent conventional loan sought by the Warrens, the Mortgage Guaranty Insurance Corporation (MGIC), which will insure acceptable conventional mortgage loans against default, levies an initial fee of 1 percent of the amount of the loan plus an annual renewal fee of one fourth of 1 percent of the amount of the unpaid balance for the first 10 years. MGIC thus provides private mortgage insurance for conventional mortgages, while the FHA and the Veterans Administration (VA) provide a government guarantee behind the borrower's obligation. FHA insures 97 percent of the first $25,000 of appraised value, then 95 percent of the remaining balance.

There are a number of additional costs (usually referred to as closing costs) associated with the making of residential real estate loans. Hardy charges a loan commitment fee of four points. Mortgage title insurance will cost an additional $520. In addition, a reserve of $850 must be set aside in escrow for property taxes and insurance. The lender must be presented at the time of closing with a mortgagee's home insurance policy whose principal value is at least equal to the amount of the mortgage loan. If the Warrens seek FHA insurance, there is an FHA appraisal charge of $90 and a mortgage discount fee of 10 points. If a 90 percent conventional loan is made, Hardy Building and Loan Association will automatically seek insurance coverage from MGIC.

If the Warrens are able to put 10 percent down, they will need to borrow $63,000 in order to purchase their new home. There are, however, some risks which need to be carefully assessed by the loan officer. First, there is some feeling among business people in the area that the local economy is due for a major downturn. To be sure, the city and surrounding county are currently in the midst of a population boom, due to the rapid influx of new residents seeking a milder climate and better job opportunities. But there are rumors of a drastic slowdown or even cutback in government employment in the near future. Indeed, the local community's unemployment rate is slightly higher today than a year ago. If the situation worsens, conditions in the local real estate market will quickly turn sour, with adverse effects on property values. Adding to the problem, a boom in apartment construction is well underway—a delayed response to the earlier growth of government jobs.

The Warren's personal financial situation raises some questions. Mr. Warren, the family's principal breadwinner, works on commission in a highly volatile industry. If the local economy turns down, auto insurance sales are likely to do the same. Moreover, his employer, the Gilbert Insurance Agency, has the reputation of frequently transferring its salespeople to new locations. Sales personnel who do not produce an adequate volume of new premiums and policy renewals are eased out; those who do perform well usually are transferred to more challenging jobs in four to five years. Mr. Warren is probably approaching a critical period in his present job, having been with the company nearly three full years. However, the Gilbert Insurance Agency indicated on the verification-of-employment form sent to it by Hardy that Mr. Warren's future employment prospects with the agency were excellent and his probability of continued employment was about 95 percent.

Loan officers at Hardy Building and Loan Association look carefully at a borrower's monthly budget, especially at the monthly installment payments to which the borrower is committed. The size of these regular payments relative to the family's monthly income reflects its capacity to handle new debt, including a home mortgage. In addition, the Federal National Mortgage Corporation (FNMA) will purchase good-quality home mortgages from savings and loans, provided the borrower's monthly payments do not exceed certain limits. For example, one FNMA operating regulation requires that the monthly mortgage payment (plus escrow payments) not exceed 28 percent of the borrower's monthly gross income, and the sum of *all* regular monthly payments (including mortgage payments) must not exceed 36 percent of monthly gross income.

If the Warren's borrow $63,000 at 16 percent to finance their new home, their monthly payments (excluding taxes and other escrow payments) will be approximately $847 for a 30-year loan.[1] Taxes and home insurance will bring this monthly levy to $915. The Warrens currently owe $2,550 to the local bank for an auto loan (monthly payments of $133), $450 to a credit card plan for vacation expenses (monthly payments of $37.50), $455 to an appliance store for a refrigerator and stove (monthly payments of $65), and $950 to a furniture company for living and dining room furnishings (monthly payments of $30). However, the report from the local credit bureau gave the Warrens a rating of good on their payment record, indicating that on only one or two occasions have late payments been made.

The substantial fixed charges incurred, coupled with the family's fluctuating income, may make it difficult for the Warrens to meet monthly mortgage payments and also to keep up the value of their property. Rising costs for fuel, taxes, and home repairs make home ownership far more expensive today than even a few years ago. However, the Warrens are anxious to purchase their new home and probably can secure the financing they need at a neighboring savings and loan or mutual savings bank which extends more liberal credit terms. You must, therefore, consider the Warren's mortgage credit application with great care.

---

[1]This is the initial monthly payment. Actually, Hardy uses a form of variable-rate mortgage adjusted upward or downward with market conditions on June 30 of each year. The rate adjustments follow the Federal Home Loan Bank Board's interest-rate index. Borrowers must be notified within 30 days of the amount of the annual rate adjustment. If the initial borrower sells his or her home, a new buyer may assume the loan balance but a new adjustable-rate mortgage must be written on the property at that time. Hardy also reserves the right to impose limits—loan-rate ceilings and rate floors—on any mortgage granted.

14. *Mutual Savings Banks*

ONE OF THE MOST IMPORTANT THRIFT INSTITUTIONS in the United States, particularly along the eastern seaboard, is the mutual savings bank. Begun early in the 19th century to encourage savings on the part of low- and middle-income individuals and families, mutuals have grown into a major financial intermediary, not only in the United States but around the globe. In the United States, mutuals have become an extremely important lender of funds in the nation's capital market, purchasing annually a large volume of mortgages, corporate bonds, and corporate stock. Thus they intermediate essentially between households with modest amounts of savings and corporations in need of large amounts of long-term funds to support residential and commercial construction and growth.[1]

As we will see, mutual savings banks are quite similar to the savings and loan associations discussed in the preceding chapter. Like savings and loans, they were started to encourage family thrift, but their incoming deposits are not as heavily committed to residential mortgage loans as is true of S&Ls. This intermediary is a strong financial-service innovator and is continually unveiling new services to appeal to individual and family savers and borrowers. Unfortunately, as we will note also in this chapter, many mutuals share with savings and loans the dubious distinction of serious financial problems spawned by an era of record high-interest rates and intense competition for savings funds.

---

[1]In terms of total assets held by the industry, mutual savings banks rank seventh—behind commercial banks, savings and loan associations, pension funds, life insurance companies, finance companies, and money market funds. However, the industry ranks much higher in the particular markets where it is most active. For example, mutuals rank fourth in total mortgage loans—behind savings and loans, commercial banks, and life insurance companies, principally because of their heavy commitment in supporting residential construction. The industry ranks third among depository institutions in total savings deposits held, preceded only by commercial banks and savings and loans. (See United States League of Savings Associations [15].)

STRUCTURE OF THE INDUSTRY

The first mutual savings banks were chartered in Scotland in 1810. Designed to channel the savings of low- and middle-income families into loans and high-grade securities, the concept of savings banking spread rapidly to other countries. In fact, the United States was one of the earliest and most successful locations for mutual savings banks. In 1816, the cities of Boston and Philadelphia saw the chartering of two savings banks—the Provident Institution for Savings and the Philadelphia Saving Fund Society—which are still in operation today. Many other savings banks soon appeared in the New England and middle Atlantic regions. By year-end 1981 there were 435 U.S. savings banks, holding close to $176 billion in total assets. These mutual associations offered savings and credit services through more than 3,600 offices in 17 states (see Table 14–1).

The mutual savings bank industry is concentrated both geographically and by size of institution. The majority of mutuals are situated along the East Coast of the United States, principally in the six New England states and in New Jersey, New York, and Pennsylvania. Massachusetts has the largest number of savings banks, with New York second, followed by Connecticut, Maine, and New Hampshire (see Table 14–2). The mutuals located in Connecticut, Massachusetts, and New York represent almost three quarters of all U.S. savings banks and hold more than 80 percent of industry resources. About 90 percent of all deposits held by mutuals are accounted for by savings banks headquartered in only five states—Connecticut, Massachusetts, New Jersey, New York, and Pennsylvania.[2]

Table 14–1 Number, Total Assets, and Average Assets of Mutual Savings Banks: Selected Years, 1900–1981
(asset figures in $ millions)

Year	Number of Mutuals	Total Assets	Average Assets
1900	626	$ 2,328	$ 3.7
1910	637	3,598	5.6
1920	618	5,586	9.0
1930	592	10,496	17.7
1940	540	11,919	22.1
1950	529	22,446	42.4
1960	515	40,571	78.8
1970	494	78,995	159.9
1980	461	147,287	315.4
1981	435	175,612	403.7

Source: Adapted from the National Association of Mutual Savings Banks, *Annual Report of the President*, New York, May 1981, pp. 11, 35; and *Annual Report of the President*, New York, May 1982, pp. 5, 12.

[2]See Harless [7], p. 24.

**Table 14–2   Distribution of Mutual Savings Banks
by State: December 31, 1979**

State	Number of Mutual Savings Banks
Massachusetts	163
New York	112
Connecticut	65
Maine	29
New Hampshire	26
New Jersey	20
Washington	10
Pennsylvania	9
Rhode Island	6
Vermont	6
Indiana	4
Maryland	3
Wisconsin	3
Alaska	2
Delaware	2
Oregon	2
Minnesota*	1
Total	463

*The savings bank in Minnesota was merged into a commercial bank in February 1982.

Source: National Association of Mutual Savings Banks, *1980 National Fact Book of Mutual Savings Banking*, New York, table 6, p. 14.

Most mutuals are relatively small. Nearly half (45 percent) hold deposits of under $100 million each, while only 15 percent hold deposits of $500 million or more (see Table 14–3). Though smaller savings banks numerically dominate, the average size mutual has risen sharply in recent years

**Table 14–3   Distribution of Mutual Savings Banks by
Deposit Size: December 31, 1979**

Deposit Size Category	Number of Mutual Savings Banks
Less than $50 million	83
$50–$99.9 million	127
$100–$249.9 million	130
$250–$499.9 million	51
$500–$999.9 million	39
$1,000 million and over	33
Total	463

Source: National Association of Mutual Savings Banks, *1980 National Fact Book of Mutual Savings Banking*, New York, table 6, p. 14.

to hold over $400 million in total assets, roughly three times the average asset size of commercial banks and savings and loan associations.

Mutual savings banks, as the name suggests, are mutual in form, which means their depositors are not creditors, but really owners. The mutual savings bank is supposed to operate for the benefit of its depositors. Savers who deposit their funds in a mutual receive the institution's net earnings (less any additions to reserve accounts, as required either by law or by the policies of the individual institution) in the form of quarterly or semiannual dividends. Strictly speaking, then, the return on a savings account in a mutual savings bank is a dividend rate, not an interest rate. Though the depositors legally are the owners, policy making and management control is reserved for a board of trustees who often serve without pay. New trustees may be chosen by the existing board or elected according to the dictates of state law. Whatever method of selection is used, state laws and the bylaws of each savings bank set out detailed rules to govern the board of trustees and the mutual's officers.

Regulation of the Industry

Historically, savings banks have been regulated almost exclusively by the states, with only limited involvement by the federal government. Indeed, before 1978 only the states could charter a new savings bank. However, in that year Congress passed the Financial Institutions Regulatory and Interest Rate Control Act, which created a system for federal chartering of mutuals. However, as of year-end 1980, only three savings banks (one in New Hampshire and two in New York) had completed the federal chartering process, with all three simply converting from state to federal charter. The principal federal role in the industry is still providing insurance for deposits and setting deposit-rate ceilings.

In contrast, state law encompasses nearly every aspect of savings bank operation, including the selection of management and the board of trustees, the kind and quality of assets that may be acquired, the types of customer services that may be offered, and rules for the distribution of earnings. Regular examination of individual institutions also is carried out by state agencies, though savings banks insured by the Federal Deposit Insurance Corporation, and mutuals belonging to the Federal Home Loan Bank System, are subject to examination by these federal agencies.

Responding to increasing competition for funds, the industry has sought and won important regulatory concessions within the past decade. Mutual savings banks appear to be striving toward the goal of becoming department stores of finance, offering a wide range of financial services similar to those offered by commercial banks (see Table 14-4). These services include thrift deposits, mortgage credit, family financial counseling, life insurance, safe-deposit boxes, money orders, traveler's checks, credit

Table 14-4 Number of Mutual Savings Banks Offering Selected Services
in 1979

Types of Services Offered	Number of Mutual Savings Banks Offering the Service
Automated tellers	95
Bank money orders	458
Checking accounts	217
Overdraft privileges on checking accounts and NOWs	177
Check verification	88
Club accounts	423
Collateral loans	381
Credit cards	192
Direct deposit	459
Education loans	388
Home-improvement loans	450
24-hour cash-dispensing facilities	63
Individual retirement accounts	436
NOW accounts	354
Passbook loans	461
Payroll deductions	314
Personal loans	316
Personal trust service	7
Point-of-sale services	23
Safe-deposit boxes	389
Savings bank life insurance	328
Savings payout plan	85
School savings	103
Self-employed retirement savings (Keogh)	311
Telephone bill paying	52
Traveler's checks	459
Total savings banks included	462

Source: Adapted from National Association of Mutual Savings Banks, *1980 National Fact Book of Mutual Savings Banking*, New York, p. 59.

cards, passbook loans, and, more recently, high-yield consumer repurchase agreements. The service package offered by the industry has expanded in recent years to encompass third-party payment services (particularly NOW accounts), trust services, and retirement plans. A number of states now permit the offering of credit cards and the transfer of funds to and from savings accounts for stipulated purposes.[3]

[3]The Depository Institutions Deregulation and Monetary Control Act of 1980 made automatic transfers of funds (ATS) from savings to checking accounts or vice versa a service which could be offered by any federally insured depository institution, including mutual savings banks. In effect, ATS enables the customer to earn interest on checkbook balances since funds deposited in a checking account can be moved into an interest-bearing savings deposit until needed and then transferred back to the customer's checking account to cover any overdrafts.

Moreover, there is a trend in the industry toward more effective utilization of marketing techniques, evidenced by increased use of cash-dispensing machines providing readily available money on a 24-hour basis and by the provision of financial counseling services to individuals and families. Further expansion in service offerings is expected in future years as the industry strives to retain its share of deposit and loan markets and compete successfully with credit unions, commercial banks, money market funds, savings and loan associations, and other institutions offering consumer-oriented financial services.

A Trend toward Consolidation in Savings Banking

The late 1970s and early 1980s were years of crisis for mutual savings banks. As we will note again at several other points in this chapter, savings banks experienced a serious erosion in their profit margins and equity reserves beginning in 1978. The principal cause was high and rising interest rates which had several adverse effects on the industry: (1) larger, more interest-sensitive deposits flowed out into other investment vehicles (disintermediation); (2) demand for home mortgages, the principal savings bank asset, declined significantly; and (3) operating costs, led by an upward surge in deposit interest rates, soared to record levels, far outstripping revenue gains. Faced with the prospect of several large savings banks failing, federal regulatory authorities began pushing for more mergers between ailing and healthy mutuals.

As Table 14–1 indicates, the number of mutuals dropped significantly between 1970 and 1980—from 494 to 466. However, the decline in industry numbers was even more dramatic in 1981, when the number of savings banks fell from 461 to 435. Thus there is a clear consolidation trend, spurred by federally sanctioned mergers, toward fewer and larger mutuals which, presumably, are more cost-efficient and better able to withstand risk and adverse economic conditions. However, many industry officials have frowned upon federal encouragement of mergers even though they reduce the potential drain on federal deposit insurance funds. These industry officials have argued that such mergers create a more concentrated, less competitive industry and one less concerned with local community needs.

Evidence bearing on the effects of new merger policy is nonexistent at present, and we must await further research to fully assess its implications for the future of savings banking. Nevertheless, more mergers involving savings banks are likely in future years as the industry continues to consolidate its resources and especially its supply of capital. The pressure for additional savings bank mergers may ease off somewhat in the future, however, with more stable growth in the economy and more moderate inflation, which would keep down deposit interest rates. An additional feature is the backstop to thrift institution viability provided by the 1982 Garn–St Germain Depository Institutions Act. As we noted in Chapter 13, this law permits the FDIC to accept net-worth certificates from troubled banks and thrifts (whose equity-to-asset ratio drops to 3 percent or less) and to issue promissory notes which the troubled institutions can hold as earning assets. Moreover, in an emergency, failing situation, the FDIC can authorize a closed or endangered large mutual to be acquired by another federally insured institution, either within the same state or outside the troubled institution's home state.[4] The mere presence of such backstops should make it easier for mutuals to retain their deposits and weather future financial storms.

Probably the most important new service offered by mutual savings banks is the account with third-party payment powers. The NOW account—an interest-bearing deposit permitting negotiable orders of withdrawal (checks) to be written against it—is the most well-known payments account offered by mutuals. Actually, mutuals today offer at least four different kinds of payments accounts: (1) regular checking accounts; (2) interest-bearing negotiable orders of withdrawal (NOW) accounts; (3) noninterest-bearing negotiable orders of withdrawal (NINOW) accounts; and (4) draftable, flexible-rate money market deposit accounts. However, it was the development of the NOW account that launched the mutual savings bank industry into the checking account-payments business.

SAVINGS BANKS INTRODUCE THE NOW ACCOUNT

NOWs have an interesting but brief history. In 1970, Consumer Savings Bank of Worcester, Massachusetts, submitted a plan to the Massachusetts State Banking Commission to offer interest-bearing draftable accounts. Citing federal and state restrictions, the commission denied the savings bank's request. Immediately, Consumer Savings filed suit, arguing that federal law prohibited offering the new service but that state law and regulation which govern Massachusetts' saving banks did not.[5] The Massachusetts Supreme Court upheld Consumer's suit in 1972, and the Worcester savings institution began offering NOWs. Soon, other Massachusetts savings banks joined in the competition to market NOWs. Meanwhile, the New Hampshire Savings Bank of Concord noted the fact that New Hampshire banking regulations were quite similar to those in Massachusetts. This discovery opened the door to the spread of NOWs in New Hampshire.

---

[4] In this instance, *large* is defined as a mutual savings bank holding more than $500 million in total assets.

[5] Federal law at the time prohibited any federally regulated institution except commercial banks from offering checking (demand) deposits and prohibited the payment of interest on checking accounts. However, Massachusetts savings banks were regulated by state law and thus were not subject to federal restrictions.

To no one's surprise, nonbank thrift institutions in neighboring states and federallly regulated depository institutions throughout New England began clamoring for permission to offer NOWs. Belatedly, Congress reacted in 1974, but only legitimized the new service for federal depository institutions in Massachusetts and New Hampshire, effective January 1974. In September 1975, checking-account powers were granted to Oregon savings institutions through a new law in that state—a move soon followed by the states of Connecticut, Delaware, Maine, and New York. Once again, Congress belatedly moved to catch up by permitting NOWs in Connecticut, Maine, Rhode Island, and Vermont in 1976, New York in 1978, and New Jersey in 1979. NINOWs were legalized for savings banks in Pennsylvania and Minnesota during 1977.

Then, in March 1980, the Depository Institutions Deregulation and Monetary Control Act was signed into law by President Jimmy Carter, legalizing NOWs in all remaining states of the union, effective December 31, 1980. The 1980 law specified that NOWs could be offered only to persons and nongovernment, nonprofit organizations. Shortly thereafter, in October 1980, the Depository Institutions Deregulation Committee (DIDC) published regulations establishing a uniform interest rate of 5¼ percent for NOWs nationwide.[6] Approximately three fourths of all mutuals offer NOW accounts today. Savings banks were also authorized by the Depository Institutions Deregulation Act of 1980 to offer checking accounts to their business loan customers. And the Garn–St Germain Depository Institutions Act of 1982 authorized the offering of NOWs to federal, state, and local governmental units.[7]

INDUSTRY SOURCES OF FUNDS

Savings Deposits

Historically, the major source of funds for mutual savings banks has been the savings deposits of individuals and families (see Table 14–5). The majority of these savings accounts offer a fairly modest yield but also possess the important features of liquidity and safety which are so important to savers of relatively limited means.

---

[6]The DIDC, as noted earlier in this text, was set up to phase out Regulation Q interest-rate ceilings on time and savings deposits by 1986. The committee includes the heads of the Office of the Comptroller of the Currency, Federal Reserve Board, Federal Deposit Insurance Corporation, Federal Home Loan Bank Board, National Credit Union Administration, and the Secretary of the Treasury. The Comptroller has no vote, however.

[7]Beginning on January 5, 1983, the DIDC authorized the super NOW with a minimum average balance of $2,500, but permitting an unlimited number of payment transactions by the customer. Unlike the regular NOW, the super NOW has no federally imposed deposit-rate ceiling (unless the customer's balance falls below $2,500, in which case the NOW ceiling rate applies). The super NOW carries the same reserve requirement as a regular checking account (which was 12 percent in 1983).

Table 14–5   Sources of Funds (liabilities and reserves) of the Mutual Savings Bank Industry: December 31, 1981 (amounts in $ millions)

Sources of Funds	Amount Held	Percent of Total Liabilities and Reserves
Savings deposits	$ 49,409	28.1%
Time deposits	103,425	58.9
6-month CDs	53,689	30.6
30-month CDs	21,772	12.4
Other time deposits	27,964	15.9
Other types of deposits	2,079	1.2
Total deposits	154,913	88.2
Borrowings and mortgage warehousing	8,147	4.6
Other liabilities	2,584	1.5
General reserve accounts	9,969	5.7
Total liabilities and reserves	$175,612	100.0%

Source: Adapted from National Association of Mutual Savings Banks, *Annual Report of the President*, New York, May 1982, p. 5.

Significant changes are continuing to occur in the mix of savings bank deposits. Passbook savings accounts—historically, the industry's principal and cheapest source of funds—have given way to higher-yielding time deposits, sharply increasing operating expenses. Even the small saver has become more cognizant of the alternative and frequently more profitable uses of funds available in higher-rate accounts. At year-end 1980, higher-yielding time deposits and other special thrift accounts with adjustable rates represented about 60 percent of total savings bank deposits, compared to only about 20 percent in 1971. Meanwhile, the low-yielding regular passbook savings accounts—once the mainstay of the industry—declined to just over 40 percent of the industry's total deposits.

Among the most popular high-yielding time deposits offered by savings banks are the 6-month money market CDs and 30-month small-saver CDs. Six-month money market time deposits were authorized by federal regulations in June 1978. These money market CDs (MMCs) have a minimum denomination of $10,000, with a yield indexed to the average auction discount rate on the most recently issued 26-week Treasury bills. The maturity of MMCs must be exactly 26 weeks and interest cannot be compounded. Small-saver CDs, authorized approximately one year after the MMCs, carry a minimum maturity of 2½ years, but less than 3½ years, with a rate not to exceed the average 2½-year yield for U.S. Treasury securities. These deposits have no legally imposed minimum denomination and interest earnings may be compounded. While small-saver CDs and money market CDs have variable ceiling rates, a new 3½-year, or "wild card," time deposit authorized in May 1982 carries no legal rate ceiling and no minimum denomination. Savings banks also aggressively market IRA and Keogh retirement plan savings accounts with minimum maturities of 18 months and no federal rate ceiling.

The growth in higher-yielding, longer-term savings deposits has had profound effects on the operating costs and net earnings of the savings bank industry. In general, operating costs, paced by a rapid increase in interest on time and savings deposits, have outstripped the growth of loan and investment revenues, squeezing net earnings and threatening the long-term viability of a number of mutuals.[8] The savings bank industry, like the savings and loan industry, was hard-hit by the rise of money market funds during the 1970s. It is estimated that the bulk of funds attracted by money funds in their race to become a $200 billion-plus industry consisted of savings deposits formerly held by saving banks and savings and loan associations.[9] Thus it is not surprising that the Garn–St Germain Depository Institutions Act of 1982 instructed the Depository Institutions Deregulation Committee to develop a new money market deposit account (MMDA), "directly equivalent to and competitive with money market mutual funds," which federally supervised depository institutions could offer. The new MMDA became available in December 1982 and carries federal insurance with a minimum average balance of $2,500. While the account has limited payment powers (a maximum of six transfers per month, with no more than three effected by writing checks), the MMDA's interest rate has no government-imposed interest rate ceiling.[10] Mutual savings banks moved quickly to offer the new money market accounts in order to better serve their customers and to avoid losing interest-sensitive deposits to other financial institutions.

The principal insurance fund for deposits in mutual savings banks is the Federal Deposit Insurance Corporation (FDIC), which insures individual

---

[8]The most rapidly growing higher-yielding deposits in recent years have been the 6-month money market CDs and the 30-month small-saver CDs. These instruments, as we noted above, have their rates tied to the market return on comparable-maturity U.S. Treasury securities. While these CDs are not floating-rate deposits, when a new certificate is issued, its rate is determined by the prevailing rate on U.S. Treasury securities in the same maturity category as the CD. Thus, in a period of rising interest rates, mutuals find that many of their deposits are renewed by customers at higher and higher rates. If interest rates rise far enough, the savings bank will probably gain little in new funds, but previously acquired deposits will roll over into higher- and higher-yielding accounts, squeezing net earnings.

[9]See Chapter 16 for a discussion of money market funds and their key role in the financial system in recent years.

[10]The reserve requirement on MMDAs is zero if held in a personal account. Nonpersonal MMDAs carry a 3 percent reserve requirement. Should the average maintained balance in the customer's account drop below the $2,500 required minimum, the deposit is considered equivalent to a regular NOW account, and its interest yield is subject to the current federal ceiling rate on NOWs.

accounts up to a maximum of $100,000. Few savings bank deposits remain unprotected by some form of deposit insurance. While the FDIC will insure qualified savings banks in every state, the state of Massachusetts also has set up an agency which insures 100 percent of deposits held by mutuals in that state. Federal and state deposit insurance has definitely spurred the historical growth of the industry, because this feature is particularly attractive to the small-saver—still the major source of funds for mutual savings banks.

The Impact of Deposit Interest-Rate Ceilings

Savings banks are limited by law in the interest rates they are permitted to pay on some deposits. As we noted earlier, these legal rates are set by the Depository Institutions Deregulation Committee, a creation of the 1980 Depository Institutions Deregulation and Monetary Control Act. The DIDC was assigned the task of dismantling federal interest-rate ceilings no later than 1986. The first major step affecting mutuals and other nonbank thrifts was to narrow the differential between maximum legal rates quoted by commercial banks and thrifts on the popular six-month money market certificates, bringing the two industries more into direct competition for short-term, interest-sensitive consumer savings. Maximum permissible rates on 2½-year small-saver certificates and NOW accounts were increased to more closely approximate market-determined interest yields. A major step toward equalizing nonbank thrifts' deposit rates and those offered by commercial banks occurred in 1982 with passage of the Garn–St Germain Depository Institutions Act. This law mandated an end to legally imposed differential rate ceilings between thrift institution deposits and commercial bank deposits by January 1, 1984.

The federal deposit-rate ceilings have had a profound effect on the growth of the savings bank industry. Because mutuals deal mainly in small savings accounts and therefore are more restricted by rate ceilings than are commercial banks, the ceilings have brought both benefits and problems. In the past, the rate ceilings granted a small preferential advantage to thrifts vis-a-vis commercial banks in attracting savings deposits, thus enabling thrifts to be more competitive in attracting deposits and in financing the construction and purchase of new homes, apartments, and other residential dwelling units. The ceilings have also held down the cost of deposits and therefore to some extent, protected the earnings of mutuals and savings and loans. However, when market interest rates have risen above the legal ceilings, mutuals have lost substantial deposits (i.e., disintermediation), which threatens their growth and viability. And the ceilings have discriminated heavily against the small saver.

The impact of the gradual removal of deposit interest-rate ceilings on mutual savings banks is difficult to gauge at this point. We are presently in a period of transition from the old, highly regulated system to a more deregulated, competitive environment. Certainly, without the deposit-rate ceilings, interest costs on borrowed funds will rise in a period of rising market interest rates; but does this mean the net yield *spread* between savings bank earning assets and interest-bearing sources of funds will be reduced? Obviously, much depends upon the interest sensitivity and flexibility of savings bank assets. As we will note in the next section, mutuals are increasingly diverting their incoming funds into nontraditional assets (particularly commercial and consumer installment loans) whose yields tend to be more flexible than the more traditional investments in bonds and mortgages. Moreover, with federal rate ceilings removed, mutuals choosing to compete aggressively for deposits will be more able to do so, expanding their deposit volume. With greater deposit volume, savings banks may be able to lower their operating costs through economies of scale. Still, as Moran [9] notes, interest-rate deregulation may impact more severely on mutual savings banks than on other thrifts (particularly savings and loans) because savings deposits represent such a dominant percentage of a mutual's liability portfolio.

Equity Reserves

Though mutuals are owned by their depositors, they do maintain equity accounts, usually labeled general reserve accounts, which hold earnings not paid out as dividends. In years of positive earnings, general reserve accounts grow, strengthening savings banks against future losses. However, as we will discuss later in this chapter, mutuals as a group have suffered significant deterioration in their profit margins of late and many have taken sizable earnings losses. The result has been a substantial decline in reserves relative to deposits and other liabilities as a source of funds. For example, the industry's general reserve accounts represented 6.6 percent of total liabilities and reserves in 1980 and just 5.7 percent at year-end 1981. This means that a decline in asset values of, say, 6 percent would threaten the survival of many savings banks. The principal function of reserve accounts is to keep a savings bank operating even in the face of earnings losses, until management and the board of directors can act to solve the problem.

USES OF SAVINGS BANK FUNDS

Loans and Investments

Mutuals are closely regulated in the loans and investments they are permitted to make. For example, securities purchased must come from a list sanctioned by the appropriate state supervisory agency. U.S. government securities are always acceptable as investments, as are high-quality municipal and Canadian government securities, World Bank securities, secured utility and railroad obligations of investment quality, highly rated industrial bonds or their equivalent, and high-quality common and preferred stock. Investments in open-market securities in recent years have averaged between 25 and 30 percent of industry assets, led by corporate bonds and stock, while the bulk of remaining funds has flowed into first-mortgage loans. Only a small percentage of total industry resources normally are devoted to the most liquid assets, which include U.S. government securities, federal agency obligations, mortgage-backed bonds, municipals, and cash (see Table 14–6).

Liquidity

The liquidity needs of mutual savings banks normally are relatively low because their deposits are predominantly savings whose fluctuations are usually more predictable than commercial bank demand accounts. The primary industry liquidity reserve consists of cash (including bank deposits), short-term U.S. government securities, and prime-quality marketable securities. In a pinch, savings banks can borrow short-term funds from commercial banks or other lenders, warehouse some of their loans, or sell their more marketable securities. Moreover, since passage of the Depository Institutions Deregulation and Monetary Control Act of 1980,

Table 14–6   Uses of Funds (assets) of the Mutual Savings Bank Industry: December 31, 1981 (amounts in $ millions)

Uses of Funds (assets)	Amount Held	Percent of Total Assets
Cash	$ 5,415	3.1%
U.S. Treasury and federal agency securities	9,861	5.6
State and local government obligations	2,274	1.3
Mortgage investments	113,889	64.9
Mortgage loans	100,015	57.0
GNMA mortgage-backed securities	13,874	7.9
Corporate and other bonds	20,186	11.5
Corporate equity shares	3,614	2.1
Other loans	14,740	8.4
Guaranteed education	2,247	1.3
Consumer	2,006	1.1
Home improvement	953	0.5
Other types of loans	9,534	5.4
Miscellaneous assets	5,632	3.2
Total assets	$175,612	100.0%

Source: National Association of Mutual Savings Banks, *Annual Report of the President*, New York, May 1982, p. 5.

mutuals have had access to extended reserve credit at the discount windows of the Federal Reserve banks.

Despite this new borrowing authority, savings banks have generally increased their liquid asset holdings in recent years, due, in part, to heavy deposit withdrawals (i.e., disintermediation) in the face of record high interest rates. The growth of interest-sensitive, six-month market CDs (now about 30 percent of total liabilities and reserves) within the industry's deposit structure has been particularly influential. Another factor leading to the recent growth in liquid assets may be the growth of NOWs and other payment accounts. It seems reasonable to assume that as mutuals become more like commercial banks in the deposit services they offer, their liquidity requirements will increase and the composition of their assets will change accordingly. And, as Dunham [4] notes, as the 1980s began, there was already evidence that a number of savings banks in the New England area displayed asset and liability portfolios whose composition substantially resembled those of a number of commercial banks in the same region.

Types of Loans

Mutuals are limited by state law and regulation in the kinds of loans they may grant, though, as we will soon see, major changes in federal law affecting loans by savings banks have just recently occurred. Most commonly, first-mortgage loans on improved real property are allowed as are loans to customers against their savings deposits. A few states allow savings banks to make installment and home-improvement loans but limit these to a relatively small percentage of total assets. However, the industry's major lending activity centers around mortgage credit, either originated by mutuals or purchased from other lenders. As a whole, mortgage loans represent about three fifths of industry assets. About 70 percent of these are *conventional* mortgage loans for the purchase of commercial and residential properties, and the remainder are about equally divided between government-guaranteed FHA and VA residential mortgages. Because mutuals face few significant geographic restrictions on their real estate lending, they often make loans far removed from their local market area. The added risk protection and standardization afforded by FHA- and VA-guaranteed mortgages are attractive features to mutuals, though the low interest-rate ceilings on these government-guaranteed mortgage instruments have resulted in a shift of industry residential lending more toward conventional mortgage loans in recent years. Purchases of GNMA mortgage-backed securities also have become an important element in the industry's support of the U.S. mortgage market.

Other Assets

Of course, net acquisitions of mortgage loans and other assets depend upon market conditions and the alternative investments available to savings banks. Mutuals have much greater flexibility in asset selection than savings and loans and are not restricted by law to investing mainly in mortgages. As Tables 14–7 and 14–8 reveal, industry investments in mortgage loans have not grown as fast in recent years as have investments in other assets, particularly mortgage-backed securities, cash, commercial paper, federal agency securities, short-term federal funds loans, security RPs, and other assets. A weakening market for new homes in the late 1970s and early 80s explains much of the slowdown in mortgage loans. Record high interest rates discouraged home buyers and builders and, due to rate-caused deposit losses, reduced the ability of mutuals to sustain a high level of mortgage lending.

Uncertain conditions in U.S. bond and stock markets also have limited savings bank acquisitions of corporate debt and equity securities in recent years. Another factor adversely affecting stock acquisitions by mutuals was the 1976 ruling by the Financial Accounting Standards Board that equity investments should be valued at the lower of cost or market value. The industry does not face the full corporate income tax rate that commercial banks do. Therefore mutuals normally purchase relatively few tax-exempt state and local government bonds.

Table 14–7   Net Flows of Investment Funds of Mutual Savings Banks: 1970–1980
(amounts in $ billions)

Year	Total	Mortgage Loans	Mortgage-Backed Securities	U.S. Govt. and Federal Agency Securities	State and Local Securities	Corp. and Other Bonds	Corp. Stock	Cash and Other Assets
1970	$ 4.8	$2.0	$0.1	$0.3	$ *	$1.3	$0.3	$0.9
1971	10.2	4.2	0.7	0.5	0.2	3.5	0.5	0.7
1972	10.9	5.5	0.6	0.7	0.5	2.1	0.6	0.8
1973	6.0	5.6	0.5	−1.0	0.1	−0.9	0.4	1.4
1974	3.7	2.2	0.4	−0.5	*	0.8	0.3	0.6
1975	11.5	2.3	1.1	2.8	0.6	3.5	0.2	0.9
1976	13.3	4.1	2.4	1.6	0.9	2.8	0.1	1.5
1977	12.4	6.5	2.5	0.1	0.4	1.2	0.4	1.3
1978	10.0	6.3	1.6	−1.0	0.5	*	*	2.4
1979	5.3	3.9	1.8	−0.6	−0.6	−0.8	*	1.8
1980	7.6	0.6	2.1	1.2	−0.6	0.7	−0.5	4.2

*Indicates net investment amount of less than $50 million.
Source: National Association of Mutual Savings Banks, *Annual Report of the President*, New York, May 1981, p. 10.

Table 14–8   Acquisitions of Financial Assets and Liabilities by Mutual Savings Banks: 1972–1982

Financial Assets and Liabilities	Net Flows at Seasonally Adjusted Annual Rates ($ billions)										
	1972	1973	1974	1975	1976	1977	1978	1979	1980	1981	1982
New acquisition of											
Financial assets	$11.0	$6.0	$3.8	$11.5	$13.8	$12.5	$10.9	$5.2	$8.2	$4.2	$4.4
Demand deposits and currency	0.1	0.1	*	0.1	*	*	1.0	−0.3	1.1	1.2	0.1
Time deposits	0.2	0.2	0.2	0.1	*	*	0.3	−0.3	*	−0.1	1.4
Federal funds and RPs	0.1	0.7	−0.3	−0.1	0.4	0.6	*	0.9	0.6	1.5	*
Corporate stock	0.6	0.4	0.2	0.2	0.1	0.4	0.1	−0.1	−0.5	−0.6	−0.4
U.S. Treasury securities	0.2	−0.5	−0.4	2.2	1.1	0.1	−0.9	−0.2	0.8	−0.2	0.6
Federal agency securities	1.1	0.1	0.2	1.7	2.9	2.6	1.7	1.3	2.5	1.2	1.3
State and local government securities	0.5	*	*	0.6	0.9	0.4	0.5	−0.4	−0.5	−0.1	0.2
Corporate bonds	2.1	−1.1	0.9	3.5	2.8	1.2	0.1	−1.1	0.7	−1.0	−1.2
Mortgages	5.5	5.7	2.2	2.3	4.4	6.5	7.1	3.6	0.6	−0.1	−2.2
Consumer credit	0.1	0.3	0.2	0.2	0.3	0.5	0.7	0.1	0.4	−0.3	0.3
Commercial paper	−0.1	−0.1	0.1	0.1	0.4	*	0.2	1.1	1.5	1.8	1.8
Miscellaneous assets	0.5	0.2	0.5	0.6	0.4	0.3	0.1	0.5	1.0	0.9	2.3
Net increase in liabilities	10.4	5.3	3.4	11.0	13.1	11.5	10.0	4.6	8.3	5.5	5.0
Deposits	10.2	4.7	3.1	11.2	13.0	11.1	8.6	3.4	7.5	3.0	5.4
Miscellaneous liabilities	0.2	0.6	0.3	−0.1	0.1	0.4	1.4	1.2	0.8	2.6	−0.3

*Less than $50 million.
Source: Board of Governors of the Federal Reserve System, *Flow of Funds Accounts, First Quarter 1983.*

Long-Term Trends in the Industry's Uses of Funds

Table 14–9, derived from the Federal Reserve Board's *Flow of Funds Accounts*,[11] helps to highlight a number of long-term trends in the savings bank industry's asset structure. For example, the increase in cash and demand deposit accounts in response to growing liquidity pressures clearly shows up. Funds invested in demand deposits and currency holdings in savings bank vaults rose from $1 billion in 1970 to more than $5 billion in 1982. Investments in mortgages (mainly residential) climbed from about $58 billion in 1970 to $94 billion in 1982, but fell sharply as a percentage of industry assets, from 73 percent to about 50 percent. The decline in mortgage investments reflects in substantial measure recent problems in the housing industry.

The industry's switch to more liquid open-market securities, particularly money market instruments, is also highlighted by the Federal Reserve's *Flow of Funds Accounts*. As Table 14–9 reflects, industry investments in short-term commercial paper expanded more than tenfold between 1970 and 1982, as did federal fund loans and short-term security repurchase agreements. Rapid increases were also recorded in industry holdings of

---

[11]See Chapter 2 for a discussion of the *Flow of Funds Accounts.*

Table 14–9   Financial Assets and Liabilities of Mutual Savings Banks Outstanding at Year-End: 1970–1982

Year-End Outstandings in $ Billions

Financial Assets or Liabilities	1970	1971	1972	1973	1974	1975	1976	1977	1978	1979	1980	1981	1982
Financial assets:													
Demand deposits and currency	$ 1.0	$ 0.9	$ 1.0	$ 1.1	$ 1.1	$ 1.2	$ 1.3	$ 2.1	$ 3.0	$ 2.8	$ 3.9	$ 5.1	$ 5.2
Time deposits	0.3	0.5	0.6	0.8	1.0	1.1	1.1	0.3	0.7	0.4	0.4	0.3	1.8
Federal funds and security RPs	0.4	0.7	0.8	1.5	1.2	1.1	1.5	2.1	3.0	3.1	3.7	5.2	5.3
Corporate stock	2.8	3.5	4.5	4.2	3.7	4.4	4.4	4.8	4.8	4.7	4.2	3.2	3.3
U.S. Treasury securities	3.2	3.3	3.5	3.0	2.6	4.7	5.8	5.9	5.0	3.9	5.3	5.4	6.0
Federal agency securities	2.2	3.0	4.2	4.2	4.4	6.1	9.1	14.7	13.4	15.6	17.5	18.4	17.8
State and local government securities	0.2	0.4	0.9	0.9	0.9	1.5	2.4	2.8	3.3	2.9	2.4	2.3	2.5
Corporate and foreign bonds	8.1	12.0	14.2	13.1	14.0	17.5	20.3	21.5	21.6	20.5	21.2	20.3	19.0
Mortgages	57.9	62.0	67.6	73.2	74.9	77.2	81.6	88.1	95.2	98.9	99.8	100.0	94.1
Consumer credit	1.4	1.5	1.6	1.9	2.1	2.3	2.6	3.1	3.9	3.9	4.1	4.2	4.9
Commercial paper	0.5	0.7	0.6	0.5	0.5	0.6	1.0	1.0	0.3	2.3	4.0	5.3	6.8
Miscellaneous assets	1.3	1.7	2.1	2.4	2.6	3.2	3.6	3.9	4.1	4.4	5.0	5.6	7.9
Total financial assets	$79.3	$90.1	$101.5	$106.8	$109.1	$121.2	$134.8	$147.3	$158.2	$163.3	$171.5	$175.3	$174.3
Liabilities:													
Deposits	$71.6	$81.4	$ 91.6	$ 96.3	$ 98.7	$109.9	$122.9	$134.0	$142.6	$146.0	$153.4	$156.5	$157.0
Miscellaneous liabilities	1.7	1.8	2.0	2.6	2.9	2.8	2.9	3.3	4.7	5.9	6.7	9.2	7.9
Total liabilities	$73.3	$83.3	$ 93.6	$ 99.0	$101.6	$112.6	$125.8	$137.3	$147.3	$151.9	$160.1	$165.7	$165.0

Source: Board of Governors of the Federal Reserve System, Flow of Funds Accounts, Assets and Liabilities Outstanding, 1959–1982.

U.S. government securities, federal agency obligations, state and local government bonds, corporate and foreign bonds, and consumer credit. As we noted earlier in the chapter, these long-term portfolio changes reflect the tremendous forces of change which now engulf the savings bank industry. The acceptance of higher-yielding, more interest-sensitive savings accounts, coupled with the offering of NOWs and other checkbook-like payments services, has sharply increased the industry's need for readily marketable, liquid assets. And because these developments have raised operating costs, savings banks have been forced to search the financial markets for higher yields, often only available from financial instruments outside their traditional investments in mortgages and domestic bonds. This is one of the principal reasons their holdings of both consumer installment loans and money market instruments have grown so rapidly in recent years.

Savings banks, at least those with federal charters, will be able to broaden their search for higher-yielding loans and investments in future years due to passage of the Garn–St Germain Depository Institutions Act of 1982. Title III of the 1982 law authorized federally chartered savings banks for the first time to grant overdraft loans, to make commercial loans, and to place funds in deposits offered by other insured depository institutions. They can also purchase state and local government revenue bonds and have broader powers in commercial and residential real estate lending.

Moreover, both federal and state-chartered thrifts should benefit greatly from two other provisions of the Garn–St Germain bill. One of these empowered state banks and thrift institutions to offer variable-rate mortgage instruments under the same terms as federal depository institutions. And Title II of the 1982 law preempts state-imposed restrictions on the enforcement of due-on-sale clauses in mortgage contracts. This will require, in most cases, old, low-yielding mortgages to be replaced by new mortgage loans (probably at higher rates, depending upon market conditions) when an existing home is sold. The foregoing changes in federal law offer the potential of higher gross asset yields for the savings bank industry.

REVENUES, EXPENSES, AND TAXES

Mutuals during the postwar period generally have received lower rates of return on their assets than have savings and loans, but higher returns than commercial banks. In the most recent years, however, earnings of mutuals generally have lagged well behind commercial banks. This is due to sharp increases in savings bank expenses, especially in years of rapidly rising interest rates. The earnings squeeze has been exacerbated, as we have seen, by a gradual shift of depositor funds from relatively low-yielding savings deposits to higher-yielding time deposits. Industry earnings have become much more volatile, with more expensive, interest-sensitive deposits, because the cost of industry funds now tends to shift with greater speed than do returns on assets (particularly on the industry's extensive holdings of bonds and mortgages).

A partial offset to the effect of rising costs on net earnings may be found in the relatively lenient tax situation faced by mutuals. However, there is a long-term trend toward higher effective tax rates resulting principally from provisions of the 1969 Tax Reform Act. The law requires savings banks to pay ordinary corporate income tax rates on net income left over after interest is paid to depositors. But, as in the case of savings and loans, a portion of net earnings may be sheltered through additions to bad debt reserves, based upon the savings bank's actual or estimated loss experience. For nonqualifying loans (principally loans not connected with the financing of real property), tax-free additions to reserves for losses must be related to actual loan loss experience. In the case of qualifying loans, savings banks may employ the greater of the actual loss experience or a fixed proportion of taxable income. The 1969 Tax Reform Act stipulated that by 1979 no more than 40 percent of otherwise taxable income could be used for tax-free additions to bad debt reserves.

While the industry's tax situation is lenient compared to commercial banks, the lower legal tax rate has not been enough to protect mutuals against volatile earnings and even losses in recent years. As Table 14–10 shows, the mutual savings bank industry reported negative net operating

Table 14–10   Income and Expenses of Mutual Savings Banks: 1979–1981

Item	Amount in $ Millions			Percentage of Average Total Assets		
	1979	1980	1981	1979	1980	1981
Total operating income	$13,316	$14,713	$15,996	8.26%	8.79%	9.20%
Operating expenses	2,374	2,955	3,325	1.47	1.77	1.91
Net operating income after expenses	10,942	11,758	12,671	6.79	7.02	7.29
Interest paid to depositors	9,876	11,881	14,240	6.13	7.10	8.19
Net operating income after expenses and interest	1,066	−123	−1,568	0.66	−0.07	−0.90
Taxes:	292	53	−96	0.18	0.03	−0.06
Federal	155	−78	−204	0.10	−0.05	−0.12
State and local	137	131	108	0.08	0.08	0.06
Net realized gains or losses on assets	−33	−30	68	−0.02	−0.02	0.04
Retained earnings	741	−206	−1,405	0.46	−0.12	−0.81

Note: The effective interest rate paid on mutual savings bank deposits in 1979, 1980, and 1981 was 6.80 percent, 7.96 percent, and 9.17 percent, respectively.

Source: National Association of Mutual Savings Banks, *Annual Report of the President*, New York, May 1982, p. 6.

income after expenses and deposit interest in 1980 and 1981–the first actual net losses since World War II. In 1979 mutuals as a group reported positive earnings but the net figure was well below the industry's historical average. The principal factor was the simple inability of industry revenue sources to keep pace with rapidly growing interest costs on deposits.

The earnings outlook for the industry remains highly uncertain at this point. Future decisions by the Depository Institutions Deregulation Committee in changing federal deposit-rate ceilings undoubtedly will have a profound impact on the industry's earnings picture as will the success or failure of government monetary and fiscal policy in controlling inflation and bringing about lower interest rates.[12] One hopeful feature, as noted by Moran [9], is that the capital (net-worth) position of mutuals is somewhat stronger than savings and loan associations, on the average, giving them a somewhat stronger cushion against future losses. Moreover, as 1983 began, deposit interest rates generally declined in response to slower growth in the economy and less vigorous inflation, which should provide aid to the earnings picture for savings banks.

SUMMARY

In this chapter we have taken a close look at the mutual savings bank industry, noting that mutuals depend principally upon time and savings deposits sold to individuals and families, to raise funds and employ the majority of those funds in the form of mortgage credit for residential and commercial construction. The industry is also a major investor in government securities and money market securities for liquidity purposes and is emphasizing consumer installment loans more heavily than in the past.

Over all, it must be said that the outlook for the savings bank industry is clouded at this time. A period of more moderate growth seems likely in

[12]It is interesting that a number of mutuals and savings and loans have searched for and found unique ways in recent years to offset operating losses and to protect their net worth. One of the most fascinating is the sale of their own buildings, which raises immediate cash and gives management more time to develop new strategies for long-term survival. Among the savings banks adopting such an approach were such industry leaders as Manhattan Savings Bank and Dry Dock Savings Bank of New York; and Gibraltar Savings and Home Savings of America, both headquartered in Los Angeles. These institutions leased back all or a portion of the office buildings they sold. The net result was really a sale of tax-shelter benefits, which increased sharply with passage of the Economic Recovery Act of 1981. The purchaser of such a building could depreciate its purchase price over 15 years versus 30 years or more under old tax rules. At the same time, inflation over the past two decades has sharply increased the market value of many office buildings (including savings bank office facilities) well above their historical cost, resulting in a substantial capital gain at point of sale for the buildings' owners. For example, when Dry Dock Savings of New York sold its Manhattan headquarters in 1982 it received an estimated $13 million capital gain on the sale over and above its original cost. And because the buyer receives large tax benefits from the liberalized depreciation rules, he or she may lease back the building to the savings bank at a lease rate below market.

future years, provided the industry can adapt its structure and package of services to the changing market for financial services. Among other things, successful adaptation will require even greater diversification of assets—a step recommended by numerous authorities in the field—and more aggressive use of branching, mergers, electronic equipment, and marketing of financial services. If federal regulations permit, it seems likely that mutual savings banks and savings and loan associations will look even more alike in their service offerings and portfolios in future years and that both sets of thrift institutions will more closely resemble commercial banks. The aggressiveness with which the mutual savings bank industry has penetrated the payments system, with such devices as NOW accounts and computer terminals for withdrawing and depositing funds, is a hopeful sign for the future.

Questions

14-1. Who charters mutual savings banks? Who is the industry's chief regulator?

14-2. Using historical, regulatory, and economic factors, explain why the industry draws upon the particular sources and uses of funds that it employs.

14-3. Why do you think mutual savings banks developed the NOW account? What benefits and costs can you see from the growth of this service?

14-4. The number of mutual savings banks has been declining in recent years. Discuss the reasons behind this trend. What is your best estimate regarding the industry's population of firms in the future? Defend your answer.

14-5. The growth of mutual savings banks has become more volatile recently, leading to greater uncertainty in the financial management of these institutions. What reasons can you assign for this development? If you were managing a mutual savings bank, what would you do to counteract increased volatility?

14-6. What impact did passage of the Depository Institutions Deregulation and Monetary Control Act of 1980 have upon mutual savings banks? The Garn–St Germain Depository Institutions Act of 1982? What new powers did the industry acquire? Can you foresee problems as well as benefits from these new powers? Explain your reasoning.

References

1. Benston, George J. "Savings Banks and the Public Interest." *Journal of Money, Credit, and Banking*, February 1972, pt. II, pp. 133–226.

2. Bronwyen, Brock. "Mortgages with Adjustable Interest Rates Improve Viability of the Thrift Industry." *Voice*, Federal Reserve Bank of Dallas, February 1981.

3. Carlson, John B., and K. J. Kowalewski. "Thrifts, Extended Credit, and Monetary Policy." *Economic Commentary*, Federal Reserve Bank of Cleveland, September 7, 1981.

4. Dunham, Constance. "Mutual Savings Banks: Are They Now or Will They Ever Be Commercial Banks?" *New England Economic Review*, Federal Reserve Bank of Boston, May–June 1982, pp. 51–72.

5. Federal Reserve Bank of Chicago. "The Depository Institutions Deregulation and Monetary Control Act of 1980." *Economic Perspectives*, September–October 1980, pp. 3–23.

6. Garcia, Gillian, Herbert Baer, Elijah Brewer, David R. Allardice, Thomas F. Cargill, John Dobra, George G. Kaufman, Anne Maxie L. Gonczy, Robert D. Laurent, and Larry R. Mote. "The Garn–St Germain Depository Institutions Act of 1982." *Economic Perspectives*, Federal Reserve Bank of Chicago, March–April 1983, pp. 3–31.

7. Harless, Doris E. *Nonbank Financial Institutions*. Richmond: Federal Reserve Bank of Richmond, October 1975.

8. Loeys, Jan G. "Deregulation: A New Future for Thrifts." *Business Review*, Federal Reserve Bank of Philadelphia, January–February 1983, pp. 15–26.

9. Moran, Michael J. "Thrift Institutions in Recent Years." *Federal Reserve Bulletin*, December 1982, pp. 726–38.

10. Moulton, Janice M. "Implementing the Monetary Control Act in a Troubled Environment for Thrifts." *Business Review*, Federal Reserve Bank of Philadelphia, July–August 1982, pp. 13–21.

11. National Association of Mutual Savings Banks. *National Fact Book of Mutual Savings Banking*. New York, 1980.

12. _____. *Annual Report of the President*. New York, 1981.

13. _____. *Annual Report of the President*. New York, 1982.

14. United States League of Savings Associations. *'81 Savings and Loan Sourcebook*. Chicago, 1981.

15. _____. *'82 Savings and Loan Sourcebook*. Chicago, 1982.

15. *Credit Unions*

ONE OF THE FASTEST GROWING and most unusual of all financial intermediaries is the credit union. The financial institutions we have discussed to this point are very much like other business firms in the economy—corporations or associations out to maximize the returns flowing to their owners. Though locked within a framework of close regulation by state and federal authorities, financial institutions generally hope to turn a profit from their borrowing and lending activities. This is not the case with credit unions, however, for they are nonprofit associations, operated solely for the benefit of their members. Credit unions are unique in focusing almost exclusively upon the credit and savings needs of households—individuals and families. And only qualified members of credit unions can avail themselves of credit union services.

Historically speaking, credit unions are a relatively young financial intermediary. The first U.S. credit union opened its doors to member savers and borrowers in 1909. Their basic purpose—to encourage thrift among their members and to make loans available at reasonable cost to those same members—has not changed in more than 70 years of operation.

Why did credit unions begin relatively recently? Because this financial institution caters almost exclusively to small savers and borrowers. Thus it was the rise of the middle class, especially people employed in private industry, which led to the development of credit unions. Middle-class individuals and families proved affluent enough to support a savings program and understood the benefits of using credit to improve their standard of living. Credit unions today and in the past have been one of the leading institutions in granting small loans to finance the purchase of automobiles, home appliances, and furniture, and to cover the cost of medical care, vacations, and even ordinary household expenses. Not surprisingly, with the acceptance of a buy-now-and-pay later philosophy in recent decades, the loans and other assets of credit unions have increased rapidly.

As Table 15–1 shows, there were less than 9,000 credit unions operating in the United States as World War II ended, but by 1960 their number had reached 20,000 and by 1970 almost 24,000. Thereafter, the credit union population began to decline due to consolidations and failures. In 1982, just over 20,000 U.S. credit unions were in operation, with nearly 46 million members and assets exceeding $80 billion.

HISTORY AND STRUCTURAL MAKEUP OF THE CREDIT UNION INDUSTRY

Credit unions started in Germany during the middle of the 19th century and quickly spread throughout Europe and then to Asia. In North America, credit unions came to Canada early in this century. Frequently started by church organizations in the early years, they were designed originally to protect poor families from paying usurious interest rates, offering them small loans at reasonable cost. The first U.S. credit union was started in New Hampshire in 1908. It provided savings deposit and loan services to members of a church located in the city of Manchester. In 1909, Massachusetts enacted the first credit union law at the state level.

The modern-day credit union appeals to a wide variety of social classes and income strata as reflected in a recent survey conducted by the Credit Union National Association (CUNA), the industry's trade association, and Opinion Research Corporation.[1] Credit union members tend to make greater use of credit cards, checking accounts, and home mortgage credit than do the general population. In fact, the extremely rapid growth of credit unions during the postwar era is a direct reflection of the industry's ability to offer services matching the financial needs of millions of households.

Table 15–1   Growth of the U.S. Credit Union Industry: 1945–1982, Selected Years

Year	Number of Credit Unions	Number of Members	Share Deposits ($ millions)	Loans Outstanding ($ millions)	Total Assets ($ millions)
1945	8,683	2,842,989	$ 369	$ 128	$ 435
1950	10,591	4,610,278	850	680	1,005
1955	16,201	8,153,641	2,447	1,934	2,743
1960	20,456	12,037,533	4,975	4,377	5,653
1965	22,119	16,753,106	9,249	8,095	10.552
1970	23,699	22,797,193	15,492	14,108	17,960
1975	22,703	31,151,763	33,116	28,218	37,937
1980	21,731	44,252,733	65,014	48,986	72,484
1981	20,814	45,333,000	68,871	50,448	77,682
1982*	20,481	45,839,000	72,569	50,011	81,351

*As of April 1982.
Source: Credit Union National Association, *Credit Union Report 1982*, p. 2.

---

[1]For a summary of the survey findings, see Credit Union National Association [2], pp. 4–9.

At first, credit unions were chartered only by the states. Then, in 1934, Congress passed the Federal Credit Union Act, authorizing federal charters for institutions that could qualify. Federal charters are issued by the National Credit Union Administration (NCUA) in Washington, D.C. In 1981, the 12,185 federally chartered institutions accounted for 58 percent of the total number of U.S. credit unions. There were at that time 8,934 state-chartered credit unions. The number of credit-union charters is closely linked to population size and population growth. The populous states of California, New York, Pennsylvania, and Texas have accounted for a disproportionate number of credit union charters in recent years.

The Dominance of Small Associations

SIZE DISTRIBUTION OF CREDIT UNIONS

The majority of credit unions are very small, especially when compared to other financial intermediaries. As Table 15–2 reflects, a full 60 percent held assets of less than $1 million apiece in 1981. The mean size credit union holds about $4 million in total assets. Nevertheless, there is a trend toward larger and larger credit unions, with fewer very small ones. The average size credit union is increasing rapidly under the pressure of rising costs, the need for greater efficiency, and a shortage of competent managers.

One of the reasons credit unions are so small, on the average, relative to other financial institutions, is that they cater to the small saver and not to large corporations whose average deposits run in the thousands or millions of dollars. For, example, the average size savings deposit at federal credit unions, according the the National Credit Union Administration, is about $1,270, substantially smaller than at commercial banks or savings and loan associations. Moreover, until recently, all deposits offered by U.S. credit unions were similar to passbook savings accounts at commercial and savings banks. These deposits, which could carry interest rates up

Table 15–2 Number of Credit Unions Grouped by Volume of Assets Held, 1981

Volume of Total Assets Held	Percent of All U.S. Credit Unions
Under $100,000	13.1%
$100,001–$500,000	32.9
$500,001–$1,000,000	15.7
$1,000,001–$2,000,000	13.5
$2,000,001–$5,000,000	12.2
$5,000,001 and over	12.6
Total	100.0%

Source: Credit Union National Association, *Credit Union Report 1981*, p. 7.

to 7 percent, turned over quite rapidly because they could be withdrawn virtually at will by the customer.

New Savings Instruments

The nature and average size of credit union deposits is changing rapidly in the wake of legislation passed by Congress in 1977. On December 20, 1977, federally chartered credit unions were authorized to offer variable-rate share certificates. Many state regulatory agencies followed suit in order to grant their member associations more options in raising funds. The new authority to offer higher-yielding, longer-term thrift deposits undoubtedly increased credit union operating costs. For example, in 1981 the average annual dividend rate on passbook savings accounts at federal credit unions was 6.76 percent. In contrast, the most common rate paid on all types of share certificates during 1981 was in the 12 to 15 percent range.[2] Adding to the trend toward higher interest costs, credit unions were permitted to offer money market certificates (MMCs) in 1978, to compete with commercial banks and savings and loan associations.

While it was hoped that these new savings plans would bring greater stability to credit union deposit flows and allow credit unions to make longer-term loans, these gains did not materialize. Instead, under the pressure of competition from other financial institutions and an increasingly financially sophisticated consumer, there was a dramatic shift in the composition of credit union deposits toward more expensive and more interest-sensitive accounts. Table 15–3 illustrates this trend. Regular low-yield passbook shares declined sharply in relative importance, while share certificates (including MMCs) rose rapidly, approaching one third of all federal credit union savings accounts at year-end 1981. Moreover, the more interest-sensitive of these accounts fluctuated markedly with varying interest rates and economic conditions. Credit unions experienced wide swings in deposit growth, creating substantial liquidity pressures. The problem was exacerbated by the great success of money market funds in attracting small savers in the late 1970s and early 1980s.[3]

Declining Numbers and Increasing Size

As we noted earlier, the number of credit unions is very large—about 20,000—and in total exceeds the number of commercial banks, mutual savings banks, and savings and loan associations combined. But their numbers are falling and their average size is increasing rapidly. In short, under pressure from rising costs and increased competition from other fi-

[2]See National Credit Union Administration, *1981 Annual Report* [16], p. 17.
[3]See Chapter 16 for a discussion of money market funds.

Table 15–3   Recent Changes in the Composition of Savings Accounts at Federal Credit Unions

Type of Savings Account	*Years*			
	1981	*1980*	*1979*	*1978*
Total savings held	100.0%	100.0%	100.0%	100.0%
Regular passbook shares	69.2	75.6	86.8	97.3
Share certificates, total	30.8	24.4	13.2	2.7
Money market certificates	16.3	15.1	8.8	2.4
Other certificates	14.5	9.3	4.4	0.3

Source: National Credit Union Administration, *1981 Annual Report*, p. 11.

nancial institutions, the credit union industry is consolidating into fewer but larger associations which may yield greater efficiency. Moreover, if the industry continues to expand its services at the present rate in order to compete more successfully with commercial and savings banks for consumers' funds, the pressures for consolidation into fewer but larger credit unions are likely to intensify.[4]

Despite the existence of thousands of very small credit unions, there are a few very large ones. As an example, Figure 15–1 lists the 50 largest federally chartered credit unions at year-end 1980. The largest of all, the U.S. Navy Credit Union, held $866 million in assets on December 31, 1980. Another military-oriented association, the Pentagon Credit Union, ranked second with almost $533 million in assets. Other large credit unions were centered around such major corporations as Eastern Airlines, Hughes Aircraft, Lockheed, IBM, McDonnell Douglas, Rockwell, Litton Industries, Pan American Airways, LTV, and International Harvester. And, as noted above, pressure to develop such large credit unions is likely to grow in future years as associations strive to keep unit operating expenses as low as possible, develop costly and somewhat risky new services, stabilize their cash flows, and attract increasingly scarce managerial talent.

---

[4]This trend toward credit union consolidation is reinforced by the strong competition which apparently exists between credit union thrift accounts and deposits of comparable size and maturity at savings and loans and commercial banks and between thrift accounts and marketable bonds. For example, a study by Koot [11] finds that credit union shares are competitive substitutes with savings and loan shares and time and savings deposits at banks. Share accounts also are competitive substitutes with high-quality bonds sold in the open market, but are more closely asociated with liquid deposits offered by competing intermediaries rather than open-market bonds. However, Taylor [19] finds that selected nonprice features, such as convenience for the customer and image of the credit union, are also important features in the selection of credit unions as places to save. This finding probably reflects the fact that credit unions tend to advertise heavily, sell the same group of customers many different services, and emphasize personal contact with their customers.

Figure 15–1 The 50 Largest Federally Chartered Credit Unions as of Year-end 1980

Rank 1980	Name of Credit Union	City and State	Year Chartered	Total Assets 12/31/80 ($000)
1	Navy	Washington, D.C.	1947	$866,154
2	Pentagon	Arlington, Va.	1935	532,837
3	Alaska USA	Anchorage, Alaska	1948	308,948
4	Eastern Airlines Employees	Miami, Fla.	1937	302,717
5	Hughes Aircraft Employees	El Segundo, Calif.	1940	283,738
6	Lockheed	Burbank, Calif.	1937	198,489
7	San Diego Navy	San Diego, Calif.	1953	186,067
8	Dearborn	Dearborn, Mich.	1950	178,483
9	IBM Poughkeepsie Employees	Poughkeepsie, N.Y.	1963	166,369
10	Eglin	Ft. Walton Beach, Fla.	1954	158,713
11	Lockheed Missile Employees	Sunnyvale, Calif.	1956	157,426
12	Security Service	San Antonio, Tex.	1956	147,107
13	McDonnell Douglas West	Torrance, Calif.	1935	143,213
14	Jax Navy	Jacksonville, Fla.	1952	142,936
15	Rockwell	Downey, Calif.	1937	137,651
16	Redstone	Huntsville, Ala.	1951	132,325
17	East Hartford Aircraft	East Hartford, Conn.	1935	130,722
18	Northwest	Washington, D.C.	1947	130,284
19	Bethpage	Bethpage, N.Y.	1941	129,529
20	Tower	Annapolis Junction, Md.	1953	126,409
21	California Teachers	Los Angeles, Calif.	1974	123,319
22	Lockheed Georgia Employees	Marietta, Ga.	1951	118,696
23	Andrews	Washington, D.C.	1948	117,404
24	State Department	Arlington, Va.	1935	113,981
25	Suncoast Schools	Tampa, Fla.	1978	107,557
26	Travis	Travis AFB, Calif.	1951	104,644
27	FAA Western	Los Angeles, Calif.	1949	101,256
28	Litton Employees	Canoga Park, Calif.	1957	99,535
29	Randolph Brooks	Universal City, Tex.	1952	99,126
30	Mather	Sacramento, Calif.	1953	96,721
31	Robins	Warner Robins, Ga.	1954	94,350
32	Pan American	Jamaica, N.Y.	1940	92,302
33	ENT	Colorado Springs, Colo.	1957	84,879
34	Maxwell-Gunter	Montgomery, Ala.	1955	84,423
35	IBM Endicott Employees	Endicott, N.Y.	1966	84,165
36	Chattanooga TVA Employees	Chattanooga, Tenn.	1936	83,039
37	Kern Schools	Bakersfield, Calif.	1940	83,008
38	Bank Fund Staff	Washington, D.C.	1947	81,846
39	Langely	Hampton, Va.	1936	80,987
40	Desert Schools	Phoenix, Ariz.	1939	80,865
41	SAFE	North Highlands, Calif.	1940	80,392
42	66	Bartlesville, Okla.	1939	79,906
43	Keesler	Keesler AFB, Miss.	1947	79,073
44	Pen Air	Pensacola, Fla.	1936	78,108
45	Aberdeen Proving Ground	Aberdeen, Md.	1938	77,595
46	LTV	Grand Prairie, Tex.	1936	77,100
47	ORNL	Oak Ridge, Tenn.	1948	76,553
48	Westernaire	Los Angeles, Calif.	1948	75,420
49	Los Angeles City Employees	Los Angeles, Calif.	1936	75,301
50	Charleston Naval Shipyard	Charleston, S.C.	1936	74,996

Source: National Credit Union Administration, *1980 Annual Report*, pp. 51–52.

One of the essential differences between a credit union and other financial intermediaries is that not everyone can deposit funds or borrow from a particular credit union. To avail yourself of the services offered by a credit union, you must be a *member* and there are specific qualifications for membership. Most credit unions are organized by individuals who work for the same employer or industry; that is, most credit unions are related to their members' occupation or place of work. Thus the Eastern Airlines credit union, headquartered in Miami, serves only employees of that major airline company, while California Teachers credit union in Los Angeles serves members of the teaching profession in the state of California.

As Table 15–4 shows, more than 60 percent of all credit unions have members who share a common occupation in private industry or in education. Another large group of credit unions is centered around members who belong to the same association—church, lodge, labor union, or even students in a particular school or school district. Governmental employees make up another large group which has organized several credit unions, some of which rank among the industry's largest. Examples include the Navy and Pentagon credit unions, the State Department and Chattanooga TVA Employees credit unions, and the Los Angeles and Hawaii State Employees credit unions.

Traditionally, at least 100 potential members are necessary to apply for a credit union charter. However, even small groups have been able to join the credit union movement by affiliating with an existing association. There has also been a trend in recent years toward more liberally defining

THE BASIS FOR JOINING A CREDIT UNION

Table 15–4   The Basis for Membership in U.S. Credit Unions

Membership	*Percentage of All U.S. Credit Unions Reporting Whose Members Fall in Category Shown Below*
Members sharing a common occupation in private industry or in education	62.4%
Members all belonging to the same association or service organization	17.3
Members employed by the same governmental unit	15.8
Members all residing in the same community, neighborhood, or state	4.1
Total of all credit unions reporting	100.0%

Note: Column may not add to 100.0 percent due to rounding.
*Occupation-oriented credit unions in the private sector include those whose members are employed in manufacturing, wholesale and retail trade, and other private business endeavors as well as in education.
Source: Credit Union National Association, *Credit Union Report 1981*, p. 7.

groups with a common interest or association in order to expand the credit union movement. A good example of this expanded membership idea is the chartering of a few associations based solely on the fact that members reside in the same community or state. For example, the Wisconsin credit union is designed to serve members who reside in that state. A person who believes he or she is eligible for membership in a particular credit union may apply for membership and, in most cases, must pay a small entrance fee.

HOW CREDIT UNIONS ARE ORGANIZED

Most financial institutions are organized as corporations with stockholders, boards of directors, a management team to conduct daily business, and a staff to assist management in carrying out day-to-day operations. Credit unions, however, have their own unique organizational form, which is similar to the corporate form in some respects, highly dissimilar in other respects.

The Owners and the Board of Directors

For example, the "stockholders" in a credit union—its owners—are the members who acquire a voting "share of ownership" by making deposits in and borrowing from the association. Members elect the credit union's principal officers and vote on which services to offer and the interest fees charged on loans and paid on deposits. Like a true democracy, each member has one and only one vote regardless of how much money he or she has deposited in or borrowed from the credit union. Like corporate stockholders, members receive all earnings left over after expenses and additions to equity reserves. Earnings are paid out usually in two forms—dividends on savings accounts and interest rebates on outstanding loans.

Credit union policy is set by the board of directors, who are elected by the members. It is the board which lays down the rules for accepting deposits and making loans and which determines the range of services that meet the financial needs of the membership. Generally, board members are selected once a year at the annual meeting, and both the board and the association's officers must be members. The board serves without pay, though the credit union's treasurer is usually salaried.

Credit Union Committees and Management

Much of the administrative work of a credit union is done by committee. For example, analogous to the loan committee in a commercial bank, a credit committee (selected by the membership) is used to approve or disapprove loan requests. New members are attracted through the efforts of the education committee, which is responsible for the advertising function in a credit union. An auditing committee is usually appointed by the association's board of directors to make sure that sound record-keeping practices are being followed. Committee members serve without pay, contributing their voluntary services to insure that the credit union meets the financial needs of its membership as fully as possible.

The management of day-to-day operations in a credit union is headed up by four principal officers—the president, one or more vice presidents, a secretary, and a treasurer. Particularly in smaller credit unions, these officers (with the exception of the treasurer) are often nonpaid volunteers. In fact, a significant problem credit unions have faced for many years is the lack of a sufficient supply of qualified professional managers; moreover, this shortage of qualified management seems to be growing, contributing to the consolidation trend in the industry discussed earlier.

The responsibilities of credit union officers are not significantly different from those of similar officers in most private corporations. The president has overall responsibilities for day-to-day management of the credit union and conducts board meetings. The credit union vice president normally chairs one or more standing committees and fills in when the president is not available to fulfill his or her responsibilities. The secretary of a credit union assists in the preparation and distribution of reports to members and prepares minutes of all official meetings. Finally, one of the most important of all credit union officers is the treasurer, who as we noted above, is often the only salaried officer. He or she will oversee the association's staff of lending officers, tellers, and other staff members and maintain the credit union's books.

Organizational Structure of the Industry

There is probably minimal competition among individual credit unions for members and deposits (though, as we will see later on, competition between credit unions and other depository institutions has intensified in recent years). This lack of strong competition among members of the same industry, reinforced by membership requirements and voluntary service, has resulted in a tradition of close cooperation among individual credit unions—sharing ideas, advertising programs, and operating information.

As a whole, the industry is well organized at local, state, and national levels, making individual credit unions part of a national credit union system. The industry's chief organization at the national level is the Credit Union National Association (CUNA). Established in 1934, CUNA is literally the voice of the industry with regard to national or international issues affecting credit unions. Through its offices in Madison, Wisconsin, CUNA provides a substantial volume of educational materials to its member associations (which include more than 90 percent of U.S. credit unions) and to the public and represents the industry before legislative bodies and governmental commissions. CUNA conducts research on the

impact of new laws and other recent developments on credit union operations. It also pursues an aggressive public relations campaign in support
of the credit union movement. While CUNA's activities center upon the
United States, there is also a World Council of Credit Unions, which performs some of the same functions for the credit union movement around
the globe.

Credit unions are also well organized at local and state levels. For example, credit unions in the local market area or region may pool some of
their activities (such as advertising or education of employees) through a
chapter. Chapters and individual associations, in turn, usually join at
least one of two (and sometimes both) state or regional organizations
known as corporate credit unions and leagues. In 1981, 42 corporate credit unions provided a source of loans for credit unions in need of liquidity.
In addition, individual credit unions can pool their investment funds
through a corporate credit union and earn prevailing interest returns in
the nation's money market. Credit union leagues, on the other hand, provide operating information, educational services for employees, advertising, and legal advice for individual credit unions in a particular state. The
state leagues represent the industry on issues coming before state legislatures and commissions and aid in the chartering of new credit unions. In a
majority of states, the leagues operate service corporations which supply
products and services needed by individual associations. All 50 states as
well as the District of Columbia have credit union leagues.

DEPOSITS, LOANS, AND OTHER SERVICES PROVIDED BY THE INDUSTRY

New Services and Advantages over Other Lenders of Funds

An almost bewildering array of new services, mainly centered around
the taking of deposits and the making of loans, have been offered by credit
unions in recent years. In their lending activities, credit unions appear to
have some definite advantages over other consumer lending institutions,
particularly commercial banks, finance companies, and savings banks.
Because their loans average much smaller than those granted by other institutional lenders, are generally secured credit, and are confined to members, many financial analysts contend that credit unions have less need for
extensive credit files on their customers. Moreover, in most cases the rate
of default on installment loans appears to be lower at credit unions compared to loan default rates experienced by many other consumer installment lenders (particularly finance companies).

There is some research evidence that the average cost of making and
servicing installment loans is lower for credit unions than for many other
lenders. One reason is the extensive volunteer management assistance
provided by members. This lower level of management overhead fre-

quently results in lower loan rates.[5] However, credit unions, like other financial intermediaries today, increasingly are diversifying the services they offer the public, and this movement has profound implications for their cost structure.[6] If the experience of the commercial banking industry is an appropriate indicator, diversification into new service lines typically brings rising unit costs, greater volume, and often a declining profit margin.

Increasingly, the services offered by credit unions are bringing them into direct competition with commercial banks, savings and loan associations, mutual saving banks, and other depository institutions. For example, like many commercial banks, larger credit unions frequently operate automated teller machines which are available to members around the clock. The industry is working on a nationwide ATM system which would allow credit union members to access their accounts at thousands of different locations across the contry.

Beginning in the 1970s, credit unions began to offer credit and debit cards for the convenience of their customers in making purchases in retail stores. Credit cards allow the customer to postpone payment for the purchase of goods and services, while debit cards merely allow the customer to pay for a purchase now by either serving as identification to guarantee a check or to transfer funds electronically from the customer's account to the store's account. At first, few credit unions ventured into the plastic card field, but now thousands offer either credit or debit card services or both. More recently, associations have competed with banks and other thrift institutions in bidding aggressively for Individual Retirement Accounts (IRAs), which permit members to place a portion of their current income in savings for retirement and to shelter that income from taxes until it is actually withdrawn from the IRA.

Role in the Payments System

For many years, commercial banks faced little or no competition in the payments field because only they possessed the power to accept demand deposits (checking accounts). In 1981, about 3,700 U.S. credit unions

---

[5]Flannery [7] estimates that the average annual cost of making and servicing an installment loan is $20 for credit union, $48 for a commercial bank, and $51 for a consumer finance company.

[6]One example of service diversification is the offering of insurance policies. Credit life insurance and disability insurance is frequently offered in association with the granting of loans. A number of credit unions have developed life insurance programs for their depositors in cooperation with a life insurance company. Typically, the amount of life insurance offered to a customer is tied to the value of the customer's share deposit up to a predetermined maximum amount.

were offering so-called *share draft services* through nearly 4 million accounts. These permit depositors to write drafts against their account balances and to pay bills just as they would with a bank check. Share drafts were authorized for federal credit unions with passage of the Depository Institutions Deregulation and Monetary Control Act of 1980. Many states have granted similar authority to the credit unions they charter.

In 1981, U.S. credit union members held $3.3 billion in share draft balances. The new service is expected to spread rapidly as more credit unions see tangible benefits from entering the nation's payments system and attracting transactions accounts. In an important sense, credit unions are being forced into the share draft business by the pressure of competition. Commercial banks, savings and loans, and mutual savings banks are offering interest-bearing checkable deposits (principally NOW accounts and money market deposits) in great numbers, a step which forces many credit unions to act or lose some of their deposit customers to another financial institution.

In the competition for checking account business, credit unions would appear to possess some important advantages over banks, savings and loans, and other competing institutions.[7] For example, when a share draft is written by a credit union member in payment for goods and services, a carbonless duplicate is automatically created, lessening the importance of the customer remembering to write down every item in a check register. Share drafts are usually truncated so that when the draft reaches the final bank, the essential information is microfilmed. All further processing is handled by computer and the paper draft is not returned either to the customer or to his credit union. Instead, the credit union and customer receive a printout of all drafts written against their accounts, thus providing a convenient summary of all financial transactions but minimizing the transfer of paper items.

Probably the most significant advantage to the customer of the share draft account is that it generally pays dividends (interest) on the average or minimum balance remaining on deposit during the dividend period. Thus share drafts are a combination of savings and checking accounts. Moreover, the yield is often quite high, offering the customer an advantageous return on balances held mainly for transactions purposes. However, this can also be a real disadvantage for credit unions not operating at a high level of efficiency, because share drafts, with higher activity levels than ordinary savings accounts, can significantly increase operating costs. The cost of processing share drafts, including return-item charges,

---

[7]The discussion of share drafts in this and subsequent paragraphs is based, in part, upon an article by one of the authors appearing in *The Canadian Banker & ICB Review* (see reference [17]).

account maintenance fees, and data transmission charges, has been variously estimated at 6 to 10 cents per draft. Yet many credit unions have adopted extremely liberal service fees and low charges for each draft written.

In their penetration of the payments system through share drafts, credit unions appear to be looking ahead to an era when most payments are made electronically via computer terminal and perhaps even home TV screen rather than through pieces of paper. As we will discuss in Chapter 23, the United States is rapidly moving forward with plans to link computers and provide electronic clearance of drafts against financial institutions involved in the payments process. This is already well on its way for transactions between financial institutions through automated clearing houses (ACHs) and for large payroll firms that often use computer tapes to automatically deposit employee paychecks—so-called wholesale electronic funds transfer systems. Moving more slowly, but gradually becoming a reality, are electronic transfers of funds (EFTS) between customers and their financial institutions, such as through point-of-sale terminals (POS), telephone transactions, and, more distantly, home computer terminals and TV screens. The new payments technology will all but erase the traditional distinction between checking and savings deposits, since funds can be moved from one account to another instantaneously. However, the managers of many credit unions, savings and loans, and savings banks feel they must gain access to the nation's payments system through NOW accounts, share drafts, checkable money market deposits, telephone transfers, and the like if they hope to be able to protect their share of the deposit market.

Of particular concern to credit union managers is what will happen to the consumer's dollar when automatic electronic deposit of payrolls spreads nationwide. Deposit of payroll checks in a financial institution via computer tape instead of pieces of paper will give a strong competitive edge to those institutions that are already part of the payments process, especially commercial banks. The customer's entire paycheck is likely to be automatically deposited with one financial institution, resulting in a potential loss of deposit funds to other financial intermediaries. Today, credit unions are participating in the direct deposit of federal social security payments and military payrolls. Direct computer deposits of payrolls from *private* employers is a growing service offered by credit unions.[8] At

---

[8]To some extent, credit unions have sheltered themselves over the years from losses of deposits to institutions with direct computer deposits by aggressively advertising payroll savings plans. In fact, approximately 95 percent of all U.S. credit unions have a program in which members can automatically have a predetermined amount deducted from each paycheck and placed in a credit union share deposit or applied to repayment of a credit union loan.

the so-called wholesale level of electronic banking, credit unions were granted access in the late 1970s to the nationwide system of automated clearinghouses, which provide for electronic transfer of funds among financial institutions. At the retail level of electronic banking, some credit unions have introduced automated tellers and point-of-sale terminals in stores and shopping centers.

Related to the share draft, credit unions were authorized (along with other U.S. depository institutions) to offer money market deposit accounts (MMDAs) beginning in December 1982. Issued in accordance with provisions of the Garn–St Germain Depository Institutions Act of 1982, MMDAs were designed to be competitive with share accounts offered by money market mutual funds. As we noted in earlier chapters, MMDAs have no legally imposed interest-rate ceilings for accounts maintaining an average balance of at least $2,500, though the interest rate can be guaranteed for up to a month. Up to six automatic or telephone transfers from the account are permitted per month and up to three of these may be effected by check. However, the customer appearing in person may make an unlimited number of withdrawals from an MMDA. Following their introduction, MMDAs grew rapidly as substantial amounts of funds were shifted by depositors from other time and savings accounts, money market mutual funds, and even from investments in bonds, stocks, and money market instruments.

Credit Function

Credit unions are also moving rapidly into the mortgage loan field. Prior to 1977 only state-chartered credit unions could engage in long-term mortgage financing in those states specifically authorizing the service. However, following Congressional action in that year, the National Credit Union Administration issued new regulations permitting federally chartered credit unions to grant up to 30-year home mortgage loans to members. In 1981, NCUAs board ruled that federally chartered credit unions could make home mortgages with variable interest rates.

A further step was made to liberalize the rules surrounding real estate lending by credit unions when Congress passed the Garn–St Germain Depository Institutions Act of 1982. As we noted in the previous chapter, this law sharply reduced the proportion of total assets which savings and loan associations—the nation's number one home mortgage lender—were required to devote to residential mortgage loans. Concerned that this step might significantly curtail the flow of loanable funds into housing, Congress, through the 1982 law, granted federally chartered credit unions much broader real estate lending authority, expanding their ability to make longer-term mortgages. Refinancing loans and mortgage credit not secured by first liens were permitted. Restrictions on the median sales price of residences against which a credit union can lend money were significantly liberalized. While only a minority of credit unions actually hold a significant quantity of first-mortgage loans, the volume of such loans is expected to increase significantly over the next decade, bringing credit unions into direct competition with commercial banks, savings and loans, and mutual savings banks in the financing of family dwellings.

Other Services

Other services offered by U.S. credit unions include money orders and traveler's checks—where they compete directly with banks—as well as travel planning and financial planning. Regardless of future developments, the present array of services offered by the industry represents a radical change in the role of credit unions within the U.S. financial system. Just as other financial intermediaries have broadened their services, so must the credit union if it is to survive and grow in the increasingly intense competition now shaping up for the consumer's credit and deposit needs.

In the preceding paragraphs we have focused upon the many new services credit unions have developed in recent years. These new services have begun to have a significant impact upon the composition of assets (uses of funds) and liabilities (sources of funds) drawn upon by the industry, as our discussion in this section will show.

PRINCIPAL SOURCES AND USES OF FUNDS FOR THE INDUSTRY

Sources of Funds

Table 15–5 presents a picture of the principal sources and uses of funds for federally chartered credit unions in 1970, 1980, and 1981 and the changes which occurred over the intervening decade.[9] It is clear that the industry's principal source of funds is and always has been the share accounts (deposits) of members. As shown in Table 15–5, members' savings accounts provided 90 percent of industry funds sources in 1980 and 1981 and 86 percent in 1970.

The growth of credit union shares has been especially rapid since insurance, through the National Credit Union Share Insurance Fund (NCUSIF), was set up in 1970. Larger-size deposits have flowed in since the creation of NCUSIF, particularly those over $5,000, which accounted for just over half of the dollar volume of credit union deposits as the 1980s began. However, it should be noted that credit unions experienced substantial

---

[9]The data presented in this section on credit union industry funds sources and uses encompass only federally chartered credit unions due to the lack of complete information on state-chartered credit union activities.

Table 15–5   Distribution of Sources and Uses of Funds in Federal Credit Unions:
1970, 1980, and 1981

	Years			Change	
Item	1970	1980	1981	1970–80	1980–81
Sources, total	100.0%	100.0%	100.0%	—	—
Members' savings	86.1	90.4	90.2	4.3	−0.2
Reserves and undivided earnings	10.3	5.5	6.1	−4.8	0.6
Notes payable:	2.6	2.1	1.7	−0.5	−0.4
Certificates of indebtedness	0.7	0.8	0.8	0.1	—
Other	1.9	1.3	0.9	0.6	−0.4
Other sources	1.0	2.0	2.0	1.0	—
Uses, total	100.0	100.0	100.0	—	—
Cash	5.1	1.7	2.2	−3.4	0.5
Loans to:					
Members	78.7	65.7	64.9	−13.0	−0.8
Other credit unions	1.2	*	0.1	−1.2	—
Liquid assets, total:	13.7	30.0	30.1	−16.2	0.1
U.S. government securities	10.2	10.1	8.7	−0.1	−1.4
Share/deposits at S&Ls and banks	2.6	11.3	11.0	8.7	−0.3
Shares/deposits in other CUs	0.9	7.9	9.8	7.0	1.9
Other investments	NA†	0.7	0.6	—†	−0.1
Other uses	1.3	2.6	2.8	1.3	0.2

Note: The figures for U.S. government securities include federal agency securities and common trust investments. The figure for shares/deposits at S&Ls and banks includes only savings and loan shares for 1970. The figure for share deposits in other credit unions (CUs) includes deposits at corporate centrals, while other investments contain deposits at the Central Liquidity Facility (CLF).
*Less than 0.5.
†Not available.
Source: National Credit Union Administration, *1980 Annual Report*, p. 13; *1981 Annual Report*, p. 14.

outflows of larger size deposits during the late 1970s and early 1980s to money market funds, which offered rates on share accounts not restricted by legal interest-rate ceilings.[10] In fact, the proportion of credit union deposits accounted for by large ($5,000-plus), interest-sensitive deposits began falling in 1979. Credit unions appear to have little difficulty competing for small size deposits, but have not been as successful in attracting and retaining larger size accounts.

The average size credit union deposit is very small compared to deposits in banks. This is not surprising since credit unions are exclusively household financial intermediaries, while banks can draw on large corporate accounts. At year-end 1981, federal credit unions held 28.6 million in savings accounts, and over 24 million of these held $2,000 or less in average balance. Fewer than 2 million savings accounts at federal credit unions exceed $5,000, and only a very minor portion of credit union deposits are so large that they exceed federal deposit insurance limits.

---

[10]See Chapter 16 for a discussion of money market mutual funds.

Reserves and undivided capital—the cushion of capital held by credit unions to help protect depositors—have fallen as a proportion of total sources of funds over the past decade. Like commercial banks, credit unions have relied more heavily in recent years upon borrowed sources of funds (principally in the form of certificates of indebtedness and borrowing from other depository institutions) to finance their operations. The relative decline in reserves and undivided earnings is partly the result of lower reserve requirements imposed on federal credit unions after 1970. Under the law, federal associations must set aside at least 6 percent of the amount of their "risk" assets (defined as loans to members minus government-guaranteed loans and those secured by share deposits) as a reserve for losses. This reserve is built up over time by diverting a portion of each year's gross income into the regular reserve account.

A major change was made in federal regulations applying to credit union reserves in 1980 when Congress passed the Depository Institutions Deregulation and Monetary Control Act. Reserve requirements determined by the Federal Reserve Board were imposed on all depository institutions, including credit unions that are federally insured or eligible to apply for federal insurance. However, these reserve requirements applied only to transactions accounts, such as credit union share drafts. For transactions deposits amounting to less than $28.9 million (which would include virtually all credit unions), the reserve requirement is 3 percent. The purpose of these requirements is to grant the Federal Reserve Board closer control over the growth of transactions deposits—the principal component of the nation's money supply.

Uses of Funds

Credit unions exist principally to offer savings accounts and make loans to their members. Therefore, it should not surprise us to learn that on the asset side of their balance sheet, loans to members rank first. For example, as Table 15–5 shows, loans to members accounted for about 65 percent of federal credit union assets in 1981. Investments in marketable securities—generally highly liquid U.S. government securities and deposits at banks, savings and loans, and other credit unions—have always run a distant second in importance. In 1981, for example, liquid assets of this sort accounted for only about 30 percent of industry assets.

Still, there is an interesting trend in loans and security investments now underway. The growth of credit union loans has become more volatile and uncertain in a more volatile economy. Until 1979, loans generally increased as a percentage of industry assets, while investments in marketable securities generally declined. As the decade of the 1980s began, however, the reverse trend set in. Loans dropped sharply under the influence of two factors: (1) legal interest-rate ceilings frequently prevented credit unions from lending at high enough rates to offset rising costs, and (2) economic recession and rising unemployment (especially among members of industrial credit unions) reduced the demand for loans. In addition, as unemployment rose in the early 1980s, many consumers began to use installment loans more conservatively while trying to expand their savings as a precaution against possible loss of a job. This combination of a softening economy and restrictive loan-rate ceilings forced many credit unions to divert more of their incoming deposits into government securities and other liquid assets.

Interestingly, after years of gaining on other consumer lending institutions—increasing their market share of total consumer installment credit—the industry began to lose some of its market share as the 1980s began. As Table 15–6 indicates, despite their extremely rapid growth in recent years, credit unions still hold a fairly small share of the nation's installment loan market, representing only about 14 percent of all such consumer loans outstanding in 1983. More recently, however, finance companies (many of these controlled by bank holding companies) and savings and loan associations have gained in the consumer credit market at the expense of credit unions and commercial banks. The gains scored by savings and loans are not surprising in view of major federal legislation (particularly the Depository Institutions Deregulation Act of 1980 and the Garn–St Germain Depository Institutions Act of 1982) granting S&Ls much broader consumer loan powers, making them more effective competitors with credit unions.

Just as the loan total has changed in recent years, the *composition* of industry loans is also undergoing some interesting changes. While credit un-

Table 15–6 Market Shares of the Consumer Installment Loan Market Accounted for by Major Institutional Lenders: July 31, 1983

Type of Lender	Amount Outstanding ($ millions)	Percent Distribution
Total, all lenders	$358,020	100.0%
Financial institutions, total	$330,120	92.2
Commercial banks	159,666	44.6
Finance companies	97,319	27.2
Credit unions	49,139	13.7
Miscellaneous lenders*	23,996	6.7
Retail stores†	27,900	7.8

*Includes savings and loan associations, mutual savings banks, and gasoline companies.
†Includes auto dealers, but 30-day charge accounts held by travel and entertainment firms are excluded.
Source: Board of Governors of the Federal Reserve System.

ions can lend money to other credit unions, as Table 15–7 shows, the bulk of their loans (over 90 percent) goes to members. Of the loans made to members, the single most important form of credit goes to support the purchase of new and used automobiles. Historically, auto loans have dominated credit union loan portfolios, but this dominance is fading. The reasons are well known: (1) auto sales slowed in the late 1970s and early 1980s due to a soft economy and foreign competition, (2) consumers bought smaller autos for fuel efficiency, and (3) many consumers were literally priced out of the auto market by high prices and high interest rates. As Table 15–7 indicates, "other" consumer loans now account for more than half of consumer credit held by credit unions. Leading loan categories today include credit to cover household expenses and home repair, boat loans, recreational vehicle loans, medical loans, and debt consolidation loans.

The majority of credit union loans are secured. The principal security used is automobiles, followed by member deposits pledged behind the loans. Most loans are comparatively short in maturity, with about half carrying maturities of two years or less. Most short-term credit union loans cover personal, family, and household expenses. Loans on durables, real estate, and business loans generally are the longest-term loans in a credit union's portfolio.

Under federal and most state laws, credit unions may charge no more than 15 percent per year on the unpaid balance of a loan, including all

Table 15–7 Changes in Types of Credit Union Loans Outstanding: 1975 to 1981 ($ millions)

| | | | | *Type of Credit* | | | |
| | | *Total Consumer Credit Outstanding Held by CUs* | | *Automobile* | | *Other* | |
Year	*Total Loans Outstanding at Credit Unions*	*Amount*	*Percent of Total CU Loans*	*Amount*	*Percent of Total Consumer Credit Outstanding*	*Amount*	*Percent of Total Consumer Credit Outstanding*
1975	$28,168	$25,666	91.1%	$12,741	49.6%	$12,925	50.4%
1976	34,310	31,169	90.8	15,238	48.9	15,931	51.1
1977	41,845	37,605	89.9	18,099	48.1	19,506	51.9
1978	50,269	44,334	88.2	21,200	47.8	23,134	52.2
1979	52,224	46,517	89.1	22,244	47.8	24,273	52.2
1980	48,983	44,041	89.9	21,060	47.8	22,981	52.2
1981	50,877	45,954	90.3	21,975	47.8	23,979	52.2

Source: Board of Governors of the Federal Reserve System and National Credit Union Administration.

charges incident to granting the loan.[11] The majority of credit unions give their members credit life or other insurance protection free. Default and delinquency rates on credit union loans generally are low compared to other lending institutions. However, as the 1970s drew to a close and the 1980s began, delinquency rates rose significantly. During this period, economic conditions deteriorated, resulting in substantial unemployment, especially in the manufacturing sector served by many credit unions. By year-end 1980, approximately 4.5 percent of the number and 3.3 percent of the dollar volume of loans granted by federal credit unions were reported as being delinquent two months or longer. This represented roughly a 25 percent increase in the loan delinquency rate between 1977 and 1980. In 1981, however, loan delinquency rates dropped slightly, to 4.3 percent of the number and 2.9 percent of the volume of loans outstanding.

Smaller credit unions generally have a greater problem with delinquencies and defaults since many are manned by volunteers or part-time employees who frequently have less expertise in credit analysis. For example, in December 1981 almost 13 percent of loans insured by federally chartered associations with assets below $50,000 were delinquent two months or more. Interestingly, the delinquency rate has been rising faster at larger credit unions in recent years. Still, the number of credit union failures is comparatively small. For example, 265 federal credit unions underwent liquidation in 1980, or between 1 and 2 percent of the industry's total population. Of this total the majority—236 associations—were placed in involuntary closings since deposits were first federally insured in 1970. Thus, while the failure rate in the industry remained comparatively low, a definite upward trend set in as economic conditions deteriorated. Moreover, the number of new charterings reached record lows as the 1980s began, and cancellations of charters—especially among industrial credit unions—posted record highs for the post–World War II era.

THE INDUSTRY'S STATEMENT OF EARNINGS AND EXPENSES

Industry Revenues

We observed earlier that loans to members are the number one item on the asset side of the credit union's balance sheet. Not surprisingly, then, interest revenues earned from lending to members account for the largest share (about two thirds) of the industry's gross revenues. A distant second in importance is income from investments in securities and deposits, accounting for about one third of total industry revenues. Due to recent

---

[11]The official credit union loan-rate ceiling as established under the Depository Institution: Deregulation and Monetary Control Act of 1980 is 15 percent per annum. However, the industry's federal regulatory agency—the National Credit Union Administration—was granted authority to increase this ceiling for periods of 18 months. The federal ceiling rate was first moved to 21 percent in December 1980 to deal with an upward surge in money market rates which, in the view of the NCUA, endangered the safety of some credit unions.

weaknesses in loan demand, the proportion of revenues accounted for by investment has increased, while loan income generally has declined in relative terms.

Expense Items

Credit union expenses have increased rapidly in recent years, squeezing net income at times. As reflected in Table 15–8, the wages, salaries, and fringe benefits paid to employees were by far the most important expense category for federal credit unions (accounting for about 40 percent of total expenses). Other major expense items include insurance services provided members who borrow, office operations, and interest on borrowed money. Note that interest paid on deposits is *not* technically an expense item for a credit union, since the depositor is really an *owner* and receives a portion of the association's net income after expenses.

Dividends Paid Out to Members

The majority of credit union income (almost 60 percent in 1981) is returned to members in the form of dividends. Indeed, the percentage of in-

Table 15–8   Revenues, Expenses, and Net Income of Federal Credit Unions: 1981

Revenue, Expense, and Income Items	Dollar Volume ($ millions)	Percentage Distribution
Total revenues	$5,072	100.0%
Revenue sources:		
Interest on loans*	3,347	66.0
Income from investments	1,643	32.3
Other income sources	81	1.6
Total expenses†	$1,676	100.0
Expense categories:		
Employee compensation	662	39.5
Association dues	21	1.3
Examination and supervision fees	20	1.2
Interest on borrowed money	99	5.9
Office occupancy expense	62	3.7
Educational and promotional expense	34	2.0
Office operations expense	222	13.3
Professional and outside services	112	6.7
Conventions and conferences	29	1.7
Annual meeting expense	11	0.7
Members' insurance	163	9.7
Other expenses	240	14.3
Net income	$3,396	

*Figure is net of interest refunds to borrowers.
†Figure excludes year-end dividend payments.
Source: *Annual Report of the National Credit Union Administration, 1981*, Washington, D.C., p. 17.

come accounted for by dividends has risen in recent years, reflecting a shift of member deposits to higher-yielding accounts and more frequent crediting of dividends. In 1974, federal credit unions were permitted to credit members with savings dividends as frequently as daily, instead of quarterly, as called for by earlier provisions of the Federal Credit Union Act. Average savings dividend rates paid by U.S. credit unions have risen sharply in recent years. For example, in 1981 federally chartered associations paid an average dividend of 7.76 percent on regular share accounts, compared to only 6.15 percent in 1976. The higher rates paid are traceable to greater competition from other financial institutions, a shift by credit union members toward savings certificates paying higher rates, and an attempt by credit union managers to protect their deposits against disintermediation due to higher prevailing interest rates.

Many credit unions pay interest refunds to their borrowing members, which lowers the individual borrower's net-interest cost. Refunds in the 11 to 20 percent range are the most prevalent. There is a trend toward lower interest refunds or none at all due to increased pressure on credit union earnings from rising expenses and the need to pay higher dividends on savings accounts in order to keep credit unions competitive with other thrift institutions.

FEDERAL AND STATE REGULATION OF THE CREDIT UNION INDUSTRY

Credit unions are a heavily regulated industry at both federal and state government levels. Their chartering, lending, and deposit taking are all subject to close supervision through state commissions and a federal regulatory board—the National Credit Union Administration.

State Regulations.

At the state level, a banking or credit union commission normally is set up by the legislature to regularly examine state-chartered credit unions, establish and enforce operating rules, and issue new charters or cancel existing charters. Forty-six of the fifty states have statutes on the books which authorize charters for new credit unions. Only Alaska, Delaware, South Dakota, and Wyoming have no state or local chartering law, though, of course, the federal government can charter new credit unions in these states.[12]

State-issued charters have been on the decline in recent years, and, in fact, the number of operating state-chartered credit unions has declined for several years. More recently, the number of federal credit unions has been falling as well, though credit union membership has been increasing rapidly. As we noted earlier in this chapter, the declining numbers of credit

---

[12]There are also no credit union statutes in the District of Columbia and in the U.S. possessions of Guam and the Virgin Islands.

unions reflect the pressure of rising costs, heavy competition from other thrift institutions, and the need to offer many new services to compete more effectively.

Federal Regulations

At the federal level, the National Credit Union Administration, established in 1970, now is the dominant regulatory authority. The governing body within NCUA is the National Credit Union Board, composed of seven members appointed by the president of the United States. NCUA's board has played an increasingly important role in the industry in recent years because it has acted frequently to liberalize rules and regulations restricting the development of new credit union services. Federal insurance of deposits up to $100,000 is provided by the National Credit Union Share Insurance Fund administered by NCUA. Associations chartered by the states may also apply for NCUSIF deposit insurance. By year-end 1980, nearly 5,000 state-chartered credit unions and all federally chartered credit unions—about 80 percent of the industry population—had NCUSIF insurance coverage on their deposits. Each insured credit union is assessed an annual insurance premium based on the total amount of member accounts.

Lenders of Last Resort for the Industry

Until recently there was no institution to serve as a lender of last resort to the industry in order to deal with short-run cash shortages. Credit union leagues had lobbied for several years for the creation of a federal credit agency that would supply such funds in time of need. In 1978, Congress passed new legislation authorizing the creation of a Central Liquidity Facility (CLF) within the National Credit Union Administration which would act as a lender of last resort for emergency credit needs and which would interface with the CCU system. Then, in 1980, credit unions along with other depository institutions offering payments accounts or nonpersonal time deposits were granted access to the discount windows of the Federal Reserve banks.[13]

---

[13]Recall from the discussion earlier in this chapter that the industry itself has also organized a source of liquid reserves with the development of the corporate central credit unions (CCUs). The first CCU was chartered in Kansas in 1974. CCUs channel short-term funds and provide cash-management services to individual associations through 42 designated corporate central credit unions. The need for improved access to liquidity has arisen in the industry due to the proliferation of services, especially services such as credit cards and share draft accounts which give customers instant access to credit union funds. The result is frequent swings between liquidity surpluses and liquidity shortages. The CCUs moderate the effects of such swings in liquidity by investing surplus funds when credit unions are flush with liquidity and by raising cash at the lowest possible rates or liquidating marketable securities when additional liquidity is needed.

Regulation of Loans and Investments

Perhaps no single activity of credit unions is more closely regulated than how they lend and invest their funds. The basic regulatory standard for the industry is the Federal Credit Union Act, passed in 1934. The act authorizes each federally chartered credit union to grant both secured and unsecured loans to its members.[14] Selected investments may also be acquired, but the list of permissible investments is rather limited. Direct debt obligations of the United States government are acceptable, and, as we saw earlier, credit unions do hold a substantial volume of U.S. government and federal agency securities. Interest-bearing deposits (including CDs) issued by commercial banks, mutual savings banks, savings and loan associations, and other credit unions that carry federal insurance are also permissible investments. A few states allow their associations to acquire high-grade corporate bonds and certain state and local government (municipal) securities.

The lending powers of federally chartered credit unions were increased significantly when Congress passed Public Law 95-22 on April 19, 1977. Permissible maturities for most loans were increased from 5 years to 12 years. Residential real estate loans to finance one- to-four-family dwellings could have maturities out to 30 years, instead of the previous limit of only 10 years.[15] Further liberalization of real estate lending rules occurred in 1982 with passage of the Garn–St Germain Depository Institutions Act. Mobile home and home-improvement loans can now be granted on more lenient terms. Self-replenishing lines of credit may also be granted members, and credit unions may participate out loans with other credit unions or other financial intermediaries.

Tax Rules

Do credit unions pay income taxes? The answer is no, provided each association conforms to all the operating rules of state and federal authorities and thereby qualifies as a nonprofit association. As such, both state

---

[14]Prior to 1981, credit union loans generally had fixed interest rates, but the NCUA board okayed variable-rate consumer loans in that year.

[15]Following the passage of Public Law 95–22, the NCUA issued new regulations governing real estate lending by federal credit unions. Such loans must be a first lien against residential property no larger than a one- to four-family dwelling, and the dwelling must be the principal residence of the member-borrower. The original loan must be limited by either 80 percent of the purchase price of the property or 80 percent of its appraised value, whichever is less. The remaining amount may also be secondarily financed by a credit union so long as the institution's total indebtedness does not exceed 95 percent of the property's value. In 1981, as we saw earlier, variable rate mortgages were allowed at federal credit unions. And the 1982 Garn–St Germain Depository Institutions Act further broadened real estate lending, allowing second mortgages, higher-priced loans, and longer maturities.

and federal credit unions are exempt from federal income tax levies and from state income taxes where these exist. In essence, for tax purposes a credit union is viewed merely as a conduit for earnings from loans and investments, with all earnings (less permissible additions to contingency and equity reserves) flowing through to their members. Of course, credit union members must pay personal income tax rates on any dividends received.

The tax-free status of credit unions has been a center of controversy in recent years. Commercial banking groups have vigorously objected to the exemption privilege, pointing out that banks are subject to the full corporate tax rate. In earlier years, when credit unions offered few bank-like services, commercial banks were not as much concerned with taxing credit unions. However, with the development of share drafts that compete directly with commercial bank checking accounts, and with broader lending authority for credit unions bringing them into direct conflict with bank lending, bankers have begun to take notice. The banking community has called forcefully for a truly "level playing field" in which credit unions would face the same regulatory restrictions (including tax rules) that banks do. It is unlikely, however, that any major change will be made in credit union tax rules for the foreseeable future.

SUMMARY

Credit unions have been one of the most rapidly growing of all financial institutions since World War II. By offering loans at reasonable interest rates and many new deposit services to their members, credit unions have captured a growing share of both consumer savings and credit markets in the United States.

Structurally, credit unions are nonprofit associations owned by their members, and only members may deposit funds or receive loans from a credit union. The majority of credit unions draw their members from industry, but in recent years associations (such as labor unions, churches, lodges, and other social groups) have also organized substantial numbers of credit unions. Regardless of the source of their membership, however, all credit unions are nonprofit, tax-exempt associations, paying out the bulk of their earnings to members in the form of dividends.

The credit union industry has been highly innovative in recent years, offering many new services. Prominent among these are share drafts, which are the equivalent of interest-bearing checking accounts, variable-rate residential mortgages, higher-yielding savings certificates, and consumer credit lines. It is anticipated that such service innovations will continue in the future, bringing credit unions into increasingly intense competition with commercial banks, savings and loan associations, and savings banks for consumer accounts.

Questions

15–1. In what ways is the credit union different from other financial institutions previously discussed, especially commercial banks and savings banks?

15–2. Discuss the reasons behind the recent growth of U.S. credit unions.

15–3. What do the abbreviations *CUNA, CCU, NCUA,* and *NCUSIF* stand for? Describe the functions of these institutions.

15–4. What advantages do credit unions have over other consumer lending institutions (especially commercial banks and finance companies) in their lending activities? In attracting savings deposits? Which of these advantages appear to be long lasting and which only temporary?

15–5. What are share drafts? What advantages do they offer the customer? The individual credit union? Can you foresee any significant financial management problems for a credit union stemming from the offering of share drafts?

15–6. List the principal sources and uses of funds for a credit union. What are the major sources of revenue and expenses? Cite any recent trends which appear to have influenced the pattern of funds flows through credit unions.

15–7. Why is the population of U.S. credit unions declining? What are the probable consequences of this for credit union management?

References

1. Cargill, Thomas F. "Recent Research on Credit Unions: A Survey." *Journal of Economics and Business*, no. 2 (winter 1977).

2. Credit Union National Association. *1979 Yearbook,* Madison.

3. Credit Union National Association. *1980 Yearbook,* Madison.

4. Credit Union National Association. *Credit Union Report, 1981.*

5. Croteau, John T. "A 'New' Financial Intermediary: The American Credit Union." *Rivista Internazionale di Scienze Economia Commerzial* XVIII, no. 9 (1971), pp. 896–905.

6. Dougall, Herbert E., and Jack E. Gaumnitz. *Capital Markets and Institutions.* 3d ed. Englewood Cliffs, N.J.: Prentice-Hall, 1975.

7. Flannery, Mark J. "Credit Unions as Consumer Lenders in the United States." *New England Economic Review,* Federal Reserve Bank of Boston, July/August 1974.

8. Harless, Doris E. *Nonbank Financial Institutions.* Richmond: Federal Reserve Bank of Richmond, 1975, chap. 10.

9. Hempel, George H., and Jess B. Yawitz. *Financial Management of Financial Institutions.* Englewood Cliffs, N.J.: Prentice-Hall, 1977, pp. 129–31, 148–52.

10. Kidwell, David S., and Richard L. Peterson. "A Close Look at Credit Unions." *The Bankers Magazine*, no. 1 (January/February 1978), pp. 71–80.

11. Koot, Ronald S. "The Demand for Credit Union Shares." *Journal of Financial and Quantitative Analysis*, March 1976, pp. 133–41.

12. McConnell, M. M. "Meanwhile, Back at the Credit Unions." *Golembe Reports* 1982–9. Washington, D.C.: Golembe Associates, 1982.

13. Jacobs, Donald, et al. *Financial Institutions*. Homewood, Ill.: Richard D. Irwin, 1972.

14. National Credit Union Administration. *Annual Report, 1977*. Washington, D.C., 1978.

15. National Credit Union Administration. *Annual Report, 1980*. Washington, D.C., 1981.

16. National Credit Union Administration. *Annual Report, 1981*. Washington D.C., 1982.

17. Rose, Peter S. "The NOW Row." *The Canadian Banker & ICB Review* LXXXV, no. 4 (1978), pp. 68–71.

18. Smith, Paul F. *Economics of Financial Institutions*. Homewood, Ill.: Richard D. Irwin, 1971.

19. Taylor, Ryland A. "The Demand for Credit Union Shares: A Cross-Sectional Analysis." *Journal of Financial and Quantitative Analysis*, June 1972, pp. 1749–56.

20. "The Depository Institutions Deregulation and Monetary Control Act of 1980." *Economic Perspectives*, Federal Reserve Bank of Chicago, 1980, pp. 3–23.

21. United States League of Savings Associations. "Garn–St Germain Depository Institutions Act of 1982." *Special Management Bulletin*, November 5, 1982.

22. U.S. House of Representatives. Garn–St Germain Depository Institutions Act of 1982. *Conference Report*, 97th Congress, 2d session, September 30, 1982.

Problem for Discussion

CREDIT UNIONS GRANT A LARGE NUMBER of different kinds of loans to their members. The majority of loans are relatively small and cover household expenses, medical and dental bills, debt consolidation, home and auto repairs, vacation and other travel costs, purchases of home appliances, and moving costs. However, the single most important loan granted by a credit union is financing to support the purchase of new and used automobiles. Indeed, credit unions are among the leading auto lenders in the United States. A recent study by the Credit Union National Association indicates that credit unions account for about 18 percent of the U.S. auto loan market (measured by dollar volume of loans), placing them in third place behind commercial banks and finance companies in this particular financial service.

In this particular discussion problem, assume that you are the treasurer and chief lending officer of a moderate size credit union, the Tri-City Credit Union, which had about $2 million in assets as of year-end 1983. The membership consists of the employees from several large steel and metalworking plants in the surrounding area. Like many other industrial credit unions in the northeastern section of the country, Tri-City's growth has slowed significantly and some sizable deposits have been withdrawn recently. Unemployment is high in the local metropolitan area due to numerous plant closings and layoffs. An estimate by the U.S. Bureau of Labor Statistics placed the local unemployment rate at 16 percent. Few new jobs are available and the local housing market is down about 40 percent in sales volume from its peak three years ago. Recently, a number of families have moved to the Sun Belt or to the West Coast, seeking employment opportunities there. Still, there are some hopeful signs for the local economy. Two new electronic/computer firms have new plants under construction, with projected employment over the next 18 months of 2,700. Moreover, both major banks in the downtown area are constructing new office buildings and expanding their ATM networks.

Estimated population for the greater Tri-City area is 600,000. The local market is served by eight commercial banks (which operate an average of six manned branch offices apiece), five savings and loan associations (which have three to four branches each), four finance companies, and three credit unions (including the Tri-City association). Assets and deposits in these local financial institutions were essentially flat this past year and have increased at a 5-percent average annual rate for the past four years.

As treasurer and loan officer for Tri-City, you enjoy working with people (even though your salary is modest) and responding to their needs for small-denomination, liquid savings instruments and for credit. With an uncertain economic environment enveloping the local economy, those credit needs seem to have increased in recent months. Indeed, many members of the Tri-City association have been drawing down their share (deposit) balances and increasing their loan requests to supplement declining incomes. For many of these association members, particularly younger families with children, their savings balances are significantly less than their outstanding debt and current loan requests.

This morning you received an auto loan request from Mr. and Mrs. Frank Houser, residents of the Tri-City area for the past seven years. Frank Houser is an assistant supervisor at the largest petrochemical plant in the city where he earns $3,500 per month (gross). His wife does not work at present but is at home caring for three children, one of whom is a preschool youngster, four years old. The Housers already have one car, a 1983 Buick, valued at $8,200, which Mrs. Houser drives to school and to shopping. Frank, who used to ride the bus to work, now finds that form of transportation unreliable from their new residential location. He feels the need for a second, more fuel-efficient car to get to work everyday. The Housers are asking Tri-City Credit Union to lend them $6,500 for 36 months to purchase a 1984 Plymouth Reliant—a six-cylinder automobile with air conditioning, power steering, power brakes, and AM/FM stereo radio. The purchase price is $7,500.

About seven months ago, the family moved into a new rented house after living for six years in a small home they were buying. They still own that original home, which is rented to another family for $650 per month. The Housers owe $45,700 on the mortgage against their former home to Equitable Savings and Loan Association of Tri-City and are making payments of $552 per month. The family also owes $515 to Tri-City Finance Company, $7,700 on their Buick auto to a local auto dealership, and $240 on a bank credit card. Their outstanding debt obligations and monthly payments are summarized in Exhibit 15–1.

As loan officer, you must consider the Housers credit request with care. Loans to members at reasonable interest rates are one of the basic functions of credit unions and one of the principal reasons they are chartered by federal and state governments. The Housers are bona fide members of the association, with a savings account (share) balance of $500. The current annual percentage charged by Tri-City on such loans is 15 percent, with loan maturities extending out to 42 months.

Exhibit 15–1 Schedule of Debt Obligations and Monthly Payments

Creditor	Balance Remaining on Loan	Monthly Payments
Bay City Finance Company	$ 515	$190
Elkins Motor Company	7,700	197
Equitable Savings and Loan Association	45,700	552
First National Bank	240	20

16. Money Market Funds

THE MONEY MARKET MUTUAL FUND represents one of the most important developments in the financial system in many decades. In the short space of a 10-year period, from 1973 to 1983, assets under the management of money market funds grew from almost nothing to more than $200 billion, an amount far surpassing the assets of all other mutual funds combined and approximating the assets of state and local government pension funds and property-casualty insurance companies. The growth of money market funds is important not only because of the size they have achieved but also because of the massive changes which have occurred in the regulation and operation of financial institutions due to the successful competition offered by money market funds.

The present chapter concentrates on the following aspects of money market fund: (1) the nature of money market funds and the services performed by these financial institutions, (2) the development of money market funds and the implications of such developments for the financial system, (3) financial management in the operation of money market funds, and (4) the outlook for the future of money market funds. An understanding of these aspects of the money market fund phenomenon is important to understanding recent developments within the financial system and important to personal financial planning as well.

THE NATURE OF THE MONEY MARKET FUND

It is important to recognize that money market funds are merely a specialized form of mutual funds.[1] As such, they sell their shares to the public at a specified price—most frequently one dollar per share—either with a sales commission (in which case the fund is referred to as a *load fund*) or without a sales commission (in which case the fund is referred to as a *no-load fund*). Almost all money market funds are sold without a sales com-

---

[1]See Chapter 21 for a more extensive discussion and analysis of the character of mutual funds.

432

mission. The holder of shares in a money market fund is an owner, not a creditor, and stands to lose if the fund has financial difficulty. The money obtained through the sale of shares is then invested in money market instruments, such as certificates of deposit, commercial paper, Treasury bills, and bankers' acceptances. The maturity of these money market instruments is usually quite short, with the average maturity of the portfolio of a money market fund seldom exceeding four to six months.

The portfolio of assets chosen by a money market fund—the average maturity of the assets of the fund and the particular types of money market instruments included in the fund's portfolio—are determined by an investment adviser. The adviser is often a large mutual fund management company that manages a number of mutual funds in return for a management fee. This management fee, coupled with other operating expenses of the fund, is deducted (usually on a daily basis) from the total income of the fund, and the remaining income is distributed to the fund's shareholders. The return paid to investors varies daily (in contrast to a guaranteed return paid by a depository institution) with changes in the earnings of the fund on its portfolio and also with changes in operating expenses, though the principal source of variation in investor returns is changes in the level of interest rates on money market instruments.

Money market funds are commonly divided into three groups, based upon the nature of the management and investors of the fund: broker/ dealer, general purpose, and institutional. Broker/dealer funds are affiliated with stockbrokers and are open to the general public. General purpose money market funds are offered to the general public by management companies not affiliated with stockbrokers. Institutional funds are available only to or through institutional investors. Initially, the money market mutual fund industry was dominated by general purpose funds, though broker/dealer funds became the largest subcomponent of the industry by the late 1970s.

Reasons for Growth

Money market funds have experienced phenomenal growth because they offer financial services with desirable characteristics. The desirability of these financial services may be discussed within a general or a specific context. Within a general context, money market funds have prospered because they offer an efficient means of financial intermediation. Within a more specific context, money market funds have attracted shareholders through offering high yields, check writing, wire transfer, float, liquidity, and other services.[2]

---

[2]See Fraser [8] for a more complete discussion of the reasons for the growth of money market funds.

Money Market Funds as Financial Intermediaries

Money market funds provide financial intermediary services in a manner similar to other financial intermediaries. These include *denomination intermediation*, whereby the fund offers shares in smaller denominations to investors than the denominations available on the securities purchased by the funds. In the case of money market funds, shares are offered in low minimum denominations (often as little as $500), while the money market instruments themselves are available only in large denominations, frequently $1 million or more in order to get the best price. Denomination intermediation has been a very important factor in the growth of money market funds. Money market funds have allowed access to the yields available in the open competitive money market for those investors who previously were unable to obtain such yields.

In addition to denomination intermediation, however, money market funds also offer *default-risk* and *maturity* intermediation. With regard to default-risk intermediation, money market funds offer to investors securities which represent part of a pool of assets selected by investment experts. The pooling of risk itself, completely apart from professional management, should reduce the riskiness of a portfolio through asset diversification. The significance of professional management in creating further risk reduction is difficult to assess, though it has been shown in the case of equity mutual funds that professional management has added little beyond the benefits available through portfolio diversification. In any case, the significance of default-risk intermediation should perhaps not be overemphasized, as the degree of default risk in money market instruments is quite small. The importance of *maturity intermediation*, however, should not be ignored. Maturity intermediation refers to the money market fund offering shares that have a shorter maturity than the assets held by the fund. In fact, the money market fund offers shares with almost instant liquidity, since shares may be redeemed through wire transfer following telephone instructions to the fund, while the assets of the fund have 30, 60, 90 days or longer average maturity. This liquidity dimension of the intermediation function of money market funds has undoubtedly been of substantial significance in contributing to the industry's growth.

Money market funds also offer economies of scale in the pooling of short-term funds. This function has been especially important in attracting funds from wealthy individuals and particularly from corporations and bank trust departments. These larger investors do have access to the open market and could purchase Treasury bills and other money market instruments directly. However, they choose to purchase money market fund shares because the economies of scale of money market fund operations, along with the liquidity and other desirable characteristics of the shares of money market funds, allow them to obtain a higher return per unit of risk than would be the case through other vehicles of direct investment in the money market. While little is known about the relative costs of money market funds versus the costs of direct investment in money market instruments, Cook and Duffield [3] have shown that the average costs of money market funds decline at least until the fund reaches an asset level of about $50 million. This would imply that money market investors who have access to the money market but do not have very large quantities of funds might be better off to invest in money market funds.

Specific Services of Money Market Funds

To this point our discussion has viewed the money market funds from a broad social perspective. However, it is also important to understand the operations of the money market funds in terms of the specific services they offer to investors. Of course, the high liquidity of fund shares is of significance, especially to smaller investors without direct access to the money market. For these smaller investors, the liquidity of the money market fund may be compared to the liquidity of a NOW account (high liquidity but low return) or the liquidity of a 3-month, 6-month or 30-month certificate at a depository financial institution (high return but low liquidity). As compared to these alternatives for the small investor, the money market fund offers a financial instrument with high return *and* high liquidity.[3] Moreover, this liquidity comes with convenience. The shares may be redeemed generally through telephone or wire communication, and the funds can be provided with a very short delay. Also, the funds may be redeemed by check, though generally with a substantial (often $500) minimum per check.[4] Redemption by check has particular advantages in the time delay between writing the check and the presentation of the check for payment, at which time sufficient shares of the fund are sold to provide cash to pay the check. The float created by this time delay can be substantial if the check is drawn on a bank located at a considerable distance from the fund.

Many money market funds have been created by stock brokerage firms and by equity-oriented mutual fund management companies. In fact, roughly one half of the assets of all money market funds in late 1981 were held by these so-called broker/dealer funds (see, Dotsey, Englander, and

---

[3]The phenomenal success of the money market fund contributed to the 1982 authorization by the Depository Institutions Deregulation Committee of two deposit instruments that offered both high liquidity and high yield: the money market deposit, effective December 14, 1982, and the super NOW, effective January 5, 1983. Neither carries a federal interest rate ceiling on the rate offered depositors, but both require a minimum average balance of $2,500. Both accounts are accessible by check or automatic transfer of funds.

[4]The purpose of such a minimum is to prevent the money fund account from being used as a general purpose checking account. However, not all funds impose such a minimum.

Portlan [5]). For the stock brokerage firm, the money market fund is another service available to its customers. In some cases (Merrill Lynch being the most notable) the money market fund provides the core of a complete cash management service provided its customers. It also is available as a temporary place for customers of securities brokerage firms to "park" their funds and wait for more desirable investment opportunities. For mutual funds management companies, the funds serve as a means of retaining assets under their management when customers withdraw from stock and/or bond funds. Without the money market funds in the range of services offered, such an action on the part of their customers would result in a reduction in the size of their assets under management and in their income. With the money market funds, however, investors may simply switch from one fund to another within the same mutual funds management group. This action is encouraged, since the management companies generally allow transfers from one company to another without imposing any transfer fee.

Purchasers of Money Market Funds

Information on the ownership of money market funds is less complete than would be desired. However, it appears (see Cook and Duffield [2]) that money market fund ownership is concentrated among individuals and bank trust departments. There appears to be some ownership of money market funds by corporations, though the amount is small compared to that held by individuals and bank trust departments. Access to money market yields for those without direct access to the money market seems to have been the principal explanation for individual ownership of money market funds, especially for individuals of relatively modest financial means. This motivation may be less significant in explaining the holdings of money market fund shares by bank trust departments and by corporate accounts. According to Cook and Duffield [2], however, the principal motivation for these investors relates to economies of scale in managing a portfolio of money market instruments. Except for very large organizations, money market funds appear to offer a better alternative than does direct investment in money market instruments.

Distribution of Assets of Money Market Funds

Money market funds invest in money market instruments. Yet the mix of assets held by money market funds varies over time.[5] As shown in Table 16–1, the most important money market fund asset during most of the

---

[5]Some money market funds invest in the short-term debt of state and local governments. These funds exist to provide liquidity and high after-tax income for those in high tax brackets. The total assets of these funds represent a very small fraction of the total assets of the entire mutual fund industry.

Table 16-1 **Distribution (in percent) of Assets of Money Market Funds: 1974–1982**

	1974	1976	1978	1980	1981	1982
Domestic time deposits	67%	41%	42%	28%	24%	20%
Foreign time deposits	—	—	5	9	10	12
Repurchase agreements	4	3	3	8	8	8
U.S. government securities	4	30	14	11	18	26
Commercial paper	25	24	34	42	39	33
Other assets	—	2	2	2	1	1
	100%	100%	100%	100%	100%	100%

Source: Board of Governors of the Federal Reserve System, *Flow of Funds Accounts.*

industry's history has been the time deposit, both domestic and foreign, issued by major banks. Usually, these interest-bearing deposits are large ($100,000 and over) negotiable certificates of deposits. As of the end of 1974, domestic and foreign time deposits accounted for 67 percent of the total assets of money market funds. At the end of 1982, domestic and foreign time deposits accounted for 32 percent of the total assets of money market funds (and, of course, the total assets of money market funds had expanded dramatically over the period, so that money market fund holdings of time deposits were much larger in dollar terms in 1982 than in 1974). However, time deposits obviously had declined sharply in relative terms in money fund portfolios over the 1974–82 period. In large part, their dominant position was taken over by investments in commercial paper—short-term IOUs issued by major corporations—which rose to 33 percent of money fund assets in 1982, though holdings of U.S. government securities also increased in the early 1980s, principally reflecting an uncertain financial environment.

Variations in the composition of the portfolio of money market funds over time reflect a number of considerations. The most important factor is the changing relationship among yields on different money market instruments. At one point in time, CD rates may be very attractive relative to commercial paper rates, and money market fund managers may shift their assets toward CDs. At another point in time, commercial paper rates may be attractive relative to CD rates, and the opposite flow of funds should occur. Relevant also would be the outlook for credit-risk developments in each sector. For example, both the commercial paper and CD markets have suffered from time to time from credit-risk shocks, such as the bankruptcy of the Penn Central Corporation in 1969; the failure of Franklin National Bank in 1974; and, more recently, financial problems at Chrysler, International Harvester, Braniff, and other major corporations. These developments should be expected to influence the portfolio preferences of investors. It must also be kept in mind that some money market funds are restricted to certain kinds of securities; the most notable of the types of specialized funds would be those that invest in U.S. government securities. To the extent that these funds grow in investor favor, which is likely during periods of financial uncertainty, the composition of assets held by the money market industry will be affected.

THE DEVELOPMENT OF MONEY MARKET FUNDS

As pointed out above, money market funds are a very recent phenomenon, tracing their origins back only to the early 1970s. Yet the growth of the industry has been phenomenal, more rapid than has been experienced by any other financial institution over the same time period. As shown in Figure 16-1, money market funds grew from almost nothing in 1973 to over $200 billion in 1982, though the assets declined to under $200 billion in 1983, reflecting falling interest rates and competition from the newly authorized money market deposit accounts. It is also interesting to observe that assets of money market funds grew most rapidly during the 1979–81 period, one of extremely high short-term interest rates.

While explosive, the growth of money market funds has not been steady. Rather, money market funds have increased their total shares outstanding and total assets during periods of rising interest rates, while falling interest rates have tended to lead to a plateau or decline in the amount of assets. From virtually nothing in 1973, money market fund assets expanded to $2.4 billion by the end of 1974 and to $3.7 billion in 1975, a period of rising interest rates. At that time, the rates paid on money market fund shares seemed quite attractive as compared with the low rates available to savers on savings and time deposits offered by depository financial institutions. In large part, this favorable situation for the money funds was due to the severely limiting Regulation Q interest-rate ceilings on deposits offered by banks, savings and loans, and other depository institutions. However, during the period of declining interest rates in 1976 and 1977, the assets of money market funds remained roughly unchanged. In contrast, with rising interest rates in 1978, and particularly in the period from 1979–81, money market fund assets literally exploded, reaching more than $200 billion in 1982. Not only did interest rates rise to historically unprecedented levels in this period, but they remained at extremely high levels for an extended period. Moreover, by the late 1970s, individuals were becoming more knowledgeable about the services offered by money market funds and more sophisticated in the use of the financial services provided by these funds.

INTEREST RATES AND THE GROWTH OF MONEY MARKET FUNDS

Cook and Duffield [2] have conducted an extensive analysis of the relationship between the growth of money market fund assets and the interest rate available on money market funds during the period 1975–79. This relationship is shown in Figure 16-2. Since yields quoted in the financial press refer to *expost*, realized yields over some past period (generally seven days), while the passbook savings rate is a *promised* rate over some fu-

Figure 16–1 The Growth of Money Market Funds: 1973–1983

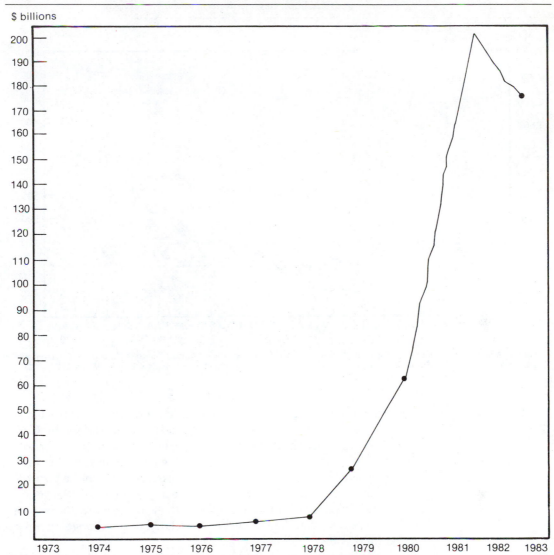

Source: Data obtained from Board of Governors of the Federal Reserve System, *Flow of Funds Accounts.*

Figure 16-2 Change in MMF Assets and Spread between MMF Ex Ante Yield and Passbook Savings Rate

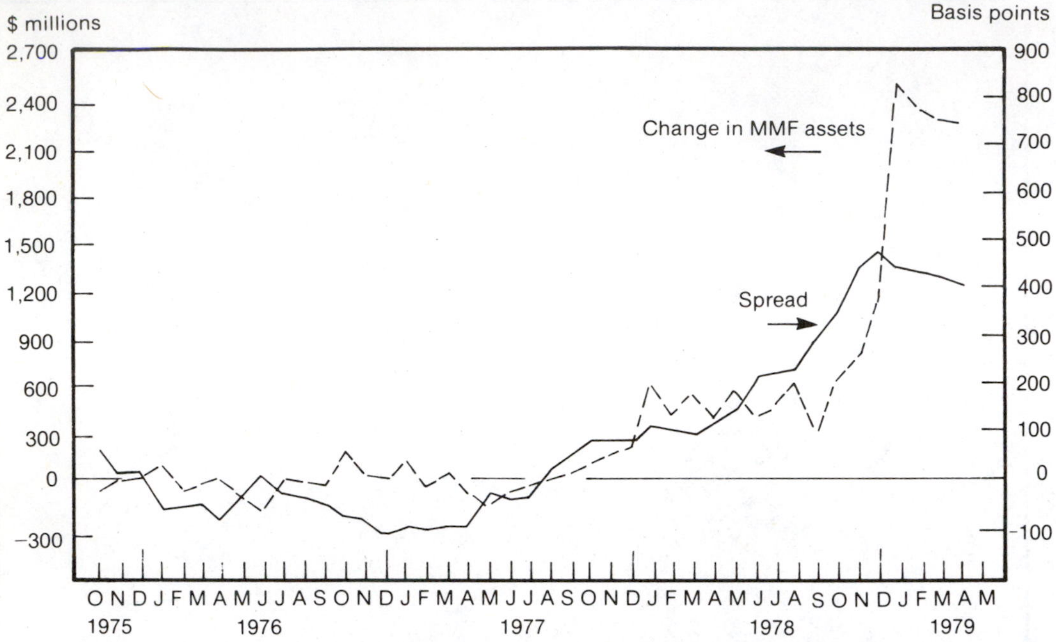
$ millions
Basis points
2,700
2,400
2,100
1,800
1,500
1,200
900
600
300
0
−300
900
800
700
600
500
400
300
200
100
0
-100
Change in MMF assets
Spread
O N D J F M A M J J A S O N D J F M A M J J A S O N D J F M A M J J A S O N D J F M A M
1975
1976
1977
1978
1979

Source: Adapted from Timothy Q. Cook and Jeremy G. Duffield, "Money Market Mutual Funds: A Reaction to Government Regulations, or a Lasting Financial Innovation," Federal Reserve Bank of Richmond *Economic Review*, July/August 1979, p. 27.

ture period, it is necessary in making such a comparison to construct an *ex ante*, or expected rate for money market funds. This was done by Cook and Duffield [2] through calculation of the yield to maturity on a portfolio with the same composition as that held by five large money market funds at the relevant point of time, assuming that each security in the portfolio matured in the number of days equal to the average maturity of money market fund assets. This *ex ante* yield was then compared with the passbook savings rate, and the difference was related to the change in money market fund assets.

The solid line in Figure 16-2 relates to the difference between the money market fund yield and the passbook savings account yield in the period from October 1975 to May 1979, while the dotted line refers to the change in money market fund assets during the same period. As shown there, money market fund yields were generally below yields available on passbook savings accounts from October 1975 through July 1977. Not surprisingly, money market fund assets declined, though only slightly, over that period. In contrast, beginning in late 1977 the spread turned in favor of money market funds, and the assets of money market funds began to grow again. In late 1978 and during 1979, the spread widened considerably (to 400 basis points, or 4 percentage points, at one point), and money market fund assets grew even more rapidly. Although not shown in Figure 16–2, the spread expanded even more in the period from 1979 through 1982, leading to an explosion in the size of money market funds. While there is some question as to whether the passbook savings rate best measured the alternatives available to individuals and whether the six-month money market CD might be a more meaningful comparison in recent years, these results by Cook and Duffield at least provide considerable support to the expectation that interest-rate levels influenced strongly the flow of funds into and out of money market funds. It must also be remembered, of course, that these results from past periods may not be applicable to future years due to the development of the money market deposit account offered today by banks and thrifts.

Implications of Money Market Funds' Growth

The surge in money market fund assets has substantial implications for the operations of individual financial institutions and the regulation of the financial system. The development of money market funds has created a powerful new competitor for existing financial institutions. This competition appears to be greatest for depository institutions, though the availability of a high-yielding, highly liquid financial instrument undoubtedly provides competition for nondepository financial institutions as well. The competition has produced serious strains at depository financial institutions during periods of high interest rates and has, through pulling deposits away from these institutions, contributed to intense liquidity pressures at some institutions. Moreover, there is some indirect evidence that the growth of money market funds has come especially at the expense of small and medium size depository institutions. Recall the information in Table 16–1 that shows that a substantial amount of money market fund assets have historically been held in the form of time deposits at depository institutions. Yet most of these CDs are held at a very few, very large institutions. Hence large institutions that lose deposits to money market funds are likely to get some or all of those funds back as the money market funds buy CDs from the depository institutions, though the cost of those funds to the depository institution may rise. However, small depository institutions are unlikely to get their lost deposits back from money market funds.[6]

---

[6]Some money market funds did attempt in 1981 and 1982 to invest a portion of their funds in smaller depository institutions. The success of this program is difficult to evaluate.

The phenomenal growth of money market funds has also had an important effect on the regulation of financial institutions. The growth of money market funds outside of the framework of regulation was one of the major factors producing the trend toward deregulation of the financial sector of the economy. While it is likely that financial deregulation and other regulatory changes embodied in the Depository Institutions Deregulation and Money Control Act of 1980 and the Depository Institutions Act of 1982 would have occurred regardless of whether money market funds had ever been developed, it is also likely that the growth of money market funds stimulated and speeded up that change. The phasing out of Regulation Q under a specific timetable as mandated by DIDMCA of 1980 is at least partially the result of the success of money market funds. The regulatory authorities sought throughout the 1970s to create innovations in order to allow depository institutions to compete more effectively with money market funds and other types of competitors. These innovations included six-month money market certificates as well as the 2½-year certificates of deposit, with both having interest-rate ceilings tied to open, competitive money market rates. Also, the regulatory authorities substantially reduced the minimum deposit level necessary in order to open these higher-yielding accounts. Yet, it became increasingly evident that these were stopgap measures and that the growing competition from money market funds and other competitive vehicles required the complete dismantling of Regulation Q ceilings, as has been done (though perhaps not fully until 1984) with the passage of the Depository Institutions Deregulation and Monetary Control Act of 1980. To a considerable extent the authorization in late 1982 of the money market deposit and the Super NOW account represents a reaction to the growth of money market funds.

One important aspect of the growth of money market funds concerns their implications for the conduct of monetary policy. In particular, the growth of money market funds raises important questions as to the proper definition of money. Should all, or at least a significant portion, of money market fund balances be included within the transactions (M1) definition of the money supply? The answer to this question depends upon the extent to which investors use their money market fund holdings for transactions purposes. While little information is available on this question, Dotsey, Englander, and Portlan [5] present evidence on turnover rates on money market fund balances which suggests that, in past years at least, they have not been serving primarily as transactions vehicles. The turnover rate for money market funds has been much below that of demand deposit accounts and much closer to that of savings deposits. Yet, with the rapid evolution of money market funds, what has been true of the past may not be true of the future.

The financial management of the portfolio of a money market fund involves two key decision variables: (1) what *maturity* the portfolio should have and (2) what *mix* of different money market instruments should be included in the portfolio. There are, of course, limitations imposed by regulation and by the prospectus of the individual fund which place some restrictions on the discretionary authority of the money market fund portfolio manager. Yet, within external constraints, the portfolio manager has considerable discretion over the maturity and mix of assets. Moreover, analysis of the maturity and mix of assets of different funds at the same point in time show considerable differences in the ways in which individual fund managers have made these decisions. Figure 16–3 shows the average maturity of a number of money market funds, while Figure 16–4 shows the portfolio mix of six large funds, as an example of differences in the way portfolio management decisions are made at different money market funds.

FINANCIAL MANAGEMENT OF MONEY MARKET FUNDS

Maturity

The maturity decision encompasses the range of maturities of assets in the portfolio as well as the average maturity of those assets. At any point in time the portfolio manager would have a desired average maturity as well as a desired distribution of the maturity of individual assets in the

---

Figure 16–3 Average Maturity of Assets of Selected Money Market Funds: February 5, 1982

Fund	Average Maturity in Days
Capital Preservation 2	3
Current Interest	32
Delaware Cash Reserve	38
Dreyfus Liquid Asset	43
Fidelity Cash Reserve	32
Financial Planning Federal Securities	4
Fund For Government Investments	10
Kemper Money Market	34
Liquid Cash Trust	1
Mutual of Omaha Money Market	20
Oppenheimer Money Market	27
Reserve Fund	43
Rowe Price Prime Reserve	24
St. Paul Money	18
Security Cash Fund	18
Webster Cash Preservation	30

Source: *The Wall Street Journal*, February 10, 1982.

Figure 16–4   Portfolio Composition of Selected Money Market Funds: October 29, 1982

Deposits	Portfolio Mix (in percent)						
	Domestic Time Deposits	Foreign Time Deposits	Repurchase Agreements	U.S. Government Securities	Bankers' Acceptances	Commercial Paper	Other Assets
Fidelity Cash Reserves	53%	21%	—%	—%	5%	11%	10%
Inter-Capital Liquid Assets Fund	40	—	—	21	2	37	—
Merrill Lynch Ready Asset Trust	22	—	6	41	7	24	
Money Market Trust	16	4	3	—	23	—	9

Source: Wiesenberger Financial Services, Investment Companies, New York.

portfolio. As with all portfolio management decisions, there would be different risk/return dimensions to each portfolio. A longer maturity portfolio would, assuming that the yield curve was generally upward sloping within the relevant maturity range for money market funds, produce a higher yield than would a shorter maturity portfolio. However, in periods of changing interest rates, the longer maturity portfolio faces the potential both of greater variability in market price and less liquidity.

These considerations are quite important to the managers of money market fund portfolios whose obligations are payable on demand. The portfolio manager of a fund alters the fund's portfolio maturity based upon *expectations* of changes in interest rates. Expectations of *falling* rates should produce a *lengthening* in the maturity structure in the attempt to lock in the currently higher yields and perhaps obtain some capital gain from appreciation in the market value of securities as interest rates fall. In contrast, expectation of *rising* interest rates would produce a shortening in the maturity of the portfolio as fund managers attempt to cushion the value of the portfolios against capital depreciation due to rising rates and as they attempt to roll over their portfolios more quickly into higher-yielding securities. Such portfolio adjustments in expectation of changing rates, however, must be tempered by the realization that expectations may not be realized. In 1980, for example, the Institutional Liquid Asset Fund held long-maturity assets at a time when interest rates unexpectedly increased, causing severe financial difficulty for that particular fund.

There is little information available on how effective managers of money market funds have been in their maturity management decisions. One study, by Ferri and Oberhelman [7] attempted to determine if money market fund managers, taken as a group, can correctly anticipate the future movement of interest rates. While the success of interest rate forecasters generally has been quite poor, it might be anticipated that forecast accuracy would be greater for those intimately involved in the money market as money market fund managers must be. The Ferri and Oberhelman study compared expected changes in interest rates as reflected by changes in money market fund maturity within a month with actual changes in rates in the following months. Hence an increase in average maturity of money market funds during a given month would be taken as evidence of a forecast of falling rates later, and vice versa for a decrease in average portfolio maturity. Somewhat surprisingly, the comparison suggested that money market fund managers were able to *anticipate* interest rate movements: "The tests of this paper indicate that money fund managers have a fairly consistent record of shortening maturity before rates rise and lengthening maturity before rates fall" [7, p. 29].

Credit Risk

Fund managers must also make important decisions as to credit risk. The return expected from a portfolio of financial assets varies with the degree of credit risk as well as with the average maturity of the portfolio. The portfolio manager must decide whether to invest only in gilt-edge securities, such as Treasury bills, and to accept the lower returns associated with such an investment or to reach for higher yields in CDs, commercial paper, and other money market instruments which do carry some degree of credit risk. The choice presented between domestic and foreign CDs is a good example of this problem. The fund may invest in the domestic CDs of a U.S bank or in the CDs of the London branch of that same bank (in which case the CD would legally be a foreign one). The CD of the London branch would generally pay a higher return to the investor than would the CD of the domestic bank, due to differences in perceived credit risk as well as differences in liquidity and other factors.

Little information is available on the effectiveness of money market fund managers in controlling credit risk.[7] Up to the time at which this book was written, there had been no serious problems in money market funds due to default on assets held in their portfolios. Whether this absence of credit risk problems reflects skill in portfolio management or the fact that most money market instruments inherently carry only very limited default risk is not known. However, with the size to which the money market fund industry has grown, it would not be unexpected to find default risk problems becoming significant at some funds. In evaluating the success of money market fund managers in controlling credit risk,

---

[7]Davis [4] did find excess returns over and above those expected, given the risk level of the assets for a small sample of funds. Also, Shawky, Forbes, and Frankle [9] found, using the capital asset pricing model, that money market funds obtained slight excess returns. However, much remains to be learned about the effectiveness of money market funds in managing risk.

it should be remembered that the openly competitive financial markets appear remarkably efficient in pricing risk; such that fund managers should not expect excess returns, beyond those attributable to accepting additional risk, from increasing the credit risk of their portfolio.

THE FUTURE OF
MONEY MARKET
FUNDS

One of the most interesting and important issues concerning money market mutual funds is their future performance. More specifically, is the explosive growth of money market funds a *temporary* phenomenon, produced primarily by government regulations which have prevented depository institutions from offering financial instruments fully competitive with the instruments available in the openly competitive money market? Or does the growth of money market funds represent a permanent change in the flow of funds in the U.S. financial system? There is little doubt that a sizable proportion of the growth of money market funds represents the support of investors who do not have direct access to the money market and who traditionally have been denied, by government regulations, access to high money market yields, indirectly, through their depository institutions. On the other hand, there also may be a substantial portion of investors in money market funds who do have access to the financial instruments of the money market but who choose because of economies of scale, liquidity, or other considerations to invest in money market funds. The essence of the question of permanence of money market funds concerns the relative sizes of these two groups. Of course, it must be recognized that the permanence of money market funds depends to a very considerable extent on the implementation of future reforms in the regulation of financial institutions, though it is equally true that many future regulatory reforms depend upon the competitive position of money market funds as compared to depository institutions.

The future course of government regulation of financial institutions is of vital consequence for the permanence of money market funds. The phasing out of Regulation Q limitations on the interest rates on deposits at depository institutions as well as other reductions in the restraints on the services offered by depository institutions should produce a reduction in the size of money market funds. Certainly the implementation in late 1982 of the money market deposit and in early 1983 of the super NOW account will substantially increase the degree of competition by depository institutions for funds that have gone to money market funds. It is significant to note that in countries such as Canada, where depository institutions have not been constrained by regulation on rates paid to obtain funds, the money market fund industry is almost unknown. This industry is essentially an American innovation. Moreover, the growth of money market funds will undoubtedly be affected by any constraints placed on their behavior or by additional regulations which increase their costs. For example, it has been proposed that money market funds be prohibited from offering checking account privileges against their shares. More importantly, it has also been proposed, as was discussed earlier in the chapter, that money market funds should be subject to the same reserve requirements as are imposed against depository institutions. Also, as more investors obtain larger wealth positions, they will gain direct access to the money market and may have less need of money market funds.

These arguments would suggest that the money market fund industry would decline in the future, at least relatively and perhaps absolutely. In fact, money market fund assets fell by roughly $50 billion in the period from late 1982 through mid-1983. There is another argument, though, that suggests any decline in the industry may be modest. This argument, as made by Cook and Duffield [2], stresses the *multiple uses* of money market funds by a variety of investors. Hence, while the usefulness of money market funds to investors without direct access to the money market will diminish as depository institutions pay market rates of interest for funds, the usefulness of money market funds to other investors will remain. Remember that ownership of money market funds includes individuals, bank trust departments, and corporations. While many individuals hold money market funds only because they do not have direct access to the money market, many also hold money market fund shares because of convenience, liquidity, and other considerations. Those who hold shares for convenience—for example, as a place to "park" funds between stock and bond market investments—are less likely to abandon money market funds as depository institutions offer higher rates. Also, bank trust department and corporate investors in money market funds are probably even less likely to shift their investments out of money market funds.

The relative importance of these different factors is difficult to weigh. It seems reasonable to expect that the money market fund movement has offered sufficient innovations in financial services such that it will continue to play a role in the financial system in the future.[8] Yet, there are powerful regulatory and market forces which are increasing the competition for short-term funds. As such, while the industry may be permanent, its relative significance in the financial system may decline in forthcoming years.

Money market funds are mutual funds which invest in short-term, highly liquid money market instruments. Holders of money market fund shares are owners, not creditors, and are entitled to all income earned by

SUMMARY

---

[8]This assumes that the industry continues its record of safety for investors' funds. Since shares at money market funds legally represent an ownership interest for the investor and carry no deposit insurance, financial problems within the industry could seriously harm its long-term viability.

the fund minus the operating costs of the fund. This income fluctuates daily with changes in the interest income earned on the portfolio of the fund as well as with changes in operating costs. Money market funds have developed since the early 1970s; they have experienced explosive growth, especially in the period of exceptionally high interest rates in the 1979–82 period; and they have become a major factor in the financial system. To a considerable extent, the growth of money market funds prompted the financial reforms of the late 1970s and early 1980s.

Money market funds have grown because they offer financial services desired by the public. These include their role as a financial intermediary offering denomination intermediation, default risk intermediation, and maturity intermediation. In addition, money market funds offer high liquidity and economies of scale in the management of a portfolio of financial assets. Money market funds also offer a variety of specific services which enhance their attractiveness. These include redemption by check or wire transfer, as well as exchange privileges with other funds within a group of mutual funds. While the investments of money market funds vary over time with changes in the relative pattern of interest rates, the largest percentage of the assets of the industry have generally been held in time deposits, usually certificates of deposit, and commercial paper.

Most money market fund shares are purchased by individuals and bank trust departments, with a smaller but significant amount of shares held by corporate accounts. Many individuals have held money market fund shares because of lack of access to the higher yields available through direct ownership of money market instruments due to modest financial wealth and also because depository institutions have been constrained (by Regulation Q) from offering money market rates. However, many individuals, bank trust departments, and corporations purchase money market funds because of the economies of scale available through the funds.

The financial management of a money market fund involves the control of both the maturity and credit risk of its portfolio of securities. Both maturity management and credit-risk management decisions have been made differently by different funds, as shown by the makeup of each fund's portfolios. There is little information available on the efficiency of portfolio management of money market funds, though limited evidence does suggest that money market funds have been reasonably successful in altering the maturity of their portfolios in anticipation of changing interest rates.

The fact that some of the growth of money market funds reflects regulatory restrictions (such as Regulation Q) on depository institutions and that these restrictions are being eliminated would suggest a reduced role for these funds. Yet, the multiplicity of services offered by money market funds and the fact that a substantial amount of fund shares are held by bank trust departments and corporations would suggest a more permanent role for money market funds within the nation's growing financial system.

Questions

16–1. What is a money market fund? What services does it offer?

16–2. How does denomination, maturity, and default-risk intermediation relate to money market funds? Liquidity? Economies of scale?

16–3. Why did money market funds experience explosive growth in the 1979–81 period?

What factors bear upon the future growth of money market funds?

16–4. Who are the principal buyers of money market fund shares? Is their motivation the same?

16–5. Under what condition would it be possible to use the maturity of money market funds as a predictor of future interest rates? Does that condition exist?

References

1. Anreder, Steven S. "Liquidity Plus Return Adds Up to a Fresh Surge in Money Market Funds." *Barrons*, June 5, 1978, pp. 4–5.

2. Cook, Timothy, and Jeremy Duffield. "Money Market Mutual Funds: A Reaction to Government Regulations or a Lasting Financial Innovation." *Economic Review*, Federal Reserve Bank of Richmond, July/August 1979, pp. 15–31.

3. Cook, Timothy, and Jeremy Duffield. "Average Cost of Money Market Mutual Funds." *Economic Review*, Federal Reserve Bank of Richmond, July/August 1979, pp. 32–39.

4. Davis, Carolyn Dubose. "Money Market Mutual Funds: An Arbitrage Pricing Theory Performance Evaluation." *Staff Papers*, Comptroller of the Currency, Washington, D.C., 1982.

5. Dotsey, Michael; Steven Englander; and John C. Portlan. "Money Market Mutual Funds and Monetary Control." *Quarterly Review*, Federal Reserve Bank of New York, Winter 1981–82, pp. 9–17.

6. Dunham, C. "The Growth of Money Market Funds." *New England Economic Review*, Federal Reserve Bank of Boston, September/October 1980, pp. 20–34.

7. Ferri, Michael, and H. Dennis Oberhelman. "A Study of the Management of Money Market Mutual Funds: 1975–1980." *Financial Management*, Autumn 1981, pp. 24–29.

8. Fraser, Donald. "The Money Market Fund as a Financial Intermediary." *MSU Business Topics*, Spring 1977, pp. 5–12.

9. Shawky, Hany; Robert Forbes; and Alan Frankle. "Liquidity Services and Capital Market Equilibrium: The Case for Money Market Mutual Funds." *The Journal of Financial Research*, Summer 1983, pp. 141–152.

Problem for Discussion

THE INSTANT LIQUIDITY FUND (ILF) is a large money market fund, with over $1 billion in assets. The fund is operated by a mutual fund management company which has a diverse group of funds under its control, including three different stock funds and two bond funds. The management company also serves as an adviser to a number of pension funds throughout the nation as well as to some individuals with substantial inherited wealth. Within the trade, the management company is known as "solid but not spectacular, perhaps a little staid." The performance of its funds has generally been below the average for comparable funds, though the fund managers have explained this performance as reflecting the conservative, low-risk nature of the portfolios of the funds. As one manager put it, "Better to be safe than sorry."

The ILF was a comparative latecomer to the money market fund industry, having been founded in 1979. Reflecting the conservative nature of the mutual fund management company, the ILF had been started principally as a defensive measure. Other mutual fund management companies had started money market funds some years earlier and were openly advertising the usefulness of being able to transfer money from one type of fund to another easily and without charge. It was feared that unless a similar money market fund were started there might be a drain of investment money away from the stock and bond funds of the organization. Somewhat to the surprise of the fund managers, the ILF had grown rapidly so that it now was one of the more profitable funds in the entire organization, though most of the money had come from transfers from other funds within the group rather than from new money from outside. The management fee was 0.5 percent of total assets, and, with the economies of scale involved in managing financial assets, the fund had become quite profitable after its total assets exceeded $500 million. There was, in fact, pressure from consumer groups generally and from some shareholders specifically for ILF to reduce this management fee.

The ILF offered essentially the same services as other money market funds. Shareholders could contact the fund by toll-free telephone. Once in contact with the fund, they could redeem their shares for cash with wire transfers directly to their bank if they desired, or they could transfer their investment (the total or any portion) to any of the other funds within the same management group without any transactions costs (there was a transaction fee assessed if the number of transactions exceeded 10 in any 12-month period). In addition, the shares could be redeemed by check (with a minimum amount of $500). The check could be drawn either on a New York bank or a bank in California, at the option of the shareholder. By allowing such a choice, the fund offered to its shareholders the possibility of greater float, during which time the shareholders earned interest on their share accounts. The ILF was also qualified for custodial accounts under the Uniform Gift to Minors Act, for Keogh plan retirement contributions, and for IRA retirement accounts. The fund assessed no additional maintenance charge for participation in these plans.

Managers of the fund had recently become concerned about their lack of success in obtaining money from new clients outside of the mutual fund management group. This lack of success was attributed to the fact that the return on shares of the fund had been below those of competing funds during most recent periods. The differences in returns among the funds were not great, but it was recognized that institutional investors such as bank trust departments were extremely sensitive to small differences in yield. It was just these institutional investors that the ILF fund wished to attract, for their large account balances with low servicing costs could prove to be very profitable.

Management of the fund recognized that a complete change in portfolio management might be necessary in order to produce the kind of track record that would attract new business. It therefore decided to reevaluate its portfolio management strategy that had guided investments of the fund since its inception. A summary of these policies is provided in Exhibit 16–1. It was anticipated that this reevaluation would emcompass the desirability of changing portfolio management policies, the advantages and disadvantages of any proposed changes, and the desirability of instituting such changes at present. In order to make such an analysis, the management of the fund also reviewed its present portfolio and the most recent interest-rate structure as shown in Exhibits 16–2 and 16–3. The consensus of forecasters was for a moderate decline in economic activity and interest rates during the next 12 months.

Exhibit 16–1   Portfolio Management Policies of ILF Fund

Maturity:
1. No security may have a maturity more than 180 days.
2. Not more than 25 percent (by value) of the securities in the portfolio may have a maturity greater than 120 days.
3. The average maturity (weighted by the value of the securities in the portfolio) may not exceed 60 days.
4. At least 20 percent of the assets of the fund must have a maturity of less than 10 days.
5. The average maturity of the fund should not vary by more than 10 days during any given month.

Credit Risk:
1. The assets of the fund should be diversified over a range of types of securities and issuers of any given type of security.
2. At least 25 percent of the assets of the fund should be in U.S. government securities or government agency securities.
3. No more than 20 percent of the assets of the fund should be invested in any particular kind of security, and no more than 10 percent of the assets of the fund should be invested in the securities of any issuer, except for issues of the U.S. government.
4. No foreign time deposits should be held.
5. Domestic time deposits should be held only in commercial banks whose bonds carry the highest credit rating by Standard & Poor's and Moody's.
6. No commercial paper held by the fund should carry less than a prime-1 rating.
7. No security repurchase agreements should be held.

Exhibit 16–2   Portfolio Dimensions of ILF Fund

Mix of Assets:
1. U.S. government securities   = 50 percent
2. Commercial paper   = 15 percent
3. Prime certificates of deposit   = 15 percent
4. Bankers' acceptances   = 20 percent

Maturity of Assets:
1. Average maturity of portfolio   = 60 days
2. Average maturity of U.S. government securities   = 40 days
3. Average maturity of commercial paper   = 80 days
4. Average maturity of CDs   = 60 days
5. Average maturity of bankers' acceptances   = 40 days

Exhibit 16-3   Selected Money Market Rates

Prime rate	= 15¾–16½ percent
Federal funds rate	= 14½ percent
Call money	= 15¾–16 percent
Commercial paper	= 15⅛ percent, 30 days 15⅛ percent, 60 days 15 percent, 90 days 14½ percent, 90–270 days
Bankers' acceptances	= 14.75 percent, 30 days 14.70 percent, 60 days 14.65 percent, 120 days 14.40 percent, 150 days 14.20 percent, 180 days
Eurodollars	= 15¾ percent, 30 days 15⅞ percent, 60 days 15¾ percent, 90–180 days
Domestic CDs	= 14⅞ percent, 30 days 15 percent, 60–90 days 15⅛–15¼ percent, 90 days–1 year
U.S. government securities	= Bills: 13.47 percent, 3 months 13.60 percent, 6 months 13.43 percent, 9 months Notes: 14.87 percent, 1 year 14.41 percent, 5 years 14.60 percent, 10 years Bonds: 14.22 percent, 15 years 14.67 percent, 20 years 14.09 percent, 25 years

PART FIVE

Contractual Financial Institutions

17. *Life Insurance Companies*

LIFE INSURANCE COMPANIES number among the leading institutions in the financial system. Life insurance in force totaled more than $4 trillion in 1981, with 86 percent of all families in the United States holding policies from one or more legal reserve companies. U.S. families held an average of $53,200 in life insurance protection.

Life insurance companies are true financial intermediaries. Policyholders pay premiums to receive protection against the risk of financial loss associated with death, disability, or old age. In turn, those premiums are loaned out by the insurance company to corporations and governments. When a policyholder has a claim against the company, the life insurer will either liquidate some of its assets, draw upon current cash flow, or both to pay the claim. The strong predictability of most insurance claims has allowed life insurers to commit billions of dollars in funds to the capital market to support the economy's growth.

In this chapter we examine recent trends in the life insurance industry in the United States. We will focus first upon the types of risk protection sold by life insurers today and upon how the mix of policies bought by the public is changing. Then we turn our attention to the portfolio investment strategies of life insurance companies which have changed markedly in recent years under the pressure of inflation and high and volatile interest rates. The chapter concludes with an analysis of the structure of the life insurance industry and a look at recent innovations in insurance services.

SELLING RISK-PROTECTION SERVICES

The life insurance business has a long and distinguished history in the United States. Life insurers were one of the first intermediaries actively marketing financial services in America. A company known today as the Presbyterian Ministers Fund holds the distinction of being the oldest life insurer in the world having an unbroken record of service to its policyholders. The Ministers Fund was incorporated in Philadelphia in 1759. A few decades later the state of New York established itself as a leader in the supervision and regulation of the life insurance business, passing the first comprehensive insurance law in 1849 and setting up the first insurance department in 1859. Today there are insurance departments in all 50 states and the District of Columbia, each charged with the responsibility of regulating nearly 2,000 life insurance companies, whose combined assets now exceed $500 billion. Approximately 400 million life insurance policies are currently in force in the United States.

Risks Covered by Life Insurance

One of the most serious financial losses a family can incur is the premature death of one of its members, especially the principal wage earner. Life insurance policies are designed to minimize the financial impact of such an event by providing a supplemental source of income to a policyholder's designated beneficiaries. With an adequate size policy, the family's standard of living is protected until other sources of income can be developed.

Over the decades since the industry's inception, life insurance has evolved into a highly complex business, providing protection against a wide array of financial risks, not all of which are related to the death of a policyholder. In fact, there are three major forms of risk covered by life insurance company policies today—death, old age, and medical disability. In 1981, payments to beneficiaries associated with death claims reached nearly $14.2 billion, while cash awards and annuities paid during the lifetime of policyholders, many of whom had reached retirement age, amounted to almost $30 billion (see Table 17–1). These figures do not include health and medical benefits, which exceeded $24 billion in 1981.

Table 17–1 Benefit Payments and Premium Receipts for U.S. Citizens and U.S. Life Insurance Companies: 1981

Benefit Payments by U.S. Life Insurance Companies

Payment Recipients	*Amount ($ millions)*
Payments to beneficiaries	$14,154
Payments to policyholders	17,309
Payments to annuitants	12,021
Total payments	$43,484

Premium Receipts of U.S. Life Insurance Companies

Source of Premium Receipts	*Amount ($ millions)*
Life insurance policies	$ 47,356
Annuity policies	28,582
Health insurance policies	31,803
Total premium receipts	$107,741

Source: American Council of Life Insurance, *Life Insurance Fact Book, 1982*, Washington, D.C., p. 5; and Life Insurance Marketing and Research Association.

The life insurance business is founded on the principal of *sharing risk*. No one knows for sure when his or her death will occur. The same uncertainty exits in the case of medical disability and other events resulting in serious financial loss. However, with the purchase of an insurance policy, certainty is substituted for uncertainty. The certainty consists of premiums paid by the policyholder to the insurance company which purchase financial protection against an uncertain future loss. Thousands of policyholders pool their funds in an insurance company, each sharing in a portion of the loss which will be incurred by a few policyholders each year.

Why does insurance work? Simply because the risk of financial loss associated with death, disability, retirement, and so forth is highly predictable for a large group of individuals. Life insurance companies have no way of knowing, for example, who will die or be disabled in a given year. However, actuarial tables constructed from information obtained over a long period of observation tell the companies with a great deal of precision how many policyholders will incur losses and file legitimate claims each year.

Knowing how many claims are likely to be submitted by policyholders or their beneficiaries each year allows life insurers to derive a fairly precise estimate of their annual cash outflow. That outflow is an expense which, along with operating costs and a reasonable profit, must be covered by premiums charged policyholders and by investment income. In the life insurance business, annual premiums received from policyholders each year usually far exceed annual outgoing payments to policyholders or their beneficiaries. In other words, the companies experience a strong net cash *inflow* each year. However, the excess of cash received over cash outflow is not profit because life insurers know that, sooner or later, policyholder claims will roughly match any premiums paid in. Thus, incoming funds must be invested at adequate rates of return in preparation for the day when claimants must be paid off. If income from life insurance company investments is high enough, it will cover all legitimate claims, generate adequate profits for the company and, in some cases, yield extra funds to reduce insurance rates or increase the services available to policyholders.

Types of Policies Sold

The modern life insurance firm sells many different kinds of policies. The oldest and most traditional form of insurance is the *whole-life policy*, sometimes referred to as straight, ordinary, or permanent life insurance. The word *permanent* is particularly relevant in this case because a whole-life policy covers the policyholder for a lifetime as long as premiums are paid on schedule. A whole-life policy offers both risk protection and savings. Over time, the policy accumulates a cash value because a portion of annual premiums are set aside in a savings fund. If the policyholder decides to surrender his or her policy, that individual is entitled to receive back the policy's accumulated cash value. The policyholder can also borrow against a whole-life policy at a guaranteed rate of interest.

Whole-life policies offer benefits to the insurance company as well as to the policyholder. The amount of risk protection is usually a fixed dollar amount. For example, a policyholder might be insured for $50,000. In the event that policyholder dies, his or her designated beneficiaries would receive a death benefit of $50,000 (less any policyholder borrowings against the policy's cash value and accumulated interest expense on those borrowings). Thus, regardless of inflation or other developments, the insurance company would owe the deceased's beneficiaries no more than $50,000. This fixed-claim feature of traditional whole-life policies, coupled with the fact that most death claims occur years after a policy is first issued, has allowed life insurers to grow rapidly and to invest billions of dollars in long-term assets, such as corporate bonds and mortgages. As indicated in Table 17–2, whole-life insurance represented nearly 40 percent of life insurance policies purchased in 1981.

Another major form of life insurance is *term insurance*. As the name implies, risk protection is provided only for a specific time period, or

Table 17–2   Types of Policies Purchased from U.S. Life Insurance Companies: 1971 and 1981

Type of Policy	Policies Purchased (percent)		Amount of Policies in Force (percent)	
	1971	1981	1971	1981
Permanent insurance	32%	39%	27%	24%
Limited payment life	19	13	9	4
Endowment policies	6	1	3	*
Retirement income	3	1	2	1
Modified life	4	5	4	5
Modified term	†	2	†	10
Level or decreasing term	11	21	22	40
Family plan (FP)	4	1	3	*
(with additional term)	3	*	5	*
Regular policy with FP rider	4	6	5	5
(with additional term)	2	2	4	3
Combination policies	10	8	13	8
Progressive and other policies	2	1	3	*
Totals	100%	100%	100%	100%

Note: Figures in the table exclude credit life insurance.
*Less than 0.5 percent.
†Figure not available separately.
Sources: American Council of Life Insurance, *Life Insurance Fact Book, 1981,*Washington, D.C., p. 14; and *Life Insurance Fact Book, 1982,* Washington, D.C., p. 11.

term. For example, a customer might take out a term policy paying his or her beneficiaries $50,000 if the policyholder dies within the next 10 years. Term insurance is *much* cheaper than whole-life insurance. As a result, term policies have been expanding at a significantly faster pace than whole-life contracts, though the latter still have a good lead. In 1981, for example, term policies accounted for almost 40 percent of the amount of ordinary life insurance in force in the United States, while whole-life policies represented nearly 60 percent. As Table 17–3 indicates, the proportion of term insurance in all life policies outstanding has steadily climbed for about three decades.

The life insurance industry has been very much concerned about term insurance growth at the expense of sales of whole-life policies. The simple fact is that term policies do not generate as large a cash flow for investment purposes as do whole-life policies, since premiums associated with term policies are much lower. There is a clear threat to the long-term growth rate of the life insurance business. Many former whole-life customers have simply surrendered their more expensive permanent policies in favor of term protection and placed the difference in premium costs into other savings instruments—notably money market funds and bank CDs.

Of course, whole-life policies do build up cash values (savings) over time, which provide a liquid reservoir of funds for the policyholder to meet financial emergencies or to be used at retirement. The interest income which accumulates in a whole-life policy grows tax-free. Term insurance has no savings component.

A popular and more recent form of insurance with a substantial element of saving is the *annuity*. An annuity policy will pay out either death benefits, or, if the policyholder is still alive after a designated period, the

Table 17–3 Distribution of the Amount of Ordinary Life Insurance in the U.S. by Type of Insurance Plan (percent of policies in force)

Year	Whole-Life Policies	Other Types of Permanent Insurance Policies*	Term Insurance	Total
1954	65.5%	18.3%	16.2%	100.0%
1957	65.8	13.9	20.3	100.0
1962	66.1	9.5	24.4	100.0
1966	65.9	7.3	26.8	100.0
1970	64.3	7.2	28.5	100.0
1974	63.0	6.0	31.0	100.0
1977	60.9	5.8	33.3	100.0
1981	58.0	3.5	38.5	100.0

*Figures in this column include endowment and retirement income policies.
Source: American Council of Life Insurance, *Life Insurance Fact Book, 1982*, Washington, D.C., p. 25.

policy pays living cash benefits. The fundamental objective of an annuity policy is to guarantee income in the future. These policies build up tax-deferred interest on monies invested by the policyholder until he or she draws upon the account for current income, often at retirement. Sales of annuity contracts have been increasing rapidly in recent years because of a growing number of persons approaching retirement and their high tax-deferred yields which are competitive with municipal bonds and money market funds. Nearly seven million individual and supplemental annuity contracts were active at year-end 1981, while actual or owed annuity payments by life companies exceeded $10 billion during that year.[1]

Still another policy sold by U.S. life insurers is designed to pay a predetermined amount of money at policy maturity. This type of policy is known as an *endowment*. Endowment policy sales in the United States are limited; for example, they represented only about 1 percent of the policies purchased in the United States in 1981 (see Table 17–2). Some policyholders would prefer to pay off the cost of insurance protection early, perhaps while their incomes are high. In this instance, the policyholder may want a *limited payment* insurance contract. Premiums are paid for a specific time interval or until the policyholder is deceased. Limited payment contracts accounted for 13 percent of policy sales and 4 percent of the amount of policies issued in 1981, as indicated in Table 17–2.

Group life insurance provides coverage under a master policy for employees of business firms or governmental units and for union members as well as those belonging to professional organizations. This form of coverage has grown dramatically in recent years and in 1981 represented about 46 percent of the amount of all life insurance in force in the United States (see Table 17–4). *Industrial* life policies are small term insurance contracts with premiums collected weekly or monthly. The roughly $35 billion in industrial life policies carried by U.S. companies at year-end 1981 represented just under 1 percent of the amount of all outstanding life policies. Another form of term insurance is *credit* life, taken out when money is borrowed. Banks, credit unions, and other installment lenders sell credit life insurance in order to guarantee repayment of a loan in the event the borrower dies prematurely. While dwarfed in importance by individual and group policies, credit life insurance has been increasing rapidly and, as reflected in Table 17–4, totaled $162 billion by year-end 1981. As the composition of the types of policies written by life insurance companies

---

[1]Major changes in the tax status of annuity policies held mainly for retirement purposes were brought about by passage of the 1982 Tax Equity and Fiscal Responsibility Act. Prior to the new law, it was assumed that the initial withdrawals a policyholder made from an annuity were part of the accumulated principal and therefore tax-exempt. After the 1982 act, however, initial withdrawals are presumed to come from accumulated interest earnings and therefore are taxable. There is also a penalty tax rate for early withdrawals.

Table 17–4 Total Number of Life Insurance Policies and Amount of Life Insurance Protection for American Families: Selected Years, 1900–1981
(figures in millions of policies and $ millions)

| | Types of Insurance Policies | | | | | | | | | |
| | Ordinary Life Insurance | | Group Life Insurance | | Industrial Policies | | Credit Life Insurance | | Total | |
Year	No.	Amt.	No.	Amt.	No.	Amt.	No.	Amt.	No.	Amt.
1900	3	$ 6,124	—	$ —	11	$ 1,449	—	$ —	14	$ 7,573
1920	16	32,018	2	1,570	48	6,948	*	4	66	40,540
1940	37	79,346	9	14,938	85	20,866	3	380	134	115,530
1960	95	341,881	44	175,903	100	39,563	43	29,101	282	586,448
1981	149	1,978,080	123	1,888,612	55	34,547	73	162,356	400	4,063,595

*Less than 500,000.
Source: American Council of Life Insurance, *Life Insurance Fact Book, 1982,* Washington, D.C., p. 15.

changes, this changing mix affects the growth and composition of their loan and security investments. We will explore in more detail the effects of policy mix upon life insurance company investment policies at a later point in this chapter.

Characteristics of Life Insurance Customers

It is interesting to examine the basic characteristics of life insurance customers. A survey conducted by the Life Insurance Marketing and Research Association in 1981 indicated that about three fifths (55 percent) of all new policies were written for individuals between the ages of 15 and 34 (see Table 17–5). Much of this activity among younger age groups reflects the efforts of heads of households to protect their families against financial loss in the event a principal breadwinner dies. Younger families usually do not have sufficient accumulated assets to sustain family income when a principal earner in the household passes on. Moreover, more women are purchasing life insurance, undoubtedly reflecting their expanding role in the labor force and the increasing divorce rate. For example, the American Council of Life Insurance estimates that the ratio of male adults to female adults purchasing life insurance declined from 60 to 24 in 1971 to 52 to 33 in 1981. The average American family had almost $46,000 in life insurance[2] in 1981 and there were approximately 150 million policyholders—about two out of every three U.S. citizens and two out of every three households. The preponderance of policies are sold to middle- and upper-income individuals. As Table 17–5 indicates, almost 90 percent of insured individuals have annual incomes of $10,000 or more.

---

[2]As we noted at the beginning of this chapter, the average amount of life insurance coverage per *insured* U.S. family was $53,200 in 1981.

Table 17–5   Analysis of Insured Individuals and Life Insurance Policies Purchased in the United States: 1971 and 1981

Characteristics of Insured Individuals	Percent of Policies		Percent of Amount	
	1971	1981	1971	1981
Sex of Insured				
Male insureds under 15	9%	8%	3%	2%
Female insureds under 15	7	7	2	2
Male adults	60	52	83	75
Female adults	24	33	12	21
Totals	100%	100%	100%	100%
Age of Insured				
Under 15	16%	15%	5%	5%
15–24	33	23	28	14
25–34	25	32	36	40
35–44	14	16	20	27
45 or over	12	14	11	14
Totals	100%	100%	100%	100%
Income of Insured†				
Under $5,000	12%	*	6%	*
$5,000–$7,000	31	4	19	2
$7,500–$9,999	25	8	21	3
$10,000–$24,000	27	60	38	42
$25,000 or over	5	28	16	53
Totals	100%	100%	100%	100%
Mode of Premium Payment				
Annual	18%	17%	25%	26%
Semiannual	6	5	6	7
Quarterly	12	10	13	11
Monthly debit‡	22	22	9	5
Bank plan§	17	31	21	35
Other monthly	20	10	21	11
Salary savings	5	5	5	5
Totals	100%	100%	100%	100%

Note: Figures exclude credit life insurance.
*Less than 0.5 percent.
†Excluded from income figures are individuals 0 to 14 years of age and those without gainful income.
‡Includes a small amount of weekly premium ordinary.
§Under bank plan, the most common frequency of premium payments is monthly.
Source: American Council of Life Insurance, *Life Insurance Fact Book, 1982*, Washington, D.C., p. 11.

Recent Growth of the Life Insurance Industry

Total assets of U.S. life companies have grown rapidly in recent years. In 1981 the industry's total resources stood at $526 billion, which was more than double the $207 billion asset figure in 1970. In fact, the industry has roughly doubled its assets every decade. For example, in 1960 life insurers held $120 billion in assets and $64 billion in 1950. Paralleling the growth in assets, life insurance in force has increased from $242 billion in

1950 to more than $4 trillion in 1981. Purchases of new life insurance soared as the 1980s began. For example, policy purchases climbed more than 40 percent between 1980 and 1981, after a 16-percent rise between 1979 and 1980.

Policyholder Premiums and Investment Income

FUNDS RAISED BY LIFE INSURERS

Historically, the two most important sources of incoming funds for life insurers have been cash premiums paid by policyholders plus earnings from securities and other investments. As Table 17–6 reflects, these sources of cash inflow still dominate the industry's fund-raising picture. For example, in 1981 industry income from insurance premiums totaled almost $108 billion, or about 70 percent of income from all sources. Earnings from investment holdings brought in nearly $40 billion, a little over one quarter of all cash inflows.

What is particularly interesting about these two primary sources of industry cash receipts, however, is their comparative rates of growth. For example, income from insurance premiums between 1975 and 1981 rose a healthy 84 percent, due principally to rapid growth in health insurance and annuity policy premiums. In contrast, investment earnings much more than doubled. This sharp upward surge in investment income reflects, in part, the high interest rates generally prevailing in recent years which have significantly increased the industry's average rate of return on its securities portfolio. For example, during 1981 the net rate of investment income for U.S. life insurers was 8.53 percent (excluding capital gains or losses and separate accounts) versus just 6.44 percent in 1975.

Table 17–6   Income Received by U.S. Life Insurance Companies ($ millions)

Year	Premiums Received from:			Total Income from Insurance Policies	Earnings from Investment Holdings*	Income from Other Sources†	Total Income from All Sources
	Life Insurance Policies	Annuity Policies	Health Insurance Policies				
1945	$ 4,589	$ 570	—	$ 5,159	$ 1,445	$1,070	$ 7,674
1955	8,903	1,288	2,355	12,546	2,801	1,197	16,544
1965	16,083	2,260	6,261	24,604	6,778	1,785	33,167
1975	29,336	10,165	19,074	58,575	16,488	2,959	78,022
1980	40,829	24,030	29,366	94,225	33,928	4,336	132,489
1981	47,356	28,582	31,803	107,741	39,773	4,351	151,865

*Beginning in 1951 the industry recorded investment income net of investment expenses.
†Beginning with 1975 the figures from other income sources include commissions and expense allowance on reinsurance ceded.
Source: American Council of Life Insurance, *Life Insurance Fact Book, 1982*, Washington, D.C., p. 55.

The higher investment earnings also reflect, as we will soon see, a more aggressive investment posture by the industry which stresses more flexible returns and greater short-run earnings.

Separate Accounts and General Accounts

Another interesting and highly important development in industry fund raising is concealed by the foregoing figures—the rapid growth of a new source of cash inflow known as the *separate account*. The figures shown in Table 17–6 reflect only earnings from the industry's *general accounts*, which arise mainly from sales of life and health insurance policies. Separate accounts, on the other hand, are a separate legal entity from traditional insurance selling and investing. They represent investment accounts managed by a life insurer on behalf of corporate pension plans, mutual funds, partnerships, and so forth in return for a fee for expert management advice and portfolio trading. The concept of a separate account first arose in the early 1960s when life insurance companies offered to manage the pension plans of several corporations. Assets acquired in a separate account on behalf of the customer must be held apart from all other insurance company assets and are subject to much less restrictive investment regulations than is true of assets held in the insurance company's general accounts. While a company's general accounts are normally invested in a widely diversified portfolio of bonds, mortgages, and some equity shares, separate accounts often emphasize maximum current earnings, and their portfolio may be devoted exclusively to common stock or to some other high-yielding investment.[3]

Separate accounts have been growing rapidly. For example, in 1981 these accounts held assets valued at more than $44 billion, compared to just under $13 billion in 1975. Equally important, however, is the rapid growth of industry cash inflows from separate accounts. As recently as 1975, income receipts from separate accounts represented less than 10 percent of the industry's investment earnings, whereas in 1981 such accounts brought in close to one third of the investment earnings of all U.S. life insurers. As might be expected, the average yield on investments held in separate accounts substantially exceeds the average return on life insurers'

---

[3]The predominant use of separate accounts today is in the annuity field, mainly pension plans. However, an interesting recent development is the use of separate accounts to fund variable life insurance plans. In such a plan the policyholder's beneficiaries would receive, not a fixed cash benefit (as is true of most ordinary life policies), but benefits dependent upon the value of assets pledged to the variable life contract at the time those benefits are actually paid. Most such contracts would be invested in inflation-hedged assets such as common stock.

general accounts.[4] Recent figures released by the American Council of Life Insurance reveal that nearly 40 percent of the assets held in separate accounts at year-end 1981 were in common stocks and about 11 percent in real estate, both percentages substantially higher than is true of common stock and real estate holdings in the companies' general accounts.

Changing Mix of Premium Receipts

As we have seen, premiums paid by policyholders have dominated the cash inflows of life insurers from the industry's beginnings. However, the composition or mix of premium income has changed significantly in recent years with changing customer demand for different types of risk protection. For example, premiums from the sale of ordinary life insurance policies represented only 44 percent of total premium receipts in 1981, compared to 56 percent in 1971. Premium receipts from annuity contracts represented only 10 percent of premium income in 1971, but grew to 27 percent in 1981. Only health insurance premiums maintained a relatively constant share of the industry's premium receipts, accounting for about 30 percent of life insurer's premium income. Further relative gains in annuity premiums, due to burgeoning retirement income needs, are likely. And many experts predict that, due to rapidly growing medical costs, health insurance premiums may indeed increase their share of insurance company sales in future years.

When premiums flow in, insurers must invest those funds immediately in preparation for the day when benefits must be paid to policyholders or their beneficiaries. And payment of legitimate policyholder claims cannot be postponed. They must be paid in full and in timely fashion as agreed upon in the policy contract. For this reason, insurance companies must place a high priority on *safety*—minimizing risk—when premium receipts are invested. Moreover, tradition, law, and regulation all emphasize safety in the industry. The common law and the courts hold life insurers to the standard of the "prudent man," where the investment of funds is concerned. Pursuit of the highest available returns in the market, regardless

CHANGING INVESTMENT STRATEGIES OF LIFE INSURERS

---

[4]Some indication of the difference in returns from the very large general life insurance accounts versus the smaller separate accounts is provided by the broad average net return on the industry's total investment portfolio. In 1981 the net investment return, including earnings from separate accounts, was 8.57 percent, compared to an 8.53 percent overall return on all investments, excluding the separate accounts. While this is a difference of only 4 basis points across the whole industry's securities portfolio, it represents a substantial difference in the earnings flow from general versus separate accounts, since the industry's investment portfolio in 1981 exceeded $400 billion.

of the risk involved, is *not* considered prudent. However, purchases of highly rated bonds (preferably investment-grade issues of at least Baa or BBB rating), first mortgages on commercial and residential properties, and top-quality common and preferred stocks generally fulfill the requirements of the prudent-man rule.

Until recently, the industry's investment strategy could be described quite simply: *Buy* long-term securities in the capital market (preferably bonds, mortgages, and some stock) and *hold* them until maturity. Life insurance benefit claims are long-term in nature; most policyholders take out policies when they are young, but claims will not arise for several years in most cases. Moreover, inflows of policy premiums are highly predictable; they are fixed by the policy contract. Putting all this together, most life insurers concluded their investments needed to be predominantly long-term financial instruments, promising a stable and predictable flow of income in the form of interest and dividends. Marketability was a secondary consideration because it was unlikely that an investment would have to be sold prior to its maturity. In brief, the industry's investment strategy could be described as one of buy and hold.[5]

If the industry was going to buy and hold and the marketability of most of its securities was not a major consideration, investment officers of life insurance companies reasoned that they need not purchase all their investments from the highly competitive open market. Higher yields could often be obtained in off-the-market transactions (often called *private* or *direct placements*) in which borrower and insurance company directly negotiated a loan. Then the insurance company simply acquired all the borrower's IOUs (bonds or mortgages). Moreover, there is a clear advantage for the security issuer since there is no need to register a privately placed issue with the Securities and Exchange Commission as is true of bonds offered in the open market. In addition, with private placements, life insurers avoid early *calls* and can hold the securities acquired until they mature, consistent with their traditional buy-and-hold strategy.

The volatile economic environment of recent years has brought about significant changes in the industry's investment strategy, especially among the larger companies. Rapidly rising interest rates sharply reduced the value of many long-term, fixed-rate corporate bonds and mortgages held in life

---

[5]In a recent article, O'Leary [13] notes that many investment officers of life companies argued that interest rates were, in general, *unpredictable*. Therefore the safest investment strategy was simply to employ a dollar-averaging technique which called for long-term investments in bonds and mortgages offering a variety of long-term fixed interest rates. On the average, presumably, the insurance company would earn an acceptable long-run rate of return even if there were highly volatile, short-run changes in interest rates due to cyclical changes and inflation.

company portfolios.[6] At the same time, the relatively modest yields on older investment securities limited the growth of life insurance company income and, therefore, the ability of these companies to offer new services and more attractive terms to customers. Adding to the problem, the quality of some corporate securities declined due to deepening financial problems experienced by the issuing firms.

The larger insurers responded to these pressures with a more flexible, market-sensitive investment policy. The average maturity of life insurance company investments was shortened significantly and many life insurance company investment officers refused to purchase debt securities above 10 to 15 years to maturity. At the same time, investment portfolios began to turn over more rapidly. The total-performance or total-return concept was developed in which the performance of securities already owned was evaluated on a continuing basis. Poorly performing securities were replaced with newer, more promising investments. A number of the largest companies created securities trading departments to keep close track of daily developments in the financial markets and to actively buy and sell securities. *Portfolio switching*, rather than a simple buy-and-hold strategy, became the centerpiece of financial management for many insurance firms. Today, *both* investment strategies—the traditional and the total-performance or total-return concept—exist side by side in the industry. Most life insurance managers seem to feel they are more able to deal with changing economic circumstances than was true a decade ago.

Along with greater emphasis on portfolio switching to seek higher returns, the use of private placements of securities has declined in the industry. A greater number of securities are purchased today in the more competitive open market. The principal reason is a greater need for the more readily marketable and liquid securities sold in the open market; in contrast, privately placed securities are generally nonmarketable and, therefore, are not liquid investments. Life insurers' increased need for liquidity stems from greater uncertainty surrounding the predictability of their cash flows. Customers who take out whole-life cash-value insurance policies are more likely today to borrow against them or cash these policies in, draining investment capital from the industry. At the same time, the growth of separate accounts, alluded to earlier, creates a potential cash outflow less predictable than conventional life insurance claims, increasing the need for more liquid, more marketable investments.

---

[6]Many of the bonds and mortgages held by life insurance companies were purchased during the 1960s and early 1970s when interest rates were much lower. Rapidly rising rates in the late 1970s and early 1980s sharply reduced the market value of these older investment securities.

DISTRIBUTION OF ASSETS IN THE LIFE INSURANCE INDUSTRY

The marked changes in investment strategies pursued by life insurance companies have had a profound impact on the assets these companies hold. As suggested by the figures given in Table 17–7, holdings of liquid assets (especially U.S. government securities and short-term, open-market paper), corporate stock, and real estate investments (included under miscellaneous assets) have gained at the expense of long-term bonds and mortgages. In the ensuing paragraphs of this section we take a close look at each of the major investment assets held by U.S. life insurance companies.

Liquid Assets

The need and demand for liquidity—readily available purchasing power—has increased sharply in recent years due to a more volatile economy and the changing preferences of insurance customers. One way to meet this burgeoning demand for liquidity would be to hold cash—currency and checkable bank deposits. However, life insurers, like most investors, do not like to hold substantial amounts of cash since it earns little or nothing. Indeed, as indicated in Table 17–7, the industry's cash holdings have fluctuated around 1 percent of total assets over the past two decades.

Table 17–7   Financial Assets and Liabilities of U.S. Life Insurance Companies: 1960, 1970, and 1982 (year-end outstandings in $ billions)

	Amount and Percent of Total for:					
	1960		1970		1982	
Asset or Liability Item	$	%	$	%	$	%
Financial Assets						
Demand deposits and currency	$ 1.3	1.1%	$ 1.8	0.9%	$ 5.9	1.0%
Corporate stock	5.0	4.3	15.4	7.7	58.6	10.4
U.S. government securities	6.5	5.6	4.6	2.3	33.5	5.9
State and local government securities	3.6	3.1	3.3	1.6	8.1	1.4
Corporate and foreign bonds	48.1	41.5	74.1	36.9	198.6	35.2
Mortgages	41.8	36.1	74.4	37.0%	141.9	25.2
Open-market paper	0.3	0.3	2.1	1.0	22.6	4.0
Policy loans	5.2	4.5	16.1	8.0	53.1	9.4
Miscellaneous assets	3.9	3.4	9.2	4.6	41.3	7.3
Total financial assets	115.8	100.0	200.9	100.0	563.6	100.0
Liabilities						
Life insurance reserves	78.8	72.6	123.1	65.6	234.6	43.8
Pension fund reserves	18.9	17.4	41.2	21.9	228.8	42.7
Profit taxes payable	0.4	0.4	0.8	0.4	4.2	0.8
Miscellaneous liabilities	10.5	9.7	22.6	12.0	68.1	12.7
Total liabilities	$108.5	100.0%	$187.7	100.0%	$535.6	100.0%

Note: Columns may not add to totals due to rounding.
Source: Board of Governors of the Federal Reserve System, *Flow of Funds Accounts, Assets and Liabilities Outstanding, 1957–80.*

Instead, life insurers have met their increased need for liquidity by holding more money market assets and U.S. government notes and bonds which have the best resale (secondary) markets. For example, during 1981 four fifths of all industry new investments were in short-term (under one year) securities—an unprecedented proportion of funds flowing into near-term security obligations. Most of the new money flowed into the commercial paper market and into other short-term corporate IOUs. However, a substantial portion also flowed into U.S. Treasury notes, bonds, and bills—the life insurance industry's traditional liquid reserve. As shown in Table 17–8, industry investments in U.S. Treasury securities climbed to over $8 billion in 1981, while holdings of securities issued by federal agencies climbed even higher, to more than $14 billion.[7] Life insurers also hold small amounts of state and local government securities for their tax-exempt and liquid character and a sizable portion of foreign government securities. Included among the latter are mainly obligations of Canadian central and provincial governments as well as bonds from governmental units in France, Israel, Japan, Mexico, and Sweden, and obligations of the World Bank.

Corporate Stock

Relative to their other assets, life insurance companies hold a limited amount of common and preferred stock. For example, at year-end 1981 stock holdings represented only about 9 percent of industry assets. In dollar terms, however, the industry's stock investments were a substantial

Table 17–8   Government Securities Held by U.S. Life Insurance Companies: Selected Years, 1945–1981 ($ millions)

Year	United States Issues			Foreign Govt. and International Agency Securities	Total Amount Held	Percent of Total Industry Assets
	U.S. Treasury Securities	Federal Agency Securities*	State and Local Govt. Securities			
1945	$20,583	$ —	$ 722	$1,240	$22,545	50.3%
1955	8,576	—	2,038	1,215	11,829	13.1
1965	5,119	167	3,530	3,092	11,908	7.5
1975	4,736	1,419	4,508	4,514	15,177	5.2
1980	5,838	11,144	6,701	9,332	33,015	6.9
1981	8,167	14,293	7,151	9,891	39,502	7.5

*The first year in which life insurance companies held federal agency securities was 1956; estimated holdings that year were $50 million, and that amount was recorded in other accounts at that time.

Source: American Council of Life Insurance, *Life Insurance Fact Book, 1982*, Washington, D.C., p. 75.

[7]Among the most popular federal agency securities held by life insurers are notes issued by the Federal National Mortgage Association ("Fannie Mae") and the Federal Home Loan Banks. The majority have maturities of one year or less.

sum—$48 billion (see Table 17–9). Roughly three quarters of all stock investments are in common equity and the rest are preferred shares. During the 1970s, investments in stock fluctuated widely and often declined; however, as the 1980s began, the industry's interest in the stock market revived.

In terms of the whole market for stock in the United States, life insurers are not a dominant factor. They rank third among all institutional investors in corporate equities. State laws, historically, have severely restricted the industry's stock investments, and, as we saw earlier, the industry's traditional investment strategy has emphasized guaranteed income rather than speculative investments. However, the role of life insurers in the stock market is growing due to the expansion of insured pension and variable annuity plans. State laws generally allow substantial purchases of equity securities for pension and annuity plans, provided these securities are placed in a separate account. About half of all common stock held by life insurers today is in separate accounts.

Corporate Debt Securities

Life insurance companies have been major investors in bonds and notes issued by corporations almost from their inception. And the industry remains the largest institutional purchaser of corporate IOUs. In fact, roughly 40 percent of corporate bonds outstanding today are held by the life insurance industry. As Table 17–10 shows, domestic and foreign bonds issued by corporations made up about 37 percent of the industry's assets in 1981. Holdings of corporate bonds by life insurers cover a wide spectrum of industries. However, in recent years industrial bonds and notes have grown rapidly, reflecting the dynamic growth of the U.S. man-

Table 17–9 Corporate Stock Held by U.S. Life Insurance Companies: Selected Years, 1945–1981 ($ millions)

Year	Common Stock	Preferred Stock	Total Amount Held	Percent of Total Industry Assets
1945	$ *	$ *	$ 999	2.2%
1955	1,889	1,744	3,633	4.0
1965	6,263	2,963	9,126	5.7
1975	20,304	7,757	28,061	9.7
1980	35,571	11,795	47,366	9.9
1981	35,408	12,262	47,670	9.1

*Breakdown of these figures is not available.
Source: American Council of Life Insurance, *Life Insurance Fact Book, 1982,* Washington, D.C., p. 77.

Table 17–10   Corporate Bonds Held by U.S. Life Insurance Companies: Selected Years, 1945–1981 ($ millions)

Year	Bonds Issued by U.S. Corporations	Foreign Corporate Bonds	Total Amount Held	Percent of Total Industry Assets
1945	$ *	$ *	$ 10,060	22.5%
1955	34,629	1,283	35,912	39.7
1965	54,835	3,409	58,244	36.7
1975	99,993	5,844	105,837	36.6
1980	169,699	9,904	179,603	37.5
1981	182,613	11,193	193,806	36.8

*Breakdown of these figures is not available.
Source: American Council of Life Insurance, *Life Insurance Fact Book, 1982*, Washington, D.C., p. 77.

ufacturing and industrial sector and its burgeoning demands for long-term credit. Life insurers also hold significant quantities of public utility bonds, communications industry bonds, railroad bonds, and securities of foreign corporations.

One of the most interesting features of life insurance company investments in long-term corporate securities—both bonds and mortgages—is the *forward commitment* process. In the past the cash flows of life insurers were so regular and predictable they would commit themselves to loans, especially those loans needed to support large construction projects, far in advance of the actual receipt of funds. Such loans would normally be made to developers of income properties (such as hotels, shopping centers, office buildings, and apartment complexes) and for many years carried a fixed, guaranteed interest rate. If the life insurance company found itself temporarily short of funds when a commitment had to be honored, it would typically borrow short-term funds (usually from a bank) or would "warehouse" securities with another lender in return for temporary financing.

As the 1980s began, life insurers discovered quite painfully that the old forward commitment process was simply not flexible enough to deal with volatile interest rates and major shifts in economic conditions. While advance commitments used to be made at fixed interest rates, many companies still giving commitments tie the interest rate on the loan pledge to a variable market rate. At the same time, forward commitments have shortened drastically in average maturity from two to three years—very common in the past—to a few weeks or months. And the maturity of the bonds and mortgages taken on have been shortened significantly (frequently to 10 years or less).

Commercial, Residential, and Farm Mortgages

Mortgages are secured by a lien on real property, including family residences, apartment houses, condominiums, hotels and motels, shopping centers, office buildings, and manufacturing and service establishments. Life insurance companies have always been significant investors in financing these forms of real property, though their mortgage holdings have declined relative to other assets in the most recent period. At year-end 1981, $137 billion was invested by U.S. life insurance firms in mortgages, representing about one quarter of all assets industrywide. Life insurers' heavy investments in real estate mortgages over the years may be explained by their relatively high yields and good investment quality.

Total mortgage holdings have actually been declining as a percent of industry assets since 1976, when nearly 40 percent of total assets were invested in this financial instrument. Life insurers prior to the 1960s provided roughly one fourth of all capital in the U.S. flowing into the financing of single-family homes. However, industry investments in home mortgages peaked in the mid-60s and have been declining as a proportion of the industry's portfolio ever since. For example, mortgage loans on one- to four-family dwellings represented about 13 percent of total real property loans made by the industry in 1981, compared to 32 percent only 10 years earlier. However, other—principally multifamily apartments, commercial, and farm—mortgages have generally increased. The most dramatic gains have been in industry holdings of nonfarm, nonresidential mortgage loans, which rose from 38 percent in 1971 to 64 percent in 1980. The reasons for the decline in home mortgage investing are manifold. Most home mortgage securities are relatively small and costly to administer. Moreover, there are interest-rate ceilings on FHA-VA home mortgages, which have held their yields below market levels frequently in recent years. Yields on commercial mortgages, on the other hand, are not constrained by legally imposed rate ceilings and they fluctuate with market conditions. At the same time, there is strong competition from other lenders (such as banks and savings and loans) for home mortgages, but less competition for commercial and farm mortgages. Recent changes in industry holdings of mortgages are illustrated in Table 17–11.

A major shift in the industry's mortgage and corporate bond investment policies occurred during the 1960s and 1970s and intensified as the 1980s began. This shift was toward greater *equity participation* in commercial projects like office buildings, shopping centers, and apartment buildings. In prior periods, life companies were usually quite content to accept long-term, fixed-rate bonds and mortgages to finance large-scale commercial projects. However, years of rapid inflation and volatile interest rates caused portfolio managers to look for more flexible returns from their

Table 17–11   Mortgages Held by U.S. Life Insurance Companies: Selected Years, 1945–1981 ($ millions)

| Year | Farm Mortgages | Nonfarm Mortgages | | | Total Amount Held | Percent of Total Industry Assets |
		FHA-Insured	VA-Insured	Conventional Mortgages		
1945	$ 776	$ *	$ *	$ *	$ 6,636	14.8%
1955	2,273	6,530	6,074	14,568	29,445	32.6
1965	4,823	12,538	6,286	36,366	60,013	37.8
1975	6,753	8,502	3,903	70,009	89,167	30.8
1980	12,958	6,066	2,781	109,275	131,080	27.4
1981	13,100	5,651	2,590	116,406	137,747	26.2

*Breakdown of these figures is not available.
Source: American Council of Life Insurance,
Life Insurance Fact Book, 1982, Washington, D.C., p. 79.

bond and mortgage commitments. The result was greater use of "equity kickers," with the life insurance company lending money to a project on condition that it would receive a share of the returns normally flowing to the project's owners. Thus a life insurance company financing the construction of an office building might insist on a share of the building's rental income and/or a portion of the expected appreciation in the building's market value in addition to receiving interest payments on a loan. Through the use of equity kickers, life insurance companies hoped to protect their earnings from the impact of inflation by turning fixed income flows into variable income flows possessing greater upside potential.

Direct Real Estate Investments

Faced with the prospect of continuing inflation, life insurance companies have increased their direct ownership of real property in recent years. As interest rates rose repeatedly to record levels during the 1970s and early 1980s, insurance companies saw the value of their bonds and stocks fall, but, spurred by inflation, the market value of buildings and land continued to spiral upward. Not surprisingly, then, many insurers increased their involvement in the construction and direct ownership of apartment complexes, shopping centers, and office buildings. For example, as shown in Table 17–12, U.S. life insurance companies by year-end 1981 had invested more than $18 billion (3.5 percent of their assets) in real property. Today life insurers maintain substantial equity interests in high-rise buildings in most major U.S. cities. More recently, they have purchased substantial ownership interests in suburban shopping centers, buying these properties from real estate developers and leasing them back to the devel-

Table 17-12   Real Estate Owned by U.S. Life Insurance Companies:
Selected Years, 1945–1981 ($ millions)

Year	Total Amount Held	Percent of Total Industry Assets
1945	$ 857	1.9%
1955	2,581	2.9
1965	4,681	3.0
1975	9,681	3.3
1980	15,033	3.1
1981	18,278	3.5

Source: American Council of Life Insurance, *Life Insurance Fact Book, 1982,*
Washington, D.C., p. 83.

opers or to other firms who manage and service the property. More than 98 percent of the real estate ventures of U.S. life insurers are located in the United States, with most of the remainder in Canada.

In recent years, a number of life insurers have entered the real estate development field either by themselves or in partnership with established developers. Some of the largest companies in the industry today act as both lender and developer on such large commercial projects as apartment complexes, retail shopping centers, and office buildings. In some cases the insurer both builds and then owns and operates the new facilities, while in others the insurance company builds and then sells the property to a new owner. Major life insurers involved in real estate development activity today include Aetna Life and Casualty Company, Equitable Life Assurance Society, Metropolitan Life, and Prudential.

Loans Advanced to Policyholders

Another asset—loans to policyholders—more than doubled in dollar amount during the 1970s. These loans have represented about 8 percent of industry assets for several years running but moved above 9 percent in 1981 to nearly $49 billion (see Table 17–13). The substantial growth in the dollar value of policy loans during the past few years is a response of policyholders to the high and rising rates of interest on other sources of loanable funds. Conventional whole-life policies build up cash value which the policyholder can draw upon through a policy loan, usually at a fixed rate of interest. Until recently, the maximum loan rate on most policies issued was in the range of 5 to 6 percent, which was far below the cost of borrowing funds elsewhere. Not surprisingly, whenever interest rates rise to high levels, policy loans increase, draining funds from insurance companies. Today, on new policies, loan rates average much higher and the industry has asked state regulators to allow flexible policy loan rates tied to market conditions. In any event, loans against whole-life insurance policies have

Table 17–13   Policy Loans Issued by U.S. Life Insurance Companies: Selected Years, 1945–1981 ($ millions)

Year	Total Amount Held	Percent of Total Industry Assets
1945	$ 1,962	4.4%
1955	3,290	3.6
1965	7,678	4.8
1975	24,467	8.5
1980	41,411	8.6
1981	48,706	9.3

Source: American Council of Life Insurance, *Life Insurance Fact Book, 1982,* Washington, D.C., p. 85.

been a relatively cheap source of funds for individual policyholders over the years.

Most policyholders drawing loans anticipate earning more on those borrowed funds than the policy loan rate. This expectation of a surplus return over cost usually increases, of course, when interest rates in the economy rise, such as occurred during the 1973–74 and 1978–80 periods. Interestingly enough, policyholders who borrow against their whole-life policies are also more likely to cash their policies in early, receiving in a lump-sum payment whatever the cash-surrender value of their policies happens to be. The result of this increased borrowing by policyholders is, of course, a smaller volume of funds available for investment by the industry at a time when much higher returns are generally available in the financial markets. This form of *disintermediation* also has had profound implications for the investments made by life insurers. No longer can the manager of a life insurance company investment portfolio assume that all policies sold represent long-term claims against the company. Some policies will result in short-term claims, which may well necessitate selling securities to raise cash. This encourages life insurers to emphasize shorter-term, more highly marketable, and more liquid security investments.

Factors Affecting Life Insurers' Net Income

INCOME AND TAXATION OF THE INDUSTRY

The life insurance business is reasonably profitable. But where do the profits come from? Premiums paid in by policyholders will eventually be returned to them or to their beneficiaries in the form of cash benefits. If the industry is to turn a profit, it must rely heavily upon its earnings from investments. In 1981 the net rate of return on the industry's invested assets was 8.57 percent, up substantially from 1980's 8.02 percent return. Soaring interest rates during the 1970s and early 1980s caused the rate of return on invested assets to climb sharply. For example, in 1970 the net rate of investment income was 5.3 percent and in 1975, 6.36 percent.

The majority of net earnings from industry investments flow into capital accounts serving as a reserve against future needs for funds. Most premiums collected from policyholders flow initially into *policy reserves*. State laws regulating the industry mandate that policy reserves must be high enough to cover all benefit claims in timely fashion. Policy reserves reached $428 billion in 1981. Other reserves, which result mainly from net earnings, flow into various equity accounts to cover future expenses and investment risk.

Taxation of the Industry

Life insurance firms are taxed at all three levels of government—state, local, and federal—in the United States. In the case of federal taxation, effective income tax rates are significantly lower than rates paid by other U.S. corporations, though the industry's effective income tax rate has roughly tripled since 1960. State and local governments frequently impose taxes on the gross premium receipts of life insurers selling policies in their locale. However, two thirds of the aggregate taxes paid by life insurance companies take the form of federal income taxes levied against earnings from investments and from operations. The tax burden of the industry has increased significantly in recent years, particularly following passage of the Life Insurance Company Tax act of 1959 and the Tax Equity and Fiscal Responsibility Act of 1982. U.S. life insurance companies paid federal, state, and local fees, licenses, and taxes of about $4 billion in 1981. However, federal income taxation actually became less significant for the industry in 1980 and 1981. Many insurance companies have saved a substantial amount in federal tax liabilities in recent years due to so-called modified coinsurance contracts. Under these contracts, income from investments flow into special funds with lower tax rates. However, this tax loophole was sharply reduced in 1982 with passage of the Tax Equity and Fiscal Responsibility Act.

GOVERNMENT SUPERVISION AND CONTROL

State laws and rulings by federal and state courts have profoundly influenced the way life insurers operate over the years. Virtually every aspect of the business, from selling and writing policy contracts to paying claims, is regulated at the state level. Interestingly enough, except for tax laws and laying down the rules for offering new securities, *federal* involvement in the life insurance business is slight. This minimal role for federal authorities differs substantially from that encountered by depository intermediaries, where the federal government often dominates the regulatory process.

State insurance commissions or departments represent the cutting edge of government insurance regulation in the United States. Each of the 50 states (and the District of Columbia) has a regulatory official or group overseeing the industry's activities within its borders. The names vary: For example, Colorado has an insurance commissioner; Arizona, a director of insurance; and Maine, a superintendent of insurance. However, regardless of what label is used, state regulators tend to look at the same facets of industry operations: (1) promoting the safety of policyholder funds by regulating the quality of investments made, (2) insuring an adequate volume and mix of insurance services for the public, (3) regulating entry and exit from the industry, and (4) setting premium rates at reasonable levels to insure adequate company profits without gouging the public. When premium rates are changed or the content of services is altered, public hearings are usually held with both industry officials and consumer groups often represented.

THE STRUCTURAL MAKEUP OF THE LIFE INSURANCE INDUSTRY

Like the savings and loan industry discussed in an earlier chapter, life insurance firms encompass both stockholder-owned corporations and mutuals. A *mutual* company is owned by its policyholders and operated for their benefit. A *stock* insurer is owned by its stockholders; the policyholder in this case is a customer and a creditor once a claim is filed. As of year-end 1980 there were 1,958 U.S. life insurers of which 135 were mutuals and 1,823 were stock companies. The number of stock companies is growing quite rapidly, however, though the mutuals are, on average, both older and larger (see Table 17–14). The amount of policies written is about equally split between the stocks and the much larger mutuals, but the mutuals hold about three fifths of the assets.

As the 1980s began, a new structural trend began to unfold among major life insurance companies. A new type of insurance organization—the symbiotic financial firm—appeared, offering a wide array of financial ser-

Table 17–14   Life Insurance Companies Operating in the U.S. and the Year These Companies Commenced Business

Year Companies Commenced Business	Stockholder-Owned Companies	Mutual Companies	Total in Industry*
1875 and earlier	9	22	31
1876–1925	94	34	128
1926–50	174	39	213
1951–60	348	20	368
1961–70	482	20	502
1971–80	716	0	716
Total operating in 1980	1,823	135	1,958

*Totals are numbers of companies at year-end 1980.
Source: American Council of Life Insurance, *Life Insurance Fact Book, 1982*, Washington, D.C., p. 90.

vices, many of which are designed to compete with commercial banks and brokerage companies.[8] A good example was the 1981 acquisition of Bache Group, Inc., a major securities broker, by Prudential Insurance Company, a leading mutual. In 1982 Prudential began to sell shares in mutual funds through its insurance agents. This is in addition to a cash-management service offered through Prudential's Bache affiliate. Another example of life insurance expansion into the securities business is provided by the New Equitable Life Assurance Society with a money market fund already in operation. In addition, Equitable recently asked the New York State Insurance Department for permission to begin offering cash-management services to corporations. Such services enable a customer to combine checking-account powers with access to a credit account, a money market fund, and a stock market margin account. Thus the nation's largest life insurance companies appear determined to expand their activities into securities trading and brokerage in order to attract both commercial and consumer funds. It is an attempt to diversify their operations, open new avenues for growth in funding, and become less dependent on conventional insurance services for their future income.

NEW SERVICES IN THE INDUSTRY

In recent years, life insurance companies have been under tremendous pressure to innovate and offer new services with higher returns or lower costs to the customer. Evidence of newly emerging customer demands is provided by the growth of policy loans and surrenders of whole-life policies for cash as well as the shift by customers from whole-life to cheaper term insurance. Threatened with a significant loss of premium income, most life insurers have responded with innovative new programs.[9]

Innovation of this sort opens up new sources of revenue and promotes the long-term growth of the industry. New types of policies have appeared which offer the policyholder a greater return (often tax-deferred) on his or her savings as well as lower or more flexible premium payments. As interest rates soared in the late 1970s and early 1980s, life insurers were able to earn more on their investments and pass more of those extra earnings on

---

[8]See Chapter 8 for a more detailed discussion of symbiotic financial firms.

[9]The demand for traditional life insurance policies was also adversely affected with passage of the Economic Recovery Act in 1981 and by other changes in federal and state tax rules, especially those applying to estates. Beginning in 1982, federal and state taxes against estates were slated to decline over a six-year period, eventually permitting the passage of up to $1.2 million tax-free to a person's designated heirs. Frequently in the past, life insurance was purchased to wholly or partially offset estate taxes. However, life insurance can still be advisable to sustain family income after the death of a primary breadwinner or due to the impact of inflation on the value of an estate.

to their customers. The result is a menu of new policy packages which attempt to combine the savings feature of whole-life plans with the risk protection offered in conventional term policies, while offering a savings interest rate that compares favorably in some instances with money market securities or deposits.

One example of a recent innovation is the development of *variable annuities* for individual retirement programs. Offering a hedge against future inflation, variable annuities eventually pay out a stream of earnings based on the performance of an investment portfolio. These annuity contracts are used widely for group retirement programs. Some variable annuities are tied to an index of living costs (such as the consumer price index). Income flows then will be sensitive to inflation, unlike the traditional forms of insurance which, as we have seen, are generally fixed-rate contracts.

Related to variable annuities is *variable life insurance*. There are several varieties, including variable life, adjustable life, and variable-premium life. Under a variable-life plan, benefits are related to the market value of an investment portfolio. Assets backing such a policy normally are equity securities held in a separate account. Often there is a policy contract provision that death benefits will not be allowed to go below some minimum guaranteed amount. Adjustable life permits a policyholder to shift to term insurance or to permanent (whole-life) insurance based on the customer's financial situation and preferences. In addition, the customer may be allowed to change benefits, premium payments, or policy maturity dates consistent with contract specifications. Variable premium policies, in contrast, permit variation in premium rates based on the life insurer's earnings. If inflation results in higher interest rates, increasing an insurer's income, policyholder premiums would fall. Policies whose death benefit varies with market conditions are more like direct purchases of stocks and bonds and therefore must be sold with a prospectus.

A major new type of policy appeared as the 1970s drew to a close and the 1980s began. Responding to the brilliant success of money market funds, life insurance companies developed *universal life* policies. A portion of incoming premium payments are invested in a money market mutual fund and are also employed to purchase term insurance protection for the policyholder. Thus a universal life policy combines insurance coverage for a fixed period with flexible short-term investments to build up a savings fund for the policyholder. Universal policies accumulate interest income tax-free until the policyholder draws on the accumulated savings. As a result, the rate of return to the policyholder usually exceeds that earned from conventional whole-life policies. Moreover, universal life insurance carries variable premiums, permitting the policyholder to decide how much to pay and therefore how much insurance protection and savings to acquire.[10]

Developed originally by E. F. Hutton Life Insurance Company, universal policies really resemble a money market account more than a life insurance plan. For example, when premiums fall due the insurer merely deducts the required amount from the policyholder's money market fund account. Moreover, the customer can draw on his or her money market account at any time. When the balance in the money fund gets low, the policyholder can reduce the premium costs. Yields on the new policies have been quite high because the savings flow into separate accounts.

SUMMARY

Life insurance companies are rooted deep in American history, offering their risk-protection services in the United States for more than 200 years. Today the industry offers an incredibly wide array of consumer and commercial-oriented financial services ranging from conventional life insurance policies and health insurance and retirement plans to cash-management and security brokerage services. However, the fundamental product line offered by the industry is still protection of families against financial loss from the death or disability of one or more family members.

The life insurance business is passing through a period of transition in its operating methods and service offerings. Traditional policy lines are not as well received by the public in an age of inflation, volatile economic conditions, and high interest rates. One evidence of this is the rapid increase in policyholder borrowings against life insurance policies. Life insurers have been forced to offer new types of policies with greater capital gains potential and higher rates of return on accumulated savings. New products offered by the industry in recent years include variable life insurance, variable annuities, and universal life insurance, which provide an investment outlet for the policyholder.

Investment strategies of life insurers have changed markedly in recent years. Short-term, more marketable, and more liquid securities and real estate equity investments are increasingly important to the industry today, giving life insurers greater flexibility in responding to changes in interest rates and changes in economic conditions. However, still dominating the industry's asset portfolio are commercial and residential mortgages, corporate notes and bonds, and U.S. government and federal agency securities.

---

[10]Under many universal life insurance plans, the policyholder is guaranteed a minimum interest rate on accumulated savings, usually 4 to 5 percent. In June 1982 the IRS threatened to tax any interest earnings above the guaranteed minimum rate. However, the Tax Equity and Fiscal Responsibility Act of 1982 permits insurers to deduct at least 85 percent of any extra interest earnings.

Questions

17–1. Against what kinds of financial losses do life insurance companies provide compensation?

17–2. Explain the differences between permanent or ordinary life insurance and term insurance. What is a life insurance annuity? An endowment policy? Limited-pay insurance? Group insurance? Industrial life? Credit life? In what ways do these different policies influence portfolio management practices at life companies?

17–3. What are the principal assets held by a life insurance company? How has the composition of life company asset portfolios changed in recent years?

17–4. What are the principal sources of funds drawn upon by U.S. life insurance companies?

17–5. Why do many insurance companies prefer private placements in acquiring corporate bonds rather than purchasing bonds in the open market?

17–6. List the types of regulations involved in the operation of a life insurance company. Why is this industry so heavily regulated? What are the principal goals of regulation?

17–7. What are policy loans? Explain how fluctuations in these loans affect the growth and investment policies of life companies.

17–8. Discuss recent trends in the profitability and growth of life insurance companies. Try to explain the factors behind these trends.

17–9. Why is innovation important today in the life insurance business? Explain why innovation may be even more important to the long-run viability of life companies in future years.

17–10. What is variable life insurance? Variable annuities? Universal life insurance? Why do you think these new forms of insurance protection were developed?

References

1. American Council of Life Insurance. *Life Insurance Fact Book, 1981.* Washington, D.C.

2. American Council of Life Insurance. *Life Insurance Fact Book, 1982.* Washington, D.C.

3. Benston, George J. "Economies of Scale of Financial Institutions." *Journal of Money, Credit and Banking*, no. 2 (May 1972), pp. 312–41.

4. Board of Governors of the Federal Reserve System. *Flow of Funds, Assets and Liabilities Outstanding, 1957–80.* September 1981.

5. Dougall, Herbert E., and Jack E. Gaumnitz. *Capital Market and Institutions.* 2d ed. Englewood Cliffs, N.J.: Prentice-Hall, 1980.

6. Geehan, Randall. "Returns to Scale in the Life Insurance Industry." *Bell Journal of Economics*, no. 2 (Autumn 1977), pp. 497–514.

7. Harless, Doris. *Nonbank Financial Institutions*. Richmond: Federal Reserve Bank of Richmond, 1975.

8. Hempel, George H., and Jess B. Yawitz. *Financial Management of Financial Institutions*. Englewood Cliffs, N.J.: Prentice-Hall, 1977.

9. Hirshorn, R., and R. Geehan. "Measuring the Real Output of the Life Insurance Industry." *Review of Economics and Statistics*, no. 2 (May 1977), pp. 211–19.

10. Houston, D. B., and R. M. Simon. "Economies of Scale in Financial Institutions: A Study of Life Insurance." *Econometrica*, no. 6 (November 1970), pp. 856–64.

11. Life Insurance Association of America. *Life Insurance Companies as Financial Institutions*. Englewood Cliffs, N.J.: Prentice-Hall, 1962.

12. Noback, Joseph C. *Life Insurance Accounting*. Homewood, Ill.: Richard D. Irwin, 1969.

13. O'Leary, James J. "How Life Insurance Companies Have Shifted Investment Focus." *Bankers Monthly Magazine*, June 15, 1982.

14. Robinson, Roland I., and Dwayne Wrightsman. *Financial Markets: The Accumulation and Allocation of Wealth*. 2d ed. New York: McGraw-Hill, 1980.

15. Shott, F. H. "Disintermediation through Policy Loans at Life Insurance Companies." *Journal of Finance*, June 1971.

16. "The Changing Life Insurers: New High-Yield Products Mean High-Risk Investments." *Business Week*, September 14, 1981.

Problem for Discussion

IN THIS CHAPTER we have discussed the nature of financial services offered and investments made by life insurance companies. We have noted that life insurance companies today are active lenders in the fields of commercial, multifamily, and single-family mortgage lending and in providing long-term and short-term capital funds to corporations for the purchase of equipment. Life insurers frequently make commitments of large amounts of funds to commercial or housing projects on the basis of expected net cash flows and then make fine adjustments in their cash position as projections are translated into realized revenues and expenses.

In this problem, imagine that you are a credit analyst and investment specialist for Mutual Insurance Company—a life insurer active for more than 50 years in the market for both commercial and residential mortgage loans. A group of organizers led by J. D. Reynolds has been planning for the past eight months to build a new office building and commercial complex in North Bend to house small retail businesses, doctors, lawyers, and dentists. Your company has been asked to take on the permanent financing of the project in the form of a 10-year loan in the amount of $5 million.

North Bend is a rapidly growing suburban area adjacent to Center City—a standard metropolitan statistical area (SMSA) with a population in excess of 300,000. Population growth in the area has been above the national average for the past two decades, due principally to the influx of electronics and aircraft firms into the greater metropolitan area. In addition, a large military base operated by the Strategic Air Command lies on the southern fringe of the community. The need for office space has been acute in some sections of the metropolitan area, particularly in those locations near the air base, the larger manufacturing and assembly plants, and the downtown area. In other parts of the city, the demand has been much less strong and the commercial real estate market more uncertain. It is in one of these latter areas that the proposed office complex would be constructed.

Construction of the complex would begin in 90 days, provided both construction financing and a permanent takeout commitment for a mortgage loan is granted. The Reynolds group has applied to First State Bank for construction financing at an interest rate of 16 percent. The project's organizers are hoping the insurance company will agree to taking on the permanent mortgage financing at an interest rate of about 15 percent.

A number of recent developments have raised some serious questions concerning the appropriateness to the insurance company of granting the commercial mortgage loan as requested. There appear to be substantial risks associated with the project and with local business conditions. For one thing, the federal government plays a substantial role in North Bend's economy, and the future magnitude and direction of government spending in the area are highly uncertain. For example, three years ago the air base employed 2,500 people, including service personnel and local firms under contract for construction and maintenance of base property. Currently, less than 2,000 are employed there, due to government cutbacks and curtailments. Last month, the Department of Defense announced that some military bases were being considered for possible closing or further cutbacks in personnel. Speculation has been rampant in the local business community that the SAC base might be on the Defense Department's cutback list.

Private business activity in the area tends to be highly volatile. Electronics and construction firms account for at least 30 percent of the local labor force and both industries typically experience marked fluctuations in sales coincident with movements in interest rates, government spending, and foreign imports. During the most recent recession, unemployment in the local construction industry approached 25 percent due to record high interest rates and a severe drop in the demand for new mortgage loans. The failure rate for local retail establishments has doubled in recent years due to fluctuations in spending and employment.

In the wake of these recent developments a careful review of this credit application seems in order. The proposed commercial complex would be located three miles from a freeway and within a mile and a half of two shopping centers. Due to the rapid growth of North Bend the adjacent freeway is highly congested, especially in the morning and after 5 o'clock with commuter traffic from outlying areas. Reynolds and his group have argued that a substantial number of businesses would be interested in the new office facilities because of their proximity to the city, the air base, local industrial firms, shopping centers, and the freeway. There are several other commercial buildings located in this particular area and a number under construction nearby. Right now, there appears to be a seasonal low in rentals of office space, with a number of commercial complexes in the area reporting a vacancy rate of about 12 percent.

A construction loan of $5 million for a year is requested from First State Bank in order to build the three-story structure and adjacent parking facilities. When completed, the building would include about 100,000 square feet of floor space. Building costs in the area are rising rapidly—the Chamber of Commerce says 1 percent a month—so that reliable figures on the cost of the proposed project are somewhat difficult to obtain. Based upon estimates and architect's plans submitted by the organizers, it appears that construction costs will be about $4.19 million. Interest costs and other financial charges associated with the construction phase will be approximately $810,000. Other miscellaneous costs (including architect's fees, building permits, utility assessments, and city service fees) will probably total about $50,000. First State Bank has agreed to make the construction loan of $5 million, provided a commitment for permanent financing is secured from another qualified lender of funds. Reynolds and the other project organizers already own the land needed for the structure, having purchased it last year for $650,000 with a 60-percent loan from another bank. This loan is to be paid out in five years and bears an interest rate of 12 1/2 percent.

The project organizers have estimated that annual gross revenues from the project will be about $1.45 million, provided all office suites and shop space are completely rented. Annualized operating expenses are estimated at $310,000. Mortgage costs will vary, of course, with the interest rate awarded on the loan, but the organizers have assumed a 15 percent annual interest rate in their cash-flow calculations. As the credit analyst for Mutual Insurance Company, you must resolve a number of important issues associated with this loan application. Among the most important are the following:

1. Have the developers adequately researched the market for commercial office space?
2. Should the interest rate on the loan be higher or lower or the maturity shorter or longer?
3. Is the amount of credit requested too much, considering the earnings potential of the project?
4. How much weight should be given to the volatile nature of conditions in the local economy?

Try to formulate answers to these questions and then reach a decision on whether to recommend this project for permanent mortgage financing.

18. Property and Casualty Insurance Companies

INSURANCE COMPANIES SELL POLICIES to the public for protection against financial loss associated with death and old age, disability and ill health, negligence, bad weather, crime and vandalism, and other adverse developments. As we saw in the preceding chapter, life insurance companies are organized principally to protect against losses related to death, old age (retirement), and illness. That is, life insurers focus mainly on risks to the well-being of the individual *person*. In contrast, property-casualty insurance companies are concerned principally with risks involving the ownership of *property*—aircraft, motor vehicles, homes and commercial buildings, business equipment, agricultural products, boats and recreational vehicles, money, and other valuables.

Property-casualty insurers, like life insurance companies, are true financial intermediaries. They raise funds by selling protective policies to the public and receive premium income, which is invested mainly in securities acquired from the capital market—bonds, stocks, and mortgages. While they share the common characteristic of financial intermediation with life insurers, property-casualty insurers differ markedly from life insurance firms in several major respects. For one thing, protection services sold by property-casualty companies cover a much wider span of potential losses, nearly as many and varied as there are types of personal and business property. The term *insurance supermarket* might well be applied to the assorted package of policies sold by a large property-casualty insurer, covering risks to home, office, and factory and the risks of traveling by motor vehicle, boat, and airplane.

Another crucial difference between property-casualty insurers and life insurers lies in the predictability of claims each must honor. As we saw in the preceding chapter, claims filed by life insurance customers are highly predictable and generally fixed in amount. Most life insurance claims come due when a policyholder dies, reaches retirement, or his or her policy contract matures—all events which are known well in advance (often for several years) or which can be accurately predicted from actuarial tables. In the case of property-casualty policy claims, however, predictive accuracy is far lower and the claims are not usually fixed in amount. Inflation plays a key role here because of rising property repair costs and rapidly increasing medical costs. Moreover, a property-casualty claim may arise at any time.

A good example of the basic problems faced by property-casualty insurers in marketing their services is provided by *auto insurance policies*— their leading service line. Once an individual contacts an auto insurance agent, pays all or a portion of the required annual premium, and signs a policy contract, he or she is granted financial protection up to a specified limit against personal and property damage from owning and operating an automobile. The moment the new policyholder walks out of the insurance agent's office and climbs into the automobile, a claim against the insurance company may arise. Thus the property-casualty insurer must be liquid and ready to pay from the moment a new policy is issued and cannot devote virtually all of its incoming premium receipts to long-term investments as many life insurers can.

PROBLEMS FACED BY PROPERTY-CASUALTY INSURERS IN RECENT YEARS

Note too that the driver of an automobile can be involved in a minor accident (a "fender bender") involving a claim of only a few hundred dollars; or involved in an accident where personal injury or death occurs, resulting in a claim of several hundred thousand dollars. Moreover, the cost of repairing automobiles and other properties as well as medical expenses have soared in recent years, meaning that policyholder claims are highly sensitive to inflation. Thus, in making its investments, a property-casualty insurer must select securities with significant appreciation potential that can serve as an inflation hedge.

Added to the foregoing problems faced by property-casualty insurers is a heavy federal income tax burden. Property-casualty insurers, like commercial banks and industrial corporations, are subject to the full corporate income tax rate. Therefore they typically seek to acquire a substantial amount of investments generating tax-exempt income (most notably municipal bonds). A further constraint on their activities centers upon changes in the basic risk parameters associated with property-casualty coverage. For example, a rising crime rate (particularly burglary, arson, and drunk driving) has at times resulted in a significant increase in claims, well beyond what had been expected on a historical basis. Liability suits stemming from injury caused by alleged negligence on the part of manufacturers of such diverse products as automobiles, tires, sports equipment, asbestos insulation, and drugs have resulted in huge insurance claims in recent years.[1] Legal actions against alleged professional negligence on the part of bankers, investment advisers, lawyers, physicians, and teachers have also mushroomed. Damage due to earthquakes, floods, hail, hurricanes, and even volcanoes has risen in dollar value due, in part, to increased population density in the affected areas. The net result of all these changes is not only a larger volume of policy claims, but also greater instability and unpredictability in the volume of claims and, therefore, in insurance underwriting losses. In fact, in the most recent periods, losses and loss-adjustment expenses have tended to grow faster than aggregate premiums written.

Exacerbating the property-casualty industry's problems traceable to rising claims is the pressure on profits brought about by increased *competition* (especially in the commercial insurance field). Insurance premium rates have been under considerable downward pressure in recent years from both foreign and domestic competition. There are about 3,000 property-casualty insurers headquartered in the United States. While the 100 largest of these write about 85 percent of all premiums written by domestic property-casualty insurers, competition among the largest domestic companies in what essentially is a nationwide market is intense. Adding further to this highly competitive environment is a growing cadre of foreign insurers selling their policies in the United States. Moreover, many established foreign underwriters previously active in the United States have stepped up their U.S. underwriting operations. In many foreign markets, inflation and unemployment are far more serious than in the United States, and there is often the added problem of political instability (risk) abroad. The United States, in contrast, has offered the prospect of a more stable economic environment and greater expected gains in insurance sales. Moreover, adding to domestic insurers' competitive problems are a growing number of the largest American businesses which have set up

---

[1]An interesting example of the tremendous increase in product liability claims is provided by the sports equipment field. In 1982, injuries blamed on faulty sports equipment led to liability awards larger than sports-equipment manufacturers' total sales. See, in particular, Insurance Information Institute, *Insurance Educators Newsletter* (New York), January 17, 1983.

Another product-liability area generating huge casualty claims is the asbestos industry. Recently, major asbestos insurers in the United States and Lloyds of London agreed to set up the Asbestos Claims Council after thousands of suits were filed against asbestos makers (principally in the states of California, New Jersey, Pennsylvania, and Texas). Current estimates suggest that former asbestos workers and families of deceased asbestos workers have filed about 20,000 legal actions for recovery of medical costs, lost income, and negligence, and thousands more are anticipated in the future. Considering attorneys' fees, court costs, and other expenses incurred defending asbestos companies as well as jury awards, the final insurance bill from asbestos-related legal actions may well mount into the billions of dollars before all claims are settled.

their own captive insurance affiliates and expanded their self-insurance programs.[2] Competitive pressures of this magnitude have slowed the growth of net premiums written by domestic companies each year to no more than (and sometimes less than) the economy's inflation rate.

As we will note later in this chapter, property-casualty insurance firms in recent years have developed some new strategies to deal with these problems. They have grown in size and further diversified their services to withstand some of the risks inherent in the business. Furthermore, the structure of the industry appears to be changing in an effort to meet the public's burgeoning needs for insurance protection. Heavier use is being made of reinsurance plans in which an insurance company will share the risk of, and premium income from, certain policies with other companies.

RISK-PROTECTION SERVICES SOLD BY PROPERTY-CASUALTY INSURERS

As we noted earlier, nearly 3,000 companies headquartered in the United States sell policies protecting their customers against some form of property or casualty loss. Every state in the union houses one or more property-casualty insurers, though more than 1,100 companies are headquartered in five leading states—Illinois, Texas, New York, Wisconsin, and Pennsylvania (see Table 18–1). In total, the industry held $212.3 billion in assets at year-end 1981 and wrote almost $100 billion in premiums during 1981 (see Table 18–2).

The largest property-casualty insurer is the State Farm group of companies (measured by net property-casualty premiums written), followed by Allstate, Aetna Life and Casualty, CIGNA, and Travelers. Other well-known casualty insurers in the industry's top 100 firms include Farmers Insurance, Continental Insurance, Liberty Mutual, Fireman's Fund, and Hartford Fire. A number of mergers and acquisitions have taken place among major companies in an effort to lower unit operating costs (through economies of scale), to better undertake the risks of offering new services, to reduce exposure to cyclical fluctuations, and to branch into new product lines. Examples of recent notable mergers or acquisitions in-

---

[2]Examples of major U.S. corporations owning captive insurance firms include Gulf Oil Corporation, Minnesota Mining and Manufacturing Company, Mobil Oil Corporation, and Phillips Petroleum Company. It has been estimated that close to 40 percent of the largest 500 corporations in the United States operate captive insurance subsidiaries or affiliates. Many of the captive insurers are situated offshore (for example, in Bermuda) in order to avoid certain U.S. regulations on investments and required reserves and to provide insurance policies to other companies, including overseas firms. Major U.S. corporations organizing captive insurers argue that they can save on insurance premiums; moreover, insurance premiums paid to a captive normally would qualify as a tax-deductible business expense. However, the IRS has occasionally challenged such deductions in those cases where the premium payments appeared to be unreasonable or the risk allegedly insured against was not really shifted away from the parent company.

Table 18-1   Number of Property-Casualty Insurers by State

State Where Home Office Is Located	Number of Home Offices	State Where Home Office Is Located	Number of Home Offices
Alabama	23	Missouri	86
Alaska	9	Montana	5
Arizona	21	Nebraska	36
Arkansas	25	Nevada	8
California	123	New Hampshire	33
Colorado	48	New Jersey	42
Connecticut	36	New Mexico	9
Delaware	102	New York	212
District of		North Carolina	25
Columbia	12	North Dakota	40
Florida	49	Ohio	151
Georgia	36	Oklahoma	61
Hawaii	12	Oregon	13
Idaho	5	Pennsylvania	200
Illinois	292	Rhode Island	19
Indiana	111	South Carolina	23
Iowa	50	South Dakota	56
Kansas	34	Tennessee	59
Kentucky	34	Texas	225
Louisiana	23	Utah	9
Maine	25	Vermont	14
Maryland	29	Virginia	40
Massachusetts	47	Washington	24
Michigan	50	West Virginia	18
Minnesota	180	Wisconsin	202
Mississippi	5	Wyoming	3

Sources: State insurance departments and Insurance Information Institute, *Insurance Facts*, 1982–83 edition, p. 10.

clude Connecticut General and INA (forming CIGNA), Baldwin-United and MGIC Insurance Group, and American General and NLT Corporation.

The principal service line for property-casualty insurers is the sale of automobile insurance, covering autos, trucks, and other motorized vehicles (see Tables 18–3 and 18–4). As Table 18–4 indicates, just over 40 percent of the net insurance premiums written each year by the industry involve policies protecting the customer against financial losses due to property damage and personal injury stemming from operating a motor vehicle. As Table 18–5 suggests, the bulk of auto insurance coverage is for private passenger autos owned by individuals and families. Insurance covering commercial vehicles accounted for only about 18 percent of all auto insurance premiums written in 1981, for example, with the remainder—more than 80 percent—covering liability and physical damage claims arising from driving a *private* passenger vehicle. It is interesting, too, that about 40 percent of auto insurance premiums are designed to

Table 18–2   Total Assets and Net Premiums Written by U.S. Property-Casualty Insurers ($ billions)

	Years							
Item	*1975*	*1976*	*1977*	*1978*	*1979*	*1980*	*1981*	*1982*
Total assets held by property-casualty insurers	$88.1	$105.6	$126.6	$149.1	$174.2	$197.7	$212.3	NA
Net premiums written	50.0	60.8	72.4	81.7	90.1	95.6	99.3	104.3*

NA = Not available.
*Estimated.
Sources: Insurance Information Institute, *Insurance Facts*, 1982–83, 1981–82, 1980–81, 1979, and 1978 editions; and *Best's Review* [15].

cover any physical damage caused by the operation of motor vehicles, while roughly 60 percent of the auto premiums paid by the public go for liability claims (mainly personal injuries).

Although auto insurance policies dominate the property-casualty industry's sales each year, other forms of insurance coverage are growing more rapidly. In fact, as Table 18–4 shows, the auto premiums' share of industry sales has declined slightly since the mid-1970s, from about 45 percent of all premiums written in 1975 to about 41 percent in 1981. One fac-

Table 18–3   Net Premiums Written by U.S. Property-Casualty Companies
(percentages of total premiums written for all insurance lines)

Principal Insurance Lines	*1981*	*1980*	*1978*	*1975*
Automobile insurance	41.4%	41.0%	43.8%	44.8%
Medical malpractice	1.3	1.3	1.6	1.9
General Nonauto liability	6.1	6.7	10.2	6.6
Fire insurance and related lines	4.9	5.0	6.2	7.9
Homeowners multiple-peril	10.9	10.3	10.3	10.1
Farmowners multiple-peril	0.6	0.6	0.6	0.6
Commercial multiple-peril	6.9	7.2	7.7	6.8
Workers' compensation	14.7	14.9	14.9	13.2
Inland marine	2.4	2.4	2.5	2.7
Ocean marine	1.1	1.1	1.3	1.8
Surety and fidelity	1.4	1.3	1.4	1.7
Burglary and theft	0.1	0.1	0.2	*
Crop-hail	0.5	0.4	0.5	0.1
Boiler and machinery	0.3	0.3	0.3	0.3
Glass	*	*	0.2	*
Aircraft	0.2	0.2	—	0.3
Accident and health	3.6	3.4	—	†
Miscellaneous lines	3.9	4.1	—	†
Total, all insurance lines	100.0%	100.0%	100.0%	100.0%

*Less than 0.05 percent.
†Figure not given separately in indicated years.
Note: Net premiums written represent premium income retained by insurance companies, direct or through reinsurance, less payments made for business reinsured.
Sources: *Best's Aggregates & Averages*; National Crop Insurance Association; and Insurance Information Institute.

**Table 18–4   Auto Insurance Premiums Written by U.S.
Property-Casualty Insurers: 1981**

Types of Auto Insurance Coverage	Volume of Premiums Written ($ millions)	Percentage of Total
Auto liability insurance:		
Private passenger	$19,649.9	47.8%
Commercial	4,745.3	11.5
Auto physical damage insurance:		
Private passenger	14,033.9	34.1
Commercial	2,713.9	6.6
Total auto premiums written	$41,143.0	100.0%

Sources: *Best's Aggregates & Averages*; and Insurance Information Institute, *Insurance Facts*, 1982–83 edition, p. 22.

tor accounting for the relative slippage of auto insurance sales is the growing proportion of compact and subcompact automobiles on the road and a slowing in the rate of growth of auto sales. Individuals and families, on the whole, are driving smaller cars due to energy shortages and higher gasoline prices, requiring a lesser amount of coverage per vehicle. And, with rapidly rising car prices, fewer new cars and more older vehicles are on the road today. As might be expected, personal injury rates have risen

**Table 18–5   Principal Insurance Lines Sold by U.S. Property-Casualty Companies Ranked
by Volume of Premiums Written: 1981**

Insurance Line	Volume of Premiums Written ($ millions)	Rank
Auto liability and physical damage coverage for private passenger and commercial vehicles	$41,143.0	1
Multiple-peril insurance for homes, businesses, and farms	18,269.5	2
Workers' compensation insurance	14,616.3	3
General liability insurance	7,384.6	4
Fire insurance and allied lines	4,817.0	5
Inland marine insurance	2,427.7	6
Surety and fidelity bonds	1,351.2	7
Medical malpractice insurance	1,338.3	8
Ocean marine insurance	1,126.8	9
Crop-Hail insurance protection	504.5	10
Boiler and machinery insurance	298.3	11
Burglary and theft insurance	127.5	12
Nuclear insurance protection	102.8	13
Glass insurance protection	31.1	14

Source: Insurance Information Institute, *Insurance Facts*, 1982–83 edition, p. 13.

due to the smaller vehicles. Large claims (over $1,000 per accident) are more common when smaller autos are involved in an accident, but this inflating factor has not been enough to offset slumping auto sales.[3]

As auto insurance sales have declined in relative importance, other policy sales have spurted ahead. Among the leading insurance lines in recent years have been homeowners' multiple-peril insurance to cover personal injuries and property damage incurred mainly at the policyholder's place of residence. Such a policy frequently covers damage to the home and other structures on the policyholder's land, plus personal property such as furniture, home appliances, and sports equipment. The insurance company may also pay the policyholder's living expenses if forced out of a home due to covered damages. Multiple-peril policies, as the name implies, insure against many different perils faced by the homeowner, including damage due to crime and civil disturbances, fire and smoke, storms (including ice, snow, and hail), negligent operation of motor vehicles and aircraft, falling objects (such as trees and telephone poles), glass breakage, flooding or plumbing problems, explosions and heating system problems, and electrical malfunctions. Moreover, a multiple-peril policy may also protect the homeowner against negligence and medical claims from outsiders due to bodily injury incurred on the homeowner's property, damage to adjacent property, and the cost of defending the homeowner in court. The specific coverages included in a homeowner's multiple-peril policy, of course, vary from company to company and from policy to policy. Certainly the growth of multiple-peril policies reflects the spiraling upward trend in the cost of medical and hospital care and soaring repair and building costs. Many homeowners, for example, have discovered

---

[3]One interesting trend in the insurance business which became especially intense in 1983 was the drive by various consumer groups to institute *equal* insurance and pension rates for men and women. Traditionally, insurance companies have charged women lower rates for life insurance than men in the same age group and also lower auto insurance rates. In contrast, however, women have generally received smaller annual payments from pension and annuity plans than men, though over the whole term of a pension program they may receive equal total dollar payments because women usually live longer. The traditional distinction between men and women in auto insurance rates became the initial target of various consumer groups and, by 1983, four states—Hawaii, Massachusetts, Michigan, and North Carolina—had acted to forbid the use of the policyholder's sex as a basis for setting auto premium rates. Montana followed with a broader law outlawing sex discrimination in posting rates for both insurance and pensions. Bills were soon introduced in both houses of Congress to promote unisex insurance pricing, but these bills faced strong opposition from insurance underwriters who argued that there is an actuarial basis for both sex- and age-linked premium rates. To the companies, differential insurance rates based on such factors as age, sex, and health status reflect observed differences in the risk of underwriting insurance for various groups of people. To those who argue for *equal* insurance rates, however, the principle involved is one of antidiscrimination and equal protection under law. The result is a conflict between basic insurance principles and social values—not an easy issue to resolve.

that insurance policies written several years ago are simply inadequate to cover the repair of a home damaged by storm, vandalism, or other cause and have sought new policies more responsive to changing costs and property values.

Many years ago, before automobiles became so popular, fire insurance led the list of policies marketed by property-casualty companies. However, more stringent building and fire codes and the development of better fire-fighting equipment have helped to lower the cost of fire insurance protection relative to other risk-protecting policies. Among the leading insurance lines today are workers' compensation insurance, which protects employees on the job; nonauto general liability insurance protecting individuals and businesses in a variety of situations; marine insurance to protect ships and goods in transit on both inland waterways and on the high seas; and surety and fidelity bonds, protecting business firms against losses due to employee negligence, fraud, or theft. Somewhat less important but still active insurance lines today include policies covering boilers and other forms of business machinery and equipment, crop and hail damage for farms, medical malpractice suits against doctors and hospitals, aircraft accidents, glass breakage (particularly for high-rise buildings), nuclear accidents (coverage today written by a handful of large companies), and burglary and theft of homes and businesses.

Who buys more property-casualty insurance coverage today—businesses or households? The answer is, they are almost equal, measured by premiums written, with a slight edge to households (individuals and families). In 1981, for example, households accounted for 51 percent of premiums written by the property-casualty industry, while commercial customers accounted for 40 percent. Not surprisingly, the mix of policies sold in these two sectors is quite different. Auto insurance accounts for almost exactly two thirds of household coverage, and homeowners' policies another fifth of all consumer premiums written. In the business sector, on the other hand, workers' compensation leads the list (about 30 percent of total business premiums), followed by motor vehicle coverage (about 15 percent) and commercial multiple-peril policies (about 14 percent). Household policies have been growing much faster than business coverage, which often declines in recessionary periods.

A substantial share of business insurance coverage is sold through *insurance brokers* today. These firms perform a variety of insurance-related, property-management, and consulting jobs today, but their traditional function is to purchase at the lowest possible cost property-casualty insurance protection on behalf of corporate clients. For this service, the insurance broker may collect a commission from the corporation that hires him from the insurance company chosen to write the policy for the broker's client. Traditionally, insurance brokers collected most of their income from insurance companies to whom they directed client business and were usually paid fixed commissions based on the amount of insurance premiums written. Recently, however, with intense competition for commercial insurance accounts and falling premium rates in the commercial insurance field, brokers have increasingly emphasized negotiated commissions. Moreover, more of the insurance broker's income today comes from direct charges to corporate customers and less from property-casualty insurers. In addition, many brokers have branched out to offer additional services, such as claims processing and the management of captive insurance companies owned by large manufacturing and industrial corporations.

What do property-casualty companies do with the insurance premiums they collect from policyholders? These incoming funds, of course, must be invested in anticipation of the day when some policyholders will file claims against the company. Literally, the insurer must hold onto the policyholders' premium payments by making sound investments until that income is fully "earned" by providing risk protection throughout the term of an insurance policy.[4]

However, not just any investment will do, as we saw in the early part of this chapter. Property-casualty companies must hold a substantial portion of readily marketable and relatively safe securities due to the volatile nature of policyholder claims, which may turn out to be much larger than anticipated and may occur from day one of each policy contract sold. Due to rapid increases in the dollar value of claims associated with the rising cost of property repairs and medical care, property-casualty insurers must also hold a substantial share of investments having good capital appreciation potential. Finally, the industry is subject to the full federal corporate income tax rate. As a result, property-casualty firms are eager to place a significant portion of their resources in tax-sheltered investments.

As Table 18–6 shows, investments held by property-casualty insurers reflect the industry's needs for investments possessing marketability, safety, capital appreciation potential, and tax benefits. The principal asset held is bonds issued by federal, state, and local units of government and by corporations. These fixed-income, relatively safe, and often highly marketable securities make up about three fifths of the industry's asset total.

INVESTMENT PORTFOLIOS OF PROPERTY-CASUALTY INSURERS

---

[4]Each month that passes results in the insurer "earning" more of the premiums already paid in by the policyholder. Should a policy be canceled before it matures, the policyholder is entitled to a refund of those premiums not yet earned by the insurance company unless there is a contractual agreement specifying otherwise.

Table 18–6   **Composition of Investments Held by Property-Casualty Insurers: 1971 and 1981**

Types of Investments	*Percentage of Industry's Investment Portfolio in:*	
	1981	*1971*
Bonds:		
U.S. government securities	11.7%	8.9%
Other government securities	0.8	0.6
State and municipal securities	14.9	18.1
Special revenue government securities	33.2	17.9
Railroad bonds	0.3	0.6
Utility notes and bonds	3.6	4.7
Miscellaneous bonds	9.8	9.1
Securities of parent companies, affiliates, and subsidiaries	0.4	0.5
Total of bonds	74.8%	60.3%
Common stock:		
Railroads	0.2%	0.2%
Utilities	1.5	3.6
Banks	1.0	2.1
Savings and loan associations	NA	0.0*
Insurance companies	0.9	0.4
Miscellaneous common stock	10.5	19.5
Common stock issued by parent companies, affiliates, and subsidiaries	4.7	9.9
Total for common stock	18.7%	35.7%
Preferred stock:		
Railroads	0.1%	0.0%*
Utilities	3.3	2.5
Banks	0.1	0.0*
Insurance companies	0.0*	0.0*
Miscellaneous preferred stock	1.4	1.0
Preferred stock issued by parent companies, affiliates, and subsidiaries	0.1	0.1
Total for preferred stock	5.0%	3.6%
Other investment holdings:		
Mortgages	0.8%	0.4%
Collateral loans	0.1	0.1
Other invested assets	0.7	0.0
Total for other investments	1.6%	0.5%

*Less than 0.05 percent.
Sources: A. M. Best Company; and Insurance Information Institute, *Insurance Facts*, 1982–83 edition, p. 20.

We note that, dollarwise and percentagewise, the principal type of bond held is state and local government (municipal) bonds. These include both general obligation bonds and revenue bonds issued by special governmental districts or units.[5] The interest earned on state and local gov-

[5]General obligation municipal bonds are backed by the "full faith and credit" of the issuing unit of government. As we noted in Chapter 4, this means that local citizens can be taxed (normally through property and income taxes) to service (i.e., meet interest and principal

ernment bonds is exempt from federal income taxation, and most states exempt government securities issued within their own jurisdiction from state and local income taxation.[6]

Bonds issued by private corporations represent the second most important type of fixed-income security held by property-casualty insurers. Such bonds, like municipals, are fully taxable, but their before-tax yields have been quite attractive in recent years (especially during those periods when the earnings of insurance firms are low and there is less need for tax shelters). The same is true of investments in mortgages, of which property-casualty insurers hold a modest amount. Property-casualty insurers purchase primarily commercial mortgage loans used to finance office buildings, shopping centers, and other business projects. However, the industry has been expanding its holdings of residential mortgages on single-family homes, condominiums, and apartments in recent years, particularly in some of the nation's largest cities. Construction of new residences and refinishing of old residential structures in major metropolitan areas (such as Chicago, New York, and Philadelphia) have increasingly attracted the attention and support of property-casualty companies.

Like so many other financial institutions, property-casualty firms hold substantial quantities of bonds and notes issued by the U.S. Treasury and federal agencies. Securities that are direct obligations of the federal government (principally Treasury bonds, notes, and bills) are preferred because they are free of credit risk, carry relatively stable prices as a rule, and are the most readily marketable and liquid of all fixed-income debt se-

---

payments on) the bonds. General obligation bonds (usually called GOs) are issued mainly by state, city, and county governments and school districts. Revenue bonds, in contrast, are somewhat more risky than GOs because they are serviced only by the revenue generated from a governmental project, such as a toll charged drivers who use a particular highway or bridge. If the project generates significantly less revenue than anticipated, the bonds may become in default; the bondholder's realized yield would be substantially below the expected yield to maturity. Revenue bonds are employed most frequently to finance the construction of airports, harbors, bridges, sewer lines and treatment plants, street lighting, municipal auditoriums, convention facilities, city transportation systems, and facilities to provide utilities such as water and electric power.

[6]Although interest income from state and municipal bonds is tax-exempt, capital gains are not. A short-term capital gain arising from buying and selling a state or local government security within one year is taxed at the taxpayer's marginal tax rate (i.e., income-tax rate applying to the taxpayer's particular tax bracket determined by his or her level of taxable income). A long-term capital gain (i.e., more than one year between purchase and sale) on state and local government securities is taxed at the more favorable capital gains rate. Under the terms of the Economic Recovery Act of 1981, the maximum capital gains tax rate for an individual investor is 20 percent of the long-term gain. *Some* capital gains on municipals are tax-exempt. This occurs when new bonds are issued at a discount from par. The price appreciation up toward par which occurs as the bond approaches maturity or as interest rates fall is considered part of the investor's interest return and is tax-exempt. However, any price gain over and above the original issue discount is taxable as ordinary income.

Table 18–7   Financial Assets Held and Liabilities Issued by U.S. Property-Casualty Insurers: 1970–1982 (year-end outstandings in $ billions)

Financial Assets and Liabilities	1970		1971		1972		1973		1974		1975	
	$	%	$	%	$	%	$	%	$	%	$	%
Financial assets held:												
Demand deposits and currency	$ 1.4	2.8%	$ 1.5	2.6%	$ 1.5	2.2%	$ 1.5	2.2%	$ 1.6	2.4%	$ 1.7	2.2%
Corporate stock	13.2	26.5	16.6	28.9	21.8	32.3	19.7	28.3	12.8	18.9	14.2	18.4
U.S. Treasury securities	3.4	14.7	3.2	5.6	2.9	4.3	2.8	4.0	2.9	4.3	4.7	6.1
Federal agency securities	1.6	3.2	1.9	3.3	2.3	3.4	2.3	3.3	2.7	4.0	3.3	4.3
Municipal bonds	17.0	34.1	20.5	35.7	24.8	35.6	28.5	41.0	30.7	45.3	33.3	43.1
Corporate bonds	8.6	17.2	8.9	15.5	8.1	12.0	8.0	11.5	10.0	14.7	12.2	15.8
Commercial mortgages	0.2	0.4	0.2	0.3	0.2	0.3	0.2	0.3	0.2	0.3	0.2	0.3
Trade credit	4.4	8.8	4.7	8.2	5.8	8.6	6.5	9.4	7.0	10.3	7.7	10.0
Total financial assets	$49.9	100.0%	$57.5	100.0%	$67.5	100.0%	$69.5	100.0%	$67.8	100.0%	$77.3	100.0%
Liabilities issued:												
Policy payables	34.2	99.4	37.8	99.5	42.6	99.3	47.4	99.4	52.3	99.4	58.5	99.5
Profit taxes payables	0.2	0.6	0.2	0.5	0.3	0.7	0.3	0.6	0.3	0.6	0.3	0.5
Total liabilities	$34.4	100.0%	$38.0	100.0%	$42.9	100.0%	$47.7	100.0%	$52.6	100.0%	$58.8	100.0%

Source: Board of Governors of the Federal Reserve System, *Flow of Funds Accounts, Assets and Liabilities Outstanding, 1957–82.*

curities. As we have noted, the ready marketability and high liquidity are especially important to property-casualty insurers because policyholder claims must be paid quickly in most instances and may flow in in unexpectedly large volume at times.

Substantial amounts of common and preferred stock are also held by the industry, especially common equity. In 1981, as Table 18–6 shows, property-casualty insurers held almost one quarter of their total assets in common and preferred equities, with common stock alone representing about 19 percent of total assets. Most equities held were issued by industrial and manufacturing corporations, with a lesser amount invested in stock issued by banks, insurance companies, and other financial institutions. Preferred stock and some common shares issued by utility companies accounted for most of the remaining equity holdings. As we noted earlier, property-casualty insurers often look for stock with strong capital gains potential to offset the impact of inflation on policyholder claims.

The investment portfolios of property-casualty insurers have undergone some interesting and important changes in recent years. These changes are reflected in the Federal Reserve's flow-of-funds data shown in Tables 18–7 and 18–8. Cash holdings (i.e., demand deposits and currency) have generally declined in relative terms as the industry sought to mini-

	1976		1977		1978		1979		1980		1981		1982
$	%	$	%	$	%	$	%	$	%	$	%	$	%
$ 1.9	2.0%	$ 2.2	1.9%	$ 2.6	1.9%	$ 2.9	1.9%	$ 2.9	1.7%	$ 3.1	1.7%	$ 3.2	1.6%
16.9	18.0	17.1	15.1	19.4	14.5	24.8	16.0	32.3	18.5	32.4	17.6	41.5	20.4
7.3	7.8	9.8	8.7	10.5	7.8	10.7	6.9	12.2	7.0	11.8	6.4	13.3	6.6
3.9	4.2	4.4	3.9	4.9	3.7	6.0	8.9	6.2	3.6	7.0	3.8	9.5	4.7
38.7	41.2	49.4	43.4	62.9	47.0	72.8	47.0	80.5	46.2	84.5	45.9	87.0	42.9
16.1	17.1	19.8	17.5	21.6	16.1	23.6	15.2	23.6	13.5	25.8	14.0	26.4	13.0
0.3	0.3	0.4	0.4	0.4	0.3	0.7	0.5	1.0	0.6	1.3	0.7	1.8	0.9
8.9	9.5	10.2	9.0	11.7	8.7	13.6	8.8	15.6	9.0	18.2	9.9	20.3	10.0
$93.9	100.0%	$113.2	100.0%	$133.9	100.0%	$154.9	100.0%	$174.3	100.0%	$184.2	100.0%	$203.0	100.0%
68.8	99.4	81.4	99.4	95.4	99.3	110.2	99.2	122.6	99.0	132.0	99.1	143.1	99.2
0.4	0.6	0.5	0.6	0.7	0.7	1.0	0.9	1.3	1.0	1.2	0.9	1.1	0.8
$69.2	100.0%	$ 81.9	100.0%	$ 96.1	100.0%	$111.1	100.0%	$123.9	100.0%	$133.2	100.0%	$144.2	100.0%

mize zero-yielding cash balances and remain as fully invested in income-earning assets as possible. Holdings of corporate stock also trended downward, especially in the late 1970s, reflecting the stock market's floundering performance, before recovering somewhat in 1982. Offsetting declines in these assets was a rapid increase in property-casualty purchases of tax-exempt municipal bonds, which rose from approximately one third to close to one half of all financial assets held by the industry. The increasingly high after-tax yields on municipals, coupled with the industry's need for tax-sheltered earnings, explain much of the relative increase in municipal investments.

Property-casualty insurers have experienced rapid growth in insurance sales in recent years, but this growth in revenues (policy premiums) has not always been translated into higher net earnings. Industry profits are determined by the interplay between insurance underwriting losses and investment earnings.[7] When underwriting losses grow faster than invest-

OPERATING PERFORMANCE OF PROPERTY-CASUALTY INSURERS

---

[7]Profits are also affected by size of company because there is recent evidence of significant cost savings (economies of scale) in favor of larger property-casualty insurers. See especially Doherty [5] and Skogh [16].

Table 18-8 Flow of Funds through Property-Casualty Insurance Companies: 1975–1982 (dollar figures in $ billions)

Source or Use of Funds	1975 $	1975 %	1976 $	1976 %	1977 $	1977 %	1978 $	1978 %	1979 $	1979 %	1980 $	1980 %	1981 $	1981 %	1982 $	1982 %
Sources of funds:																
Equity issues	$1.0	13.9%	$ 0.9	8.0%	$ 1.4	9.9%	$ 0.8	5.3%	$ 0.9	5.7%	$ 1.1	8.0%	$ 1.1	10.4%	$ 2.8	20.9%
Profit taxes payable	*	*	0.1	0.9	0.1	0.7	0.2	1.3	0.3	2.0	0.4	2.9	-0.2	—	*	—
Policy payables	6.2	86.1	10.3	91.1	12.6	89.4	14.1	93.4	14.7	92.5	12.4	89.9	9.5	89.6	10.6	79.1
Net increase in liabilities	$7.2	100.0%	$11.3	100.0%	$14.1	100.0%	$15.1	100.0%	$15.9	100.0%	$13.8	100.0%	$10.4	100.0%	$13.4	100.0%
Uses of funds:																
Demand deposits and currency	$0.1	1.3%	$ 0.2	1.3%	$ 0.3	1.5%	$ 0.4	2.0%	$ 0.3	1.6%	$ 0.1	0.7%	$ 0.2	1.7%	$ 3.9	25.0%
Corporate equities	-0.7	—	0.9	6.0	1.2	5.9	2.0	9.8	3.2	17.0	3.1	20.7	1.6	13.6	2.7	17.3
U.S. Treasury securities	1.9	23.8	2.6	17.4	2.5	12.4	0.7	3.4	0.2	1.1	1.6	10.7	-0.5	—	1.5	9.6
Federal agency securities	0.6	7.5	0.6	4.0	0.5	2.5	0.5	2.5	1.1	5.9	0.2	1.3	0.8	6.8	2.5	16.0
Municipal bonds	2.6	32.5	5.4	36.2	10.7	53.0	13.5	66.2	9.9	52.7	7.7	52.3	4.0	33.9	3.0	19.2
Corporate bonds	2.2	27.5	3.9	26.2	3.7	18.3	1.8	8.8	2.0	10.6	*	*	2.2	18.6	-0.5	—
Commercial mortgages	0.1	1.3	0.1	0.7	0.1	0.5	*	*	0.3	1.6	0.3	*	0.4	3.4	0.3	1.9
Trade credit	0.6	7.5	1.2	8.1	1.3	6.4	1.5	7.4	1.9	10.1	2.0	13.3	2.6	22.0	2.1	13.5
Net increase in financial assets	$7.3	100.0%	$14.9	100.0%	$20.2	100.0%	$20.4	100.0%	$18.8	100.0%	$15.0	100.0%	$11.3	100.0%	$15.6	100.0%

*Less than $0.1 billion.
Source: Board of Governors of the Federal Reserve System, Flow of Funds Accounts, 1982.

ment earnings, the industry's profitability suffers. If investment returns outstrip the growth of underwriting losses, profits tend to rise. Generally speaking, premium rates are set at levels calculated to grant property-casualty insurers a 3 to 5 percent underwriting profit.

Profits are important to property-casualty insurers for several reasons. Profits provide funds for long-term growth in facilities and insurance sales. They also support the growth of policy reserves, which serve as a cushion for the risk of loss from insurance underwriting. The policyholder gains additional protection against the possibility the insurance company might fail.

As Table 18–9 shows, income from industry *investment holdings* (net of investment expenses and before taxes) increased rapidly between 1970 and 1981 and accounted for a growing share of the industry's total return on invested capital. However, losses from insurance underwriting activities fluctuated around a generally upward trend as well. In 1981, for example, the industry's statutory underwriting loss was about $4.5 billion. After policyholder dividends were paid out, the 1981 net insurance underwriting loss exceeded $6 billion. Combining investment income and the net underwriting loss yields 1981 before-tax net income for the industry of just under $7 billion. In 1982, investment earnings hit a record $14.9 billion, according to preliminary estimates—about 12 percent higher than in 1981. However, underwriting losses rose more than 60 percent between 1981 and 1982, to $10.4 billion (based on preliminary figures), eating further into industry after-tax operating profits.[8]

In recent years the industry has moved aggressively in an effort to protect its remaining profit margin. Tax-management and investment strategies have become more skillful and aggressive as an offset to underwriting losses and burgeoning competition. A good example is the property-casualty industry's financial report for 1982, which revealed that, in addition to investment earnings of $14.9 billion, capital gains income and asset appreciation netted an additional $3.2 billion. This resulted in an 11 to 12 percent gain in the policyholders' surplus accounts (reserves), providing added strength for both the companies and their customers.

---

[8]The interplay of underwriting losses and investment income in shaping property-casualty insurance profits implies that the industry's earnings are highly interest-sensitive. Rising interest rates typically widen the spread between investment cash inflows and underwriting costs, offering the potential for greater profits. Falling interest rates dampen investment returns, narrowing the spread between investment cash inflows and costs. Profits tend to decline and a smaller volume of funds is available for future investment.

The industry is also sensitive to business-cycle fluctuations. Recessions, for example, lead to declining demand for policies (especially commercial contracts). This problem is exacerbated by the fact that insurance premium rates sometimes rise at such times as companies try to make up for declining sales by charging higher prices.

Table 18–9   The Operating Performance of U.S. Property-Casualty Insurers: 1970–1981 ($000)

Years	Underwriting Performance			Income from Investment Holdings	Combined Before-Tax Net Income
	Statutory Underwriting Gain or Loss	Policyholder Dividends	Net Underwriting Gain or Loss		
1970	$ 77,776	$ 503,558	$ − 425,781	$ 2,005,081	$1,579,229
1971	1,381,800	555,629	826,172	2,421,495	3,247,667
1972	1,797,934	736,283	1,061,651	2,799,737	3,861,388
1973	791,761	785,698	6,063	3,325,344	3,331,408
1974	− 1,878,371	766,527	− 2,644,898	3,832,669	1,187,771
1975	− 3,593,959	632,838	− 4,226,798	4,150,204	76,594
1976	− 1,558,551	630,100	− 2,188,652	4,808,939	2,617,287
1977	1,926,315	814,513	1,111,803	5,815,788	6,927,591
1978	2,548,143	1,251,811	1,296,332	7,289,554	8,585,886
1979	23,606	1,324,377	− 1,300,772	9,279,235	7,978,463
1980	− 1,712,423	1,621,545	− 3,333,968	11,063,492	7,729,524
1981	− 4,463,888	1,823,748	− 6,287,636	13,248,495	6,960,859

Sources: *Best's Aggregates & Averages*; and Insurance Information Institute, *Insurance Facts*, 1982–83 edition, pp. 16–17.

The rapid growth of property-casualty investment income has generated considerable controversy in recent years. Some critics of the industry believe that investment earnings should be considered by state insurance commissions in setting insurance rates. However, many insurers point out that investment income *does* play a direct role in the rate-setting process. When investment earnings exceed targeted profit margins, the balance frequently flows into reserves to protect policyholders or is passed back to the customer in the form of either insurance rate adjustments or improved service. This is especially true in the commercial insurance field, where competition between underwriters is intense and underwriting losses are often substantial. In fact, commercial insurance rates fell sharply in the early 1980s due to intense competition from both domestic and foreign underwriters. Many insurers argue that they need significant investment income to absorb losses and to compensate for increased risk.[9] A few state insurance commissions have begun to include formulas for investment income in their rate-setting calculations. However, most states still appear to be using a rate-setting method laid down in the 1920s which grants

---

[9]Some analysts believe that the attractively high interest rates on investment securities in recent years have encouraged insurance underwriters to make greater use of *cash-flow underwriting* techniques. Such techniques call for the insurer to: (1) lower its premium rates on policies (especially large commercial contracts) to the break-even or loss point to increase sales and market share, and (2) count on substantial investment earnings to make losing policy contracts profitable on balance. Thus funds are attracted at high cost to the insurer, who hopes to earn a cost-plus return in the investment market.

property-casualty insurance companies a 5-percent underwriting profit before investment income is taken into account.

As Table 18–10 shows, the bulk of premiums received from policyholders flow back to those policyholders filing claims for reimbursement. Approximately 75 cents out of each dollar of premium receipts is paid out in the adjustment of claims. Another 23 to 24 cents of each premium dollar is absorbed by advertising and company administrative expenses. The smallest amount—just under 2 cents of every premium dollar—is returned to owners (including policyholders in a mutual insurance company) in the form of dividends.

The fact that such a high percentage of property-casualty insurance premiums are absorbed by claims and operating expense reflects the effects of inflation on property repair costs and on the cost of medical care. As Table 18–11 indicates, medical care costs have climbed much faster in the United States than has the overall cost of living as measured by the consumer price index. The same is true for auto and home repair and construction costs. These spiraling human and property repair costs have created a serious financial problem for property-casualty insurers because insurance premium rates have generally lagged behind. Premium rates on existing policy contracts cannot be increased until the policies are renewed, meaning that in many cases an upward adjustment of premium rates will not significantly affect insurance profits for at least a year. As a result, premium receipts frequently fall far short of the cost of claims, and the industry's net underwriting loss climbs sharply.[10]

Table 18–10 Distribution of Premium Receipts by U.S. Property-Casualty Companies: 1979–1981 (percent of each premium dollar)

	1981	*1980*	*1979*
Payment of policyholder claims and expenses associated with adjusting claims	76.8%	74.9%	73.1%
Selling and administrative expenses	24.5	23.7	23.2
Federal, state, and local taxes	2.8	2.7	3.8
Dividends paid to policyholders	1.9	1.7	1.5

Sources: A. M. Best Company; and Insurance Information Institute, *Insurance Facts*, 1982–83 edition, p. 15.

---

[10]One popular measure of insurance underwriting success and efficiency is the *combined ratio*, or ratio of losses from claims and operating costs to premiums written. In recent years the combined ratio for property-casualty insurers has been increasing to well above 100 percent (for example, in 1982 it reached 109.5 percent), suggesting that the industry as a whole is absorbing losses on each policy taken on (investment earnings excluded).

A recent article by Ancipink [1] points out that in only five years over a period of three decades during the post–World War II era did the underwriting profit margin of U.S. property-casualty insurance companies approximate the 5-percent profit margin typically figured into premium rates charged the public.

Table 18–11   Rate of Inflation in Living Costs, Medical Care, Home and Auto Repair and Maintenance, and Construction Costs in the United States: 1967–1981
(consumer price index value for selected years)

Year	Cost of Living (all items)*	Medical Care	Auto Repair and Maintenance	Home Repair and Maintenance	Residential Construction Costs	Nonresidential Construction Costs
1967	100.0	100.0	100.0	100.0	100.0	100.0
1970	116.3	120.6	120.6	124.0	115.9	126.9
1975	161.2	168.6	176.6	187.6	173.6	198.0
1980	246.8	265.9	268.3	285.7	300.1	311.1
1981	272.4	294.5	293.6	314.4	324.3	324.6

*Cost-of-living index assumed to be 100 in 1967.
Sources: U.S. Department of Commerce; Bureau of the Census; U.S. Department of Labor; and Insurance Information Institute, *Insurance Facts*, 1982–83 edition, p. 41.

The foregoing analysis of insurance costs and underwriting losses reminds us of another important ingredient of the insurance business: *Premiums paid by insurance policyholders really represent the estimated cost of transferring future risk from the policyholders to the insurance company*. However, while the policyholder pays a *fixed* premium based on *expected* costs to the insurance company until his or her policy must be renewed, the *true* cost to the insurance company of the transferred risk is uncertain until all claims are in. If underwriting losses turn out to be larger than expected, the difference between actual premiums paid in and claims paid out must be covered by additional investment earnings, policy reserves, or both. If substantial underwriting losses continue for a prolonged period, the insurer may be driven into bankruptcy.[11]

SUMMARY

Property-casualty insurance companies protect their policyholders against financial losses associated with personal or professional negligence, bad weather, crime, and a wide range of other risks connected primarily with the ownership of property. Among their principal products are automobile liability and physical damage policies, homeowners' multiple-peril policies, workers' compensation insurance, general liability coverage, fire and marine insurance, surety and fidelity bonds, medical malpractice insurance, business machinery and equipment coverage, and insurance protection of agricultural products. Collecting premium receipts from policyholders, property-casualty insurers reinvest those premiums in a wide variety of financial instruments, mostly securities sold in the long-term capital market. Included among the principal investments

[11]The states generally maintain insurance guaranty funds to protect those holding policies with a bankrupt insurance company.

of property-casualty firms are state and local government (municipal) bonds, common and preferred stock, U.S. government securities, corporate and public utility bonds and notes, and commercial mortgages.

The property-casualty industry has faced serious problems in recent years, especially in preserving its profit margin in an era of inflation and rising costs, increasing competition, and new types of insurance claims. For example, the industry has witnessed a sharp increase in product liability suits due to personal injuries or disease associated with the use of such diverse products as asbestos, automobile tires, compact cars, drugs, nuclear power, sports equipment, and toys. Added to this trend is a rising tide of insurance claims due to arson, medical malpractice suits, and floods and other weather-related damage. Competition for policyholders is also intense because nearly 3,000 firms sell one form or another of property-casualty protection, with close to 900 companies active in national and regional markets. The industry's future growth and profitability will rest largely on its ability to win regulatory approval for more flexible insurance rates, innovations in new policyholder services, and efficiency in keeping costs under control.

Questions

18–1. What types of risk do property-casualty insurers protect their policyholders against? How do these insurance firms compare with life insurance companies?

18–2. Why do property-casualty insurers have to be more concerned about liquidity and inflation than life insurance companies?

18–3. List the five principal types of insurance coverage offered by property-casualty insurers.

18–4. What has happened to the profitability of property-casualty insurers in recent years? Can you explain why? What remedies would you suggest to deal with the industry's recent earnings problems?

18–5. Property-casualty insurers are most active in the nation's capital market. What kinds of financial assets do they prefer to purchase? Explain why. What recent changes have occurred in the industry's investment portfolio? Explain the reasons for these recent changes.

References

1. Ancipink, Patricia. "Insurer Profit: What It Really Means to You." *The Journal of Insurance*, November–December 1982, pp. 2–7.

2. Board of Governors of the Federal Reserve System. *Flow of Funds Accounts, Third Quarter 1982*. Washington, D.C.

3. _____. *Flow of Funds Accounts: Assets and Liabilities Outstanding, 1957–80*. Washington, D.C., 1981.

4. Cummins, J. David, and David J. Nye. "The Stochastic Characteristics of Property-Liability Insurance Company Underwriting Profits." *Journal of Risk and Insurance*, no. 1 (March 1980), pp. 61–77.

5. Doherty, Neil A. "The Measurement of Output and Economies of Scale in Property-Liability Insurance. *Journal of Risk and Insurance*, no. 3 (September 1981), pp. 390–402.

6. Dougall, Herbert E., and Jack Gaumnitz. *Capital Market Institutions*. 2d ed. Englewood Cliffs, New Jersey: Prentice-Hall, 1980.

7. Forbes, Stephen W. "Capital and Surplus Formation in the Nonlife Insurance Industry, 1956–70." *Quarterly Review of Economics and Business*, Autumn 1974, pp. 15–34.

8. _____. "Capital Gains, Losses, and Financial Results in the Non-Life Insurance Industry." *The Journal of Risk and Insurance*, December 1975, pp. 625–38.

9. Harless, Doris E. *Nonbank Financial Institutions*. Richmond: Federal Reserve Bank of Richmond, 1975.

10. Hertzberg, Daniel. "Prices, Rivals Vex Insurers Casualty Lines." *The Wall Street Journal*, June 12, 1981.

11. Insurance Information Institute. *Insurance Facts*, 1978, 1979, 1980–81, 1981–82, and 1982–83 editions, New York.

12. _____. *Insurance Educators Newsletter*, various editions.

13. Long, John D., and David W. Gregg, eds. *Property and Liability Insurance Handbook*. Homewood, Ill.: Richard D. Irwin, 1965.

14. Polakoff, Murray E., et al. *Financial Institutions and Markets*. 2d ed. Boston: Houghton Mifflin, 1980.

15. "Review and Preview." *Best's Review*, January 1983, pp. 12–14 and 94–98.

16. Skogh, Goran. "Returns to Scale in the Swedish Property-Liability Insurance Industry." *Journal of Risk and Insurance*, no. 2 (June 1982), pp. 218–28.

17. Smith, Barry D. "An Analysis of Auto Liability Loss Reserves and Underwriting Results." *Journal of Risk and Insurance*, no. 2 (June 1980), pp. 305–20.

18. Vogel, Gloria L. "Market Conditions: A Survey." *Best's Review*, May 1983, pp. 14, 16, 44, and 48.

**Problem for
Discussion**

AS WE HAVE SEEN IN THIS CHAPTER, financial management of property and casualty insurance companies has been quite difficult in recent years. One of the major outlets for funds—the equity market—stagnated until late 1982, while escalating inflation substantially increased the cost of claims. Moreover, the sharp fluctuations in the stock market caused earnings to be erratic, making planning for purchases and sales of tax-exempt municipal securities especially difficult. In the problem situation discussed below, the student is asked to determine the investment strategy of a property and casualty insurance company in a period of great uncertainty. After reviewing the material below, the student should address the following questions:

1. Under what conditions would a property and casualty insurance company devote a substantial fraction of its assets to municipal securities? Does the coming year appear to present such conditions?
2. What are the alternative investment opportunities? What are the risk and return characteristics of each of these?

Old Reliable Casualty Company is a full-line insurance company specializing in property and casualty insurance. Established originally to write fire insurance for the New England textile industry in the late 19th century, the company had grown substantially, if irregularly, throughout the years and had gradually expanded into other lines of casualty insurance. Moreover, in the early post–World War II period, Old Reliable (a motto used extensively in its advertising) had established a life insurance subsidiary. However, writing life insurance policies remained a minor part of the total premium income of the firm and was generally unprofitable. Indeed, there had been rumors that senior management of the company planned to sell the life insurance business to another firm.

Perhaps the most significant development in the recent history of Old Reliable occurred in 1966 when the company was purchased by a large conglomerate heavily involved in international and domestic manufacturing, real estate development, and oil and gas exploration. At the time, the founding family of Old Reliable, which did not play an active role in management, had viewed the exchange of its stock in Old Reliable for the stock of the conglomerate as an ideal way to diversify its investments, obtain greater liquidity, and perhaps achieve substantial capital gains. The stock of the conglomerate was selling at 43 times its expected earnings and had appreciated substantially in the recent past. Moreover, the majority owners of Old Reliable believed that affiliation with the conglomerate might increase the insurance company's access to the capital market, especially in times of adversity. There was no public market for the shares of Old Reliable, and the firm's bankers had been placing increasing pressure on the firm to expand its equity base.

Unfortunately, affiliation with the conglomerate did not achieve the desired benefits either for the founding family or for Old Reliable. The fascination of the stock market with the conglomerate movement collapsed shortly after the acquisition, so that within a year the market value of the conglomerate's stock had been reduced by more than 50 percent. Moreover, the conglomerate was unable to provide any capital to Old Reliable and, indeed, had a severe capital deficiency of its own. Perhaps most significantly, the conglomerate substantially altered the senior management of Old Reliable and also expanded markedly the regional coverage of the firm and the number of different types of insurance lines offered. As a result, costs increased dramatically—operating costs associated with a more extensive network of branch offices and the cost of claims alike—but the revenues derived from these expanded operations did not rise proportionately.

The years following the acquisition of Old Reliable turned out to be very difficult ones for the company and the economy. Severe economic and financial instability occurred, including the most severe recession since the Great Depression of the 1930s. The equity market—in which Old Reliable had more than one half of its total investments—fluctuated substantially, with no apparent trend. And, perhaps most important, inflation had become institutionalized in the economic system and had reached double-digit levels in the late 1970s. These developments had a substantial and adverse effect on Old Reliable. The stagnating stock market throughout the 1970s made it difficult for the company to earn a reasonable rate of return. Moreover, declining stock values reduced the capital position of the company. Indeed, the severe stock market decline in 1974 had lowered the capital position of Old Reliable to the point where it was in violation of the minimum statutory capital position required by state law. Further, the inflation produced escalating claims at a time when consumer pressure and intensified competition made it more difficult to obtain higher rates for policies, especially for automobile insurance and for commercial property-casualty coverage.

It was within this general background that the management of Old Reliable pondered its municipal investment strategy. The year which was about to close had been one of substantial losses for the company. However, stock prices increased substantially. The coming year was expected to be one of positive profitability, so that the attractiveness of municipal bonds would be greater. But, should the coming year be one with an operating loss, then tax-exempt municipal income would be particularly unattractive. Furthermore, depreciation of the value of investments made by Old Reliable—either in the equity market or in debt securities—could severely harm the weakened capital position of the firm.

Exhibit 18–1   Common Stock Prices

	19XX–2	19XX–1	19XX
New York Stock Exchange			
(December 31, 1965 = 50)	68.9	80.3	90.6
Industrial	78.2	92.0	104.5
Transportation	60.4	73.4	85.3
Utility	39.8	42.9	46.2
Finance	72.0	86.2	90.3
American Stock Exchange			
(August 31, 1973 = 100)	282.6	333.4	405.0

Source: *Federal Reserve Bulletin*, various issues.

Exhibit 18–2   Forecasts Made by Experts

The coming year should be one of intense pressure in the money and capital markets. Interest rates in the money market should advance by 100–150 basis points and by 50–100 basis points in the capital market.

The inflation outlook is unfavorable. The rate of inflation should accelerate from an annual rate of 4 percent late in the current year to an annual rate of over 7 percent toward the end of the coming year.

It appears likely that commercial banks will be under intense pressure by their business customers for loan accommodation. Deposit inflows should be limited, but loan demand from all types of customers should be substantial.

Stocks are cheap. Now is the time to buy. The price-earnings ratio on the Dow Jones Industrials is at historically low levels. The risk-reward ratio is presently exceedingly attractive. We are at the beginning of a decade long bull market.

19. *Pension Funds*

ONE OF THE MOST IMPORTANT FUNCTIONS performed by financial intermediaries and financial markets is to give economic units an opportunity to more closely match the time distribution (temporal allocation) of actual expenditures with desired expenditures. The receipt of cash by individual economic units frequently occurs in a discontinuous fashion, while desired expenditures are often more continuous. Moreover, over a longer time perspective, there is frequently a substantial mismatch between the receipt of income and desired expenditures.

FUNCTIONS OF PENSION FUNDS

In the lifetime earnings of an individual, the typical pattern is for earnings to mount rapidly during the early working years, reach a peak in late middle age, decline slightly from late middle age until retirement, and then fall precipitously at retirement. Yet, desired expenditure patterns need not conform to this time series at all. Desired expenditures may rise throughout the working life of the individual (although not necessarily at a constant rate) and increase sharply in later years and following retirement. Without financial markets and institutions, individuals could earn no return on their invested savings from surplus years (periods when income exceeded desired consumption) and would not have the opportunity to borrow against future income in years when desired consumption exceeded income. Without financial institutions and financial markets, the individual economic unit would be forced to constrict expenditures to match income. In contrast, with financial institutions and the system of financial markets, the individual should be able to invest surplus funds today for greater consumption tomorrow and borrow today against future income for greater consumption today. With this intertemporal shifting of such flows, the individual more closely matches desired and actual consumption patterns over his or her entire lifetime. Hence, with financial institutions and markets, the individual should be able to achieve a higher level of economic well-being (utility) than if no financial institutions and markets existed.

While all financial institutions and markets play a role in the reallocations of individual expenditures over time, the pension fund is an especially important financial institution from this perspective. The pension fund as a financial intermediary exists to bridge the gap between rising desired expenditures for most individuals following retirement and the abrupt decline in income at the cessation of the individual's work career. This gap is closed (partially or fully) by the accumulation of funds (savings) over the working lifetime of the individual (through both employer and employee contributions) and the investment of these funds in a portfolio of financial assets (stocks and bonds) and sometimes in real assets (real estate). With knowledge of the amount of funds contributed, it is possible to determine fairly precisely the amount of retirement income. With this knowledge, the individual can plan more effectively his or her current expenditures.

It must be admitted, however, that rapid inflation makes this planning process much more difficult. It is possible to actuarially determine the amount of retirement benefits in money income from information on the volume of contributions and the earnings on those contributions, but it is not possible from this information to ascertain the amount of retirement benefits in real income or constant dollar terms. Unfortunately, many individuals who planned carefully for retirement have found that rising prices have made their incomes far too small.

EVOLUTION OF PENSION FUNDS

Pension funds as important financial intermediaries are principally a post–World War II phenomenon. With rising incomes, the breakdown of the extended family, and increasing concern over financial security throughout an individual's lifetime, there developed both in private business and the government the feeling that contributions should be made toward providing an actuarially sound benefit program for employees at the termination of their working lives. This attitude produced, in the 1930s, the social security program, which was designed to establish a floor under retirement income for many individuals and which since has been broadened substantially; there was a proliferation of employer-sponsored plans both in the public and private sector after World War II in order to provide more substantial retirement benefits. Indeed, pension programs now cover most of the labor force even without considering the extensive coverage provided by social security. For example, private pension plans covered more than 50 million people in 1980, while government-administered plans provided potential retirement benefits for more than 20 million additional individuals. And the social security system encompassed over 10 million people in 1980.

With large contributions from participants in the various plans and with relatively few retirees in the early years of most retirement plans to draw funds out, the size of pension assets has grown at an enormous rate. For example, total noninsured assets held by both private and state and local government pension funds amounted to less than $7 billion in 1946. In contrast, by year-end 1982 total assets of these funds exceeded $600 billion (and these figures do not include the pension fund assets which are administered by life insurance companies and which are themselves substantial, at more than $200 billion).

The rate of growth has been so rapid and the assets of pension funds have become so large that it has been suggested by some that pension funds are becoming dominant owners of American business due to their heavy purchases of corporate stock, a development which may have substantial implications for the saving behavior of individuals. Higher savings through pension funds may reduce saving through other means. In any case, pension funds have become a major force in the financial markets, especially in the stock market, where for many years they have been the largest single purchasers of equity securities.

CHARACTER-ISTICS OF PENSION FUNDS

Funded versus Unfunded

Pension funds may be classified in a number of ways. One especially important distinction when pension funds are viewed from the perspective of the financial intermediation process is between *funded* and *unfunded* plans (or some mixture of these two which would be a *partially* funded pension program). A funded pension program is one in which the sponsor places some amount of assets under the control of a trustee after it has been determined that—at some appropriate rate of return on the assets—this contribution would produce a sufficient amount of assets at retirement in order to meet the benefits promised to member employees. In contrast, an unfunded pension program is one in which the employer accepts the responsibility to provide retirement benefits to employees but does not set aside adequate funds today to meet those future obligations. Of course, many plans lie somewhere between these two extremes and thus are termed partially funded programs. In past years, many pension programs have been unfunded or only partially funded. For example, the social security program is only partially funded (actually a very small fraction of total benefits are funded), while many state and local retirement plans have been completely unfunded. However, recent pension reform legislation has placed increasing emphasis on the funding of such programs, especially in the private sector. Only funded (or partially funded) pension programs qualify as financial intermediaries and play a role in the saving and investment process.

Insured versus Noninsured

Funded pension programs may be further classified as *insured* or *noninsured*. An insured pension program is one in which administration of the program is under the control of an insurance company. The employer agrees to provide a certain amount of funds each year, and the insurance company agrees to provide a retirement annuity to the employees in the program beginning at the time of retirement. The amount of the annuity is based upon some assumed rate of earnings on the fund during the time of accumulation prior to the beginning of retirement pay. These insured pension programs may take a variety of forms. Some are conventional group annuities in which the annual contributions purchase paid-up annuity units for those participating in the plan. Others are programs in which the annual contributions accumulate funds, and the cost of retirement benefits to individual members are charged to that fund at the time of retirement. Still another variety is a program in which a separate annuity contract is offered to each employee. But all of these programs have a common feature in that they are usually fully funded or almost fully funded. Insured pension fund programs comprise a substantial and growing share of the assets of life insurance companies, as we noted in Chapter 17.

Noninsured (not administered by a life insurance company) pension funds, in contrast, are administered by trustees chosen by the employer. And, as revealed in Table 19–1, noninsured pension funds are much larger than insured pension funds. The trustees may be employees of the firm or of some other individual or institution. The investment policies of the fund are then determined by the trustees, subject to the influence of the employer. In many cases, the trust departments of commercial banks serve as trustees for noninsured pension funds during the accumulation period and also administer payment of benefits during the retirement period. Indeed, commercial bank trust departments compete vigorously to obtain management of large noninsured pension funds. Trusteed pension funds also come in a variety of forms. They may represent corporate pension funds established voluntarily for executive and nonexecutive employees. As another possibility, the fund may be established because of union pressure, and the trustees may, in fact, be officers of the union. This would be most common in an industry in which there are a large number of small employers but one large labor union as the bargaining agent for those employees. Still other trusteed plans have been established for employees of state and local governments.

Public versus Private

Pension programs also may be separated into those sponsored by the federal government, either for its own workers or for the general popula-

Table 19-1　Assets of All Private and Public Pension Funds—
Book Values, End of Year ($ billions)

	1970	1982
Total private	$151.6	$570.5
Insured pension funds	41.2	228.9
Noninsured pension funds	110.4	341.6
Total public	87.8	362.1
State and local government	60.3	264.2
U.S. government	27.5	97.9
Total private and public	$239.4	$932.6

Source: Board of Governors of the Federal Reserve System, *Flow of Funds Accounts*.

tion, and those sponsored by the private sector (including state and local governments). The U.S. government has sponsored a number of pension programs. The best known, Social Security, is more accurately termed the Old Age, Survivors, and Disability Insurance Fund (OASDI). This program is funded only to a small extent. Indeed, one of the most important developments in the pension system in recent years has been the growing financial difficulties of the social security system. The social security trust fund shrank dramatically during the decade of the 1970s despite large increases in social security taxes. Moreover, with a growing number of retired persons, compared to the total work force, expected in coming decades, the financial problems of the social security system appear yet to be solved. While social security is the largest and best known of the retirement programs of the U.S. government, there are a number of other government-sponsored retirement programs which should also be noted. For example, the Civil Service Retirement Program covers federal government employees. It is also only partially funded and depends upon Congress for a substantial share of the benefits paid to civil service employees. Also, the Railroad Retirement Fund is a special fund established by the federal government in order to provide retirement benefits to employees of the railroad systems of the United States.

Keogh and IRA Plans

Some pension plans are established by individuals through Keogh and IRA programs. Both are fully funded, though they may be either insured or noninsured. Under the Keogh program, an individual who has income in addition to his or her regular job (a university professor engaged in consulting, for example) may establish a separate retirement program for that income. Deductions to the retirement plan may be made against current taxable income on a dollar-for-dollar basis, subject to a limitation (effective in 1984) per year of 20 percent of the outside income or $30,000 whichever is smaller.[1] Under the IRA (Individual Retirement Account) program, any individual covered by a pension program at his or her place of work may contribute an amount up to $2,000 per year into an IRA pension program and deduct the amount of the contribution from current taxable income. Hence it is possible for an individual to have three separate retirement programs (exclusive of social security): one at the regular job, another for outside income through a Keogh plan, and a third in the form of an IRA pension plan. Moreover, an individual may set up any number of separate Keogh and IRA accounts provided his or her total annual contribution to all such plans does not exceed the maximum allowed by federal law.

The investment policies of pension funds are influenced by a number of factors. These include the following:

FACTORS WHICH INFLUENCE PENSION FUND INVESTMENT POLICIES

Stability of Sources of Funds

The pension fund has one of the most stable sources of funds of all financial intermediaries. Inflows into the fund from the contributions of the employer and employee are contractual in nature and, therefore, highly predictable. Moreover, outflows from the fund in the form of retirement benefits are also highly predictable and can be anticipated well in advance of the date of the need for funds. Premature death and other causes for withdrawal from the fund prior to retirement are less predictable uses of funds, but these demands represent a small fraction of the cash flow for most pension funds. Moreover, during the beginning years of a growing pension fund, the stability is even more pronounced, since benefits can frequently be paid from the cash contribution from future beneficiaries without liquidating existing assets or even using the earnings of the existing assets for the necessary cash.

Examination of data on the receipts and disbursements of private noninsured pension funds provides some interesting information on these points. As shown in Table 19–2, in 1982 total receipts of private noninsured pension funds were $56.0 billion. Of this total, employer contributions were $44.2 billion, employee contributions totaled $2.2 billion, and investment income was $9.6 billion. Yet total benefits paid out were only $27.8 billion. Not only did the pension funds not need liquid assets in order to pay benefits, since employer and employee contributions together amounted to almost double total benefits paid out, but investment income

---

[1]This limitation is relevant under defined *contribution* programs, where the contribution is fixed and the benefit (pension payment) is variable. Under the defined benefit plan, where the benefit is fixed and the contribution is variable, the maximum contribution could exceed this amount.

alone on accumulated assets would have provided about one third of the funds needed to pay the benefits required.

The extreme stability of sources of funds, coupled with the fact that the pension fund's time horizon is quite long, means that these intermediaries are not active in short-term or even very much in intermediate-term investments. The pension fund has little need for liquidity. It is essentially an investor in capital market instruments and, within the capital market, in the longest segment of the maturity structure of these instruments: long-term bonds and equity securities—both preferred and common stock. Indeed, as will be discussed more fully below, the pension fund has

Table 19–2 Sources and Uses of Funds: Private Noninsured Pension Funds ($ billions)

	1977	1978	1979	1980	1981	1982 (estimated)
Sources of funds:						
Employer contributions	$26.5	$30.5	$34.0	$38.0	$41.5	$44.2
Employee contributions	1.8	1.9	2.0	2.1	2.2	2.2
Investment income	7.2	7.6	8.0	8.4	9.3	9.6
Total receipts	35.5	40.0	44.0	48.5	53.0	56.0
Benefit payments	16.5	18.2	20.0	22.5	25.0	27.8
Net receipts	$19.0	$21.8	$24.0	$26.0	$28.0	$28.2
Uses of funds:						
Investment funds:						
Corporate bonds	$ 6.2	$ 7.4	$ 4.7	$ 3.1	$ 2.9	$ 5.0
Corporate stocks	4.4	5.3	6.0	9.6	7.3	9.0
Total securities	10.6	12.8	10.7	12.7	10.2	14.0
Home mortgages	2.7	2.1	1.3	1.3	1.1	1.2
Multifamily, commercial, and farm mortgages	.1	.4	.3	1.0	.4	.3
Total mortgages	2.9	2.5	1.6	2.3	1.5	1.5
Total	13.5	15.2	12.5	15.0	11.7	15.5
Open market paper	.3	.8	1.0	1.3	.7	
U.S. government and agency securities:						
U.S. government securities	2.1	.1	1.4	4.1	7.6	9.0
Federal agency securities	.6		1.0	.4	1.5	.7
Total	2.7	− .1	2.4	4.5	9.1	9.7
Total funds	16.5	16.0	15.9	20.9	21.5	25.2
Cash	1.5	4.4	.5	.7	1.0	—
Other—net	1.0	1.4	7.6	4.5	5.5	3.0
Total uses of funds	$19.0	$21.8	$24.0	$26.0	$28.0	$28.2

*Includes minor amounts of other income.
Sources: Securities and Exchange Commission and Institute of Life Insurance.

become the dominant purchaser of equity securities in the U.S. capital market.

Taxes

Taxes are a factor in influencing the policies of pension funds. Taxes affect both the mix of contributions by employer and employee and the nature of fund investments. Since contributions to pension funds by the employer are not taxable to the employee as earned income until actually received, there is an incentive for pension fund contributions to come primarily from the employer. In fact, employers have contributed about 80 percent of combined employer-employee contributions in recent years. Moreover, the fund itself pays no taxes. Generally, the money paid into the fund is before taxes (at least in the case of the employer's contribution) and the funds accumulate within a tax shelter. When benefits are paid to the employee at retirement, these benefits are taxable at whatever individual income tax rate is applicable to the beneficiary at the time he or she receives payment. The lack of taxation on the earnings of the fund during the accumulation period has a number of important influences on the investment policies of pension funds. While pension funds are principally capital market investors, their interest in municipal securities is virtually nil since municipals are valuable only to investors in high, marginal income tax brackets. In addition, the pension fund need not differentiate between returns on investment in the form of ordinary income or capital gains, since it pays no taxes on either. The return to the pension fund which is significant is the *total return*, the sum of dividend or interest income plus capital gains. In contrast, many investors in high, marginal income tax brackets prefer a portion of their return in the form of capital gains—either on equity securities or deep discount bonds, since this increases their after-tax income.

Management Pressure

One important factor influencing the investment policy of many pension funds is pressure by management for a high return on the funds placed with the pension program in order to insure the payment of promised retirement benefits at minimum cost to the employer. While this would be most relevant to private pension funds administered by employers, it would also have significance for state and local government retirement funds. After all, contributions by the employer—and in most private pension funds most of the contributions are made by the employer—are expenses of the firm. The employer would like to reduce these expenses as much as possible. Yet, from a labor-relations perspective, the employer seeks to promise as high a schedule of benefits as possible. These conflicting goals can be made compatible (to a degree) if the rate of return on the fund can be increased. The amount of the retirement benefit which can be actuarially promised to employees is a function of the amount of funds during the accumulation period. To the extent that the employer is able to obtain higher returns on the fund's assets, the employer is able to reduce contributions and thereby expenses. In recent years, this factor has resulted in substantial investments in common stock.

Nature of Obligations

The types of investments which pension funds make will, of course, be determined to some extent by the nature of the obligations which have been promised to beneficiaries at retirement. There are two basic types of obligations: the fixed annuity and the variable annuity. The fixed annuity is one in which the amount of a beneficiary's retirement income is fixed at the time of retirement and remains unchanged during the payment period. Traditionally, the fixed annuity has been the dominant form of pension fund obligation. With the rapid increase in prices in recent years, many individuals have become concerned about the prospect that inflation during retirement years would reduce the value of retirement income from adequate to subsistence level or even below. As a result, the variable annuity was developed, in which payment to the beneficiary at retirement is variable and depends upon the investment performance of the contributions made prior to retirement and in subsequent years.

A fixed annuity obligation on the part of the pension fund would suggest an investment policy which concentrates on fixed-income instruments such as bonds and mortgages. In contrast, the variable annuity obligation would suggest investment in equity securities such as common stock. There are, of course, combinations of programs. The variable annuity need not have all of its investments in equities; it could be a "balanced fund," with part debt and part equity. Moreover, the fund could be devoted to equity securities during the accumulation period and then transferred to a fixed annuity at retirement. Such a policy would dictate investments in common stock during the accumulation period and in bonds and mortgages after retirement.

Limitations on Trustee Investment Policies

The investment policies of pension funds are frequently constrained by limitations in the contract establishing the fund. This is most common in public investment programs where there are substantial restraints designed to reduce the risk exposure of the fund. For example, it is often required that public pension funds invest no monies in land. In addition, at one time many public pension funds were required to invest some fraction of their assets in the bond issues of the state or local government for whose employees the fund was established. While economically this requirement has little merit (and it did reduce the returns available to the beneficiaries at time of retirement), the restriction was usually justified with the argument that public employees should support their employer with the investment of their accumulated retirement savings, a substantial part or perhaps all of which might have been contributed originally by the government employer. Certainly such a requirement should have made it easier for some governmental units to sell their debt issues.

Private Pension Funds

Private pension fund investments are heavily concentrated in two types of capital market securities: corporate equities and corporate bonds (see Table 19–3 and Figure 19–1). Indeed, as of the end of 1982, corporate equities accounted for more than 50 percent of total financial assets, and corporate bonds totaled another 20 percent for private noninsured pension funds. This concentration on equities is a relatively new development. In 1956, for example, the investment in equity securities by private pension funds amounted to only about one third of the total financial assets held by this financial intermediary. This increase in investments in the equity market reflects a number of factors. Certainly, the growth of variable annuity retirement funds has played an important role. Moreover, the pressure by management to expand the assumed earnings used in calculating the contribution necessary to make the pension program actuarially sound is also important. But perhaps most significant was the change in attitude on the part of many investors toward the risk/return opportuni-

PENSION FUND INVESTMENTS

Table 19–3 **Financial Assets of Noninsured Pension Funds: 1982 ($ billions)**

	Private	State and Local Government
Demand deposits and currency	$ 2.1	$ 5.5
Time deposits	9.3	—
Corporate equities	200.4	60.2
U.S. government securities	38.9	35.0
Agency issues	14.7	34.1
Corporate bonds	65.1	112.0
Mortgages	4.1	14.0
Municipals	—	3.4
Other	7.0	—
Total financial assets	$341.6	$264.2

Note: Columns may not add to totals due to rounding.
Source: Board of Governors of the Federal Reserve System, *Flow of Funds Accounts*.

Figure 19-1   Principal Earning Assets of Pension Funds
(amount outstanding, end of quarter)

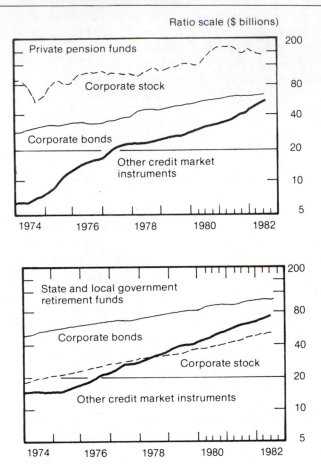

Source: Board of Governors of the Federal Reserve System, *Federal Reserve Chart Book*, Washington, D.C., 1982.

ties available in equities. The post–World War II bull market in equities convinced many investors that the risks in equity securities were relatively limited (at least for the long-term investor), while the returns were substantial.

The amount of funds contributed by private funds to the equity market in recent years has become enormous. Indeed, it has been argued that one of the main reasons for the post–World War II bull market in equities was the substantial amount of funds contributed by pension funds. For example, in 1956 private pension funds committed $941 million to the equity market—representing less than one half the net acquisition of financial assets by private pension funds and about one fourth the net new funds committed to equity securities. In contrast, in 1966 private pension funds committed $3.5 billion to the purchase of equities, representing about 50 percent of their net acquisition of financial assets and more than 75 percent of the net increase in funds committed to equities. Hence private pension funds were increasing their influence on the equity market not only because their total assets were expanding (and at a very rapid pace) but also because the proportion of that expansion in available funds that was devoted to equities was rising.

The enormous concentration of pension fund investments in equities in this period reflects a number of factors. First, the excellent performance of the stock market in the immediate post–World War II period encouraged many fund managers to believe that returns on equities would be substantially higher than returns on fixed-income securities. Given the greater risks assumed by the investor in equity securities, it would be expected that the return would be higher. In addition, many studies in the academic community of realized rates of return over a large number of past periods suggested long-run returns from equities that were considerably in excess of returns on long-term bonds. For example, Fisher and Lorie [6] investigated the average annual return which could have been obtained through a random selection of stocks listed on the New York Stock Exchange in the period from 1926 to 1965. On a before-tax basis, the average annual return over the entire period was 9.3 percent. Moreover, variable annuity policy sales were increasing as investors looked to equities as a means of hedging against inflation. Finally, while the pension funds were pulled by the apparent attractiveness of the yields available in equities, they were pushed by the pressure of management seeking to lower pension costs through increasing the assumed rate of earnings on investments made by the pension fund.

Concentration of new money in equities has diminished in recent years as the relatively poor performance of the stock market in the 1970s resurrected the fact that equity prices could fall as well as rise. For example, in 1974 private pension funds committed less than 25 percent of their net acquisition of financial assets to equities. The year 1974, of course, was a period of high interest rates with attractive returns in the corporate bond market, so that almost half of the total flow of funds at private pension funds was devoted to corporate bonds. However, even in 1981 equities absorbed less than 50 percent of the net new funds invested by private pension funds. It seems unlikely if private pension funds will again devote most of their funds to equities. Rather, it seems likely that many private pension funds will seek roughly a 50-50 split in investment of new funds between equities and fixed-income instruments.

State and Local Government Pension Funds

Investment policies of state and local government pension funds, as revealed in Table 19–3, have been quite different from the investment policies of private pension funds. Primarily because of more detailed regulation and control over investment policies, and perhaps because of less pressure for higher returns, state and local government pension funds have not invested as greatly in equity securities as have private pension funds. In recent years, the restrictions on the investment policies of these institutions have been relaxed to a considerable extent so that increasingly both private and public noninsured pension funds are following similar types of investment policies. Private pension funds appear to be reducing their contributions to equities, while public pension funds seem to be increasing their contribution to the corporate stock market.

At the end of 1982, state and local government pension funds held over $200 billion in financial assets. Most of these assets were held in the form of fixed-income instruments, principally corporate bonds ($112 billion). A small amount of these funds were devoted to municipal securities, despite the unattractiveness of this kind of security for a tax-free investor, probably reflecting the hangover of previous restrictions which forced these funds to support the bond issues of local governmental units. Yet, if we look at the Federal Reserve's *Flow of Funds Accounts*, we see some important changes in the investment policies of these institutions. For example, in 1971 state and local government retirement funds committed almost 50 percent of their net flow of funds to equities, and in 1979 the percent committed to equities was about 25 percent, a much larger share than had been common in many earlier years.

Federal Government Pension Funds

The retirement programs established by the federal government have been less significant from the perspective of financial intermediation, for two important reasons. First, since the programs have been only partially funded, the amounts accumulated in the funds have been relatively small. As Table 19–1 shows, total assets of all federally sponsored retirement programs (including disability plans) amounted to less than $100 billion in 1981. Moreover, in recent years, benefits paid have exceeded contributions so that the sizes of many of the funds have diminished. Second, the funds have been invested entirely in government securities (special issues of the U.S. Treasury). Because of concern for safety as well as the possibility that, should these funds ever become large enough they might dominate American business through stock ownership, their policies have been to invest most funds in special U.S. Treasury issues. Hence the direct result of federal government retirement programs has been to reduce the amount of funds that must be borrowed in the nation's credit markets by the U.S. Treasury.

One of the most significant events in the recent history of pension funds occurred in 1974 when the Employee Retirement Income Security Act (ERISA) became law. This law, which resulted from intensive investigation of abuse in the administration of private pension plans, made a number of changes in the existing law regulating pension programs. These changes covered such important items as determining which employees are eligible to enroll in a pension program, what length of service is necessary before the individual has vested benefits, and what kind of funding requirements are imposed on the employer.[2] The general purpose of these changes was to make sure that individuals who work for a company for some considerable number of years do, in fact, receive pension benefits. If the employer chooses to sponsor a pension program, ERISA makes certain demands on the employer in order to ensure fair treatment of the employee.

ERISA

ERISA covers a wide variety of items relevant to pension programs and is highly technical in nature. While it would be impossible to present the complete details of the act, it may be desirable to focus on some of the more significant changes which ERISA has brought about. The ERISA requirements include the following: Any employee who is at least 25 years of age and has at least one year of service with an employer must be permitted to enroll in the company's pension plan. Employees have a number of options in vesting, ranging from full vesting after a specified number of years (with no vesting prior to that point) up to partial vesting when the sum of an employee's age and years of service add up to 45, and additional vesting beyond that point. Minimum funding schedules are established, with requirements for gradual funding of unfunded past liabilities (pension promised for which no funds have been set aside). In addition, a federal pension insurance plan, the Pension Benefit Guaranty Corporation, was established to guarantee a portion of vested benefits and is financed by employer contributions. This corporation (somewhat similar to the FDIC and known widely as "Penny Benny") exists to provide insurance for employee pension benefits in the case where the employer cannot honor its commitment. Additional fiduciary responsibilities were placed on the managers of pension fund assets by ERISA. It applies the prudent-man rule (so well-known to insurance companies, as we saw in Chapter 17) to

---

[2]Vesting refers to the right of the employee to obtain the pension. A pension is fully vested if the employee has complete rights to obtain the pension regardless of future employment.

pension fund portfolio managers. In fact, as Blair [3] observes, ERISA as interpreted by the courts in recent years appears to apply a "prudent expert" rule to pension fund management. Such a rule is in conflict with the diversification precepts of portfolio theory and would be expected to reduce the risk-adjusted returns available through portfolio management.

The Pension Benefit Guaranty Corporation has itself experienced some difficulty—particularly with the bankruptcy of some large corporations in the late 1970 and early 1980s. From its beginning through 1981, the corporation assumed benefit liabilities in terminated pension plans equal to $680 million. However, of this amount, $275 million was provided by the assets of the terminated plans and $60 million from employer liability payments, so that the net claims on the Pension Benefit Guaranty Corporation were only $345 million. Yet, a very large part of this claim arose in 1980 and 1981, and further pressure on Penny Benny occurred with the 1981–82 recession.[3]

ERISA has been an extremely controversial piece of legislation. It has been charged that ERISA has caused many smaller pension programs to be discontinued because of the large amount of paperwork necessary to meet the requirements of the law. Opponents of ERISA argue that many employees are now worse off than before. While before they had an imperfect pension plan, now they have no plan at all. Moreover, the Labor Department and the Internal Revenue Service were quite slow in developing detailed guidelines to implement the act. One noticeable development was the shift of many plans from self-management by the employer to management by a financial institution due to the increased liability imposed on pension fund managers by ERISA.

THE INVESTMENT PERFORMANCE OF PENSION FUNDS

The investment performance of pension funds has been subject to detailed analysis.[4] While there is some degree of conflict in the results of these studies, the general finding is that pension fund performance has not exceeded the returns that would be expected, given the degree of risk in the portfolios held by various funds. In fact, after deducting the operating and management costs of pension funds from their gross returns, most studies find that the performance of the portfolios held by pension funds is generally worse than would be expected, given the riskiness of the portfolios held. This result is not too surprising, especially for portfolios which have concentrated in the stocks and bonds of large, well-known companies; extensive research by security analysts would apparently make per-

---

[3]"Pension Guarantees: How Well Are They Working?" *The Morgan Guaranty Survey*, March 1983, pp. 12–15.

[4]See, for example, Malca [8].

formance which is better than the market performance for a given portfolio quite unusual.

Another interesting comparison is that between alternative investment managers of pension funds. Bogle and Twardowski [4], for example, compared the investment performance of banks through their trust departments (much of which would reflect the management of pension funds), insurance companies (including their pension fund assets), investment counselors (who would manage pension funds and other types of assets), and mutual funds. This comparison included a number of different periods ending in 1977. By far the best performance (in terms of annualized total returns before expenses) was given by the mutual fund group. Investment counselors ranked second, though, with returns well under those provided by mutual funds. Insurance companies followed well behind the counselors, with banks placing last in the rankings.

FUTURE TRENDS

As discussed earlier, pension funds have grown enormously in recent years and have moved from a relatively small force in the financial spectrum prior to World War II to become one of the major financial intermediaries. Moreover, their influence in the equity market has been especially notable. Yet, it is unlikely that this rapid growth in assets under management will continue in the future. The extremely fast expansion of pension fund assets has been fueled by two factors, both of which appear to be weakening. First, there have been a substantial number of employees contributing to the programs and yet few beneficiaries in the past. Moreover, many funds attained relatively high rates of return, at least until the difficulties in the stock market in the late 1960s and 1970s. It is not surprising that pension funds grew rapidly when there existed both a large net inflow of funds and high earnings on the fund's assets. But in recent years there has occurred a significant upward shift in the ratio of beneficiaries to contributors, and this shift should become even more pronounced in the future. Indeed, the age structure of the population is projected to change dramatically in the coming decades, with fewer workers relative to retired persons. Undoubtedly, this will have a major influence on the growth of pension fund assets.

A second and perhaps more significant factor from a long-run perspective is the growing realization of the immense cost of pension benefits. In the early post–World War II period, with rapid growth in the economy, tight labor markets, and limited inflationary effects on employee compensation, employers liberalized pension benefits to a very considerable extent. Moreover, with the expectation of a high return on funds contributed to the pension program, pension benefits could be improved to a substantial extent without boosting pension costs by an appreciable amount. But, in recent years, with pressure on profits from rising labor costs and with poor performance in the equity markets, employers have begun to resist increases in pension benefits. It appears likely that employer contributions to pension funds will grow less rapidly in future years than in the recent past.

SUMMARY

Pension programs play an important role in the United States economy. From the perspective of the financial system, pension plans have accumulated massive amounts of stocks and bonds to be used for future pension benefits. This accumulation of funds has had a substantial effect on the total flow of funds and undoubtedly will continue to influence the flow of funds in the nation.

Pension plans may be classified in a variety of ways. These classifications include *funded* plans in which assets are placed in the fund today in order to pay expected future benefits; they also include *unfunded* plans in which no assets are established today against future benefits. Only funded plans may be viewed as financial institutions. Funded plans may further be classified as *insured* or *noninsured*. Under an insured plan, an insurance company administers the plan, while under a noninsured plan a trustee, often the trust department of a commercial bank, administers the plan. Pension programs also may be classified into those sponsored by the federal government or those sponsored by the private sector (including state and local governments).

The investment policies of pension programs are influenced by a variety of factors, including stability of sources of funds; taxes; management pressure; nature of obligations; and limitations on investment policies, such as legal limitations through the Employee Retirement Income Security Act (ERISA). Reflecting these factors, most private noninsured pension funds invest in corporate equity securities and corporate bonds, with the preponderance of assets held in the form of equity securities. In contrast, the investments of state and local government retirement funds are more heavily concentrated in bonds, especially corporate bonds, than in common stock, though the private and public pension funds have become more alike in investment holdings in recent years. Regardless of the investment strategy followed, however, pension funds do not appear to perform better than the market on a consistent basis.

Questions

19-1. Discuss methods by which variances in income levels and consumption levels over time are accommodated. What exactly is a pension fund? How does it operate?

19-2. Differentiate between funded and unfunded pension programs. Between insured and uninsured. Which type is most significant as a financial institution?

19-3. What are the major assets and liabilities of a typical pension fund? Differentiate according to the kind of pension funds. What factors explain these differences?

19-4. What tax advantages do pension funds enjoy?

19-5. What factors are expected to influence the future growth of pension funds?

19-6. What is ERISA? What are its principal purposes and likely effects?

References

1. Andrews, Victor, ed. "Noninsured Corporate and State and Local Governments Retirement Funds in the Financial Structure." In *Private Capital Market*. Englewood Cliffs, N.J.: Prentice-Hall, 1964.

2. Bernstein, Merton C. *The Future of Private Pensions*. New York: Free Press, 1964.

3. Blair, Eric. "ERISA and the Prudent Man Rule: Avoiding Perverse Results." *Sloan Management Review*, Winter 1979.

4. Bogle, John C., and Jan M. Twardowski. "Institutional Investment Performance Compared." *Financial Analysts Journal*, January–February 1980. pp. 33–41.

5. Ehrlich, Edna E. "The Functions and Investment Policies of Personal Trust Departments." *Monthly Review*, Federal Reserve Bank of New York, October 1972, pp. 255–70.

6. Fisher, Lawrence, and James H. Lorie. "Rates of Return on Investments in Common Stock: The Year-by-Year Record, 1962–1965." *Journal of Business*, July 1968, pp. 291–315.

7. *Funding Pensions: Issues and Implications for Financial Markets*. Boston: Federal Reserve Bank of Boston, 1976.

8. Malca, Edward. *Pension Funds and Other Institutional Investors*. Lexington, Mass.: Lexington Books, 1975.

9. McCandlish, Raymond W. "Some Methods For Measuring Performance of a Pension Fund." *Financial Analysts Journal*, November–December 1965.

10. McGill, D. M. *Fundamentals of Private Pensions*. 2d ed. Homewood, Ill.: Richard D. Irwin, 1961.

11. Allen, Everett T., Jr.; Joseph J. Melone; and Jerry S. Rosenbloom. *Pension Planning*. 4th ed. Homewood, Ill.: Richard D. Irwin, 1981.

12. Murray, Roger F. *Economic Aspects of Pensions: A Summary Report*. New York: Columbia University Press, 1960.

13. Pozen, Robert. "The Prudent Person Rule and ERISA: A Legal Perspective." *Financial Analysts Journal*, March–April 1977.

14. *The Private Pension Controversy*. New York: Bankers Trust Company, 1973.

15. Schotland, Roy A. "Divergent Investing For Pension Funds." *Financial Analysts Journal*, September–October 1980, pp. 29–39.

Problem for Discussion

THE IMPORTANCE OF BEHAVING AS A "PRUDENT MAN" is fundamental to the investment policy of pension funds. In practice, prudent investment policy has traditionally meant the acquisition of high-quality stocks and bonds and substantial diversification of the portfolio within each of these broad categories of financial assets. Yet, in a period of inflation, is it really prudent to confine the pension fund portfolio to financial assets, or should various real assets (such as ceramics, gold, paintings, and real estate) also be acquired? The problem for discussion described below deals with this question.

1. After reviewing the material, the student should make a list of the advantages and disadvantages of such a change in investment policy and should evaluate such a policy from the perspective of the employer and employee.
2. Should the pension fund buy real assets and, if so, which assets and how much?

The ABC Pension Fund is a company-sponsored plan for the employees of ABC Manufacturing Corporation. Contributions to the fund are made only by the employer (noncontributory plan), while the trustees are selected by the company. Major investment decisions for the pension fund are made by the treasurer of ABC Manufacturing Corporation with the advice of staff personnel in the treasurer's department and with additional information provided by the management of a local security broker. The level of contributions by ABC Manufacturing Corporation to the plan is determined each year during an annual review of the plan by a consulting actuary.

The ABC Pension Fund is reasonably typical of most pension funds. The program was begun by the employer in the early 1950s as an aid in obtaining skilled employees in a labor-short environment. With few employees retiring in the 1950s, 1960s, and throughout the 1970s, the total assets of the fund expanded sharply. By early 1982 the assets of ABC Pension Fund exceeded $90 million. Moreover, the investment strategy of the fund was also fairly representative of the pension fund industry. In the early 1950s, the trustees were reluctant to commit a substantial share of the fund's assets to common stock. The memory of the 1930s was too strong, along with the forecasts of another depression following the end of World War II. Yet, as equity prices moved sharply upward during the 1950s and early 1960s, the trustees became increasingly interested in common stock. In fact, by 1965 over 50 percent of the portfolio of the fund was invested in common stock, most of which was regarded as emerging growth stocks. And in the early 1960s this portfolio mix proved quite successful as the fund averaged a total return (dividends plus capital appreciation) of 12.2 percent per year.

Unfortunately, the ABC Pension Fund increased its equity commitments toward the end of the postwar bull market in common stocks. In the 15 years ending in 1981, the total return on the pension fund was only 3.4 percent, not particularly poor as compared to the performance of other pension funds but certainly unsatisfactory in a period of high inflation rates. The performance of the fund was especially troubling to the trustees, as it was less than the assumed return used by the actuaries in calculating the annual contributions made by the company in order to maintain the fund on a sound financial basis. Moreover, employees of the ABC Manufacturing Corporation were pressing for liberalization of benefits, since those previously promised were now inadequate due to rising prices. In fact, the company was voluntarily supplementing the pension payments to its retired employees, since the benefits under the existing program had been so seriously eroded by inflation.

Given this environment, the trustees were intrigued by the idea that pension funds perhaps should diversify outside of the traditional stocks and bonds (financial assets) into a variety of real assets which might appreciate more rapidly during inflationary periods. In this regard, the trustees noted that investors in paintings, gold, diamonds, land, and other real assets had done much better in some past years then had investors in stocks and bonds. For example, as Exhibit 19–1 shows, common stocks achieved a compound annual growth in value of only 3.9 percent in the 1972–82 period, yet Chinese ceramics grew in value 15.3 percent per year in the same period and gold returned an annual gain of 18.6 percent to the investor. Farmland appreciated at an annual rate of 13.7 percent and housing at an annual rate of almost 10 percent. In that period, the inflation rate was more than double the return on common stock. It seemed as if the pension fund could preserve the purchasing value of its funds only by investing a portion of its portfolio in real assets. Yet, questions of liquidity, prudence and price volatility were certainly of importance in the decision to diversify into real assets. Moreover, the trustees and their investment adviser lacked expertise in evaluating the merits of these real assets.

Exhibit 19–1   Annual Returns on Alternative Investments, 10 Years and 1 Year: June 1, 1982

Category	10 Years	1 Year
Oil	22.9%	6.3%
U.S. coins	22.5	−27.8
Oriental rugs	19.1	−16.2
Gold	18.6	−34.0
Chinese ceramics	15.3	−0.5
Farmland	13.7	−0.9
Silver	13.6	−44.5
Housing	9.9	3.4
Old masters	9.0	−22.0
Consumer price index	8.6	6.6
Stocks	3.9	−10.5
Bonds	3.6	11.4

Source: Salomon Brothers, Inc.

PART SIX

Other Financial Institutions

20. *Finance Companies*

IN THIS CHAPTER we examine a set of financial intermediaries, commonly called finance companies, that specialize in loans to businesses and consumers. As we will soon see, there have been substantial changes in both the sources and uses of funds in the finance industry in recent years. Moreover, finance companies today face increasing competition from commercial banks, credit unions, savings and loan associations, and other lending institutions. As a result of both competitive and cost pressures, finance companies of all kinds have diversified their functions, reaching simultaneously into both business and consumer loan markets. There also has been a trend toward consolidation and merger within the industry, considerably reducing the number of independent firms. The foregoing structural changes all have occurred against the backdrop of increasing penetration of the industry by affiliates of bank holding companies. Finance companies face intense competition from other financial institutions today for both business and consumer loan accounts. This competition is a great stimulus for the industry to become more cost-efficient and more innovative in services offered to the public.

THE CHANGING COMPOSITION OF THE FINANCE INDUSTRY

Finance companies have gone through remarkable changes in recent years. The dominant trend has been toward larger, more highly diversified financial organizations whose credit services span both small loans to consumers and often extremely large loans and leases to major corporations.

Until the decade of the 1970s it was fairly easy to separate finance companies into three distinct types—consumer finance companies, sales finance companies, and commercial finance companies. Though these distinctions are now far less useful, with most major finance companies offering credit services in all three areas, it is still helpful to be aware of the differences between each of the three types of companies. The reason is that each company type represents a range of services offered to a group of customers still served by the industry.

A *consumer finance company*, historically speaking, is a financial firm devoting most of its resources to small loans granted to individuals and families. Most of these loans are of the installment variety, covering a period of several months and used to purchase consumer durables (e.g., automobiles, motor homes, boats, furniture, and appliances) or to meet household expenses (e.g., dental and medical bills, home and auto repairs, and vacation costs). Many are unsecured, signature loans, though security in the form of a chattel mortgage is usually taken when a loan is made for the purchase of consumer durable items. It is generally acknowledged that interest rates charged on small loans by consumer-oriented finance companies are *higher* than loans granted for similar purposes with comparable maturities by commercial banks, savings and loans, and credit unions. However, many households borrowing from finance companies carry more risk than banks and nonbank thrifts find acceptable.[1] The making of small loans by consumer finance companies normally is regulated by small-loan laws of the various states, which generally limit the maximum rate of interest charged and the permissible size of such loans.[2]

Closely related to consumer finance companies are *sales finance companies* which lend *indirectly* to households. The traditional role of sales finance companies is to provide funding for purchases of consumer durable goods, especially automobiles, recreational vehicles, furniture, home appliances, and mobile homes. Retail stores and showrooms where such items are sold will offer their customers installment contracts, calling typically for repayment of the purchase price plus interest in monthly installments. These contracts are sold to sales finance companies. So close is the

---

[1]An interesting study by Benston [1,2] finds that consumer finance company loan losses (net of recoveries as a percent of outstanding loans) were about three times the net loan loss rate at banks and about six times the net loss rate at credit unions. Moreover, Benston points out, finance company operating costs are roughly half again as great per loan as experienced by commercial banks. He finds that a substantial proportion of the higher operating costs experienced by finance companies reflect efforts to work out and recover delinquent loans.

[2]See especially the study by Sartoris [17]. Interest-rate ceilings imposed on small loans by the various states have been of particular significance in recent years, especially where those legal rate maximums have lagged behind rising interest rates in the open market. As theory would suggest and also as found by Greer [9,10], consumer finance companies will accept less risky personal loans when rate ceilings are set low. Thus legal interest-rate ceilings appear to limit the supply of personal cash loans to consumers and are especially restrictive on the growth of the smallest size consumer loans, which tend to carry the highest risk levels. When governments set low interest-rate ceilings on consumer loans compared to market interest rates, finance companies (and probably other lenders as well) tend to reject more loan applications, particularly those judged to be more risky.

relationship between many retail stores and the sales finance company purchasing their installment paper that the finance company often supplies the contract forms and specifies what contract terms are acceptable to it. A retail dealer may sell *all* of his or her installment contracts to a single finance company with whom he or she has a close working relationship covering many years.

An interesting phenomenon in the sales finance business is the use of so-called *captive* finance companies by a number of large manufacturing firms. Probably the best known example is GMAC, the General Motors Acceptance Corporation, which accepts installment contracts from dealers selling General Motors automobiles and trucks. The obvious purpose of a captive finance company is to promote sales of a particular manufacturer's product by offering convenient and affordable credit.

The third major type of finance company, which emerged early in the industry's history, is the *commercial finance company*. In reality, there is a close historical connection between sales finance and commercial finance activities. Many companies that got their start in sales financing soon added commercial financing services and vice versa. But what does a pure commercial finance company do? It finances businesses that need either working capital or long-term investment capital or both. Working capital needs center mainly upon business purchases of inventory. Manufacturing and industrial corporations need funds to acquire raw materials, and businesses selling goods directly to the public require funds to restock their shelves. In addition to recurring inventory purchases, both types of business frequently must commit themselves to long-term investments in new machinery, office equipment, delivery vehicles, warehouse and production space, and thousands of other productive assets. These assets are typically labeled "fixed assets" or "plant and equipment."

Commercial finance companies over the years have developed a number of innovative ways for financing business inventory purchases and new plant and equipment. For example, an automobile dealer may contract with a commercial finance company to pay for a shipment of new autos. The contract's terms may simply specify that the finance company will pay the auto manufacturer for the cars which are directly shipped to the dealer's lot. The finance company retains title to the new vehicles and holds a trust receipt. Hopefully, the auto dealer will find buyers, generating either a cash flow or buyer installment contracts which can be used by the dealer to gradually pay off the promissory note held by the finance company. The rate of interest charged the auto dealer by the finance company will reflect not only the finance company's cost of raising loanable funds, but also the risks inherent in the auto dealership business. Experience has shown, for example, that when the economy is in a recession, new car sales often plunge, crippling a dealer's ability to move inventory and repay drawings on the line of credit granted by the finance company. Ultimately, in a severe economic slump, the commercial finance company may be forced to sell off the dealer's inventory at distress prices.

Lending against automobiles or other goods held in business inventories is really a form of *asset-based financing*. Commercial finance companies lend against many other kinds of business assets to provide short-term working capital. One of the most widely known forms of asset-based funding is a loan against a firm's accounts receivable (i.e., credit sales). Quite obviously, when a business firm sells goods on credit it is extending a short-term, working-capital loan to its customer. That loan temporarily ties up the selling firm's cash until the account balance is paid off. In the meantime, the seller must pay workers, acquire more inventory to replace the goods sold, and meet other near-term demands for liquid funds. This short-term need for liquid funds can be met by pledging the seller's accounts receivable as collateral for a finance company loan. This type of loan in which the borrowing firm still retains control of the credit accounts is known simply as *accounts receivable financing*.

A slightly different arrangement, known as *factoring*, calls for the finance company to purchase the borrower's credit accounts outright. The finance company would, of course, offer only a fraction of the receivable's book value because some of the accounts may become bad debts and uncollectible. In addition, customers buying on credit may not pay for a considerable period of time—often for 30, 60, or 90 days. Therefore the present value of accounts receivable is less than their book value even if all charge-account customers pay on time.

Many business assets other than accounts receivable may be used in asset-based lending by commercial finance companies. A loan may be secured by a mortgage against a firm's fixed assets (plant and equipment) or a pledge of inventories. Sometimes inventories of raw materials are used as collateral for a short-term loan, but most lenders prefer inventories consisting of finished goods as collateral since these are easier to sell in case the loan is not repaid. Leases granted by finance companies to business firms are also usually tied closely to the assets they finance. Under the terms of a typical *financial lease*, the finance company will purchase business equipment and machinery for its lease customers (leasees), turning these assets over to the customer's control and use. Typically, the leasee will be responsible for repairing and servicing the equipment or machinery until the lease term expires.

RECENT CHANGES IN LENDING BY FINANCE COMPANIES

The distinctions drawn in the preceding section between consumer, sales, and commercial finance companies are fading into history. These distinctions, to be sure, are still useful because many finance companies today still specialize in one or another of these activities. Some still prefer making small personal loans, while others still prefer providing working capital to businesses. However, companies of any size now deal in both commercial and consumer credit markets. The trend of recent changes may be seen by examining the nationwide surveys of finance companies carried out by the Federal Reserve System in 1955, 1960, 1965, 1970, 1975, and 1980. During the 1950s and 1960s, the Federal Reserve Board surveyed separately the three major categories of finance companies. By 1970, the Board reported that "this distinction was no longer meaningful because the trend toward diversification—already important in 1965— had broadened the activities of many companies substantially further."[3]

Types of Credit Extended by Finance Companies

Business credit represents the largest share of gross receivables in the finance company industry today. At mid-year 1980, for example, according to data released by the Federal Reserve Board, *business receivables*[4] of U.S. finance companies totaled $86 billion, compared to $77 billion in receivables associated with consumer credit. Moreover, business and miscellaneous receivables have grown much faster than consumer credit in recent years—a reflection of both increased competition for consumer loans from other lenders (especially commercial banks and credit unions) and greater diversification of services offered. As Table 20–1 indicates, between the 1970 and 1980 Federal Reserve surveys of the industry, consumer receivables fell from 56 percent of total credits to 42 percent in the latter year. Business credit climbed from 40 to 47 percent of the total and "other" receivables advanced from 4 to 11 percent over the decade ending in 1980, when the most recent Federal Reserve survey of the industry was completed. The growth in dollar volume in all categories of receivables is impressive. Total credit extended by finance companies advanced from $57 billion in 1970 to $138 billion in 1980—more than tripling in a decade.

Considerable diversification has occurred within the various credit categories over the past two decades, reflecting a strong emphasis upon innovation in the industry. As the Federal Reserve Board noted in its 1970 survey, "Even within the traditional types of specialization, lending had

---

[3]See especially Board of Governors of the Federal Reserve System [5], p. 958. The Federal Reserve System surveys finance companies at five-year intervals. The five surveys beginning with 1955 were each based upon the financial reports of finance companies as of a single day, June 30. As a result, the findings are subject to considerable variation, characteristic of single-date reports, and also reflect, to some extent, differences in economic conditions around the time of each survey. Nevertheless, each survey provides a reasonable benchmark for broad trends in portfolio composition and sources of financing in the industry as a whole.

[4]According to the Federal Reserve Board, business receivables include direct loans and paper purchased from manufacturers, retail firms, and wholesale trade firms (including bulk purchases of paper from vendors). Reserves for unearned income and losses are *not* deducted from the receivables total. See [7], p. 408.

Table 20–1   **Types of Credit Extended by U.S. Finance Companies: 1970–1980**

	Amount of Credit ($ billions)			Percentage Change between Federal Reserve Board Surveys		Share of Total Receivables		
Types of Credit	1970	1975	1980	1970–75	1975–80	1970	1975	1980
Consumer	$31.8	$40.8	$77.3	28%	89%	56%	48%	42%
Business	23.0	39.3	86.1	71	119	40	46	47
Other	2.3	5.8	20.0	NA*	NA*	4	7	11
Total receivables	$57.1	$86.0	$183.3	51%	113%	100%	100%	100%

Note: Figures are as of June 30 for each indicated year. Columns may not add to totals due to rounding.
*Not available.

Source: Adapted from Board of Governors of the Federal Reserve System, references [4], [5], and [6] at end of chapter. Some calculations are made by the authors.

grown most rapidly in those areas where finance company participation had been on a small scale in 1965—such as mobile home financing and leasing—and the tendency to move into nonbanking operations—already evident in 1965—had also continued."[5] The 1975 Board survey indicated "a slower but continuing trend of finance companies to move into areas such as financing of revolving credit, second mortgages, mobile homes, and leasing, and out of the financing of passenger cars."[6] And, in the 1980 survey, the Federal Reserve Board observed: "Between 1975 and 1980 finance companies accelerated their lending activities in relatively new areas, such as revolving credit, loans secured by junior liens on real estate, and leasing."[7]

Business Loans

In the business loan sector one of the most notable developments was the expansion of leasing activities. While figures on the volume of leases granted by finance companies were not reported in the 1955 and 1960 Federal Reserve surveys, data covering the 1965–80 period showed dramatic increases in this form of financing (see Table 20–2). The long-term growth in lease financing reflects efforts by various businesses to curtail capital expansion, reduce the proportion of business debt, and secure tax advantages by sharing a portion of tax benefits with the lessor. During the early 1970s and again early in the 1980s, a serious recession developed which reduced demands for consumer and other goods and created a shortage of liquidity in the corporate sector. To firms caught in this situation, leasing appeared to represent a more attractive and less costly alternative than

[5]See [7], p. 958.

[6]Board of Governors of the Federal Reserve System [6], pp. 197–98.

[7]Board of Governors of the Federal Reserve System [7], p. 399.

Table 20-2 Business Receivables Held by U.S. Finance Companies: 1970–1980 (figures are for mid-year)

Types of Business Credit	Amount of Credit to Businesses ($ billions)			Percentage Change between FRB Surveys		Share of Business Receivables		
	1970	1975	1980	1970–75	1975–80	1970	1975	1980
Wholesale paper	$ 7.5	$10.9	$21.7	46.6%	98.6%	32.6%	27.9%	25.3%
Automobiles	5.1	7.7	12.4	52.6	60.4	22.2	19.6	14.4
Business, industrial, and farm equipment	1.7	2.0	5.1	12.7	158.8	7.4	5.0	5.9
All other	0.7	1.3	4.3	88.3	237.5	3.0	3.2	5.0
Retail paper	6.6	11.1	26.3	68.6	137.8	28.7	28.2	30.6
Commercial vehicles	3.1	5.0	10.1	62.2	101.3	13.5	12.8	11.7
Business, industrial, and farm equipment	3.5	6.1	16.2	74.3	168.0	15.2	15.4	18.9
Lease paper	3.8	8.1	23.3	112.1	188.4	16.5	20.5	27.0
Automobiles	1.4	2.3	6.2	67.0	164.4	6.1	6.0	7.2
Business, industrial, and farm equipment	2.3	4.0	16.9	71.8	328.8	10.0	10.1	19.7
All other	0.1	1.8	0.1	1,689.9	−92.7	0.4	4.5	0.2
Other business credit	5.2	9.2	14.7	78.2	60.2	22.6	23.4	17.1
Short-term	3.0	5.0	8.3	67.8	66.8	13.0	12.7	9.7
Intermediate-term	2.2	4.2	6.4	92.4	52.2	9.6	10.7	7.5
Totals for business credit	$23.0	$39.3	$86.1	70.8%	119.1%	100.0%	100.0%	100.0%

Note: Columns may not add to totals due to rounding.
Source: Board of Governors of the Federal Reserve System, *Survey of Finance Companies, 1980*. [7].

either borrowing or equity financing. Lease receivables[8] increased more than 350 percent between 1965 and 1970, to almost $4 billion (or from only 7 percent of all business receivables to 17 percent); and rose further, to over $8 billion, by 1975 (or to 21 percent of total business receivables). The growth in leasing was even more dramatic between 1975 and 1980, climbing to $23 billion in the latter year and accounting for 27 percent of all business receivables held by U.S. finance companies.

The dominant type of business credit extended by finance companies throughout the post–World War II period is represented by *wholesale and retail paper*, which arises principally from the manufacture and sale of business, industrial, and farm equipment and motor vehicles.[9] Wholesale and retail paper declined in relative importance to make room for newer and more innovative forms of business financing (such as leasing) during the 1960s and early 1970s and then stabilized as the decade of the 1980s approached. Wholesale and retail paper combined represented about 60 percent of total business credit extended by domestic finance companies in 1970, dropped to 56 percent in 1975 and held at that level in 1980 (see Table 20–2). However, the *composition* of wholesale and retail paper acquired by U.S. finance companies has changed markedly. Loans on commercial vehicles have generally fallen in relative importance as auto dealers scaled back their inventories in a sluggish market. In contrast, some of the more traditional types of asset-based business financing—factored accounts and loans against pledges of accounts receivable—have held up well.

Consumer Loans

In the consumer loan field, the most dynamic element was the industry's leading consumer credit line—loans to finance the purchase of *automobiles*. Loans on passenger cars dropped precipitously in percentage terms during the early 1970s then climbed sharply late in the 70s. By mid-1980, retail automotive credit granted by domestic finance companies totaled $27 billion, representing 35 percent of outstanding consumer credit

---

[8]The Federal Reserve Board defines wholesale and retail paper as contracts arising from transactions between manufacturers and dealers that are secured by passenger cars, commercial vehicles, mobile homes, boats, airplanes, helicopters, and business equipment; retail credit stemming from sales of business equipment and commercial vehicles; and other wholesale operations not elsewhere classified. See, in particular, Board of Governors of the Federal Reserve System [5], [6], and [7].

[9]Included in business lease receivables are auto leases (including leases on passenger cars and commercial land vehicles); business, industrial, and farm equipment; and airplanes, helicopters, and boats designed for business use. Vehicles and equipment such as mobile homes, campers, motor trailers, airplanes, and boats leased for personal or family use are not included in the above figures.

held by the industry. The recent gain scored by finance companies in the auto credit field reflected a variety of forces at work. Commercial banks, their biggest competitor for auto loans, cut back on auto lending in favor of more business loans (particularly in the energy field) and because of state usury ceilings on interest rates attached to auto loans made to consumers. At the same time the captive finance companies owned by automobile manufacturers (such as GMAC) expanded their auto lending activities to offset slumping auto sales, often offering below-market rates of interest to stimulate sales.

Mobile home loans climbed rapidly through 1975, representing 8 to 9 percent of industry consumer receivables. The same was true of loans to purchase other retail consumer goods—principally apparel, merchandise, furniture, appliances, and recreational equipment. However, these trends appeared to moderate during the late 1970s due to competition from other lenders and a shift of emphasis by finance companies toward greater lending to businesses. The growth of mobile home loans and credit extended for other retail consumer goods leveled off.

The most rapidly growing form of consumer credit extended by finance companies in the late 1970s and early 1980s was real estate credit and, in particular, *second mortgage loans*. While credit extended through real estate loans represented only a modest percentage of finance-company loans—just 6.5 percent in the 1980 Federal Reserve Board survey, this percentage had expanded almost threefold from the 1975 industry survey. Only a small proportion of this gain could be traced to first mortgages on commercial and residential properties; instead, most of the growth in mortgage lending by finance companies consisted of second mortgages on homes. As the Board states in the 1980 survey report: "One reason for the growing popularity of second mortgage loans may have been that consumers were able through these secured loans to borrow larger sums of money than most state laws governing traditional forms of consumer credit permit; moreover the secured nature of these loans generally permit them to bear lower interest rates."[10]

As second mortgage loans climbed rapidly, the bread-and-butter loan of consumer-oriented finance companies in years past—the personal cash loan—declined substantially in relative significance. As Table 20–3 reflects, personal cash loans dropped from 36 percent of consumer receivables in 1975 to 28.5 percent in the 1980 survey. In part, this decline in cash loans (most of which are very small) reflected finance companies making more room in their portfolios for second mortgages, which offered security through a lien on appreciating real estate plus higher yields. However, cash loans also fell in relative importance due to intense compe-

---

[10]Board of Governors of the Federal Reserve System [7], p. 399.

Table 20–3   Consumer Receivables Held by U.S. Finance Companies: 1970–1980
(figures are for mid-year)

Types of Consumer Credit	Amount of Credit to Consumers ($ billions)			Percentage Change between FRB Surveys		Share of Consumer Receivables		
	1970	1975	1980	1970–75	1975–80	1970	1975	1980
Retail passenger cars	$ 9.3	$ 9.9	$27.1	7.4%	172.9%	29.1%	24.3%	35.1%
Mobile homes	2.3	3.5	4.8	48.7	39.6	7.3	8.5	6.3
Revolving credit	NA	5.8	16.8	NA	191.2	NA	14.1	21.7
In personal cash loans	NA	NA	0.6	NA	NA	NA	NA	0.8
In other consumer goods	NA	NA	16.2	NA	NA	NA	NA	20.9
Other personal cash loans	12.4	14.8	22.0	19.3	49.1	39.0	36.2	28.5
All other consumer loans	7.8	6.9	6.5	−11.8	−5.1	24.6	16.9	8.5
Totals for consumer credit	$31.8	$40.8	$77.3	28.5%	89.3%	100.0%	100.0%	100.0%

Note: NA means not available. Columns may not add to totals due to rounding.
Source: Board of Governors of the Federal Reserve System, "Survey of Finance Companies, 1980," *Federal Reserve Bulletin*, May 1981, pp. 398–409. See [7] at end of chapter.

tition from such credit-granting institutions as banks, credit unions, and savings and loans. These depository institutions through their branch offices and remote teller units were able to reach the consumer cash-loan market more easily, offering greater convenience to the borrowing customer than many finance companies were able to do.

SOURCES OF FUNDS DRAWN UPON BY FINANCE COMPANIES

Not only have the loans made by finance companies changed, but their sources of loanable funds also have shifted in recent years. Finance companies are sometimes called *secondary intermediaries* because they depend mainly on other financial institutions for their sources of funds. In contrast, a primary intermediary, such as a commercial bank, derives its funds principally from ultimate savers (i.e., businesses and households).

Historically, finance companies have relied upon a comparatively small equity capital base, depending mainly upon debt as a source of funds. The most important sources of their borrowed funds are commercial paper, long-term senior debt obligations, bank loans, and other short-term notes. However, as Table 20–4 reflects, the relative importance of these different funds sources has varied considerably over time as long- and short-term interest rates have changed relative to each other and as the mix of finance company loans has changed. For example, during the late 1970s and early 1980s, finance companies placed heavier emphasis on long-term lending—principally through second mortgages on residential properties and business equipment lease contracts. This shift toward longer-term financial assets permitted the companies to place more reliance on longer-term borrowings.

Table 20–4   Sources of Funds Drawn upon by U.S. Finance Companies: 1970–1980*

Funds Sources	Amount Outstanding ($ billions)			Percentage Change		Percentage of Total Liabilities and Capital		
	1970	1975	1980	1970–75	1975–80	1970	1975	1980
Liabilities:								
Bank loans	$ 7.6	$ 8.6	$ 15.5	14.1%	79.4%	8.9%	9.7%	8.8%
Short-term	6.6	7.9	7.9	20.0	− 0.2	4.5	8.9	4.5
Long term	1.0	0.7	7.6	− 25.9	954.7	4.3	0.8	4.3
Commercial paper	22.1	25.9	52.3	17.4	102.0	29.9	29.2	29.9
Directly placed	19.2	23.7	43.2	23.1	82.5	24.7	26.7	24.7
Dealer-placed	2.8	2.2	9.1	− 21.5	310.1	5.2	2.5	5.2
Other short-term debt	1.0	2.8	10.6	188.7	277.5	6.1	3.2	6.1
Other long-term debt	15.5	29.0	52.9	87.2	82.3	30.2	32.7	30.2
All other liabilities	4.5	8.4	18.4	85.7	118.2	10.5	9.5	10.5
Equity capital:								
Capital and surplus	9.9	14.0	25.4	40.3	81.7	14.5	15.7	14.5
Total liabilities and capital	60.6	88.7	175.0	46.5	97.3	100.0%	100.0%	100.0%
Memo items:								
Short-term debt	29.6	36.6	70.8	23.6%	93.4%	48.9%	41.3%	40.5%
Long-term debt	16.5	29.7	60.5	80.5	104.4	27.2	33.5	34.5
Total debt	$46.1	$66.4	$131.3	43.9%	97.9%	76.1%	74.8%	75.0%

*Figures are as of June 30 for each indicated year. Columns may not add to totals due to rounding.
Source: Board of Governors of the Federal Reserve System, "Survey of Finance Companies, 1980," *Federal Reserve Bulletin*, May 1981. See [7] at end of chapter.

Long-Term versus Short-Term Funds Sources

During the early 1960s, long-term and short-term borrowings of finance companies grew at approximately the same pace. By mid-1965 the aggregate liabilities of domestic finance companies were almost evenly divided between short- and long-term debt. However, in the period from 1965 through 1970, long-term borrowings increased only 27 percent, while short-term debt more than doubled. By mid-1970 commercial paper (short-term, unsecured corporate IOUs) was by far the largest source of funds for the industry, followed at some distance by long-term debt and bank loans. In fact, short-term obligations accounted for nearly two thirds of all debt owed by finance companies in 1970; and commercial paper represented close to three quarters of all short-term borrowings. This heavy emphasis upon short-term debt was a negative response to the record-high long-term interest rates prevailing in the economy during this period. In their rush to enter the commercial paper market on a large scale, finance companies also reduced their reliance on commercial banks as a source of loanable funds. Indeed, banks became a much less reliable source of industry financing during the late 1960s and early 1970s due to tight credit conditions and a resulting shortage of reserves. As a result, finance companies turned increasingly to short-term borrowing in the open market.[11] Moreover, investors willingly absorbed the large increase in finance company short-term IOUs due to the comparatively high yields available in the commercial paper market.

By the mid 1970s the primary sources of funds used by finance companies had changed again. With more favorable long-term rates prevailing, the industry returned to the financing mix employed a decade earlier, with a more nearly equal balance between long-term and short-term borrowings. Stockholders' equity, as in previous years, provided only about one sixth to one seventh of total funds. Debt—both short-term and long-term—accounted for about three quarters, with miscellaneous liabilities making up the remainder of total funds needed. As in prior years, most finance company debt was short-term, accounting for about 40 percent of total funds raised in 1975, down from about 50 percent in 1970. But long-term debt had climbed to 34 percent of total sources of funds in 1975, from only 27 percent in 1970.

The late 1970s and early 1980s brought a sharp rise in interest rates, both long- and short-term. Depository financial institutions found their deposits under siege from money market mutual funds which offered attractive short-term interest rates on share accounts, subject to immediate withdrawal by wire and also accessible by check. Thousands of individual and institutional investors converted their CDs into money market share accounts, with commercial banks, savings and loans, mutual savings banks, and credit unions losing billions of dollars in deposited funds. Simultaneously, the banks' prime loan rate soared to record levels.

Confronted with these developments, finance companies de-emphasized short-term bank borrowing and reduced their long-term bond offerings in favor of the commercial paper market and long-term loans from banks. As Table 20–4 reveals, by 1980 total bank loans had fallen as a percentage of finance company funds sources, from about 10 percent to less than 9 percent. However, term borrowings from banks (ranging from loans of about one year in maturity out to perhaps seven or eight years to maturity) soared from less than 1 percent to just over 4 percent of finance company fund raising. Commercial paper borrowings approached 30 percent of industry financing sources, with roughly 180 of the largest finance companies actively borrowing in the paper market during 1980. Bond issues fell from about 33 percent to 30 percent of all funds raised. Overall,

---

[11]Fluctuations between long-term and short-term debt in response to relative interest rates, changes in monetary policy, and so on are centered primarily in the larger finance companies. Smaller companies generally have much higher ratios of equity to total sources of funds and have displayed a greater dependence on long-term debt and bank credit, even in recent years.

as Table 20–4 reveals, long-term indebtedness, spurred by the growth in term loans from banks, rose slightly while short-term indebtedness fell slightly. Equity financing in a floundering stock market dropped back to its 1970 level, accounting for 14.5 percent of finance companies' available funds in 1980.

Commercial Paper Issues

One of the most important and, at times, one of the most volatile of the industry's financing sources is commercial paper. The so-called credit crunches of the late 1960s, 1970s, and early 1980s heightened finance company interest in this short-term IOU. Long-term rates had risen to historic highs, and commercial banks were having trouble making and keeping commitments on their credit lines, due principally to massive disintermediation of deposits and heavy loan demand. By mid-1970, commercial paper represented 36 percent of all funds raised by domestic finance companies, and total commercial paper borrowings stood at $22 billion, compared to less than $9 billion in 1965. Five years later, in June 1975, commercial paper accounted for about 29 percent of all funds raised by the industry. A further gradual rise ensued in the late 1970s, with open-market paper reaching 30 percent of industry funds sources ($52 billion outstanding) in June 1980. Another important reason for this rapid gain in commercial paper borrowings was the frequency with which interest costs on paper were substantially below major banks' prime lending rate.

Only a minor proportion of all finance companies issue commercial paper. Due to the fact that commercial paper is unsecured, only the largest and best-known companies can attract investors. Also, most paper issued by finance companies (between 80 and 90 percent) is directly placed rather than marketed through securities dealers. That is, the company posts the rates it is willing to pay on various maturities and sells the paper directly to interested investors. No securities dealer or other intermediary is used to identify buyers or arrange sales. On June 30, 1980, directly placed finance paper outstanding totaled $43.2 billion, while dealer-placed issues by finance companies amounted to only $9.1 billion.

Companies adopting the direct placement method must be large firms with an efficient marketing program and established contacts in the financial community. Not surprisingly, directly placed paper usually can be sold at a lower rate (higher price) than paper sold through dealers, who normally charge a commission in the vicinity of one eighth of a percentage point.[12] As the Federal Reserve Board notes: "Selling indirectly through dealers usually is the method used by issuers with only seasonal needs for

---

[12]See especially Board of Governors of the Federal Reserve System [7], p. 420.

funds or with a name not well enough known to sell without dealer contacts. In general, such paper carries a somewhat higher interest yield than paper placed directly, and in addition, the issuer always pays ⅛ of a percentage point to the dealer for his services."[13]

The industry's heavy reliance upon short-term financing is not without its dangers. It tends to make finance companies highly susceptible to fluctuations in credit conditions and particularly to changes in short-term interest rates. Heavy reliance on short-term debt introduces greater volatility into the earnings of finance companies, increasing the degree of investor risk and further increasing their borrowing costs. Moreover, the higher cost of borrowed funds typically is translated into higher loan charges to consumers and other users of finance company services. Of course, the interest rates and fees paid by customers also are influenced by the labor and administrative costs of making loans. The costs of credit examination, collection, and related administrative expenses are included in the rates charged by these companies, as is an acceptable rate of return on invested capital relative to the risks assumed by the company. However, these administrative and operating expenses are not nearly as volatile as are the costs of borrowing in the open market.

STRUCTURE OF THE INDUSTRY

Number and Size Distribution of Firms

The total number of all types of finance companies in the United States—consumer, commercial, and sales—is unknown, principally because many firms are extremely small and cater exclusively to local markets. The Federal Reserve Board's survey of the industry in 1980 received responses from 2,775 companies, down from 3,376 in 1975. While most of these companies are small, there is considerable concentration at the national level, with a few firms operating hundreds of offices across the nation through local or statewide subsidiaries and accounting for the bulk of total loans outstanding. The Federal Reserve estimated in 1980 that only about 11 percent of all domestic finance companies held about 79 percent of total consumer receivables and 98 percent of total business receivables (see Table 20–5). These leading companies each held $25 million or more in business and consumer loans. In contrast, the smallest size category in the industry—companies with less than $5 million in receivables—represented 80 percent of the number of firms answering the Federal Reserve's industry survey, but held just 2 percent of the dollar volume of consumer loans and less than 1 percent of all industry business loans.

The size of a finance company has an important influence upon its oper-

---

[13]See Board of Governors of the Federal Reserve System [6], p. 200.

Table 20–5   Number and Size Distribution of U.S. Finance Companies: 1970, 1975, and 1980

Size of Company in Total Business and Consumer Loans Outstanding ($ millions)	Number of Finance Companies Responding to Federal Reserve Survey: *		
	1970	1975	1980
Under $1 million	2,315	2,482	1,749
$1–5 million	399	500	484
$5–25 million	112	204	239
$25–100 million	77	102	156
Over $100 million	58	88	148
Total number responding to FRB survey	2,961	3,376	2,775

*Number of finance companies represents the number responding to the nationwide survey conducted by the Federal Reserve Board in the indicated years.
Source: Board of Governors of the Federal Reserve System, see references [5], [6], and [7] at the end of this chapter.

ations and, in particular, upon its sources and uses of funds. The largest companies generally hold more diversified portfolios of loans than do the smallest and are more actively involved in diversifying their activities. In contrast, the smallest firms tend to concentrate their activities on consumer loans, especially personal cash loans. Moreover, business credit extended by the smaller firms tends to be in the more traditional fields of accounts receivable financing and factoring, while the larger companies place considerably more emphasis on new types of commercial lending, such as leasing. Of course, larger finance companies have better access to the capital markets than do smaller firms and therefore are more able to vary the volume and mix of their borrowings to suit financial conditions. Also, the smaller companies are forced to use more equity capital and less debt in financing their operations (i.e., are less heavily leveraged), due to their heavier use of more risky short-term financing and less diversified loans.

For the industry as a whole, it is widely believed that competition for funds and for loan customers is intense, at least in local markets where national, regional, and local companies may all be represented and engage in direct competition with each other. Beside the half-dozen major national companies, there are numerous smaller chain organizations specializing principally in small loans to individuals and families.[14] Smaller, independent firms apparently are able to compete effectively with the larger national and regional companies, at least for consumer credit. This may reflect the fact that effective scale economies are relatively modest in this

---

[14] See especially Michelman [14] and Chapman and Shay [8].

industry, and its product is regarded as relatively homogenous by the individuals and families who regularly use the industry's financial services.[15]

Recent Structural Changes

There is evidence of considerable structural change going on in the finance company field. One important facet of this change is diversification into more profitable credit lines, as mentioned earlier. In 1970 the Federal Reserve Board reported that

> Two of the largest . . . consumer finance companies have entered the field of commercial financing on an important scale. Another company has purchased a furniture business, some have entered the field of commercial financing, wholesale financing is being carried on by some companies, and the insurance business is becoming more common as well.[16]

Several factors account for this trend toward diversification. One is the purchase of small loan companies by larger conglomerates or congeneric organizations which have the resources necessary to carry out large-scale diversification. For example, bank holding companies have purchased or started *de novo* both small loan companies and credit insurance affiliates to open up new markets for loans. Moreover, recent increases in borrowing costs (especially in 1974–75, 1978–79, and again in the early 1980s) have squeezed earnings, encouraging the search for more profitable product lines as well as the absorption of smaller companies.

Competition has also played a key role in the finance industry's trend toward diversification. Commercial banks and credit unions pose a serious threat to finance company participation in the consumer lending field

---

[15]Benston [2], in a study of three consumer finance companies operating about 2,500 branches, finds moderate-scale economies. He notes that "were a branch to service 2000 rather than 1000 loans a year, average operating costs might be $5 a loan less" at two of the three companies analyzed and $11 a loan less" at a third company ([2], p. 1,191.). Such economies of size have been used to justify state usury laws placing legal interest ceilings on small loans so that finance companies will be encouraged to pass cost savings from growth on to their customers in the form of lower loan rates. Believing in economies from fewer but larger size finance companies, many states have also used restrictive licensing of new companies to restrict entry into the industry.

Interestingly, while finance company operating costs per loan do appear to decline as the number of loans serviced is increased, operating costs do not appear to change much at all with the *size* of loans made. This means that very small loans cost about the same to make as larger loans, so that the cost per dollar of loan is much greater for small loans. As expected, very small loans (say, in the $100-to-$500 range) are often unprofitable. Similarly, the risk level does not appear to vary significantly with the size of finance company loans. Thus some finance companies may be encouraged, as Benston argues, to " 'push' larger loans on borrowers than the borrowers might wish, since the largest loan that a borrower can repay is the most profitable" ([2], p. 1,193).

[16]See Board of Governors of the Federal Reserve System [5]. p. 958.

today. In fact, the share of the nationwide consumer installment loan market accounted for by finance companies has declined sharply during the postwar period. Commercial banks, credit unions, and, more recently, savings and loans and mutual savings banks have moved in to take over a substantial portion of finance companies' lost share of the consumer credit market. These intermediaries, like finance companies, have faced a profits squeeze, brought on by the rising cost of borrowed funds. As a result, they have aggressively and successfully sought out installment credit customers. The increased competition for installment credit has caused net rates of return in the market to fall and the quality of credit receivables available for purchase to decline. Confronted with lower profit margins and increased risk in the installment loan field, finance companies (particularly the sales finance variety) have turned to other types of loans to protect their earnings, including mobile home loans, leasing, and factoring. Several companies have acquired or launched new nonfinancial subsidaries, in both domestic and foreign markets, in such widely diverse areas as insurance, manufacturing, and retailing.[17]

During the 1960s the number of U.S. finance companies declined dramatically, while the average size of individual companies remaining in the industry rose substantially. For example, in 1960 the Federal Reserve Board counted slightly more than 6,400 companies. By 1965 the industry population was under 4,300; by 1970 it was under 3,000; and, as we noted earlier, by 1980 there were fewer than 2,800 firms responding to the Federal Reserve's survey. Thus the industry has been subject to much the same pressures for consolidation and merger as have many other financial institutions during the postwar period. It is significant to note, however, that the number of companies increased by more than 400 between the 1970 and 1975 Federal Reserve surveys. A substantial part, if not most, of this growth could be attributed to entry into the field by bank holding companies which opened large numbers of *de novo* finance companies.[18]

Competition with Other Financial Intermediaries

There is an overlap of markets served by commercial banks, credit unions, savings banks, and finance companies. Each institution has tended to concentrate on that sector of the market for loanable funds where it has the greatest comparative advantage in offering its services. Commercial banks generally prefer to make larger, less risky loans which carry lower average yields. Credit unions extend loans to members only and are able to charge lower rates, in part because they draw their funds from relatively

---

[17]See especially Board of Governors of the Federal Reserve System [5], p. 959.

[18]See Chapter 8 for a discussion of bank holding company activities in various nonbank business fields, including finance companies.

small personal savings accounts. In contrast, finance companies stress convenience and the ability to extend more risky loans than any of the other competing institutions usually are willing to make. Still, many of the consumer loans extended by finance companies are acceptable to commercial banks, credit unions, and savings and loan associations. While consumers (unlike most business borrowers) are often ignorant of the credit alternatives open to them, many *are* aware and will shop around for credit. In this instance, banks and finance companies are in direct competition with each other, especially where each institution aggressively solicits consumer accounts.

There is some evidence that the "typical" household customer borrowing at a consumer finance company today is changing. Historically, the image most people have had of the typical finance company customer is that of a person down on his luck, perhaps out of a job or mired hopelessly in debt. Banks and other installment lenders frequently refuse to loan money to such an individual and, therefore, one of the few credit alternatives left is to borrow from a finance company which charges rates high enough to compensate for the risk involved in such a loan. Surprisingly, in recent years finance companies have found themselves vying with banks and other installment lenders for middle-income customers—for example, professional managers and office workers. These individuals frequently have been hard hit by soaring prices for new cars, entertainment, vacations, medical care, and home furniture and appliances, which have sharply reduced their liquid savings. At the same time, loan rates of finance companies, which once looked so high in comparison to bank rates, look somewhat more reasonable in an era where market interest rates are frequently near historic highs. In response to a growing market for loans to middle-class consumers, some finance companies have begun to look more like banks, offering credit cards and operating automated tellers for greater customer convenience.

Future competition between finance companies and other financial intermediaries should intensify as a result of changes now occurring in the U.S. financial sector. Finance companies increasingly are looking for new product lines and investments to diversify their operations and stabilize their cash flows. At the same time, deposit-type financial intermediaries, offering new services, continue to penetrate the markets for consumer loans and consumer savings. These intermediaries should continue to wrest a larger share of the consumer loan market from finance companies in the years ahead. At the same time, commercial banks through their holding company organizations undoubtedly will enlarge their foothold in the finance industry through both acquisitions of existing companies and *de novo* entry. The result will be increased pressure on independents in the finance company field to further diversify their operations and to find new sources of profitability. It is quite likely, however, that the public will be a net beneficiary of increasing competition from within and without the finance industry. In a free-market economy, competition ensures that the consumer of financial services will be served effectively and efficiently.

Finance companies specialize in granting loans to business firms and consumers. Many of their loans are designed to provide working capital, particularly to aid in business inventory purchases and to meet short-run expenses incurred by businesses and households. Finance companies also provide long-term financing for purchasing business equipment, rolling stock, family autos, and household furniture and appliances.

SUMMARY

The number of finance companies operating in the United States is close to 3,000, including small, locally oriented lenders as well as very large firms providing credit in regional and national markets. The industry population has been declining through much of the post–World War II period, however. In fact, there were more than 6,000 finance companies in operation as recently as 1960; however, mergers, absorptions, liquidations, and failures have whittled the number down to about half that figure today. Rising costs (especially the cost of borrowed funds) and intense competition from banks, credit unions, and other lending institutions have placed finance companies under intense pressure to grow into larger size institutions with broader markets.

Diversification of services and innovation in new service offerings have been taking place at a record pace in recent years. Among the most rapidly growing new services offered by finance companies in recent years are business equipment leases, revolving credit lines, second mortgages, and mobile home loans. To finance the growth of these and other loans, finance companies have drawn heavily in recent years on bank loans, commercial paper issues, and offerings of bonds.

Questions

20–1. Name the three different types of finance companies. What are the essential characteristics that differentiate one type of finance company from another?

20–2. What changes have occurred recently in the sources and uses of funds of finance companies? Try to explain why these changes have occurred.

20–3. Explain how it is possible for a finance company to charge a higher interest rate on a loan than a commercial bank located just across the street.

20–4. What is a captive finance company? What advantages and disadvantages would such a firm have relative to independent finance companies?

20–5. Examine some of the recent structural changes occurring in the finance industry. Why has the number of finance companies declined in recent years? Can you explain why diversification has become so dominant a trend among finance companies?

20–6. Differentiate between dealer-placed and directly placed commercial paper. Which type is used mainly by the larger finance companies? Why?

20–7. In what areas do finance companies compete directly with commercial banks, credit unions, and savings banks? Do you think this competition will increase or decrease in future years? Explain why.

References

1. Benston, George J. "Risk on Consumer Finance Company Personal Loans." *Journal of Finance*, May 1977.

2. _____. "Rate Ceiling Implications of the Cost Structure of Finance Companies." *Journal of Finance*, no. 2 (September 1977), pp. 1169–94.

3. "Big Change in Small Loans." *Business Week*, June 13, 1970.

4. Board of Governors of the Federal Reserve System. "Survey of Finance Companies, Mid-1965." *Federal Reserve Bulletin*, April 1967.

5. _____. "Survey of Finance Companies, 1970." *Federal Reserve Bulletin*, November 1972.

6. _____. "Survey of Finance Companies, Mid-1975." *Federal Reserve Bulletin*, March 1976.

7. _____. "Survey of Finance Companies, 1980." *Federal Reserve Bulletin*, May 1981.

8. Chapmen, John M., and Robert P. Shay. eds. *The Consumer Finance Industry: Its Costs and Regulation.* New York: Columbia University, 1970.

9. Greer, Douglas F. "Rate Ceilings and Loan Turndowns." *Journal of Finance*, no. 5 (December 1975), pp. 1376–83.

10. _____. "Rate Ceilings, Market Structure and the Supply of Finance Company Personal Loans." *Journal of Finance*, no. 5 (December 1974), pp. 1363–82.

11. "Finance Companies: An Era of Change." *Banker's Monthly*, July 1975.

12. Harless, Doris E. *Nonbank Financial Institutions.* Richmond: Federal Reserve Bank of Richmond, 1975.

13. Jacobs, Donald P., Loring C. Farwell, and Edwin H. Neave. *Financial Institutions.* 5th ed. Homewood, Ill: Richard D. Irwin, 1972.

14. Michelman, Irving S. *Consumer Finance: A Case History in American Business.* New York: Augustus M. Kelley, 1970.

15. Miller, Richard J., Roberta A. Skelton, John R. Swift, and Richard E. Edwards. "The Finance Industry and the Banks." *Journal of Commercial Bank Lending*, April 1976, pp. 27–43.

16. "The Finance Industry—A Review of the Decade." *Banker's Monthly*, April 1970.

17. Sartoris, William L. "The Effect of Regulation, Population Characteristics, and Competition on the Market for Personal Cash Loans." *Journal of Financial and Quantitative Analysis*, September 1972, pp. 1931–52.

18. Swift, John R. "Consumer Finance Companies: A Step Back and a Look Forward." *Journal of Commercial Bank Lending*, January 1982, pp. 50–55.

Problem for Discussion

IN THIS CHAPTER we have seen that finance companies make a wide variety of credit plans available to individuals, households, and businesses. These firms are most familiar to consumers for the relatively small loans they make to individuals and families for living expenses, moving costs, medical care, and purchases of consumer durables such as automobiles, furniture, and appliances. Operating out of convenient, locally based offices, consumer-oriented finance companies frequently take on credit customers that other lenders, such as commercial banks, refuse to accommodate.

In this problem for discussion, imagine that you are the manager and principal credit officer in the local office of Gulf Finance Company. Ralph Williams earlier this week submitted an application for a personal loan to consolidate some outstanding debts and make some repairs on the family car and home. In total, Williams has asked to borrow $3,375 for one year. Williams estimates that his gross earnings and those of his wife will total about $21,250 this year. Out of this, Williams projects the family will spend about $5,000 for transportation, clothing, medical care, and other personal expenses. Federal and state income and employment-related taxes will be about $3,750. Williams hopes to save about $500 in the coming year and make a few small charitable contributions.

Williams is a high school graduate and attended college for two years before dropping out. He is presently employed as a clerk in Ward's Hardware Store, where he works about 45 hours a week, including Saturdays. Frequently, he does odd jobs to supplement the family's income, such as selling shoes and men's clothing during the Christmas season and working at the neighborhood gasoline station. The hardware store hired Williams nearly two years ago, and the manager rates his probability of continued employment as "good," but there is apparently little or no opportunity for advancement in that position. The store is owned and managed by a small family corporation. Williams' previous employer was ABC Salvage Company, where he worked for a year and half until the firm closed its local office.

The Williams family has four children, including three school-age girls (ranging in age from 8 to 11) and 4-year-old boy. His wife, Jacquelyn, also a high school graduate, works as a secretary and file clerk 40 hours per week at a local aluminum siding company. During casual conversation in the finance company's office, Williams mentioned that he and his wife were thinking about having another baby.

The Williams family has few liquid assets or other savings. They hold no bonds or stocks, but have a $400 deposit in a local credit union. Williams has a $25,000 life insurance policy, but each year he has borrowed against its cash value and now has a policy loan in the amount of $1,220. There is no remaining cash value in the policy at present. Neither Williams nor the children have any life insurance in force. The family has medical insurance coverage through Ward's Hardware Store, but neither Williams nor his wife have any disability income insurance protection.

A check with the credit bureau showed that the Williamses have a "fair" credit rating. Approximately eight months ago, the family was slow in making payments on some charge accounts. This occurred after Mrs. Williams lost her job with a local department store due to a dispute with her supervisor over some missing merchandise. The department store indicates they would not hire her back, but her present employer, Hardy Aluminum Products, considers her prospects for continued employment as "good."

The Williamses own their own home, which is mortgaged to Mutual Building and Loan Association. Monthly mortgage payments are $344, including property insurance coverage. Utility costs average $125 per month on this 1,400 square foot home, while property taxes are $875 per year. The house was appraised two years ago at $37,500, when the Williamses purchased it for $36,875 with a 95-percent mortgage loan. The Williamses have taken on a number of installment obligations in recent years to upgrade their standard of living. On the credit application filed by Williams, the debts shown in Exhibit 20–1 were listed.

The family auto is a Dodge Crestwood station wagon, now five years old with about 75,000 miles on the speedometer. The car is in need of several repairs and is having transmission problems, one of the reasons for Williams' loan request. The Williamses still owe $565 on the vehicle to

---

Exhibit 20–1   Debt Obligations and Monthly Payments

Lender	Monthly Payments	Balance on Loan
Mutual Building and Loan Association (home mortgage)	$344.00	$33,750
Cooperative Employees Credit Union	137.50	375
First State Bank and Trust	39.57	565
Quinlan Furniture Company	53.75	574
Mitchell's TV and Stereo Shop	43.88	450
Dr. S. R. Kemp (pediatrician)	Open	156
Bank Credit Card	Open	812

First State Bank. The family's home also needs some new flooring in the kitchen and den, repairs to the backyard fence, and a new heating unit.

Given the foregoing facts, would you make this loan to the Williamses as requested?

If not, are you prepared to offer them a loan on terms perhaps more suited to their credit needs?

21. *Investment Companies*

INVESTMENT COMPANIES—or investment trusts, as they are often known—are financial institutions that obtain funds from a large number of investors through the selling of shares. These funds are then placed in a pool under professional management, and securities (financial assets) are purchased for the benefit of all the shareholders. While investments in the fund may be made by either large or small savers, the investment company exists primarily to offer the small saver a means to diversify asset portfolios in a manner unattainable except with a very large portfolio.[1]

Investment companies have a long and checkered history, although their existence as a significant financial institution in the United States is relatively recent. The Société Générale de Belgique, formed in 1822, is generally credited as the first investment company. Investment companies spread throughout continental Europe during the 19th century and reached special importance in England toward the close of the century. In the United States, the period from the end of World War I until the stock market crash of 1929 represented the initial period of investment company growth. However, investor experience with the returns provided by this financial institution during the 1920s was quite poor not only because of the problems in the equity market during the period but also because many of the investment companies were poorly managed and were organized more for control of the firms in which they invested than simply as passive investors. Not until after World War II did the investment company occupy a significant place quantitatively in the galaxy of American financial institutions. Conditions were favorable for the development of the investment company movement after World War II with the expansion of money incomes as well as the spread of this income among many people who were relatively unsophisticated financially. Moreover, the upsurge in the equity markets in the immediate postwar period also contrib-

---

[1]This chapter deals with all types of investment companies except money market funds, which were the subject of Chapter 16.

uted to the growth of funds under management by investment companies. As a result, the number of shareholders expanded from about 3 million in 1945 to over 50 million in 1967, and the total assets of investment companies grew from $2 billion to almost $50 billion during the same period.

Types of Investment Companies

While all investment companies have a number of common characteristics, there are substantial differences in goals and form of organization. Most (measured in terms of total assets) have the growth of capital as their primary objective. Others exist for the purpose of maximizing current income subject to reasonable stability of principal. Still others, as discussed in Chapter 16, are established to invest exclusively in money market instruments. And, recently, a large number of investment companies have been formed to invest in tax-exempt municipal bonds. Moreover, some investment companies stand ready to buy and sell their shares to potential investors in any amount at the request of their customers. Others have a fixed number of shares and buy or sell these shares to their investors only infrequently. Still other investment companies have two sets of shares (income and capital); one set obtains all the capital gains and the other receives all the income. Finally, some investment company shares are sold in the secondary market at a price below the value of underlying assets.

Comparison with Other Financial Institutions

Regardless of these differences, all investment companies do have a number of features in common with other financial intermediaries. They provide a variety of important services to the public—such as risk, denomination, and maturity intermediation as well as convenience—and it is these services which have accounted for their rapid growth since World War II. Risk intermediation is performed through the administration of the portfolio of the institution by skilled analysts and portfolio managers and also through the ability of the investor to achieve a more broadly diversified portfolio by investing indirectly through an investment company rather than by investing directly in primary securities. Even if it can be shown (and there is substantial evidence to support this view) that professional management is of little value in making equity investments (i.e., that professional investors cannot obtain a higher return than the market portfolio without taking on greater risk), still, through the greater diversification made possible by indirect investing in the investment company, the individual investor should be able to obtain a higher rate of return for a given risk level or a lower risk for a given rate of return. This should be especially important for the small investor who finds adequate diversification without excessive transaction costs virtually impossible to achieve.

Individual investors should benefit from denomination intermediation whereby they are able to obtain equity investments in denominations which are more suitable to their individual needs than is possible through direct investments in equity securities. Many investment companies permit initial investment of as little as $50 or $100. In addition, maturity intermediation is of some consequence. Through an investment company, the investor is able to obtain an indirect financial asset which has greater liquidity than individual primary securities. The importance of this maturity intermediation is intensified when that liquidity is viewed not only as the ability to turn an asset into cash quickly but also to do so at little loss in value. The diversified portfolio offered by the investment company should have greater price stability than the portfolio which the investor could construct for himself or herself from primary securities or any individual security which might represent the investor's undiversified portfolio.

Management of Investment Companies

Investment companies are managed by professional management companies which arrange for the clerical and record-keeping services necessary for the fund and which also supervise the portfolio management decisions. These management companies are often affiliated with large life insurance companies (for example, Prudential Insurance Company has almost 10 mutual funds under its management) or are independent of other financial institutions (Dreyfus Corporation, for example). These management firms receive a fee for their portfolio management services—usually something less than 1 percent per year of the assets of the fund. It is interesting to note that the fee is usually a function of the size of the fund rather than of the performance of the fund. Since there are large economies of scale in managing financial assets, this type of fee structure particularly encourages a proliferation of different types of funds under one corporate management umbrella.

As with other financial institutions, these management companies exist to achieve profit and/or wealth-maximizing goals. However, there are a number of differences between this type of organization and other financial institutions which sets the mutual fund apart. Most financial institutions can be viewed simply in terms of the model presented in Chapter 1. The institutions have a capital base on which they seek to borrow funds by offering financial assets to the investor which have desirable risk, denomination, and return characteristics. These funds (from stage I production) then become loanable funds (the output from stage I), and these loanable funds are invested following asset portfolio management decisions (stage II production). But with the mutual fund and its management company, stage II (the management of assets) is the primary stage. The fund exists to manage assets. The sources of funds represent the investors' ownership interests, about which no specific promises have been made. In fact, most mutual funds cannot—with but minor exception—use borrowed money. Yet, it is the success of the management company in devising a portfolio strategy which determines the ability of the mutual fund to compete for savings in the marketplace and thereby to generate revenues for the fund management company.

Open End versus Closed End

Investment companies may be classified either as *open end* or *closed end*. Open-end investment companies, generally referred to as mutual funds, stand ready to repurchase shares from the holders in any quantity and whenever the holder should desire. In addition, the open-end investment company will sell shares in any amount to prospective investors at whatever time the investor should determine. The price of shares in the open-end investment company is determined by the net asset value of the fund's shares, where *net asset value* refers to the total market value of the assets in the fund's portfolio less any fund liabilities divided by the number of fund shares outstanding. The fund may be offered at the net asset value per share or at the net asset value per share plus a sales charge, which may be as high as 10 percent of the net asset value (the sales charge generally goes to brokers involved in the distribution of the fund's shares). Such funds are referred to as load funds, and a large percentage of mutual funds are load funds. In contrast, the funds may be offered at the net asset value. Such funds are referred to as no-load funds. The preponderance of growth in the mutual fund industry in recent years has been among no-load funds, despite the fact no-load funds are bought directly from the fund rather than from a broker.

The enormous growth in the post–World War II period in the volume of assets under management by the investment company industry has centered among the open-end funds, and today total assets of open-end funds are many times the total assets of closed-end funds. As pointed out in Table 21–1, total assets of open-end investment companies (mutual funds) were almost $90 billion at the end of 1982. At the same time, closed-end, equity-oriented funds had total assets of about $5 billion.

Closed-end funds are quite different in many respects from open-end mutual funds.[2] The most important distinction is in terms of the number of shares outstanding. Closed-end funds issue a *fixed* number of shares. The shares are traded in the open market, and supply and demand for the funds' shares determines their price. Purchases of shares by the funds or

[2] In Great Britain, open-end funds are referred to as unit trusts, while closed-end funds are called investment trusts.

TYPES OF INVESTMENT COMPANIES

Table 21-1   Distribution of Mutual Fund Assets: 1965–1982 ($ billions)

Year	Total Net Assets	Cash and Equivalents	Corporate Bonds	Municipal Bonds	Equities
1965	$35.2	$ 1.0	$ 2.6	$ —	$30.9
1970	46.8	2.8	3.5	—	39.7
1975	43.0	2.6	5.6	—	33.7
1980	63.7	4.6	8.5	6.4	42.4
1982	89.5	9.2	10.2	21.2	48.9
		Percent			
1965		2.8%	7.4%	0%	87.9%
1970		6.0	7.5	0	84.8
1975		6.0	13.0	—	78.4
1980		7.2	13.3	10.0	66.5
1982		10.3	11.4	23.7	54.6

Source: Board of Governors of the Federal Reserve System, *Flow of Funds Accounts.*

the sale of additional shares by the funds are quite infrequent. There is only a loose association between the net asset value of the closed-end fund and the market price of the shares of the fund. Most closed-end funds which invest in equity securities have sold at discounts from net asset value in recent years. Indeed, in some cases, there is a very substantial discount, sometimes as large as 30 percent or more. These discounts have given rise to the notion that the investor could obtain a greater return by investing in the closed-end funds since the investor is purchasing $1 worth of earning assets but paying substantially less than that in many cases.[3] One explanation for the persistence of the discounts is that there is no one (i.e., no broker) to sell shares in closed-end funds as compared to open-end funds. In contrast to equity closed-end funds, some closed-end funds which invest in bonds sometimes sell at premiums over net asset value. Another difference between closed-end and open-end investment companies concerns capitalization. Open-end investment companies generally choose a simple capital structure with little or no use of financial leverage. In contrast, closed-end investment companies often have a complex capital structure with securities convertible into capital stock and with substantial amounts of financial leverage.

Objective of the Fund

Investment companies also differ widely in their objectives. Most mutual funds have an increase in the capital value of the shares of the fund as their principal objective. This objective may be approached through a variety of different kinds of equity securities. Hence these are known as

---

[3]See especially Malkiel [7] and Richards, Groth and Fraser [8].

common stock funds. Some of these funds specialize in blue chip common stocks, buying the shares of firms which are established lenders in their fields and have a long history of paying cash dividends. Others may specialize in so-called growth stocks, which pay relatively modest cash dividends, have low payout ratios (i.e., high earnings-retention ratios), and are located in areas where the demand for their product or service is expanding very rapidly. Some investment companies specialize in the issues of a particular industry, such as the utility, airline, or chemical industries, while others concentrate in specialized kinds of stocks (natural resource-related, for example), regardless of industry. As examples of the different types of common stock funds, the Dreyfus Fund, with total assets of over $2 billion, had the following companies as its five largest holdings as of the end of 1981: Texas Oil and Gas (4 percent of assets), Philip Morris (3.4 percent), Warner Communications (2.7 percent), G. D. Searle (− 2.3 percent), and R. J. Reynolds (2.0 percent). In contrast, the Rowe Price New Horizons Fund, a smaller, high-risk type fund, had the following companies as its five largest holdings at the end of 1981: Datapoint (4.2 percent of assets), Wal-Mart Stores (3.6 percent), Diebold (2.5 percent), Tom Brown Inc. (2.4 percent), and Helmerich and Payne (2.2 percent).[4]

The common stock fund accounts for the great bulk of the total assets under the control of investment companies (especially mutual funds) and has been the basic source of growth of the industry in the post–World War II era. This is made clear by reference to Table 21–1, which provides the distribution of assets in open-end investment companies for a number of years. However, the funds with other objectives—generally more conservative objectives—have become of growing importance in recent years. One of these types of funds is the *balanced fund.* The balanced fund emphasizes both appreciation of capital and income and seeks these objectives through a balanced portfolio of equities and fixed-income instruments. The portfolio of such a fund might contain a mixture of the following: common stock, preferred stock, bonds, and convertible bonds. Given such a portfolio, it might be expected that in an efficient financial market both the return and risk to the investor would be less than with a common stock fund. For example, the American Balanced Fund had 58 percent of its portfolio in common stock, 24 percent in bonds and preferred stocks, and 18 percent in cash and cash equivalents as of the end of 1981.

There is also a wide variety of *specialty funds.* One of these—the bond fund—has shown substantial growth in recent years. The bond fund is primarily concerned with the generation of current income through investing in fixed-income securities, although frequently this type of fund

---

[4]*Investment Companies,* Wiesenberger Financial Services, New York, 1982 .

seeks capital appreciation by active management of the portfolio. In recent years, there have been a large number of new bond funds brought to market. These include both open-end and closed-end funds, although a particularly large amount of these types of funds have been closed end in nature. While the open-end bond funds usually stress the advantage of active portfolio management, the closed-end bond funds often have a fixed portfolio. These closed-end bond funds hold both corporate and municipal securities. Prior to late 1976, the law did not allow open-end funds to pass through tax-free income to shareholders. However, following legislative changes, open-end mutual funds were formed in large numbers for the purpose of investing in municipal securities. The poor performance of the stock market since the mid-1960s and the high interest rates of the period have been of considerable significance in fostering the growth of bond funds. The rapid rate of inflation which has pushed people of relatively modest means into high tax brackets also has played an important role in the development of tax-exempt bond funds.

Another interesting, although quite small, investment company group is the *dual-purpose fund*. Started in 1967, all dual-purpose funds (which are entirely closed-end funds) have two shares of stock: income and capital. Moreover, there is a termination date for the existence of the fund, at which time the assets will be liquidated and the funds distributed to shareholders. The income shareholders receive all the dividends earned on the contributions by both income and capital shareholders plus a promised amount of liquidating dividend. The capital shareholders obtain no income distributions but are entitled to all capital gains distributions during the life of the fund plus, at the termination of the existence of the fund, distributions equal to the difference between the liquidating value of the fund and the promised payment to income shareholders. The basic idea behind the dual-purpose funds, which number less than a dozen, is that each shareholder—whether income or capital—obtains leverage through having $2 at work for each $1 invested. However, the performance of the dual-purpose funds after their beginning in 1967 has not been very favorable. Most of the funds have sold at substantial discounts in the secondary market. Part of the explanation is the poor performance of the stock market in the years immediately following the founding of these funds. There also appears to be an inherent contradiction within the fund between the goals of the income shareholders and those of the capital shareholders, which may cause portfolio management problems.

MANAGEMENT, SIZE, REGULATION, AND TAXATION

Investment companies, whether closed end or open end, have their portfolio and other policies determined by an investment adviser. This investment adviser may be an insurance company or its subsidiary—in recent years there has been a substantial penetration of the mutual fund management business by life insurance companies—or a firm which specializes in money management through mutual funds and other devices. Due to the economies of scale involved in managing funds, there is some advantage to the mutual fund management company in offering a variety of funds, thereby seeking to obtain a large amount of assets under control. Hence there are a number of mutual fund management companies, such as Dreyfus, Fidelity, T. Rowe Price, and Scudder, which offer quite a variety of funds with different objectives to the public and which have billions of dollars under management. For these services, the mutual fund management company receives a management fee, which constitutes its income and which is one of the principal operating costs of the fund itself. The management fee is completely separate and distinct from the load. The management fee is paid to the company regardless of whether the fund is load or no-load and is usually stated as some percent of the assets of the fund, regardless of the performance of the fund. Hence benefits to the mutual fund management company accrue from increasing the size of the fund rather than maximizing the rate of return to fund shareholders, although conceptually these factors should be related.

Size

Table 21–2 presents information on the number of open-end mutual funds and the total assets in these funds in the period from 1945 through 1982. The total asset numbers reflect net sales of the funds (sales minus redemptions) as well as changes in the market value of the securities in the portfolios of the funds. In short periods, change in market conditions may

Table 21–2   **Number of Mutual Funds and Total Assets under Management: 1945–1982 (excludes money market funds)**

Year	Number of Funds	Total Assets ($ billions)
1945	73	$ 1.3
1950	98	2.5
1955	125	7.8
1960	161	17.0
1965	170	35.2
1970	361	47.6
1975	390	42.2
1981	486	55.2
1982	539	76.8

Source: *Mutual Fund Fact Book*, Washington, D.C.: Investment Company Institute, 1983.

dominate net sales, since most of these assets consist of common stock, subject to wide fluctuations in value.

A number of important facts are highlighted by Table 21–2. First, as discussed earlier, the mutual fund industry is essentially a post–World War II phenomenon. In 1945, total assets under management for all open-end funds amounted to only slightly more than $1 billion. Second, the bulk of the growth in the mutual fund industry occurred in the 1950s and the 1960s, which were periods of generally rising stock prices. Third, since 1970, there has been less rapid growth in assets under management. Part of the recent development reflects the poor market conditions for common stock which have depressed total asset values. (As shown in Table 21–2, however, mutual fund assets increased substantially in 1982, principally reflecting the upward surge in stocks that began in August 1982.) Sales of bond funds and money market funds have been substantial, while common stock funds have suffered from net redemptions of considerable magnitude. Fourth, despite the impression of many that mutual funds dominate the equity market, in fact, mutual funds are a relatively small proportion of total equity holdings. As discussed in Chapter 18, pension funds are a much more significant influence in quantitative terms than are mutual funds. However, as a general rule, turnover of shares by mutual funds is more rapid than for pension funds, so that the significance of mutual funds in the trading of securities is greater than their share of total common stock holdings would indicate.

Regulation

There is substantial regulation of investment companies at federal and state levels. The major acts which relate to mutual funds are the following: the Securities Act of 1933, the Securities Exchange Act of 1934, the Investment Company Act of 1940, and the Investment Advisers Act of 1940. The Securities Act of 1933 requires registration with the Securities and Exchange Commission (SEC) for an offering of new securities and requires that the offering firm provide extensive information to the SEC and to shareholders. Since open-end investment companies offer shares continuously, they are always legally in registration under the rules of the Securities and Exchange Commission. The Securities Exchange Act of 1934 requires periodic reports of the investment companies and also requires that the funds provide shareholders with a prospectus before soliciting the purchase of shares. But perhaps the Investment Company Act of 1940 is most significant in its impact on mutual fund management. This act regulates the composition of the boards of directors of investment companies and the nature of the contract between each investment company and its management company. The mutual fund must file with the Securities and Exchange Commission a statement indicating its investment policies, and these policies may be changed only through a vote of the shareholders. Shareholders must be allowed to elect at least two thirds of the directors of the fund. The management contract between the fund and the management company cannot exceed two years in duration and must be approved by shareholders. Moreover, there are substantial limitations on the capital structure of the funds, especially with regard to the amount of financial leverage (i.e., borrowed funds) that may be used.

Taxation

Investment companies conforming to the appropriate statutes do not pay taxes on their dividends or capital gains. The investment company must meet a number of conditions, including paying out each year at least 90 percent of net ordinary income. Moreover, at least one half of the assets of the fund must be in cash or diversified securities, and no more than 25 percent of the assets may be invested in the securities of any one issuer. Investment companies are viewed as conduits which simply flow the dividends and realized capital gains through to shareholders. The shareholders rather than the fund itself then become responsible for the taxes on the dividends and capital gains at their individually appropriate income tax rates.

RATES OF RETURN ON MUTUAL FUND SHARES

Table 21–3 provides information on the percentage change in net asset value per share for selected types of mutual funds, as well as for two market indicators—the Dow Jones Industrial Average and the Standard & Poor's Index. The first two types of funds—maximum capital gains and long-term growth—are common stock holding funds. The balanced funds would mix common stock, bonds, and preferred stock, while the income funds would principally invest in long-term debt securities.

The information in Table 21–3 on the total changes in net assets per share (excluding dividends) for the 1-, 5-, and 10-year periods ending

Table 21–3 Performance of Selected Types of Mutual Funds
(percent change in net asset value per share)

Type of Fund	1 Year Ended 1981	5 Years Ended 1981	10 Years Ended 1981
Maximum capital gains	−3.5%	143.1%	150.6%
Long-term growth	−2.3	96.6	100.6
Balanced	−0.4	39.7	78.3
Income	5.3	22.8	69.4
Dow Jones Industrial Average	−3.5	12.5	47.7
Standard & Poor's Index	−4.9	40.2	65.1

Source: *Management Results*, Wiesenberger Financial Services.

December 1981 seem to indicate substantial volatility in net asset values. This volatility reflects general marketwide movements over the period studied as well as differences in the nature of the funds included. Not surprisingly, the common stock funds performed the best over both the 5 and 10 years ended December 1981, periods of rising market prices. Common stocks, though, performed the worst in the one year ended December 1981, a period of generally falling market prices.

It is also interesting to note that the common stock funds outperformed the market indices for the 5 and 10 years ended December 1981. Yet, it should be kept in mind that this is an average for all funds in a particular fund. The real question of interest to investors in mutual funds is whether a particular fund can do better on a consistent basis than the market indices, given comparable levels of risk.

The rate of return earned by shareholders in a mutual fund has been examined in great detail by a number of researchers. Results of this research have been relatively consistent and have not been favorable to the mutual fund industry.[5] In particular, most studies show that investors usually could have achieved as good a rate of return by purchasing and holding a market portfolio (perhaps selecting the individual securities in the portfolio by a random process) as by investing in mutual funds. These studies suggest that over periods as long as a decade, it is not likely that a single fund can consistently exceed the market returns without exceeding the risk levels of the market.

There appear to be reasonable explanations for these findings. First, it is argued by some that investment analysts employed by mutual funds for individual security selection are not able to pick securities with exceptionally high returns for a given amount of risk. For example, security analysts generally employ two different approaches to select securities with the potential for above-average returns: fundamental analysis and technical analysis. *Fundamental analysis* attempts to examine the fundamental earnings growth of a firm by looking at the products of the company, their markets, and potential. The traditional approach used in fundamental analysis would be to project the economy, the industry, and the firm's market share and, from these, to project the earnings of the firm. Based upon earnings potential, the fundamental analyst would determine the intrinsic worth or value of the company's stock by capitalizing its expected earnings at some appropriate multiple. If the intrinsic value exceeded the current market price, then the security is undervalued and is a candidate for inclusion in the fund's portfolio. Conversely, if the intrinsic value was less than the current market price, then the security is overvalued and is a candidate for exclusion from the fund's portfolio. If that security is cur-

---

[5]See Friend, Blum, and Crockett [2] and Williamson [11].

rently held in the institution's portfolio, then it should be sold as soon as possible. In contrast to this extensive analysis of the characteristics of the company used by fundamental analysts, the *technical analyst* relies only upon past price behavior of the company's stock. The technician argues that all relevant information is embodied in the movement of the price of the shares of stock. By examining these past movements, the financial analyst is able (supposedly) to predict future movements and know whether to buy or sell the security.

The notion that fundamental and/or technical analysis can predict individual securities with excess returns has been challenged by the efficient-markets literature. The *efficient-markets* hypothesis argues that all relevant information which should influence the price of the stock of a firm is quickly embodied in that price so that there is —without inside information—no opportunity for the analyst to pick securities with above-normal returns.[6] The efficient-markets hypothesis would argue that the intrinsic value and the current market price of a security are identical; that there are neither undervalued nor overvalued securities. A large number of studies have indicated that the equity market is relatively efficient; much less is known about the efficiency of the bond market. In the equity market, evaluation of various decision rules based upon technical analysis has not disclosed consistent evidence of excess returns produced by technical analysis over more random selection implied by the efficient-markets hypothesis.

The evidence seems to indicate that portfolios of securities selected by mutual funds are not able to consistently outperform the market. Yet, there are costs involved in administering these portfolios. Brokerage and other costs are substantial since the portfolio turnover of mutual fund assets is often quite high. Moreover, there is some evidence that mutual funds hold more securities than necessary in order to approach the performance of the markets. This extreme diversification which seems to produce no tangible benefits is, of course, achieved at some cost to the investor. Hence it is not surprising that the return on many mutual funds is less than the market return.

These findings of academic research, along with the disillusionment of the investor with the actively managed fund, have resulted in the creation of another type of mutual fund: the *index* fund. The index fund is a passively managed mutual fund in which the objective is not to beat the market but to equal the market. The objective is sought by structuring a portfolio of securities which is representative of the entire market. If this portfolio allocation is successful, then the fund will do as well as, though no better than, the overall market except for the cost of management.

---

[6]See Malkiel [6] for a useful discussion of the implications of efficient markets.

With passive rather than active management, the management fee should be less than for most mutual funds.

This discussion is not meant to imply that mutual fund shares may not be beneficial to the investor. Clearly, for the small investor, investment companies do offer degrees of diversification that are impossible to realize through direct investment. But these results do indicate that, under most circumstances, the investor should not expect to achieve abnormally high returns through mutual fund shares. There is one important exception to this generalization. Returns above the market return should be possible if the investor is willing to accept a risk level above that of the market. If investors wish to achieve excess returns, they should then choose a fund with excess risk.

The ability of mutual funds to sell their shares is principally a function of their performance, which, in turn, is a function of market conditions. Stock-oriented mutual funds had a difficult time selling their shares throughout the 1970s, since their performance was quite poor. As shown in Table 21–4, net sales were generally over $1 billion each year from the late 1950s until the early 1970s. But in 1972, 1973, and 1974 there were net redemptions exclusive of the sale of money market funds. Given the poor performance of the equity market, it is not surprising that the performance of mutual funds also was disappointing and that investors sold more fund shares than they bought. With the strengthening in the market beginning in August 1982, equity funds found it easier to raise funds.

Table 21–4   Sales and Redemption of Mutual Fund Shares ($ billions): 1950–1982

Year	Sales of Own Shares	Repurchase of Own Shares	Net Issuance
1950	$ 518.8	$ 280.7	$ 238.1
1955	1,207.5	442.6	764.9
1960	2,097.2	841.8	1,255.4
1965	4,358.1	1,962.4	2,395.7
1970	4,625.8	2,987.6	1,638.2
1971	5,147.2	4,750.2	397.0
1972	4,892.5	6,562.9	(1,670.7)
1973	4,359.3	5,651.1	(1,291.8)
1974	3,091.5	3,380.9	(289.5)
1975	3,307.2	3,686.3	(379.1)
1976	4,360.3	6,801.2	(2,440.9)
1977	6,399.7	6,026.0	373.7
1981	9,710.4	7,469.6	2,240.8
1982	15,738.3	7,571.8	8,166.5

Note: Excludes money market funds.
Source: *Mutual Fund Fact Book*, Washington, D.C., Investment Company Institute, 1983.

There is more to the difficulty of raising funds than the poor performance of the market. Many investors were sold mutual fund shares with the unrealistic expectation of returns substantially higher than the market. Research associated with the efficient-markets literature suggests that these expectations were unreasonable and should not have been created in the first place. The mutual fund investor must recognize that return is a function of risk and that in our efficient securities market there is no free lunch.

SUMMARY

Investment companies pool the contributions of many investors, generally those of relatively modest means, and invest in a diversified portfolio of stocks and/or bonds. The investor receives shares in the fund which entitles the investor to all returns earned on the fund minus the operating costs and management fee. By purchasing shares in a fund, the investor obtains risk, denomination, and maturity intermediation as well as convenience.

Investment companies come in a variety of forms. The most common form is the open-end investment company, commonly referred to as a mutual fund. In this form, the investment company stands ready to buy or sell fund shares with the investor at the net asset value of the fund (if a no-load fund) or the net asset value plus a fee (if a load fund). In contrast, with a closed-end fund, there is a fixed number of shares, and purchase or sale of fund shares occurs in the open market (such as on the New York Stock Exchange) at prices determined by supply and demand. Not only does the form of organization differ, but the types of investments also differ from fund to fund. Most assets of investment companies are invested in common stock, though an increasing fraction of total assets is held in fixed-income instruments. The growth of funds which specialize in investments in tax-exempt state and local government bonds has been quite rapid since legislation authorized such funds in 1977. In addition, some investment companies are known as dual-purpose funds because they have two kinds of stock, income and capital.

Investment companies are managed by professional investment advisors who often manage a large amount of funds as well as other investment vehicles. The industry experienced very rapid growth in the early post–World War II period, reflecting its concentration in equity investments at a time when equity prices were rising rapidly. In recent years, however, the total assets of investment companies have grown more slowly, and the industry has diversified into fixed-income investments in order to increase total funds under management.

The performance of mutual funds has been the subject of a large number of studies. The results generally support the argument that mutual fund managers do no better than would be expected, given the riskiness of their portfolios. Moreover, considering the reduced returns to the investor (as a result of operating costs) from shares of investment companies, it is generally found that returns to the investor will be less than the average for the securities in which they invest.

Questions

21–1. What is an investment company? What are the different kinds of investment companies? What are some of the areas of specialization that investment companies have developed?

21–2. In terms of risk and rate of return, what might be the advantages for a small investor to purchase shares in an investment company?

21–3. With regard to investment companies, what is the advantage of maturity intermediation?

21–4. What is a mutual fund? Differentiate between load and no-load funds. Differentiate between open-end and closed-end funds.

21–5. What is a balanced fund? What is a specialty fund?

21–6. What is the difference between an active portfolio and a fixed portfolio?

21–7. Examine different aspects of investment companies in terms of management, size, regulation, and taxation.

21–8. Differentiate between fundamental analysis and technical analysis as attempts to select securities with the potential for above-average returns.

References

1. Baumol, William J. *The Stock Market and Economic Efficiency.* New York: Fordham University Press, 1965.

2. Friend, Irwin; Marshall Blum; and Jean Crockett. *Mutual Funds and Other Institutional Investors.* New York: McGraw-Hill, 1970.

3. Investment Company Institute. *Mutual Fund Fact Book.* Published annually.

4. Jensen, Michael D. "The Performance of Mutual Funds in the Period 1954–1964." *Journal of Finance*, May 1968, pp. 389–416.

5. Litzenberger, Robert, and Howard Sossin. "The Structure and Management of Dual Purpose Funds." *Journal of Financial Economics*, March 1977, pp. 203–30.

6. Malkiel, Burton. *A Random Walk Down Wall Street.* New York: W. W. Norton, 1965.

7. _____. "The Valuation of Closed-End Investment Company Shares." *Journal of Finance*, June 1977, pp. 847–59.

8. Richards, Malcolm, John Groth, and Donald Fraser. "Closed-End Funds and Market Efficiency." *Journal of Portfolio Management*, Fall 1980, pp. 50–55.

9. Securities and Exchange Commission. *A Study of Mutual Funds.* Washington, D.C.: U.S. Government Printing Office, 1967.

10. _____. *Public Policy Implications of Investment Company Growth.* Washington, D.C.: U.S. Government Printing Office, 1961.

11. Williamson, J. Peter. "Measuring Mutual Fund Performance." *Financial Analysts Journal*, November/December 1972, pp. 78–91.

Problem for Discussion

GEORGE SMITH, portfolio manager for the New Opportunites Fund, faced the quarterly review and outlook conference with the fund's executive committee with some degree of apprehension. The meeting, scheduled for next Monday morning, would initially be devoted to reviewing the performance of the portfolio of the fund over the most recent few quarters and also from a longer-term perspective. Such a review would encompass comparisons of the performance of the fund with general market indices such as the Dow Jones Industrial Average, the Standard & Poor's Composite Index, and the New York and American Stock Exchange Indices. These comparisions were usually provided in the fund's quarterly report to shareholders and were therefore of some value from the perspective of marketing the shares of the fund, though neither Smith nor the members of the executive committee believed that these indices were the most relevant ones for evaluating the performance of the fund. Rather, for internal use, the management of the New Opportunities Fund compared the performance of the fund with a selected group of 10 other funds which were thought to be comparable in purpose to New Opportunities.

Once the review of past events was completed, the meeting would be devoted to formulating an investment strategy for the next quarter. This strategy did not include the specific securities to be selected for inclusion or elimination from the fund's portfolio. This decision was left to Smith and the investment managers—each specializing in a different type of security—who reported to him. Rather, the concern of the executive committee was with establishing broad guidelines within which specific investment decisions could be made over the next few quarters. These guidelines encompassed the percentage of assets of the fund which would be held in cash (actually in short-term money market instruments). This decision principally reflected the outlook for the securities markets within which New Opportunities Fund generally invested. Expectations for rising security prices during the coming quarter would lead to a reduction in the cash position of the fund, while expectations of falling security prices would lead to a more defensive position either through the sale of existing securities or using the net inflow of cash from the sale of shares of the fund to purchase money market instruments. As with most mutual funds, the New Opportunities Fund was prohibited from selling short, that is, selling securities which the fund did not own but had borrowed in the hope that those securities could be repurchased later at a lower price.

The formation of investment strategy also included a discussion of the proportion of the securities of the fund that should be held in securities outside the United States and a discussion of the division of the portfolio into the securities of different industries. These decisions were, of course, interrelated to some degree. The decision as to how to spread the investments of the fund internationally depended on the outlook for the performance of different national economies and on expectations for exchange-rate movements. Substantial appreciation in the securities of one country *in that country's currency* could be completely negated by adverse movements of that country's currency against the United States dollar. The decision as to how to spread the investments over different industries primarily reflected the outlook for sales, earnings, and other factors affecting the fortunes of individual corporations. Also, the management of the New Opportunities Fund was especially sensitive to the effects of changes in the outlook for inflation and changing levels of interest rates as they affected the prices of financial assets.

The New Opportunities Fund had been established in 1978 in order to offer to investors, especially those of relatively modest means, a vehicle to participate in the new opportunities available through the enormous changes taking place in the world's economy. As stated in the prospectus of the fund, these opportunities derived from three interrelated developments: (1) the differing cyclical and especially secular growth rates for different countries and regions of the world. In that regard, the prospectus highlighted the growth rates in such Pacific nations as Japan, Korea, Malaysia, Hong Kong (a British Crown Colony rather than a nation), Australia, and New Zealand; (2) the sharp instability in currency values since the move to floating exchange rates in the early 1970s;[1] and (3) the substantial changes in the relative importance of different industries. In that regard, the prospectus of the fund emphasized the importance of investments in the energy industry and precious and nonprecious metals. The argument here was that the supply of each of these assets was limited and

---

[1] For example, it was pointed out in the prospectus that an investment made in a company in Great Britain in 1976 and sold in 1981 could have produced a 53 percent return from currency value changes, independent of capital appreciation and dividends on the security bought.

that their value would rise as the demand for the assets increased with growing population, income, and especially with inflation.

The New Opportunities Fund was one of a number of funds sponsored by a large mutual fund management group. The management group offered almost every conceivable type of fund, following the argument that it could only realize economies of scale in money management by becoming very large. Funds offered by the management group included portfolios of U.S. government securities, municipal bonds, corporate bonds, equities of various characteristics, funds with very active management and funds with little management except the attempt to match the market (often referred to as an index fund), and a money market fund. While quite new, the New Opportunities Fund had been very successful, particularly in its first two years of operation, 1979 and 1980. In these years the prices of energy companies, both domestically and internationally, appreciated considerably as did the prices of precious and nonprecious metals mining companies. Moreover, the foreign currencies of the countries in which New Opportunities had substantial commitments appreciated against the dollar. These results were reflected in an inflow of money into the fund, so that by early 1981 the New Opportunities Fund was the second largest (next to the money market fund) of all the funds controlled by the management company, with total assets of almost $1 billion.

The performance of the fund in the period from early 1981 through early 1982, however, had deteriorated substantially. The world-wide inflation in basic commodity prices appeared to have ended, at least temporarily. In fact, the prices of many basic commodities had declined substantially as had the profitability of many mining companies. Moreover, the dollar had appreciated against many foreign currencies, with the result that although the domestic currency performance of the investments of the fund had been reasonably good, their value in dollars had fallen considerably. For example, the price of the British pound had declined from over $2.40 per pound in 1981 to less than $1.90 per pound in early 1982, thereby reducing the dollar value of investments of the New Opportunities Fund in the United Kingdom.

In preparing for the quarterly review meeting on Monday, George Smith decided to draw upon the experience and expertise of the managers under his supervision. Specifically, he asked that each investment manager make a recommendation through a written memorandum to him (by Friday afternoon) about the fund's portfolio management for the coming quarter. He asked for recommendations on the desired cash position of the fund and on the distribution of funds among areas of the world and industries. In each case, the investment manager was asked to list the advantages and disadvantages of his or her recommendation. Mr. Smith provided the information in Exhibits 21–1 through 21–5 to the investment managers to be used in preparing their recommendations.

Exhibit 21–1 Performance of New Opportunities Fund and Stock Indices (%)

Year	New Opportunities Fund	Standard & Poor's	New York Stock Exchange	American Stock Exchange	10 Similar Funds
1979	42%	12%	3%	29%	44%
1980	58	10	22	62	64
1981	−15	1	2	3	−20
1982	−20	−4	−6	−18	−25

Notes: Performance for New Opportunities Fund and 10 similar funds reflects dividends and price changes. Performance for Standard & Poor's, the New York Stock Exchange, and American Stock Exchange Indices only reflect price changes. Data for 1982 are only through June 1.

Exhibit 21–2 Sales and Redemptions of New Opportunities Fund

Year	Sales (number of shares)	Redemptions (number of shares)	Net Sales or Redemptions (number of shares)
1979	41,820	18,220	23,600
1980	58,430	12,430	46,000
1981	43,200	56,800	(13,600)
1982	20,200	34,200	(14,000)

Note: Data for 1982 are only through June 1.

Exhibit 21–3 Portfolio of New Opportunities Fund: June 1, 1982

	By Percent
Classified by industry:	
Oil and gas exploration and development	26%
Oil and gas servicing	14
Gold and silver mining	15
Nonprecious metals	10
Finance	8
Durable goods manufacturing	12
Utilities	5
Cash	10
	100%
Classified by country:	
United States	46%
United Kingdom	15
West Germany	10
Japan	8
Hong Kong	5
Australia	4
New Zealand	4
Mexico	4
Brazil	4
	100%

Note: All cash asset investments are made in securities denominated in U.S. dollars.

Exhibit 21–4 Foreign Currency Rates: May 30, 1982

	Spot	One Month (forward)	Three Months (forward)
United Kingdom	1.775	.07 Discount	.17 Discount
West Germany	0.415	0.70 Premium	0.25 Premium
Japan	0.004	1.50 Premium	4.5 Premium
Hong Kong	0.173	NA	NA
Australia	1.041	NA	NA
New Zealand	0.754	NA	NA
Mexico	0.021	NA	NA
Brazil	0.006	NA	NA

Note: NA means not available. Foreign currency values are expressed as the amount of U.S. dollars necessary to purchase one unit of the foreign currency.
Source: *The Financial Times*, May 31, 1982.

Exhibit 21–5 Stock Market Indices: January 26, 1982

	January 26	1981–82 High	1981–82 Low
Australia	559.9	787.3	539.9
Germany	225.2	245.5	215.9
Hong Kong	1399.2	1810.2	1115.7
Japan	7883.4	8019.2	6956.5
Singapore	775.6	973.3	773.7
South Africa	524.9	797.8	476.2
Switzerland	256.0	304.2	242.9
World	140.0	162.8	133.9

Source: *The Financial Times*, January 27, 1982.

22. *Other Financial Institutions*

PREVIOUS CHAPTERS HAVE DISCUSSED a number of major financial institutions in considerable detail in terms of sources and uses of funds, industry characteristics, management-decision problems, and other important features. This chapter attempts to touch briefly upon five financial institutions—federal agencies, security brokers and dealers, mortgage banks, leasing companies, and real estate investment trusts (REITs)—which play important roles in specialized parts of the economy. With the exception of federal agencies, the overall quantitative significance of these organizations in the total flow of funds is relatively minor. Yet some, such as security brokers and dealers, play roles in the economy which are much greater than the dollar value of their total sources and uses of funds would indicate.

There are both important similarities and important differences in the characteristics and functions of the financial institutions discussed in this chapter. Most are quite specialized in function, generally providing funds for the purpose of making purchases of capital goods such as new homes, machinery, and transportation equipment. Most of the funds provided by federal agencies support agriculture and housing. Security brokers and dealers are intimately involved and vital to the capital accumulation process. Mortgage bankers and real estate investment trusts are generally associated with the financing of housing, with the former widely involved in the financing process for single-family residences and the latter involved in the financing of apartments and other income-producing property. Leasing companies also frequently engage in the financing of income-producing property, such as office buildings, although their financial activities tend to be more diversified than those of either mortgage banks or REITs.

While similar in terms of providing specialized financial services, the financial institutions discussed in this chapter also exhibit considerable differences among themselves. Federal agencies, leasing companies, and real estate investment companies essentially lend their own funds and act as principals in financial transactions. Each of these financial institutions has an equity base upon which it pyramids large amounts of financial leverage (debt). The funds provided by owners are combined with the funds provided by creditors, and the financial institution acquires for itself either financial assets (such as mortgages) or real assets (such as an office building, which is then leased). It is important to note here, however, that the motivation of such activities often varies considerably among these organizations, with federal agencies oriented more toward fulfilling a social role with less emphasis on profitability; earning a return on invested capital should be more important at leasing companies and real estate investment trusts. In contrast to these lending organizations, however, security brokers and dealers and mortgage bankers are perhaps better viewed as agents rather than as principals in financial transactions. Security brokers and mortgage bankers both are involved in bringing buyers and sellers together—in the first case for the purchase and sale of stocks and bonds and in the second for the purchase and sale of real estate—though both do also take a position in financial and/or real assets in their role as dealers.

The financial institutions discussed in this chapter also differ considerably in terms of recent growth and future prospects. Federal agencies have experienced enormous growth, especially in the decade of the 1970s as the federal government extended its financial support to specific sectors of the economy. However, with the reordering in federal priorities which occurred in the early 1980s, there is uncertainty as to whether the growth of these agencies will continue. Security brokers and dealers, taken as a group, have also experienced rapid growth, though the growth has been interspersed by periods of substantial financial distress and consolidation in the industry. Mortgage banking and the leasing industry have experienced impressive growth and are likely to continue to grow, though the recent financial problems of the housing industry have affected mortgage banking considerably. In contrast, real estate investment trusts have experienced considerable financial difficulties, with large numbers of bankruptcies.

FEDERAL AGENCIES

The United States government itself is a major financial institution through the borrowing and lending activities of its agencies. In fact, during the 1960s and 1970s, the federal agencies were among the most rapidly growing of all financial institutions in the United States. These agencies are principally concerned with reducing the cost of funds and/or increasing the availability of funds to two sectors of the economy—agriculture and housing—though government agencies exist for other purposes also. The principal justification for these government agencies lies in the fact that certain activities in the American economy, particularly farming and the provision of adequate housing, are regarded as vital to the nation's well-being and deserving of special treatment. Moreover, it is widely argued that, left to itself, the financial marketplace would not provide an adequate volume of credit at reasonable cost to support these vital activities.

Most government agency borrowing has been done by the sponsored agencies rather than by the government-owned agencies, though, in either case, the agencies obtain their funds primarily through borrowing from the financial markets, either directly or indirectly, and then lend these funds to economic participants in the sectors they serve. In addition to these activities of government agencies, there are some agencies which substantially affect the flow of funds in the financial system by providing guarantees of loans made by private organizations.[1]

Federally Sponsored Agencies

Federally sponsored agencies are technically private organizations but in many ways can be considered public in nature. They include the Federal National Mortgage Association (a New York Stock Exchange–listed firm), the Federal Home Loan Bank system, the Federal Home Loan Mortgage Corporation, all of which are concerned with the support of the housing industry; and the Farm Credit system with its three component parts, the Federal Land Banks, the Federal Intermediate Credit Banks, and the Banks for Cooperatives.[2] Each of these agencies borrows in the financial markets by selling debt securities of various maturities, denominations, and security, and in turn makes loans to participants in designated sectors of the economy or acquires securities from those participants. The debt issues sold by the sponsored agencies do not carry the guarantee or backing of the United States government. Yet the securities generally sell at yields reasonably close (though higher) than U.S. government debt of comparable maturity, suggesting that investors expect support from the federal government if a federally sponsored agency gets into trouble. The sponsored agencies themselves are self-supporting and receive no tax money from the U.S. Treasury. Their revenues come from the interest received on their loans and other fees.

Mortgage Credit Agencies

The mortgage credit agencies account for most of the debt of the federally sponsored agencies, as shown in Table 22–1. (Additional information

---

[1]See Hand [4] and Schwartz [7] for more detailed reviews of the activities of federal agencies.

[2]There is also a small amount of debt outstanding from the Student Loan Marketing Association. This organization guarantees loans made by private lenders to individuals for educational purposes and also creates a secondary market in these loans.

Table 22–1 Debt Obligations of Federally Sponsored Agencies: July, 1982
($ billions)

Agency	Debt Outstanding
Federal Home Loan Banks	$ 62.1
Federal Home Loan Mortgage Corporation	3.1
Federal National Mortgage Association	65.6
Federal Land Banks	7.7
Federal Intermediate Credit Banks	0.9
Banks for Cooperatives	0.2
Farm Credit Banks	65.7
Student Loan Marketing Association	5.0
Total debt obligations	$210.3

Note: In the late 1970s, the Farm Credit system began to issue consolidated bonds to replace the individual issues of the components of the system.
Source: *Federal Reserve Bulletin*, November 1982, A35.

is provided in Figure 22–1.) The Federal National Mortgage Association (sometimes known as "Fannie Mae") was established in the 1930s in order to improve the liquidity of the mortgage market by creating a secondary market for U.S. government-insured (FHA) and guaranteed (VA) mortgages. Fannie Mae has provided this liquidity by purchasing mortgages from mortgage bankers, savings and loan associations, and other originators of mortgages. While, in concept, Fannie Mae should serve both as a buyer (in periods of excess supply of mortgages) and a seller (in periods of excess demand for mortgages) it has generally bought rather than sold mortgages, reflecting recent problems in the mortgage market. As a result, the portfolio of FNMA has grown enormously and exceeded $60 billion by late 1982. This portfolio is financed by the sale of debt instruments in the financial markets.

The Federal Home Loan Bank system and the Federal Home Loan Mortgage Corporation are two closely related federal agencies involved in the support of housing. The Federal Home Loan Bank system resembles the Federal Reserve System in that it is, in a sense, a central bank for savings and loan associations. While it regulates individual savings and loans it also lends money to them. These loans usually increase in periods of diminished private sources of funds at the savings and loans (generally periods of high interest rates) and decrease in periods when private sources of funds (usually during periods of low interest rates) are more adequate. However, the volume of lending by the Federal Home Loan Bank system to savings and loans expanded sharply in the late 1970s and early 1980s (as shown in Table 22–2), reflecting the persistence of high interest rates and serious financial problems within the savings and loan industry. These loans are financed by borrowings in the financial markets. In contrast to the large volume of lending by the Federal Home Loan Bank system, the

Figure 22–1   Federally Sponsored Credit Agencies (seasonally adjusted annual rates, quarterly)

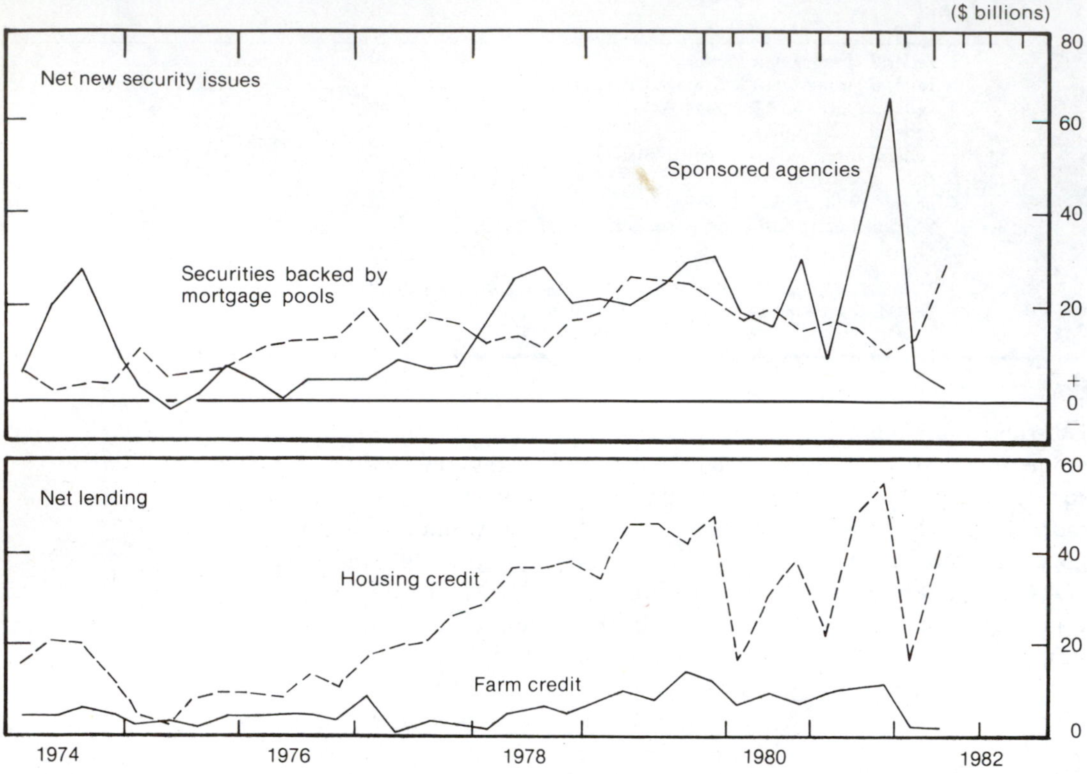

Source: Board of Governors of the Federal Reserve System, *Federal Reserve Chart Book*, August 1982.

Federal Home Loan Mortgage Corporation plays a much smaller role as a direct lender, as shown in Table 22–1. This organization exists to improve the secondary market for conventional mortgages (savings and loans have traditionally specialized in conventional mortgages). As such, it plays a role quite similar to that performed by FNMA for insured and guaranteed mortgages. However, the FHLMC (or "Freddie Mac," as it is sometimes called) is perhaps more significant in terms of its creation of mortgage pools, a role which will be discussed below, rather than for its permanent lending.

Agriculturally Related Agencies

A smaller though quite significant part of the debt of federal agencies comprises that of the Farm Credit system. This organization is composed

**Table 22–2   Federal Home Loan Bank System Loans to Savings
and Loan Associations: 1960–1982 ($ billions)**

1960	$2.0	1968	$ 5.3	1976	$15.9
1961	2.7	1969	9.3	1977	20.2
1962	3.5	1970	10.6	1978	32.7
1963	4.8	1971	7.9	1979	41.8
1964	5.3	1972	8.0	1980	49.0
1965	6.0	1973	15.1	1981	65.2
1966	6.9	1974	21.8	1982	66.0
1967	4.4	1975	17.8		

Source: Board of Governors of the Federal Reserve System, *Flow of Funds Accounts*, 1983.

of three lending agencies, each serving a different role within the financing of agricultural production. The Federal Land Banks make loans to farmers for the purchase of land and other similar permanent assets. The Federal Intermediate Credit Banks make loans to production credit associations, which, in turn, make loans directly to farmers and ranchers. In contrast to the Federal Land Bank loans, which tend to be quite long-term in nature, the loans of the Federal Intermediate Credit Banks generally carry a shorter maturity. The Banks For Cooperatives provide loans to agricultural marketing and cooperative organizations. The loans are generally fairly short-term in nature. At one time each of the components of the Farm Credit system financed itself separately. Beginning in the late 1970s, however, the Farm Credit system began to issue debt instruments for the entire system.

Federally Owned Agencies

The federally owned agencies are quite distinct in many ways from the federally sponsored agencies. In contrast to the federally sponsored agencies, which are self-supporting, the federally owned agencies usually receive direct support from the U.S. Treasury. This difference in funding reflects differences in purpose. The federally sponsored agencies provide an indirect subsidy to the sectors of the economy that they serve. This indirect subsidy comes primarily through their ability to borrow at lower rates due to the market perception of implied U.S. government support. The lower borrowing costs are then passed through to their customers in the form of lower lending rates. In contrast, the subsidy provided by the federally owned agencies is a direct one. As such, it is generally impossible to cover the total costs of the program, with the result that a portion of the costs must be financed from Congressional appropriations.

The federally owned agencies provide direct loans to various sectors of the economy. These include loans by the Agency for International Development (as a part of foreign aid), Commodity Credit Corporation loans to farmers as a part of agricultural price supports, loans by the Farmers Home Administration to individuals in rural areas in order to finance the purchase of homes, Small Business Administration loans, Export-Import Bank loans, and a variety of loans from other units of the federal government. These loans have a direct impact on the flow of credit just as does any loan by a private or public financial institution. In addition, many of these agencies provide extensive government guarantees of loans made by private organizations. These guarantees do not directly provide government funds, until and unless there is a default by the borrower, though the impact on the flow of funds may be as important as through direct-lending programs.

The largest government guarantee programs are the mortgage pools sponsored by the Government National Mortgage Association, Federal Home Loan Mortgage Corporation, and the Farmers Home Administration. While differing to some extent in detail, these pools essentially package a group of mortgages into a pool, place a guarantee of the government agency on the pool and sell interests in the pool to investors. As shown in Table 22–3, the growth of these pools have been extremely rapid, from less than $50 billion in 1970 to almost $200 billion in 1982. The financial innovation represented by these mortgage pools has undoubtedly had a substantial effect on the flow of funds. Yet, it is not clear for this program or other programs of federal agencies whether the programs have in fact achieved the goal of expanding the flow of funds into targeted sectors of the economy. It may be that much of their efforts have been negated by the higher interest rates created, in part, by an expanded volume of agency borrowing.

Beyond the funds provided by Congressional appropriations and fees charged for their services, the federally owned agencies raise funds by borrowing. In past years, agencies borrowed directly from the open market. As shown in Table 22–4, public holdings of agency debt totaled over $30 billion in July 1982. However, most such borrowing today is done

---

Table 22–3 Mortgage Holdings of Federal Mortgage Pools: 1970, 1975, 1980, and 1982 ($ billions)

Type of Mortgage Holdings	Amount			
	1970	1975	1980	1982
Home mortgages	$3.0	$25.3	$107.1	$174.1
Multifamily mortgages	0.1	1.2	6.0	3.8
Farm mortgages	1.7	2.0	0.9	0.7
Total	$4.8	$28.5	$114.0	$178.5

Source: Board of Governors of the Federal Reserve System, *Flow of Funds Accounts*, 1983.

Table 22–4   Debt Obligations of Federally Owned Agencies: July 1982 ($ billions)

	Debt Outstanding
Defense Department	$ 0.5
Export-Import Bank	13.9
Federal Housing Administration	0.3
Government National Mortgage Association participation certificates	2.2
Postal Service	1.5
Tennessee Valley Authority	13.8
United States Railway Association	0.2
	32.1
Federal Financing Bank Debt	$121.3

Note: Debt owned by the agencies to the Federal Financing Bank is excluded from the debt given for each agency in order to avoid double counting.

Source: Board of Governors of the Federal Reserve System, *Federal Reserve Bulletin*, November 1982.

through the Federal Financing Bank. This U.S. government agency borrows directly from the Treasury in order to lend to other agencies. As such, increases in borrowing requirements of the government-owned agencies now appear as increases in Federal Financing Bank debt and then increases in U.S. government debt.

SECURITY BROKERS AND DEALERS

Security brokers and dealers play a vital role in the financial system, a role which is much greater than their total assets would suggest. As shown in Table 22–5, the total assets of security brokers and dealers amounted to less than $50 billion in 1982, a quantity of assets which would rank their industry well below other types of financial institutions in terms of size. Yet security brokers and dealers are the go-betweens without which the financial markets would not operate efficiently; in a sense, they are the oil that allows the machinery of the financial system to operate. Moreover, security brokers and dealers have been quite innovative in providing new financial services. Many brokers and dealers have been on the leading edge of the enormous changes that have occurred and that are continuing to occur within the financial system.

Broker versus Dealer Functions

Security brokers and dealers provide a number of diverse financial services. However, their principal functions are given by the terms *broker* and *dealer*. A broker is one who earns a commission or fee for bringing buyers and sellers together. Brokers do not take an ownership position in an asset and therefore do not accept the risk of fluctuating asset prices. In

Table 22–5   Assets and Liabilities of Security Brokers and Dealers:
1982 ($ billions)

Financial assets	
Demand deposits and currency	$ 4.3
Corporate equities	4.0
U.S. government securities	4.8
State and local obligations	1.0
Corporate and foreign bonds	4.9
Security credit	24.3
Total financial assets	$43.3
Liabilities	
Security credit	$37.9
From U.S. chartered banks	$20.5
From foreign banks	1.2
Customer credit balances	16.0
Other liabilities	0.6
Total liabilities	$43.3

Source: Board of Governors of the Federal Reserve System, *Flow of Funds Accounts*, 1983.

contrast, a dealer takes an ownership position, either with the intent of immediately disposing of the asset or with the intent of holding it for a more extended period. Along with ownership of the asset, of course, comes the risk of price fluctuation. This risk is very important for security brokers and dealers as their capital base (as a fraction of their total source of funds) is quite small. Small declines in the prices of securities held by these firms can easily result in insolvency.

As brokers, these firms provide a conduit through which individuals, businesses, and governments may purchase or sell bonds, stocks, commodities, financial futures, limited partnerships in oil and gas and real estate ventures, and other types of securities. Those who wish to purchase or sell these securities may, of course, do so without the intervention of a broker, thereby avoiding the fee charged by this agent. Yet such a direct sale or purchase may take days, weeks, or months to arrange and may involve large amounts of time. In the words of the economist, the *search costs* of such an undertaking may be very substantial. In contrast, the broker has a well developed set of relationships with organized markets such as the New York Stock Exchange or a communications system for trading in securities over the counter, for which the broker receives a commission or fee.

Dealer Function

In their function as dealers, these firms provide a variety of services. Extremely important from the perspective of the efficient operation of the financial system, many of these firms serve as market makers. They serve in this capacity both for debt securities, such as corporate, municipal, and U.S. government bonds and also for equity securities. In this role, the dealer holds an inventory of securities and is prepared to sell the securities at one price (the ask price) and to purchase those securities at another and lower price (the bid price). Naturally, the ask price exceeds the bid price such that the dealer expects to make a profit on the complete transactions of buying and selling the security (referred to as a turn). Of course, such a profit on the spread between bid and asked prices could easily be eliminated by adverse price movements in the securities held by the dealer. By serving as market makers, the dealers are effectively creating the market in these securities. Virtually all debt securities are traded over the counter, so that the existence of a secondary market depends on the function of the dealer as a market maker. Also, many equity securities are traded over the counter so that here also the role of the dealer is crucial. In contrast, the listed exchanges such as the New York Stock Exchange are auction markets rather than dealer markets.

U.S. Government Security Dealers

The role of dealers is especially important in the market for U.S. government securities. A small group of large dealers, generally referred to as primary government security dealers, is accredited by the Federal Reserve for open-market trading with the Fed. These dealers dominate the U.S. goverment securities market and provide the excellent liquidity in that market. Located at the center of the financial markets, they play an extraordinarily important role in the entire financial system. Other participants in the financial markets frequently look to these firms for information and advice on financial market developments. While these dealers also take positions in other money and capital market instruments, their role in the government market is central to their operation and also essential to the functioning of the government securities market.

Dealers in the Primary Market

The role of dealers as market makers principally relates to the secondary market. However, dealers also are important in the primary market where new securities are sold. In this market, dealers participate in *underwriting* securities. In the underwriting function, dealers purchase securities from the issuer with the intent of selling them to the permanent investor at a higher price. This anticipated markup provides the dealer's profit from the underwriting. Here again, though, as in market making, the dealer risks loss due to adverse price movements in the securities during the time that they are held by the dealer. In the corporate market, the dealer often purchases the securities from the issuer through a negotiated

Part Six

price arrangement. More commonly, in the municipal market and always in the U.S. government market, the dealer obtains the securities through a competitive bidding process.

Other Dealer Activities

Security brokers and dealers are engaged in a wide variety of other security-related businesses. Some provide very extensive financial advice and detailed information on individual companies and securities, sometimes referred to as the research function. Some also manage a number of mutual funds. Others have diversified into a large number of related financial services such as insurance and real estate. The extent of innovation in financial services offered by brokers and dealers is substantial.

As with most financial institutions, brokers and dealers vary widely in the portion of the market they seek to serve. The primary government security dealers tend to be wholesale-oriented, servicing business customers exclusively or principally, and quite specialized in the services they perform. Other firms do little in the way of dealing in securities but rather emphasize the brokerage function. Some of these brokers are retail-oriented, seeking business in a state, region, or from the entire nation while still others are wholesale-oriented and emphasize brokerage services for large institutional customers. Some brokerage firms—referred to as discount houses—concentrate on providing transactions services only, without the other services offered by brokerage firms, and do so at reduced commission rates.

Sources and Uses of Funds

As shown in Table 22–5, the largest single asset of the industry is security credit. This represents the funds that brokers and dealers have loaned to their customers for the purchase of securities under margin-account arrangements. With a margin account, the customer is allowed to borrow a fraction of the funds for the purchase of the security. A broker will loan to a customer a specified fraction (the maximum is set by the Federal Reserve's margin requirements) of the amount needed to purchase a security (the amount is different for stocks than for bonds). The other principal assets of brokers and dealers are various types of securities held by the firms in their role as market makers and underwriters. The funds for the loan from the broker to the customers are usually borrowed, generally from commercial banks, so that the largest single source of funds for brokers and dealers is security credit in the form of short-term borrowings from commercial banks. The other principal liability of the industry is customer credit balances, which represent funds owed by brokers and dealers to their customers following the sale of customer securities or for other reasons.

The revenue structure for brokers and dealers reflects the functions performed by individual firms in the industry. The brokerage function gives rise to commissions, and the largest single source of revenue for the industry is commission income. Naturally, the proportion of commission income will range widely from company to company. The market making and underwriting function produces interest and dividend income, trading income, and underwriting fees. Still, however, market making and underwriting revenue represents the second largest source for the industry, after the income generated from commissions. Naturally, for some large wholesale firms that emphasize market making and underwriting, these sources of income will be much larger than commission earnings.

Trends

Security brokers and dealers have experienced enormous changes in recent years. While a complete review of these changes is beyond the scope of this discussion, two striking developments should be mentioned. The first is the *consolidation* in the number of firms, and the second is *proliferation* in the number of services offered by individual firms. Consolidation may be traced back to the financial difficulties that were encountered by many firms in the late 1960s and early 1970s and also to the abolition of fixed commission rates in 1975. The expansion in volume of trading in equities in the late 1960s caused enormous clerical problems for many firms, ultimately leading to financial difficulties in some cases. In addition, the increasing volatility in stock and bond prices produced financial problems at many firms that "guessed wrong" about the future levels of prices and took incorrect positions in their portfolios. Equally significant, however, was the abolition by the S.E.C. of fixed-minimum commission rates, effective May 1, 1975 (known as May Day in the industry). As a result, commission rates for large transactions (though not for small transactions) fell substantially, making many firms not viable. As a result of all these factors, the number of firms in the industry has declined substantially and the average size of surviving firms has increased dramatically.

A development related to this consolidation has been the acquisition of broker/dealer firms by companies outside the industry. The trend accelerated in 1982 and 1983 as rising volume in the stock market and the resultant higher profitability for brokerage firms made them more attractive as acquisition candidates. The acquisitions of Shearson by American Express and Bache by Prudential Insurance intermingled the brokerage function with other financial institutions, though the aquisition by Sears of Dean Witter Reynolds, Inc. was especially significant in terms of size and in terms of mixing companies from different industries.[3]

---

[3]See Chapter 8 for further discussion of the reasons for and impact of these newly created symbiotic financial firms.

The second major development is the proliferation of services. This proliferation appears to reflect both the pressures of declining profitability associated with greater competition and also the stimulus of developing opportunities in a rapidly evolving financial system. The abolition of fixed commission rates, in particular, was an important reason for firms in the industry to seek new revenue sources, but the enormous changes in the demands for financial services and the growth of computer technology which made it feasible for many brokers and dealers to meet that demand have produced opportunities for new financial services. As a result, many brokerage firms are well on their way to becoming department stores of finance in direct competition for funds with commercial banks and other depository institutions as well as with many nondepository institutions, such as life insurance companies.

MORTGAGE BANKING

Functions

Mortgage banks (or mortgage companies, as they are frequently called) are not easy firms to define because the industry encompasses firms which differ greatly in both size and function. Moreover, in contrast to the financial institutions discussed earlier, the degree of regulation of the industry is very slight. Indeed, one of the reasons for the rapid growth of mortgage banking in recent years is the comparative absence of regulation. In the broadest sense, a mortgage bank is any firm which both lends money on improved real estate and offers the securities to other investors as a dealer, or is an investor in real estate securities, or is an agent of an insurance company or other purchaser of first-mortgage securities. Such a definition would cover a multitude of individuals and corporations. But, in its essence, the basic function of the mortgage bank is to originate and service mortgage loans for institutional investors. Mortgage banking firms must then be greatly concerned with finding sources of demand for mortgage loans and simultaneously with finding a source of funds to meet that demand. Funds are obtained from life insurance companies, mutual savings banks, savings and loan associations, and other long-term investors. Once the loans have been originated and financed, the mortgage banker provides (for a fee) the servicing functions of collections, paying insurance, and taxes for the institutional investor.

The mortgage banker is first concerned with the *origination* of the loan. As such, prospective borrowers must be found. The successful mortgage banker usually will develop close relations with real estate brokers and builders, both of whom are likely to have intimate knowledge of the needs of individuals for financing real property. In this regard, many mortgage bankers employ solicitors whose function (either on a commission or a salary basis) is to obtain loan applications for the firm. Once loan applications are obtained, the financing of the loan must be secured. Most mortgage bankers have relationships, carefully cultivated and developed over the years, with institutional investors. Since the supply and demand for funds in the United States is not balanced geographically, these institutional investors are often located some distance from the office of the mortgage banker. For example, rapidly growing areas in the West, Southwest, and Southeast would be expected to have a capital deficit while slowly expanding areas such as the Northeast would be expected to have a capital surplus. The flow of money then is often from the Northeast to these more rapidly growing parts of the nation.

Mortgage bankers may place a loan with an institutional investor in one of several different ways. First, the loan may be made only after the investor has approved the transaction. While this is the safest approach from the perspective of the investor, it is also the most cumbersome. Since the process necessarily is quite slow, it risks loss of the borrower to another lender. As another possibility, the mortgage bank may make the loan out of its own funds (usually borrowed from commercial banks) and then offer the loan for sale to one or more institutional customers. Obviously, the latter approach provides the customer with a more rapid decision on the credit application, although with limited funds the mortgage banker generally cannot handle all its operations in this manner. In either case, the mortgage banker must be quite careful of the credit quality of the prospective customer.

Once the loan is closed, the mortgage banker handles all the details of the loan until the maturity of the financial instrument. Such details involve processing current payments, inspecting the property at reasonable intervals, changing records when the property is sold, and protecting the owner of the mortgage in case of a delinquency. For this service, the mortgage banker receives what is referred to as a servicing fee, which is the principal source of income for many companies.

Sources of Income

The mortgage banking firm generally obtains its income from three sources. First, as already mentioned, it earns a servicing fee on loans placed with institutional investors. Institutional investors, who are often located at a considerable distance from the property financed, have neither the expertise nor the inclination to service the loans and would prefer to see the mortgage banker engage in this necessary function. Mortgage banking firms argue that they can perform this function more efficiently than institutional investors because of economies of scale and because they have additional sources of income besides the servicing fee. Mortgage bankers also may earn income from selling mortgages to an institutional investor (on those mortgages where the mortgage company acts as a principal) at a price higher than the mortgage company paid. In a period of falling interest rates this can be a source of sizable profit. Finally, the mortgage banker may obtain income from the sizable fees associated with change of title, commissions from writing insurance on property, and in some cases, property management fees.

Dimensions of the Industry

The dimensions of the mortgage banking industry are difficult to determine. The firms range in size from one-man operations to national firms with branches in most major cities of the nation. Some mortgage banking firms are indeed very large. Table 22–6 provides information of the 10 largest mortgage banking firms, based upon information of the volume of mortgages serviced as of mid-year 1982. Lomas and Nettleton Financial Corporation serviced over $12 billion in mortgages representing over 400,000 individual mortgages. Perhaps the most striking aspect of the industry is its recent growth. There has been more than a doubling of the number of mortgage companies since World War II. Moreover, the assets of mortgage banking firms expanded even more rapidly, and, perhaps most significantly, the share of single-family mortgages serviced by mortgage banking firms rose dramatically. While there are a number of reasons for this growth, one in particular stands out—the postwar expansion in insured mortgage operations of the U.S. government, especially the program sponsored by the Federal Housing Administration. The insured mortgage contract provided a financial instrument which was suitable for investment by capital market institutions. These institutions sought the yields available on mortgages but were unwilling to accept the risks of conventional mortgages on single-family homes. At the same time, these

Table 22–6   Ten Largest U.S. Mortgage Companies: June 30, 1982

	Dollar Volume of Mortgages Serviced ($ billion)	Number of Mortgages Serviced
Lomas and Nettleton Financial Corp.	$12.1	488,675
Weyerhaeuser Mortgage Co.	7.8	193,948
Banco Mortgage Co.	6.1	119,000
Manufacturers Hanover Mortgage Corp.	6.0	203,614
Mortgage Associates Inc.	5.9	214,458
Suburban Coastal Corp.	5.3	109,462
Advance Mortgage Corp.	4.7	186,131
Colonial Mortgage Service	4.5	124,878
Wells Fargo Mortgage Corp.	4.3	74,784
Kissell Co.	4.1	152,705

Source: *The American Banker*, October 12, 1982.

institutional investors were often located at some distance from where property expansion was occurring and did not wish to set up their own facilities for investigation of a large number of small loans. The mortgage banker fulfilled the needs of the large institutional investors by offering insured mortgages and taking care of the servicing of these mortgages.

One of the most significant recent developments in the mortgage banking industry has been its penetration by commercial banks. Many commercial banks have owned mortgage banking subsidiaries for some years. But with the development of the bank holding company movement and the approval by the Federal Reserve Board of mortgage banking activities for bank holding companies, many commercial banks shifted their mortgage banking firms from bank subsidiaries to holding company subsidiaries. Moreover, many bank holding companies have acquired independent mortgage banking firms and have started *de novo* mortgage banks. Bank holding companies today are estimated to control a substantial fraction of the total dollar volume of mortgages serviced by the largest mortgage banking firms.

LEASING

As an alternative to lending funds to businesses and others so that they may acquire tangible assets such as machinery, financial institutions may acquire the assets themselves and lease the equipment to the user. With such an arrangement, the financial institution retains ownership of the equipment. This type of financing is often referred to as asset-based lending.

Advantages of Leasing

Leasing as a means of obtaining the use of capital equipment has grown enormously in recent years. There are a number of reasons for this interest. From the perspective of the lessee, leasing may sometimes be transacted at a lower rate than borrowing. Since the lessor is often able to obtain substantial tax benefits from accelerated depreciation and the investment tax credit, the lessor often passes a part of these benefits on to the lessee in the form of a lower implicit rate of interest on the lease contract. Lease payments can often be structured so that they approximate the useful life of the asset more closely than loan payments. Leasing can be construed as a hedge against inflation for the lessee, since lease payments will be paid with dollars having reduced purchasing power.[4] Capital limitations may prevent a purchaser from making the down payment associated with a purchase. Leasing may allow for off–balance sheet financing—the lessee

---

[4]Any type of borrowed funds would, of course, provide a similar type of protection.

can charge the use of the equipment as a current operating expense rather than capitalizing the asset, thereby avoiding the appropriate liability on the balance sheet, and depreciating the equipment on the income statement. Recent pronouncements from the Financial Accounting Standards Board make it increasingly difficult to follow this procedure.

In the early years of the lease, the lease process may provide a more desirable cash flow than purchasing, and it may be especially desirable as compared with other forms of borrowing (such as term loans) which do not provide 100 percent financing. Leasing may also minimize reductions in book earnings, especially during the early years of the lease. The Economic Recovery Tax Act of 1981 also added to the desirability of leasing through allowing companies to sell their "tax losses" to profitable companies through sale and leaseback arrangements.

From the perspective of the lessor, financial institutions (especially commercial banks), have found leasing to be an attractive endeavor for several reasons. For a bank especially, leasing can benefit the institution indirectly through the attraction of new customers and thereby increase deposits. By filing consolidated tax returns and taking advantage of the investment tax credit, financial institutions are often able to shelter substantial amounts of nonleasing income through benefits from leasing. Moreover, it is sometimes argued that a commercial bank can accept loans of greater risk through a leasing subsidiary rather than directly through the loans of the bank.

Nature of Lease Contracts

Lease contracts can be immensely complicated and vary in a number of ways. However, certain generalizations can be made. One approach is to classify leases according to the method of origination. By this approach, leases may be *dealer-generated* or *direct*. The dealer-generated lease involves a procedure whereby a lender purchases leases generated or originated by dealers. The dealer negotiates the lease, delivers the asset, and then assigns the lease paper to the lessor. The lessor makes title application and notifies the lessee that the lease has been assigned to the lessor to whom lease payments must be made. In contrast, a direct lease refers to an arrangement in which the customer comes to the lessor with the motivation to lease. The lessor refers the customer to a dealer for equipment selection and, after this selection, buys the asset. Subsequently, the dealer makes delivery to the lessee.

Another method of classification is by *bearer of risk*. By this classification a lease may be either open end or closed end. In an open-end lease, the lessee assumes the risk of damage or loss and the responsibility for repair and maintenance. The lessee is required to make monthly rental payments plus final payment. By requiring the lessee to guarantee the residual value of the property to the lessor, the lessor is guaranteed its investment in the assets, recovery of its cost of financing, and its profit. The principal difference between a closed-end and open-end lease is that the lessee does not guarantee the residual value of the property under a closed-end arrangement.

Leases may also be categorized as *operating* or *financial leases.* The operating lease is a short-term transaction akin to a rental of property. In contrast, the financial lease is long-term and can best be compared to a secured term loan. The financial lease is the most appropriate type of lease for commercial banks. This lease may not be cancelled without full payment of all amortized costs to the lessor, so that the bank receives assurance of the return of its funds plus an annual return on funds invested, provided of course that the lessee fulfills all promises. A financial lease is actually the functional equivalent of a loan in that the lease payments are spread over the useful life of the asset. At the end of the lease, the lessee has the option to purchase the asset at its fair market value. Responsibility for taxes, insurance, and maintenance rests with the lessee.

Leases may also be classified either as *nonleveraged* or *leveraged.* A nonleveraged lease is an arrangement in which the lessor finances the lease with its own funds. In contrast, with a leveraged lease, the lessor provides only a portion of the required investment for the equipment, with the rest being borrowed from other lenders usually on a nonrecourse basis. The lender has recourse only to the asset financed in the case of a default on the lease, in which case the lessor can lose only that equity invested. The originator of a leveraged lease usually invests 20 to 40 percent of the asset cost and must contribute a minimum of 20 percent for it to qualify as a lease within the rules of the Internal Revenue Service. Leveraged leases are most common on larger capital items, such as railroad cars, airplanes, and ships. The mechanics of the leveraged lease are somewhat complicated and usually involve trustees for both lenders and equity participants. The resulting yields are significant in relation to the size of the equity investment, since the lessor still claims all the tax benefits from the entire investment. However, some of these benefits may be passed through to the lessee in the form of lower rental payments.

It is interesting to note that the leveraged lease may provide a substantial return to the investor and yet the cash flow to the investor may be negative over the life of the asset. Cash flows are usually positive in the early years of the lease (negative in later years), and the differential time value of money produces a positive time-adjusted rate of return. Calculations of the true rate of return on these types of transactions are fairly difficult, since conventional calculations of the rate of return when the cash flows alternate in sign over the time horizon of the investment will produce more than one estimate of the true rate of return.

Characteristics of the Industry

As with the mortgage banking industry, there is limited information available on the structure of the leasing industry. The leasing market appears to contain several layers of firms. At the top is a group of firms serving a nationwide market and competing for large corporate accounts. Below these are smaller leasing companies serving local and regional markets and in competition with only a few firms. One factor which heightens competition in the industry is the number of different firms that provide leasing services. These services are offered by banks and bank holding companies, consortiums of banks, pension funds, insurance companies, financial lessors, lease brokers, and captive leasing companies. In addition, some major manufacturing companies have expanded their leasing operations from a merchandising activity into a dual profit center arrangement, with merchandising as one focal point and the investment of funds as another. The volume of annual leases is not known with certainty. Estimates place the annual amount of equipment leases written at well over $10 billion and growing at a rate of 10 to 30 percent per year.[5]

Trends

Perhaps the most significant development in the leasing industry in recent years has been the entry by banks and bank holding companies. Ownership and leasing of real property (excluding certain well-defined items) is still prohibited to most banks, although not to bank holding companies. However, banking organizations cannot stock inventories of property to satisfy demand. Property may be purchased by banking organizations only after the leasing customer makes an application. The lease arrangement must be, in effect, a credit transaction arranged at the request of the lessee, much as a bank loan is extended in response to a credit application from a customer. Leases prepared by bank holding company subsidiaries must provide for full payout through rentals, salvage value, and tax benefits. The Federal Reserve System seems determined to keep banks and bank holding companies out of the riskier aspects of leasing.

REAL ESTATE INVESTMENT TRUSTS

The real estate investment trust (or REIT) is a financial institution which was created in order to permit many small investors to pool their funds (as in the mutual fund industry) and to invest these funds in commercial real estate. REITs were designed to allow the individual investor who has neither the time nor the knowledge to manage real property to

---

[5]Weiss and McGugh [8].

participate in the potential tax advantage and inflation-hedging characteristics associated with income-producing property. The REIT industry is a relatively recent and controversial institution. Created by Congress through the Real Estate Investment Trust Act of 1960, REITs grew rapidly, especially during the tight-money period of 1969. In the early and mid-1970s, substantial difficulties with loan quality began to develop, many REITs (including some of the largest affiliated with bank holding companies) were forced into bankruptcy, and a number of observers began to question the viability of the industry as an effectively functioning financial intermediary. Moreover, many of the largest REITs were sponsored by major commercial banks, and the financial difficulties of the REITs brought into question the soundness of some of the nation's largest banks.

REITs operate under the Real Estate Investment Trust Act of 1960, which exempts the individual trust from income taxes if it complies with certain provisions of the internal revenue code. As such, the REITs are able, as with investment companies which commit funds to stocks and bonds, to flow income through to shareholders and thereby act as a conduit. The most important of the provisions required for a REIT to be treated as a conduit are the following:

1. At least 90 percent of the net income of the trust must be distributed to shareholders.
2. The trust must be a passive investor and cannot manage its own properties. The trust must exist primarily as a conduit for investment capital and must hire property managers on a fee basis.
3. The trust must have at least 100 shareholders, and no group of five individuals or less can own more than 50 percent of the shares.
4. The income that the trust may receive in capital gains from the sale of a particular parcel of property is limited to 30 percent of the gross income of the trust.

As of year-end 1982, the REIT industry had total assets of about $12 billion (see Table 22–7). The largest single financial asset held was commercial mortgages ($1.4 billion). The uses of funds were financed from a variety of sources. Bank loans and revolving credit provided $3.3 billion, while mortgages provided an additional $2.0 billion. At one time, a number of REITs relied heavily upon the commercial paper market for short-term financing. However, the financial problems of the industry effectively precluded the REIT from gaining additional access to this market.

REITs are classified into three basic groups: equity trusts, short-term mortgage trusts, and long-term trusts. REIT equity trusts are engaged primarily in the ownership of real property. The most common form of equity trusts pay off long-term mortgages out of rental or lease income while also passing along part of this income to shareholders. The reduction of

Table 22-7   Assets and Liabilities of Real Estate Investment Trusts: 1970–1982 ($ billions)

	1970	1972	1973	1974	1975	1976	1977	1982
Total assets	$4.8	$13.9	$20.2	$21.8	$21.3	$18.7	$15.8	$11.9
Physical assets	0.9	2.5	3.2	4.3	7.3	8.9	8.6	4.2
Multifamily	0.3	0.8	1.1	1.4	2.4	3.0	2.8	1.4
Nonresidential	0.6	1.7	2.1	2.9	4.9	5.9	5.7	2.6
Financial assets	3.9	11.4	17.0	17.5	14.0	9.8	7.2	7.7
Home mortgages	0.6	1.2	1.9	1.7	1.4	1.1	0.9	0.1
Commercial mortgages	2.0	5.0	7.5	7.7	7.0	5.2	3.8	1.5
Multifamily mortgages	1.3	4.2	6.6	6.8	4.8	3.1	2.3	0.8
Other	—	1.0	1.0	1.3	0.8	0.5	0.2	5.3
Total liabilities	$2.2	$ 8.8	$14.4	$16.6	$17.8	$16.0	$13.0	$ 8.4
Mortgages	0.5	1.2	1.5	1.6	2.0	2.4	2.4	2.0
Corporate bonds	0.6	1.4	1.9	2.1	2.1	1.9	1.8	0.7
Bank loans	0.1	3.2	4.0	1.5	2.9	2.8	2.3	3.3
Other liabilities								2.4

Source: Board of Governors of the Federal Reserve System, *Flow of Funds Accounts*, 1983.

debt along with an anticipated inflation-aided increase in property values may give shareholders substantial real estate equity.

Equity Trusts

Typical holdings of equity trusts include office buildings, apartment houses and condominiums, and commercial property such as shopping centers. In addition, some trusts have holdings in more diverse properties like college dormitories, motels, indoor tennis courts, and even oil wells.

One of the key elements in the operation of an equity trust is the use of depreciation as a tax deduction. The following example shows how these depreciation charges may benefit shareholders. Assume that a trust-owned apartment house cost $1 million and yields $125,000 a year in rental income. Operating expenses (maintenance, utilities, taxes) are $40,000, and the mortgage, $30,000 ($7,500 principal and $22,500 interest). Subtracting the $70,000 total of expenses and mortgage payments, a cash flow of $55,000 is left that the trust can pass on to its shareholders. Only part of this $55,000 cash flow is considered taxable income. For IRS purposes, the $40,000 operating expenses plus the $22,500 interest are added to the depreciation for the year. Assuming that yearly depreciation is straight line at $55,000, then total expenses on the tax form add up to $112,500. Subtracted from the $125,000 rental income, this leaves a taxable income of $12,500. Shareholders then pay taxes on the $12,500 while actually obtaining the right to a cash flow of $55,000. While the REIT industry has had enormous financial problems in the 1970s, the equity trusts were least affected.

Short-Term Mortgage Trusts

These trusts do their investing in construction and development loans of less than one year to maturity. While mortgage trusts do not have the benefits of depreciation write-offs, they have another valuable tool to increase income to shareholders—leverage. These trusts make their money on the difference between the cost of borrowed funds and the rate at which they lend out these funds. However, in periods when yield relationships are unfavorable, the short-term investment trust finds profitable operation quite difficult. Many trusts, especially short-term trusts, have been able to grow without borrowing by selling new shares at a price higher than book value, referred to a *contradilution*. This was one of the favorite techniques used by real estate investment trusts to expand during the period when their stocks were selling at high price-earnings ratios. Moreover, the sale of new stocks increases the equity base and provides the opportunity for additional financial leverage.

Long-Term Trusts

These long-term mortgage trusts are the most recent type of REIT. Their loans may run for up to 30 years and are often made at rates substantially lower than short-term construction and development loans. The spread between short- and long-term rates reflects the added risk the short-term lender takes that the project may never be completed or that takeout money (long-term funds used to pay off the short-term construction and development debt) might never be obtained by the builder.

Long-term trusts have little use for conventional forms of leverage, because the spread between the long-term bond rate and the long-term mortgage loan rate is usually quite small. Even though financial leverage works in only a small fashion for these types of organizations, long-term trusts can raise their return by adding extras into the agreement with builders such as *equity kickers*. These agreements can take the form of either an ownership interest in the property (office buildings, shopping center, or apartment house) or a percentage of the rental income above a certain level.

Industry Trends

While the REITs are generally organized under the Real Estate Investment Trust Act of 1960, rapid expansion of the industry did not occur until the late 1960s. The breakthrough for REITs came in 1968 and 1969, when a severe credit crunch curtailed almost all sources of funds for mortgage loans. As a result, REITs were able to commit large amounts of funds at attractive rates, and the value of their shares of stock moved upward rapidly. During 1969 and 1970, REITs were started by major financial institutions such as the Bank of America, Chase Manhattan Bank, and Connecticut General Life Insurance Company. Approximately 31 public offerings of REITs, with assets of $10 million or more, occurred during the first nine months of 1971. With increasing competition for available properties and declining interest rates on available investments, the REITs began to have difficulties in maintaining profit margins. Moreover, the stock prices of the REITs declined, making it more difficult to raise additional equity as a base for more financial leverage and setting the stage for financial disaster in the mid-1970s.

It was the 1974–76 period which really exposed the problems of the industry. Profit margins continued to erode. Also, more and more developers were forced into default because of high interest rates and escalating materials costs. Hence not only were the REITs making fewer loans, but also many existing loans were becoming problems. Many short-term trusts experienced especially large losses. These losses were accentuated by the accrual accounting system whereby many trusts continued to accrue interest on their loans even though no cash interest payment had been made for some time and even though it was highly doubtful if such interest payments would be made in the future. Finally, the cash drain on these REITs became so intense that major default occurred on the debt of the REITs, and many of the largest REITs became bankrupt. While the industry stabilized in the late 1970s, it remains uncertain what the future of this financial institution will be.

The significant trends in the REIT industry are illustrated by the information provided in Table 22–7. The rapid growth of the industry through the mid-1970s is evident, with total assets expanding from $4.8 billion in 1970 to $21.8 billion in 1974. As discussed earlier, most of this expansion was concentrated in multifamily and commercial mortgage lending. Commercial mortgages held by REITs rose from $2.0 billion in 1970 to $7.7 billion in 1974; and holdings of multifamily mortgages expanded from $1.2 billion to $6.8 billion in the same period. Yet, what is most vividly revealed by the information in Table 22–7 is the severity of the financial problems which have plagued the industry, beginning with the 1974–75 recession. Total assets fell from $21.8 billion in 1974 to $11.9 billion in 1982. Moreover, physical assets—property owned by the REITs—rose from $3.2 billion in 1973 to $8.9 billion in 1979. Most of this property acquired by the REITs reflected the foreclosure on defaulted loans. In fact, by 1980 physical assets exceeded financial assets, a most unusual development for a financial institution.

This chapter has presented information on five specialized financial institutions. Except for the federal credit agencies, these financial institutions are quantitatively of minor importance in the financial system. Yet, they play important roles within their specialized components of the economy. Moreover, with the exception of the real estate investment trust, each of these financial institutions has shown considerable growth in recent years.

The federal government has stimulated the flow of credit into selected portions of the economy—primarily agriculture and housing—through its federally sponsored agencies, such as the Federal National Mortgage Association, as well as through its federally owned agencies, such as the Government National Mortgage Association. This stimulation has taken the form both of direct loans at attractive terms and of guarantees of loans made by other financial institutions.

Security brokers and dealers serve a variety of specialized roles in the economy. As brokers, these firms bring buyers and sellers together for a commission fee. As dealers, these firms take a position in individual securities and thereby risk their capital. As dealers, they "make the market" in some stocks and bonds, thereby creating liquidity in the secondary market. They also serve to underwrite new securities in the primary market. Security brokers and dealers have been among the most innovative of all financial institutions in recent years.

Mortgage banking firms play a role somewhat comparable to security brokers and dealers, though they specialize in the mortgage market. Their principal function is to originate mortgages, to place them with a permanent investor, and to earn fees for servicing the mortgages. However, mortgage bankers also take an ownership position in mortgages, though the position is usually temporary, and perform a number of other real estate-related functions.

Leasing companies acquire real assets, such as durable equipment and office buildings, and lease these assets to a variety of users. Due to tax factors as well as accounting and other considerations, the volume of leasing has expanded considerably. Commercial banks and bank holding companies have become very active in leasing as they have also in mortgage banking.

The real estate investment trust industry consists of long-term credit trusts. After early success, the industry experienced substantial financial problems in the 1970s, from which it has never fully recovered. The financial problems were concentrated among trusts which concentrated in lending rather than in the ownership of property.

Questions

22–1. Distinguish between a federally owned and a federally sponsored agency.

22–2. Discuss the functions of security brokers and dealers.

22–3. Discuss the similarities of mortgage banks, leasing firms, and real estate investment trusts with reference to the long-term commitment of funds, real estate financing, and historical development.

22–4. What is it exactly that a mortgage bank does? Does the mortgage bank generally act as a principal or as an agent in financial transactions?

22–5. What is leasing and what are its advantages? When is it used? Differentiate between dealer-generated, direct, open-end, closed-end, and financial leases.

22–6. What are REITs? Of what significance is the Real Estate Investment Trust Act of 1960?

22–7. REITs are classified into what three basic groups? Give a definition of each group.

References

1. Anderson, Paul F. "Financial Aspects of Industrial Leasing Decision." In *MSU Business Studies.* Michigan State University, 1977.

2. Colean, M. L. *Mortgage Companies: Their Place in the Financial Structure.* Englewood Cliffs, N.J.: Prentice-Hall, 1962.

3. De Hurzar, William I. *Mortgage Loan Administration.* New York: McGraw-Hill, 1972.

4. Hand, John H. "Government Lending Agencies." In *Financial Institutions and Markets,* ed. Murray Polakoff et al. Boston: Houghton Mifflin, 1981.

5. Pease, Robert H., and Lewis O. Kerwood. *Mortgage Banking.* 2d ed. New York: McGraw-Hill, 1965.

6. Schulkin, Peter A. "Real Estate Investment Trusts: A New Financial Intermediary." *New England Economic Review,* November/December 1970.

7. Schwartz, Harry. "The Role of Government Sponsored Intermediaries in the Mortgage Market." In *Housing and Monetary Policy.* Federal Reserve Bank of Boston, 1970.

8. Weiss, Steven J., and Vincent J. McGugh. "The Equipment Leasing Industry and the Emerging Role of Banking Organizations." *New England Economic Review,* 1973, pp. 3–30.

PART SEVEN

Current Issues in the Evolution of the Financial System

23. *Electronic Funds Transfer Systems (EFTS), the Payments Mechanism, and the Role of Financial Institutions*

MODERN ELECTRONIC COMPUTERS AND COMPUTER SOFTWARE have brought about fundamental changes in the way banks and other financial institutions offer and deliver services to the public. And evidence is rapidly accumulating that future advances in electronic circuitry and communications will result in even more sweeping changes in the nature and delivery of financial services to both businesses and consumers. Historically, financial institutions have regarded themselves as people-to-people businesses with a strong personal (human) element involved in making loans, accepting funds, and dispensing payments. However, the rising costs of commuting and scarcity of time in a highly competitive environment have encouraged many customers of financial services to prefer the accuracy, speed, and convenience of electronic transfers of financial data. Indeed, the basic nature of the financial services' business is simply one of *information transfer*—amounts of funds are credited or debited to various accounts—a task which is easily accomplished by electrical impulses transmitted by wire, tape, or through microwave transmissions. Electronic funds transfer equipment is expensive, to be sure, but its average cost has been dropping in recent years and it is laborsaving and efficient in handling a high volume of financial transactions.

In this chapter we take a close look at the trend toward greater use of EFTS by banks and other financial institutions. As we will see, this trend has profound implications for virtually all aspects of the financial services business. EFTS impacts the profitability, cost structure, hiring policies, service mix, market share and structure, and viability of nearly all financial intermediaries, whatever their size and location.

THE NEED FOR COMPUTERS AND ADVANCED ELECTRONIC TECHNOLOGY IN THE FINANCIAL INSTITUTIONS' SECTOR

Any discussion of the origins and utility of EFTS begins with the making of payments. At the heart of every business transaction is a flow of funds from buyer to seller and from lender to borrower. In an earlier era, business transactions generally involved a face-to-face meeting between buyer and seller, and goods were often bartered or paid for in metallic coin. Little paper money was used prior to the beginning of the Industrial Revolution of the 17th, 18th, and 19th centuries. Indeed, for the most part, the public in that earlier era would have been hesitant to accept pieces of paper in exchange for goods and services. However, governments and commercial banks soon helped to change the public's attitude toward paper as a medium for making payments. Paper bank notes were issued, with banks and governments guaranteeing their value in exchange for goods, services, and, for a time, metallic coins.

Later, banks introduced checks—an innovation which in the United States really caught on during the Civil War era. Checkbook (demand) deposits offered the public several advantages over other means of payment. Checks were more convenient than coins or barter, possessed less risk of loss or theft, and made for easier record keeping—a feature which became increasingly important with the advent of income taxes in the present century.[1] Public acceptance of checks spread rapidly after the Civil War. And what began as a trickle of payments by check in the 19th century became a flood of paper transactions in the 20th century. In the United States, the public wrote an estimated 8 billion checks in 1952; about 25 billion in 1972; and about 34 billion in 1980, though no one knows *for sure* how many paper drafts are written each year. In recent years, check volume in the United States has been growing about 6 percent annually, roughly doubling every dozen years or so. While the increasing use of electronic money machines should slow that growth substantially in the future, Americans will probably be writing 40 billion checks a year before the

---

[1]No one knows for sure when checks first began to be used. Some historians find evidence of the use of these payment-on-site drafts as early as the 4th century B.C. in Rome. Another historical account goes back to 16th century Amsterdam, when goldsmiths and other businessmen agreed to act as depositories for metallic coins and other valuables. The depositors could then issue to anyone they desired (such as a merchant or bill collector) a written order to pay which would be presented to the depository for collection. The practice spread to England, where goldsmiths allegedly offered a similar service to their customers. In the United States the first significant use of checks occurred in 1681, when a shortage of coins resulted in the creation of the Fund at Boston in New England. The Fund was a cooperative effort by Boston merchants who mortgaged their property in favor of the Fund and received accounts against which checks could be written. Due to the subsequent growth of government and bank-issued currency, however, checks did not achieve significant popularity with the U.S. public until well over a century later. In fact, as the Federal Reserve Bank of New York [11] notes, it wasn't until the Civil War that the volume of U.S. checkbook money exceeded the amount of paper currency in circulation.

decade of the 1980s comes to a close. The Federal Reserve System estimates that better than 90 percent of the dollar volume of business transactions in the United States are accomplished by writing checks. In 1980 about $30 trillion dollars of checkbook money changed hands in the United States. The well-known M1 definition of the nation's money supply shows that checking accounts (demand deposits) represent about 70 percent of the U.S. money stock.[2]

The dominance of checks as a means of payment has brought greater convenience and safety to both buyers and sellers, but increasingly bad news to those institutions (mainly commercial banks and the Federal Reserve System) who must process and clear those checks. Gradually, the technology of the computer and automation has expanded the capacity of the nation's check-clearing system in a desperate race to keep up with the growth of business transactions. A number of needed improvements *have* been made; however, our paper-based transactions system, as it has grown, has placed an increasing strain on the financial system. It absorbs tremendous quantities of scarce resources—buildings, processing machines, and people—to insure that payments eventually find their way to the right accounts at the right institutions. And with payments by paper there remains always the danger of collapse—a flood of transactions so huge as to break down the entire system with chaotic consequences for the nation's commerce and industry.

Tremendous growth in the volume of checks has been paralleled by a rapid increase in the cost of clearing (i.e., posting, routing, and collecting) checks. Current estimates of the cost of clearing each check written vary widely (and of course are influenced by the source and destination of each check), but 30 cents to 50 cents per check appears to be a reasonable estimate. And, these figures do *not* include the costs of paper, printing, and mailing cleared checks and bank statements back to the customer. Added

---

[2]The M1 definition of the U.S. money supply includes currency in circulation (outside Treasury, Federal Reserve, and bank vaults), traveler's checks of nonbank issuers, demand deposits at all commercial banks (excluding interbank, U.S. government, and government institutions, deposits, cash items in the process of collection, and Federal Reserve float), negotiable orders of withdrawal (NOW) and automatic transfer service (ATS) accounts at banks and thrift institutions, credit union share draft (CUSD) accounts, and demand deposits at mutual savings banks. In January 1983, M1 totaled about $480 billion (on a seasonally adjusted basis) of which demand and other checkable deposits totaled $344 billion, or 72 percent.

A somewhat broader definition of money, including liquid savings, is M2, which equals M1 plus savings and small-denomination time deposits at all depository institutions, overnight RPs at commercial banks and Carribean branches of member banks, and balances in money market funds (general purpose and broker/dealer). In January 1983, M2 stood at $2,007 billion (seasonally adjusted), with demand and other checkable deposits accounting for about 17 percent of that total.

to these expenses is the opportunity cost of *time*—the time it takes to deliver and clear checks and receive credit for the face amount of each check. Time, indeed, is money because each day that passes until a check is finally cleared and collected is lost interest income which the check's recipient (payee) could have earned by investing, even temporarily, the face amount of the check.

The burgeoning cost of payments by checks, coupled with fear of a collapsing payments system, prompted Congress in 1974 to enact the Electronic Funds Transfer Act. This law represented a belated attempt to organize and systematize thinking and action concerning the development of new payments delivery systems, especially those centering on the electronic transfer of funds and financial data. As the Federal Reserve Board observed not long ago:

> Just as the electronic calculator has replaced the slide rule, EFT seems destined to displace many current check uses because electronic technology can be a more efficient, secure, convenient, and less costly method of transferring funds than is the check.[3]

Among other things the 1974 law set up a National Commission on Electronic Funds Transfer (NCEFT)—a 26-person, federally-sponsored study group. Its constituency includes federal and state government officials, bankers and managers of other financial institutions involved in the payments process, representatives from firms relying on credit card sales (such as retail stores and credit card companies), and individuals representing the consuming public. In addition to studying the nation's options for expansion of electronic payments systems, the commission also was directed to consider the risks and dangers to business and consumer welfare inherent in centralized computer processing and control of the payments process.

The Electronic Funds Transfer Act made the Federal Reserve Board, Federal Deposit Insurance Corporation, Federal Home Loan Bank Board, Comptroller of the Currency, and National Credit Union Administration responsible for enforcing the act. Pursuant to this law, Regulation E was drafted. It contains rules governing unsolicited issuance of payment orders and privacy of customer accounts, and it prescribes the limits of customer liability when unauthorized transfers or errors are made. (A summary of some of the important provisions of the EFT Act and supporting regulations affecting the EFT customer is shown in Figure 23–1.) Ultimately, the Federal Reserve, working together with the National Commission on Electronic Funds Transfer and institutions and industry groups, hopes

---

[3]Board of Governors of the Federal Reserve System [5], p. 280.

Figure 23–1   Important Provisions of the Electronic Funds Transfer Act and Supporting Regulations of the Federal Reserve Board

• Customers using electronic terminals, preauthorized transfers, or telephones to transfer funds must receive periodic statements showing all funds transfered into and out of their accounts, identifying the individuals and institutions receiving payments, any charges for transfer services, and beginning and ending account balances.

• When informed by a customer of a possible error in his or her EFT-accessed account, the financial institution holding the account must promptly investigate the problem and try to resolve it within a period of 45 days. If an error is found, the institution must correct it promptly and credit the customer's account for the proper amount. If no error is found, this must be explained to the customer in writing.

• The financial liability of the customer holding an EFT or debit card resulting from unauthorized use of the card is limited to a modest amount, provided the customer notifies the financial institution involved in timely fashion. Specifically, liability is limited to $50 if the issuing institution is notified within two business days after a customer becomes aware of the loss or theft of an EFT card or code number. Longer periods without notification after a customer becomes aware of unauthorized transactions (such as through receipt of a monthly account statement) subject the customer to the risk of greater losses (perhaps up to the full balance in the account plus the amount of any overdraft credit line).

• Customers cannot be sent unrequested EFT cards. Any cards sent must be accompanied by information on the extent of any customer liability, how to report the loss or theft of a card, how errors can be dealt with, and who may be entitled to receive information concerning the customer's account.

• Payments already preauthorized by the customer may be stopped if the customer orders his or her financial institution to do so a minimum of three business days before the date payment was supposed to be made.

---

to establish a computer-based payments mechanism which speedily routes payments data, reduces or eliminates float time, minimizes the need for more capital investment and human resources in the payments process, reduces the problem of fraudulent checks and processing errors, and simultaneously preserves and protects the customer's privacy and security. This is no small task!

THE CURRENT PAYMENTS SYSTEM AND PAYMENTS METHODS

The payments system in the United States today is a hodgepodge of old and new transactions methods. Indeed, the present system is really in transition to something new and, hopefully, faster, safer, and more efficient. Gradually, the United States is moving toward a payments system which substitutes electronic signals for checks, currency, and coin.

Currency and Coin (Pocket Money)

Currency and coin are still widely used for small transactions. Indeed, the growth of coin-operated vending machines which dispense everything from cigarettes, coffee, and soft drinks to toothpaste and insurance policies has supported and expanded the need for pocket money. At year-end 1973, currency and coin in circulation in the U.S. economy totaled about $60 billion. By June 1983, however, currency and coin in circulation exceeded $140 billion—a dramatic rate of growth in this legal tender form of money[4] (see Figure 23–2). However, many analysts believe that this traditional means of payment will grow more slowly in the future and should decline in relative importance as electronic methods continue to increase in popularity.

Payment by Check

Checks are still the most important means of executing payments for goods and services in the United States. As we noted earlier, roughly 70 percent of the money supply held for transactions purposes consists of demand deposits in commercial and savings banks as well as NOW accounts, share drafts, ATS, and other accounts subject to immediate withdrawal by draft, wire, or telephone in order to make payments. Well over 90 percent of the dollar volume of American business transactions are still carried out by check.

As we have also seen, the familiar checking account has deserved the popularity it has held for many decades. It is relatively safe, convenient, and provides a useful record of business and consumer transactions for bookkeeping purposes and for tax audits. Indeed, in a smaller, less urbanized setting where the overwhelming bulk of transactions are *local* in

Figure 23–2   Growth of Various Payments Instruments in the United States
($ billions; averages of daily figures)

Payments Instrument	Amounts Outstanding for:					
	December 1978	*December 1979*	*December 1980*	*December 1981*	*December 1982*	*June 1983*
Currency and coin in circulation	$ 97.4	$116.1	$116.2	$123.1	$132.8	$140.3
Traveler's checks	3.5	3.7	4.2	4.3	4.4	4.9
Demand deposits (regular checking accounts)	253.9	262.2	267.2	236.4	239.8	242.1
ATS, NOWs, credit union share drafts, and demand deposits at mutual savings banks	8.4	16.9	26.9	77.0	101.3	121.0

Source: Board of Governors of the Federal Reserve System, *Federal Reserve Bulletin,* selected issues.

---

[4]Currency and coin are the only forms of money in use that represent legal tender for payment of amounts owed to someone. The term *legal tender* simply means a form of money acceptable for all debts, public and private. If a seller or creditor refuses to accept legal tender, the buyer or debtor is not obligated to offer any other form of payment (unless, of course, a legal contract between buyer and seller calls for payment in something other than money— e.g., barrels of oil, diamonds, etc.). However, the purchaser's debt is not cancelled; it remains on the books (though not accruing interest charges) until the seller agrees to accept payment. Checks are *not* legal tender nor are electronic means of payment.

character (i.e., involve financial institutions in the same city or county), the check probably would have served the nation's transactions needs extremely well for a long period into the future.

The fundamental problem, of course, is that markets are far broader today than in the past and are continuing to expand in size. Local markets have given way to huge regional, national, and even international markets for exchanging goods, services, and financial claims. A good example of this *market-broadening* phenomenon was provided by the rise of money market mutual funds during the 1970s.[5] Prior to the appearance of the money funds, most observers of the savings deposit market assumed it was primarily *local* in character. It seemed clear that savers preferred to hold their savings deposits in a bank, savings and loan, or credit union within the same city or county because of convenience. However, using the lure of high interest rates plus the convenience of check writing and telephone or wire transfer of funds, money market mutual funds—most of them located in or adjacent to the New York money market—were able to attract billions of dollars in small-denomination savings deposits away from local financial intermediaries. Money funds proved that, through technological improvements in communication and transfer of data, even the market for household financial services was regional, perhaps national in scope.

The lesson taught by money market mutual funds has not been lost on the banking community. The convenience of financing purchases by writing a check might well be supplanted by purchases made or facilitated through computer terminals and cash-dispensing machines. And the financial institution offering electronic payments services might well be located hundreds or thousands of miles from the customer. Thus, as the money market funds grew rapidly during the 1970s, so also did automated teller machines and deposit accounts accessed via computer terminal.

Most checks today are cleared and collected through the private banking system. Checks written in the local area are usually first deposited in a local bank. That bank adds the amount of the check to the depositing customer's account (sometimes with a time delay) and then sends the check to the bank on which it was drawn through the local clearinghouse, which may be an automated computer facility jointly owned by local financial institutions. Checks drawn on out-of-town banks may be sent to large upstream correspondent banks which route them to the paying banks through the private banking system. Alternatively, checks drawn on out-of-town banks may be sent to the Federal Reserve banks for clearing and

---

[5]See Chapter 16 for a discussion of the history, growth, and characteristics of money market mutual funds.

collection. For such out-of-town cash items the Federal Reserve System has been the principal clearinghouse for decades. And, by any measure, the Fed processes, speedily and efficiently, a huge volume of checks each year. In 1980, for example, the Fed's check-clearing system processed 15.7 billion checks having a total face value of $8 trillion.

One reason the Fed has been so popular as a conduit for out-of-town checks is that, prior to 1981, it cleared checks for free. As long as a bank (even those banks not members of the Federal Reserve System) kept a clearing account on deposit with the Federal Reserve Bank in the region, it could use the Fed's nationwide clearing service at no charge. This situation changed dramatically in August 1982 when, under authority granted by the Monetary Control Act of 1980, the Federal Reserve banks began charging on a per-item basis for all cash items collected. The Fed's check-clearing volume declined about 20 percent as correspondent banks across the nation offered competing check-clearing services.

In effect, the Monetary Control Act set up two *competing* nationwide check-clearing networks—one operated by a government agency, the Federal Reserve System, and the other by a private system dominated by the largest commercial banks situated in metropolitan areas across the nation. Even a disinterested observer could have predicted trouble for such a system, pitting government against private enterprise. And, of course, that is just what has happened. For example, in 1982 and 1983 the Fed proposed changes in its rules for check clearings in order to speed up the process and reduce "float" (i.e., the volume of uncollected checks outstanding at any one time). The Fed doesn't give banks immediate credit for checks deposited with it but usually waits one or two days (figuring that, on the average, most checks will be collected by that time) before giving a depositing bank credit for any checks it has brought to the Federal Reserve banks. However, due to various delays in the payments system (often caused by bad weather or delays in transportation schedules), some checks remain uncollected even after the Fed has given the depositing bank credit for them. In effect, the Federal Reserve bank grants an *interest-free loan* to the depositing bank when it gives credit for an uncollected check, creating the potential for further expansion of bank loans. If this is undesirable—perhaps because of the presence of serious inflation—the Fed may have to offset the volume of float by using its open-market operations. Unfortunately, successful operations to combat the buildup of float require accurate forecasting of changes in float—a highly volatile item.

Recently, the Fed has decided that a good method of dealing with checkbook float is simply to reduce or eliminate it. Proposals brought forward in December 1982 would permit the Fed to collect payment for many outstanding checks left with it within 24 hours rather than as long as two days. Because many banks and large corporate depositors would object to such a speedup in collections,[6] the Fed also proposed lowering its prices for clearing cash items. Almost immediately, many large correspondent banks across the country vigorously objected to the Fed's price reductions, fearing a substantial loss of check-clearing business. Several air courier services which earn substantial revenues transporting checks for private banks filed suit in federal court to block the Fed's new pricing and collection scheme. Many private companies see the Fed's efforts to speed up check collection, along with lower prices, as "predatory pricing" and a violation of the federal law which requires full-cost pricing of Federal Reserve services.

There is little question that the current mix of government and private check-clearing services will continue to be a source of controversy until, perhaps, Congress changes the basic rules of the game. One beneficiary, however, should be the consumer, because competition between the Federal Reserve and large private banks in offering check-clearing services should keep the cost of checking services lower than would otherwise be the case. Such competition may also foster more rapid development of advanced EFT systems, which would further reduce the volume of resources devoted to making payments.

Preauthorized Automatic Transfers and Automatic Payroll Deposits

The past decade has ushered in important precursors to a completely automated national deposit system. One of these precursors was ATS—automatic transfers of funds into and out of transactions (checking) accounts in order to make payments or access savings accounts (see Figure 23–3). For many years now, most bank customers have been able to sign authorization forms which give their banks permission to automatically draft their checking accounts for payments on a mortgage or installment loan or to meet premiums due on insurance policies or, in some cases, to pay gas, electric, and other utility bills. Other preauthorized transfers of funds make possible automatic deposit of social security or stock dividend payments.

The growth of checking-savings transfer arrangements has been modest due to the strong competition offered by NOW accounts (negotiable orders of withdrawal) and, in 1983, by super NOWs and Money Market De-

---

[6]One of the Fed's problems in handling float has been the rise of controlled disbursement accounts set up by large U.S. corporations. Frequently a company issuing many checks will place its checking account with a bank in a remote location to increase check-collection delays, thus giving the company use of its deposit for a longer period of time.

Figure 23–3   The Terminology of EFTS

ATS	Automatic transfers of funds, usually between checking and savings accounts or into bill-paying accounts; often used to pay recurring expenses, such as utility bills, mortgage payments, and insurance premiums through customer preauthorization of an automatic draft against his or her account.
ATM	Automated teller machine, which dispenses cash and accepts deposits, usually available for customer use 24 hours a day.
RSU	Remote service unit, an automated teller machine located away from the main bank building, typically in a shopping center or free-standing structure, and usually directly accessible by automobile or pedestrian traffic.
POS	Point-of-sale computer terminal, located in stores and shopping centers, permitting instant customer payment for purchases of goods and services by transferring funds from the customer's account to the store's account.
ACH	Automated clearinghouse, a computer facility serving several financial institutions and used mainly to clear checks and other cash items.
TBP	Telephone bill paying, a service offered principally by large banks and savings and loan associations through which the customer can pay bills by telephone, authorizing his or her financial institution to transfer funds to another individual or institution.
APD	Automatic payroll deposit, a method for speeding payment of salaries and wages from businesses and governments to their employees by placing the amounts due employees each pay period on a computer tape and delivering the tape to a depository institution or automated clearinghouse, where a computer transfers payroll amounts to each employee's deposit account.

posit Accounts (MMDAs), which pay interest on transactions balances. Super NOWs offer the combined features of an unregulated interest rate and access by written draft.[7] The unregulated interest rate was a particularly significant advance because the yield on regular NOWs was then subject to federal interest-rate ceilings controlled by the Depository Institutions Deregulation Committee (DIDC). In March 1983, NOWs were limited to a maximum interest return of 5¼ percent, while many super NOWs and MMDAs were paying interest rates in the 9 to 10 percent range. Confronted by these new hybrid checking-savings deposits and full-cost pricing of automatic transfer services, ATS diminished in attractiveness to consumers.

A precursor to nationwide electronic payments systems, which *has* continued to grow in popularity, however, is the *automatic payroll deposit* (APD). Used mainly by large businesses and governmental units, APD involves putting a firm or governmental unit's payroll on computer tape instead of issuing a separate paycheck to each employee. The tape is then delivered to a depository institution or automated clearinghouse, where a computer transfers the payroll information to all depository institutions

---

[7]As we saw in Chapters 8, 13, and 14, legal clearance to develop super NOWs and MMDAs was granted by the Garn–St Germain Depository Institutions Act of 1982 to the Depository Institutions Deregulation Commission (DIDC). Regular NOW accounts were first authorized nationwide by the Depository Institutions Deregulation Act of 1980.

holding employee checking or savings accounts. Each employee receives automatic credit in his or her account for the amount of salaries or wages earned. Thus a payroll can be met without the use of paper, except that many banks still send a written notice of the date and amount of the automatic deposit to each employee—thus replacing one paper document (a payroll check) with another.

In recent years the U.S. Treasury has become a positive force in developing direct-deposit banking. At the end of 1982, approximately 37 percent of all social security pension and benefit checks issued to retirees and other recipients were made by automatic electronic deposit. And the Treasury's accomplishments in this field have been a catalyst for private pension plans to do the same. For example, as noted in *The Wall Street Journal* in February 1983, Equitable Life Assurance Society was making electronic pension payments to approximately 76,000 individuals.[8] At the same time Connecticut General Insurance Company was making approximately one quarter of its pension payments by direct deposit. Yet, many pensioners still prefer paper checks, which give the recipient tangible evidence of money received.

Payments by Wire

Many businesses make payments today through automatic wire transfers. These payments typically include purchases of inventories, interest and dividend payments, purchases of securities, and, as we noted earlier, payrolls. These payments may be carried out via the Federal Reserve System's nationwide electronic wire transfer system (known as Fed Wire) or through private wire transfer systems. Payments made through the Fed's wire transfer network are moved instantaneously from one reserve account to another within the same Federal Reserve district or between districts.

The Fed's wire transfer network is an old, established conduit for making large intercorporate or government payments. It began in 1915, two years after passage of the Federal Reserve Act, as a telegraphic communications network and is today a computerized information and data transfer system used not only for instantly recording payments in the proper bank reserve accounts but also to assist the Fed and securities dealers in trading U.S. government securities. When a depository institution makes a loan to another depository institution (such as through the federal funds market) or a customer asks his or her bank to move a sizable amount of funds to another institution, Fed Wire is usually the chosen conduit for

---

[8]See [25] at the end of this chapter.

transfering the funds. Even the U.S. Treasury and a variety of federal government agencies use Fed Wire to make payments and to collect funds owed them. When a depository institution must report its deposit balances to the Fed for monetary policy purposes, Fed Wire is also used. Direct deposit information and bill payments between automated clearinghouses (to be discussed later) typically move via transfers of reserve balances on Fed Wire. The Fed's wire network can be accessed by written requests on paper or via transfers of reserve balances on Fed Wire via computer terminal or telephone. As Allison [1] points out, in 1980 alone 43 million transfers of reserve balances, amounting to $78 trillion, took place over Fed Wire.

While automatic payroll-deposit and wire-transfer devices are convenient and far less time-consuming than comparable paper-based payment systems, their use nationwide is still of relatively modest proportions. Such devices are employed mainly by the largest companies, which are in the minority. However, greater use of this service is expected in the future. In fact, Humphrey [17] notes in a recent study for the Federal Reserve Board that wire transfer volume has been rising about 20 percent a year, or roughly three times the rate of growth in check volume. Humphrey also observes that wire transfers "supported a total expenditure flow of $102 trillion" in 1979, or about five times the expenditure flow supported by checks. [9]

One form of wire transfers which appears to have a very bright future is *cash-management services*. Corporations working through banks and insurance companies (or, in a few cases, corporations working on their own) monitor their checking or transactions accounts continuously via wire and computer terminal. When surplus funds are found, those funds can be invested by wire in the form of temporary loans to security dealers, banks, and other financial intermediaries, and to large nonfinancial corporations. Then, when the lending corporation needs its funds once again, they can be quickly wired back into its transactions accounts and used to pay bills. Interestingly, many large nonfinancial companies now have electronic links between themselves, permitting instantaneous payments between corporate buyers and sellers and bypassing the banking system.

Credit Cards

Credit cards have been very popular payments devices since their inception during the 1950s. Spurred by the success of American Express,

---

[9]See Humphrey [17], p. 2

Master Charge (now MasterCard), and BankAmericard (now VISA), use of plastic cards to buy goods and services on credit has become a worldwide phenomenon. More than 700 million such cards have been issued. At year-end 1982, bank credit card balances totaled about $110 billion. Roughly 12,000 U.S. banks offer the service today. Moreover, the Depository Institutions Deregulation Act of 1980 authorized the offering of credit cards by credit unions and savings and loan associations. The use of a plastic card to buy now and pay later has become a major alternative to check writing.

Regrettably, the plastic credit card has unleashed its own paper tiger. When a customer makes a purchase using a credit card, the store involved gives the customer a receipt for the transaction. The store also keeps a receipt, which is passed on to the store's bank in order to receive credit for the deposit. Another copy of the receipt may be returned to the customer when he or she receives a monthly account statement. Many card plans have bypassed this last paper transfer, however, by sending the customer an abbreviated monthly statement consisting of a computer printout which lists all recent transactions in chronological order. Still, the volume of paper associated with credit card transactions is substantial. We must add to this tally the disturbing fact that consumers who actively use their credit cards also seem to write more checks than people who don't actively rely on the convenience of credit cards.[10]

Debit Cards

Related to the credit card is another piece of plastic known as the *debit card*. While credit cards permit a user to purchase goods and services on credit (i.e., buy now and pay later), debit cards are simply an alternative form of immediate payment, similar to a check. In fact, in many places debit cards encoded with the customer's name and deposit number simply serve as identification to make check cashing easier. However, debit cards can also be used to make payments or receive currency. In this instance, the customer inserts the card into a computer terminal, which automatically deducts the amount spent or withdrawn from the customer's deposit account.

---

[10]An interesting and perplexing problem with credit cards appeared as the decade of the 1980s began—counterfeiting. Banks and credit card companies lost an estimated $40 million in 1982 and $15 million in 1981 from counterfeit cards. Counterfeiters have been using discarded charge slips to get a valid number and name and to imprint that information on a new plastic card. Manufacturers and card systems are currently developing new kinds of cards which will be more difficult to duplicate.

Automated Teller Machines

Over the past decade, banks and other depository institutions began taking a close look at their expenses, especially those associated with daily paying out and receiving funds through their teller windows. Wage and salary costs for human tellers and other bank employees were soaring. Added to this was a huge volume of paper consisting of checks and deposit slips to be processed. In major, rapidly growing metropolitan areas long lines of cars often backed up at bank drive-in windows, while in bank lobbies there were often long lines of customers waiting to transact business with a human teller. Despite frequent complaints about customer delays and soaring costs, many depository institutions were hesitant to trade in a time-honored, people-to-people system for a coldly efficient and speedier computerized system offering automated teller services.

Nevertheless, a few innovative financial institutions in large metropolitan areas where teller congestion had become a major problem began installing automated teller machines (ATMs). These machines permit the customer to insert a plastic card (often called an EFT or debit card) into a designated slot and punch a special code number (usually called a PIN, or personal identification number) into a keyboard. By pressing a transaction button, the customer can then receive cash, pay bills, or move funds from one account to another electronically. The customer may receive a printed receipt of the transaction which indicates the amount of the funds transferred, account number, and date. ATMs are now the most popular EFT device, with 35,721 money machines in operation in the United States at year-end 1982, compared to just 13,800 in 1979. In 1982 alone, 3.1 billion transactions (not counting account-balance inquiries) took place through ATMs.[11]

The first faltering steps in the automated teller field were generally side-by-side arrangements. ATMs appeared in bank lobbies or in the form of drive-in stations within sight of human tellers offering the same services. Many of the early ATMs did little more than dispense cash. Not surprisingly, many depository institutions were disappointed with their performance. The majority of customers seemed to prefer the human touch. Often the machines stood idle while long lines backed up at regular teller windows, particularly on Fridays when people normally cash a large volume of checks to get pocket money for the weekend. Like most pieces of capital equipment, efficient use of ATMs requires a large volume of trans-

---

[11]See Federal Reserve Bank of Dallas [33]. Seventy-six percent of the recorded transactions were withdrawals of funds, and 19 percent, deposits. An average of 7,200 transactions passed through each machine each month, with withdrawals averaging $37 each and deposits about $267 each.

actions just to break even on the cost of each machine. In numerous instances, customer use of ATMs was well below the break-even point.[12]

The few studies in existence generally find that customer acceptance of ATMs over human tellers depends upon a number of different customer characteristics: (1) age group, (2) level of education, (3) job or profession, (4) sex, (5) level of income, and (6) the relative preference of the customer for self-service versus having service provided by someone else. For example, Hood [16] finds that young, upper-income, white-collar males are more likely than any other group to make use of ATMs. This group can be attracted to a new ATM facility through advertising which has specific meaning and identification to that group. Nonusers from other socioeconomic groups can also be encouraged to use ATMs by advertising programs designed to fit their background, needs, and values.

Subdued customer acceptance of ATMs is still a feature of the banking landscape in many parts of the nation. Banking is still thought of as a people-oriented business, and old habits are hard to break. Then, too, ATMs are sometimes prone to errors, and breakdowns are by no means uncommon. One of the authors of this book still remembers his recent visit to a shopping center in a large Midwestern city where an automated teller station stood in the middle of the parking lot. A large, irate crowd was gathered around the ATM, some of whom were kicking and others beating on the machine with their fists. Closer inspection revealed that this particular ATM had failed to dispense the right amount of currency to some customers and had shortchanged others who were trying to make a deposit. Attempts to call the emergency number posted on the wall were frustrated by a phone that also was out of order!

Machines can go awry, just as human tellers sometimes make unintentional errors. Moreover, computer fraud can be as damaging to a financial institution as outright fraud or theft by its employees. Added problems center upon the possible vulnerability of ATMs to crime. For example, during 1983 a couple of ATM burglaries occurred in Texas when explosives were used to gain access to cash stored in the money machines. On other occasions, customers have been robbed just after receiving cash

---

[12]There is evidence that the *composition* of transactions through an automated teller machine can have as much of an impact on its profitability or lack thereof as the total *volume* of transactions. Moreover, both the volume and composition of transactions are highly sensitive to machine location. Kutler [21], in a study of ATM activity for the First National Bank of Atlanta, found that approximately half (52 percent) of all ATM transactions were withdrawals of cash; about one fifth (22 percent) represented customers checking the balance in their accounts; about one eighth (13 percent) represented deposits made into existing accounts; and minor fractions of total transactions were accounted for by the transferring of funds between accounts (about 2 percent of the total).

from an ATM. Stolen EFT or debit cards have also resulted in substantial losses from some money machines.

A number of important lessons have been learned from early experiences with ATMs, however. One is that, given a choice and with all other factors (especially convenience and cost) held constant, most consumers prefer dealing with human tellers rather than ATMs. Yet, ATMs require a large volume of transactions to be profitable. To overcome this dilemma, money machines have to possess a distinct advantage over human tellers in either convenience or cost, and preferably both. Not surprisingly, therefore, a few banks began during the 1970s and early 1980s either to charge their customers for using human tellers, restricting hours of customer access to human tellers, or assessing lower service charges for customers willing to conduct their business with a self-service ATM. Not long ago, Citizens and Southern Bank in Atlanta, for example, experimented with a promotional program where cash withdrawals from an ATM carried lower service charges than cashing a check through a teller window. Other institutions have been phasing out no-service-charge or minimum-service-charge demand deposit accounts, so that customers come closer to paying the full cost of paper-based transactions and can therefore make a more rational comparison between use of EFT and check writing.[13]

Additional incentive to use ATMs is also being provided today by a gradual expansion in the range of services available through money machines. Newer ATMs issue traveler's checks, dispense cash from checkbook accounts or from preauthorized credit lines, take deposits, accept bill and loan payments, dispense information on account balances, and move funds from one account to another. Other ATMs are being developed to dispense coins as well as paper currency so that exact change can be given for cashed checks. In addition, many financial institutions have set up shared ATM systems covering a state or region, so that a customer traveling to a distant city can access an ATM there to secure additional funds.

Point-of-Sale (POS) Terminals

ATMs represent a form of *retail* EFTS—that is, electronic systems reaching the bank customer directly, facilitating the customer's access to a financial institution. Another form of retail EFTS is point-of-sale (POS)

---

[13]See especially Johnson and Arnold [18]. Because ATMs can be operated 24 hours a day, they reduce the number of hours banking offices need to be kept open for routine transactions (especially on weekends). The result is a substantial savings in labor and overhead costs which may be passed along to the customer in the form of more advanced ATM equipment or lower service fees.

terminals, situated in stores and shopping centers where consumers purchase a large volume of goods and services. Through a POS computer terminal, the customer can pay for a purchase simply by inserting a debit or EFT card into the terminal and punching in the amount of the purchase. This information is immediately transferred to a computer which adds the amount to the store's deposit account and deducts it from the customer's account. Other than a receipt of the transaction given to the customer, no paper changes hands.

Through POS, the store selling goods and services clearly benefits from rapid (instantaneous) collection of funds. The banks involved benefit in reduced check-processing volume. The customer also gains in convenience from not having to write a check. Unfortunately, the customer loses *float time*, since he or she gives up funds immediately rather than being able to retain funds on deposit until a check clears. POS terminals are especially at a disadvantage with respect to credit card purchases because the credit card user does not have to pay for a purchase until the end of a billing period (if he or she desires to avoid paying interest charges). This, not surprisingly, is why consumers usually regard POS terminals with mixed feelings and one of the reasons the use of POS devices is not nearly as widespread as the use of ATMs and ACHs.

Many businesses also have mixed feelings about the desirability of POS terminals. Instantaneous payment of bills speeds up a firm's cash collections from sales (i.e., increases the rate of turnover or velocity of accounts receivable) but also tends to accelerate the payment of trade debt (i.e., increases the turnover rate or velocity of accounts payable). Thus the attractiveness to a business firm of making payments via computer terminal depends on the relative importance to the firm of accounts receivable versus acounts payable. One often forgotten advantage of POS terminals for merchants, however, is the growing use of POS devices to verify that a customer's check is good or that a credit card is not stolen or from a delinquent or closed account. Thus POS terminals can cut down on business losses due to fraud or slow-paying accounts.

The growth and expansion of POS terminals has been retarded somewhat by cost and customer resistance. Nevertheless, progress *is* being made. Leading New York banks, such as First National City Bank (Citibank) and the Chase Manhattan Bank, have pioneered in setting up POS systems in retail stores and branch offices. Similar experiments have also been conducted in the Midwest—notably in Lincoln, Nebraska, and Columbus, Ohio. The key to increased customer acceptance of POS terminals and probably of many other EFT devices as well seems to be an *economic* one—will customers find a significant economic advantage from using EFT equipment over older methods of funds transfer? In particular, will the loss of float time be fully offset by advantages associated with the speedy investment of collected funds and greater accuracy and convenience? Many financial institutions are finding that customer acceptance of POS terminals and other EFT equipment requires the full-cost pricing of the older, paper-based payments services such as checks and credit cards.

Telephone Bill-Paying (TBP) and Transfers

An increasingly popular form of prearranged banking is bill paying and other transfers of funds authorized by a telephone call. The customer opens an account with a bank or nonbank thrift institution which allows him or her to designate which bills need to be paid via telephone. The customer's financial institution then handles the transaction from this point, transferring funds to those individuals and institutions receiving payments. Customers can also move funds from a savings to a checking account or vice versa through a telephone order. Telephone payments and transfers normally do not generate paper receipts and thus alleviate the problem of a growing volume of paper transactions. Most TBP systems offer the customer access to his or her account 24 hours a day, seven days a week.

Telephone banking seems to be spreading rapidly in some areas. A majority of billion-dollar U.S. banks are expected to offer the service sometime during the 1980s. The U.S. League of Savings Associations recently found that, as of year-end 1981, 167 commercial banks and 168 savings and loan associations were offering bill paying by telephone to their customers. In May 1982 the Federal Reserve Board reported that just over 400 financial institutions offered TBP services during 1981.[14] However, TBP can be quite expensive. One research organization, Payment Systems, Inc., estimates that the average cost per customer transaction is probably in the range of 60 to 70 cents—a figure clearly favoring more conventional methods of funds transfer (such as checks). Adding to the cost of TBP is the fact that the "average" TBP customer calls frequently, authorizing only a few transactions on each call, rather than waiting to conduct all of his or her transactions in one phone call. For example, a study by the Bank Administration Institute found that in December 1981, TBP customers averaged two or less transactions per telephone call.[15] Among the most significant costs involved are the expense of acquiring computer hardware and software, personnel costs, and advertising expenses. Reflecting the high

---

[14]See Board of Governors of the Federal Reserve System, *Annual Report to Congress on the Electronic Funds Transfer Act, 1981* [7].

[15]See Van der Velde [32].

cost of TBP, over 80 percent of the financial institutions offering the service in 1981 charged for it.

There is also some evidence of customer resistance to TBP, making it more difficult to reach the break-even point. For example, Van der Velde [32] notes that, nationwide, less than half (43 percent) of the customers of financial institutions offering TBP have signed up to use the service on a monthly basis. Moreover, less than a third of customers dealing with commercial banks offering TBP use the bank's telephone service.

As we noted earlier, people would normally prefer to conduct their banking business with a human being—someone they can interact with—rather than merely feeding information into a computer. There is apparently a strong need for consumer education in the TBP field—admittedly a costly venture—before the majority of customers readily accept dealing on-line with the bank's computer system. Recognizing this, most TBP systems offer human teller assistance whenever the customer requires it.

In-Home TV Banking

Telephone banking is one facet of *home banking*—the service which enables a customer to transact business in his or her place of residence at times convenient to the customer, usually through phone lines or computer terminals. Another growing facet of home banking is *video banking*—using a home television screen to display current account information and a terminal to transact banking business. In 1980, Banc One in Columbus, Ohio, began experimenting with a system (known as Channel 2000) in which subscribing customers could determine the status of their bank accounts merely by calling up their account file from the bank's computer and displaying the results on a home television set. A computer terminal in the home is linked both to a TV set and to the bank's computer through telephone lines. (Recently similar systems have been set up in customer business offices, thus electronically linking both home and office to the banking system.) The customer can check his or her account at any time and authorize transfer of funds out of that account in order to pay bills or move money into another account. The convenience of home banking clearly reduces the need to visit a bank personally, thus saving time and money.

The concept of in-home banking was given a substantial boost in February 1983 with the announcement that four major banking organizations—Banc One Corp of Columbus, Ohio; Southeast Banking Corporation of Miami, Florida; Wachovia Corporation of Winston-Salem, North Carolina; and Security Pacific Corporation of Los Angeles—were forming a joint venture to offer in-home TV banking. The new venture is named

Video Financial Services and uses both home TV sets and telephone lines to transmit signals. Initially, 16 banks in South Florida were linked to the system. Customers were offered an American Bell Telephone terminal which translates telephone signals into color graphics on a home TV screen. Customers can also get the latest news, order merchandise, and purchase tickets to sporting events through the video service.

A number of problems have appeared recently with home TV banking, and they pose significant barriers to its growth and expansion. One problem centers on delivery systems—whether telephone lines, satellites, or cable TV networks should be employed to transmit financial data and customer instructions.[16] Moreover, there is considerable uncertainty surrounding the nature and cost of in-home banking equipment. Computer terminals look expensive to many households, and it is not clear the customer would incur the extra cost of an in-home terminal merely to conduct banking transactions. Other in-home TV services, particularly information retrieval systems, will probably have to be developed in parallel to justify the cost of installation. These services are likely to include videotex copies of the telephone book, classified advertisements, shoppers' catalogs, local and national news stories, and library card catalogs. One promising prospect is that future home TVs will probably be manufactured with built-in home banking capabilities.

Automated Clearinghouse (ACH)

As we have seen, ATMs and POS terminals represent alternative forms of *retail* EFTS, reaching the customer directly. Equally, if not more, impressive progress has been made in developing *wholesale* EFTS, which links financial institutions to one another. The dominant form of wholesale EFTS technology today is the automated clearinghouse (ACH). An automated clearinghouse is simply a computer facility linked by wire and computer tape to all the financial institutions served by the clearinghouse. ACHs also permit automatic bill paying and direct deposit of payrolls, government payments to businesses and individuals, and payments of insurance premiums and retirement benefits. Figure 23–4 illustrates the typical channels through which direct payroll deposits and prepayments of insurance premiums find their way into and out of an ACH.

The first ACH appeared in California in the late 1960s, and today close to 40 ACHs serve the U.S. banking system. Most are designed to serve one region of the nation. However, the system is being gradually expanded to integrate all major ACHs into a nationwide payments network—a joint project of the private banking system and the Federal Reserve System. ACHs have been handling a substantial volume of electronic payments in

---

[16]See, for example, Van der Velde [32].

Figure 23–4   Typical Transactions Handled through an Automated Clearinghouse

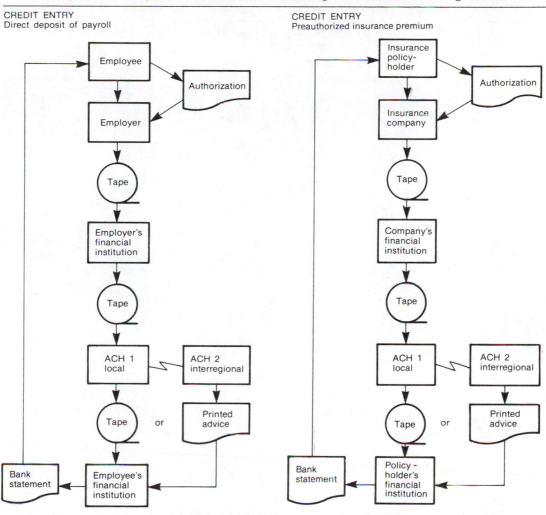

Source: Earl G. Hamilton, "An Update on the Automated Clearinghouse," *Federal Reserve Bulletin*, July 1979, p. 526.

recent years. For example, Allison [1] points out that the ACH system processed about 160 million U.S. Treasury payments and 60 million commercial transactions in 1980. More than 13,000 financial institutions and about 7,000 corporations participate regularly in ACH transactions. Figure 23–5 indicates the volume of commercial and government transactions through ACHs in April 1979. As that figure shows, government is the biggest user of ACH services.

Figure 23–5 The Volume of Different Types of Commercial and Government Transactions Handled through Federal Reserve-Operated Automated Clearinghouses

Number of Commercial ACH Items Processed at Federal Reserve Banks, April 1979, by Type

Federal Reserve District	Number			Percent of District Total		
	Debits	Credits	Prenotifications	Debits	Credits	Prenotifications
Boston	21,756	146,542	5,748	12.5%	84.2%	3.3%
New York	189,771	16,685	23,925	82.4	7.2	10.4
Philadelphia	2,204	11,442	516	15.6	80.8	3.6
Cleveland	145,582	147,449	5,439	48.8	49.4	1.8
Richmond	141,417	89,922	11,927	58.1	37.0	4.9
Atlanta	119,171	49,015	15,825	64.8	26.6	8.6
Chicago	51,937	97,427	8,362	32.9	61.8	5.3
St. Louis	40,119	24,445	2,046	60.2	36.7	3.1
Minneapolis	20,405	65,407	2,102	23.2	74.4	2.4
Kansas City	158,103	64,489	10,586	67.8	27.7	4.5
Dallas	4,835	25,897	1,187	15.1	81.1	3.8
San Francisco	102,652	203,122	35,433	30.1	59.5	10.4
Total	997,952	941,842	123,096	48.4%	45.7%	5.9%

Number of Government ACH Items Processed at Federal Reserve Banks, April 1979, by Type

Federal Reserve District	Number		Percent of District Total	
	Social Security Payments	Other Government Payments	Social Security Payments	Other Government Payments
Boston	512,920	104,893	83.0%	17.0%
New York	928,767	115,573	88.9	11.1
Philadelphia	357,453	83,972	81.0	19.0
Cleveland	402,604	192,174	67.7	32.3
Richmond	474,771	296,828	61.5	38.5
Atlanta	865,409	392,282	68.8	31.2
Chicago	1,117,741	164,216	87.2	12.8
St. Louis	404,429	122,391	76.7	23.3
Minneapolis	300,015	106,899	73.7	26.3
Kansas City	554,995	249,084	69.0	31.0
Dallas	488,239	327,847	59.8	40.2
San Francisco	1,608,971	560,119	74.2	25.8
Total	8,016,314	2,716,278	79.9%	20.1%

Source: Earl G. Hamilton, "An Update on the Automated Clearinghouse," *Federal Reserve Bulletin*, July 1979, pp. 525–31.

The ACH system is tied closely to the Fed's wire transfer network discussed earlier. This network really includes three wire channels—Interdistrict Fed Wire, Interdistrict Bulk Data, and Local District Networks. The last of these wire networks serves payment and financial data needs within each Federal Reserve district. The first two wire networks move data between the Federal Reserve banks and the Federal Reserve Board and are used to make ACH payments.[17] Additional ACH services are also available through (1) CHIPS, the Clearing House Interbank Payment System, which is part of the New York Clearing House Association and is set up to process payments affecting bank reserve accounts; (2) SWIFT, which is an international payments system serving foreign and U.S. banks organized by the Society of Worldwide Interbank Financial Telecommunications; and (3) Bank Wire, which is an interbank system serving about 200 U.S. commercial banks.

The ACH system has several important advantages for the customer over the older paper-check system. For one thing, errors are less likely and more easily resolved. Moreover, reversal of transactions can be made, and depositors can be assured of funds availability on a particular business day, in contrast to the delays often involved in clearing and verifying checks.[18]

The revolution represented by electronic banking has raised a number of important issues in the public policy field. As discussed below, these issues center on the right of the customer to protect his or her privacy, how much competition should be permitted in the provision of EFT facilities, what institutions should have access to EFT systems, who should pay for the installation and operation of those facilities, the proper roles of federal and state regulatory agencies, and the implications of the spread of EFTS for the conduct of monetary policy.

KEY ISSUES IN EFTS

---

[17]The Fed is currently updating its communications network to a system labeled FRCS-80, an acronym for Federal Reserve Communications System for the 80s. It will consolidate all three wire networks into one with greater capacity, security, and speed at lower cost. One important advantage of the new system is greater use of check truncation in which data on paper checks is translated into electronic signals to speed up check collection. In effect, FRCS-80 represents the most recent and significant step in the development of a nationwide automated clearinghouse, which links—through the Federal Reserve banks—all major regions of the nation.

[18]See Hamilton [15], p. 525. There may also be substantial cost savings to taxpayers because of the government's heavy use of the ACH system. When the government can pay its bills through an ACH instead of a check, it saves an estimated 12 cents per payment (Hamilton [15], p. 529). Business users also save significantly on labor time, capital, and postage. The cost advantage of ACH funds transfer over the writing of checks depends, of course, upon the volume of transactions processed. A detailed scale-economies study by Humphrey [17] shows that at low processing volumes the average cost of regular check clearings through Federal Reserve offices is substantially below the average cost of images processed through an ACH. However, Humphrey finds that average production costs *fall* at an ACH when processing volume rises, but check processing costs rise significantly with increases in processing volume. Interestingly, Humphrey finds that wire-transfer costs tend to remain constant as processing volume rises.

Customer Privacy

Computers in the financial services field permit the recording of more detailed information on each customer and ready access to that information on the part of those able to tap computer files. This opens up a variety of possibilities for the use of such information, not all of which are in the best interest of customers. For example, if funds can be moved from one account or location to another electronically, they can be stolen by well-trained individuals who can gain access to computer files.

Examples of computer fraud and electronic theft abound. Not long ago, after precoded checks and deposit slips first appeared, bearing account numbers in magnetic ink for automated processing, a clever individual worked out a system for stealing deposits as they came into a local bank. This individual simply removed blank deposit slips from the bank's lobby and replaced them with slips imprinted magnetically with his own account number. The result was that customers coming into the bank to make a deposit were unknowingly contributing their funds to this particular individual's account. A few days later, after the thief had left town, the bank was deluged with calls from irate customers who had not received proper credit in their accounts for their most recent deposits.

No electronic funds system is completely and totally safe from tampering by someone with the necessary skill and desire to profit from the information it contains. Just as fraudulent checks and counterfeiting have plagued the paper money system for decades, so the electronic money system will have its own inherent weaknesses which those who elect to evade the law can use to their advantage. The best that can be done is to make unauthorized invasion of the system both difficult and costly.

More significant to some observers is the prospect that various groups and government agencies (such as the IRS, for example) will use computerized banking files to snoop on the private financial affairs of individuals and businesses. The basic concern here is a philosophical one—that the advent of a world analogous to George Orwell's *1984* will emerge in which Big Brother (presumably, a big, all-emcompassing government overseer) knows so much about everyone that individual freedom, privacy, and initiative will be trampled.

The esoteric nature of such fears makes them particularly difficult to analyze and assess. Computerized files containing financial data on businesses and households certainly make it easier to tap pertinent information (some of which may be incriminating). However, *if* the customer knows of such activities, there *are* legal remedies and protections offered by federal and state laws to deal with them. One source of concern is that EFTS makes it easier to access such information without the customer knowing. While there are no easy answers to this problem, it is important to point out that concern for privacy of personal records was one of the key reasons Congress created the National Commission on Electronic Funds Transfer (NCEFT) in 1974. It is charged with the responsibility of finding ways to expedite the development of nationwide EFTS, while simultaneously protecting the rights of the public to be secure from unreasonable and unnecessary invasions of personal privacy.

Acting under directives from the NCEFT, the Fed maintains ACH computer records containing individual and business names no longer than 30 days after a transaction has taken place through an ACH. Microfiche transactions data showing individual transactions are kept no longer than 60 days after settlement. The Federal Reserve refuses to disclose the content of individual financial transactions to anyone except to parties involved in the transaction or in response to a court order.

Fostering Competition and Efficiency

Another key issue surrounding the development of EFTS centers on the often conflicting goals of increased *competition* to protect the consumer of financial services, and greater *efficiency* in providing EFT services at minimal resource cost. The goals of minimizing the cost of resources used in constructing and operating EFT systems would appear to be best handled by limiting the number of competing systems. Thus it might be better to install only one ATM in a shopping center with lines to all area financial institutions rather than for each institution to install its own ATM in the same shopping center. Similarly, one automated clearinghouse serving a region seems preferable to several, each one serving one or a few institutions. The problem with this limited-alternative, "public utility" approach to EFTS is that it may discourage competition in providing more and better EFT services at lower prices to the customer. The public-utility approach may inhibit innovation in developing and using *new* EFT technology. For example, if a group of banks in the local area decide to share in a single automated teller or point-of-sale terminal, there may be great hesitation to upgrade the facility with better equipment until the existing equipment is fully paid for.

While this controversy between the public-utility approach—shared EFT facilities—and the competitive approach—several parallel EFT systems—is likely to go on for some time, a partial resolution seems to be emerging. Many *retail* EFT systems (principally ATMs, RSUs, and POS terminals) are following the *competitive* model, with depository institutions competing with each other to find prime locations for their respective machines (though some sharing, especially in shopping centers, is also going on). In contrast, *wholesale* EFT systems (principally automated clearinghouses) appear to be following the public-utility model. (Indeed, if as Humphrey [17] suggests, the average cost curve for ACH transactions declines continuously as the volume of transactions increases, the production of ACH services may be a *natural monopoly*. This would suggest that a *single* firm or government agency (such as the Federal Reserve System) should provide ACH facilities for the nation's payments system.) Competing financial institutions typically are all served by one basic ACH system, operated by the Fed. The National Commission on Electronic Funds Transfer has argued that the Fed *must* play a prominent role in operating ACHs because the private sector cannot yet do so efficiently.[19]

The role of the Federal Reserve as the principal "public utility" in the nation's payments system dates from the Fed's earliest days. The Federal Reserve Act of 1913 spelled out Congress' desire that the Fed assume ultimate responsibility for the efficiency and integrity of the country's payments system. The 1913 law directed that reserve accounts held at the Fed by depository institutions be employed to clear payments transactions among institutions participating in the system. This responsibility was reaffirmed when Congress passed and President Carter signed into law the Depository Institutions Deregulation and Monetary Control Act of 1980. The 1980 law charged the Fed with the mission of promoting competition, improving efficiency, and insuring a sufficient quality of payments services throughout the United States. All depository intermediaries must be granted access to the Fed's payments system, and the charges for services rendered must be uniform and high enough to cover the total cost of providing those services.

The Fed now charges for *all* payments services. This includes check processing, wire transfers, cash settlement, transfer of securities, ACH transactions, and shipments of currency and coin. As we noted earlier, the Monetary Control Act of 1980 requires the Fed to charge prices high enough to cover full service costs (including an allowance for finance charges and taxes which a private firm would normally have to carry to provide comparable, competing services). This is to give private companies an opportunity to compete with the Fed in both check processing and funds transfer.

Branch Banking

Branch banking—whether it should be permitted and where—has been the center of a storm of controversy in U.S. banking for more than a century. Proponents of allowing individual banks to set up branch offices whenever and wherever there is sufficient public need argue that the consumer is better served (especially more conveniently) and that branch banks are more stable and less prone to failure. Opponents of branching

---

[19]See Allison [1], p. 23.

stress the danger of excessive power concentrated in a few hands, since branch banks average much larger than unit (single-office) banks and often buy out smaller banks, converting them into branch offices. Moreover, it is alleged, branch banks often ignore the small customer (particularly individuals and small businesses) in favor of large corporations and siphon funds away from local communities into major money centers. Opponents of branching have generally held sway in the state legislatures, so that many states prohibit or at least limit bank-branching powers. Federal law, principally the McFadden Act (1927), prohibits branching across state lines.[20]

EFTS has brought a whole new dimension to the age-old branch banking question. Essentially, antibranching laws erect geographical barriers to the growth of individual banks. A bank may desire to set up offices in a distant city, but state law and possibly also federal law may prevent it from doing so. But what if the bank decides to set up automated teller machines in that same city—remote service units (RSUs) which accept deposits and dispense cash? Alternatively, POS terminals could be installed in the city's retail stores? Would this be a violation of federal and state antibranching laws?

The courts have given mixed signals in response to this question. Some have ruled that limited-service facilities such as RSUs and POS terminals in stores are *not* the equivalent of full-service branches. Others have argued, to the contrary, that terminals and teller machines are an extension of branch banking. Since deposits can be accepted and credit card loans often can be granted through terminals and teller machines, they are, in effect, branches and therefore subject to federal and state antibranching laws. In Texas, for example, it was ruled that ATMs in locations remote from a bank's main building were in violation of that state's constitution, which allows a bank to offer its services through one and only one office. It took a statewide referendum in 1978 to exempt ATMs and RSUs from Texas' constitutional prohibition against branch banking. The EFTS-branching controversy reminds us of an important truth about electronic money systems today: *the principal barriers to EFTS growth and expansion are legal and social, not a matter of lacking the necessary technology.*[21] If public fears about snooping into private affairs and about computer fraud, along with the fears of some banker groups over the spread of branch banking, can be dealt with adequately, there are few remaining obstacles to a national or even international electronic payments system involving both customers and the financial institutions that serve them.

---

[20]See Chapter 8 for a more complete discussion of the branch banking issue.

[21]See, for example, Rose [27].

What Financial Institutions Should Have Access to EFTS?

Branch banking and EFTS are a *market structure* issue: How many financial institutions should be allowed to offer EFT services in a given market area? Who should be permitted to enter a new market with EFT services? These questions apply not only to the branching powers of banks, but also to the entry of nonbank financial institutions into the payments mechanism. For example, suppose we live in an area where local commercial banks have set up an automated clearinghouse to handle interbank transactions and have agreed to share in a network of ATMs and POS terminals housed in local retail stores and shopping centers. Suppose, too, that local credit unions, savings banks, and savings and loan associations begin offering checkable deposits (such as NOWs, share drafts, and money market accounts). Should these nonbank depository institutions be allowed access to the automated clearinghouse? The ATMs? The POS terminal network? If the answer is yes, on what basis should access be granted? Who will pay the cost of those facilities?

These questions have cropped up all over the United States in recent years. And, in most instances, nonbank institutions *have* gained access (sometimes only after a long battle in the courts) to existing EFT facilities or have set up parallel facilities of their own. The result, quite obviously, has been accelerated competition for the customer's payments account. In turn, the resulting intense competitive struggle has caused institutions offering payment and credit services to pay more attention to the costing and pricing of those same services.

EFTS and Monetary Policy

There is some concern on the part of bankers, economists, and government officials that the spread of EFTS may make it harder for the Federal Reserve to manage the nation's supply of money and credit. In other words, the Fed's job of carrying out monetary policy might just be more difficult because the spread of EFT devices will result in less Fed control over the money supply and the economy. To take just one example: The Fed must keep track of the flow of funds between checkbook deposits and savings deposits (including CDs and money market accounts) in order to control the growth of bank reserves—the principal determinant of money and credit growth. If the volume of funds flowing from checking accounts to savings balances goes up, the banking system gains more excess reserves for lending, *ceteris paribus*, because reserve requirements are much lower on savings accounts. In the absence of countermoves by the Fed, the banking system will manufacture additional credit, perhaps fueling the fires of inflation.

But EFT blurs the distinction between checking and savings accounts. EFT makes it possible to move funds into and out of money balances instantaneously and therefore consumers and businesses can minimize their transactions balances and stay more fully invested in higher-yielding assets. The Fed may have great difficulty deciding exactly how much money is in the system and what its rate of growth is. Thus the Fed cannot base its estimate of the public's spending power solely on the size of checking accounts and other transactions deposits. A broader definition of the nation's money supply (such as M2 or M3, for example) would be needed.[22]

Unfortunately, it is not clear at this juncture that the Federal Reserve can as accurately control broader measures of money as it can a more narrowly defined money measure such as M1. One obvious problem is that, with different reserve requirements on different kinds of transactions and savings accounts, as funds shift from one type of account to another there are differential effects on the banking system's reserve balances and therefore on the system's ability to create money and credit. Because most of the growth in the nation's money supply normally comes from credit creation—lending and investing by banks and other depository institutions—the Federal Reserve could be confronted with a far more difficult money management problem than in the past.

Another concern linking EFT and monetary policy concerns the *velocity* (i.e., rate of turnover) of the nation's money supply. The particular focus of this issue centers upon the behavior of money-income velocity (V_Y)—that is,

$$V_Y = GNP/MS \qquad (23\text{--}1)$$

where MS measures liquid transactions balances (such as those included in the M1 definition of the U.S. money supply) and GNP is, of course, the dollar value of the nation's annual output of new goods and services. Presumably, the widespread use of EFT will increase the velocity or turnover rate of money balances. Each dollar of money can be employed more intensively during the year, leading perhaps to more spending. Thus, since

$$MS \times V_Y = GNP \qquad (23\text{--}2)$$

a rise in money-income velocity (V_Y), without a corresponding reduction in the money stock (MS), will produce an increase in money GNP. Unless there is substantial unemployment and underutilization of productive capacity in the economy, prices of goods and services will rise, leading to more rapid inflation. Equally damaging, income velocity might become more *unstable*, making it difficult for the Federal Reserve to predict velocity and offset its effects by making appropriate changes in the rate of

---

[22]See Chapter 5 for a discussion of the various definitions of the U.S. money supply now in use.

growth of the nation's money supply. This would make the Fed's monetary policy tools (such as open-market operations) less effective.

There are no easy answers to such policy problems. Indeed, the EFT-monetary policy issue is part of a larger field of study and of public policy centering upon the changing nature of payments methods and technological innovation.

WHAT THE FUTURE EFT FINANCIAL SYSTEM MAY LOOK LIKE

As the foregoing discussion in this chapter suggests, the nation's payments system is in turmoil and is passing through an era of transition. The broad outlines or features of the future electronic payments system are discernible, but many of the casualties and consequences are difficult to assess at this time.[23]

Certainly funds and financial data will move more rapidly from payments accounts to savings and back again. Businesses, consumers, and governments are becoming more sensitive to the idea of *continuous money management*. This means constantly monitoring money balances, keeping only a minimal amount of money in a transactions account, and quickly moving surplus balances into the highest available investment vehicles until more transactions funds are needed. More and more financial institutions will find themselves under pressure to join the developing electronic payments network just to get a piece of the action.

One of the exciting and potentially fruitful transactions systems of the future is *home and office banking*. Earlier in this chapter we noted that limited experiments with banking information transmitted into homes via TV sets were being conducted. Actually, the customer may not only shop for banking services through a home or office TV, but for other things as well (such as information from a local library or inventories of goods available in stores). Indeed, TV banking *and* telephone banking, by reaching into the home or place of work, in effect makes each customer a branch office.[24] The result is less need for brick-and-mortar buildings, hopefully less need for paper, and perhaps even less need down the road for other EFT devices such as ATMs, RSUs, and POS terminals. Deposits, bill payments, and transfers of funds into investments can be accomplished readily at home or at the office without the necessity of driving to the bank or to a security broker's office. It may even be possible to take out a loan via telephone and video screen. In some cases, such loans will represent automatic drawings on a line of credit previously arranged between customer and bank. However, it should be possible eventually to

---

[23]The discussion in this section depends, in part, on an earlier article by Rose [27] in *The Canadian Banker and ICB Review*.

[24]See Kemmer and Smith [20].

apply for a new loan (or seek an extension of an old loan) by electronically transmitting the loan application and supporting financial statements to the loan officer. Once the loan is approved, the loan officer can electronically credit the customer's transactions account for the approved loan amount.

All in all, people will have less need for personal contact with the financial institutions that hold their accounts. Time is the most precious resource for most people (particularly in families where all adults work) so that speed, convenience, and accuracy are highly valued and eagerly sought after. In recent years, relatively high energy costs have placed a significant premium on minimizing travel time. With telephones, terminals, and, on an international scale, microwave transmissions and communications satellites, the necessity for expensive travel to negotiate and finalize financial transactions will be greatly diminished. Indeed, several motel chains have recognized this of late and are now installing teleconference facilities which permit busy executives to gather at local motels and confer with other executives hundreds or thousands of miles away, each without leaving their own home town.

Most certainly, *competition* among financial institutions will intensify in the developing EFT environment. Greater convenience for the customer in carrying out financial transactions will also make it easier for that same customer to shop around for financial bargains. Those institutions offering more investment options, greater ease of access to their systems, and superior accuracy and record-keeping services will have a clear competitive advantage. The *price* of financial services will become even more important to the average customer because it will become increasingly easier to *compare* both service packages *and* prices. Loyalty to a single financial institution, already eroding in an inflation-plagued, high-interest-rate environment, should be greatly diminished. The customer will be able to quickly search out the best deal—lowest loan rate, highest investment yield, lowest service fees or commissions, etc.—and patronize the particular institution offering the best deal at any particular time. The next time the same customer enters the financial marketplace seeking the same services, he or she may readily switch to another financial institution whose prices and service package look better at that time.

As they have in the 1970s and early 1980s, markets for financial services will continue to broaden, covering wider and wider geographic areas. Already the so-called national market for large corporate loans has become a true international market, centering on Eurocurrency credits and Eurocurrency interest rates (such as LIBOR—the London interbank offer rate—on short-term Eurodollar deposits, which serves as a base rate for many large business loans today). Dramatic improvements in communications have broadened the financial markets to a global scale, necessarily bringing into the common competitive fray many new suppliers and customers. Hopefully, out of this increasingly intense competitive struggle will emerge solid benefits for customers—a wider array of better-quality financial services at more reasonable prices.

There are also major implications from the spread of EFTS for the cost structure of participating financial institutions and for the kinds of employee skills that will be needed in the future. For one thing, the provision of important financial services—especially the making of payments and financial record keeping—will require greater use of capital equipment, which generally carries heavy fixed costs and less use of labor time, a variable-cost resource. This shift towards greater fixed and less variable costs has critical implications for the profit margins and viability of individual financial institutions. In general, the industry's changing cost structure calls for larger financial institutions which can bear the cost of electronic services. Perhaps, however, smaller financial institutions will be able to develop better cost-sharing arrangements with other institutions. Those institutions unable to offer competitive EFT service packages alone or in combination with other financial intermediaries will find themselves in danger of losing key customers and, increasingly, in risk of failure.[25]

What does EFTS mean for the kinds of employee skills banks and other financial institutions will need in the future? There is little doubt that individuals skilled in credit analysis and financial counseling will continue to be in demand because the credit function will still be at the heart of financial operations. Similarly, financial intermediaries will continue to be heavy purchasers of debt securities, requiring continuing expertise in investment analysis and security trading. However, routine, everyday transactions in banking—accepting deposits, dispensing cash, collecting loan payments, and transferring funds between transactions and investment accounts—should continue their drift away from human processing towards machine processing. Those individuals skilled in computer soft-

---

[25]One factor which may blunt the economies-of-scale advantages possessed today by large financial institutions is the tendency for computer equipment costs to fall in recent years. Smaller and cheaper computers with capacity and versatility rivaling much larger machines are continually emerging. If these costs continue to fall, even the smallest institutions can still get a piece of the action. Then, too, there may still be important channels open to the smallest financial intermediaries, even in an EFT-dominated financial system. There will still be, presumably, a sizeable cadre of customers preferring personalized service over the speed and efficiency of computers. Beyond this, small institutions can join together through consortiums and pool their available resources or purchase membership in a funds-transfer system run by larger financial institutions. Indeed, there is already a history of joint computer ventures by banks and savings and loan associations, some of these in the form of local clearinghouses. Moreover, just as there was strong incentive in the past for larger, upstream banks to attract the correspondent deposit accounts of smaller, downstream banks, there may continue to be such an incentive for the marketing of EFT services among smaller institutions' clientele.

ware and hardware, therefore, will be in heavy demand, along with those attuned to communications technology. There will be more room for employees who have creative skills in designing service packages for customers and organizational skills in managing human and material resources, but less room for those who perform the more routine tasks requiring little creativity or organizing ability. In brief, among financial institutions, we are moving rapidly toward an era of intense competition which favors the technically well-trained, yet creative individual who possesses a strong desire for professional success and personal fulfillment.

SUMMARY

EFTS—the use of computers and other electronic devices to speed the transfer of funds and other financial data—is gaining widespread public notice and attention today. Many EFT devices have become popular with selected groups of businesses and consumers. Particularly noteworthy today is the growing use of automated teller machines (ATM), remote-service teller units (RSUs), wire transfers of large business payments, automatic deposits of payrolls and government checks, and automatic transfers between checking and savings deposits. These electronic devices are often referred to as *retail* EFTS since they reach the customer directly. Increasingly popular on the *wholesale* EFTS level—that is, electronic transfers between financial institutions—is the automated clearinghouse, replacing the transporting of checks and other paper items between financial institutions with transfers of accounting information via computer tape. Thus the clearing of checks and other cash items is accomplished with greater speed and accuracy.

The soaring costs of paper, transportation, and labor time suggest that EFTS will become an ever more popular, cost-effective alternative to writing checks and other paper-based payments methods in the future. An added plus factor for EFTS is greater *convenience*, saving customers time and trouble and providing handy records of transactions via computer printouts. However, the EFT revolution now engulfing the banking industry is not without its problems and pitfalls. Funds can be stolen by those individuals skilled enough to manipulate computer files. Moreover, a computer-based information system makes it easier for government and other institutions to snoop on the private financial affairs of businesses and households. Individual privacy becomes more vulnerable to attack by those with vested interests in such information.

There are also growing problems in the area of banking structure— should all financial institutions in a given market be permitted to develop competing EFT systems? Or should EFT facilities be *shared* to minimize the quantity of scarce resources used by the nation's payments system? Who should make that decision? And, if at least some EFT facilities are to be shared, who should pay for them and on what basis? Moreover, are

EFT facilities (particularly ATMs and RSUs) branch offices, and, therefore, in violation of state and federal antibranching laws? The courts and legal authorities are divided on such questions.

Beyond these issues is a broader question of how EFTS might affect the government's pursuit of economic policy, particularly monetary policy carried out by the Federal Reserve System. Perhaps more widespread use of EFT devices will alter the velocity and rate of growth of the nation's money supply, adding to the Federal Reserve's already difficult problems of trying to control the growth of the nation's supply of money and credit. Ultimately, the nation as a whole might suffer from less satisfactory control of inflation, unemployment, and economic growth. On this and other important issues surrounding the growing use of EFTS, we must await the verdict of detailed research and observation. One point is certain, however—the future holds greater and greater use of electronic means to move financial data between one financial institution and another and between customer accounts. For better or worse, electronic forms of money are alive and spreading rapidly.

Questions

23–1. What factors in the banking system and the economy are stimulating the development of EFT systems?

23–2. How are checks usually cleared? Explain how EFTS can improve upon conventional check-clearing processes. Be sure to consider the costs of conventional clearing methods.

23–3. Under what circumstances would full electronic processing of payments be economically viable? What does research evidence have to contribute in answering this question?

23–4. Explain the difference between wholesale and retail EFTS. What is an ACH? POS terminal? ATM? RSU?

23–5. What are the principal barriers to the widespread use of EFTS at the retail level? In your opinion, how serious are these barriers likely to be in the future?

23–6. Explain the links between EFTS and the branch-banking issue. Do you think the coming of EFTS would hasten the adoption of interstate or even nationwide branch banking? Why?

23–7. What is the access issue in the EFTS field? Explain why it is important and to whom.

23–8. How, in your opinion, will the widespread adoption of EFTS affect the pricing of financial services? Will it benefit the consumer? Why or why not?

23–9. What factors appear to affect customer acceptance of EFT facilities? Devise a simple marketing plan to promote greater customer usage and acceptance of electronic money machines.

23–10. Is there a possible link between EFTS and monetary policy? Explain. Would nationwide EFTS make the Federal Reserve's job of regulating money and credit easier or harder?

References

1. Allison, Theodore E. "The Federal Reserve's Role in the Payments Mechanism and Its Communications Plan." *Economic Review*, Federal Reserve Bank of Richmond, LVXVIII, no. 2, pp. 21–25.

2. "Bank One of Ohio to Launch Test of In-House Video Banking." *The American Bankers*, January 22, 1980, pp. 1, 16.

3. "Bankers Hope EFTs Can Melt Industry's Blizzard of Paper." *Financial Trend*, March 20–26, 1982, p. 10.

4. Bequai, August. "Legal Liabilities of EFT System." *Magazine of Bank Administration*, January 1983.

5. Board of Governors of the Federal Reserve System. "EFT and Privacy." *Federal Reserve Bulletin*, April 1978, pp. 279–84.

6. _____. Press release. Washington, D.C., March 8, 1983.

7. _____. *Annual Report of Congress on the Electronic Funds Transfer Act, 1981.* Washington, D.C., May 10, 1982.

8. "City National Makes Electronic Banking Work." *Business Week*, February 27, 1978, p. 76.

9. Cohen, Allen M. "The Growth of Corporate Electronic Banking." *Bankers Monthly*, June 15, 1982, pp. 20–23.

10. Damon, Davlin. "Home-Banking Network Due in Florida in September, but Cost May Limit Appeal." *The Wall Street Journal*, February 23, 1983, p. 10.

11. Federal Reserve Bank of New York, Public Information Department. *The Story of Checks and Electronic Payments.* New York: 1981.

12. Fielitz, Bruce D., and Daniel L. White. "An Evaluation and Linking of Alternative Solution Procedures for the Lock Box Location Problem." *Journal of Bank Research*, Spring 1982, pp. 17–27.

13. Goodfriend, Marvin, James Parthemos, and Bruce Summers. "Recent Financial Innovations: Causes, Consequences for the Payments System and Implications for Monetary Control." *Economic Review*, Federal Reserve Bank of Richmond, March/April 1980, pp. 14–27.

14. Grandstaff, Mary G., and Charles F. Smaistrla. "A Primer on Electronic Funds Transfer." *Business Review*, Federal Reserve Bank of Dallas, September 1976.

15. Hamilton, Earl G. "An Update on the Automated Clearinghouse." *Federal Reserve Bulletin*, July 1979, pp. 525–31.

16. Hood, Jerry M. "Demographics of ATMs." *The Bankers Magazine*, November–December 1979, pp. 68–71.

17. Humphrey, David B. *Cost, Scale Economies, Competition and Product Mix in the U.S. Payments Merchanism*. Staff economic study no. 115. Board of Governors of the Federal Reserve System, Washington, D.C., April 1982.

18. Johnson, J. G., and E. C. Arnold. "EFT—Changes That May Shape Its Future." *Bankers Monthly*, June 15, 1979, pp. 14–16.

19. Keith, Robert W., and Alfred O. Stromquist. "Bank Personnel Forecast: A Background for Planning for the '80s." *ABA Banking Journal*, November 1979, pp. 77, 80, 82, 85, 86.

20. Kemmer, Rick, and David M. Smith. "Telephone Banking—Careful Planning Can Make It Work." *The Magazine of Bank Administration*, January 1980, pp. 25–27.

21. Kutler, Jeffrey. "Pioneer Takes a Closer Look at EFTs." *American Banker*, January 31, 1980.

22. Martin, Stan, and Don Clark. "Moving to ATM's: An Analytical Approach." *Magazine of Bank Administration*, December 1982, pp. 28–38.

23. "MasterCard Introduces a Card That's Designed to Stop Counterfeiters." *The Wall Street Journal*, March 2, 1983, p. 30.

24. Padilla, Marie T. "Home-Banking Tests Begin in a Few Places, but the New Systems May Be Slow to Spread." *The Wall Street Journal*, January 27, 1983.

25. "Pension Payers Move to Eliminate Paper Checks." *The Wall Street Journal*, February 24, 1983, p. 1.

26. Randle, William M. "ATMs Are Properly a Full Component of Any Strategy for Retail Banking." *The American Banker*, January 9, 1980, p. 47.

27. Rose, Peter S. "People, Machines, and the Future of Banking." *The Canadian Banker and ICB Review*, no. 6 (December 1980), pp. 56–61.

28. Smaistrla, Charles F. "Electronic Funds Transfer and Monetary Policy." *Business Review*, Federal Reserve Bank of Dallas, August 1977, pp. 6–12.

29. Snellings, Aubrey N. "The Financial Services Industry: Recent Trends and Future Prospects." *Economic Review*, Federal Reserve Bank of Richmond, January/February 1980, pp. 3–8.

30. Stone, Bernell K., and Ned C. Hill. "Alternative Cash Transfer Mechanisms and Methods: Evaluation Framework." *Journal of Bank Research*, spring 1982, pp. 7–16.

31. Van der Velde, Marjolijn. "EFT Transactions: Growth and Direction." *Magazine of Bank Administration*, December 1982, pp. 36–38.

32. _____. "Home Banking: Where It Stands Today." *Magazine of Bank Administration*, September 1982, pp. 16–19.

33. Varvel, Walter A., and John R. Walter. "The Competition for Transactions Accounts." *Economic Review*, Federal Reserve Bank of Richmond, March/April 1982, pp. 2–20.

34. White, George C. "Electronic Banking and Its Impact on the Future." *The Magazine of Bank Administration*, December 1979, pp. 39–42.

24. *International Financial Institutions: Growth and Implications*

T HE OPERATIONS OF FINANCIAL INSTITUTIONS have increasingly become international in scope. Larger depository institutions—especially commercial banks—have sought funds from "off-shore" sources and often placed these funds with "off-shore" borrowers. United States commercial banks have expanded overseas through numerous branches and affiliates, while foreign commercial banks have established offices in the United States and have also acquired a number of U.S. banks. Nondepository financial institutions, such as life insurance companies, pension funds, and investment companies, have spread internationally through acquiring the securities of foreign firms and governments worldwide. Brokers and dealers have increasingly performed their market-making and underwriting functions within a multinational framework. The spread of domestic financial institutions throughout the world has, indeed, internationalized the nature of financial institutions and has made it difficult to understand the role of financial institutions without adopting a worldwide perspective.

The present chapter discusses selected aspects of the internationalization of financial institutions. It concentrates on commercial banks because this largest of all financial institutions has been extremely active in international activities, though international activities of other important financial institutions are discussed where appropriate. The chapter concentrates on the following topics: (1) the importance of U.S. banks abroad and of foreign banks in the United States,[1] (2) multinational banking, encompassing a discussion of retail and wholesale activities of multinational

---

[1]It is necessary to recognize that commercial banks outside the United States are generally allowed to perform a much wider range of financial functions than banks operating in domestic markets. For example, the separation in the United States between commercial banking and investment banking is not a common practice internationally. Hence the discussion of the international activities of commercial banks is actually broader in scope than the term *commercial banking* would indicate.

banks, (3) Eurodollar borrowing and lending, (4) the evaluation of risk in international lending, and (5) issues in the internationalization of financial institutions.

U.S. Banks Abroad

U.S. banks play a vital role in providing funds for international commerce and investment. They have led in the growth and development of multinational banking facilities to serve foreign governments, agencies, and multinational corporations, especially corporations based in the United States. Until the mid-1970s, the foreign banking activities of U.S. banks were centered mainly in their overseas offices due to federal government controls. Beginning in 1963 the federal government restricted foreign lending from domestic banking offices in order to reduce the outflow of capital from the United States and strengthen the American balance-of-payments position. However, in 1974 the Nixon Administration relaxed government controls on foreign loans. The result has been an aggressive expansion of international banking services provided by the domestic offices of American banks as well as by their foreign offices and subsidiaries. And, as we will see shortly, there is a trend today toward more international financial services provided by domestic offices and fewer provided by offices located in overseas markets.

U.S. bankers have developed a number of different organizational forms to aid them in overseas operations. The larger American banks typically operate branch offices in major financial centers, where the host country permits them to offer a full line of conventional banking services. However, in many countries (Mexico is a good example) U.S. banks and other foreign-based banking organizations are not permitted to operate full-service branches. In these instances or where the risks or costs of a full branching system appear to be too high, U.S. banks have used other organizational devices to secure a foothold. One such device is the representative office, which makes contacts with potential loan and deposit customers in the host country and refers identified customer leads back to the home office. Where risks or competition appears to be particularly steep, U.S. multinational banks frequently will cooperate with foreign banks through joint ventures, consortiums, or correspondent arrangements. If host-country laws prohibit majority control of a domestic firm by U.S. banks, a minority ownership interest in a foreign bank or other business may be sought to give U.S. banks at least a toe-hold in a desirable overseas market.[2]

---

[2]Houpt and Martinson [8] provide an extensive treatment of the reasons for growth of foreign subsidiaries of U.S. banking organizations.

Smaller U.S. banks frequently carry on international operations principally through their domestic offices. However, if a bank hopes to achieve a high volume of international transactions with a secure position in foreign markets, it is virtually a must to have office facilities, staffed by well-trained professionals, present in the market area to be served. Local customers often demand to have a point of convenient contact with their principal banks. While U.S. banks have been represented in foreign markets (particularly in Western Europe) for many decades, the international activities of U.S. banks really gathered momentum after 1960 due to strong demands for credit abroad and foreign interest rates relatively higher than those in the U.S. During the late 1960s and 1970s, the U.S. economy expanded at a rapid pace with burgeoning credit demands. Larger U.S. banks began viewing foreign markets (especially the Eurodollar market) as a prime source of loanable funds to supplement domestic deposits in order to accommodate customer demand for loanable funds. This was also a period during which the Federal Reserve System pursued tight credit policies which restricted the growth of domestic deposits by making bank reserves more scarce, not allowing federal deposit interest-rate ceilings (such as Regulation Q) to be raised fast enough to keep up with market interest rates, and occasionally raising reserve requirements on domestic sources of funds. Thus many U.S. banks, especially the largest, turned to the Eurodollar markets, where ample dollar-denominated deposits were available due to huge American balance-of-payments deficits and the complete absence of interest-rate ceilings. Borrowings of Eurodollar deposits by domestic banks increased sharply in periods when U.S. interest rates rose toward record levels such as during the late 1960s and early 1970s and again late in the decade of the 70s.

Assets of Foreign Offices of U.S. Banks

International banking data provided by the Federal Reserve System shows that the assets held by foreign branches of American banks reached $463 billion in 1982 (see Table 24–1). Though just 13 U.S. banks operated foreign branches in 1965, the number had jumped to over 100 by year-end 1982. Latin America and the Caribbean basin still lead the list of nations providing a home for the branches of U.S. banks, partially because of their advantageous position as a base for access to the worldwide Eurodollar and Eurocurrency markets. However, other market areas are experiencing at least as rapid a growth as the Caribbean basin in U.S. banking facilities, including the Middle East, West Germany, London, Asia, and the Pacific basin. Latin American and the Caribbean basin account for more U.S. branch offices than any other region, but only in numbers, not dollar volume of assets. Here, the United Kingdom heads the U.S. branch list with the highest portion of total assets—clear testimony to the dominance of London as the centerpiece of Eurodollar and foreign ex-

Table 24–1   Assets and Liabilities of Foreign Branches of U.S. Banks: March 1982 ($ millions)

Assets		
Claims on United States		$ 72,927
Parent bank	$ 48,648	
Other	24,279	
Claims on foreigners		371,045
Other branches of parent banks	89,371	
Banks	146,976	
Nonbank foreigners	108,384	
Other assets		19,204
Total assets		$463,176
Liabilities		
To United States		$149,996
Parent bank	58,439	
Other banks in United States	24,404	
Nonbanks	67,153	
To foreigners		293,705
Other branches of parent banks	85,864	
Banks	117,095	
Official institutions	23,008	
Nonbank foreigners	67,738	
Other liabilities		19,475
Total liabilities		$463,176

Source: Board of Governors of the Federal Reserve System, *Federal Reserve Bulletin*, June 1982.

change trading activity. Of course, we must keep in mind that branching is only one facet of U.S. banking and financial-services activity abroad. Through bank holding company affiliates and bank subsidiaries, U.S. banking organizations operate business finance companies (such as their well-known commercial finance operations in Canada), consumer-oriented finance companies (prevalent in Western Europe), and investment banking houses (many of which are oriented toward the offering of Eurobonds).

Edge Act Banks and International Banking Facilities

Some of the most significant expansions in the role of U.S. banks internationally has come under the power of the 1919 Edge Act (an amendment to the Federal Reserve Act). This act allowed the Federal Reserve Board to permit the establishment of corporations for the purpose of engaging in international or foreign banking. With the passage of the Edge Act, U.S. banks were thereby permitted to engage in foreign banking, either through indirect ownership of foreign banking subsidiaries or through U.S. domestic offices directly related to foreign operations. A large number of banks have now established domestic Edge Act corporations with branches in many cities of the United States in which foreign commerce is important (the Federal Reserve allowed interstate branching for Edge Act corporations beginning in 1979).

The International Banking Facilities (IBFs) represent a very recent and yet potentially very important development in the international activities of US. banks. The Federal Reserve Board authorized—effective in December 1981—U.S. banks to establish separate organizations, referred to as International Banking Facilities, that will be located in the United States but not subject to domestic reserve requirements or interest-rate ceilings. These IBFs may offer time deposits of at least $100,000 with a minimum maturity of only two days, though only to foreign nonbank residents. They can also offer time deposits with a one-day minimum maturity to foreign banks and foreign offices of U.S. banks.

The authorization for U.S. banks to establish IBFs was prompted by the desire to attract a significant share of Eurodollar trading from London and especially from the Caribbean where U.S. banks have established shell branches. IBFs located in the United States are able to offer Eurodollar deposits with less perceived political risk than in many other areas of the world. While foreign investors may have some reluctance to place Eurodollar deposits in U.S. IBFs after the United States froze Iranian assets in the late 1970s, a similar fear may exist with regard to placing Eurodollar funds in London after the British government froze Argentinian assets in London in 1982.[3]

A number of the largest U.S. money-center banks in recent years have generated a majority of their net earnings from overseas lending and from providing other international banking services. In some foreign markets, regulations are less restrictive, competition less intense, and profit opportunities more attractive than is true in domestic banking markets. However, as U.S. banks have expanded abroad, this expansion has added a new dimension to regulatory policy and created a major regulatory problem, particularly for the Federal Reserve. The Fed regulates activities of member banks abroad and of bank holding companies. The Fed must approve foreign bank branches of member banks or of bank holding companies. Nonmember banks, on the other hand, must follow the regulations of their own state banking commission, though most states have not exerted effective control over international banking operations.

In addition to being confronted with different assets and liabilities held by banks active abroad the Federal Reserve also faces a *regulatory equity* problem. Often U.S. banks would be allowed to offer services abroad that they could not offer in the United States, such as purchasing the stock of other business firms and underwriting equities. In contrast, U.S. banks have been forbidden to engage in investment banking for corporate secu-

---

[3]By mid-year 1981 the total assets of International Banking Facilities exceeded $150 billion.

rities since passage of the Glass-Steagall Act in 1933. The Federal Reserve Board, therefore, typically allows U.S. banks to offer a greater variety of services in foreign markets than permitted them inside the United States. This regulatory strategy has been referred to as the *principle of mutual nondiscrimination*—foreign banks should be allowed to operate under basically the same regulations and offer the same array of financial services as domestic banks. Such a regulatory strategy is economical because it eliminates the necessity for establishing a different set of rules for domestic banks than that faced by foreign banks.

Foreign Banks in the United States

Just as U.S. banks have chosen to penetrate foreign markets in growing numbers, foreign banks have come to U.S. shores in ever-increasing numbers over the past several decades. At year-end 1981, total assets of foreign banks chartered and licensed within the continental U.S. exceeded $117 billion (see Table 24–2). The latter figure represents almost 10 percent of all U.S. bank assets. Commercial loans made by foreign banks in the U.S. represent an even larger share of the domestic commercial loan market. British banks (which rank third in number of banking offices in the United States) have set up full-service banking facilities by creating branches and purchasing domestically chartered banks. Canadian banks (which rank second behind Japanese banks in both assets and number of U.S. offices) have used at least three different organizational forms to conduct their operations in the United States: (1) trust companies to provide

Table 24–2   Assets and Liabilities of Foreign Banking Offices in the United States: December 31, 1981 ($ millions)

Financial assets	
U.S. government securities	$ 3,581
State and local government obligations	397
Corporate bonds	1,096
Bank loans	81,688
Open-market paper	5,250
Corporate equities	97
Security credit	1,306
Miscellaneous assets	24,040
Total assets	$117,455
Liabilities	
Demand deposits	$ 4,216
Time deposits	31,503
Net interbank liabilities	58,551
Miscellaneous liabilities	23,685
Total liabilities	$117,455

Source: Board of Governors of the Federal Reserve System, *Flow of Funds Accounts*, 1982.

for safekeeping and for the processing of security payments, (2) agencies, and (3) wholesale-retail affiliates. Banks in Switzerland and Germany have established branch offices and securities affiliates operating in the U.S. money market, and they rely heavily on that market for liquidity. Japanese banks have created wholesale banking affiliates, retail banking outlets, and agency offices which deal in securities and the financing of international commerce, playing a particularly strong role in dollar lending abroad.

Canadian banks saw the potential inherent in U.S. financial markets a century ago and began setting up affiliates and agencies, mainly centered in the New York area and along the U.S.-Canadian border. The main attractions to Canada's chartered banks were two in number: (1) the availability of a large commercial loan market and (2) the huge size of the American money market, which offered a convenient vehicle for adjusting bank liquidity positions. Loans to American security dealers have become especially popular along with foreign-exchange trading between American and Canadian banks. During the 1920s a number of branches were opened by Canadian and other foreign-based banking organizations in the western part of the United States and in the state of Illinois. However, many state governments were disturbed by the invasion of foreign banks into local banking markets and enacted laws forbidding branching by foreign-owned banks. Gradually, however, the idea of comparative advantage—the marketing of services in the domestic economy by outside firms promotes efficiency and competition—began to emerge. A few states moved to lift their restrictions against foreign bank entry.[4]

Reasons for Entry

Foreign banks have entered the United States for a wide variety of reasons. Three key factors dominate—the rapid expansion of international commerce, the enormous size of the U.S. market, and the relative stability of the U.S. economy and political environment. Then, too, many foreign banks have followed their own corporate customers to U.S. shores just as U.S. banks have pursued their customers abroad. Having gained a foothold in the United States, however, foreign banks grew rapidly by attracting deposit and loan business from *both* foreign and domestic companies and from individual depositors. In general, the United States has experienced more stable growth, milder recessions, and less severe inflation than has been true in a number of other industrialized nations.

While foreign bank entry into the U.S. seems rapid at times, it is dwarfed in importance by the spread of U.S. banks overseas. For example, in the London money market, U.S. banks, seeking both corporate loans and

---

[4]For an in-depth analysis of the scope and growth of foreign bank operations in the United States, see Edwards [5] and Klopstock [10].

Eurodollar deposits, are more numerous than British banking institutions and account for the majority of Eurodollar loans. London branches of U.S. banks hold an estimated 10 percent of all bank loans in pounds sterling extended to residents of Great Britain. Assets held by U.S. bank branches in Britain approached $60 billion in 1983. Foreign branches of U.S. banks have approximately four times the assets of all branches and affiliates of foreign banks active in the United States. In addition, the equity interests of U.S. banks in financial institutions overseas—particularly commercial banks, finance and leasing companies, and merchant banks—are significant. Obviously, U.S. commercial banks play a greater and more significant role in overseas markets than do foreign banks offering their services in the states, though lately their growth abroad has slowed significantly.

Whatever the facts, the perception of many legislators, regulators, and bankers in recent years has been that the invasion of foreign banks into U.S. domestic markets has become significant enough to demand regulation. Indeed, many domestic bankers saw it as an issue of *regulatory equity*. U.S. banks were more closely regulated and restricted than were the foreign banks competing with them in domestic markets. Fairness seemed to demand a common set of rules for all. Accordingly, after much debate (including an expression of fear by some of the largest American banks that too strict regulation of foreign-bank operations in the U.S. would invite regulatory retaliation against U.S. banks overseas) Congress passed the International Banking Act of 1978. Known as IBA, the new law brought the domestic agencies, branches, and commercial lending affiliates of foreign-owned banks under federal supervison and federal regulation. Federal branches and agencies of foreign banks with total worldwide consolidated bank assets exceeding $1 billion were made subject to required reserves on deposits and Regulation Q deposit interest-rate ceilings as imposed by the Federal Reserve. (Now, of course, deposit rate ceilings are set by the DIDC.[5]) The act also authorizes the Federal Reserve Board to levy reserve requirements and impose rate ceilings on state agencies and branches of foreign banks in cooperation with state bank supervisory authorities. Moreover, no foreign bank may establish a federal branch office which accepts deposits of less than $100,000 without securing insurance from the Federal Deposit Insurance Corporation. In those states requiring deposit insurance for the banks they charter, state authorized branches of foreign banks which accept deposits of less than $100,000 also must be insured. Foreign banks that operate U.S. offices other than branches or agencies must register with the Secretary of the Treasury. Finally, any foreign bank operating an agency, branch, or commercial lending company within U.S. borders or territories is defined as a bank hold-

---

[5]See Chapter 8 for a discussion of the activities and powers of the DIDC.

ing company and comes under the Bank Holding Company Act. Such a foreign affiliate must register like all domestic holding companies with the Federal Reserve Board and is subject to Board supervision.

To many observers, the IBA appeared to be an overreaction to the foreign-bank invasion, and some feared foreign retaliation. But the 1978 law turned out to be less stringent than many had feared. It brought greater regulatory equity since foreign and domestic banks face similar regulations now, consistent with the doctrine of *national treatment*. Moreover, for the first time, non-U.S. citizens are permitted to serve as directors of Edge Act corporations, and foreign banks can acquire majority ownership in these corporations which aid in carrying out international transactions. Recent Fed regulations now require foreign banks to designate a home state, and their banking offices are not allowed to branch outside their home state. This provision parallels the McFadden Act of 1927 which prohibited U.S. banks from branching across state lines.

TYPES OF MULTINATIONAL BANKING ORGANIZATIONS

Multinational banking—usually defined as the ownership of banking facilities in one country by residents of another country—has assumed a variety of forms around the globe. The most common forms are multinational retail banking and multinational wholesale banking. In some cases, one banking organization performs each of these different types of banking services; in others, a banking organization specializes in one of these functions. In any case, the nature of multinational retail and wholesale banking is quite different. The degree of competition, regulation, and anticipated profitability vary widely for these different types of banking organizations.

Multinational Retail Banking

Multinational retail banking refers to the ownership in one country of consumer-oriented banking facilities by residents of another country. This type of banking would generally include deposit taking from household accounts as well as lending to individuals for ordinary consumption purposes. Since convenience is extremely important in retail banking, it would also generally involve a large number of branches with a substantial number of employees. Multinational retail banking, as with domestic retail banking, is costly in terms of people and facilities, though the development of electronic technology promises to reduce the cost of retail banking.

Multinational retail banking has been perhaps the least successful of the various types of multinational banking. There has been some penetration of the California retail markets, especially by British and Japanese banks. United States and Canadian banks have established a number of retail branch systems in South America, though the rising tide of economic nationalism has reduced the importance of these organizations. Also, some United States banks have established retail-deposit and lending organizations in Great Britain, though with limited success. As a general rule, attempts by banking organizations to use their marketing and management skills to establish retail banking organizations in other countries have been unsuccessful in achieving market penetration.

Multinational Wholesale Banking

Multinational wholesale banking refers to the ownership in one country of business or wholesale-oriented banking facilities by residents of another country. It includes the traditional deposit-taking and lending functions of commercial banks but also frequently is much broader in scope, encompassing many investment banking functions. As with domestic wholesale banking, multinational wholesale banking involves large amounts of funds but few people (at least relative to retail banking) and only a small number of facilities. Large loans are made by banking professionals operating out of relatively small physical facilities, and large amounts of funds are purchased through telephone or electronic communication with the depositor. Large numbers of branch banking facilities are not needed and are not cost-efficient.

Multinational wholesale banking has been quite successful and is the principal reason for the spread internationally of banking organizations. (The growth over time of foreign banks in New York and London—two important centers of multinational banking—is shown in Table 24–3.) Major multinational wholesale banks, buying large denomination deposits from multinational corporations, governments, and government agencies, and making large denomination loans to these same organizations

Table 24–3   Foreign Banks with Offices in New York and London

Year	New York	London
Before 1971	75	163
1971	81	176
1972	85	215
1973	98	232
1974	114	264
1975	127	263
1976	144	265
1977	177	300
1978	208	313
1979	244	330
1980	253	353
1981	255	355

Source: Carol Parker, "New Names in New York," *The Banker*, February 1982, p. 97.

are at the core of the multinational banking system. Through these multinational banks, massive amounts of capital are moved internationally every day. Balance-of-payment adjustments for individual countries are smoothed, and multinational corporations are able to allocate funds efficiently through their many subsidiaries.

Multinational wholesale banks buy and sell funds in massive quantities. The size of loan requests from individual borrowers is frequently beyond the capacity of the individual multinational bank to prudently make. As a result, various types of partnerships have become common in multinational banking. The most common of these arrangements is a *consortium* of banks. These consortiums allow the multinational banks to provide an extremely large loan to one borrower without any individual multinational bank accepting excessive risk.

Some of the consortiums are informal in nature. However, many are formal and legal organizations established for the purpose of providing credit beyond that which is possible or desirable for the individual members of the consortium. When formalized, a consortium is a joint venture between two or more multinational banks of (usually) different nationality. The consortium obtains potential borrowers from the individual banks that own and thereby control the consortium. The consortium itself then attempts to meet the credit needs of the borrower by arranging a syndication of many banking organizations to provide credit and often to provide investment banking functions such as underwriting securities.

Consortiums among multinational banks are especially important in London, the principal center for multinational banking. By the early 1980s, more than 25 consortium banks were established in London. These consortium banks often have a regional or national orientation in which ownership is dominated by banks from one country or from one area of the world (for example, Europe).

It is important to note when discussing multinational wholesale banking (but not when discussing multinational retail banking) that most borrowing (through issuing deposit liabilities) and lending is done with only a few currencies. In fact, the United States dollar is by far the dominant currency by which deposits and loans are denominated in multinational wholesale banking transactions, reflecting the massive size of the Eurodollar market.

It is also significant to recognize that multinational wholesale banks vary widely in terms of their motivation for participation in the international wholesale market and in their position in the market. Some multinational wholesale banks—generally associated with the very largest banks in each country—view their international operations as a separate profit center, in which operations have considerable independence from the home office. Others—usually the smaller organizations—view their international operations as much as a service center as it is a profit center. These organizations may establish foreign operations in order to service their domestic customers who have established manufacturing, wholesale, retail, or service organizations abroad. They may also be used to attract foreign investment into the market area served by the home office bank. These organizations will often participate in a lending consortium but normally in a very minor way. They are unlikely to be the lead bank in a syndicate established by any of the consortiums. An example of different types of multinational banks represented in one market is shown in Table 24–4.

A Eurodollar is a dollar-denomiated deposit (almost always a time deposit) at a bank outside the United States. These deposits are bought and sold in what is known as the Eurodollar market. The Eurodollar market is a portion of the Eurocurrency market. A Eurocurrency deposit is a deposit on a bank's balance sheet that is denominated in any currency other than that of the country in which the bank is located, and the Eurocurrency market is the market in which Eurocurrency deposits are bought and sold.

EURODOLLAR BORROWING AND LENDING

A relatively recent development (since World War II and primarily since the early 1960s), Eurodollar deposits have exploded in amount, and are estimated to exceed $1 trillion. The phenomenon of buying and selling Eurodollars is an important one in international financial history. The enormous growth of Eurodollars clearly raises the question of why banks choose to lend dollars rather than their own home currency and why borrowers choose to borrow dollars rather than their own home currency; that is, why should a British bank choose to lend dollars rather than pounds; and, similarly, why should a European borrower choose to borrow dollars in Britain rather than in the United States? To some extent, answers to these questions reflect differences in government regulation. Yet, answers to these questions basically explain the phenomenal growth of the Eurodollar market.

The basic reason for the growth of the Eurodollar market is the ability of depositors to receive a higher rate of return on a dollar deposit in the Eurodollar market than in the domestic market and yet the simultaneous ability of the lender to borrow at a lower rate in the Eurodollar market than in the domestic market. In other words, the growth of the Eurodollar market may be attributed to the ability and willingness of multinational banks to operate with lower spreads between interest paid on deposits and interest earned on loans than is possible on domestic borrowing and lending operations. There are a number of reasons for this phenomenon. Most can be grouped under the heading of regulation and competition.

Regulation

Multinational banks are able to offer higher rates on Eurodollar deposits and lower rates on loans because they have less regulation and lower

Table 24–4   Foreign Banks with Houston Offices: December 31, 1982

Bank	Total Deposits (U.S. $ billion)	Bank	Total Deposits (U.S. $ billion)
Australia		**Japan**	
Australia and New Zealand Banking Group	$11.4	Bank of Toyko	$38.3
Bank of New South Wales	12.7	Dai-Ichi Kangyo Bank	62.9
		Daiwa Bank	31.4
Brazil		Fuju Bank	56.5
Banco do Brasil	27.1	Hokkaido Takushoku·Bank	15.4
Banco do Estado de Sáo Paulo	3.5	Industrial Bank of Japan	48.3
Banco Real International	2.1	Mitsubishi Bank	54.4
		Mitsui Banks	37.7
Canada		Sanwa Bank	51.9
Bank of Montreal	35.6	Sumitomo Bank	55.6
Bank of Nova Scotia	33.2	Taiyo Kobe Bank	34.5
Canadian Imperial Bank of Commerce	41.6	Taiko Bank	37.3
Royal Bank of Canada	47.9	**Korea**	
Toronto Dominion Bank	24.8	Bank of Seoul and Trust Co.	4.6
		Cho Heung Bank	2.4
Denmark		Korea Exchange Bank	3.6
Den Danske Bank	5.9		
		Netherlands	
England		ABN Bank International	39.2
Barclays Bank International	76.5	Algenmene Bank Nederland	45.2
Barclays International Banking Corp.	43.0	**Norway**	
Lloyds Bank International	16.6	Bergen Bank	2.5
National Bank of North America	4.7	Christiania Bank og Kreditkasse	NA
National Westminster Bank	76.1	Ken norske Credit Bank	NA
Standard Chartered Bank International	32.3	**Philippines**	
		Philippines Commercial and Industrial Bank	0.3
France			
Banque de L'Indochine et de Suez	14.8	**Scotland**	
Banque de Paris et des Pays-Bas	93.6	Bank of Scotland	6.7
Banque Francaise du Commerce Exterieur	6.9	Clydesdale Bank	3.4
Banque National de Paris	2.6	Royal Bank of Scotland	7.0
Credit Lyonnais Southwest	88.5	**Sweden**	
Paribas North America	NA	Post-och Kreditbanken	16.4
Société Générale	82.6	**Switzerland**	
		Credit Suisse	31.5
Germany		Swiss Bank Corporation	36.7
Bayerische Hypothekenund wechselbank	41.0	Union Bank of Switzerland	36.5
Dresdner Bank	58.9	**Taiwan**	
		International Commercial Bank of China	1.1
Hong Kong			
Hong Kong Bank Group	43.2		
Italy			
Banca Nazionale del Lavoro	42.6		
Banco di Roma	25.0		
Credito Italiano	28.6		

taxes than is generally true of their domestic operations. As a general rule, multinational banks operating in the Eurodollar market are not subject to reserve requirements on their Eurodollar deposits. Because the reserve requirement is appropriately viewed as a tax on the operations of a financial institution (though perhaps a justifiable tax for monetary policy purposes), the Eurodollar bank has a smaller tax burden than the domestic bank. This reduced tax burden allows operation with a smaller spread, either through higher rates paid for deposits or lower rates charged for loans. Multinational banks also have greater flexibility in their deposit offerings. For example, a multinational bank may offer a customer a Eurodollar CD with no minimum maturity.

Competition

Reduced spreads in the Eurodollar market may also be attributable to greater competition than in the domestic markets of many countries. It is common in a number of countries, especially in Europe, for domestic banks to engage in limited degrees of competition among themselves in order to increase their profit margins. In contrast, the worldwide Eurodollar market has so many participants that either explicit or implicit collusion is difficult, if not impossible. This situation intensifies the extent of competition and further reduces spreads. In effect, borrowing and lending in the Eurodollar market is done by multinational banks almost completely free from regulatory constraints and in a market intensely competitive due to the larger number of competing firms. Domestic banking in most countries still faces substantial regulation and has a much smaller number of competitors.

Multinational commercial banks compete for funds in the Eurodollar market primarily through offering time deposits, including large CDs, to large multinational corporations, governments, government agencies, and other multinational commercial banks. These time deposits are quite short-term in maturity, seldom more than one year and usually only a few months. A substantial fraction of these time deposits are sold to other multinational banks so that the Eurodollar market may be viewed to a considerable extent as an interbank market. The deposits are usually quite large in denomination—millions of dollars—and are obtained from the depositors through telephone contact directly or through the intermediation services of a broker or dealer.

Most of the funds raised are then loaned to multinational corporations, governments, government agencies, and multinational banks. Again, the loan market is to a considerable extent an interbank market. The loans vary in maturity, though they are generally established with floating rates, with the rate reestablished every three months. The benchmark for the loan is the London Interbank Offering Rate (LIBOR), which is a rate established for trading of Eurodollars among multinational banks in London, the focus of the Eurodollar market. The LIBOR is analogous to the federal funds rate in the United States. Default-risk premiums are then established on individual loans by setting the loan rate at LIBOR plus a premium (for example, LIBOR plus 1 percentage point).

Evaluating Risk in International Lending

U.S. commercial banking organizations have become very active in international lending. As discussed earlier in this chapter, total assets held by foreign branches of U.S. banks are approximately $500 billion. Of that amount, claims on foreigners exceeded $300 billion, of which claims on foreign banks (exclusive of other branches of the parent bank) and on nonbank foreigners each exceed $100 billion.

Additional information on international lending by U.S. banks is provided in Table 24–5. This table provides data on cross-border and nonlocal currency lending. These result from a U.S. bank's office in one country lending to residents of another country or lending in a currency other than that of the borrower's country. The data in the table are broken down geographically and by maturity. For example, the group of 10 and Switzerland—which encompassed Belgium, Luxembourg, Canada, France, the Federal Republic of Germany, Italy, Japan, the Netherlands, Sweden, Switzerland, and the United Kingdom—owed over $100 billion to U.S. banks. Of that amount, most (over $90 billion) was owed by banks, and

Table 24–5   Amounts Owed to U.S. Banks by Foreign Borrowers: June 1982
(data by type of borrower and maturity distribution; $ millions)

County	Total	Portion of Total Owed by			Maturity Distribution of Amounts Owed		
		Banks	Public Borrowers	Private Nonbank Borrowers	One Year and under	Over One to Five Years	Over Five Years
Group of 10 and Switzerland	$131,422.9	$ 91,505.1	$ 8,552.9	$31,363.9	$110,846.3	$14,005.7	$ 6,569.7
Nongroup of 10 developed countries	29,479.1	10,217.7	6,590.2	12,671.0	16,408.1	8,696.1	4,373.7
Eastern Europe	8,053.5	3,994	3,148.6	910.5	3,865.2	3,465.7	723.4
Oil-exporting countries	23,010.8	6,254.6	8,012.6	8,743.5	16,301.9	5,252.9	1,455.9
Non-oil-exporting developing countries—Latin America and Caribbean	61,979.1	19,324.5	19,579.6	23,074.6	34,520.4	17,845.0	9,615.0
Non-oil-exporting developing countries—Asia, China, Taiwan	21,208.1	10,878.0	6,706.3	8,622.7	18,388.9	5,184.9	2,638.2
Non-oil-exporting developing countries—Africa	4,641.1	1,394.4	2,363.6	883.0	3,110.1	1,131.5	399.4
Offshore banking centers	46,663.3	36,049.5	1,007.2	9,606.5	40,434.8	3,668.4	2,560.0
International and regional organizations	603.5	0	219.6	383.9	231.3	214.2	158.0
Totals	$332,061.6	$179,608.2	$56,180.9	96,260.1	$244,107.4	$59,464.1	$28,493.6

Source: Federal Financial Institutions Examinations Council, *Statistical Release*, June 3, 1982.

almost all of the total was due within one year. In contrast, Mexico (classi-fied in the non-oil-export developing countries group for Latin America and the Caribbean) owed $21.5 billion to U.S. banks, of which one half was owed by private borrowers and almost one half was due in over one year.

The existence of massive amounts of credit by U.S. banks to foreign borrowers (public and private) raises questions of credit evaluation and appropriate control of risk. In many ways, the evaluation and control of risk in foreign lending is similar to risk management in domestic lending. Such an evaluation involves the determination of the degree of credit risk in each loan application with the use of the Cs of credit as discussed in Chapter 10. Once the degree of credit risk is ascertained, it is then possible to determine whether that credit risk falls within the limits allowed by bank policy and whether market conditions will allow adequate pricing of the loan to compensate for the degree of credit risk. While similar in this respect to domestic lending, there are other considerations which make in-ternational lending quite different from domestic lending. These involve differences in the *legal systems* of different countries and *country risk* con-siderations.

In contrast to domestic lending where there is a well-established legal framework for the collection of debts, in international lending there is no uniform legal system to settle disputes and no system for enforcement of decisions made by the courts. Such differences are especially important for the Eastern bloc countries and for countries whose cultural and legal heritage vary widely from those of the United States. The differences mean, of course, that one of the Cs of credit—collateral—is much less im-portant in much international lending than in domestic lending. An inter-national loan may involve the pledge of collateral, but that collateral may, in fact, not be available to settle the obligation in the event of default by the borrower.

Country risk is perhaps even more important than different legal sys-tems in affecting the riskiness of international lending. Country risk in-volves exchange-rate risk, capital-control risk, and sovereign risk. Ex-change-rate risk exists wherever cross-currency loans are made and results from potential and actual fluctuations in exchange rates. For exam-ple, if a United States bank made a loan to a Mexican company that was denominated in pesos, the bank would lose from any devaluation of the peso (of course it would gain from any upvaluation of the peso). The bank would receive the same number of pesos but a devaluated peso would translate into fewer dollars. This problem is less significant for U.S. banks than for banks of other nations, since many loans throughout the world are denominated in dollars. However, even for dollar-denominated loans there exists currency risk to the U.S. bank. For example, suppose that the loan to the Mexican company is denominated in dollars rather than pesos.

The problem then is for the Mexican company to get enough dollars to re-pay the loan. A devalued peso makes it more difficult for the Mexican company to obtain enough dollars and thereby increases the credit risk to the U.S. lenders.

There also exists the possibility of capital controls imposed by the gov-ernment of the borrowing country. The foreign borrower may have suffi-cient funds to repay the loan but may be prohibited from doing so through government-imposed capital controls. Most commonly, such capital con-trols are imposed in order to reduce balance-of-payments deficits. How-ever, such controls may also be imposed due to armed conflict between two nations or other political problems. In any case, such capital controls make it impossible for the borrower to repay the lender and thereby in-crease the credit-risk to the lender.

Perhaps the most important—though highly unpredictable—type of credit risk involved in international lending is *sovereign risk*. Sovereign risk refers to the possibility that a sovereign government will refuse to ac-cept its obligation under the debt. This is especially important in interna-tional lending since much such lending is to governments and government agencies and since many portions of heavy industry in many countries are state-owned. At the extreme, sovereign risk involves the repudiation of existing debts. It might also include unilateral delay in payments, as well as government policies to prevent private borrowers from repaying for-eign lenders.

ISSUES IN THE INTERNATIONAL-IZATION OF FINANCIAL INSTITUTIONS

The expansion of U.S. banks abroad and of foreign banks in the United States and the associated growth in foreign lending has raised a number of important issues. Two in particular have become especially significant in recent years: the regulation of the activities of banks internationally and the degree of credit risk accepted by the banking system in its internation-al lending.

Domestic banks in the United States are regulated by domestic laws in the United States. Similarly, British banks are regulated by British laws, German banks by German law, and so forth for other countries. Yet as banks become international (or multinational), they become subject to a conflicting set of regulations that restrict and guide their activities. For ex-ample, regulations affecting commercial bank participation in underwrit-ing and other investment banking functions, as well as a bank's ability to own equity securities, differ considerably among countries. These differ-ences have usually been handled by each country requiring the foreign banks that operate in the country to conform to domestic banking laws. Yet such approaches contain inherent problems of equity. As banks be-come truly international in their operations, it may become necessary to develop a consistent set of regulatory guidelines to control their behavior.

The potential and actual problems with the credit quality of international loans is also an issue of great importance. Many countries which expanded their borrowing rapidly during the 1970s have experienced considerable difficulty in servicing their debt in recent years. Mexico and Poland are two examples of the debt-servicing burden that face a number of countries.[6] These problems have led to restructuring the debt, to delays in payment of interest and principal, and to fears that larger amounts of defaults would threaten to destroy the integrated structures of banking throughout the world.

Such problems have raised a number of issues and questions. One of these issues concerns the adequacy of risk evaluation by the major international banks of the world. If, in fact, a large number of borrowers are unable to service their debt to international banks, questions may be raised about the judgment of these banks in extending the loans initially. How could sophisticated bankers with the assistance of specialists in petroleum, agriculture, and other industries available to assist in the decision process make billions of dollars of questionable loans? An answer to that question is not easy to provide. Partially, the problem may stem from pressure from governments of the developed nations to finance the developing countries and to recycle the surplus of petrodollars that existed in the 1970s. Partially also, the problem reflects the worldwide economic contraction that occurred in the early 1980s. But it may also be that part of the problem is attributable to poor procedures at the large banks for evaluating credit risks.

Regardless of the cause of the problem, the question remains of how to deal with the inability of large numbers of borrowers to service their international debts and how to protect the stability of the world financial system. Of course, a return to noninflationary economic growth with falling unemployment would assist markedly in increasing the ability of international borrowers to service their debts. But it may be that government action, perhaps a coordinated effect of many governments, will be necessary to protect the stablity of the international financial system. In any case, the credit quality of international loans remains an important and unresolved problem.

Commercial banks as well as other financial institutions have increasingly become international in their operations. Large banks gather deposits from throughout the world and make loans in many countries. U.S.

SUMMARY

---

[6]Gasser and Roberts [7] report a vulnerability index for developing countries. By that index, Poland, Mexico, and Argentina evidenced high vulnerability for liquidity problems and sensitivity to unexpected economic shocks as of 1982. In contrast, Taiwan evidenced low vulnerability.

banks have spread abroad as a means of servicing their domestic customers who have expanded internationally. Similarly, foreign banks have penetrated the U.S. banking market by branching and also by acquiring a number of domestic banks. U.S. banks have also increased their international operations through Edge Act subsidiaries and also through International Banking Facilities (IBFs).

Multinational banking organizations may be classified into retail and wholesale organizations. Multinational retail banks essentially serve the consumer market and have done so only with limited success. Multinational wholesale banking, which is designed to obtain deposits from and make loans to businesses, is the dominant form of multinational banking. Many of the multinational wholesale banks are consortiums.

The Eurodollar market plays a fundamental role in international banking. Multinational banks buy and sell dollar-denominated deposits at banks outside the United States (Eurodollars) in massive quantities. The absence of regulation makes it possible for multinational banks to offer high rates on deposits and relatively low rates on loans. Also, the intense degree of competition in the Eurodollar market has made it attractive to participants.

Multinational banks face the risk-evaluation problem in international lending just as they do in domestic lending. While the Cs of credit are important in international lending, the lender must consider a number of complications not present in domestic lending. These include differences in legal systems and country risk (exchange rate, capital controls, and sovereignty risks).

The spread of international banks has raised a number of issues. Two issues of substantial importance concern equity in the regulation of banks and the problem with credit quality, as many nations have experienced considerable difficulties in servicing their debts.

Questions

24–1. Why have U.S. banks expanded abroad? Why have foreign banks expanded in the United States?

24–2. What are Edge Act corporations? What are International Banking Facilities? Are they similar in purpose?

24–3. Distinguish between multinational retail and wholesale banking. Why has multinational wholesale banking dominated?

24–4. What is a consortium bank? Why is it created?

24–5. What is a Eurodollar? How do multinational banks use the Eurodollar market? What accounts for the rapid growth of the Eurodollar market?

24–6. Compare and contrast the risk-evaluation process in domestic and international lending.

References

1. Aliber, Robert Z. "International Banking: Growth and Regulation." *Columbia Journal of World Business*, Winter 1975, pp. 9–15.

2. Davis, Steven. "How Risky is International Lending?" *Harvard Business Review*, January–February 1977, pp. 135–43.

3. Dod, David P. "Bank Lending to Developing Countries." *Federal Reserve Bulletin*, September 1981, pp. 647–56.

4. Edwards, Franklin. *Regulation of Foreign Banking in the United States: International Reciprocity and Federal-State Conflicts.* Columbia University Graduate School of Business. Research paper no. 64. New York: Columbia University, 1974.

5. Edwards, Franklin R. "The New International Banking Facility: A Study in Regulatory Frustration." *Columbia Journal of World Business*, Winter 1981.

6. Federal Reserve Bank of Boston. *Key Issues in International Banking.* Proceedings of a conference held in Boston, October 1977.

7. Gasser, William J., and David L. Roberts. "Bank Lending to Developing Countries: Problems and Prospects." *Quarterly Review*, Federal Reserve Bank of New York, Autumn 1982, pp. 18–29.

8. Houpt, James T., and Michael G. Martinson. *Foreign Subsidiaries of U.S. Banking Organizations*, Staff study no. 120. Washington, D.C.: Board of Governors of the Federal Reserve System, October 1982.

9. Jacobs, Klaas Peter. "The Development of International and Multinational Banking in Europe." *Columbia Journal of World Business*, Winter 1975, pp. 33–39.

10. Klopstock, Fred H. "Foreign Banks in the United States: Scope and Growth of Operations." *Monthly Review* 55, no. 6, 1973, Federal Reserve Bank of New York, pp. 140–54.

11. Korth, Christopher M. "Risk Minimization for International Lending in Regional Banks." *Columbia Journal of World Business*, Winter 1981, pp. 21–28.

12. _____. "The Management of International Lending Risk by Regional Banks." *Journal of Commercial Bank Lending*, October 1981, pp. 27–36.

13. Longbrake, William, Melanie R. Quinn, and Judith A. Walter. *Foreign Ownership of U.S. Banks: Facts and Patterns.* Office of the Comptroller of the Currency, Washington, D.C., 1981.

14. Quinn, Melanie R. *A Selected Bibliography on the Topic of International Banking Supervision and Risk*. Office of the Comptroller of the Currency, Washington, D.C., 1982.

15. Rabino, Samuel. "The Growth Strategies of New York Based Foreign Banks." *Columbia Journal of World Business*, Winter 1981, pp. 29–35.

16. Rudy, John P. "Global Planning in Multinational Banking." *Columbia Journal of World Business*, Winter 1975, pp 16–22.

17. Sterling, J. F. "A New Look at International Lending by American Banks." *Columbia Journal of World Business*, Fall 1979, pp. 61–70.

18. Teeters, Nancy H. "The Role of Banks in the International Financial System." A paper presented to the International Conference on Multinational Banking and the World Economy, Tel Aviv, Israel, June 14, 1983.

25. Reform of the Financial System

THE PRESENT CHAPTER reviews the proposals for reform of the financial system that have been put forward in recent years. These proposals reflect the growing inadequacy of the regulatory structure of financial institutions and of the limits on the functions of individual institutions in a world of rapid changes in technology, shifting consumer demands for financial services, and extremely volatile interest rates. Most of the proposals for reform reviewed in this chapter were never enacted into law. However, many of the proposals contained similar and overlapping provisions, and many of these provisions were contained in the major revisions of the financial system brought about by passage of the Depository Institutions Deregulation and Monetary Control Act of 1980 and the Garn–St Germain Depository Institutions Act of 1982. These two laws undoubtedly will have profound effects on the financial system in the years ahead. As such, the principal orientation of this chapter is towards the implications of that legislation. The chapter concentrates on the reasons for financial reform proposals and on some of the major implications of that reform for managers of financial institutions and for the public. Also, since it is quite likely that passage of the Depository Institutions Deregulation and Monetary Control Act of 1980 and the Depository Institutions Act of 1982 represent the *beginnings*, rather than the end of financial reform, the chapter closes with a few tentative conclusions about future reforms. Throughout the chapter the emphasis is on reform measures affecting depository institutions, though major changes at nondepository institutions are treated where appropriate.

No economic entity is static in its functions. Rather, the role played by economic entities evolves, reflecting changes in the demand for financial services, changing technology, regulatory factors in industries such as financial services in which government policy has a major influence, and

REASONS FOR FINANCIAL REFORM

various other considerations. Economic entities flourish under one set of external factors and diminish in importance under another. The evolving role of different financial institutions and proposals for financial reform reflect a number of different considerations.[1]

Interest Rates and Disintermediation

One of the principal factors that has produced pressure on the profitability and market shares of some financial institutions—especially savings and loan associations and mutual savings banks—has been the persistence of rising interest rates, both in secular and cyclical terms. In periods of high and rising interest rates, the ability of some financial institutions to attract funds is severely eroded. The effect is especially strong on depository financial institutions which have traditionally been restricted by Regulation Q on the maximum interest rates they could pay to obtain deposit funds. Since there were no such limits applicable to securities offered by nondepository financial institutions and by nonfinancial institutions, savers naturally placed their funds with these other institutions by directly acquiring corporate bonds, U.S. government bonds, state and local government bonds, and other such securities rather than acquiring the deposit liabilities of financial institutions. In contrast, when interest rates fell, such as in 1967, 1970, and 1976, Regulation Q became less constricting, the flow of funds was *reintermediated*, and the market share of depository financial institutions increased. Historical perspective on the flow of funds through the different financial intermediaries is provided in Figures 25–1 and 25–2.

There is another aspect of the high interest-rate levels that persisted throughout most of the 1970s and early 1980s that also profoundly affects the need for financial reform. High interest rates and the inverted, or negatively sloped, yield curve that frequently is associated with very high interest rates has called into question the basic viability of some traditional financial institutions. Again, the effects have been most pronounced on savings and loan associations and mutual savings banks. Most of the asset portfolios of these institutions have traditionally been held in long-term, fixed-rate mortgages. These mortgages, as with all fixed-income securities, depreciate in market value as interest rates rise, reducing the solvency position of institutions in these two industries. In fact, in the early

---

[1]Colton [2] points out that pressures for change in the financial system have originated from (1) the federal government, especially the legislative branch and the Congress; (2) regulatory agencies; (3) concerned industries (including financial institutions and the housing industry); (4) technological innovation; (5) public and consumer pressure; and (6) changing economic and market conditions. In contrast, Silber [15] attributes recent financial innovation to (1) inflation, (2) the volatility of interest rates, (3) changing technology, (4) legislative factors, and (5) internationalization of financial institutions.

Figure 25–1   Net Funds Supplied by Type of Lender (annually)

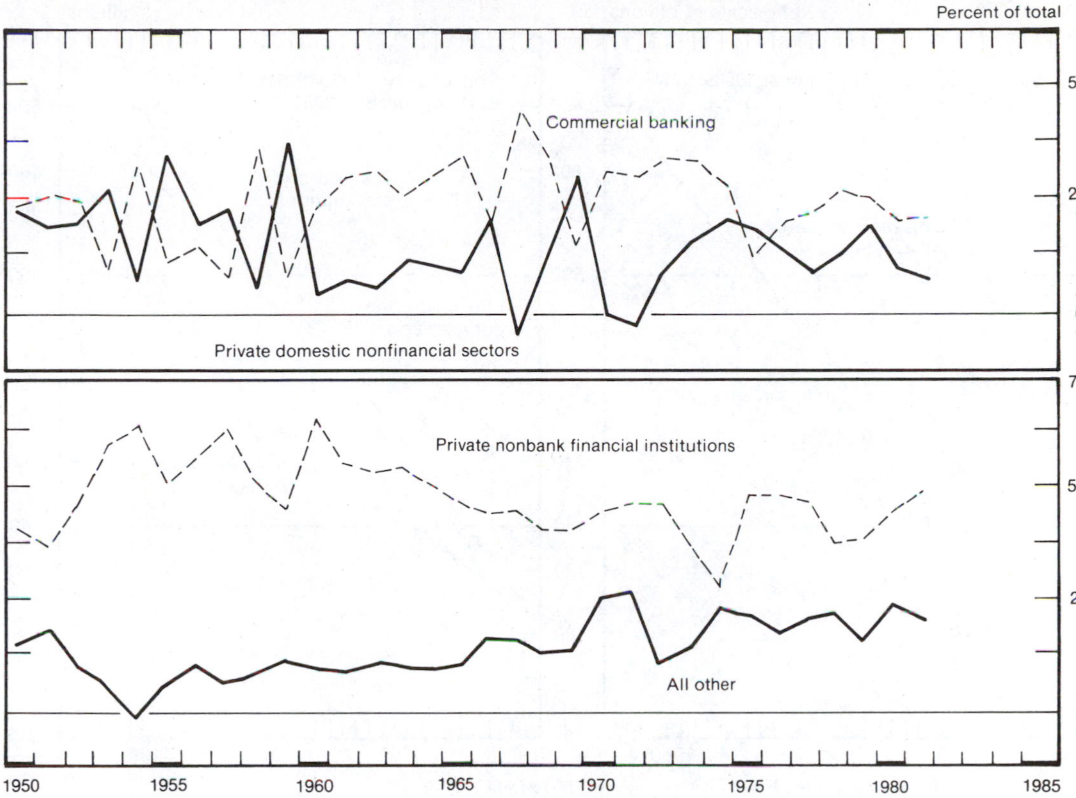

Percent of total

Source: Board of Governors of the Federal Reserve System, *Historical Chart Book.*

1980s a very large fraction of the savings and loans and mutual savings banks in the United States would have been insolvent if their assets had been valued at market.[2] In addition, the profitability of savings and loans and mutual savings banks has been sharply and negatively affected by periods of inversely shaped yield curves, when the price of funds rises until it exceeds the revenue on earning assets, creating a negative spread. A large number of savings and loans and mutual savings banks experienced negative profitability in 1981 and 1982.

These periods of high interest rates created pressure from the managers of financial institutions as well as from some members of Congress and

---

[2]Debt securities held by financial institutions are traditionally valued at cost rather than market as long as their credit-risk levels are satisfactory.

Figure 25–2 Assets of Selected Financial Institutions (amount outstanding)

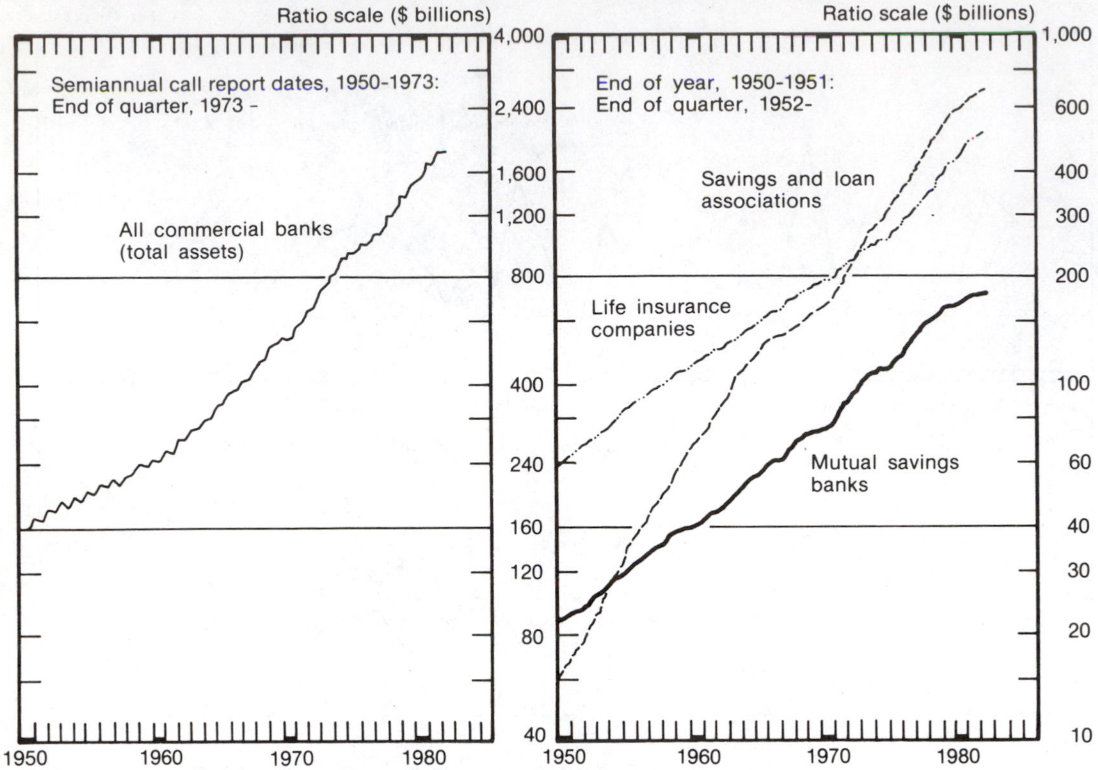
Ratio scale ($ billions)
4,000
2,400
1,600
1,200
800
400
240
160
120
80
40
Semiannual call report dates, 1950-1973:
End of quarter, 1973 -
All commercial banks
(total assets)
1950
1960
1970
1980
Ratio scale ($ billions)
1,000
600
400
300
200
100
60
40
30
20
10
End of year, 1950-1951:
End of quarter, 1952-
Savings and loan
associations
Life insurance
companies
Mutual savings
banks
1950
1960
1970
1980

Source: Board of Governors of the Federal Reserve System, *Historical Chart Book.*

other participants in the financial system for substantial changes in the powers allowed different financial institutions. In the case of thrift institutions, the pressure was for changes in the basic purposes and functions of these institutions. In particular, the suggestions for financial reform centered on diversifying the asset and liability structure of thrift institutions, generally by shortening the maturity of their assets and lengthening the maturity of their liabilities. Specific recommendations included allowing savings and loans and mutual savings banks to make consumer and business loans and allowing these institutions to offer mortgages in which the rates were fully adjustable.[3] On the liability side of the balance sheet, the

[3]A fully adjustable mortgage preserves the value of the institution in periods of high interest rates, thereby preserving its solvency, and also automatically increases the revenue of the lending institution as interest rates rise. It, in effect, reduces the maturity of the assets in the portfolio by bringing in more revenue earlier in the life of mortgage.

various proposals to remedy the problems created by high interest rates and disintermediation usually involved allowing thrift institutions to offer checking accounts; the proposals involved also the gradual elimination of Regulation Q so that the institutions could compete on a price basis with the open competitive marketplace. More generally, many of these proposals would, in effect, turn thrift institutions into commercial banks.

Competition from Unregulated Institutions

A second major factor pushing financial reform was the intense competition offered to depository financial institutions by new and unregulated (or, at least, less regulated) financial institutions. Two excellent examples of this growing competition for depository institutions from nontraditional sources are brokerage firms and money market mutual funds. While brokerage firms have existed for many years as major financial institutions, the proliferation of their services in recent years has been substantial. Moreover, many brokerage firms have been affiliated with insurance companies and some with nonfinancial firms. In the case of the money market fund, this new financial institution has been phenomenally successful in a very short time, as was discussed in Chapter 16.

Many nondepository financial institutions have begun to offer financial services in direct competition with depository institutions. In addition, many services offered by nondepository institutions have been prohibited to depository institutions. Perhaps the best example of competition from nondepository financial institutions is offered by Merrill Lynch, the largest brokerage firm in the United States. Figure 25–3 presents a list of financial services offered by this brokerage firm. It is important to note that many of these services are directly competitive with depository financial institutions. For example, Merrill Lynch offers credit for real estate and re-

---

Figure 25–3   Services offered by Merrill Lynch, Pierce, Fenner & Smith, Inc.

Securities services	Insurance services
Broker and dealer	Mortgage cancellation life insurance
Commodity futures and options brokers	Other life insurance
Security underwriting	Annuities
Investment banking	Insurance to real estate lenders against default risk
International merchant banking	"Directed" life insurance
Leasing	
Dealer in U.S. government agency securities and in money market instruments	**Real estate and related services**
Margin lending	Real estate financing
Securities research	Mortgage banking
Investment counseling	Real estate management services
Sale and management of mutual funds	Brokerage
Cash management account	Employee relocation

Source: Merrill Lynch.

lated purposes and for the purchase of securities. Moreover, with its Cash Management Account (CMA), Merrill Lynch created a financial instrument which is directly competitive with checking accounts offered by depository financial institutions. Yet, Merrill Lynch is able to offer investment banking and insurance services to customers—functions prohibited to depository financial institutions.

In the case of money market funds, much, though not all, of the growth of these types of mutual funds may be attributed to the restrictions on depository financial institutions that prevented them from offering market rates of interest on savings vehicles. In virtually all aspects of their operations, the money market funds did not face the same degree of regulation as is the case for depository financial institutions. As such, they were free to innovate new financial services more quickly and with less cost than for depository institutions.

The growth of this competition from brokerage firms, money market funds, and other types of providers of financial services has placed substantial pressure on depository institutions. These institutions have responded by creating new financial services where permitted by regulation. However, regulatory restrictions have made many kinds of innovations costly and difficult to implement. This has led many observers to promote financial reform through reducing the limits on different kinds of services at depository institutions. For example, some observers have argued that the separation between commercial banking and investment banking that goes back to the Glass-Steagall Act of the early 1930s should be removed. To these observers, depository institutions must be allowed to offer services similar to those offered by brokerage firms and money market funds if they are to prevent the erosion of their importance in the financial system.

Blurring and Overlapping of Function

Perhaps equally important in affecting the proposals for financial reform is the increasing homogenization of sources and uses of funds at depository institutions. This homogenization occurred throughout the 1960s and 1970s in response to market forces and in some cases was prodded by administrative decisions by the regulatory agencies. It is often referred to as a "blurring of function." Whatever it is called, it represents a remarkable change in the role of individual financial institutions. The traditional separation of functions between commercial banks, savings and loan associations, mutual savings banks, and credit unions was already being eroded well before passage of the Depository Institutions Deregulation and Monetary Control Act of 1980. Commercial banks which were founded as specialized lenders to commerce had already become department stores of finance. Savings and loans, which were originally formed as temporary cooperative building societies in order to channel funds into home ownership, were rapidly diversifying. Mutual savings banks, which were formed during the 19th century in order to provide an outlet for savings of the new immigrants, were also substantially changing their sources and uses of funds. Even credit unions, one of the smallest of the nation's financial institutions, were shifting their portfolios into nontraditional uses and sources of funds. In fact, these institutions had broken the traditional monopoly of transactions accounts in some parts of the nation well before passage of the Depository Institutions Deregulation and Monetary Control Act of 1980.

This blurring and overlapping of function had enormous significance for the need for financial reform. Despite the growing similarity in function among these institutions, their methods of regulation and the rules governing their operations were quite different. For example, reserve requirements varied for commercial banks, savings and loan associations, mutual savings banks, and credit unions. In fact, credit unions generally had no reserve requirements. Moreover, capital requirements differed substantially among different kinds of depository institutions. These differences (inequities in the view of many) led to a number of proposals for reform, including unification of the supervision of all depository institutions and uniform and universal reserve requirements for all depository institutions.

The Fed Membership Problem

The Fed underwent a period—following World War II until 1980—of decline in the proportion of commercial banks (both in terms of number of banks and total assets) that are members of the Federal Reserve System. This decline was especially pronounced during the 1970s. The exodus from the Fed was viewed as a problem by the Federal Reserve (though not by all outside observers) in that the withdrawal of membership made it more difficult for the Fed to control the money supply and thereby to implement monetary policy.

The principal reason banks were leaving the Fed was the higher reserve requirements levied by the Fed against deposits as compared to most states. Reserve requirements for *nonmember* banks prior to the passage of the Depository Institutions Deregulation and Monetary Control Act of 1980 were not set by the Fed but rather by the state where each bank was headquartered. These state-imposed requirements varied significantly from state to state. However, the critical distinction between Federal Reserve and state-required reserves was not in the percentage requirement but in the definition of those assets eligible to be counted as legal reserves. For Federal Reserve member banks, only vault cash and deposits at the Fed—both of which are nonearning assets—count toward meeting legal reserve requirements. In contrast, most states allow reserves to be held in interest-earning form such as time deposits at other banks.

The differential reserve requirements for member versus nonmember banks was a major factor in producing pressure for financial reform. The Fed, of course, was very anxious to eliminate such differences and to end the Fed membership problem. As a result, it had introduced into the Congress in 1975, 1978, and 1979 various bills which would have made identical the reserve requirements for member and nonmember banks. Pressure for change also came from member banks, especially national banks which are forced to be members of the Federal Reserve, who found it more difficult to compete due to the higher effective reserve requirements. Not until the passage of the Depository Institutions Deregulation and Monetary Control Act of 1980, however, did these pressures produce legislation.

Changing Technology

The development of new technology for the delivery of financial services has also had a profound influence on the need for financial reform. To a considerable extent, the historical evolution of the nation's financial institutions reflects the limitations on transportation and communication that confined businesses and economic transactions to a fairly limited geographical scope. Yet, as transportation has become easier and faster and with the explosion in the ability to communicate over vast distances, the extent of feasible economic transactions has broadened considerably. Moreover, the development of sophisticated data processing and electronic funds payment systems have profoundly affected both the demand for financial services and the ability of financial institutions to provide those services.[4] As a result, it became more difficult to justify severe limitations on the geographic location of depository institutions through branching. In addition, the large investment in fixed assets required by the electronic technology invading the financial institutions' arena raised questions about the survival of small institutions and also about the need to allow more services to be offered by financial institutions in order to fully utilize these expensive facilities.

PROPOSALS FOR REFORM

There have been numerous proposals for reform extending back over 20 years. The principal proposals are those of the President's Commission on Financial Structure and Regulation (better known as the Hunt Commission) in the late 1960s and early 1970s, and the study of Financial Institutions and the Nation's Economy (FINE), produced in the mid 1970s by the House Banking Committee. Many of the proposals embodying these

---

[4]See Chapter 23 for a comprehensive discussion of electronic payment systems and their implications for financial institutions and the public.

attempts to create financial reform were later included in the Depository Institutions Deregulation and Monetary Control Act of 1980 and in the Depository Institutions Act of 1982.[5]

These previous attempts to reform the financial system reflect the pressures that had been building for changing the structure of financial institutions in the United States. Indeed, a strong argument could be made that changing economic and financial conditions, coupled with advances in technology, had already forced major structural changes in the nation's financial institutions—changes which Congress, after considerable delay, legitimized in 1980.

The Hunt Commission

The Hunt Commission recommended, among other proposals, that nonbank depository institutions be allowed to offer transactions accounts and receive broader lending authority. In addition, the commission recommended that Regulation Q be eliminated, though only gradually and over a 10-year period. With regard to reserve requirements, the Hunt Commission recommended mandatory membership in the Federal Reserve System for all state-chartered commercial banks and for savings and loans and mutual savings banks which offered transactions accounts.

The FINE Recommendations

Many of the recommendations of the Hunt Commission were subsequently incorporated into the Financial Institutions and the Nation's Economy discussion principles prepared by the House Banking Committee in 1975. Hearings were held in 1975 on these proposals to reform the financial structure, and the Financial Reform Act of 1976 was introduced into the House of Representatives. The very broad provisions of this proposed legislation included the following: (1) permission for all depository institutions to offer transactions accounts; (2) broader powers for thrifts, particularly in making consumer loans, in issuing credit cards, and in offering trust services; (3) Federal Reserve requirements applicable to all depository institutions, though imposed over a 5-year transition period; and (4) elimination of Regulation Q deposit interest-rate ceilings, with no more than a 5-year delay from the passage of the proposed legislation. The similarity between this proposed legislation and the major provisions of the Depository Institutions Deregulation and Monetary Control Act of 1980 is striking. However, the very broad nature of the provisions of this proposed legislation, coupled with the limited external and financial pressures for reform at that time, prevented final passage of these proposals.

---

[5]See Fraser and Rose [5] and Mayne [13] for some of the specific proposals for financial reform contained in the Hunt Commission and FINE reports.

Background to DIDMCA of 1980

External pressures for financial reform were increased when, on April 20, 1979, the U.S. Court of Appeals for the District of Columbia Circuit ruled that the federal financial institutions' regulatory agencies—the Federal Reserve Board, the Federal Home Loan Bank Board, and the National Credit Union Administration—had exceeded their authority in allowing depository financial institutions to offer interest-bearing transactions accounts (such as automatic transfers from savings to checking for commercial banks, share drafts for credit unions, and remote service units for savings and loans). The court allowed Congress until January 1, 1980, to pass legislation which would give the financial regulatory agencies appropriate authority. If not authorized by that date, the activities would be prohibited.

Responding to the pressure of this court ruling, the House passed, on September 11, 1979, the Consumer Checking Account Equity Act. This proposed legislation expressly gave authority to the financial regulatory agencies to authorize the various forms of interest-bearing transactions accounts. It also extended NOW accounts to all depository institutions nationwide. The Senate then passed, on November 1, 1979, the Depository Institutions Deregulation Act. This more comprehensive act included the following: authorization of those practices banned by the Court of Appeals; authorization of NOW accounts nationwide; approval for savings and loans to invest up to 10 percent of their assets in unsecured consumer loans, commercial paper, and corporate debt securities; authority for savings and loans to invest in real estate on the same terms as national banks; the phase-out of Regulation Q ceilings over a 10-year period; and the preemption of state usury ceilings on mortgage interest rates.

The two bills were sent to a conference committee. However, unable to agree on a compromise prior to adjournment, Congress did not authorize the court-banned practices until March of 1980. Finally, just prior to the March 31, 1980, deadline Congress passed the Depository Institutions Deregulation and Monetary Control Act (DIDMCA). It is perhaps significant to note that the final bill which emerged from the conference committee was somewhat different from either the Senate or House versions of this reform measure.

MAJOR PROVISIONS OF THE DEPOSITORY INSTITUTIONS DEREGULATION AND MONETARY CONTROL ACT OF 1980 (DIDMCA)

Signed into law by President Carter on March 31, 1980, this act sets the legal framework for the future evolution of depository financial institutions. While the act represents the beginning rather than the end of financial reform, it does represent an important culmination of more than a decade of proposals for financial reform.

The Act

The Depository Institutions Deregulation and Monetary Control Act of 1980—sometimes referred to as the Omnibus Banking Act or the Monetary Control Act—contains nine titles, each dealing with a separate aspect of reform of the financial system.[6] Taken as a package, the provisions of the legislation sought to improve both the implementation of monetary policy and the degree of equity in the regulation of financial institutions. Title I related to the problem of declining membership by commercial banks in the Federal Reserve System and to the different reserve requirements among the different types of depository institutions. Title II dealt with Regulation Q, which limits the rates depository financial institutions may pay for time and savings deposits and provides for the gradual elimination of such limitations. Title III granted to all depository institutions nationwide the right to offer to individuals some form of interest-bearing checking accounts. Title IV increased the lending powers of thrift institutions, primarily by giving savings and loans the legal right to increase the proportion of consumer loans in their portfolios. Title V sharply reduced the applicability of state usury laws. Title VI provided for simplification of the truth-in-lending legislation applicable to depository financial institutions. Title VII made a number of changes in the national banking laws relating to the operating authority of national banks and the supervisory authority of the Comptroller of the Currency. Title VIII related to the simplification of the laws under which depository financial institutions are regulated. Title IX related to the acquisition of domestic financial institutions by foreign organizations.

The first five titles of the legislation are most relevant for discussing the implications of the act for the financial system. A brief summary of the major changes embodied in the legislation is contained in Figure 25–4.

Title I—the Monetary Control Act of 1980—established new reserve requirements and extended their applicability to all depository institutions. This title provided for identical reserve requirements for member and nonmember commercial banks, thereby sharply reducing any incentives for commercial banks to withdraw from the Federal Reserve System. It further establishes the same reserve requirements for commercial banks as for savings and loans, mutual savings banks, and credit unions. After 1985, the year of full implementation of the legislation, changes in reserve requirements by the Federal Reserve System will affect the level of required reserves at all depository institutions simultaneously and to the same degree.

---

[6]For a more extensive discussion of the provisions of the legislation, see Fraser and Uselton [6] and McNeill [12].

Figure 25–4   Regulation of Depository Institutions before and after the Depository Institutions Deregulation and Monetary Control Act of 1980

Before	*After*
No uniform reserve requirements for depository financial institutions. No uniform reserve requirements even for commercial banks. No reserve requirements at all for credit unions.	Reserve requirements for all depository financial institutions established at uniform levels by the Federal Reserve.
Federal Reserve provided services only to member commercial banks and generally without charge (excepting interest on borrowing).	Federal Reserve provides services, including access to the discount window, to all depository institutions, although on an explicit fee basis.
Interest-rate ceilings established separately by each regulatory agency, although with mutual consultation and coordination.	Power to control interest-rate ceilings transferred to deregulation committee with instructions to eliminate ceilings gradually, completely by 1986.
Interest-bearing transactions accounts (NOW accounts, share drafts, and so forth) generally available at all depository institutions only in the northeastern United States.	All depository institutions nationwide allowed to offer interest-bearing transactions accounts.
Transactions accounts generally available at all depository institutions only in the northeastern United States.	All depository institutions nation-wide allowed to offer transactions accounts.
Savings and loans generally not allowed to make consumer loans, except those related to housing, and not allowed to offer trust services. Mutual savings banks not allowed to make business loans or accept demand deposits.	Savings and loans allowed to make large amounts of consumer loans and to offer trust services. Mutual savings banks allowed to make business loans and to accept demand deposits from their business customers.
State usury laws had substantial effect on flow of credit in different states.	Application of state usury laws virtually eliminated.

Source: Fraser and Uselton [6].

Title I also instructed the Federal Reserve to adopt a set of pricing principles and a schedule of fees for services performed for depository institutions. The fees to be charged are to be based upon the cost of providing those services.

Title II—Depository Institutions Deregulation—provided for the gradual elimination of the limitations on interest rates payable on accounts in depository institutions covered by the legislation. The phasing-out of the interest-rate controls is scheduled to occur over a six-year period ending no later than March 31, 1986.

The timing of the elimination of Regulation Q is under the control of the Depository Institutions Deregulation Committee, comprising the Secretary of the Treasury, the chairperson of the Board of Governors of the Federal Reserve System, the chairperson of the Board of Directors of the Federal Deposit Insurance Corporation, the chairperson of the Federal Home Loan Bank Board, and the chairperson of the National Credit

Union Administration. This group was instructed to eliminate interest-rate ceilings while observing the effects on the housing market and small savers as well as the viability of depository institutions in general.

Title III—the Consumer Checking Account Equity Act of 1980—authorized all dipository financial institutions to provide what are in effect checking account services. It authorized automatic funds transfer from interest-bearing savings accounts to demand deposits. It also authorized negotiable order of withdrawal (NOW) accounts and share drafts for individual depositors and religious, charitable, and philanthropic organizations. These accounts, while not legally checking accounts, are functionally the equivalent of demand deposits, although paying interest. Prior to passage of the legislation, depository institutions in only a few states (primarily in New England) were legally able to offer these services. This section of the legislation also raised federal deposit insurance coverage for individual accounts in all insured depository institutions from $40,000 to $100,000.

Title IV deals with the operating powers of nonbank depository financial institutions. Federally chartered savings and loans were authorized to issue credit cards and to expand consumer lending substantially. Savings and loans were authorized to invest up to 20 percent of their assets in consumer loans, commercial paper, and corporate debt securities. Authority of savings and loans to make real estate loans was also sharply increased. Mutual savings banks were authorized to make commercial, corporate, and business loans, but not more than 5 percent of total assets may be loaned for such purposes. Mutual savings banks were also authorized to accept demand deposits in connection with a commercial, corporate, or business loan relationship.

Title V relates to state-imposed usury laws. The provisions of state laws limiting the interest rate on first mortgage loans made after March 27, 1980, were preempted. Similar restrictions were placed on state usury laws governing certain types of business and agricultural loans. Also, any state restrictions on the interest rates paid on deposits at depository institutions were eliminated.

What Was Left Out

While the Depository Institutions Deregulation and Monetary Control Act of 1980 was quite comprehensive in scope, there were a number of recommendations that had been incorporated in earlier financial reform proposals that were not included in the bill. These involved branching, the regulatory framework, equality of regulation, and the availability of mortgage credit.

Both the Hunt Commission and the FINE study recommended increased branching authority for commercial banks. In fact, it would seem that expanded branching powers for financial institutions would be an integral part of financial reform. Yet, the legislation made no mention of altering the nation's branching laws. Developments since passage of the act, especially the growing amount of interstate branching by savings and loans through the rescue of financially troubled institutions by stronger out-of-state institutions, increased the importance of changes in the branching statutes, some of which were incorporated into the Depository Institutions Act of 1982.

The Hunt Commission and the FINE study recognized that it was illogical to have similar types of depository financial institutions regulated by different agencies. Both proposed consolidating the overlapping and confused system of federal financial regulation. The FINE study went furthest by proposing that regulation, supervision, and examination of all federally chartered depository institutions be handled by a single commission. This would merge into one agency the functions of the Comptroller of the Currency, the Federal Deposit Insurance Corporation, the regulatory and supervisory functions of the Federal Home Loan Bank Board, and the National Credit Union Administration. Despite the logic of such reform, the Depository Institutions Deregulation and Monetary Control Act of 1980 made no mention of reform of the federal regulatory structure.

Both the Hunt Commission and the FINE study dealt with the functions of depository financial institutions and the need for equality of regulation. The FINE study favored creation of a set of depository institutions that were virtually indistinguishable in function. Yet such equality of function requires equality of taxation, equality of capital adequacy guidelines, and equality of other important regulatory factors. The Depository Institutions Deregulation and Monetary Control Act of 1980 attempted to bring greater similarity of function to the nation's depository institutions, but it did not deal with equality of taxation or other such matters of law or regulation.

Perhaps the most important omission from the provisions of the Depository Institutions Deregulation and Monetary Control Act of 1980 concerns the availability of mortgage credit. To a considerable extent, passage of the legislation in 1980 involved the intent to save the thrift industry and the mortgage market from a financial crisis. Yet when the Hunt Commission and the FINE study approached the same problems, they recognized that broadening the powers of the thrifts might reduce the flow of credit to the mortgage market; they therefore proposed a mortgage subsidy. Since no such subsidy was incorporated into the Depository Institutions Deregulation and Monetary Control Act of 1980, the effects of reform on the availability of mortgage credit remained an open issue.

Pressures for additional financial reform continued to exist during the high interest rate environment of the early 1980s. Partially, these pressures emanated from the regulatory authorities, concerned about their ability to deal with the increased incidence of failure at depository institutions, especially at thrift institutions. The pressures also reflected concern that the Depository Institutions Deregulation and Monetary Control Act of 1980 had not done enough to broaden the powers of thrifts in order to make them viable institutions. These pressures finally culminated in passage of the Depository Institutions Act of 1982 (often called simply the Garn bill), signed into law by President Reagan on October 15, 1982.

The legislation gave the Federal Deposit Insurance Corporation and the Federal Savings and Loan Insurance Corporation additional authority to arrange interstate acquisitions of failed and failing firms by more solvent institutions. In previous years, efforts by these organizations to arrange such acquisitions had been hampered by restrictions on the interstate operations of depository institutions. Title II of the legislation (the Net Worth Certificate Act) was designed to bail out floundering and failing depository institutions, especially the thrift institutions. Under this act, the FDIC and the FSLIC may maintain the capital position of distressed institutions by making periodic purchases of net-worth certificates.

Under the new rules, the FDIC and the FSLIC can arrange for the acquisition of a large closed or floundering commercial bank, mutual savings bank, or savings and loan by an out-of-state organization. In arranging for such an out-of-state acquisition, the regulators must attempt to minimize their own loss and to recognize the following priorities in the bidding process:

1. Alike in-state financial institutions; for example, a commercial bank for a floundering commercial bank.
2. Alike out-of-state financial institutions.
3. Different in-state financial institutions.
4. Among out-of-state bidders, priority must be given to financial institutions headquartered in adjacent states.

The Garn–St Germain Act is built upon the reforms incorporated into the Depository Institutions Deregulation and Monetary Control Act of 1980. It, among other things, increased the ability of thrifts to make consumer and business loans and also allowed them to offer demand deposit accounts to commercial, corporate, and agricultural borrowers. More specifically, the legislation authorized savings and loans and mutual savings banks for the first time to make overdraft loans, to invest in the accounts of other insured institutions, and to make commercial loans. The legislation broadened the power of savings and loans and mutual savings banks to invest in state and local government debt, to make residential and nonresidential real estate loans, and to make consumer and educa-

MAJOR PROVISIONS OF THE GARN–ST GERMAIN DEPOSITORY INSTITUTIONS ACT OF 1982

tional loans. In addition, the Depository Institutions Act of 1982 allowed federally chartered savings and loans to provide demand deposits to customers that have a business loan relationship with the organization.

Perhaps the most important provision of the act relates to the deposit powers of these institutions. The act instructed the Depository Institutions Deregulation Committee (DIDC) to establish a deposit account that was equivalent to and competitive with money market mutual funds. Responding to these instructions, the DIDC authorized depository institutions, on December 14, 1982, to offer a money market deposit account that, with $2,500 minimum, had no interest-rate ceiling, provided instant liquidity, was insured by the appropriate insurance agency, and had limited check-writing privileges. Going beyond the reforms mandated by legislation, the DIDC also shortly thereafter authorized depository institutions to offer, beginning January 5, 1983, a super NOW account, similar in features to the money market deposit except that an unlimited number of checks could be drawn against the account. The DIDC also announced an acceleration in the timetable for the phase-out of Regulation Q ceilings, with complete elimination of interest ceilings on deposits to take place in the spring of 1984, barring unforeseen complications.

IMPLICATIONS OF FINANCIAL REFORM

The reforms initiated by the Depository Institutions Deregulation and Monetary Control Act of 1980 and the Depository Institutions Act of 1982, will, when fully implemented, profoundly affect the role and function of individual depository institutions. Moreover, as it appears likely that the acts will be the beginning rather than the end of legislative change associated with financial reforms, the ultimate effects may be even greater. Yet, projecting the ultimate effects of these reforms is quite difficult, especially since the shape of future legislation cannot be projected with any degree of certainty. Nevertheless, there is available enough information from a number of studies about the effects of financial reform, both potential and actual, so that some general projections may be made. These are presented below, though it is important to recognize the tentative nature of the projections.[7]

Competition

It would appear that much of the ultimate impact of financial reform will flow from the greater degree of competition associated with that re-

---

[7]The discussion is in terms of the effects on the operations of individual financial institutions rather than on the effectiveness of monetary policy, though financial reforms may have significant effects on monetary policy. For example, the provision for uniform and universal reserve requirements for all depository institutions that was contained in the Depository Institutions Deregulation and Monetary Control Act of 1980 would appear to improve to some degree the ability of the Federal Reserve to control the supply of money.

form. As individual financial institutions are allowed to increase the number and variety of services offered and as they are allowed to offer those services over wider geographic areas (provided that future financial reform includes reduced restrictions on branching and holding company affiliations), the extent of competition seems certain to increase. Moreover, the removal of Regulation Q ceilings on rates paid for deposits will lead to greater competition. Competition among depository institutions will intensify as will competition among depository institutions and nondepository institutions, such as life insurance companies, pension funds, mutual funds, and other types of nondepository financial institutions.

The greater competition should produce benefits to consumers of financial services, just as would intensified competition in any industry. The interest rates received by depositors should rise relative to what they would have been without financial reform. This development may have little significance for large depositors, who already are able to receive market rates of interest on their deposits. However, the benefits should be much larger for smaller depositors, who have received lower interest rates in the past due to Regulation Q ceilings. Greater competition should also produce benefits for borrowers in the form of lower interest rates as compared to those which would have been available without financial reform. Again, though, the effects may be uneven throughout different classes of borrowers. Larger borrowers, most of whom would be from the business sector, usually have substantial alternative sources of credit both from bank and nonbank suppliers. As such, intensified competition may produce limited benefits for these borrowers. Small borrowers who operate in less competitive financial markets may be benefited to a much greater extent by the increase in competition. This benefit may be especially pronounced for small consumers (as opposed to business borrowers) due to the entry of large numbers of new firms into the industry as savings and loans and mutual savings banks take advantage of their expanded powers.

Profitability

Rising interest rates paid for funds and diminished interest rates on loans would suggest reduced profitability for financial institutions, especially for depository financial institutions. Again, however, it must be remembered that the reduced profitability is as compared to what the level of profitability would be without financial reform. In fact, the level of profitability of individual financial institutions at any point in time is determined by other factors in addition to the degree of competition. As has been shown by events in the late 1970s and early 1980s, the level of interest rates is also a powerful factor in affecting the profitability of individual financial institutions. It must also be recognized that financial institutions may, to some degree, be able to blunt the effects of increased competition on their profitability by cost-reduction measures. The availability of more advanced data processing equipment and of electronic funds transfer systems may provide one way for financial institutions to effect cost reductions. Indeed, it may be that a more rapid introduction of advance technology will be one of the major consequences of financial reform.

Consolidation

To the extent, however, that financial reform reduces the profitability of financial institutions, certain projections follow from the competitive model. Higher competition and diminished profit margins usually lead to exit from an industry and to consolidation of existing firms. It is not unlikely, therefore, that the number of failures among financial institutions will rise. These failures may not actually involve large numbers of bankruptcies but rather may produce mergers whereby a strong financial institution takes over a weak one. In any case, the number of independent financial institutions, especially depository financial institutions, should decline, perhaps substantially. In fact, some observers have estimated that the number of commercial banks may fall to about 10,000 (a decline of about one third), while the number of savings and loans may fall even more dramatically. This reduction in the number of independent organizations may be especially profound among credit unions, due to the existence of a very large number of quite small organizations in that industry.

The potential effects of financial reforms, while generally positive, do have some features that have raised concern, for instance, the consolidation of the structure of the financial institutions sector and the potential for failure for large numbers of institutions. Also, the effects on the mortgage market of reducing the extent of specialization among the traditional mortgage lenders have raised questions among many observers as to the effects of financial reform on the availability of mortgage credit. While there are few easy answers to these questions, there is fortunately considerable evidence that is helpful. Not surprisingly, the results of these studies are mixed, though at least they provide identification of the relevant issues and variables for further analysis.

The New England Experience

One way to project the effects of financial reform is to view New England as a laboratory and to extract from the New England experience generalizations that may be applicable for the remainder of the country. The advantage of this approach is that NOW accounts have existed for more than 10 years in that area. Moreover, even broader financial reform has occurred in the state of Maine. However, this approach is not without its difficulties. With the exception of Maine, the financial reforms have been limited to legalization of NOW accounts. Other dimensions of the reforms authorized by the Depository Institutions Deregulation and Monetary Control Act of 1980 are absent from the New England experience. Also, the economic and financial characteristics of the New England economy are quite distinctive. In addition, mutual savings banks are extremely important in New England relative to commercial banks and savings and loans associations.

The experience in New England seems to suggest that savings and loans and mutual savings banks are able to obtain a significant, though not a dominant, share of the NOW account market. Balance per account at savings and loans and mutual savings banks, though, seems to be much less than at commercial banks. The increased competition associated with the introduction of NOW accounts does, as expected, seem to have reduced the profitability of financial institutions, especially commercial banks, though the effects at most banks have been quite modest, generally well under a 10 percent reduction in profitability. In some financial institutions, however, especially mutual savings banks, the introduction of NOW accounts has led to higher profitability.

Hayssen [8] reported results from a study in Maine which perhaps has more relevance to the potential effects of financial reform. Maine enacted legislation which was applicable to all state-chartered financial institutions and which embodied most of the recommendations of the Hunt Commission. It permitted all commercial banks, savings and loan associations, and mutual savings banks to branch statewide, equalized reserve requirements for all depository institutions, and allowed thrift institutions to compete directly with commercial banks for consumer loans and demand deposits. As of 1976, the time of the study, many thrift institutions had not yet entered the consumer loan market. Twenty-three percent of the mutual savings banks and 50 percent of the state-chartered savings and loans did not make new auto loans, while 10 percent of the mutual savings banks and 42 percent of the state-chartered savings and loans did not make unsecured consumer installment loans. To the extent that these results may be generalized, they suggest that the degree of competition arising from liberalized powers for savings and loans and mutual savings banks may not be increased as much as it might appear, at least with regard to lending. As such, the diversion of credit from mortgage to consumer loans by savings and loans and mutual savings banks may be quite limited.

Studies of Previous Proposals for Financial Reform

Jaffee [10] analyzed the potential impact on the mortgage and housing markets of the Hunt Commission proposals. The impact of these proposals was examined with the use of the Federal Reserve-MIT-Penn Econometric model. Simulations were made of the volume of deposits and mortgages at commercial banks, thrift institutions, and life insurance companies (reserves rather than deposits for life insurance companies) under the Hunt Commission proposals. To the extent that the results of these simulations are relevant for present-day conditions, there appears to be little concern about the impact of financial deregulation on the availability of mortgage credit. In fact, Jaffee's simulations indicate that the Hunt Commission proposals would help rather than hurt the housing and mortgage markets. Mortgages made by savings and loans and mutual savings banks were projected to be substantially higher with the Hunt Commission proposals than without them.

In a related study, Hendershott [9] simulated the impact of another set of regulatory reforms. These included allowing savings and loans and mutual savings banks to offer demand deposits and NOW accounts and to allow these institutions to increase their commitment of funds to consumer loans and corporate debt instruments. In addition, this set of recommendations would have altered the tax laws to raise the effective tax rate paid by savings and loans and mutual savings banks, but this disincentive to investment in mortgages would be replaced by a mortgage-interest tax credit.

Simulations of the impact of these proposals were done with the use of a flow-of-funds model. The time period selected was the first quarter of 1966 through the fourth quarter of 1974. The results suggest that, with the inclusion of the mortgage-interest tax credit, savings and loans's share of the home mortgage market would decline but that decline would more than be compensated for by increased purchases of mortgages by mutual savings banks and commercial banks. With no mortgage subsidy, however, the results are not quite as optimistic.

A more recent study by Jaffee and Rose [11] concentrated on the impact of money market certificates on the availability of housing credit in 1978 and the first half of 1979. Their simulations showed that the money market certificates, by increasing the flow of funds to savings and loans, sharply increased the availability of credit to the mortgage market. Indeed, the results indicated that money market certificates provided sufficient funds to build 300,000 houses in the first half of 1979 that would not have been built without the certificates.

Projections of the Effects of DIDMCA

Fraser [3] conducted a mail survey to determine the perceptions of managers of depository financial institutions as to the effects of the Depository Institutions Deregulation and Monetary Control Act of 1980. Senior managers of over 1,000 depository financial institutions nationwide were asked to evaluate the effects of the legislation. Such a survey not only provides an independent verification of the reasonableness of projections made by econometric models and by other techniques but also provides important information on the perceptions of managers about the effects of financial reform. These perceptions have importance in and of themselves. Yet, it is significant to recognize that these perceptions may be influenced by the financial pressures faced by the managers of depository financial institutions at the time of completion of the survey in June, 1981, a period of exceptionally high interest rates.

Results from the survey would suggest a profound effect of the legislation on depository institutions, especially savings and loans and mutual savings banks. Most savings and loans indicated that they had already taken advantage of the new powers authorized by the Depository Institutions Deregulation and Monetary Control, a finding in sharp contrast to that of Hayssen in Maine. Moreover, both savings and loans and mutual savings banks expected NOW accounts and consumer loans to be of substantial importance in their portfolios within only a few years.

Perhaps the most important part of the survey related to the views of the managers of depository institutions with regard to the effects of the legislation on profitability, the number of institutions, and the availability of mortgage credit. Managers expected the legislation to have a very strong effect on the profitability of their institutions. While this view was held by a majority of the managers of all types of depository institutions, there did appear to be greater concern among managers of savings and loans and mutual savings banks than among managers of commercial banks. There also appeared to be more concern among managers of smaller institutions—a not surprising result. In addition, most of the respondents indicated that financial reform would have a very important impact on the *number* of institutions, with a sharp decline expected in the number of independent institutions. Finally, most of the respondents were pessimistic as to the effects of financial reform on the availability of residential real estate credit. These pessimistic views were particularly pronounced at the major residential lenders, the savings and loans and mutual savings banks.

In contrast to these pessimistic views, a study done by the Federal Home Loan Bank Board [14] provides more optimism, providing that interest rates recede to more normal levels. Econometric projections were done in this study of the balance sheet and income statements of the savings and loan industry through 1988 under various interest-rate assumptions. While savings and loans are projected to reduce their concentration in mortgages and to increase their holdings of consumer loans, the growth in funds available to the industry should be adequate to offset this diversification in terms of its effects on mortgage lending.

While these results would not seem to indicate any great concern about the effects of financial reform on the availability of real estate credit, there is one aspect of the study that does raise some important questions. This relates to the level of profitability of the industry. In the FHLBB study, savings and loan profitability is satisfactory under the assumption of falling interest rates. However, under the assumption of a constant level of interest rates, the industry experiences alternating years of negative earnings, and its financial health is weakened considerably. Under the assumption of rising interest rates, the industry experiences negative earnings each year, and the net worth of the industry becomes negative in 1985.

FUTURE DIRECTION OF FINANCIAL REFORM

Any conclusions about the future directions of financial reform must be guarded and tentative. However, many of the same pressures that culminated in the passage of the Depository Institutions Deregulation and Monetary Control Act of 1980 and the Depository Institutions Act of 1982 remain significant sources of additional reform. The economic and financial world is everchanging and producing the need for adaptation in the role of financial institutions. Given these limitations applying to any projections we might make, however, the following future changes seem likely:

Reduced Restrictions on Branching.   As noted earlier, the Depository Institutions Deregulation and Monetary Control Act of 1980 did not address the branching issue, despite recommendations in previous proposals for marked reductions in the restrictions on the geographic expansion of banking organizations. Savings and loan associations have already achieved a degree of interstate branching. Some bank holding companies have expanded nationwide through their nonbank subsidiaries. It appears very likely that this aspect of financial reform will be dealt with by Congress in the near future and that limitations on the geographic expansion by depository institutions through branching and holding company acquisitions will be reduced considerably.

Rationalization of the Structure of Regulation.   Again, as noted earlier, despite the inclusion in previous proposals for financial reform of the structure of financial regulation, no such changes were included in either the Depository Institutions Deregulation and Monetary Control Act of 1980 or the Depository Institutions Act of 1982. Yet, with depository institutions becoming more alike in function and thereby more competitive, it is more important that their regulation be coordinated. Such coordination might be achieved by vesting all supervisory power in a new federal agency or allowing one of the existing federal agencies to take on such powers for all federally insured depository institutions. As part of this process, it appears increasingly likely that the deposit insurance system will be fundamentally altered, perhaps with a shift to variable-rate insurance premiums (in which the insurance rate is a function of the risk of the institutions) and with a merging of the deposit insurance funds. In any case, future legislation to rationalize the structure of regulation seems quite possible.

Broader Powers for Depository Institutions. It seems likely that even broader powers will be granted to depository institutions. The Depository Institutions Deregulation and Monetary Control Act of 1980 allowed savings and loans and mutual savings banks to act a great deal like commercial banks. These powers were broadened again with the 1982 legislation, yet not all the powers of banks were granted to the thrifts. It appears likely that many of these powers will be given to the thrifts in the future. Perhaps, at the same time, the powers of commercial banks may be extended. The separation between commercial and investment banking created by the Glass-Steagall Act of 1933 may be ended and commercial banks may be allowed to offer money market funds and other innovative financial services, such as limited trading in corporate debt and equity securities.

Affiliations of Financial Institutions. It seems likely that, as financial pressures mount, there will be greater affiliation among previously separate financial institutions. Such affiliations have already occurred between the insurance and the brokerage industries. Legislation may be produced which would allow such affiliation between commercial banks and nonbank financial institutions, perhaps through the holding company device.

Mortgage Subsidy. Many proposals for financial reform have contained a mortgage subsidy. Whether future financial reform contains such a subsidy depends upon two factors: (1) the extent to which the availability of mortgage credit is affected by existing financial reforms (as discussed above, the results of previous research are in conflict on this issue) and (2) the political commitment to the housing industry. Throughout the 1960s and 1970s there was strong political pressure to support the housing industry. This pressure seemed to have diminished in the early 1980s.

SUMMARY

There have been many reasons for the existence of financial reform legislation. The principal reasons are interest rates and disintermediation, competition from unregulated institutions, blurring and overlapping of functions of financial institutions, the Fed membership problem, and changing technology. Reflecting these factors have been a large number of reform proposals, the best known of which are the Hunt Commission and the House Banking Committee's study of Financial Institutions and the Nation's Economy. While neither of the reform packages was enacted into law in their entirety, many of their individual provisions were incorporated into the Depository Institutions Deregulation and Monetary Control Act of 1980 and the Depository Institutions Act of 1982.

The 1980 legislation contained the following provisions: uniform reserve requirements for depository institutions, gradual elimination of Regulation Q, authority for all depository institutions to offer interest-bearing transactions accounts nationwide, greater lending powers for savings and loans and mutual savings banks, and reduction in the scope of state usury laws. The 1980 legislation left out references to branching, the regulatory structure for financial institutions, and the increased availability of mortgage credit—proposals which had been included in previous financial reform measures. Additional reforms were included in the Depository Institutions Act of 1982, most notably authority to allow depository institutions to compete directly with money market funds.

The long-term implications of financial reform are difficult to see with any clarity at this point. Neither the results of the New England experiment nor econometric forecasts based upon previous proposals for financial reform suggest any great upheaval in the operation of financial institutions. However, while greater competition may produce benefits for users of financial services, it may also produce an increase in the number of failures and a sharp consolidation in the financial services industry. The results of a 1981 survey of managers of depository institutions suggest a strong impact on profitability and the number of institutions as well as on the availability of mortgage credit.

It is unlikely that the recent acts represent the end of financial reform legislation. Indeed, future legislation, which appears quite likely, may deal with the branching issue, the rationalization of the structure of regulation, the powers of depository institutions, the affiliation of financial institutions, and the mortgage subsidy issue.

Questions

25–1. What were the principal factors that produced the need for financial reform? Do those factors still exist?

25–2. What was the Hunt Commission proposal? The FINE proposal? Why did these proposals not produce legislation?

25–3. List the major provisions of the Depository Institutions Deregulation and Monetary Control Act of 1980. Relate them to the factors that produced the need for financial reform.

25–4. What factors were left out of the 1980 legislation? Why?

25–5. What are the major provisions of the Depository Institutions Act of 1982?

25–6. What do the results of previous research suggest as to the implications of financial reform? Why are they in conflict?

25–7. What are the major factors on the agenda for additional financial reform?

References

1. Carron, Andrew S. *The Plight of the Thrift Institutions*. Washington, D.C.: The Brookings Institution, 1982.

2. Colton, Kent W. *Financial Reforms: A Review of the Past and Prospects for the Future*. Washington, D.C.: Office of Policy and Economic Research, Federal Home Loan Bank Board, September 1980.

3. Fraser, Donald R. *The Changing Role of Depository Financial Institutions and the Availability of Funds to the Real Estate Industry*. College Station, Tex.: Texas Real Estate Research Center, Texas A&M University, 1982.

4. Fraser, Donald R. "DIDMCA and the Savings and Loan Industry: Evidence from a Survey." *Journal*, Federal Home Loan Bank Board, January 1982, pp. 2–10.

5. Fraser, Donald R., and Peter S. Rose. "The Hunt Commission Report: Implications for Banking." *Journal of Commercial Bank Lending*, November 1972, pp. 20–27.

6. Fraser, Donald R., and Gene C. Uselton. "The Omnibus Banking Act." *MSU Business Topics*, Autumn 1980, pp. 5–14.

7. Garcia, Gillian, et al. "The Garn–St Germain Depository Institutions Act of 1982." *Economic Perspectives*, Federal Reserve Bank of Chicago, March–April 1983, pp. 3–31.

8. Hayssen, Jonathan. "Competition among Financial Institutions: A

Survey from Maine." *Issues in Bank Regulation*, Summer 1977, pp. 13–20.

9. Hendershott, Patric H. *The Impact of the Financial Institutions Act of 1975*. Washington, D.C.: Department of Housing and Urban Development, 1975.

10. Jaffee, Dwight M. "The Extended Lending, Borrowing, and Service Function Proposals of the Hunt Commission Report." *Journal of Money, Credit and Banking*, November 1972, pp. 990–1000.

11. Jaffee, Dwight, and Kenneth T. Rose. "Mortgage Credit Availability and Residential Construction." *Brookings Papers on Economic Activity* 2 (1979), pp. 333–76.

12. McNeill, Charles R. "The Depository Institutions Deregulation and Monetary Control Act of 1980." *Federal Reserve Bulletin*, June 1980, pp. 444–53.

13. Mayne, Lucille S. "The Deposit Reserve Requirement Recommendations of the Commission on Financial Structure and Regulation." *Journal of Bank Research*, Spring 1973.

14. "The Savings and Loan Industry in the 1980s." *Journal*, Federal Home Loan Bank Board, May 1980, pp. 2–15.

15. Silber, William L. "The Process of Financial Innovation." *American Economic Review*, May 1983, pp. 89–95.

16. U.S. Congress, House Committee on Banking, Currency, and Housing. *Financial Institutions and the Nation's Economy: Discussion Principles*. Washington, D.C.: 94th Congress, 1st session, November 1975.

17. Waite, Donald C. "Deregulation and The Banking Industry." *The Bankers Magazine*, January–February 1982, pp. 26–35.

Index

This book has been set by Compugraphics 8600, in 10 and 9 point Palatino, leaded 2 points. Part numbers are 9 point Palatino Bold. Part titles and chapter numbers are 18 point Lubalin Graph Medium. Chapter titles are 24 point Palatino. The size of the overall type page is 34 by 44 picas.